RELIGIOUS OFFENCE AND CENSORSHIP OF PUBLICATIONS

This book analyzes the role of laws and the judiciary in the process of censorship in India. It examines the rationales and observations produced by the judiciary when demands for censorship are directed against publications that allegedly offend religious sentiments. Focusing on a micro-level analysis of censorship of publications, it presents a hard case to understand the limitations of freedom of expression and the role played by the judiciary in defining its boundaries. The volume traces the evolution of laws governing freedom of expression since the colonial period and the context in which these laws were amended after Independence. It also explicates how the legal process – the structural and functional aspects of working of judiciary – affects the fate of freedom of expression in India. Employing comparative legal analysis, it tries to understand and situate the Indian case within the larger discourse of censorship and freedom of expression around the world, thereby marking its similarities and differences. In unravelling the politics of censorship, the author also examines the interaction among different stakeholders like government, non-state actors and the judiciary.

A tract for our times, this book will be of great interest to scholars and researchers of law, especially constitutional law and fundamental rights, politics, especially political theory and Indian politics, modern India and South Asian studies.

Nishant Kumar teaches Political Science at Dyal Singh College, University of Delhi, India. After finishing his undergraduate studies from Hindu College (DU) and postgraduate studies from the Centre from Political Studies (JNU), he completed his PhD from King's College London, UK, as Commonwealth Scholar. His areas of interest include political theory, constitutional law in South Asia and intellectual history. He is currently also the coordinator of IHRG (Intellectual History Research Group), an international group of scholars working in the field of the history of ideas in India.

RELIGIOUS OFFENCE AND CENSORSHIP OF PUBLICATIONS

An Enquiry through the Prism of Indian Laws and the Judiciary

Nishant Kumar

Routledge
Taylor & Francis Group
LONDON AND NEW YORK

First published 2023
by Routledge
4 Park Square, Milton Park, Abingdon, Oxon OX14 4RN

and by Routledge
605 Third Avenue, New York, NY 10158

Routledge is an imprint of the Taylor & Francis Group, an informa business

British Library Cataloguing-in-Publication Data
A catalogue record for this book is available from the British Library

ISBN: 978-1-032-38499-3 (hbk)
ISBN: 978-1-032-43892-4 (pbk)
ISBN: 978-1-003-36925-7 (ebk)

DOI: 10.4324/9781003369257

Typeset in Sabon
by SPi Technologies India Pvt Ltd (Straive)

Dedicated to *Naima*

CONTENTS

ACKNOWLEDGEMENTS

Writing this book was the most beautiful and adventurous journey I have ever undertaken. It therefore becomes imminent to express my gratitude towards all individuals and institutions, which in different roles, either became co-travellers or facilitators in this journey. I wish to first thank Commonwealth Scholarship Agency for providing me the required funding as Commonwealth Scholar to undertake this research in London. I would also like to thank my PhD supervisors, Sunil Khilnani and Christophe Jaffrelot, and my examiners, Bhikhu Parekh and Rochana Bajpai, without whom this project would not have seen the light of the day. Words are not enough to express my gratitude for the office staff at various institutions: King's College London, SOAS, LSE, British Library, Nehru Memorial Museum and Library, and National Archives of India, who graciously offered all help possible to locate archival sources and other materials for research. There are some, without whom this journey would not have even started. Smita for being such a wonderful life partner, and my parents for doing whatever they could to make me whatever I am today. Last, but not the least, I would like to acknowledge the contribution of Naima, who in several undefined ways, remained a constant source of strength and motivation. My special thanks to the entire Routledge team, including the reviewers and editorial board, for making this dream come true.

LIST OF ABBREVIATIONS

AIMF	All India Minority Forum
AIR	All India Reporter
CAD	Constituent Assembly Debates
CPI (M)	Communist Party of India (Marxist)
CriJL	Criminal Law Journal
CrPC	Code of Criminal Procedure
CSDS	Centre for the Study of Developing Societies
DMK	Dravida Munnetra Kazhagam
ECHR	European Convention on Human Rights
ECtHR	European Court of Human Rights
ICCPR	International Covenant on Civil and Political Rights
IPC	Indian Penal Code
LSD	Lok Sabha Debates
MIM	Majlis-e-Ittehadul Muslimeen
NMML	Nehru Memorial Museum and Library, Delhi
PUCL	People's Union for Civil Liberties
RSD	Rajya Sabha Debates
RSS	Rashtriya Swayamsevak Sangh
SAHMAT	Safdar Hashmi Memorial Trust
SCC	Supreme Court Case
SCR	Supreme Court Reporter

LIST OF CASES

Arun Ghosh v. State of West Bengal, (1969) 1970 3 SCR 288.
Baba Khalil Ahamad v. State, A.I.R. 1960 All. 715.
Baragur Ramachandrappa & Ors. v. State of Karnataka & Anr., (1998) CriJL 3639.
Beauharnais v. Illinois, (1952) 343 U.S. 250.
Bhagwati Charan Shukla v. Provincial Government, (1947) A.I.R. 1947, Nagpur 1.
Brij Bhushan v. State of Delhi, (1950) AIR 37 SC 129.
Chaplinsky v. New Hampshire, (1942) 315 U.S. 568.
Choudhury v. United Kingdom, (1991) Application No. 17439/90, ECommHR.
Devi Sharan Sharma and another v. King Emperor, (1927) 14 AIR 594 (Lahore).
Devidas Ramachandra Tuljapurkar v. State of Maharashtra & Ors., (2015) (Criminal Appeal No. 1179 of 2010).
Dr. Ram Manohar Lohia v. State of Bihar and others, (1965) 1966 AIR 740.
Gopal Vinayak Godse v. Union of India and others, (1971) AIR BOM 56.
Harnam Das v. State of Uttar Pradesh, (1961) A.I.R 1662.
I.A. v Turkey, (December 13, 2005) Appl. No. 42571/98).
Kasem Said Ahmad and Asmaa Abdol-hamid v. Denmark, (18 April 2008) Communication no. 1487/2006, CCPR.
M/S Prakash Jha Productions vs. Union of India, Writ Petition (Civil) No. 345 of 2011.
Manzar Sayeed Khan v. State of Maharashtra (2009) 12 S.C.C. 157
Maqbool Fida Hussain v. Raj Kumar Pandey, (2008) Crl. Revision Petition No. 114/2007.
Master Amanpreet Singh and Others v. Government of India and others, (1996), AIR PH 284.
Mohammad Khalid v. The Chief Commissioner, Delhi, (1967) A.I.R. 1968 Delhi 13.
N. Veerabrahmam v. State of Andhra Pradesh, A.I.R. 1959 A.P. 572.
Nand Kishore Singh v. State of Bihar, AIR 1986 Pat 98.
National Socialist Party of America v. Village of Skokie, (1977) 432 U.S. 43.

New York Times Co. v. Sullivan, (1964) 376 U.S. 254.
Police Dept of Chicago v. Mosley, (1972) 408 US 92 96.
Public Prosecutor v. P. Ramasamy Nadar, Case Number - Crl. App. No. 125 of 1962.
R. V. Bhasin v. 2 Marine Drive Police Station, (2010) Criminal Application No. 1421 of 2007.
R. v. Chief Metropolitan Stipendiary Magistrate, ex p. Choudhury (Queen's Bench Division) (1991), 1 QB 429 (1990)
R.A.V. v. City of St. Paul, (1992) 505 U.S. 377.
Raj Pal v. King Emperor (1927) 14 AIR 590 (Lahore)
Ram Manohar Lohia v. State of Bihar, (1966) AIR SC 740.
Ramji Lal Modi v. State of Uttar Pradesh, (1957) AIR 620.
Ramlal Puri vs. State of Madhya Pradesh (1970) AIR 1971 MP 152
Ranjit Udeshi v. *State of Maharashtra*, (1965) A.I.R. 881.
Rigsadvokaten (Director of Public Prosecutions), (2006) J. Nr. RA-2006-41-0151.
Romesh Thapar v. State of Madras, (1950) AIR 37 SC 124.
S. Rangrajan v. P. Jagjivan Ram, (1989) 2 SCC 574.
S. Tamilselvan and other v. The Government of Tamil Nadu and others, (W.P. No. 1215 of 2015).
Shiv Ram Dass Udasin v. The Punjab State, (1954) A.I.R. 1955 P H 28.
Shreya Singhal v. Union of India, Writ Petition (Criminal) No. 167 of 2012.
Sri Baragur Ramachandrappa & Ors. v. State of Karnataka & Anr, (2007) 5 S.C.C.11.
State of Bihar v. Shailabal Devi (1952) AIR 329 SCR 654
State of Gujarat v. Mirzapur Moti Kureshi Kassab Janat (2005) 8 SCC 534, 567
State of Maharashtra & Ors. v. Sanghraj Damodar Rupawate & Ors. (2010) Civil Appeal of 2010 (Arising out of S.L.P. (C) No. 8931 of 2007)
State of Uttar Pradesh v. Lalai Singh Yadav (1976) 1977 AIR 202
Sujato Bhadra v. State of West Bengal (2006) 39 A.I.C. 239
Superintendent, Central Prison, Fatehgarh v. Ram Manohar Lohia (1960), 2 SCR 84
The State of Madras v. V. G. Row (1952) AIR 196 SCR 597
The State of Mysore vs. Henry Rodrigues And Anr. (1961) 1962 CriLJ 564
The Trustees of Safdar Hashmi Memorial Trust v. Govt. Of NCT of Delhi (2001) CriLJ 3689
Virendra v. State of Punjab (1957) AIR 896 SCR 308
Whitehouse v. Lemon (1977) (1979) 2 WLR 281
Zac Poonen v. Hidden Treasure Literature (2001) 2002 CriLJ 481

INTRODUCTION

"The writer Perumal Murugan is dead."

This announcement was made by Perumal Murugan, a Tamil writer, in his Facebook post on 12 January 2015 (*The Indian Express*, 15 January 2015). It reflected the state of the writer's mind after one of his popular novels, *Madhorubagan* (One Part Woman), first published in December 2010 and a recipient of several prizes and accolades, suddenly became the subject of controversy in 2015. *Madhorubagan* was set in a village near Tiruchengode (Namakkal district) during the colonial period, and it told of the social stigma faced by a childless couple.[1] The controversy over Murugan's novel erupted when, in December 2014, some pages of the novel were photocopied and distributed along with a handbill that accused the author of demeaning women belonging to the Kongu Vellala community (also called Gounders) and of vilifying an old tradition attached to the village temple. The accusation took a dramatic turn after around 40 different caste-based outfits, mobilized by the local leaders, decided to launch an agitation against the author for presenting in poor light the character of Gounder women and the old temple ritual, which, they held, brought a bad name to Tiruchengode. The town was shut down in protest, and the author received threats to his life from the local community. Though no formal ban was placed on the book, the attitude of the district administration created a sense of forced censorship. On 12 January the District Revenue Officer, V. R. Subbulakshmi, who also served as Additional District Magistrate, convened a 'peace committee meeting', to which Murugan along with his lawyer were also invited. However, in the meeting, Murugan and his lawyer were not allowed to present his case, nor was he allowed to meet the protesting groups. Rather, authorities ordered him to sign a statement, as had been demanded by the protesting groups. It stated that the author wished to apologize unconditionally, agreed to recall all copies of the book, change controversial references and paragraphs, and never in the future to write anything connected with Tiruchengode. In order to buy peace, the district administration had sacrificed, it would seem, the freedom of speech and

DOI: 10.4324/9781003369257-1

expression of P. Murugan. Murugan's subsequent Facebook post claiming his death as a writer was a reaction to these events, which he claimed had left him 'insecure and disgusted'.[2]

This episode is just one among many that illuminate forms of censorship that are operational in Indian society. The case of Murugan also exposed different layers involved in the process of censorship. Let me highlight some of the important issues involved in this case. First, when the book was originally published in the local language (Tamil) more than four years before the incident, there was no protest against the content of the book. In fact, it became a bestseller, with the publisher selling more than 5,000 copies before the controversy began.[3] The gap between the time of publication and the claims about hurt sentiments suggest other intervening factors at play. Second, the attitude of the government authorities of Tamil Nadu was open to question. The district administration claimed that its action was best to control a potentially disruptive law-and-order situation in the town. In the 'peace-meeting', the administration brokered a one-sided deal which not only legitimized the claims of hurt by the protestors, but also ensured that their demands were met. Neither did the administration investigate who was responsible for the circulation of photocopies of selective portions from the book that had incited the harassment of Murugan, nor did the police try to find out the people who had threatened Murugan and his family members. The message was clear: the district administration wanted to avoid public-order problems, and it was convinced that the freedom of expression of the author was a small price to be paid to secure that.

The third important aspect related to the case, which has often been ignored by analysts and commentators, was the role of the court. After Murugan was forced to sign a compromise letter by district authorities, several organizations including the People's Union for Civil Liberties (PUCL) filed writ petitions in the Madras High Court highlighting two issues: first, continuous harassment of Murugan by 'caste and religion based groups'[4] and, second, the role of state authorities in pressuring Murugan to sign the agreement. Based on these grounds, the court was requested to hold the agreement 'illegal, unconstitutional, and not being enforceable'. The first petition in this regard was filed on 26 January 2015 in the High Court. Petitions were also filed by the protesting groups, requesting the court to order the government to ban the book and bring criminal proceedings against Murugan for vilifying religious practices and disturbing communal harmony. Within a month, Murugan submitted his reply in the form of an affidavit, where he spoke out about his experiences as well as his discomfort with the attitude of the state authorities. However, it took more than one-and-a-half years for the court to pronounce its final judgement on the subject.[5] Such delays in judgements create uncertainty as far as the issue of legality is concerned and have proved detrimental to the defender's right to freedom of expression. Scholars and commentators on free speech have held that cases like that of Murugan have a tendency to produce a 'chilling effect' that acts as an informal mode of censoring freedom of expression.[6] Further, it exposed a looming complexity in the response of the Indian state when claims of religious offence are directed against freedom of speech and expression.

Such incidents, however, are not new for Indian society. A survey of case laws and archives of newspapers and periodicals suggests that a fundamental right to freedom of speech and expression has routinely faced challenges. When the constitution of independent India was being drafted and the provisions concerning fundamental rights were being discussed, the constitution makers assigned a special role to the judiciary: that of safeguarding citizens' fundamental rights from encroachment by individuals, groups or the executive. It was assumed that in case of contradictions and controversies, the judiciary would act to protect the rights of citizens. But how far has the judiciary succeeded in upholding this expectation of the constitution makers? In the present work, I examine this aspect through an analysis of the role that law and the legal process have played when freedom of expression is threatened by the claims of religious offence or hurt sentiments. Central to this is the judiciary's role as the interpreter of the constitutional provisions that guarantee freedom of speech and expression and the laws that allow for its restrictions.

As the field of freedom of speech and expression is too broad, the scope of this study has been confined specifically to censorship of publications. Focus is on those publications which invoked religious issues and became contentious as they were claimed to be 'offensive' to religious sensibilities by socio-religious groups. Commentators on censorship in India have claimed that since Independence there have been many publications that became party to such controversies, and were either banned or censored by authorities citing reasons like a threat to public order or the hurt caused to the religious sentiments of different communities (Dhavan 2008; Kumar 1997). Censorship of publications becomes a representative case to analyze and understand the scope of freedom of speech and expression due to various reasons. First, in India, where the average literacy rate is low, it is striking to note how a publication could generate controversy over hurt caused by the publication's content. Moreover, most books that attracted controversy were not even aimed at public consumption. The price of the book and the specificity of the subject (especially in cases of academic publications) should have acted as hurdles to broader public reception or awareness. Therefore, the chances of publications being a cause of hurt sentiments are much less than in cases of other modes of expression. It is easier, for example, in the case of visual representation, like films and cartoons, to reach a wider audience and attract opposition if it is controversial. However, it is often seen that in controversies related to publications, rumours and hearsay play important roles in spreading the content and its interpretation. The fact remains that publications, like any other visual forms of expression, are equally vulnerable to the claims of hurt sentiments and they are indicative of the scope of freedom of expression. Second, censorship of publications also helps to clarify the legal boundaries of freedom of speech and expression. Section 295(A) of the Indian Penal Code (IPC), related to hurting religious sentiments, and section 153(A), related to promoting enmity between two classes of citizens, have been routinely used by government authorities as well as non-state actors in their efforts to censor different forms of expression. In 2001, authorities in Delhi used the provisions under section 153(A) and 295(A) of IPC to disallow a public exhibition arranged by the Safdar Hashmi Memorial Trust (SAHMAT) group.[7] Similarly, in case of the artist M. F. Hussain, the petitioners filed criminal charges against the painter under the same statutory laws.[8] Third, controversies related to censorship of publications also explicate the interplay of power relations between important stakeholders – government agencies, courts and non-state actors. Hurt caused to religious sensibilities has been one of the most potent reasons invoked for censoring and banning publications in India. Although government authorities have also exercised their legal powers against publications that were adjudged to be against national interest, defamatory of individuals or obscene, the contentions based on religious subjects have been vital. One important reason for this is the fact that claimants of hurt sentiments have often used the logic of another fundamental right – that is, the right to freely profess, practice and propagate their religion, guaranteed by article 25 of the constitution.[9] So, focus on the subject also enables a broad understanding of how legal processes in India deal with situations where two different fundamental rights are in contention – freedom of speech and expression guaranteed under article 19(1)(a) and freedom of religious practice guaranteed under article 25.

Freedom of Speech and Expression and Legal Intervention: A Comparative Perspective

Freedom of speech and expression has always enjoyed a special value within liberalism. On the one hand, almost everyone seems to agree that freedom of speech and expression is important, and it ought to enjoy special legal protection that does not extend to any other class of acts in society; on the other hand, there is no real agreement amongst philosophers, lawyers, legislators and citizens as to why such freedom is important and how much freedom might be too much freedom. Historically, the primary justifications put forward in favour of freedom of speech fall in one of these four categories – (1) for the purpose of promotion of truth (or the marketplace of ideas theory) (Emerson 1966; Mill 1978); (2) its benefits to democracy and self-government (Meiklejohn 1966); (3) its role in promotion of other virtues that survive society (Bollinger 1988); and (4) its contribution to individual's self-realization and self-determination (the autonomy-based defence of free speech) (Baker 1989). Interestingly, none of the advocates dismisses the need for state intervention. For example, though J. S. Mill (1978) advocated that freedom of speech was important to produce a marketplace of ideas which could get us closer to truth, he also devised the 'harm principle' and argued that government interventions could be valid if they aimed to neutralize speech acts that had high potential to cause harm to others. With respect to state intervention, however, most advocates of freedom of speech and expression suggest that the principles of 'neutrality' be followed – both 'content-neutrality' and 'viewpoint neutrality'. It is claimed that state action should neither be based on the content of the speech acts nor on the viewpoint that the speech acts represented. Similarly, there remains scepticism about the nature and scope of the state's interventions. For example, there is wide acceptance that 'child pornography' should be banned, but there are continuing debates about whether the state is justified in making laws to regulate adult pornography, blasphemy and forms of speech which are widely referred to as hate speech. Regardless of the theoretical debates on the subject, most governments across the world have provisions in law to restrict free speech in some form or other.

International law, which appears to vociferously defend the right to free speech, also recognizes the need to allow some liberty to member states to legislate in order to balance free speech against its harms. For example, article 19(2) of the International Covenant on Civil and Political Rights (ICCPR) of the United Nations provides for the right to freedom of expression. However, it also allows the member states to restrict free speech by law under clause 3 of the same article, if such restrictions are meant to protect the 'rights' or 'reputations' of others or for national security, public order or public health and morals. It is further specified under article 20(2) that 'any advocacy of national, racial or religious hatred that constitutes incitement to discrimination, hostility or violence shall be prohibited'. Similarly, article 10 of the European Convention on Human Rights (ECHR) protects freedom of speech subject to certain restrictions that the member states could by law deem necessary

> in the interests of national security, territorial integrity or public safety, for the prevention of disorder or crime, for the protection of health or morals, for the protection of the reputation or rights of others, for preventing the disclosure of information received in confidence, or for maintaining the authority and impartiality of the judiciary.

It is evident that even international organizations like the UN and the EU observe the rights of its member states to restrict free speech on some important grounds.

If we look at the legal provisions devised by individual countries to control the harms of free speech, we find a wide disparity. At one end of the spectrum stands the US legislation under the First Amendment, which allows strong protection to freedom of speech, and at the other end appear laws devised under the German system, where article 130 of the Strafgesetzbuch

(German Criminal Code) adopted in 1960 prohibits attack on human dignity, which includes: (1) inciting hatred against a certain part of the population, (2) inciting to violent or arbitrary acts against such part of the population, or (3) insulting, maliciously ridiculing or defaming such part. Bhikhu Parekh has rightly pointed to the diversity of issues that have prompted legal restrictions in different countries:

> Britain bans abusive, insulting, and threatening speech. Denmark and Canada prohibit speech that is insulting and degrading; and India and Israel ban speech that incites racial and religious hatred and is likely to stir up hostility between groups. In the Netherlands, it is a criminal offence to express publicly views insulting to groups of persons. Australia prohibits speech that offends, insults, humiliates, or intimidates individuals or groups, and some of its states have laws banning racial vilification. Germany goes further, banning speech defining and diminishing hate speech that violates the dignity of an individual, implies that he or she is an inferior being, or maliciously degrades or defames a group.
>
> (2012: 37)

Case laws in different countries appear to define the scope for government regulation based on the challenges and potential threats that extreme defence of free speech could pose in that society. For example, in the US case, Samuel Walker (1994) argues that the Supreme Court has shown a significant shift in its position from the early 20th century to the 1940s, and then from the 1950s to the 1980s. This shift could occur because the civil rights movement in the US recognized that free speech was the only resource available for the powerless and the excluded, and so always stood in its favour, as it served broad social and political needs in the struggle for racial equality (Walker 1994: 160). One can definitely locate a shift in the courts' position from the early 20th century, when hate crimes of the white supremacist group the Ku Klux Klan were widely reported, to the post–Second World War period of ideological opposition to communist and fascist ideologies. A shift in the judiciary's attitude is clearly visible from cases like *Chaplinsky* (1942) and *Beauharnais* (1952), where it upheld laws against group libel and argued that not all speech is protected by the First Amendment, to cases like *Sullivan* (1964), *Mosley* (1972) and more prominently in the *Skokie* (1977) and *R. A. V* (1992). The debate seems to have taken a further turn with the challenge of 'campus hate speech' that became prominent from the 1980s onwards. This phase is also marked by the rapid expansion of feminist theory, critical race theory and other alternative discourses, all of which attacked mainstream and official speech as inherently oppressive and white-male-dominated discourse and argued for pluralization and fragmentation of discourse (Rosenfeld 2012: 255). As the judgements in different cases show, the court has set very high standards for free speech, and its regulation is possible only in exceptional circumstances, even in cases concerned with hate speech. However, at the same time if we look at the cases that appear in the European courts, especially, in the European Court of Human Rights (ECtHR), it appears that the court has upheld the right of the member states to use legal sanctions against the claims of free speech in a wide range of cases. For example, in *Otto-Preminger-Institut* (1994), the court held the forfeiture and seizure of the anti-religious film *Das Liebenskonsil* (Council in Heaven) did not contravene article 10 of ECtHR since it was aimed at the protection of the religious right of the majority, in that case the Christians of Austria. Similarly, in *I.A.* (2005), the court held that the case of blasphemous libel of a publisher was justified for printing a fictional work by Abdullah Riza Erguven entitled *Forbidden Verses* in which a character makes disparaging comments about Islam. It argued that the conviction was intended to protect Muslims against offensive attacks on matters regarded as sacred by the community.

These readings of the legal provisions and case laws show that there is no uniformity in the way questions surrounding the scope and limitations to free speech are handled around the world. In this respect, the case of India is no different. In India, though freedom of speech and expression is a guaranteed constitutional right, it in no way enjoys any primacy or prior preference over other rights. The Constituent Assembly Debates (CAD) clearly show the tension between different aspects of rights and the way the constitution makers tried to balance them along with the possible threats emanating from freedom of speech and expression by providing certain restrictions under article 19(2). This article, as it stands today, imposes reasonable restrictions 'in the interests of the sovereignty and integrity of India, the security of the State, friendly relations with foreign States, public order, decency or morality or in relation to contempt of court, defamation or incitement to an offence'. However, India's difference from the Western democracies is also clearly visible if we examine major legislation designed to regulate free speech, and try to identify the reasons for prosecution specified in these laws. For example, even if we argue that 'incitement to an offence' and concern for 'public order', as present in article 19(2), may reflect the debates in the West, how do we account for restrictions based on 'decency', 'morality' or 'defamation'? The broad latitude of restrictions to free speech that India allows can further be gauged from the language used to define the statutory laws. For example, section 153(A) of the IPC criminalizes the promotion of 'enmity between different groups on grounds of religion, race, place of birth, residence, language etc' or engagement in 'acts prejudicial to maintenance of harmony'. The broad scope of section 153(A) is further buttressed by section 153(B), which prohibits 'imputations and assertions prejudicial to national-integration'. The section criminalizes the use of 'words either spoken or written', signs 'or by visible representations or otherwise'. Similarly, there are other provisions like:

- Section 295, which prohibits 'injuring or defiling [any] place of worship with intent to insult the religion of any class';
- Section 295(A), which prohibits 'deliberate and malicious acts, intended to outrage religious feelings or any class by insulting its religion or religious beliefs';
- Section 298, which prohibits 'uttering words, etc, with deliberate intent to wound religious feelings';
- Section 505(1), which prohibits 'statements conducive to public mischief'; and,
- Section 505(2), which prohibits 'statements creating or promoting enmity, hatred or ill-will between classes'.

These legal provisions, unlike most European provisions, use terms like 'injury', 'insult', 'malicious act', 'outrage feelings', 'wound', 'promoting enmity' and 'ill-will', which have much wider, normative and practical connotations. These legal provisions and the historical background in which they emerged indicate that the right to freedom of speech and expression is treated differently in India. This obviously stands in contradistinction to the expectations of those advocates of free speech who assume there can be any right way to establish free speech through abstract principles, which could then be applied anywhere, regardless of local conditions. Charles Taylor (1989) has rightly questioned such assumptions based on two reasons: (1) Any regime of freedom of expression, he opined, required some broad consensus. It cannot just be imposed by law, because, if its principles are too distant from mass sensibilities, it will be rendered nugatory by all sorts of extra-legal pressures; and (2) Any regime of free expression has limits which are justified by the possibility of harm inflicted on others. This is an issue which is sensitive to cultural differences.

In the case of India, though one may disagree with the kind of regulative and restrictive mechanism allowed to be placed in the hands of government, one cannot deny that the regulations were included in a particular social and historical context. The complexities of inter-communal relationships, marred by the memory of partition, and the challenges facing the post-colonial Indian state, particularly that of national integration and nation-building, became reasons for such extensive provisions for restricting free speech in India. So as the European nations argued for regulation of hate speech in the context of the Holocaust and, later, under the pressure exerted by the 'multi-cultural' nature of the European society, and in the US in the context of racism and anti-communism, India had its own complex reality to deal with. The impact of context on legal regulation of free speech is very well reflected by Parekh in his discussion about hate speech. As he puts it:

> Western societies have several mechanisms to cope with hate speech and its consequences, such as an open and competitive economy, a vibrant civil society, a reasonably cohesive and integrated society,

> a varied media representing a wide spectrum of views, and a plural and self-limiting public culture. They can therefore afford to assign law a relatively limited role.... So far as the developing countries are concerned, the situation could not be more different. Most of them are composed of ethnic, religious, and racial groups with little experience of working together and a long legacy of mistrust, ignorance, misunderstanding, and hostility. Rumours, jokes, inflammatory or ill-conceived remarks by politicians seeking short-term gains, and even reasoned criticisms made in the course of an uninhabited exercise of free speech can arouse deep-seated fear, trigger unrest, and undo years of good work in nation building.
>
> (2012: 55)

Many scholars and legal practitioners have made critical assessments of the nature and scope of laws in India that govern free speech. One line of criticisms pertains to the continuance of laws that had colonial roots. It is argued that such laws have lost their relevance in the present era and should therefore be scrapped (Ghosh 2004; Kumar 1990; Liang 2004). This idea echoes the concern that many lawmakers had also raised on the floor of the Constituent Assembly, when the restrictions enshrined under article 19(2) of the constitution were being debated. Another set of scholars highlight how these laws do not prove effective in achieving the goal they were meant to achieve – preventing hate speech or protecting hurt to religious sentiments of the people. There are two primary apprehensions raised by scholars in this regard – the first is with respect to the way in which these laws, rather than preventing hate speech which could hurt sentiments, allow for mobilization in the name of hurt sentiments (Liang 2004); the second apprehension is about the 'slippery slope' effect of laws, concerning the misuse of laws by state agencies in promoting or enforcing a legal sanction that might create hurdles for free exercise of the right to freedom of speech and expression (Ghosh 2004; Liang 2004). Highlighting the inefficacy of the Indian statutory laws in dealing with the subject of hate speech, these scholars cast doubts about the need and presence of such laws.

Contrary to these views are the arguments of those who believe that given the nature of Indian society, where political power structures favour religious majorities, and where caste and gender inequalities render large numbers of citizens vulnerable and exposed to the threat of hate speech based on their caste, religious or gender identity, the state needs to intervene for their protection. Scholars like A. G. Noorani (1999), Rajeev Dhavan (2008), Iqbal Ansari (2008) and Rajeev Bhargava (2012) represent this view, and they constantly highlight the importance of 'reasonable restrictions' as enshrined in the constitution. However, they are cautious to suggest that the state machinery should understand that it is the fundamental right of speech and expression that is 'sacred' and not the restrictions themselves. Reports on riots in India show that most of the instances of communal violence were preceded by altercations often incited by pamphlets, booklets or other publications or even hate speech targeting the vulnerable religious group of the region, which included threats or vilification of their religious beliefs or practices. Studies such as those by Paul Brass (2003) and Steven Wilkinson (2005) support such explanations. These facts are used by human rights activists, such as Teesta Setalvad, to argue that hate-speech laws are integral to the protection of the plural and secular nature of multi-religious Indian society. In the absence of hate speech laws, Setalvad (2011) holds that the instances of hate crimes against minorities could rise.

The present study does not intend to judge whether the presence of legal provisions against free speech is a good thing or not. Rather, it tries to understand what the presence of these laws means to the discourse of freedom of speech and expression in India. Therefore, one of the focus areas is the genesis of these laws – the context in which such laws were devised and the major actors who were involved in their formulation. It includes a study of the circumstances that led to the formation of the provisions under the constitution and statutory laws as well as the amendments introduced at later stages. The legislative debates shall help us to contemplate the attitude of lawmakers towards freedom of speech and expression, both under colonial rule as well as after independence. The legal apparatus to control freedom of speech and expression was historically handed down by the British, who took it upon themselves to codify criminal and civil laws in India. They devised far-reaching laws that were considered relevant according to the needs of the colonial context. Some laws were promulgated to maintain British control over the means of free expression, especially the press, and other laws were devised to legitimize the authority of the British as neutral arbiters of diverse cultural and religious interests that communities in India represented. A study of legislative proceedings of the period reveals that some Indian representatives had raised issues with regard to British attempts to curb freedom of expression. But, as argued in Chapter 1 of this work, concerns like maintenance of public order and protecting religious sentimentalities of different communities from hurt formed the bedrock on which the edifice for the legal regime to control free speech was constructed. After independence, though the nature of Indian state and its character changed significantly, the concerns regarding probable harm of free speech remained similar as they did during the colonial period. Challenges like partition and other events that marked the birth of India as a free nation warranted a fresh consideration of the legal aspects in order to avoid crisis at the level of internal security and prevent public-order issues. The new set of challenges forced amendments to the constitution, most significantly to those articles that dealt with freedom of speech and expression, in order to strengthen the executive's control. The justification forwarded, as discussed in Chapter 2 of this book, was that the citizens of a free nation should entrust confidence in its democratic government to protect and promote the interests of its citizens. This paternal attitude is explicitly reflected in the debates of the Parliament when amendments were introduced to the constitutional provisions as well as the statutory laws.

Censorship and the Role of the Courts

Censorship is a form of suppression whereby speech considered harmful, objectionable, sensitive or inconvenient is controlled. There can be several forms of this control and several agents that might perform this act. Traditionally it was understood to be under the power of some legitimate authority, mostly the state, to decide about censorship, but the nature and forms of censorship have changed drastically in recent decades. More recently, censorship has come to be understood as a power relation operating at different nodal points in social relationships. While histories of censorship used to chronicle official legal suppression of speech, Foucault's work invited us to 'escape from the limited field of juridical sovereignty and state institutions, and instead base our analysis of power on the study of techniques and tactics of domination' (Post 1998). A set of scholars have used the Foucauldian method to develop a framework to view this power relationship, which is popularly called 'new censorship'.[10] These scholars point at the change in the practice of censorship with the growth of new power centres, sometimes visible, at other times imperceptible. So, a range of new vocabularies have entered the discourse like 'self-censorship', 'market censorship', 'social censorship' and others. All these present different notions of censorship based on the difference in the location of power. The assumption is that threats to free speech come from all directions, not just from government. To this extent, censorship has been privatized, taken out of the hands of the state and located in other sources of power (Lee 1990).

Commentators on censorship in India have primarily focussed on the role of the state in the process. Concepts like 'market censorship' and 'self-censorship' are fairly new entrants into this scholarship. It is not to say that other forms of censorship did not exist in the Indian context; it is just that the field is heavily under-researched. Moreover, the state in India still plays a dominant role as censor. The only other form of censorship that appears prominently in the literature on censorship in India is 'social censorship', or what Noorani (1995) calls 'informal censorship'. Some scholars believe that the issue of social censorship has still not acquired centrality in the discourse of free speech, even though it has greater ramifications than the traditional form of censorship practiced by the state institutions (Dhavan 2008; Kumar 1997). If this is true, what happens to the traditionally defined role of the state as the legitimate authority to take decisions regarding censorship?

The demand for censoring or banning a publication on a religious subject can be based on different grounds: feeling of offence, hate, vilification, discrimination or threat experienced by individuals belonging to the target religious groups, or the feeling of any disruption or interruption in the enjoyment of the constitutionally guaranteed freedom of religion. In such controversies it is expected that the state shall act according to rational judgement, thereby providing a balance to contradictory claims. If any party is dissatisfied with the response of the state, he or she can approach the judiciary requesting legal scrutiny of executive's action.

The pragmatic vision of the lawmakers capacitated the judiciary to review executive decisions regarding important fundamental rights and, at the same time, to adjudicate the scope and relevance of the laws with changing times. Constitutionally, the first amendment to the constitution added the clause of 'reasonability' in relation to restrictions placed on freedom of speech and expression under article 19(2) of the constitution.[11] This 'reasonability' test provided courts with a tool to keep a check on the arbitrary actions of the government and thereby to protect individual rights to free speech from regulation even in the name of public order or protecting socio-cultural rights. Other than this, as the custodian of fundamental rights, the judiciary is also empowered by the constitution to review, strike down or sit on any law that appears to be contravening provisions of fundamental rights. Further, the power to adjudicate on cases of freedom of expression also draws from the provisions of statutory laws. For example, Section 96 of the Code of Criminal Procedure (CrPC) allows for any interested person to challenge the decision of forfeiture or ban of any publication by the government in the respective High Courts. This wide-ranging space for intervention by the judiciary ensured that after Independence, courtrooms became sites for struggles to define the scope and boundaries of freedom of speech and expression.

As guardian of fundamental rights, courts enjoy considerable respect and legitimacy in the eyes of the people. For such reasons, advocates of free speech also look towards the courts with high expectations. However, the history of free speech jurisprudence in India reflects a complex dynamic emerging from a balance based on respect for group identities and individual rights (Bhargava 1999: 26–59). The balance is not fixed, and there is always a scope for its shift of prioritizing one over the other. In the context of fundamental rights, the challenge of balancing was clearly reflected in the concerns of the constitution makers. Although the constitution guaranteed individual political rights and civil liberties, all these were severely circumscribed in the name of either national interests or the need to protect interests of cultural communities (Mahajan 1998: 155–158). The same is reflected in the approach of the judiciary. For example, unlike the US judiciary, which has largely dealt with the question of 'hate speech' by means of 'fighting words' and 'clear and present danger' doctrines, the Supreme Court in India takes a wider cognizance of the test for 'reasonableness' of restrictions imposed by the state machinery by treating each case differently from the substantive as well as procedural standpoints. Although one can easily locate references to US free-speech case laws in their judgements, judges in India have consistently maintained that the context and nature of society being different, the principles and positions that the courts in other countries take may not be reproduced in India. For example, free speech scholar Daniel Hantman (2014) invokes a comparison between Indian and US Supreme Courts' approach to freedom of expression and argues that Indian courts show a higher degree of tolerance for restricting socially offensive and emotionally harmful speech. He concludes that this has been made possible due to the persisting tension present between India's Western governing system and indigenous communal social structure.

Regardless of the centrality of the judiciary in free speech discourse in India, it has (until recently) largely remained an under-studied area. Most literature available on the subject is about press freedom (S. Bhatia 1997; Sorabjee 1976). Other than this, the subjects of censorship of books, art, films or obscenity find space in journalistic writings and are primarily in the context of specific acts of censorship. Works on censorship such as Bhowmik's on film censorship (2009), Girja Kumar's on book censorship (1997), Brinda Bose's on gender and censorship (2006) and Kaur and Mazzarella's edited volume on censorship in South Asia (2009) have all avoided critical engagement with case laws. Though they use judicial pronouncements in their work, one can find only a selective use of case laws aimed to buttress their arguments. Recently some serious engagement with the topic can be seen in the works of legal scholars like Rajeev Dhavan, Gautam Bhatia, Siddharth Narrain and political scientist Pratap Bhanu Mehta. Dhavan (2008) shows that courts in India, especially higher courts, have tried to provide a strong defence to freedom of speech. However, the legal process is so exhaustive and painful that the process itself becomes a form of punishment. This point has been reiterated by Narrain in his study of hate-speech laws in India (2016a). However, with reference to case laws, Narrain has highlighted the ambiguities that exist even at the level of Supreme Court judgements, and hence he shows that the judgements even from courts at the highest level are not immune to contradictions, which makes the fundamental right to speech and expression more vulnerable in the Indian context. The issue of ambiguity in free speech–related judgements is also pointed to by Pratap Bhanu Mehta (2008), who believes that one of the reasons for such ambiguity is the concern for and the tilt of the courts towards communitarian values, especially when a fundamental right such as that of speech is posed in contention with freedom ofreligion. An approach based on values of individualism, according to Mehta, could help the courts overcome their bias against the right to freedom of speech and expression. Bhatia (2016) presents a set of contradictory streams that appear as foundational to the judiciary's position on free speech. He argues that the judges have either favoured a 'moral-paternalistic vision' or a 'liberal-autonomous vision'. The 'moral-paternalistic vision' holds that since human beings are corruptible, they may not be entrusted with extreme freedoms, and it is therefore the duty of public institutions to prevent any harm to the citizens. The 'liberal-autonomous vision', according to Bhatia, is based on the immanent faith on human judgement and choices, and any form of interference with that is seen as unwarranted. Where on the one hand, the 'moral-paternalistic' attitude limits the scope of free speech, therefore allowing wider interference from the state, on the other hand, the 'liberal-autonomous' attitude favours the claims of free speech. Bhatia argues that, based on these approaches, the courts decide the fate of free speech cases. These recent works on the subject have contributed significantly to the discourse. Such scholarship helps to grasp the multiple ways in which the role of the judiciary can be viewed. Taking cues from each of the above-mentioned scholarships, this book presents a detailed study of courts role vis-à-vis the claims of religious offence against publications. A detailed study of courts' approach towards free speech, as well as the laws and legal process that define the boundaries of free speech, reveals that there are many variables that impact the fate of the case laws. For example, the courts' generous consideration of the public-order situation and the emphasis on protecting the secular and plural credentials of Indian society has prompted moves to limit free speech. Similarly, the ambiguity in the court's decisions, as well as the operative constraints like delay in judgements, has increased the vulnerability of freedom of speech and expression in the Indian context. At such a juncture, the philosophical considerations that scholars like Bhatia impose on the judiciary might not represent the actual complexity. Mehta's opinion about an individualism-based approach might be fruitful, but the judiciary does not actually enjoy that liberty as it is guided by the constitution, where freedom of expression is not the only value that needs protection. The courts are under a lot of pressure to balance this fundamental right with others like freedom of religion, and in the process, even if the courts fail the expectations of libertarians who argue for extreme freedom of expression, it appears prepared to do that. For its justification of curbing free speech, the courts easily invoke article 19(2) of the constitution, which defines the limits to freedom of speech and expression. In the present work, I critically engage with all these scholars through the prism of case laws. However, the study is limited not only to an analysis of case laws. It also looks at the structural and operative aspects of courts' functioning, which have been overlooked by both Bhatia and Mehta. This helps to develop a broader understanding about the role of the courts in the debates over freedom of expression. For example, the duration of the time taken by the courts in India to pronounce judgements in cases related to publications claimed to be offensive shows that it usually takes long for the courts to adjudicate in the matter. This creates conditions whereby authors/publishers try to evade the legal process and agree to out-of-court settlement with the complainants, even if it hampers their free exercise of freedom of expression. Further, I also look at cases where government, non-state actors and the judiciary interact. This helps to examine the consequences of such interactions, and also to understand how courts view the role of non-state actors in censorship, an issue largely overlooked in earlier studies.

Notes

1 The novel highlights the plight of Kali and Ponna, the protagonist couple, and while discussing their attempts to conceive, it also refers to an age-old local custom of the community which, according to temple laws, allowed consensual union among consenting adults outside of marriage during the village festival to overcome the problem of childlessness. More than 5,000 copies of the novel had been sold and on popular demand a translated version with the title *One Part Woman* was published by Penguin in 2013. Two sequels to the novel have also been published.

2 Murugan expressed his anguish in an affidavit that was submitted to Madras High Court on his behalf, where a plea to dismiss the undertaking had come up (W.P. No. 2668 of 2015). Ilangovan Rajasekaran, 'Writer Speaks Out', *Frontline*, 20 March 2015, Available at http://www.frontline.in/the-nation/writer-speaks-out/article6955375.ece (accessed on 30 April 2017).

3 This is a part of the information provided by S. R. Sundaram as the publisher of Murugan's book in a counter-affidavit filed in the case *S. Tamilselvan and other v. The Government of Tamil Nadu and Others* (2015) W.P. No. 1215 of 2015.

4 The petition was filed by S. Balamurugan, General Secretary of PUCL in Tamil Nadu and appeared as *S. Balamurugan v. The Government of Tamil Nadu and others* (2015) W.P. No. 2668 of 2015.

5 The Madras High Court finally pronounced its judgement in the case on 5 July 2016, almost one and half years after the petition had first appeared in the court.

6 A chilling effect applies to cases where the state might not directly censor free speech, but its role produces conditions that lead to self-censorship. It may either be due to uncertainty in legal sanctions or an unfriendly attitude of administration or any such reasons. See LaMarche (1991: 56–58).

7 The case appeared in Delhi High Court as *The Trustees of Safdar Hashmi Memorial Trust v. Govt. of NCT of Delhi*, (2001) CriLJ3689. SAHMAT is a left-oriented cultural organization that includes academicians, artists and others, and it claims to promote the values of pluralism and secularism in Indian society.

8 The case was dealt by the Delhi High Court as *Maqbool Fida Hussain v. Raj Kumar Pandey* (2008) Crl. Revision Petition No. 114/2007.

9 Article 25 provides for freedom of conscience and free profession, practice and propagation of religion. Clause 1 of the article is most important; it reads: 'Subject to public order, morality and health and to the other provisions of this Part, all persons are equally entitled to freedom of conscience and the right freely to profess, practise and propagate religion'.

10 Advocates of this new approach include Richard Burt (1994), Sue Curry Jansen (1991) and Michael Holquist (1994), among others. However, this approach has also received severe criticism from scholars like Beate Muller (2004) and Robert Post (1998). For example, Robert Post criticises the new scholarship on censorship by arguing that it has 'flattened distinctions among kinds of power, implicitly equating suppression of speech caused by state legal action with that caused by the market, or by the dominance of a particular discourse, or by the institution of criticism itself'. This invariably makes it difficult to formulate a pointed criticism of censorship itself because it gets so difficult to locate the point of origination.

11 Article 19(2) of the constitution allows the validity of existing laws and empowers the government to make new laws vis-à-vis free speech, only if the laws impose 'reasonable restrictions' and are 'in the interests of the sovereignty and integrity of India, the security of the State, friendly relations with foreign States, public order, decency or morality or in relation to contempt of court, defamation or incitement to an offence'.

1

CENSORSHIP OF PUBLICATIONS IN COLONIAL INDIA

The Genesis of a Legal Idea

The ideas and institutions of colonial modernity were brought to India from outside – that is, by the agents of European, especially British, imperialism. This was in sharp contrast to primarily internal or indigenous processes through which Europe itself had launched its project of enlightenment and modernity (Mehta & Pantham 2006; Kaviraj 2010). The claim of monopoly and expertise over modernity was used as justification by the colonial powers to fulfil its imperial ambitions. For many, British India was a contradictory political formation. In Henry Maine's words, it was a 'most extraordinary experiment' involving 'the virtually despotic government of a dependency by a free people' (Maine 1876: 233). The colonial rule reflected dichotomies at two different levels. Firstly, liberty, which was held to be the most sacred and universal value of the enlightenment project, was being curtailed through the processes of colonialism and creation of subject peoples – another product of the same enlightenment project. Further, the same argument of modernity used to enlarge civil liberties in the West was being used to deny basic rights to the colonial masses. This contradiction was sharply reflected in the case of freedom of expression. The people who celebrated and claimed freedom of expression and the press as sacred in their own societies became, under the garb of imperial rulers, its ardent opponents in the colonies, restricting both free expression and freedom of the press for their own benefits. These dichotomies produced a new context through the interaction of 'East' and 'West', which is clearly reflected in the translation and understanding of freedom of speech and expression in India.

The power relationship operating in colonial India can be deduced, as Guha (1977) argues, by deriving a relation between dominance and subordination. The British tried to establish their hegemony by inducing changes in the institutional structures. The introduction of Western education was an important part of this strategy, with an aim to produce a rationalist intelligentsia, who could ensure a relay of ideological justification for their activities (Kaviraj 2010: 61–66). Though the class of new intelligentsia largely remained loyal to this cause, the liberal ideas based on values of rights and liberty encouraged a section of the same intelligentsia to question the

DOI: 10.4324/9781003369257-2

rationale of the colonial rule in India. The press became an effective tool to expose and criticize the British. Such interventions frustrated the attempt to generate legitimacy, which meant that the British rule had to extensively depend on coercion as the primary mode of dominance. They responded by enacting several laws to curb the freedom of the press. This was just the beginning of a series of censorship laws initiated by the British that also witnessed a parallel struggle for the demand of freedom of speech and expression by the native Indians.

Press Censorship and Its Opposition in the Early Nineteenth Century

The formal debate over freedom of speech and expression in India began to take shape from the early 19th century, which, according to C. A. Bayly, was the period of the advent of 'constitutional liberalism' in India. This development, according to him, shared some connection with the great expansion of the press and the idea of association across the world, beginning in the 1780s (2012: 28–34). The first newspaper in India was also started during this period. However, James Augustus Hickey's *Bengal Gazette* or *The Calcutta General Advertiser*, which took off in 1780, was stopped only two years after its inception as its exposure of the private lives of company servants did not go well with the British authorities (Chaudhuri 1955: 291). In 1799, the idea of press censorship became more explicit and official with the Censorship of Press Act introduced by Lord Wellesley. It brought all the newspapers under government scrutiny before their publication. Later, in 1807, it was extended to cover all kinds of press publications – newspapers, magazines, books and pamphlets. The act was revoked by Lord Hastings in 1818. However, the abolition was initiated on the terms that the editors would take responsibility to exclude matters likely to affect the authority of government or be injurious to the public interest.

During this period, Raja Rammohan Roy arose as the undisputed representative of the Indians in the struggle for freedom of speech and expression. Roy's aim was to build an Indian 'public' from the ground up, so that within a generation Indians would begin to share in power and legislative authority (Bayly 2010: 27). His concern for freedom of speech and expression is reflected in his opposition to the arbitrary deportation of editors and formal press censorship. Along with other Indian liberals of his time, like D. N. Tagore, G. C. Bonnerjee and others, Roy wrote a memorial to the Supreme Court against the ordinance initiated by the then acting Governor General John Adam in December 1823, popularly known as the Licensing Regulation Act. When the Supreme Court did not pay heed to the request and went on to register the regulation, he pursued the case further and wrote another memorial, this time addressed to King George IV in London (Roy 1925). These memorials are often cited as evidence of his undaunted love and concern for freedom of speech and expression. The comparison of this document with Milton's *Areopagiticia* seems to be valid not only because it was the first comprehensive appeal in defence of the free press in India as Milton's *Areopagiticia* was in Britain, but also because of the similarity of arguments in both documents. Although it was one of the pioneering tracts in the field, it, like Milton's, cannot be considered a strong argument for liberty per se, but a strategic response to the context in which it was written.

The memorial makes it explicit that Roy was not in support of unbridled freedom, nor was he opposed to already existing laws that limited such freedom, like laws against libel, among others. In fact, he argued that if there were objectionable or seditious publications, the judicial system should render a 'writer or publisher culpable and amenable to punishment' (Roy 1925: 60). Further, he also ensured that should the limitation of the liberty of the press become necessary if it was (1) for the sake of 'greater security and to preserve the union existing between England and this country' or (2) against a seditious attempt to excite hostility with neighbouring or friendly states, the colonial subjects would be perfectly willing to submit to additional penalties to be legally inflicted (1925: 71–72).

Rammohan Roy was sure that an Indian public could come into existence only through the expansion of public knowledge, and the press as an organ of education could play an important role in this. Importantly, there was yet another point raised in defence of a free press that is significant. It was about the role of a free press in religion. The first printing press in India was brought by the Jesuit missionaries from Portugal to Goa in 1556. The publishing of books and pamphlets helped the missionaries to promote and spread their religious viewpoints. Though the British government was largely suspicious of missionary activities, during this period liberal concessions were allowed for papers published by them. For example, the papers published by Seerampore missionaries were never targeted even after the ordinance by John Adam came into effect, whereas the government came down heavily on editors like J. S. Buckingham[1] and C. J. Fair,[2] who were deported for their activities. In the memorandum, Rammohan mentioned the presence of the ideological clash between different religions and how the free press was being used by the native religions to defend themselves from the onslaught of English missionaries, through debates and discussions. He writes:

> After a body of English missionaries have been labouring for about twenty five years by preaching and distributing publications in the native languages in all parts of Bengal, to bring the prevailing system of religion into disrepute, no alarm whatever prevails, because your Majesty's faithful subjects possess the power of defending their religion by the same means that are employed against it, and many of them have exercised the freedom of the press to combat the writings of English missionaries, and think no other protection

> necessary to the maintenance of their faith. While the teachers of Christianity use only reason and persuasion to propagate their religion, your majesty's faithful subjects are content to defend theirs by the same weapons.
>
> (Roy 1925: 60)

This, according to Roy, was a significant contribution of the free press in India, which allowed for debates over key tenets of belief and faith in a non-violent and discursive environment. It is evident that Roy and others did not contemplate that in the future the press could be used to incite communal violence. Though such concerns did not find a place in Milton's *Areopagiticia*, the fact that both were pleas against the Licence Act of their times (in the case of Milton it was to the legislature and in the case of Rammohan to the king) to reconsider the law, and return to the pre-licence phase (thereby status quo) makes them similar in many senses. But similarly in both cases, the defence of freedom of speech and expression was a weak one. It would not be wrong to say that though the Indian liberals of this phase stressed the importance of a free press, they did not include deep concern for an individual's freedom of speech and expression, nor was it seen as a necessary philosophical defence of the former. If anything, the argument for a free press was teleological and not concerned with the value of free speech as a good-in-itself. It prioritized the benefits a free press could have for society, both for the governors as well as the governed. So, the demand for a free press, it can be argued, was not a claim but a plea based on the shared notion of values that it served. Further, a need was seen to reasonably restrict this freedom under laws such as those against libel and sedition. However, Roy's memorial received no response and the act remained in place till it was abolished by Charles Metcalfe, another acting governor general, on persuasion by Lord Macaulay.

British Attitudes towards Free Expression in Colonial India

From the beginning of press culture in India, the British authorities wanted to ensure that press freedom did not pose a threat to their rule. So, though some freedom was allowed, it was always subjected to conditions that determined its scope. The legislation introduced during this period reflects this approach. In the process, the basic tenets of liberalism were modified to develop a creative logic in support of imperial control. The most important advocates of liberalism and free speech, like J. S. Mill, were also engaged in justifying the control over free speech of the colonial subjects (U. Mehta 1999; Parekh 1994: 11–13). One of the important figures who contributed in this redefinition was Thomas Macaulay, who spearheaded the formulation of the IPC.

Regulating Free Speech through Law: The Indian Penal Code (IPC) and Legal Provisions

In 1833, Thomas Macaulay was appointed India's First Law Member and Head of its first Law Commission. The legal system in India, which he inherited, was complex, pluralistic and in many respects unmanageable as it suffered from what James Fitzjames Stephen would later call 'vices of vagueness'.[3] The reference point for Macaulay was his predecessors like James Mill and Charles Grant, who claimed to have exposed the instability, injury and ignorance inherent in the Indian society and believed it to be the duty of the British to assimilate them into the civilizational umbrella and try to improve their condition. Macaulay also envisioned the British Empire as 'an enlightened and paternal despotism', morally obligated to the reform of Indian society. But such moral achievement was not the only driving force. Macaulay's vision was also guided by the material aims of the Raj. 'To trade with civilized men is infinitely more profitable than to govern savages', he maintained (Macaulay 1898: 583). To achieve such aims, Macaulay held it necessary that the language of the laws should be clear, unequivocal and concise.

The lawmaking process of this period was dominated by the Utilitarians, in particular the followers of Jeremy Bentham (Smith 1988; Stokes 1959). Macaulay tried to introduce an attitude that has been described as a 'fusion of utilitarian clarity and rigour with Burkean pragmatism' (Collini, Winch & Burrow 1984: 198). Certainty and clarity were two aspects of Benthamite tradition that remained central for Macaulay. For him, laws should resonate 'uniformity where you can have it; diversity where you must have it; but in all cases certainty' (Macaulay 1898: 578). This was also necessary to 'limit the power which the courts of justice possess of putting their own sense on the laws', rendering them uncertain and contradictory (1898: 424). The codification of penal laws in India was an attempt in this direction. The formulation of the IPC reflected not only the productive engagement of Macaulay in creating 'a concise, lucid and comprehensive code that aimed to minimize discretion, differences in legal status and concessions to local circumstances' (Wright 2011: 19) but also, as K. J. M. Smith (1989: 145) observes, it represented an important episode in the development of criminal jurisprudence and 19th-century intellectual history.

Chapter XXII of the code, entitled *Of Criminal Intimidation, Insult and Annoyance*, is entirely devoted to forms of offensive language not previously criminalized. He introduced various doctrinal innovations in this section to suit the need of the context. For example, he expanded the term 'defamation' to cover libel and slander as well.[4] Together with this, he also rejected the notion that a strict division between speech and acts could be made. He argued that offensive and insulting language should be conceived as speech acts and ought to be a subject to criminal jurisprudence (Macaulay 1898: 121–123). In many ways his idea of 'performative' speech was prescient to the contemporary understandings as reflected in Mackinnon (1996) and

Butler (1997). He proposed that defamatory spoken words should be considered an offence irrespective of whether they actually caused a breach of peace, on the ground that the mental pain they inflict is a sufficient basis for action. The reason for this proposition was also based on his reading of Indian society. He maintained, 'There is perhaps no country in which more cruel suffering is inflicted, and more deadly resentment called forth, by injuries which affect only the mental feelings' (as quoted in Ahmed 2009: 130).

He was particularly concerned about religious insults and devoted a whole chapter entitled *On Offence relating to Religion and Caste* (chapter XV). In the *Notes* he argues that in contexts such as India's, where the relationship between different religions is volatile, dangers 'can only be averted by a firm adherence to the true principle of toleration'.[5] He also emphasized that the penal codes provided an opportunity to inculcate such values in the society by including strict laws against violation. So, laws like section 298 were inserted into the IPC.[6] This understanding of toleration seems to be aimed at making religious beliefs immune to any criticism. He argued that even if the contents of any religion may be wrong, the 'pain which such insults give to the professors of that religion is real'. It cannot be dismissed that such posture was another attempt by the colonial state to boast about its capacity to impartially regulate and administer a multiplicity of particularistic communities through the rule of law, and thereby to justify its imperial mission. However, in the process, Macaulay introduced some unprecedented interventions in the discourse of free speech in India: (1) the 'volatile' context of India and the 'intolerant' public culture were used as reasons to legally limit the scope of free speech; (2) they made space for prosecution against 'mental injury' or feeling of 'offence'; and (3) at least indirectly, they made religions immune to any criticism or questioning, thereby generating a sense of autonomy which had potential to promote orthodoxy. This completely changed the nature of debate about free speech in India, and the burden of legal limitations has guided the discourse since then, which also made it very different from the West.

The legal experts of the time like John Dawson Mayne (1862) and Sir Lawrence Peel (1848) were very critical of Macaulay's approach. They believed that making wounded sentiments a cause for action was a recipe for disaster and should only be subject to sanction when it led a public disorder. Another person who criticized such an approach was James Fitzjames Stephen. Though he lauded the nature of the Codes and their success, he was particularly suspicious of the scope of such provisions like section 298 (Stephen 1883: 322). Section 298 rendered everyone liable to a year's imprisonment who,

> with the deliberate intention of wounding the religious feelings of any person, utters any word or makes any sound in the hearing of that person, or makes any gesture in the sight of that person, or places any object in the sight of that person.

Stephen believed that it would end the possibility to convince any person that his religious beliefs were untrue.

> It is impossible to convince anyone that he is in error upon religious subject without causing him great pain if he really believes in his creed, and the act of addressing cogent and earnest arguments to him on the subject must of necessity involve a deliberate intention of wounding his feelings.
>
> (1883: 312–313)

Though he believed that the intention of the lawmakers was not this and in the hands of the English magistrates it would be interpreted to apply only to wanton insults, Stephen was suspicious that in future if the power came to the hands of Hindu or Muslim government and judges it could cause havoc as it was too easy to make accusations (1883: 312–313).

Stephen was convinced that strong laws and a proactive state were required to maintain peace and order against ever-present threats of inter-communal conflict in societies like India (as quoted in O'Dowd 2013: 271). This understanding of the Indian context became the basis of his criticism of John Stuart Mill's *On Liberty*, expressed by Stephen in his seminal *Liberty, Equality, Fraternity* (1967, written during his voyage back from India. If one compares the attitudes of Stephen and Mill towards imperial policy in India, though there were great overlaps, they also exhibited significant differences. Stephen's advocacy for coercion was a universal and fundamental aspect of his political thought, unlike Mill, who considered it apt only for societies who were still in early stages of civilization (Mill 1978: 10–11).

Stephen was a firm believer that power preceded liberty and 'that liberty from the very nature of things is dependent on power; and that it is only under the protection of a powerful, well organized government that any liberty can exist at all' (Stephen 1967: 183). As far as his understanding about liberty as a value was concerned, he believed that whether liberty was good or bad depended on the particular context, time, place and circumstances. In certain cases, he believed, the curtailment of liberty was pertinent for the larger benefit of the society and cites the example of British coercion in India. He argued that coercion was extremely necessary in the British efforts to direct moral and religious changes in the Indian society in order to civilize it. Stephen notes that important coercive measures in India had proved very fruitful, and that such changes were necessary in the progress towards civilization. As such, he also claimed, coercion helped in the larger cause of human progress. On similar account, praising the British policies in India, he comments:

> 1) They have forced upon the people, utterly against the will of many of them, the principle that people of different religion are to live at peace with each other, that there is to be no fighting and no oppression as between Mahommedans and Hindoos, or different sects of Mahommedans.

2) They have also forced upon the people the principle that change of religion is not to involve civil disabilities. The Act by which this rule was laid down utterly changed the legal position of one of the oldest and most widespread religions of the world. It deprived Brahminism of its principle coercive sanction
3) They have set up a system of education all over the country which assumes the falsehood of the creed of the Hindoos and – less pointedly, but not less effectually – of the Mahommedans.
4) Whenever religious practices violate European ideas of public morality up to a certain point, they have, as in the case of suttee and human sacrifice, been punished as crimes.
5) They compel the natives to permit the presence among them of missionaries whose one object is to substitute their own for the native religion, and who do, in fact, greatly weaken the native religion. (1967: 89)

Stephen's attitude towards the state's role in freedom of speech and expression also becomes evident when he questioned Mill's assumption that compulsion was justifiable until the time 'when mankind have become capable of being improved by free and equal discussion' (Mill 1978: 10–11). He believed that in the absence of the heavy hand of the state, no society can fruitfully value its liberties, and therefore insisted that compulsion was a necessary component of any transformation, and it could never be completely replaced by discussion in any society at any time (Stephen 1967: 70). Stephen's engagement with Mill had particular relevance for India as he had been Law Member of the government of India and had introduced measures to control the press, which Indian liberals regarded as authoritarian (Bayly 2012: 11). Most significant among his contributions was the Special Act No. XXVII of 1870, which inserted section 124(A) in the IPC, and which was at par with the sedition law in England.

The period between Macaulay as Law Commissioner and Stephen as Law Member of the Council of the Viceroy (1838–1869) witnessed important shifts in the approach of the British administration – both in terms of attitude and policy imperatives. The revolt of 1857 and the transfer of powers from the East India Company to the Crown in London marked an important moment in this shift. The earlier emphasis on the universalist project of civilization based on the assumption that non-Western societies were politically dysfunctional was replaced by an aim to understand the logic of native society. There seemed to have appeared a consensus in the post-mutiny context to 'curtail the transformative ambition implied in the civilizing mission and reconstitute the imperial order on a more conservative basis, in line with the "traditional" imperatives of native society' (Mantena 2009: 5). According to D. A. Low (1973: 39–82), this initiated in India a more authoritarian insistence on efficiency and stability as the watchwords of imperial policy, and also a reversal of liberal efforts at civilizing and creative reform in favour of protecting and conserving native society. This approach was manifest when the religious causes of the revolt became evident and Queen Victoria's Proclamation made the principle of non-interference into native religious beliefs and customs the cornerstone of the post-mutiny imperial policy. The proclamation said:

> We declare it to be our royal will and pleasure that none be in any-wise favoured, none molested or disquieted, by reason of their religious faith or observances, but that all shall alike enjoy the equal and impartial protection of the law; and we do strictly charge to enjoin all those who may be in authority under us that they abstain from all interference with the religious belief or worship of any of our subjects on pain of our highest displeasure.
>
> (As quoted in Philips, Singh and Pandey 1962: 11)

The most important representative of this shift was Henry Maine, who advocated the idea of 'indirect rule'[7] based on his study of Indian society. Significant change in the understanding about law – its utility, its goal and more importantly its scope – can also be marked as a direct product of such a shift.[8] Though Warren Hastings had introduced, back in 1772, the colonial distinction between private and public laws – where 'public' applied to property and commerce and personal law pertained to the 'private' realm of women, family, religion and tradition – such classification got a new definition and importance during this period. This classification formed two different spheres of law based on the socio-cultural understanding of Indian society: on the one hand, the British administered universal law in the public sphere; on the other hand, a separate sphere was left for the administration of Hindu and Muslim 'personal law'. As Thomas Metcalf explained: 'The legal system of colonial India thus accommodated both, the assimilative ideals of liberalism, which found a home in the codes of procedure, and insistence upon Indian difference in a personal law defined by membership in a religious community' (1994: 38).

The colonial lawmakers like Maine argued that crime was universally understood, whereas the civil laws touched upon what he called 'the local peculiarity of the country', and hence it was assumed that the reform of the criminal law would meet with the least social resistance. It was not surprising that the Indian Penal Code (1860), the Code of Civil Procedure (1859) and the Code of Criminal Procedure (1861) were the first three codes enacted by the government. It can be argued that for the British Raj, it was an effective tool to manage its firm control over the administrative aspects of the society and still maintain a certain level of legitimacy. But such bifurcation also had the capacity to sanction a higher degree of autonomy to religious groups and make their internal system more closed. Non-interference in religious matters could also establish a freedom to profess and popularize one's religion, which could later be used to criticize and attack other faiths and belief systems.

The British Raj and 'Selective Censorship'

Just after the revolts of 1857, the English language press, largely owned by members of the European community, came down heavily upon the authorities for being too soft and indecisive in punishing the rebels. Lord Canning was at the centre of the wrath, and he reacted by announcing gag orders against the press that remained in force for around a year. A decade later in 1867, an Act for the Regulation of Printing Presses and Newspapers was passed to replace the Metcalfe Act from 1835. This act later came to be known as The Press and Registration of Books Act. After several modifications and amendments in 1890, 1914, 1952 and 1953, this formed a part of the formal law in post-independent India. However, the biggest and most strategic threat to the idea of free press came in 1878 in the form of the Vernacular Press Act, enacted to give better control over newspapers published in Indian languages. It appeared during the Second Anglo-Afghan War (1878–1880) in order to prevent the vernacular press from expressing criticism of British policies. It was only four years later, in 1882, that Lord Ripon repealed the act. One significant feature of the Vernacular Press Act was that it made an explicit distinction between the English language press and the vernacular press (Seal 1968: 143). The distinction was a product of two long-term developments – on the one hand, public opinion in India was largely being defined by the state as the opinions of the 'non-official' European community, which was mostly represented by the English-speaking press; on the other hand, the vernacular press was held responsible not only for supporting developments that led up to 1857 but also for engaging in statements in the years after. For example, Ashley Eden, the Bengal governor, defended the English-speaking press by 'non-official Europeans' and argued that it should be kept outside the impact of the Vernacular Press Act. He said:

> On the whole the English press of India, whether conducted by Europeans or natives, bears evidence of being influenced by a proper sense of responsibility and by a general desire to discuss public events in a moderate and responsible spirit. There is no occasion to subject that press to restraint, and therefore, naturally enough, it is exempted. It would be a sign of great weakness on the part of government to bring it within the scope of this measure merely to meet a possible charge of partiality.
>
> (As quoted in Buckland 1976: 716–717)

The nationalist movement after 1885 gave a new impetus to the development of the press in India; in fact, the press played a significant role in the movements that followed. By the 1890s, when the issues of sedition became more prominent, government geared for new laws. Most significant was the amendment of section 124(A) of the IPC, which was restructured in

1898 to include 'hatred' and 'contempt' along with 'disaffection towards the government' as being worthy of prosecution. This further limited the space for criticism of the administration. The need for the amendment was justified by the authorities in the name of judicial arguments during sedition trials, including Tilak's, which had raised questions about the validity and the scope of the impugned law (Donough 1911: 42–59). When the amendment was being discussed in the Legislative Assembly, it was proposed that promotion of religious enmity should also be included as an offence against the state under section 124(A),[9] as this period also witnessed communal violence between Hindus and Muslims in several parts of the country. However, after deliberations, the Select Committee recommended the inclusion of a separate section within the IPC to deal with such cases. This led to the formation of section 153(A), which punished anyone who with words, either spoken or written, promoted or attempted to promote feelings of enmity or ill will between different classes of subjects, based on religion, race or other factors (Donough 1911: 60–70).

Each important event in local or international politics that had the potential to engage and mobilize public opinion against the British administration was greeted with heavy censorship of the press in India. Although the press in India was never completely free, special tools were used during crisis periods. For example, the Press Act of 1910 and the Defence of India Act 1939 were promulgated against the background of the two World Wars, respectively. Similarly, the Press Emergency Act during the Salt Satyagraha (1931) and the gag orders during the Quit India Movement (1942) were evidence of this approach of the British government. The understanding of 'crisis' was political and instrumental. It lacked objective assessment and was defined primarily based on the interests of the administrators. For example, when the Cow Protection Movement peaked and took violent forms in 1893, the vernacular press in the hands of both communities – Hindus and Muslims – played an important role in sowing distrust and enmity. Yet on this occasion, the government did not respond to the situation with a sense of urgency to prevent communal clashes. A communication between Lord Lansdowne and the Earl of Kimberley, in 1893, indicates that the authorities were well aware how the communal frenzy was spreading so fast all across the country. On a question about 'why ... disturbances are becoming more frequent than in past years', Lansdowne responded:

> One of the causes to which this is due [is] in our opinion, beyond all doubt, the greater frequency of communication and the interchange of news by post and telegraph between different parts of the country.... This rapid dissemination of news and increasing activity of controversy, carried on through the Press, by public meetings, and by the addresses of itinerant preachers, is in some respects a new feature in Indian life, and is one which is likely to grow and add considerably to the difficulties of administration.[10]

Further, he also gives a detailed account of how it was happening:

> In addition to the inflammatory harangues delivered to meetings of Hindus, [wandering ascetics] have distributed throughout the country pictures of the cow, of a kind calculated to appeal strongly to the religious sentiment of the people. One of them, for instance, depicts a cow in the act of being slaughtered by three Muhammadan butchers, and is headed 'the present state'. Another exhibits a cow, in every part of whose body groups of Hindu deities and holy persons are shown, being assailed by a monster with a drawn sword entitled the 'KaliYug' but which has been largely understood as typifying the Muhammadan community.

However, no action was taken to prevent dissemination of such controversial material. Similarly, in the chromolithograph *Chaurasi Devata Auvali Gay*, published by Ravi Verma Press in 1915, which represented a cow with depictions of different Hindu gods in its body and a demon drawing its sword to sacrifice it, the demon was interpreted to be Muslim, and it led to riots in different parts of north India.[11] Such situations were further fuelled by the actions of the authorities. As one of the officers wrote,

> The whole anti-kine-killing movement is, of course, antagonistic to European and Muhammadans. That is inevitable. Therefore it may be said that the picture reflects upon these races, which is true; but *we tolerate the agitation as long as it does not become too violent*, and I should not describe the picture as a particularly violent manifestation of it.[12]

The government did not proscribe this broadside due to the fear that it would be charged of being pro-Muslim (Barrier 1974: 61).

Though the administration had such precise details, very little was done to prevent such circulations in different parts of the country. Even when some kind of censorship was imposed to prevent communal tensions, it was always on the pretext of appeals from local officers, who in most cases were natives. This prevented the British authorities from taking direct responsibility for such acts, and in many cases it led to further uproar as it was assumed that the presiding officer was supporting the cause of his own religious brethren in an indirect way. The case of Munshi Inderman of Moradabad in 1879 illustrates how the spread of print was sharpening existing cleavages and exposing new kinds of social tensions. Inderman, who was a follower/member of the Arya Samaj, had been writing and publishing extensively against Islam and practices of the Muslim community. The Muslim groups, through their press, had been continuously urging the district administration to take steps to prevent such offensive publications, but in vain.[13] Later the magistrate imposed a fine on Inderman and ordered destruction of all the copies of the objectionable books he had published. It was found that the magistrate's orders were based on evidence provided by the Deputy Collector, who happened to be a Muslim. This incident was given a communal colour and popularized to demonstrate that now Muslims in public offices were practicing 'oppression and tyranny upon the Hindus'.[14] The Lahore Hindi weekly *Mittra Vilas* regretted that a 'distinguished disciple' of Dayananda Saraswati should be treated so severely when many offensive Christian Missionary publications went unpunished (Jalal 2000: 82). Attempt was made to mobilize public opinion against both enemies simultaneously – the colonial state as well as the Muslims. In the context of the Arya Samaj movement, this strategy helped further polarization.

Commenting on the attitude of the government vis-à-vis censorship during this period, N. G. Barrier (1974) opines that it barred any title strongly critical of Western civilization or Christianity and was also very strict against any publication against the government and left no stone unturned to charge the offenders under the laws of sedition. Even the courtrooms, in cases of writings against the administration, were used only as signifiers of government's faith in the legal system and its inherent respect for freedom of the press, but in reality the government used all the possibilities at hand to punish such offenders (1974: 63). However, in the case of religious vilification and insult among Hindus and Muslims, even after being well aware of the propaganda, the colonial rulers took calculated steps, exhibiting 'selective censorship'. Robert Darnton (2001, 2002) also notes that government freely used all available means to ensure that those guilty of generating public opinion against the government's policies or actions could not escape the web of law. They had developed strict literary surveillance on the publications in India, and if anything was found to be against their liking, it was deterred and repressed, but such urgency was never visible in issues related to religious insults and offence (Darnton 2001).

It is evident from the above discussion that, on the one hand, the British authorities were not averse to the idea of framing new laws to control what they held to be misuse of freedom of speech and expression. However, they were selective in the use of these laws, especially when it involved the subject of religion, as on the one hand they wanted to project their non-interference on religious matters of the colonial subjects, and on the other hand, they feared that if they acted against members of one community, they would be blamed for favouring the other. So, unlike the political subjects, the government acted in the controversies over religion selectively, considering all the risks and benefits involved.

The Indian Nationalists' Position on the Question of Freedom of Expression

The post-mutiny period witnessed major socio-political changes within the internal structure of Indian society. In politics, a significant development was the formation of the Indian National Congress in 1885, which later led the nationalist response to British colonial rule. Similarly, in the field of religion, this phase saw a wide range of experimental explorations initiated by reformers and revivalists. There were reformers who were using liberal vocabularies to challenge the conservatives (Bayly 2012: 11). Contrarily, it also gave rise to sections of orthodox fundamentalists within each religion, who opposed any kind of attempts to revive or reform. Such conservatives sought to guard the inner citadel of their religions against any form of external intervention or interrogations. Evidently, there was a rise of new forms of communal consciousness, which by the 1880s and 1890s became an all-India phenomenon (Chandra 1990; Sarkar 1983). For example, Christophe Jaffrelot (1999: 11–12) argues that this was when Hindu nationalism was constructed as an ideology and derived from the socio-religious movements initiated by high-caste Hindus, such as the Arya Samaj. The printing press became an important site in the process of cultural self-definition, and also the realm in which 19th-century communalism developed. The early nationalists like Rammohan Roy, who argued that the freedom of the press was important for a non-violent clash of religious ideologies, had not contemplated that the same freedom would be used in the future to incite violence in the name of religion. It was obvious, therefore, that the attitude of Indians of this period towards freedom of speech and expression was different than that of Roy.

Communal Consciousness during the 1870s and the Role of Freedom of Speech and Expression

Historians have held that in India, two ideologies – nationalism and communalism – had simultaneous and parallel growth trajectories (Chandra 1990; Jaffrelot 1999; Sarkar 1983). The British policy of non-interference in the internal matters of religion further allowed a space for cultivation of communal ideologies. Sandra Freitag (1989) has shown how public arena activities like religious ceremonies among the Hindu and Muslim groups helped in consolidating communal consciousness and also became the breeding ground for violent clashes as witnessed during language controversies over Hindi-Urdu or the Cow Protection Movement. The same movements also produced local leaders who carried the baton of the nationalist response to colonial rule.

Partha Chatterjee has claimed that in the wake of colonial modernity, the 'spiritual' or 'inner' domain of culture, such as language, or religion, or the elements of personal and family life, was central to nationalists, and the

> more nationalism engaged in its contest with the colonial power in the outer domain of politics the more it insisted in displaying the marks of "essential" cultural difference so as to keep out the colonizer from that inner domain of national life and to proclaim its sovereignty over it.
>
> (1993: 26)

So, on the one hand, nationalists fought relentlessly to eradicate 'colonial difference' in the outer domain, but on the other hand, they struggled to protect their inner/spiritual domain, thereby retaining its difference. In this way Chatterjee responds to the claims of Benedict Anderson (1983) and Edward Said (1978), who suggested that the colonized people confronted their domination and imagined their nationalism through the discourses made available by the West. In his work, Chatterjee explored one of the ways in which the active and creative process of self-fashioning happened in the colonial context. But as Ayesha Jalal (2000) and Neeladri Bhattacharya (2005), among others, have demonstrated, Chatterjee's assumptions seem to be based on his study of Bengal's middle-class Hindu society. In their respective works, these scholars have shown that there were alternative strategies which were utilized by different sections of the population to counter the threat of cultural invasion. In this context, Jalal (2000) talks about the process of identity formation among Muslims and the way they had to negotiate their space in the nationalist discourse, which was overwhelmingly dominated by Hindu majoritarianism. Bhattacharya (2005) discusses the constant interaction between the 'private' and the 'public' sphere (especially between religion and law) through which the colonial subject defined itself.

Furthermore, the categories Chatterjee uses (of 'inner' and 'outer' sphere) do not seem to engage with the fact that though the 'inner' domain of the colonized was different from the colonizer, it was not homogeneous. The insistence of essential difference between the 'inner' spheres raised possibilities for a multiplicity of subjectivities which consolidated in different forms of available spaces. Hence the forms of consciousness found in this 'inner' domain took multiple forms, motivated by divergent interests – religion, caste, language, among others. Even within religious consciousness, there were several strands/layers – some dominated by the orthodox sections and the other by the revivalists and reformists. The use of modern statistical tools like the census and mapping by the British further added to this process of consolidation. So, even if it was a strategy by the nationalist elites to counter the impact of imperialism in their 'inner' or 'spiritual' domain, it made way for further disintegration and increasing differences among themselves. Also, 'private' and 'public' spheres often intermingled in multiple ways. So there were situations where components of public sphere interacted with the private and vice versa, and such interactions had the capacity to reconstitute and redefine the other sphere. Consider, for example, the sphere of religion. According to Chatterjee, it would form a part of the 'inner' or 'spiritual' domain, and this sphere was guarded by freedom of belief and faith. Similarly, freedom of speech and expression was something of 'public' or 'outer' domain as it was situated in the realm of law, and there was a constant demand to grant such equal rights as enjoyed by the European inhabitants. If the 'inner' and 'outer' spheres existed as autonomous, how do we understand the phenomenon wherein such freedom was also used by different socio-religious groups to not only profess and popularize one's own religion but in the process vilify other beliefs and encourage conversion? The role of the vernacular press, tracts and pamphlets published in the period are evidence of such strategy. In a way, it can be argued that the freedom in the 'external' domain was being used to impact belief and faith, which constituted the 'inner' domain. This form of interaction between the private and public spheres also became a problem for the British administrators, as they were not sure whether to intrude in certain domains. So, though the realm of the communal press remained embedded in the structure of colonial rules, it was relatively autonomous of the direct patronage of the colonial state (Gilmartin 1998). The communal consciousness that occurred under the effect of print during this period did not give rise to a 'public sphere' as understood by Habermas (1992) in a European context, but rather made the public space itself a site of multiple contestations and differences. 'Lay leaders'[15] played a prominent role, utilizing the new techniques of journalism, public preaching and debates, tracts and book writing to promote and profess their ideology. This process also included the invocation of 'history' to define and distinguish different communities.[16]

Initially the printing press was used by Indians to expose the role of Christian missionaries.[17] But soon these same critical tools were directed by Hindu and Muslim groups against each other, exposing the fissures in the religious organization of Indian society. The opposition in this politics was constituted through an imagination of the 'other', which changed according to the context of the clashes. So for example, in Punjab when the activities of the Arya Samaj became prominent, they were challenged by the growth of two different streams – the Sanatanis from within the Hindus and the Singh Sabhas from the Sikhs. However, when the Cow Protection Movement became popular, the natural 'other' was found in the Muslims, and on many occasions, one could see tacit understanding among the Arya Samajists, the Sanatanis and the members of Sikh Sabhas to fight against the common enemy, in this case the Muslims (Barrier 1992; Metcalf 1992).[18]

Though the literate population was still very small, one did not need to be a literate to be aware of such struggles, which often were fuelled by rumours that were transmitted by the spoken word (Bayly 2009; Guha 2009). The contents of newspapers and pamphlets were also disseminated through word of mouth at bazaars and local fairs to rouse communitarian emotions (Jalal 2000). Various newspapers and pamphlets of this period also voiced their resentment and questioned the colonial government's proclaimed policy of impartiality in the domain of religion. Some of the newspapers urged the government to ban all publications intended to inflame religious passions, but in vain. They equally opposed the virus of conversion that was infecting social peace and urged the state to take steps in this regard.[19] The demand for censorship had started to emerge from among the Indians, and it was mainly based on the logic of preventing the misuse of the freedom of press and publication to vilify and denigrate religious symbols and personage, which led to the incitement of communal hatred among different religious communities. However, such demands were largely overlooked by the British authorities.

By the beginning of the 20th century, clashing communitarian narratives, ostensibly emanating from the 'private' domain, flowed in unrestrained form into a public arena of informal politics (Jalal 2000). Freitag (1989) discusses in her work how the public arena became the site of new forms of communal consciousness that contributed both in the project of nationalism as well as communal self-definition. Many of the nationalists during this period were also deeply religious, and often the political use of religious categories blurred the line between nationalism and communalism (Metcalf & Metcalf 2012: 150). This process had two-way repercussions. On one side, the creative energy generated by such consciousness was used in the service of nationalism. For example, Tilak used Ganesh Puja as a public event to facilitate community participation and build a new grassroots unity between Brahmins and non-Brahmins, which contributed significantly to the nationalist project, especially in western India (Kaur 2003; Metcalf & Metcalf 2012). At the same time, such communal consciousness also inflamed fundamental differences and gave rise to new forms of inter-community conflicts that often took the shape of violent riots. As Barbara Metcalf (1992) notes, unlike the European experience, where national loyalty dominated, in the colonial areas, communal divisions were decisive. In India, according to her, this happened due to two significant developments. Firstly, 'representation' and 'communalism' were linked. The British had created a 'form of government structured on representation, in which leaders to be effective had to claim to speak for the interests of communities' (1992: 231). This meant that it was not individuals but communities defined by religious identities that engaged with the colonial state. This led to, as Freitag (1996) has also shown, politicization of religious identities. Secondly, Metcalf also points out that 'the colonial appropriation of public and civic institutions encouraged a kind of retreat to domestic and religious space as sites where cultural values could be reworked and renewed' (1992: 231). In this process, religious vocabulary attained the role of legitimate expression against the colonial rule. Not only this, even when spaces within civic and public institutions were later created for representation of Indian interests, these were so limited in scope that the issues of religion dominated the debates within these spaces. For example, in Allahabad, the electoral rivalry between Motilal Nehru and Madan Mohan Malviya during 1920s revolved around the question of 'who was a better Hindu?' and was dominated by issues like beef eating, organizing the Ram Lila procession and so on (Jaffrelot 2010: 350–353). This suggests how electoral mobilization, even when it involved such avowedly secular leaders as Motilal Nehru, tended to be assimilated into debates defined by communal consciousness during this period.

The practice of surveillance and control on different forms of expression by the British authorities also contributed to the process of communal consciousness. It led to a new tendency among the nationalists to use religious idioms in order to articulate their political aspirations (Pinney 2009).[20] Freitag (1989) argues that because the 'British viewed "political" activities as discrete from "religious" or cultural ones', such attempts were less susceptible to strict censorship. This gave an alternative way to convey the same idea in a covert way. However, the use of religious aspects in national consciousness also opened the dangers of misinterpretations and communal polarization as most of these new experiments used references from Hindu mythologies and tried to portray the superiority of the Hindu race. Take, for example, the religious idioms used in plays written by Indians in the late-19th century. In 1876, the government passed the Dramatic Performances Act to 'prohibit dramatic performances' that were 'seditious or obscene, or otherwise prejudicial to the public interests', 'likely to excite feelings of disaffection to the government established by law in British India', or 'likely to deprave and corrupt persons present at the performance' (Bhatia 2010: 191). The immediate reason for such legislation was the popularity and impact in Bengal of plays like Dinnabandhu Mitra's *Nil Darpan* (1860), Dakshina Charan Chattopadhayay's *Chakar Darpan* (1875), Upendra Nath Das's *Surendra-Binodini* (1875), *Ganjananda and the Prince* (1876) and *Police of Pig and Sheep* (1876). Through these performances, the playwright not only explicitly showcased the atrocities of the government, but also appealed for unity to overthrow the Raj. However, under strict censorship initiated by the new law, the writers had to change the plots and characters. So, plays were now based on mythologies, and the British characters, which were earlier at the centre of criticism, were replaced by the anglicized Indian character carved by imperial rule (Pamment 2009). This antagonized the new middle-class intelligentsia, who along with some from the Brahmin sections had even earlier objected to the plays on grounds of obscenity, to misrepresentation of women subjects and even to the stage performances by women. Further, being based on Hindu mythologies, these plays also lacked appeal to the Muslims: indeed, if anything, the call to Hindu pride put Muslims off. There is evidence that some of these plays were being used with multiple purposes – on the one hand, to expose the British and the other to counter the Muslims claims, especially during the Cow Protection Movement and the Hindi-Urdu controversy (King 1992).

The examples cited above indicate the way that religious symbols were used to speak simultaneously the language of communalism and nationalism. But such symbolism often contained communal overtones, and in the backdrop of multiple moments of religious violence and a culture of vilification of the other religion, the religious differences became more prominent. The situation worsened in the 1920s, and with the extreme political polarization of religious identities, government had to come up with new regulations, in the form of 295(A), which followed the famous *Rangila Rasul* (The Merry Prophet) case in 1927. The most significant aspect of this legislation, however, was that the demand for a law to curtail freedom of expression had emanated from Indians themselves and was passed by the

Central Legislature, which contained a reasonable number of Indian representatives. Though such demands were not new, in the charged political climate, they took on a completely new dimension.

The Rangila Rasul *Controversy and the Making of Section 295(A)*

The *Rangila Rasul* controversy was shaped and propelled in the context of 1920s Punjab. The Non-cooperation-Khilafat phase of Indian politics (1919–1921) represented an unprecedented scale of collaboration between the two largest religious communities of India – the Hindus and the Muslims. However, by 1922, after a sudden call-off of the movement by Gandhiji following the mass violence at Chauri Chaura, things began to change. The void created by the nationalistic politics was overtaken by competing religious sentiments. This was further fuelled by the Shudhi (purification) and Sangathan (organization) movement launched by the Arya Samajists in North India. This was equally and strongly reciprocated by the Muslims. The printing press again became a significant means for propaganda setting, and very soon the reports of communal clashes replaced the news about the nationalist movement as headlines of most major dailies. It turned into a bitter war of tracts and pamphlets which involved not only criticism of each other's faith but went as far as to vilify prominent figures of the other religion. It was in this context that the pamphlet *Rangila Rasul* first appeared.

The tract was published and distributed by Raj Pal, an Arya Samaj polemicist, and it was aimed to denigrate the image of the Prophet Mohammad by primarily mocking his marriages and sex life.[21] The publication appeared in response to another Urdu tract entitled *Unisveen Sadi ka Maharishi* (The Great Sage of the Nineteenth Century), penned by a Muslim fanatic to counter the alleged criticism and misrepresentation of the Prophet and Islam in Satyarth Prakash, the most revered book of the Arya Samajists. When the demand for the banning of the tract *Unisveen aid ka Maharishi* was raised, the government rejected it, citing the absence of 'any general public feeling', 'lack of any public motive' and no formal complaint, unlike *Rangila Rasul*, which 'attracted immediate attention' and received 'wide publicity and was condemned by certain Hindu as well as Muhammadan papers' (as quoted in Kumar 1997: 51). Consequently, Raj Pal was arrested under section 153(A) of the IPC. Though Raj Pal was convicted and sentenced by the lower courts, he was eventually acquitted by the Lahore High Court.[22]

The Case in the Lahore High Court

The final appeal in the case was directed to the High Court at Lahore, where Justice Dalip Singh heard it and handed down the judgement on 4 May 1927 (case details present as *Raj Pal, AIR 590 [Lahore]*). After extensive examination of the evidence and contents of the pamphlet, he concluded that the pamphlet was 'undoubtedly… a scurrilous satire on the founder of the Muslim religion'. In strong words, he maintained that it was a ridiculous piece of writing, liable to 'arouse the contempt of all decent persons of whatever community'. However, he insisted that he could not find anything that showed 'it was meant to attack the Mohammedan religion as such or to hold up Mohammedans as objects worthy of enmity and hatred'. So, he very 'reluctantly' acquitted the petitioner as he believed that the subject in question – malicious satire on the personal life of a religious teacher – was outside the purview of section 153(A). He further suggested that if such writings were to be convicted, there was a need for passage of a law to amend the code 'by which the publication of pamphlets published with the intention of wounding the religious feelings of any person or of insulting the religion of any person might be made criminal'. But because he had to base his judgement in the case upon existing law, he ordered acquittal of the appellant.

The judgement received polarized reactions. It was proclaimed as the victory of Hindu religion by the Arya Samajists. On the other hand, protest meetings were held by Muslims all over India, the one in Lahore being attended by around 10,000 Muslims. It was held that the court had failed in protecting the honour of the Prophet. This caused a serious law-and-order crisis in Punjab. Discussing the situation, Punjab governor Hailey commented:

> There was really a very serious danger of disorder, for an attack on the Prophet was a concrete offence against Islam that stung them to the quick, and they could not bear the thought that Hindus could repeat it with impunity.
>
> (Hailey to Vincent, August 11, 1927, in *Hailey MSS* [Eur. C. 152], IOL/R)

On 11 June, due to the rising fear for the law-and-order situation, Hailey moved beyond the set protocol and met a Muslim deputation.[23] He admitted to them that the judgement had left the government 'much concerned'. He said that he sympathized with those Muslims who felt 'justifiably offended' by the pamphlet, and if required, the government would also seek amendment of the law in order to extend its application as suggested by Justice Dalip Singh. Though the liberal Muslims were convinced by Hailey's promises, according to the popular press reports, these voices were silenced by the strong feeling of betrayal and sense of victimhood felt by the agitated popular Muslim response.[24]

In Punjab, a demand for the resignation of Justice Dalip Singh and reversal of the judgement delivered by him was growing. A radical opinion was expressed under the title 'Resign' in *Muslim Outlook* of 14 June 1927, in which both – the judgement in the *Rangila Rasul* case and Justice Dalip

Singh – were abusively criticized. It included grave allegations against impartiality, justice and the integrity of Justice Singh (Barrier 1974: 100).[25] The demand for his resignation was further echoed by other newspapers. Responding to the situation, government arrested D. S. Bukhari, the editor of the daily, and its printer, Nur-ul-haq, on the charges of contempt of court.[26]

The situation worsened with these arrests. Though Bukhari and Nur-ul-haq were punished under the charges of contempt of court, it was widely perceived differently in connection with the *Rangila Rasul* case. The general feeling among the Muslims was that the government had been vigilant and interested in punishing for the offence of contempt of court but was casual on the issue of the contempt of their Prophet. The sense of anger was rooted in what was seen as a case of bias in favor of Hindus and victimization of the Muslims. The news and the interpretations of the cases spread rapidly all over the country, and the press reported reactions in the form of protest meetings, *hartals* (strikes) and Hindu boycotts from different regions.

The community antagonism was at its peak, and the government was under pressure to restore the faith of protesting Muslims in the justice system. Within a few months, in another similar case involving Devi Sharan Sharma, who published a similar tract entitled *Sair-i-Dozakh* (Passage to Hell) in *Risala Vartman*, the publisher was held guilty and punished. In this case the judges argued against the logic of Dalip Singh and held that any kind of 'promotion of feeling of hatred' in any form was prohibited. Justice Broadway stated that 'any criticism of a religious leader, whether dead or alive, falls within the ambit of section 153(A) of IPC' (*Devi Sharan Sharma and another v. King Emperor* [1927] 14 AIR 594 [Lahore]). The importance the government attached to this particular case can be gleaned from the fact that Justice Broadway, then on vacation, was especially asked to return to Punjab for the court hearing in the hope that he would reverse the earlier decision.[27]

Broadway's judgement delivered what the government was expecting. But it could do nothing to improve the law-and-order situation in the country. The harsh punishment pronounced in the case was enough to alienate the Hindus, especially in United Province and elsewhere. It was argued that in each case of religious vilification it was Hindus who were prosecuted, and no action was initiated against Muslim authors who wrote similar tracts against Hindu deities. It was further held that the harsh punishment delivered in the *Vartman* case was only because of the hysteria created by Muslims after the *Rangila Rasul* case, and the government had buckled under their pressure. Mass meetings were organized all over the United Provinces to condemn and protest against the attitude of Muslims and of government officials.[28]

The Bill in the Legislature

Though the *Vartman* case went as desired by the government, it was thought that uncertainty should be avoided. There was a looming fear of a judgement like *Rangila Rasul* coming up in the future, especially, with the kind of uncertainty it had generated vis-à-vis section 153(A). The doubt over such judicial issues needed to be clarified, and the only way of doing it was by introducing a revision of the law. It was also believed to be helpful in winning back the lost confidence and goodwill among the Muslims. Unlike the popular Muslim demand for legislation, particularly against such vilification of the Prophet, Hailey recommended drafting a general section which could prohibit attack upon any sacred symbol of all religions. Hailey believed that a general law of this nature could find support both among the Muslims and the Hindus, who had been equally vocal in their criticism when the matter came to discussion in the Punjab Legislative Council.[29] The decision to legislate the Religious Insult Bill to amend the required sections of IPC was approved by the Viceroy, and the bill was put on the table for discussion in the August session of the Central Legislative Assembly.

From the time of introduction of the bill to its way through the Select Committee and its final passage, there were several dissenting voices. Most of the dissenters felt that the legislation was being pushed through hurriedly. B. P. Naidu called it a 'panicky legislation' and along with others reiterated the request for a wide circulation of the bill so that responses could be sought from all sections whose interests were at stake.[30] Some members also charged the government of appeasement by acting so hastily on the demands raised by a set of Muslims in north India.[31] Amar Nath Dutt termed it as the 'favourite wife policy'.[32] A large section of the dissenters also believed that there already existed enough such laws, and if the government truly wanted to maintain peace and order in society, it did not need an additional law.

However, the most serious questions were raised about the scope of the bill – about its aims, the fear of misuse and its failure to address the real issues. Though it was recognized that the bill that appeared after the Select Committee stage was much better than what was initially proposed, it did not end all worries. There was a general feeling among dissenters that the bill would not be able to achieve its aims as it did nothing to address the real problem – the causes of Hindu-Muslim tension – since the scurrilous writings were only a product of such tension.[33]

Significantly, there was another issue that received shared concerns from most members across religious and other affiliations. Lajpat Rai, Jinnah, Kunzru and Madan Mohan Malviya were all in support of legitimate criticism of religion or religious reform, especially if made in works of historical importance.[34] Largely it was a concern that the freedom of speech and expression should not be restrained to such an extent that it lost its meaning and true value. Though most of these members were worried about the fate of freedom of expression, the presence of contingent situations forced them to compromise. Freedom of speech and expression in the colonial context, after all, was just a desired claim and not a legal or fundamental right. The lawmakers considered it more important to counter the temporary threat that it was having on public order and tranquillity. There was also a suggestion in the form of amendment that the law be made applicable only for a limited duration, and this was widely supported by the likes of Lajpat Rai and S. Iyengar, but it lost by a close margin.[35] Section 295(A) as finally adopted said:

> Whoever with deliberate and malicious intention of outraging the religious feelings of any class of His Majesty's subjects, by words, either spoken or written, or by visible representations, insults or attempts to insult the religion or the religious belief of that class, shall be punished with imprisonment of either description for a term which may extend to two years, or with fine, or with both.
> (*The Gazette of India*, 24 September 1927)

The case further reflected what I have earlier referred to as an attitude towards using the law for 'selective censorship'. The government did not ban earlier pamphlets like *Unisveen Sadi ka Maharishi* on the pretext that 'no serious threat was visible', whereas it was evident that *Rangila Rasul* was written in reaction of those tracts. If the government would have acted earlier, it is possible that the incumbent situation could have been avoided. Such inaction encouraged aberrants like Raj Pal and raised several issues about the intentions of the government, which were also reflected in the debates in the Assembly.[36] At the same time, it can be seen as a conscious and calculated move to assert the capacity of the state to act as a neutral arbitrator of 'supposedly endemic and inevitable religious conflicts' (Ahmed 2009: 173). In this regard, one should not overlook the fact that section 295(A) was structured in the form of a law for public order and aimed at preventing vilification of religious belief and personalities of all sections. At least in this sense it was projected as a secular law, thereby also upholding its promise of neutrality on religious matters.[37] So, without direct intervention on religious matters, the British could claim to have developed a law that protected the interests of all religious communities.

But how does one understand the role of native Indian representatives in the legislature during the making of section 295(A)? Neeti Nair has argued that in the context of 'competitive communalism', this moment should be seen as a case of 'legislative pragmatism', where leaders from opposition parties came together to stop wanton attacks on religious figures and create an atmosphere for dialogue between the two communities (2013: 329). A close analysis of the Assembly debate suggests that this analysis is not entirely correct. Firstly, as discussed earlier, the primary reason cited by most of the members who were against the bill was fear of political misuse and increase in space for executive action. Secondly, the proceedings of Assembly also reflected sharp divisions on religious lines. It would not be entirely correct to claim, as Neeti Nair does, that the leaders rose above their loyalties and affiliations (2013: 317). In contrast, they seem to hold strongly religious lines of arguments.[38] Most of the Muslim legislators were in favour of the bill, and among those who voted against the bill, most were Hindus.[39] The charges levelled by several Hindu members that the bill was an extension of a Muslim appeasement policy of government has already been discussed. In fact, many of those Hindu members who supported the bill did so only because they believed that prohibition and check on scurrilous writings would be equally beneficial for all religious denominations. Thirdly, though the concern for freedom of expression was raised, it was not centrally addressed. Doubts about the bill's impact on freedom of expression largely remained confined in the arguments of professional pressmen, who feared that such law would directly impact their lives. At all other times when the concern was raised about its impact on historical research or religious reforms, it was never seriously dealt with, and no remedy was therefore suggested. It was not surprising that the claim about the bill's impact on freedom of speech and expression was easily overshadowed by the concern for the emergent communal situation and thereby the need to empower the state to maintain public order and tranquility. It is for this reason that a 'consensus', as claimed by Nair, could be reached. But the fact remains that the debates in the Assembly lacked any serious discussions about the fate of freedom of speech and expression, and at the same time the participants overwhelmingly used overtly religious arguments in order to underline the need for such laws. Law was seen as an instant means to protect emotional subjects from hurt in a context where vilification of religion and religious figures had become a regular phenomenon. I doubt that this approach can be called 'legislative pragmatism', as Nair has claimed. If anything, the role of the Indian representatives in the Assembly reflects a sense of urgency and short-sightedness. In an attempt to provide instant protection to religious sensibilities from hurt, they failed to contemplate the long-term repercussions that such a law could have on the basic rights of people.[40] The most significant aspect of the debates in the Assembly was that native leaders engaged in a process of deliberation on a law that was going to govern their lives and impact their basic liberties in a fundamental way. However, a consensus was implicit in the process of deliberation that some rational limits had to be drawn in order to check religiously offensive speech acts. This aspect dominated the proceedings of the legislature, and the importance rendered to such a law in overcoming topical issues marred the possibility of an assessment of its probable implications.

The Nationalist Discourse and the Dichotomy over Freedom of Expression

Running parallel to the attempts at censorship by British authorities was also the story of nationalists' struggle for 'fundamental rights'. The first explicit demand for fundamental rights appeared in the Constitution of India Bill, 1895. Article 16 of this bill included a variety of rights like free speech, free education and others (Rao 1967). A series of congressional resolutions adopted in the period 1917–1919 also reiterated the concern for civil liberties. During this time, the central concern was to gain equal rights as the British in India and as the Britons had among themselves in England. However, by the mid-twenties the aim was changed, and with the demand of *swaraj* taking centre-stage, the comparisons were replaced by a thesis about complete freedom (Austin 1997: 50). Mrs Besant's Commonwealth of India Bill (1925) was reflective of this spirit. It laid down that individual liberty, freedom of conscience, free expression of opinion, free assembly and equality before the law were to be ensured. The *Nehru Report*, prepared by a committee headed by Motilal Nehru and formed by a resolution by the Madras Congress, reiterated this position. It declared that the first concern of Indians was to 'secure the fundamental rights that have been denied to them'. In this report, the desire to afford protection to minorities was especially prominent. For example, the right to freedom of conscience and to the free profession and practice of religion was included explicitly to prevent 'one community dominating over another'. It declared,

> Another reason why great importance attaches to a declaration of rights is the unfortunate existence of communal differences in the country. Certain safeguards are necessary to create and establish a sense of security among those who look upon each other with distrust and suspicion. We could not better secure the full enjoyment of religious and communal rights to all communities than by including them among the basic principles of the constitution.[41]

It is explicit that in nationalists' understanding, religious and communal rights were not seen as antithetical to individual rights; rather, it was held that they could co-exist harmoniously. The Karachi Resolution of Congress (1931) on Fundamental Rights and Economic and Social Change, which was both a declaration of rights and a humanitarian socialist manifesto, took the demand forward (Austin 1997: 56). Continuing this spirit was the *Sapru Report* of 1945 that declared:

> What the constitution demands and expects is perfect equality between one section of the community and another in the matter of political and civic rights, equality of liberty and security in the enjoyment of the freedom of religion, worship, and the pursuit of the ordinary application of life.
>
> (Sapru 1945: 260)

All these were important reference points when the fundamental rights were debated in the Constituent Assembly, and freedom of speech and expression featured in all these documents, reflecting a kind of unanimity on the issue.

Situations like the *Rangila Rasul* controversy exposed the lack of clarity among the nationalists on the question of freedom of speech and expression. On the one hand, they were demanding greater freedom to criticize the colonial government,[42] and on the other hand, they were not very sure how to respond when such freedom was used for vilification of religious symbols and personalities. This was further evident when *Satyarth Prakash* (The Light of Truth), the most important book of Arya Samaj, was banned in Sind in 1944. The demand for the ban had been made time and again by several Muslim groups since its publication in 1875, as they insisted that it contained severe insulting references to the Prophet Mohammad and to Islam, which according to them was offensive to Muslims all over the country. But the British did not endorse their position. In December 1943, during a public meeting in Karachi, the Muslim League reiterated this demand and appealed for action. In 1944, due to immense pressure from Muslim public opinion, the Sind government, led by the Muslim League, announced the ban. Gandhi was distressed with the ban. He maintained, 'Satyarth Prakash enjoys the same status for 40 lakhs of Arya Samajists as the Koran for the Muslims and the Bible for the Christians' (*Harijan*, 3 November 1946). He argued in his article entitled *Sind bans Satyarth Prakash*:

> The virtue of toleration is never strained, especially in matters of religion. Differences of religious opinion will persist to the end of time. Toleration is the only thing that will enable persons belonging to different religions to live as good neighbours and friends. Religion never suffers by reason of the criticism – fair or foul of critics, it always suffers from the laxity or indifference of its followers.
>
> (*Harijan*, 3 November 1946)

Ironically, about the same book, writing in *Young India* in 1924 in an article entitled 'Hindu-Muslim Tension: Its Cause and Cure', Gandhi had said:

> I have read Satyarth Prakash, the Arya Samaj Bible.... I have not read a more disappointing book from a reformer so great.... He has unconsciously misrepresented Jainism, Islam, Christianity and Hinduism itself.... One having even cursory acquaintance with these faiths could easily discover the errors into which the great reformer was betrayed.

Although he was extremely critical about *Satyarth Prakash*, he believed the banning of the book was uncalled for. Gandhi's position with regard to *Satyarth Prakash* indicated his approach to the question of tolerance and his discomfort with the idea of banning any form of publication. Rather, the remedy he suggested to counter writings containing vilification or denigration of other religions was different. In his article 'Hindu-Muslim Tension:

Its Cause and Cure', Gandhi was particularly critical of writings – tracts and pamphlets – which according to him had played a significant role in heightening Hindu-Muslim tensions. But he believed that the best mechanism to counter this competitive vilification of each other's religion was the role that local community leaders should play, for instance, by taking measures to find ways of 'stopping these publications or, at least, discrediting them and distributing clean literature instead, showing tolerance for each other's faith' (Gandhi 1967: 261). He also insisted on creating a public opinion that could reject such incitements. He believed that the regulatory and legal mechanisms failed 'to serve the purpose intended, except temporarily, and in no case do they convert the writers.... The real remedy is healthy public opinion that will refuse to patronize poisonous journals' (*Harijan*, 28 May 1931).

Gandhi's was a moral position on the subject and also reflective of his general aversion to the role that law and government should play in an ideal society. Rather, he insisted on building local networks to counter the threat posed by offensive publications. However, many other nationalists would not uphold this position. Though they were critical of the ban on *Satyarth Prakash*, they had their own reasons. For example, Nehru claimed it to be a larger issue of religious freedom. He was worried that 'this may become a precedent for future invasions on all civil rights and liberties' (*Harijan*, 5 October 1945). Nehru asserted that 'I shall always endeavour to have civil liberties in all forms maintained and practised in India and to resist any encroachment on them'. For Nehru, to take a principled position when the ban was called by the Muslim League's government in Sind was easy, but one can contrast this view from his position in 1937 after the Indian National Congress had emerged in power in most of the provinces. When communal tensions increased in some regions and was further frenzied by vernacular press, he wrote in *Harijan* on 23 October:

> Inspite of every desire to avoid it, coercive action may become necessary and in such cases ministries will inevitably have to undertake it. Such coercive action should only be undertaken where there has been violence or incitement to violence or communal strife.

Nehru's approach was more realistic than Gandhi's, as he saw the inevitability of the state's role in regulating free speech in certain circumstances, especially when it increased communal tensions. He insisted that in such cases, governmental interferences were necessary, a position that he maintained even after India became independent. The opposition to the ban seemed to situate Nehru on the same side as S. P. Mookherjee,[43] who also criticized the ban, however, for completely different reasons. Mookherjee condemned the ban as an attack on Hinduism. He took the opportunity to appeal to the Arya Samajists to work in cooperation with other parties for the consolidation of the Hindu forces and freedom of Hindustan (Madok

2001: 53). The Arya Samajists organized a massive *satyagraha* (non-violent protest) in Sind but in vain.[44] The book remained banned even after all such agitations.

It was evident that though the ban was opposed by the nationalists, different sections had different reasons for their oppositions. It was particularly true in cases where the freedom of speech and expression was seen as being in collision with religious values and identities. So, whereas Gandhi was in principle against the use of government machinery for such a cause, Nehru's opposition was based on his arguments for religious liberties, and Mookherjee saw it as a conscious ploy by Muslim fundamentalists. The divergent arguments reveal no unanimity over the criticism of the ban, but rather ambiguities in nationalist positions regarding censorship. These issues once again came out in the open when these personalities sat down to write the Constitution for Independent India.

Conclusion

What ramifications did the debates over censorship during colonial times have on the understanding about freedom of speech and expression? On the one hand, the legal provisions and limitations introduced by the British formed the guiding principles for the free speech discourse in India, and on the other hand, in the absence of any comprehensive civil liberties movement, the mediums of nationalist responses like the vernacular press, tracts, books and iconographies became the rallying point around which the freedom of expression debate centred.[45] Freedom of expression remained largely dependent on the interpretations of law offered by the colonial authorities. Neither the British nor the Indians treated freedom of expression as a fundamental individual right. It was invoked based on the utility it served for the community at large. The British attitude to freedom of expression in relation to offence or insult to religious identities reflected a subtle dichotomy. On the one hand, in legal and legislative language, the limits to free expression were pronounced and kept on growing (in the form of section 153[A], or section 295[A] of the IPC and other similar regulations); on the other hand, post-1857 they claimed to maintain a policy of non-interference in the religious activities of the natives. The use of colonial laws, however, was subject to the interests of the imperial design, which was believed to be best served by the colonial state maintaining an image of a neutral arbitrator of religious conflicts. So, at times due to the fear of being branded as biased towards a particular community, and at other times, in order to extract maximum benefit from such antagonisms, they exercised 'selective censorship'.

On the part of the colonized Indians, the response was equally diverse. The early liberals like Rammohan Roy argued for some limits to freedom of speech and expression especially in conditions of libel and sedition but thought it to be a potent weapon to respond to the challenges of Christian missionaries. But gradually the same freedom was used by Hindus and Muslims against each other. As these antagonisms escalated and began to take violent shape, there were demands from within the Indian communities to restrict freedom of expression. There was no clarity in the position of Indian nationalists on the subject. The nationalists questioned the British claim that they had conferred religious liberty and toleration on Indian society through their policy of impartiality in the domain of religion and argued that it only allowed men of various creeds to play fast and loose with religion (Jalal 2000: 80). Though they were struggling for greater freedom of expression to criticize the authorities, they were not sure if similar freedom should be allowed in religious matters. Legislative debates of the time reveal that they were not just mute observers in the lawmaking process; rather, they participated actively in critically analysing the scope and limits of such laws. During the making of sections 153(A) and 295(A), Indian legislatures made a significant impact both in criticizing the colonial government and, at the same time, pitching a rational law that could prevent vilification of religious personalities and incitement to religious hatred.[46] Several leaders also cautioned against granting too much power to the executive, as it could impact the freedom of speech and expression in significant ways.[47] However, an overwhelming support for the proposed amendments and additions in the IPC reflected a general consensus among Indians leaders that freedom of speech and expression should be limited in cases where it could cause religious harm or incite hatred in the name of religion or other forms of community-based identity.

This analysis presents a picture of free speech debate in colonial period in a different way than the one forwarded by legal scholar Arun K. Thiruvengadam, who characterizes different historical periods in India's free speech experience and argues that during the anti-colonial struggle it presented a 'universalist' nature that subsequently got replaced by 'particularistic' concerns during the constitution-making process and led to the inclusion of several grounds of restrictions.[48] As the discussions in this chapter highlight, such a 'universalist' approach never existed. Indian leaders, in the name of harm that publications vilifying different religions had caused, aggressively advocated curtailment of freedom of expression through legal means. It can be concluded that when India became independent, it carried with itself an ambiguity, vis- à-vis the position over freedom of expression, particularly in relation to religious offence. There was, however, a looming consensus that such freedom needed to be controlled and regulated through law. This history of contradictions and the role of the vernacular press in communal violence had a significant impact on the future of freedom of speech and expression when it was being debated in the Constituent Assembly.

Notes

1 Buckingham was the editor of the *Calcutta Journal* until 1823, when he was deported.
2 Fair was the editor of the *Bombay Gazette* and was deported in 1824.
3 Henry Maine also believed that India was 'empty of laws' before the British started to legislate. He wrote, 'Nobody who has inquired into the matter can doubt that, before the British government began to legislate, India was, regard being to its moral and material needs, a country singularly empty of law'. See 'Minute on Codification in India', dated 17 July 1879, NAI, Home (Legislative) August 1879: 217–220.
4 His provision simply states: 'Whoever, by words either spoken or intended to be read, or by signs, or by visible representations, attempts to cause any imputation concerning any person to be believed in any quarter, knowing that the belief thereof would harm the reputation of that person in that quarter, is said except in the cases (hereinafter mentioned), to defame that person'. See 'Of Defamation' in *A Penal Code Prepared by the Indian Law Commissioners* (Kolkata: Bengal Military Orphan Press, 1837), p. 124.
5 See 'Notes J', in *A Penal Code Prepared by the Indian Law Commissioners*, p. 49.
6 Section 298 in the original IPC is present as section 282 in the Report in *Penal Code Prepared*, 71. It rendered everyone liable to a year's imprisonment who, 'with the deliberate intention of wounding the religious feelings of any person, utters any word or makes any sound in the hearing of that person, or makes any gesture in the sight of that person, or places any object in the sight of that person'.
7 'Indirect rule' was basically the rule through native institutions. Scholars like Maine argued that there was fundamental difference between native societies and the British. Based on this argument, he urged that the aim of British rule should be to use the internal coherence of native institutions rather than its dissolution. Indirect rule became the foundational principle of late-imperial philosophy in Asia and Africa. For a detailed analysis see Karuna Mantena (2009).
8 There are commentators like Chatterjee who don't agree with the idea of shift in the policy. He argues that the essentialized difference between colonizers and colonized justified colonial authoritarianism, and so although British administrators promised that colonialism would eventually eradicate differences, once the colonized 'other' became modern subjects, colonial control would have lost its ideological foothold. So, in *The Nation and Its Fragments* (1993) he maintains that 'colonial difference' was always at the centre of imperial policy, and the case of legal reform was no different. But even he agrees that the British maintained an essential difference between criminal and personal laws.
9 In the English law the provision for enmity between classes was included in the section dealing with offences against the state.
10 Lord Lansdowne et al., memo, 27 December 1893, *India Office Library/Records*, London (Henceforth IOL/R), L/P & J/6/365, File no. 84, p. 4.
11 'Note on the Cow Protection Agitation in Gorakhpur District', 1894, IOL/R, File no. 84, pp. 1–2 (emphasis added).
12 See Wheeler note (27 November 1913), Government of India Home Political Proceeding (GIPOL) December 1913, 9D, as quoted in Barrier (1974: 61).
13 *Lauh-i-Mahfuz*, Moradabad, 29 August 1879, Selections, L/R/5/56, IOL/R, p. 698.
14 *Samaya Vinod*, 1 November 1876, L/R/5/53, IOL/R, p. 627.

15 Barbara Daly Metcalf (1992) has argued that these were the new leaders who became experts in religious tradition, though they did not receive traditional teachings and training like the pundits or *ulemas*. They became more popular due to their use of modern techniques like print in professing and popularizing religion. An example of such leaders, according to Metcalf, was Arya Samaj founder Swami Dayanand Saraswati.

16 It was based on this recognition that Gandhi, in his attempt to bring different communities together, rejected the idea of historicization of the past as it could lead to a divisive and self-defeating project for Indian nationalism. He prioritized 'civilizational consciousness' over 'historical consciousness'. 'I believe in the saying that, a nation is happy that has no history', he maintained. As quoted in R. Iyer (1986: 187).

17 *Lauh-i-Mehfuz*, an Urdu journal, exposed that instead of using the mission funds for supporting the poor, the money was being wasted on the 'publication of books written with no other object than to expose, to ridicule and hold in contempt the Hindus and Mussalman religion'. *Lauh-i-Mahfuz*, Moradabad, 14 September 1874, Selections, L/R/5/52, IOL/R, p. 484.

18 The common enemy appeared in the form of Muslims because beef formed an important part of their diet, and the same was prohibited in both Hindu as well as Sikh religious traditions, which considered the cow to be sacred (Barrier 1992; Metcalf 1992).

19 Nizam-l-Akhbar, 27 August 1876, Selections, L/R/5/53, IOL/R, p. 471.

20 Christopher Pinney (2009) considers this phenomenon in Indian politics as 'Iatrogenesis' i.e., an illness that comes about as a direct result of the physician's intervention.

21 The real author of the tract remains unknown. However, some scholars have claimed that it was Pandit Chamupati, a popular Arya Samajist (Kumar 1997: 50; Thursby 1975: 40).

22 The main source of the case and judgments is POLITICAL/1927/File 132/I, NAI (National Archives of India). Judgement of the final appeal also was published as *Raj Pal v. King Emperor* (1927) 14 AIR 590 (Lahore).

23 This incident was widely publicized in the press. See, 'Deputation to the Governor', *Tribune*, 14 June 1927. Also see Hailey's letter to the Home Department on 23 June 1927, in POLITICAL, 1927, File No. 132.

24 Mohammad Iqbal was shouted down by an agitated crowd at Lahore on 9 June 1927. 'Muslims Climb Down', *Tribune*, 10 June 1927.

25 The article 'Resign' published in *Muslim Outlook* also tried to make sense of the judgement in the light of the religious identity of Dalip Singh, who was a Christian. See, 'Alleged Contempt of Court', *Times of India*, 17 June 1927.

26 'Clear Contempt of Court: Lahore Editor to Jail', *The Times of India*, 22 June 1927; 'Lahore Editor Jailed: "In Perfect Good Faith"', *Times of India*, 23 June 1927.

27 Telegram, Hailey to Broadway, 6 July 1927, *Hailey MSS* Eur. E 200, IOL/R, London.

28 'Hartals in UP Towns: Hindus Agitated: Aftermath of Vartman Judgment', *The Times of India*, 10 August 1927.

29 'Hailey's letter to the Home Department', 12 August 1927, in POLITICAL, 1927, File No. 132.

30 B. P. Naidu, *The Legislative Assembly Debates*, vol. 14, 16 September 1927, 4478. All volumes of *The Legislative Assembly Debates* are available at the NAI. All the citations regarding the debate follow from same source, so until mentioned, the reference remains same and only the column number will be mentioned with the names of the speakers.

31 K. C. Roy, 4468. Roy held that the demand had only come from 'a handful of men in the Punjab, thoughtful perhaps, patriotic perhaps, but really, the inner working came from a set of men who are responsible for the communal disturbances in north India'.
32 Amar Nath Dutt, 4484–4486.
33 M. K. Acharya, 3433–3436; Thakur Das Bhargava, 3951–3952; Roy, 4467–4468.
34 Lajpat Rai, 3930–3931; M. A. Jinnah, 3932–3933; Kunzru, 3941; M. M. Malviya, 3948.
35 The details of amendments that were tabled are available in The Legislative Assembly Debates, vol. 14, 16 September 1927, 4502–4584.
36 Dr. Belvi, 4469–4470. He had raised this issue in the Assembly.
37 Julia Stephens (2014) has also developed this point, arguing that the case reflects an inextricable relationship between 'religious sentiments, colonial politics and secular laws'.
38 There were attempts to derive the idea of tolerance from religious scriptures like the Koran, the Gita and others. There were also attempts to pass the buck on the other community and blame them for starting the problems. See Abdul Haye, 3928; Acharya, 3433–3436; Mohammad Shah Nawaz, 3443–3444; Malviya, 3448; Bhargava, 3451–3452.
39 None of the Muslim members voted against the bill. List of who voted 'for' and 'against' the bill is available in POLITICAL, File No. 132/27, 1927, 26.
40 Nair (2013: 331) also agrees that most of the votes in favour of the bill were 'reluctant' and only responding to the 'emergency situation'.
41 All Parties Conference, 'Report of a Committee to Determine Principles of the Constitution for India', *The Nehru Report*, pp. 89–90.
42 All the major documents brought out by the nationalists reiterated this demand like the Constitution of India Bill (1895), Commonwealth of India Bill (1925), Nehru Report (1928), The Karachi Resolution of Congress (1931) on *Fundamental Rights and Economic and Social Change*, and The Sapru Report (1945).
43 Member of the Congress Party considered very close to religious nationalists of the time, and who later founded the right-wing nationalist party Bharatiya Jana Sangh.
44 'Satyagraha in Sindh launched', *The Times of India*, 17 January 1947.
45 This, however, changed after the 1870s, when tracts, books and iconography also became sites of contestations and debates. See Pinney (1997: 834–867).
46 For example, during the discussions over the introduction of section 153(A) in the penal codes, Select Committee member P Ananda Charlu described the enactment of section 153(A) as 'a dangerous piece of legislation and has been impolitic (among other reasons) by necessitating Government to side with or to appear to side with one party as against another'. He said, 'In my humble judgment it will only accentuate the evil which it is meant to remove. Far from healing the differences which still linger, or which now and then come to the surface, it would widen the gap by encouraging insidious men to do mischief in stealth'. See, Select Committee Report, *Gazette of India*, Part V (5 February 1898), 15. Although as a member of the Select Committee he registered his dissent, he voted for the bill in the Council, and section 153(A) was passed there with 18 members in favour and 4 against the amendment to the criminal laws.
47 These concerns were raised by Indian representatives like Ananda Charlu and the Maharaja of Darbhanga during the debates over section 153(A) in 1898 and members like Lala Lajpat Rai and Mohammad Ali Jinnah among others, during the debates over section 295(A) in 1928.

48 Arun K. Thiruvengadam, 'The Evolution of the Constitutional Right to Free Speech in India (1800–1950): The Interplay of Universal and Particular Rationales', University of Washington Trans-Pacific Comparative Constitutional Roundtable on 6 December 2013; Centre for Asian Legal Studies, National University of Singapore, Working Paper Series, Available at http://papers.ssrn.com/sol3/papers.cfm? abstract_id= 2470905 (last accessed on 17 July 2017).

2

FREEDOM OF EXPRESSION AND RELIGIOUS VILIFICATIONS

Decoding the Constitutional and Legal Definition of 'Limits'

When India became independent, celebrations of the birth of a new nation were accompanied by the general feeling of hope that everything associated with colonial rule would be undone, and independence along with formation of a new state under the leadership of the nationalists would usher a fresh sense of freedom with an uncompromising respect for civil liberties (U. Mehta 2011: 17). However, the challenge of nation-making and the pressure of the context did not allow space for such ambitious intervention. This dichotomy was clearly evident in the Constituent Assembly Debates (henceforth to be called CAD) and the constitution that took shape thereafter. Sudipta Kaviraj has significantly argued that 'before independence as power was not in the hands of the nationalists, political and ideological positions could be articulated only as ideas, which allowed the liberty to think beyond barriers, almost a utopian imagery of independent India' (2011: 76). The real challenge, therefore, was visible when the same nationalists occupied positions of power and responsibility to shape the future of the nation.

The Constituent Assembly and the Idea of Freedom of Speech and Expression in the Constitution

The Constituent Assembly became the site where divergent visions about India's future interacted to produce a document which could become the 'statement of Indian identity' (Parekh 2008). The discussions in the Assembly over freedom of speech and expression lacked any political or philosophical argumentation about the importance or need for such a right in a democracy. Its inclusion in the constitution was considered sine qua non, partly because of the historical background of the struggle for Independence and more because of the fact that the most part of India's constitution was borrowed from the declarations or constitutions of the then-successful democracies. The Bill of Rights, the debates over the First Amendment in the US and others were clear in the minds of the constitution makers. But it was not an exclusive case with freedom of speech

DOI: 10.4324/9781003369257-3

and expression. Many political concepts that were used and included in the constitution were little debated or reflected upon by the constitution makers. Though Nehru claimed in the Assembly on 13 January 1946 that 'we have laid down no theoretical words', the constitution was full of political concepts and ideas that required far more clarity than was rendered (Gopal 1991: 247). Sunil Khilnani has rightly argued that such evasion 'retracted attention from how these elements might interact with one another over time, producing mutations in the forms of democracy, while also changing the internal character of the nature of representation, rights and equality' (2005: 70). However, it did not mean that the ideas were not discussed at all. For example, in relation to freedom of speech and expression, the members debated extensively about the appropriate limits to such freedom.

The issue about the restrictions and its rationale came up at an early stage when the *Draft Report* submitted by the sub-committee to the Advisory Committee for consideration subjected freedom of speech and expression to 'public order' and 'morality'. It also included provisions for action against 'publication or utterance of seditious, obscene, slanderous, libellous or defamatory matter' (Rao 1966–1968: 138). Pointing out the lacunae, members like K. T. Shah[1] argued that the limitations should be minimal and terms like 'morality' should be avoided, as they were vague and could be misused (ibid.: 157). On the opposite of the spectrum were members like A. K. Ayyar,[2] who argued that exceptions were too narrow and should be broadened in order to be used by the state for security and other emergencies. These discussions forced early amendments and the *Interim Report on Fundamental Rights* that was presented to the Constituent Assembly by the Advisory Committee read:

> 8. There shall be liberty for the exercise of the following rights subject to public order and morality or to the existence of grave emergency declared to be such by the government of the union or the unit concerned whereby the security of the union or the unit, as the case may be, is threatened:
>
> a) The right of every citizen to freedom of speech and expression: provision may be made by law to make the publication or utterance of seditious, obscene, blasphemous, slanderous, libellous or defamatory matter actionable and punishable.
>
> (CAD, Vol. III: 2)

This draft attracted severe criticism from different ends. For example, Somnath Lahiri[3] argued that the provisions seemed to have been framed 'from the point of view of a police constable'. He also warned that the phrase 'grave emergency' was one open to interpretation, and hence its misuse by the executive was possible (CAD, Vol. III: 384–385). Looking at the kind of hostility it had generated, Patel moved clause 8 the next day, omitting the provisos contained in clause 8(a). Based on the committee reports and their discussion in the Constituent Assembly, B. N. Rau[4] prepared the Draft Constitution, which was cleared by the Drafting Committee before being placed in the Assembly. Interestingly, the Draft Constitution included a set of new provisos and read as follows:

> 13. (1) Subject to other provisions of this article, all citizens shall have the right- (a) To freedom of speech and expression;
>
> (2) Nothing in sub-clause (a) of clause (1) of this article shall affect the operation of any existing law, or prevent the state from making any law, related to libel, slander, defamation, sedition or any other matter which offends against decency or morality or undermines the authority or foundation of the state.

These new inclusions received polarized reactions, some opposing the provisos and others in support. Those opposing included K. T. Shah, Damodar Swaroop Seth,[5] Mahboob Ali Baig,[6] Sardar Hukam Singh[7] and Pandit Thakur Das Bhargava,[8] among others. They invoked the Bill of Rights of the US Constitution and argued that the fundamental rights should be absolute and not subject to exceptions. It was feared that the presence of provisos made the liberty insignificant. Damodar Swaroop Seth said: 'Rights guaranteed in article 13 are cancelled by that very section and placed at the mercy of the high handedness of the legislature' (CAD, Vol. VII: 712). There was a general feeling that the presence of provisos in the article seemed as if the right was 'given by the right hand and taken away by the left'. They were concerned about the executives in the future acting like the British in the past and using laws to curb political dissent. Most of the advocates of such unconditional institutional protection for civil rights belonged to political minorities: Muslims, Communists and the Hindu Right. Based on their distrust of government's role, they argued that the decisions about regulation of freedom of speech and expression should be left exclusively for the judiciary, which could decide on a case-by-case basis.

Contrary to this view were those who believed that some form of censorship was important for government to enable it to handle the turbulent times that the country was undergoing. For example, Shri K. Hanumanthaiya[9] said:

> We went through a course of suffering and sacrifice which were imposed upon us by the repressive laws of British imperialism; this naturally made us votaries of unadulterated fundamental rights and that was our hope. But, ultimately when we emerged out of those innumerable difficulties, we are faced, within our own society, with elements who want to take advantage of those rights in order to do violence to men, society and laws.... No man who believes in

> violence and who wants to upset the State and society by violent methods should be allowed to have his way under the colour of these rights. It is for that purpose that the Drafting Committee has thought it fit to limit the operation of these fundamental rights.
>
> (CAD, Vol. VII: 754–755)

Those in favour of restrictions insisted on the need to show faith in the executive's commitment not to misuse power since it was under democratic oversight.[10] Defending the presence of provisos, T. T. Krishnamachari[11] argued that it just reflected the middle path adopted by the government to balance freedom with responsibility (CAD, Vol. VII: 770–773). There were others, like Amiyo Kumar Ghosh, who were not against the idea of including provisos, but believed that the vagueness of the terms used to limit such freedom should be avoided, as it could lead to ambiguity and misinterpretations (CAD, Vol. VII: 769–770).[12] However, there seems to have been no serious response to such arguments.

At the end only K. M. Munshi's[13] amendment to delete the word 'sedition' from article 13(2) was accepted and the re-numbered provision, finally adopted, read as follows:

> 19. (1) all citizens shall have the right- (a) to freedom of speech and expression;
>
> (2) nothing in sub-clause (a) of clause (1) shall affect the operation of any existing law in so far as it relates to, or prevent the state from making any law relating to, libel, slander, defamation, contempt of court or any matter which offends against decency or morality or which undermines the security of, or tends to overthrow, the state.

CAD and the Central Concerns regarding Freedom of Expression

The debates in the Constituent Assembly reflected three broad concerns related to freedom of speech and expression in particular: (1) there was concern about any continuity to the British form of rule and colonial laws, and at least symbolically there was a unanimous negation of it; (2) there was concern about whether the government could always be trusted on questions relating to freedom of speech and expression, and there was agreement on the need for a 'two-tiered' response system, as it was agreed that the judiciary should play an important role as the protector of fundamental rights; and (3) set against the backdrop of Partition, the constitution-makers were also taking into account and reacting to the new set of challenges connected with communal antagonisms.

The Fear of Continuing Aspects of British Rule

The concern that the restrictions on freedom of speech and expression by the government represented a continuing aspect of colonial policies of control was reflected in the way the reference to British rule was invoked to either criticize the government or question its intentionality. For example, Mr. Mohammed Ismail Sahib[14] raised his concern about the scope of the provisos and said:

> It was different when the Britisher, the foreigner was in the country and that now it's our own rule. True, but that does not mean that we can deal with liberty of the citizens as we please.... Therefore, Sir, the citizen must be protected against the vagaries of the executive in a very careful manner as other self-governing countries have done.
>
> (CAD, Vol. VII: 725)

A similar attitude was reflected when other members compared the expectations from the constitution of a new state with the history of denial of such rights by an autocratic government. For example, Somnath Lahiri in the course of debate accused Sardar Patel (then Home Minister and the Chairman of the Advisory committee on fundamental rights) of trying to arm the future legislature and executives with more powers than the British government itself, which according to him, was 'not the basis of democracy' (CAD Vol. III: 2, 384–385). It is ironic, however, that though there was a firm determination to be different from the British in forms of administration and rule in general – or to say so at least in the visible forms of governmental manifestations – the fact that more than one-third of the constitution was taken from the 1935 act and further, article 372 allowed all the then-existing laws to continue (subject to the review power of the judiciary) did not seem to be in consonance. The fear of existing laws affecting the sanctity of these rights was raised at several instances. Mahboob Ali Baig pointed out that the laws like the Press Acts, Criminal Law Amendment Acts and Security Acts were promulgated by British for repressive purposes, and the continuation of such laws was both unwarranted and useless in a democracy (CAD, Vol. VII: 728). A similar fear is reflected in Sardar Bhupinder Singh Mann's[15] claim that 'to apply the existing law in spite of changed conditions really amounts to trifling the freedom of speech and expression' (CAD, Vol. VII: 750). One could also see a fierce opposition launched to include the word 'sedition' within the provisions restricting freedom of speech and expression. The history of bitter experiences faced by the leaders of nationalist movement at the hands of the British, and the scope for its misuse in the future, were cited as primary reasons for such opposition.[16] Eventually the word 'sedition' was dropped.

A special clarification had to be offered by Nehru and Ambedkar, claiming that no such intrusion was intended. It was forcefully argued that article 8 (article 19 in the present constitution) would be a safeguard against any such attempt by future authorities in power. It was further assured that any law which was in force in any part of the land should be held as void if the judiciary found it to be inconsistent with the provisions guaranteed under fundamental rights.

Uncompromising Faith in the Judiciary

It was almost unanimously held that the judiciary should be the sentinel of the rights promised by the constitution. This confidence in the judiciary was encouraged by the concern that the executives in the future could misuse their capacities if these rights were not granted such protections. Sardar Hukam Singh and Pandit Thakur Das Bhargava argued that if the fate was left in the hands of the authorities in power, the fundamental rights would become 'illusory' and hence the Supreme Court should have the 'final say with regard to the destinies of our nationals' (CAD, Vol. VII: 733–745). There was a strong set of voices in the Assembly arguing that 'unconditional' rights be granted by the constitution, and in cases of disputes, the judiciary could judge its validity, as in the US case.

The faith in the judiciary was also shaped by two other factors: first, the positive role that the judiciary had played in preservation of civil liberties against executive excesses in other successful democracies. The US case was an instant reference point. Mahboob Ali Baig cited the Fourteenth Amendment of the US constitution and the British experience to highlight the primacy of the judiciary contrary to the German experience, where power was misused by the legislature and the executive under Hitler's rule (CAD, Vol. VII: 728). Second, the enthusiasm also flowed from the experiences of the workings of the Supreme Court at home, especially in its last phase before Independence. As legal historians like Rohit De have demonstrated, there were instances of severe confrontation between the colonial state and the federal judiciary when the latter struck down a number of emergency wartime legislations. This not only took both the colonial officials and Indian public by surprise, but also encouraged a degree of faith in the judiciary among Indians themselves (De 2012: 59–90).

All these factors invoked a deep reverence for the judiciary as the protector of such rights. However, there was a small section, mostly amongst Congress loyalists, who were not enthusiastic about giving extensive powers to the courts. For example, K. Hanumanthiya doubted the court's capacity to come to grips with rapid changes within the country. He also argued that the function of courts was only to interpret, and the legislature should therefore frame laws that could adjust according to the demands of changing times and not depend on the judiciary for its innovations (CAD, Vol. VII: 754–755). Similarly, G. B. Pant[17] was afraid that the future of the country would be determined 'not by the collective wisdom of the representatives of the people but by the fiats of those elevated to the judiciary'. 'We cannot be subject to varying court judgements, to the whims and vagaries of judges.... If we can't put mischief makers in jail, there is no end to communal disorders', he said (as quoted in Austin 2003: 85). It seems that in order to maintain a balance, although the judiciary was assigned a central role via article 13 and article 32 of the constitution, the space for such judicial intervention was in some ways limited by pronouncing provisos to freedom of speech and expression under article 19(2).

Responding to the Complicated Context

The making of the constitution took two years, eleven months and eighteen days. This period was full of turmoil and disturbances in the country. Though the period was marked by the transition from a subjugated colony to a free nation, it was accompanied by partition and widespread communal violence. Such transformation posed serious challenges to the project of nation-building facing the framers of the constitution. A central question they had to confront concerned the fate of the religious minorities who had chosen to stay back. There was, on the one hand, the fear among minorities of being suppressed by the Hindu majority, something about which the Muslim League had long been warning. On the other hand, there were expectations of some 'reward' in return for their decision to stay back – rewards in the form of institutional protection of their political and cultural rights as promised by the nationalists during the course of the freedom struggle and as they had enjoyed during the last phase of British rule (Jaffrelot 2010: 8). It was also a test for the new Indian leadership, since they were required to refute the historical claim made by the British that the British had special obligations to protect the minorities as they could not find justice if left in the hands of other Indians (Austin 2003: 59). So, Patel made it explicit in the first meeting of the Advisory committee on 27 February 1947 on minority rights that:

> It is for us to prove that it is a bogus claim, a false claim, and that nobody can be more interested than us in India, in the protection of our minorities. Our mission is to satisfy everyone of them ... at least let us prove we can rule ourselves and we have no ambition to rule others.
>
> (As quoted in Rao 1966–1968, Vol. II)

There was mounting pressure on the Assembly to handle in tandem the issues of rights and liberties and the concerns of minority protection and national integration. Though these were not mutually exclusive goals, the real challenge was to derive an acceptable and workable balance among them all. In the process, the Assembly arrived at remedies that had lasting impact on and consequences for the future of Indian democracy. At least three of these deeply affected the discourse on free speech: (1) the location of the value of liberty in relation to equality and fraternity in the democratic discourse; (2) individual versus group in the constitutional vocabulary; and (3) freedom of speech and expression vis-à-vis 'communal hatred'.

The Location of the Value of Liberty in Relation to Equality and Fraternity

In the Indian context, it seems that the values of equality and fraternity were placed at a higher pedestal than that of liberty. The constitution makers of a nation which had experienced police repression, arbitrary governmental action and brutality under the colonial regime showed little respect for civil liberties and individual freedom. The enunciation of fundamental individual rights was conjoined with a set of conditions under which the state could exercise its power and limit such liberties to realize a broader national and political vision. So, a broad understanding was achieved that individual liberties would attain a subsidiary position within the constitution, and more emphasis was rendered on the values of equality and fraternity. Ambedkar's statement in the Assembly on 4 November 1948 is significant in this regard. While distinguishing between non-fundamental rights and fundamental rights, he argued that while the non-fundamental rights are created by agreement between parties: 'Fundamental rights are gifts of the law. Because fundamental rights are the gift of the state it does not follow that the state cannot qualify them' (CAD, Vol. VIII: 40). So, if the need be, the state had every legitimate right to compromise such individual rights and liberties for larger goals. In a context marred by riots and political violence, it was considered imperative that the state should assert its prerogatives and, with extensive powers under its command, should guide the process of nation-building by inculcating a sense of trust and faith among communities which in turn required projecting the values of fraternity and promises of equality where necessary (CAD, Vol. VII: 754–755).

Broadly speaking there were two positions amongst those who supported such limitations of individual liberties: (1) The first was expressed by CAD members who argued that extensive powers in the hands of the state was required in order to control the conflictual situation that had arisen post-Independence. The state was expected to maintain peace and order in society not only by enforcing law and order but also enabling solidarities and trust to emerge among various communities, especially between Hindus and Muslims. This idea was articulated by members like Hanumanthaiya and T. T. Krishnamachari. (2) The other position was held by those CAD members who believed that by its very nature liberty was different from licence, and the role of the state was important also to ensure that clashes of different perceptions of liberty did not occur. No rights therefore could be absolute. This position was held by members like Ambedkar, Patel and others. As the proceedings of the CAD turned out, these voices were dominant in the house and led to the fact that the provisions in the constitution favouring individual rights were made conditional to the authority of the state to manage liberties to ensure equality and fraternity in society.

Individual Rights versus Group Rights in the Constitutional Vocabulary

The prevailing context and the history of national movement also had a deep impact on the way individual rights were perceived in relation to group rights in the constitution. Within the Constituent Assembly, there was a significant section who wanted individuals and not groups to be the bearers of rights. For example, G. B. Pant condemned the practice of invoking the category of 'community', thereby undermining the value of the 'individual', who was the citizen and therefore should be the centre of concern (CAD, Vol. I: 332). This attitude, as Christophe Jaffrelot argues, represented a classical 'Jacobin rejection of communities' (2010: 7). It was also reflected in the ideas of Nehru, Patel and Radhakrishnan, among others. This rejection of communities was based on two central arguments: (1) the project of nation-building required a strong unity of the nation, which could be hampered by due allegiance to intermediary forms of identity such as religion or caste; and (2) the fear that recognition of minority identities would inevitably lead to the isolation and neglect of these communities by the majorities in the future. It was reflected in Nehru's concern that '[in] a full-blooded democracy, if you seek to give safeguards to a minority, and a relatively small minority, you isolate it' (CAD, Vol. III: 330).

There was yet another section among the Constituent Assembly members who invoked individual rights and national unity considerations virtually interchangeably. This position was represented by Rajkumari Amrit Kaur,[18] Hansa Mehta[19] and Minoo Masani.[20] Their opposition to community recognition was based not only on the importance of equal rights for all citizens in nation-building, but also on a fear that if the cultural communities were thus recognized without drastic internal reform among these communities, it would mean the continuation of the subjugatory illiberal practices within each such community, which would be contrary to the interests of large sections within these communities that were vulnerable, like women.[21] So, they preferred the individual-based concept of rights, equal for all. This was reflected in their consistent support for the Uniform Civil Code and opposition to the addition of 'practice' and 'propagate' religion as a fundamental right.

Contrary to all these positions were the views of other members like K. T. Shah, K. M. Munshi and representatives of different minority communities who argued for recognition of the rights of communities based on the significance of religious identity to the self (Mahajan 2008: 300). Eventually, as it happened, this latter position was in part accepted, and space was made for recognition of groups and the claims of community rights. However, with Independence, the context had changed, and partition in the name of religion had convinced the members that though minorities' right to culture should be protected, they should have no claim to benefits in political rights either in the form of reservations or separate electorates (Bajpai 2011; Chandoke 2005). Many of the minority leaders, including several Muslim leaders, welcomed the decision.[22]

In the case of religious and cultural rights, on the one hand the leaders of religious minorities wanted no interference of the state on issues of institutional and cultural practices internal to religion, but at the same time they expected protection and support in the form of social welfare programmes that included education and propagation of cultural values. About the abrogation of political benefits and protection of socio-cultural rights, Gurpreet Mahajan (2008) is of the opinion that in the post-partition phase, minority leaders were more interested in preserving their cultural rights of their communities than in upholding the political rights that they previously enjoyed during the British rule. Rochana Bajpai (2010, 2011) adds to this understanding by demonstrating that unlike political safeguards, the language of cultural rights of minorities found support in key nationalist ideals. Preservation of such rights was seen as a part of the secularism that the new state was expected to follow, whereas political safeguards in the form of either separate electorates or reservations were considered a threat to national unity. It is not surprising therefore that unlike the standard liberal position, groups as well as individuals were recognized in nationalist opinion as the subjects of rights and entitlements (Bajpai 2010: 291). The Constituent Assembly took a balanced position on this issue: on the one hand, the right to religion – to profess, practice and propagate – was conferred to all persons; on the other hand, the freedom was not left unfettered – state intervention was authorized in the interest of protecting 'public order, morality and health' (Bajpai 2010: 293). It is equally true that cultural pluralism, rather than liberal individualism, became the operative principle of democracy, and though the constitution had guaranteed a set of individual political rights like freedom of speech and expression, almost all of these were severely circumscribed. Cultural community, on the one hand, and national interest, on the other, curtailed the free expression of these rights (Mahajan, 2008: 38). This position was indicative of the approach of the government in cases where individual rights came in collision with group rights. For example, when the claim of religious 'offence' is presented as a claim for protection promised under the right to freedom of conscience and free profession, practice and propagation of religion under article 25, and is shown to be threatened by someone's freedom of speech and expression guaranteed under article 19 (1) (a), it presents a complicated situation because though each of these rights is legally treated as an individual right, the practical implications of the former is for a wider public.

Freedom of Speech and Expression and the Issue of 'Communal Hatred'

The context in which the constitution was being drawn also brought in question the relation of freedom of speech and expression to communal harmony. The role of the press and publications as a means for propaganda to incite communal hatred had been significant. Several members were convinced that such incitement to religious and communal hatred should be prevented by the state. So, during the meeting of the Advisory Committee on Fundamental Rights, A. K. Ayyar insisted on the inclusion of the words 'calculated to promote class hatred' as a condition to limit freedom of speech and expression.[23] This idea was supported by K. M. Pannikar, who wanted the addition of 'class or religious hatred' as one of the provisos under article 19(2).[24] On this, Rajagopalachari noted that some of the provisions for such action were already present in existing laws within the IPC, especially under section 153(A); therefore, he argued that the best way to deal with it was by re-drafting the whole clause and saying – 'The right of every citizen to freedom of speech and expression, subject to criminal law'. Rajagopalachari opined that 'the fundamental peace and orderly progress' of the country depended upon 'communal peace and harmony', and if the 'speeches and utterances likely to foster communal hatred' were not prevented, 'we cannot have progress.'[25] What Rajagopalachari was suggesting was extremely dangerous, as it would have meant that the fundamental rights would become subordinate to criminal laws of the land, which incidentally were devised by the British, and were not at all amended as of then. It would have definitely made the limits placed upon such rights more central and seminal than the idea of liberty itself. It was to be expected that such attempts to curtail liberties faced severe criticism from among the members. S. P. Mookherjee thought that such expression could cut both ways. It was possible that simply expressing opinions against the party in power might be construed as class or communal hatred and punished (Rao 1966–1968: 157). Bakshi Tek Chand[26] and H. C. Mookherjee[27] pointed out that their worries about abuse were rooted in their experience under the British rule and feared that such powers in the hands of future executives could be extremely dangerous (Rao 1966–1968: 231–232). K. M. Munshi took the debate forward and argued that 'class or communal hatred' was omitted as it was feared that the state units would make drastic laws under such provisions in order to curtail even the basic forms of free expressions. For him 'breach of peace or public order' should be important for restrictions. He said:

> The right of free expression is now recognized all over the world, and it has been felt that speeches or writings tending towards

> communal or class hatred, if they do not go to the extent of causing violence or crime, may be permitted.
>
> (As quoted in Rao 1966–1968: 231)

As none of the sides was ready to relent, the amendment was put to a vote whereby the amendment proposed by Rajagopalachari was defeated. Even though the amendment failed, it seems that the framers saw some merit in the argument related to communal hatred and in the *Interim Report of the Advisory Committee on Fundamental Rights*, one could find the mention of 'blasphemy' as one of the provisos. However, in the drafting stage, when the provisos reappeared (after it was dropped by Sardar Patel during debates in the Assembly), the word 'blasphemy' was found missing. Interestingly, there is no evidence of any opposition or protest against such move, neither within the drafting committee, nor during the debates of the assembly.[28]

A similar issue appeared when, during the course of debate on the Draft Constitution, Mohd. Tahir[29] argued that invoking 'communal passion' should be made an offence against which the state should have the right to make laws to limit freedom of speech and expression. 'Communal passion', according to him, included 'agitating or exciting the minds of one community against the other'. He pointed to the great 'loss and disservice' that such offences had done to the country and to the neglect of such laws by the British as it served their interest. But after independence, he believed, such stringent laws were important (CAD, Vol. VII: 742). This initiative also found support among others like Syed Karimuddin,[30] who argued that 'whether Muslims are responsible or the Hindus are responsible for communal passions it has eaten away everything that is good in society' (CAD, Vol. VII: 757). Hence, he maintained that inciting communal passion in any form should be made an offence. This concern was reflected in the amendment suggesting the inclusion of 'inciting communal passion' as a proviso to restrict freedom of expression.[31] This amendment was vociferously opposed by members like M. A. Ayyangar,[32] who argued that there were already laws under the IPC to deal with such issues and hence such inclusions were not required. The amendment was put to a vote and was eventually defeated.

The demand for making 'promotion of communal hatred' or incitement of 'communal passion' as a proviso to limit freedom of expression was based on the premise that Indian citizens could easily be misguided by communal elements, and therefore the state needed to step in more prominently to protect them from such propaganda. Though incitement of communal passion or promotion of communal hatred did not form a part of the caveats introduced under article 19(2), it was primarily because the lawmakers showered extensive faith on statutory laws like section 153(A) and 295(A), as credible tools in the hands of the officials to deal with situations where communal hatred was being promoted. It not only hinted at their support to the statutory laws (which had colonial origins), but also gave a sense that they wanted the officials to use it extensively, in order to suppress fissiparous tendencies among some Indians to incite communal hatred.

Looking at the final draft, one can say that the opponents of the provisos failed in their efforts because not only were the provisos entered, the final clause wasvague in its content and intent, which made it open to misuse and misinterpretations by different parties. It was also clear that the lawmakers thought that though freedom of speech and expression was important, its misuse for communal polarization that led to violence was detrimental to social harmony, and hence it was necessary to curb it. A broad consensus was reached that in the interest of national integration, freedom of speech and expression should carry important provisos, which significantly limited its scope in practice. It now remained upon the courts to protect the fundamental rights of citizens from any form of intrusions by either the state or society.

Constitutional Amendments and Other Legal Apparatuses

Within a few months of its introduction, the judiciary and the parliament were at loggerheads over the interpretation of the constitution. Both these institutions seemed to have diverse views regarding some key constitutional aspects. It was felt that political stability and national integrity was in conflict with the democratic rights to freedom of expression and personal liberty. Responding to the situation, Nehru's government introduced the First Amendment Bill in 1951. The situation arose primarily because of decisions of courts in the *Crossroads* case (*Romesh Thapar v. State of Madras, [1950] AIR 37*), the *Shailabala Devi* case (*State of Bihar vs Shailabal Devi [1952] AIR 329*) and the *Brij Bhushan* case (*Brij Bhushan v. State of Delhi [1950] AIR 37*). In each of these cases, the state governments took action under some version of the 'Public Safety Act', and each defendant turned for protection to the first clause of article 19. In the *Crossroads* case, dangers of the 'communist threat' were used by the government to justify press censorship and laws of Preventive Detention against Romesh Thapar, the editor of the communist mouthpiece. The Patna High Court in the *Shailabala Devi* case rejected the contention that the pamphlet incited violence, and the Supreme Court unanimously upheld this judgement. In East Punjab, the Public Safety Act, 1950, was struck down by the Supreme Court on the grounds that pre-censorship restricted the liberty of the press. The laws were all struck down on grounds of 'over-breadth' – the courts claimed that their ambit was much greater than the exceptions provided within article 19(2).

This led to wide-ranging political reactions, some of which were particularly significant. Sardar Patel thought that the *Crossroads* decision knocked 'the bottom out of most of our penal laws for the control and regulation of the press'.[33] Ambedkar, the erstwhile Chairman of the Drafting Committee, and Law Minister at the time of the First Amendment Bill, opined that the Supreme

Court had decided the issue incorrectly.[34] Central to Nehru's arguments regarding amendment to article 19 was his unease with some of the press, which according to him seemed irresponsible: 'some two page news-sheet... full of vulgarity, indecency and falsehood'. New provisos in the form of 'public order' and 'incitement to an offence' were added as Nehru maintained that a constitution should not limit the 'power of the Parliament to face a situation'. The 'concept of individual freedom has to be balanced with social freedom and the relations of the individual with the social groups', Nehru argued.[35]

The opposition to the amendments came from different directions. There were criticisms about the high-handedness of the government thereby undermining the importance of freedom of speech and expression (S. P. Mookherjee, PD, 8838). Questions were also raised about the timing of such introduction (just before general elections) and the technical subject about whether a Constituent Assembly (largely unelected) had such rights to introduce so significant an amendment (Austin 2003: 47).

However, it was H. V. Kamath's[36] suggestion about the need to include 'reasonable' as qualifying any restrictions on speech that attracted the most attention (PD, 8913–8924). Amidst a lot of pressure, both from the opposition and from within the cabinet (especially from the Law Ministry), Nehru agreed to include this proposal, but he was not very happy as he feared that such inclusion could invite each such case to go to the courts and hence more intervention of the courts in executive decisions (Gopal 1991: 189). Finally, the Assembly passed the bill by a vote of 228 to 20. It retroactively and prospectively empowered government to impose 'reasonable restrictions' on freedom of expression 'in the interests of the security of the State (replacing the words 'tends to overthrow the state'), friendly relations with foreign states, public order, decency or morality, or in relation to contempt of court, defamation, or incitement to an offence' (Austin 2003: 49).

Other than broadening the scope for government intervention, there were three important aspects in the debates: (1) The First Amendment received, as expected, comparisons with the First Amendment in the US. It was pointed out that while the First Amendment had extended individual rights, 'our First Amendment did the opposite by curtailing individual freedom' (S. P. Mookherjee, PD: 8912–8913); (2) There was pointed discussion and criticisms about the courts. Nehru charged the courts of practicing conservatism (PD: 8818), and Congress leader N. G. Ranga extended the charge to the judges of the courts (PD: 8681). All the top leaders including Ambedkar, Patel and Rajagopalachari questioned the wisdom of the courts in interpreting the constitution and argued that the amendment was necessary as such interpretations had been made possible because of the error in the founding of the constitution itself; and (3) The addition of 'reasonable' to qualify the restrictions on freedom of expression was a significant move. It provided the judiciary with the test of 'reasonableness' in order to assess whether the action of the executive in cases dealing with freedom of speech and expression were justifiable.

Significant transformation again occurred in 1963, when both external and internal situations forced another amendment of the constitution. The threats emanating from the Chinese invasion in the northeast and concerns over the demands of regional autonomy reflected in Tara Singh's fast for the Sikh state and Dravida Munnetra Kazhagam's (DMK) call for 'Dravidanad' led to the Sixteenth Amendment to the constitution, which added that the government might place restrictions on expression in the interest of 'the sovereignty and integrity of India', the qualifier 'reasonable' remaining in place (Austin 2003: 50). After all these changes, the constitutional provision for freedom of expression as it stands today reads as follows:

> 19(1) The citizens shall have the right-
> (a) to freedom of speech and expression; and the proviso under 19 (2) reads:
>
> Nothing in sub-clause (a) of clause (1) shall affect the operation of any existing law, or prevent the State from making any law, in so far as such law imposes reasonable restrictions on the exercise of the right conferred by the said sub-clause in the interests of the sovereignty and integrity of India, the security of the State, friendly relations with foreign States, public order, decency or morality, or in relation to contempt of court, defamation or incitement to an offence.

Amendment of Statutory Laws and Its Implication for Freedom of Speech and Expression

The challenges facing Indian society in its post-Independence phase forced the government to relook into the existing statutory laws. Incidents of communal violence and the role of print media in it, especially the vernacular press, allowed interventions which ensured that the scope of sections 153(A) and 295(A) of the IPC was significantly altered. The government wanted to curb the misuse of the press to spread communal hatred, but changes initiated were also going to affect pamphlets, tracts and books, as the laws governing all these forms of publications remained the same. A strong will to introduce new changes to these laws was reflected as early as 1956, when the controversy surrounding the publication of the book *Living Biographies of Religious Leaders* and the subsequent role of some sections of Urdu press in Uttar Pradesh led to communal riots in Aligarh and surrounding areas (Brass 2003).

The book *Living Biographies of Religious Leaders* was written by Henry Thomas and Dana Lee Thomas and was originally published in the US. It was already in circulation when Bharatiya Vidya Bhawan, Delhi, decided to reprint it.[37] The protests against the book began in Aligarh with students of Aligarh Muslim University playing a pivotal role in organizing strikes and demonstrations (*The Times of India*, 14 September 1956). It was argued that the book contained a chapter on Prophet Mohammed, and it presented the Prophet in the wrong light. The protests also targeted K. M. Munshi, who was then the Governor of UP and closely associated with Bharatiya Vidya Bhawan as a founding member and one of the editors. Because of the fear that the controversy would scale up, the book was quickly withdrawn, and Munshi also published an unconditional apology along with requests to the protestors to allow the matter to rest (*The Times of India*, 7 October 1956). However, the controversy did not die down.[38] The offending passages from the book were reproduced in Urdu newspapers, and these were distributed to mobilize Muslims against the attitude of the Indian government in general and Munshi in particular. There were significant communal clashes in different parts of Uttar Pradesh (Brass 2003).

The controversy further took an international dimension. The Hindu groups argued that protesting Muslims were getting support from Pakistan as the Muslim organizations in Pakistan had voiced their concerns against the book, and thereby the protestors were also referred as 'anti-national elements'.[39] The crisis was later resolved by the involvement and interventions by Zakir Hussain, the retiring Vice Chancellor of the Aligarh Muslim University; Maulana Azad, Education Minister; and Nehru, the Prime Minister.[40]

This episode highlighted some deep concerns regarding freedom of speech and expression and the question of religious offence. Most leaders criticized the manner in which Muslim demonstrations turned violent, and a counter-movement was launched by Hindus in north India. Another important issue of concern was the role of print media in promoting communalism; objectionable portions of the book were reprinted by the vernacular press, which further escalated the feeling of offence among the Muslims in those areas. Nehru in particular saw it as a major challenge to be strongly dealt with in the future and was eager to come up with a legislation to prohibit such acts. He wrote to the Chief Ministers that if they were 'convinced that a newspaper editor or any other individual has spread communal hatred or incited people to communal violence, we should arrest him and either proceed against him in a court of law or keep him under preventive detention'.[41] In an attempt to devise a zero tolerance attitude for incitement of communal violence, Nehru also encouraged the executive to take direct action against such violators, which could be seen as a dangerous step as there was every possibility that some official could misuse this power for political ends. In another letter addressed to the Chief Ministers Nehru wrote:

> I have personally come to the conclusion that we must have fresh legislation to deal with the spread of communal hatred by newspapers, etc. I would confine this to offensive communal writings, and not extend it at all in the political or other fields.

The urgency expressed by Nehru reflects the impact the protests and the violence that followed had on national politics. Further, this attitude was also reflective of the understanding that amendment to the existing laws was warranted, and if need be, the political class was prepared to intervene in order to counter the threat of communal violence. Stronger and wider laws were seen as an important tool in the hands of the state to maintain public tranquillity. The incidents that occurred also had connotations for publications that were considered to be religiously offensive. It was clear that the book was already available in India much before the publishers decided to reprint it, and the timing of the furor could therefore be questioned. But contrary to this, the government seemed to consider removal of the book from the public sphere as an easy and instant remedy to the hurt sentiments of the protesting Muslims. This approach of the state laid the foundation of a trend in the future where claims of religious offence obtained a sense of legitimacy, and the tendency to take to the streets against publications considered offensive became a legitimate democratic means to pulp such publications.

Though Nehru wanted to strengthen statutory laws in order to counter the tendency of spreading communal tension by means of the vernacular press, government did not initiate any legislation in this regard. Things, however, changed in 1961. Recurrence of communal violence in different parts of the country, and particularly in Assam and Jabalpur, forced the Nehru government to form a special committee under Indira Gandhi to study the causes of such incidents and strategies to counter them. The Committee recommended important changes in statutory laws, including section 153(A) and section 295(A) of the IPC. These recommendations were further approved by the Conference of Chief Ministers, a forum that took the shape of the National Integration Council in 1962. Based on the suggestions from both these groups, the government introduced a bill in the Parliament which later became Act XLI of 1961.

The bill was introduced in the Lok Sabha on 11 August 1961 by Home Minister Lal Bahadur Shastri as the Indian Penal Code Amendment Bill, 1961, and a detailed discussion took place in the house on 30 August after the bill returned from the Select Committee stage. Debates in both the houses of Parliament reflected similar concerns about the scope of the amendment, the fear of misuse of extended power by the executive and the attack on freedom of speech and expression. While initiating the debate, Minister of State at the Ministry of Home Affairs, Mr. Dattar, stressed that the amendment was being introduced as a constructive step in order to assure 'the integration of the nation in the fullest sense of the term' (Dattar, LSD: 5884) by preventing 'fissiparous tendencies within different religious and other groups that impact the peace in which all religions stay together' (Dattar, RSD: 2030).

The amendment proposed some significant changes in the statutory laws, especially section 153(A) of the IPC. Firstly, it made the grounds of conviction explicit in sections 153(A) by allowing punishment for the acts that 'promote or attempt to promote feelings of enmity or hatred' on grounds of 'religion, race, place of birth, residence, language'. Further, it proposed to increase the quantum of punishment under section 153(A) and section 295(A) of the IPC from two to three years. It also proposed to insert an additional clause (c) to section 153(A), which made punishable any act that was 'prejudicial to the maintenance of harmony between different religion, racial or language groups or castes or communities and which disturbs or is likely to disturb the public tranquillity' (LSD: 5884). But the most fundamental change was the removal of the explanation that was associated with section 153(A) since its inception as a colonial law in 1898. The explanation said:

> It does not amount to an offence within the meaning of this section to point out *without malicious intentions* and with an honest view to their removal, matters which are producing or have a tendency to produce, feelings of enmity or hatred between different classes of citizens.

This explanation put the onus of proving malicious intentions on the prosecutor. However, its removal meant that the responsibility to prove innocence would completely fall on the person charged with the crime.[42]

Debates over the bill in both houses of Parliament centred around a set of issues which were very similar to the ones raised during the colonial period, when these laws were inserted to the penal codes. Opposition to the respective bills were also based on similar grounds. The opposition charge was led by Jan Sangh, leader and future Prime Minister of India Atal Bihari Vajpayee in Lok Sabha, and Communist leader Bhupesh Gupta in Rajya Sabha, who demanded that the bill should be sent for wider consultation, and public opinion should be sought before inserting amendments. Vajpayee claimed that the exercise would not only be representative of the true democratic process but also 'help in educate and train people to national integration' (LSD: 5900). But the demand to send the bill for wider consultation was defeated in the house by an overwhelming majority of 116 votes against 22 as it was seen as a delaying tactic on the part of the opposition.

One of the foremost arguments against the bill was that already-existing laws were potent enough, and there was no need for fresh amendments. A. Krishnaswamy, an independent MP from Tamil Nadu, and M. S. Aney, independent MP from Nagpur, argued in Lok Sabha that the step showed the failure of government to use the available laws properly. Krishnaswamy also pointed out that a new law would be counter-effective as it would only ensure that the oppositional and disintegrative forces go underground, and thereby it did not provide a good solution to the problem of communalism (LSD: 5924). There were other opposition leaders who strictly rejected the need for any legislation of that sort. H. Hynniewta, an independent MP in

Lok Sabha representing hill regions of Assam, along with others like Socialist leader Ramsevak Yadav considered the bill a threat to freedom of speech and expression as it widened the space for state interventions (LSD: 5998). Similar views were put forward by Communist leader Bhupesh Gupta and Republican Party of India MP B. D. Khobragade in the Rajya Sabha (LSD: 6217). There was also opposition to the removal of the explanation from section 153(A), as it was believed that the change would make the law amenable to misuse and make it difficult to prove innocence in cases where the charges were falsely implicated. Congress leaders like Mahavir Tyagi (LSD: 5937–5940) and Thakur Das Bhargava (LSD: 5945) were vehemently opposed to this move. They argued that the removal of 'malicious intentions' from the necessary requirement to convict individuals under the law as contained in the explanation to section 153(A) would be a direct attack on freedom of expression. Hridaynath Kunzru remarked in the Rajya Sabha: 'We are now trying in the name of national integration to adopt a more stringent measure than Government considered it necessary to adopt during the war' (RSD: 3166). A similar attitude was reflected by All India Mahasabha Vice President V. G. Deshpande, who in a press conference on 12 August 1961 charged that the 'section has become too wide in scope and will make innocent activities for social reform also a criminal offence' (*The Times of India*, 13 August 1961).

The Congress Party was well armed to counter these opinions and justify its decision to introduce the amendments. The foremost justification extended in support of amendments was that they were required to protect the secular character of Indian polity. Congress members like Raghubir Sahai (LSD: 5968) and Sriram Sahay (RSD: 3168) argued that it was necessitated by the activities of communal parties which tried to polarize votes by invoking religious contentions. Santosh Kumar Basu, Congress MP from West Bengal (RSD: 3194), along with other members like Kasliwal (LSD: 5922) and Akbar Ali Khan (RSD: 3174), argued that government needed such laws in order arm itself to curb the intentions of communal parties of all hues. Khan even recommended that the guilty should not just be jailed but be hanged (RSD: 3174). Reply to the opposition was led by the Minister of Home Affairs Lal Bhadur Shastri, who defended his government's position aggressively. He not only rejected the need for circulation but also argued that unlike the opposition's claims, section 153(A) was being made more pointed and grounded according to the needs of the time (LSD: 6218). On the subject of removal of explanations, he argued that the onus to prove that the intention of the accused was neither mala fide nor malicious should be the responsibility of the accused and not the prosecutor, else it was very difficult for the executive to act even in most disastrous situations. The explanations, he remarked, gave an undue advantage to the accused (LSD: 6220). The overwhelming presence of congressmembers in both houses of Parliament ensured that the bill was passed without any difficulty.

As is visible, overall debate in both houses of the Parliament concentrated on issues of communal violence and the role of the press. The question of freedom of expression remained important but was overshadowed by harms that an excess of it had caused to society. The need of the hour, it was widely acknowledged, was to curb such liberty to promote values of 'national integration' and 'toleration' (Dattar, LSD: 5884). Though the question of religious offence did not figure at all in the debates, there were clear signs that the legislation was going to have serious ramifications on the subject. So, any form of publication which could incite religious passions could face punitive action. Further the amendment to section 153(A) also meant that the scope of preventive laws under section 99 of CrPC was also widened, and hence any such publication could also be proscribed without any consideration about the intentions of the author. Furthermore, the way in which government introduced the amendments in response to communal violence in different areas meant that strengthening the laws was seen as an important and easily available remedy to counter such attempts. It was overlooked, however, that these changes would have long-term repercussions on the freedom of speech and expression, and its impact would not be limited to the communal press but could also affect other mediums of expression. The congressmembers like S. S. N. Tankha (RSD: 3174–3179) insisted that Parliament should have faith in the elected government that the laws would not be misused, but in practice it was no guarantee to the way in which the executive would translate and use such powers in its dealing with contentious subjects like publications that were claimed to be religiously offensive. At the least, an increase in the scope of sections 153(A) and 295(A) meant a direct attack on the scope of freedom of speech and expression, a relation that most lawmakers overlooked, considering it a necessary step to curb tendencies of communal disturbances.

Similarly, in 1968, after a series of communal riots, most significantly in Srinagar, Ranchi and Aurangabad, the National Integration Council recommended further amendments to these laws and recommendations the government readily accepted.[43] Following this, the government introduced the Criminal and Election Laws Amendment Act, 1969, in the Parliament, which became Act XXXV of 1969. While introducing the bill in the Rajya Sabha, Vidya Charan Shukla, Minister of Home Affairs, pronounced that the aim of the legislation was to counter 'growing trends of communalism, factionalism and regionalism' in the country (RSD: 5482). He specified the role of the communal press in disturbing the peace and harmony of the country and inciting religious hatred among common people who are easily swayed by such propaganda material (RSD: 5483). He specifically accused the RSS mouthpiece, *Organizer*, and journals like *Mother India*, of misguiding citizens on communal lines. The most significant amendments that the bill proposed to undertake in relation to freedom of speech and expression included: (1) The scope for intervention of the executive under section 153(A) was enlarged. So, unlike earlier, when promoting feelings of enmity or hatred were punishable, promotion of 'disharmony' and 'ill-will' was also added as eligible for conviction. However, the terms like 'disharmony' and 'ill-will' remained undefined, and also there was no discussion about what parameters would be used to judge a particular publication's capacity to promote 'disharmony' or 'ill-will' among different communities. (2) Along with the change in the scope of 153(A), section 196 of CrPC was also amended whereby the offence under section 153(A) was made cognizable and unlike earlier, the District Magistrate could act *suo motu* in such cases without permission of the state government or any court. As Shukla claimed on the floor of the house, the District Magistrate could now directly take cognizance of such inflammable matters to 'not only stop that sort of writing, but also seize the printing press' (RSD: 5484). It is explicit that both these measures were detrimental to the scope of freedom of speech and expression as they increased the space for subjectivity in executive action. These amendments only made the laws more prone to subjective intervention and hence available for misuse by the executive.

As in the case of the amendments in 1961, debates in both houses of the Parliament revolved around the issue of communal violence. The opposition concentrated on highlighting the failures of the Congress government to stop communal riots. It was claimed that statutory laws, if used properly, had enough scope to deal with the situation, and there was no need to increase them further. It was maintained that the continuing spree of communal violence was representative of the inability of government and not the inefficacy of laws.[44] The Jan Sangh leaders like Niranjan Verma accused government of practicing pseudo-secularism and argued that it had failed to inculcate the values of 'toleration' and 'national integration' among citizens (RSD: 5505–5507). The Communist and Socialist members doubted the intentions of government in widening the powers of local authorities.[45] On the contrary, congressmembers and other supporters of the bill defended the step of government by citing the NIC recommendations.[46] They criticized the politics of political parties like Jana Sangh and the Muslim League in religious polarization and pointed to the role of the press in corrupting the minds of vulnerable masses that fall prey to their political propaganda.[47]

The subject of freedom of speech and expression remained largely absent in these debates. Among all participants in the debates in both houses of Parliament, the only member who raised the issue of freedom of speech and expression extensively was Pranab Kumar Mukherjee, a Congress Party member and first time MP of Rajya Sabha representing West Bengal. Though Mukherjee supported the bill, he raised serious issues about the attitude of politicians regarding freedom of expression. He remarked:

> Whatever be our feelings about any particular journal, whatever be our feelings about any particular press, whatever be our sentiments about the opinions expressed in a publication, we cannot advocate on the floor of the house that the freedom of the press be curtailed. (RSD: 5548)

He was critical about any attempt by government to curtail the freedom of press, and though he belonged to the ruling party, he raised doubts about the future of freedom of expression if the power of the executive was increased. He said:

> If we want to curtail the freedom of the press only from the view of stopping communalism, it will not stop there. If we give this power to the government of India, give this into the hands of the bureaucrats, they will control them and will say what should appear. It will not stop there, will go further. So, I think there should not be that power which can control the press.
>
> (RSD: 5548)

He raised objections with clause 6 of the bill, which maintained that freedom of expression could be restricted for maintaining communal harmony. According to him, eight exceptions were mentioned in article 19(2) of the constitution, and maintenance of communal harmony did not figure there, and therefore he was not sure if the bill itself was in accordance with the spirit of the constitution (RSD: 5549). Mukherjee asked pointed and pertinent questions regarding the constitutionality of the bill as well as on the subject of freedom of expression. Unfortunately, when the concerned Minister Vidya Charan Shukla delivered his final comments on the bill, he continued his attack on leaders belonging to the Jana Sangh as well as the Communist and Socialist parties but evaded throughout his speech any discussion about the probable impact of the bill on the scope of freedom of speech and expression. Mukherjee's name or concerns raised by him did not even appear in the speech of Shukla. The context of communal violence trumped any concern for freedom of speech and expression, and as in 1961, the amendments to statutory laws in 1968 were dominated by the aim of the government to control the communal press from inciting and spreading communal hatred. It resulted in further strengthening the hands of the executive by widening the scope of statutory laws.

Attitude of the Lawmakers towards Freedom of Speech and Expression in Independent India

Two aspects dominated the attitude of lawmakers in the debates of Parliament, during the amendments of constitution and the statutory laws. The first was the sense of urgency, and the second was the sense of paternalism reflected by the lawmakers. The urgency of the context – communal violence and the role of the press in it – guided these debates. In order to respond to the threats of communal violence, the lawmakers concentrated on enlarging the space for executive action. Though a constitutional right, freedom of speech and expression was considered a threat for maintenance of communal and social harmony. The sense of urgency is reflected throughout the debates, where leaders consistently argued for the need of making laws more stringent in order to strengthen the process of 'national integration' by curtailing 'fissiparous tendencies' and enforcing 'toleration' and 'communal harmony' among the citizens through fear of punishment for deviants. In order to curb the capacity of the communal press in the context of a disturbed communal context, it was overlooked that an amendment to the law would not only affect newsprint but would be detrimental to all forms of expression, and the increased scope for applicability of such laws ensured that the right to freedom of speech and expression would remain conditional on what the executive thought was permissible within the law.

The debates also reflected another important aspect in the attitude of the lawmakers, that is, the sense of paternalism. Repeated concern was raised about the vulnerability of Indian citizens and how they were being easily misguided by the communal press. For example, during the debates over the First Amendment, it was argued that most Indians were 'ignorant and illiterate' and, therefore, 'easy to mislead' (Bhargava, PD: 9717). When the opposition criticized the government by citing examples from other democracies, it was held that other countries had a long tradition in freedom, and that had 'instilled discipline and restraint' in them. It was also argued that Indians 'respond to incitement easily', unlike citizens of other countries, and therefore the comparison was faulty (Rev. D'Souza, PD: 9692). Similarly, while introducing the amendment to the statutory laws, B. N. Dattar, the then–Minister of Home Affairs, claimed that the bill was aimed to contain 'fissiparous tendencies' and was required because 'each man often times here and there thinks more of his religion ... than common binding links of the Indian society' (RSD: 3019–3020). It was therefore considered the duty of the government to protect citizens from the impact of a communal press that was misguiding them. The above discussions reflect that in the context of urgency, the attitude of the lawmakers was paternalistic and reactionary, and a debate about the ramifications of the proposed changes to the law on the fundamental right to freedom of speech and expression was avoided.

Conclusion

In the Indian case, the right to freedom of speech and expression was considered a natural ally to independence, and therefore its inclusion in the constitution as a fundamental right was neither doubted nor debated. In the process, an opportunity was lost to seriously reflect about its importance and the role it could play in making Indian democracy more vibrant. Rather, the need for national unity and public order motivated the constitution makers to severely limit its scope. Uday Singh Mehta has very well presented the situation as an irony 'that the successful culmination to free oneself from imperial subjection led almost immediately to freedom itself becoming a subsidiary concern; that is subsidiary to national unity, social uplift, and a concern with recognition' (2011: 17). But for the constitution makers, it was not an irony, but rather an 'ideal' produced under compulsion of the complex context in which they were operating.

The Constituent Assembly faced the classic dilemma of how to preserve individual freedom while promoting the public good (Austin 1997: 50). It attempted to create a happy marriage between different ideal values, overlooking the possibilities of clashes among them. The debates that followed reflected three important strands: (1) The idea of liberty, though important, was seen as subsidiary to the promises of social equality and the need for fraternity. So although important freedoms were included as fundamental rights, they were accompanied with caveats that made space for state intervention; (2) There was an attempt to balance individual rights with community/group rights, but as was visible, in relation to freedom of speech and expression, it further increased the ambiguity of state intervention, as it did not say anything about the situation when both these aspects could clash; and (3) Though the assembly did not approve the inclusion of 'communal hatred' as a proviso for state intervention, it was not because they did not recognize it as a threat, but because they believed that other laws especially under the IPC were enough to deal with such issues. These strands made space for state intervention from three directions: firstly, through the constitutional provisions whereby laws could be made to limit freedom of speech and expression; secondly, through the ambivalence created by not considering the situation where individual and group rights might clash in the form of potential contradictions that were yet undeveloped; and thirdly, the recognition of criminal laws as a deterrent to excesses of free speech, which incidentally, were to be imported as formulated during British rule.

Soon after its formulation, the constitution faced newer contradictions, resulting in its amendment. However, again, rather than engaging in a debate about the prospects of free speech, it was posed as a threat to state capacity and hence resulted in increased powers to the state against such freedom. It can be said that different contexts call for different ways of treating the issues of rights and liberties, and it often depended on the socio-cultural and political contexts. Some scholars have pointed at the 'paradox of constitutional democracy', which assumes a strange merger of 'constitution' and 'democracy', which often stand for contradictory values and ideals (Habermas 1996; Michelman 1998). Habermas has argued that such paradox can only be settled if we try to understand the principle of 'co-originality' – that private and public autonomy require each other. The argument is not therefore that there should or should not be limitations; rather, it is about the kind of limitations forwarded and whether they improve the space for liberty or restrict it (Habermas 2001: 767). The laws in such cases should consider freedom at its core, which apparently did not happen during the CAD. The terms used to delimit the scope of freedom of speech and expression – libel, slander, defamation, contempt of court, decency, morality – are vague and uncertain; there is every possibility for multiple interpretations. This not only invited state intervention but increased the possibilities of its misuse. Adding to these were the already existing and newly developed legal instruments, be it either in the form of the IPC, CrPC or the state-based laws which did not only severely limit but also introduced similar ambiguities about the scope of free speech as experienced during colonial times.

The attitude of lawmakers and executives towards freedom of expression is equally a matter of concern. The way in which this freedom was juxtaposed to the maintenance of social harmony reduced its scope – both legal as well as substantive. As the debates in both houses of Parliament during the amendment to penal codes in 1961 and 1969 show, lawmakers were not interested in discussing the issues of freedom of expression, and even in cases where the concerns were raised; it attracted little attention due to the context in which the legislations were introduced. A series of communal violent incidents and the role of the press in escalating polarization convinced the legislators that freedom of speech and expression needed to be curbed. However, the repercussions of amendments were largely overlooked. It affected not only the communal press, but also other forms of expressions like books and others. Also, an increase in powers of the executive to act upon such laws meant that the space for freedom of speech and expression was further left conditional to the prerogative of the administrators. Two conclusions can be drawn from such exercise: (1) Freedom of speech and expression as a fundamental right did not enjoy any significant status in India. It was allowed with several caveats that defined its scope; (2) The political class was insistent in allowing greater space for government intervention in the free exercise of freedom of speech and expression. It was believed that on the one hand, it was the responsibility of the government to maintain communal harmony and social cohesion, and therefore there was the need to balance freedom of expression with such challenges; on the other hand, it was considered the duty of government to adopt a paternalistic role to inculcate values of national integration and toleration among its citizens, and therefore there was the need to allow excessive powers under its command on contentious subjects like freedom of speech and expression.

Notes

1 K. T. Shah was an alumnus of London School of Economics and a left-oriented member representative from Bombay.
2 Ayyar was a well-known lawyer from the Madras constituency and represented the liberal school within the Congress Party.
3 Lahiri was a Communist leader from West Bengal.
4 He was a civil servant and appointed as the Chief Advisor to the Constituent Assembly. He played a key role in this capacity in formulating the Indian Constitution.
5 Seth was a Socialist leader representing United Provinces.

6 Baig was a prominent Muslim representative from Madras.
7 Sardar Hukam Singh was one of the two members included as a Sikh representative. He belonged to Shiromani Akali Dal and was Secretary of the National Democratic Front formed by S. P. Mookherjee. Later he joined the Congress Party and became the Speaker of the Lok Sabha in 1962.
8 Bhargava was a representative from East Punjab. Though a congressmember, he was known for his strong critical views against the government and was largely oriented to right-wing politics.
9 Hanumanthaiya was a prominent congressmember from Karnataka, considered to be very close to Nehru.
10 Such faith was reflected in the speeches of Congress Party members like Algu Rai Shastri, among others. See CAD VII: 767.
11 Krishnamachari was a prominent congressmember from Madras and an efficient economist.
12 Ghosh was a representative from Bihar. He argued: 'one expects that so far as the rights of the people are concerned, they should be expressed in clear, simple and straight language, so that a common man when he reads the Constitution can understand exactly and precisely what are his rights and what are the checks to his rights. I do not propose to say that at times of emergencies or grave needs freedom does not require to be checked to a certain extent. I believe in checks and balances, but at the same time, I must say that those checks should be very precise, and clear and should not be couched in ambiguous language and left to courts for decisions'
13 Munshi was one of the most vocal members in the Constituent Assembly. Though a congressmember, his ideas were largely influenced by right-wing ideology.
14 Ismail Sahib was a prominent member of the Muslim League and represented the Madras Presidency.
15 Along with Sardar Hukam Singh, Mann was the other Sikh representative inducted in the Assembly.
16 Volume VII of CAD is full of such instances where leaders of different parties highlighted this issue, especially in the discussions of 1 December 1948.
17 Pant was one of the topmost leaders of the Congress Party and the first Chief Minister of Uttar Pradesh, who later became the Home Minister in Nehru's cabinet.
18 One of the most prominent women leaders in Indian National Congress, Kaur became the Union Health Minister in Nehru's first cabinet.
19 Mehta was a reformist and social activist. She was known for her strong views on the Uniform Civil Code and all forms of reservations except for Scheduled Castes.
20 Trained as a barrister at London, Masani was one of the founding members of Congress Socialist Party in 1934.
21 See Rao (1966–1968, Vol. II: 140, 165, 173, 208). Also see the note of Rajkumari Amrit Kaur, Hansa Mehta and Minoo Masani to the fundamental rights sub-committee dated 14 April 1947 in Rao (1966–1968, Vol II: 162).
22 For example, Naziruddin Ahmad considered the demand for reservations as a result of a post-partition 'fear complex', which was now fast disappearing, and the situation was improving (CAD, Vol. III: 296). Also see Tajamul Husain, CAD, Vol. III: 270; Z. H. Lari, CAD, Vol. III: 283.
23 See Ayyar's Comments on the Draft report on 10, 14 and 15 April 1947 in Rao (1966–1968, Vol. II: 157).
24 Pannikar was a well-known journalist and historian who represented Punjab. For his comments on the subject see Rao (1966–1968, Vol. II: 157). Also see *Proceedings of the Meetings of the Advisory Committee on 21–22 April 1947* in the same volume at page 231.

25 For Rajagopalachari's comments see *Proceedings of The Meetings of the Advisory Committee on 21–22 April 1947* in Rao (1966–1968, Vol. II: 232).
26 Chand was a retired judge of the High Court who represented East Punjab in the Assembly.
27 H. C. Mookherjee was the Vice President of the Constituent Assembly. He was an educationalist and a prominent Christian leader of the Congress Party from West Bengal.
28 It is significant that the Minutes of the Drafting Committee recorded only the conclusions of each meeting but did not record the discussions. However, there is no trace of any such protest even during the discussions on the draft constitution in the Assembly, which makes the case more curious.
29 Tahir was a Muslim representative from Bihar.
30 Karimuddin was a famous criminal lawyer and a congressmember from Central Province.
31 Amendment No. 477 placed on the floor of the house on 2 December 1948. For details see CAD VII.
32 Ayyangar was a lawyer representing the Madras Presidency and became the first Deputy Speaker and later the Speaker of the Lok Sabha.
33 See Patel-Nehru letter dated 3 July 1950 in Patel (1972, Vol X: 358).
34 See *Parliamentary Debates*, Vol. XII (henceforth to be called PD and all references in this chapter belong to same volume, so only the column number will be mentioned), part 2, 17 May 1951, 90067.
35 See *Statements of Objects and Reasons*, appended to the Constitution (First Amendment) Act, 1951.
36 Kamath was a Socialist leader representing All India Forward Bloc.
37 Bharatiya Vidya Bhawan is a central government–funded organization founded in 1938 by K. M. Munshi, a popular Congress leader. See 'Stray Musings', *The Times of India*, 30 September 1956.
38 Nehru wrote to the Chief Ministers: 'There were reports being spread that in Aligarh Gita was desecrated which was wrong and led to mob violence', as quoted in Gupta (2006: 273).
39 'Military Preparedness by India Suggested: Mr. Chatterjee's Address at Mahasabha Conference', *The Times of India*, 12 November 1956; 'Clenched Fist Shown at India: Karachi Protest against Book', *The Times of India*, 22 September 1956.
40 'Protest Must Stop: Bhavan's Book', *The Times of India*, 3 October 1956; 'Agitation is Condemned', *The Times of India*, 7 October 1956.
41 See letter dated 29 September 1956 in Nehru (1990, Vol. 4). Also see, 'Special Letter in Addition to Fortnightly Letter' on page 447 of the same volume.
42 This position was justified by Home Minister Lal Bahadur Shastri in his closing speech on the subject. He said: "Our intention in omitting the explanation is with a view to cast responsibility on the offender to prove that his intentions were not malafide or malicious" (LSD: 6220).
43 See 'Delhi Approves Legislation to End Communalism; Measures Suggested by Home Ministry', *The Times of India*, 3 July 1968; 'Communal Riots: Preventive Steps Favoured', *The Times of India*, 23 June 1968. The recommendations were based on a report prepared by the Sub-committee headed by Andhra Pradesh CM K. B. Reddy.
44 This position was reiterated by several opposition leaders like B. N. Mandal (RSD: 5484); S. K. Vaishampayan (RSD: 5490); Niren Ghosh (RSD: 5511); Z. A. Ahmad (RSD: 5484).

45 See Niren Ghosh (RSD: 5511); Z. A. Ahmad (RSD: 5484); Rajnarain (RSD: 5777–5783).

46 See for example Congressmember Abid Ali representing Maharastra in Rajya Sabha (RSD: 5516–5519); Forward Bloc member Sheel Bhadra Yajee (RSD: 5506–5511).

47 Yajee (RSD: 5506–5511); Shukla (RSD: 5483–5484).

3

PREVENTING RELIGIOUS OFFENCE

Law, Courts and Freedom of Expression

Many commentators on Indian politics opine that 'unlike most western democracies, liberty was neither a political nor a primary social norm' for the post-Independence Indian State (Bhowmik 2009; Mahajan 1998; Mehta 2011). One of the primary challenges before the newly formed state was to balance competing claims of liberty and social tranquillity, and as a response, it endorsed the restrictions on individual freedoms. In fact, the concern for public order 'tilted the balance in favour of policing rather than civil liberties', whereby the state used its executive powers extensively to curtail fundamental rights like freedom of speech and expression in the pretext of public interest (Mahajan 1998; Sorabjee 1976). Government's decision to curb freedom of speech is guided both by the real and imaginary fears of a threat to public order, as well as the pressure exerted by socio-religious groups so that 'social censorship' comes to be linked with 'state censorship' (Dhavan 2008; Eswaran 1992). This made the role of the courts as defender of citizens' fundamental rights especially significant in the post-Independence period. As the final arbitrator of law, the courts in India have the power to define the scope of freedom of speech and expression, and under the reviewing authority assigned by the constitution, the courts can also check the arbitrary actions of the government.[1] If that is the case, how do the courts respond to the competing claims of freedom of expression and religious offence in order to judge whether the government's action is justified under the provisions of 'reasonable restriction'?

Legal practitioners and scholars like Soli J. Sorabjee (1994) and Rajeev Dhavan (2008) have argued that though some High Courts are more prone to allow restrictions of freedom of speech on the pretext of 'offence' and threat to public order, the Supreme Court generally maintains wide protection in its favour. Ratna Kapur (1996), based on her study of case laws, has held that there is no evidence of 'either an overuse of the provisions or a judicial abuse of the power of censorship' on the part of the courts. In fact, she argues, the courts have done an excellent job of protecting minority groups from hatred of the Hindu Right, which according to her was an important objective of India's hate speech laws. Contrary to this opinion, however, Pratap Bhanu Mehta (2008) has claimed that laws on the subject

DOI: 10.4324/9781003369257-4

are so ambiguous that the courts often seem to be upholding any form of censorship by the government, particularly in relation to religiously contentious speech acts, either due to the presumed threat to public order or based on its effect on the religious sensibilities of the followers within the community in question.

This chapter aims to engage with these interpretations based on my study of court cases involving religiously offensive publications. The aim is also to highlight the contemporary debates on the issue and put India's statutory laws in perspective. For analysis, cases both from the Supreme Court as well as different High Courts in India have been used.[2] One of the general limitations with legal studies pertaining to freedom of expression in India has been exclusive dependence on Supreme Court judgements to draw conclusions, overlooking the debates in the High Courts, including their observations. High Court cases are significant because most controversies about contentious publications fall under the category of law-and-order subjects that are primarily dealt with by the High Courts. Few of these cases travel to the level of Supreme Court – only if the constitutionality of any statutory laws is challenged or if review petitions against the decision of High Courts are filed. More importantly, a review of Supreme Court cases reveals that many of these High Court judgements and observations of the judges also play a guiding role in Supreme Court decisions and are referred recurrently in the debates of the courtroom. The analysis of case laws presented in this and the next chapter is derived from study of thirty-two court cases related to contentious books claimed to be religiously offensive during the period 1947–2010. For this a search was conducted on Manupatra Database[3] for the terms '19(1)(a)'; '19 (2)'; '295(A)'; '153(A)'; and 'CrPC 95'. The reason was that these are the sections of the constitutional and statutory laws which deal with the subjects of freedom of speech and expression vis-à-vis the claims of religious offence, including issues like proscription and banning of publications. Following this, I tried to locate the original cases in various official records, like AIR (All India Reporter) and journals published by the Supreme Court and other agencies like the Indian Law Institute, at Delhi, like CriJL (*Criminal Law Journal*), SCC (*Supreme Court Case*), and SCR (*Supreme Court Reporter*). The lists of cases referred here include all cases from the Supreme Court and High Courts on the subject, which were recorded in these documents.

Religious Offence and Restrictions to Freedom of Speech and Expression

According to the Oxford English Dictionary, 'offence' means annoyance or resentment brought about by a perceived insult or disregard for oneself. The expression contains two aspects – an action and an effect. In this work, 'offence' is used to refer to the hurt or wounded feelings produced, either voluntarily or involuntarily, by speech acts, most notably books and other publications. In this context, the idea of 'offence' also implies a relationship between two parties, that is, one who offends (who gives offence) and the offended (who takes offence). The one that gives offence can be either an individual or an object (in the present case books and other publications). At the same time, the offended can be an individual as well as a group (when the offence is experienced by many individuals from the same social group or community).[4] Religious offence, therefore, refers to the hurt generated to the religious sensibilities of individuals or groups, through the invocation of contentious religious subjects like defamation of religion or promoting hatred on the basis of religion. Considering that the injury is caused by speech acts, the subject under examination here is: when should law interfere, if at all, to regulate such speech acts in cases where religious offence is claimed?

There are several advocates of absolute and universal freedom of expression. Asserting this position in relation to religious offence, legal philosopher Ronald Dworkin (2006) opines that everyone has 'the right to ridicule' and no one has the 'right not to be insulted or offended'. He is against the idea that freedom of speech should have limits or that it ought to be balanced against any other good that society aspires to achieve, like the virtues of multiculturalism. Dworkin's views are based on the basic principle of human dignity, whereby he argued that expressing attitudes, opinions, fears and even libel confirmed the speaker's standing as a responsible agent in collective action (2009: vii–viii). But Dworkin's position emphasized the dignity of the 'speaker' and did not take into consideration the dignity of his or her putative target, that is, against whom the speech act was aimed.

Jeremy Waldron (2010), for example, raises this issue and further maintains that 'freedom from censorship of someone who uses hate speech does not outweigh the freedom from defamation of his or her target'. Developing this approach, Waldron provides a liberal defence to hate speech laws. But Waldron's use of 'dignity' is very specific. He defines dignity as the confirmation of *equal membership* in a society – 'basic social standing ... as a proper object of society's protection and concern' (2012: 15). Waldron suggests that the concern for dignity should be distinguished from concern to avoid offence. He argues that the feeling of offence is highly subjective, and it is the 'public nature of hate speech – in time, manner and place – that takes it outside the realm of offense of feelings (2012: 106). The aim of hate speech laws, he contends, should not be to prevent people from being offended. As is visible, neither Dworkin nor Waldron support legal action against religiously offensive speech acts. Dworkin completely rejects any basis whatsoever to restrict freedom of speech, and Waldron's idea of 'hate speech', though it allows some forms of restrictions, does not allow religious insults and offence as a valid and justifiable ground to restrict speech acts.

Perhaps one of the most significant and enduring contributors to the debate over validity of religious offence as a reason for restrictions was John Stuart Mill. Mill in his classic *On Liberty* devised what is popularly known as the 'harm principle'. The central tenet of Mill's idea is that 'the only purpose power can be rightfully exercised over any member of any civilized community, against his will, is to prevent harm to others' (Mill 1978). In case of speech acts, Mill would not support any action solely on the basis of the content of an opinion because he defended 'fullest liberty of professing and discussing, as a matter of ethical conviction, any doctrine, however immoral it may be considered' (1978: 106). For him, the circumstances in which the opinion is expressed could only make a speech act punishable. The corn dealer example that Mill used to explain his argument is also indicative of the difference he would place between 'advocacy' and 'instigation'. 'Instigation' was different from 'advocacy' in that in the case of 'instigation', there is a direct urging to action and the action follows immediately. For example, Mill argued that it was acceptable if someone advocated through print that the corn dealer starved the poor. But when the same view is expressed in front of an angry mob standing outside a corn dealer's home, it can lead to violence and hence harm to the dealer. In this case there appears to be a direct link between the idea advocated and the action of the mob, and hence the speech act was punishable. So, according to Mill, a speech act was only punishable if it was in the form of instigation and resulted in an 'overt act' and 'at least a probable connection can be established between the act and instigation' (1978: 107). Drawing a parallel, it could be deduced that for Mill, even a religiously offensive speech act could be punished only if it was in the form of 'instigation', which means defamation of religion would not constitute a valid crime and could only be punished if, for example, it promotes hatred among the audience and instigates them to harm others as a result. Religiously offensive publications in the form of books or printed articles would similarly escape punishment, according to Mill's standards.

Some critiques feel that Mill's consequentialist argument set the bar too high, and if this principle was taken seriously, it will be difficult to constrain any form of speech. Joel Feinberg (1973, 1985), for example, argued that there were human experiences that might be 'harmless' but still so unpleasant that a demand for legal protection against them would be justified even if it was at the cost of an individual's liberty. Therefore, Fienberg formulated the 'offence principle'. The basic assumption is that offence is less serious than harm, and the offended mental state is a condition different from harm. According to Feinberg, 'offense' takes place when (1) one suffers a disliked or unpleasant state and (2) one attributes that state to the wrongful conduct of another and (3) one resents the other for his or her role in causing that state (1985: 1–2). However, Feinberg was clear that not all such claims could be legally protected at the cost of freedom of speech. Therefore, he derived certain standards for analyzing whether an action in this regard was warranted or could be justified as reasonable. These standards included: (1) the 'extent of offence' standard – in order to allow consideration of the intensity and durability of repugnance produced; (2) the 'reasonable avoidability' standard – to check whether the offensive displays could be easily avoided by the subject; and (3) the 'volenti' standards – to assess whether or not the witness has willingly assumed the risk of being offended (Feinberg 1985: 26–27). For Feinberg, an action against a speech act could be justifiable only if the witness had to face it involuntarily and was in such a position that there was no way in which the displays could be avoided and the 'offence' produced by the display was deeply hurting. This scale could be useful for all kind of offence, including that caused by religiously injurious speech.[5] Feinberg held that the offence principle is dependent on 'cultural standards' that vary greatly from place to place and within each nation 'constantly and rapidly change' (1985: 47). This stress on context-based analysis of the need and nature of law is also supported by political philosophers like Charles Taylor (1989 and Bhikhu Parekh (2012).

Modern democracies have come up with their own sets of laws to restrict freedom of speech and expression according to their specific needs and challenges (Letsas 2012). As discussed in the last chapter, in India, laws were introduced to restrain freedom of expression in the name of preventing the threats it posed to peace and tranquillity in society. The process began with the introduction of the penal codes during the colonial regime. Based on the 'unique' context of India, specific laws were created to take care of the performative dimension of speech, but more specifically, these laws were characterized by a predisposition towards protecting against mental agitation and hurt sentiments in response to loaded words, offensive gestures and transgression of hierarchical order. Gradually newer laws were added to prevent harmful impacts of religiously offensive speech acts, significant among them the addition of section 153(A) in 1898 and section 295(A) in 1927. In the post-Independence period, these laws were adopted as part of the revised penal codes. So, with regard to defamation of religion and incitement of religious hatred, other than the limits drawn under article 19(2) of the constitution, the two older, colonial-era statutory laws became particularly important. Section 295(A) aimed to prevent acts where nuisance is not the physical aspect of a communication, but arises because the message is considered provocative, indecent or denigrating. It prohibits 'deliberate and malicious acts, intended to outrage religious feelings of any class by insulting its religion or religious beliefs'. Though it is not a blasphemy law, it was meant to serve a similar purpose. It does not punish an imputation to god but to the followers, whereby the outrage and hurt felt by the followers is protected. Section 153(A) is aimed to prevent the consequences of a communication that may indirectly bring about harm to others by promoting hatred against any religious group. So, it criminalises the promotion of 'enmity between different groups on grounds of religion, race, place of birth, residence, language, etc.', or 'doing acts prejudicial to maintenance of harmony'. Both these laws form the basis of state action against offenders who indulge in any of the above-mentioned activities. Unlike Dworkin's and Waldron's propositions, where the individual is the unit of analysis, these laws are meant to respond to the threat experienced by a 'group' or 'class' of citizens. Also unlike in Mill's argument, these laws criminalized not just instigation, but any speech act that intended to outrage religious feelings or promote hatred. There is no necessary emphasis on either the consequences of the outrage or the hatred produced. Such laws allow government to criminalize a wide range of activities in the name of protecting the religious sensibilities of the citizens. The 'reasonableness' of government action was to be based on the test about how justifiably the government has used these statutory laws within the limits approved by the constitution. In order to make that judgement, the courts first needed to define the scope of these laws, which could help in understanding when and why religious offence became punishable.

Understanding 'Religious Offence' in the Light of Statutory Laws: A Perspective from Indian Courts

The present section examines what according to the courts is problematic in religious offence that warrants government's intervention either in the form of punishing the agent or in the form of censoring the speech act. Firstly, I discuss the courts' understanding about what makes a publication contentious – whether it is the 'manner' in which the opinion is expressed or the 'matter' contained in the publication. Secondly, I show how the courts further open the interpretation of statutory laws by emphasizing the essential difference between 'punitive' and 'preventive' laws. The subject-matter under consideration here shifts from the publication itself to the judgement of the government officials, thereby expanding their powers to proscribe or forfeit contentious publications without proper examination of the facts.

The Matter versus Manner Conundrum

Debates over legal intervention against freedom of expression include a vital concern about what should be the determining factor in such decisions: is it the substance of the speech or the form of expression? There is a strong belief among scholars that it should be the 'manner' in which the views are expressed and not the 'matter' that should be the basis of analysis. The expression of an opinion can be curbed, it is argued, only to the extent that offence is caused by the manner in which it is expressed (Feinberg 1973; Jones 1980). If the emphasis is shifted from 'matter' to 'manner', it allows the bar to be set higher; it hence creates a more favourable environment for a marketplace of ideas in search of truth by not interfering with people's ability to make judgements about religion, but does not allow the speech act to be deliberately offensive. Thus, it offers a balanced position to those who value freedom of expression but also want to avoid offence (Feinberg 1973). It also helps to maintain a distinction between what people disagree with or disapprove of and what causes offence. One of the extreme positions on this subject is reflected in the 'content-neutrality' doctrine popularized by American jurisprudence (Heyman 2002). The 'content-neutrality' doctrine assumes that the state would not punish or restrict speech acts on the basis of the content or the substance of the expression. Content-neutrality includes both 'subject-matter neutrality' as well as 'viewpoint neutrality', which means that speech acts could not be restricted on grounds of either the matter of the expression or the idea that the matter represented.

However, in the Indian context, the courts have emphasized the need to consider both the 'manner' as well as the 'matter' of the speech. Focus on 'manner' of speech helps in two vital aspects that substantiate the 'reasonableness' of legal intervention: (1) it helps the courts to trace the 'intention' of the accused; and (2) it helps the courts to weigh the intensity of the hurt. An important component of the punitive law under section 153(A) and 295(A) of the IPC is the aspect of *mens rea*, which emphasizes the need to examine the intention of the accused. In both the above-mentioned laws, punishment is justified only if it can be proved that the accused had 'deliberate and malicious' intentions involved in the contentious speech act. Courts analyze the 'manner' in which an idea is represented in order to test for 'deliberate and malicious' intention. They have upheld this reading of law in several judgements. For example, in 1960 the Allahabad High Court heard a case where the government of Uttar Pradesh had ordered the forfeiture of six books written by Baba Khalil Ahmad (*Baba Khalil Ahamad v. State* [1960] A.I.R. 1960 All. 715). The controversy was regarding the character of a historical figure, Muwaiya, who was considered revered by certain Sunni Muslim communities, whereas others thought him to be an evil person. The counsel for the applicant urged that the notification of the government was flawed, as any hurt caused was not intentional and the only aim of the author was to educate the masses about the negative character of Muwaiya and his role in Islamic history as a tyrant and a villain. Counsel also argued that the claims in the books were based on historical facts, and therefore it could not be seen as a deliberate attempt to hurt religious sentiments. The court held that:

> The intention of the writer of a book must be judged primarily by the language of the book itself.... If the language is of a nature calculated to produce or to promote feelings of enmity or hatred, the writer must be presumed to intend that which his act was likely to produce.

The court further remarked that 'even a true statement may outrage religious feelings', and therefore the argument about the content being based on historical facts did not really matter. In order to test whether the books were injurious in the above case, an inquiry into the language used in the publication, with reference to Muwaiya, was therefore considered important. It was reflective of the fact that court believed that the 'manner' in which ideas or arguments are presented become the primary indicator of the intentions of the author.

Secondly, the courts also examine the 'manner' in which the subject of speech is presented to differentiate between the content of speech acts that people disagree with or disapprove of and those that cause offence and are liable to legal intervention. Considering that it is impossible to quantify the feeling of hurt or offence, the courts concentrate on the intensity of offence. One of the primary tests that the courts have endorsed is that of the 'reasonable man' doctrine, which implies that only those speech acts that have the capacity to 'grossly offend' any 'reasonable man' deserve to be restricted (*Shiv Ram Dass Udasin v. The Punjab State* [1954] A.I.R 1955 P H 28). To apply this test, the court maintains that the expression 'outrage' (as used in section 295[A]) needs to be distinguished from feelings like 'wound', 'hurt' and 'injury'. In the *Sujato Bhadra* case, the West Bengal High Court differentiated between 'wounding' used in section 298 IPC and 'outraging' used in section 295 IPC. It held that the expression 'outraging' is much stronger than 'wounding', and that the term 'outrage' means 'to wrong grossly, treat with gross violence or indignity (*Sujato Bhadra v. State of West Bengal* [2006] 39 A.I.C. 239). The expression 'grossly offensive' is a natural extension of this distinction maintained by the courts.[6] Also, the courts have repeatedly asserted that the impact of a speech act should not be judged on the basis of the reaction that is expected out of a believer or an emotional person; rather the effect is 'to be judged from standard of [a] reasonable, strong minded, firm and courageous' person (*State of Maharashtra & Ors. v. Sanghraj Damodar Rupawate & Ors.* [2010] Civil Appeal of 2010 [Arising out of S.L.P. {C} No. 8931 of 2007]).[7]

The most important signifier in each of the above-mentioned tests is the language used to express the opinion, since this is considered to be an explicit indicator of both – the intention of the accused as well as the intensity of the hurt caused. Based on the emphasis on the 'manner' of expression in general, and language in particular, a study of courts' judgements provides some understanding about how they perceive the idea of religious offence. The courts have held that 'rational criticism of religion couched in restrained language' (*Lalai Singh Yadav v. State of Uttar Pradesh* 1971 CriLJ 1773) or 'doctrinal disagreement' (*Zac Poonen v. Hidden Treasure Literature* [2001], 2002 CriLJ 481) could not be considered an offence under law. However, even if the criticism of the religion is based on truth claims, the use of vile and insulting language would make the speech act eligible for punishment and prohibition (*Henry Rodrigues and Anr.* 1962 CriLJ 564). The courts went so far as to argue that if the writing in question was not intended to insult other religions or to promote hatred among different religious groups, then proselytizing writings could also not be restricted (*Ramlal Puri v. State of Madhya Pradesh* [1970] AIR 1971 MP 152). The emphasis on language to decipher the intention, however, provides an extremely subjective tinge to the analysis. It further highlights the moralizing aspect of courts' behaviour, whereby they dictate what form of expression is allowed or disallowed in a civil discourse.

It would be wrong to conclude, however, that the courts in India depend only on the 'manner' of expression or the language used in the publication to judge its legality. In different cases courts have also emphasized the need to look into the 'matter' or the content of the publications. It is maintained that in several instances, though the publication may not contain offensive language, the matter itself might be volatile and thereby attract legal injunction. Two primary reasons can be attributed to this approach: (1) the extensive scope of statutory laws, especially section 153(A) of the IPC, and (2) difficulty in deriving clear clinical tests to maintain the manner-matter distinction to contemplate religious offence. As discussed above, the emphasis on the 'manner' of speech acts helps in judging the intention of the author as well as the intensity of the 'hurt' caused by the speech. However, the statutory laws governing legal intervention to speech acts in India include section 153(A), where the subject under analysis is whether a speech act 'promotes or attempts to promote, on grounds of religion ... disharmony or feelings of enmity, hatred or ill-will' between different religious communities. In order to judge whether a publication falls under this category, the courts cannot solely depend on the 'manner' of the expression but are also required to analyze the content or the 'matter'. Consider, for example, the case of *Babu Rao Patel* in the Supreme Court, where the court was considering the constitutionality of section 153(A). An additional question under analysis was whether political writing or historical truth could attract the provisions under section 153(A) (*Babu Rao Patel v. State of Delhi* 1980 A.I.R. 763). The case was regarding the arrest of Babu Rao Patel after two of his articles – 'A Tale of Two Communalisms' and 'Lingering Disgrace of History' – were published in the political magazine edited by him called *Mother India*. These articles were considered to be a deliberate and malicious attempt to promote feelings of enmity and hatred among Hindus and Muslims. It appeared in the Supreme Court in the form of special appeal from the plaintiff after the High Court had refused to quash the arrest order.

In the first article 'A Tale of Two Communalisms', Patel discussed Muslim communalism and argued that communalism in India was an instrument employed by political minorities. The central thesis of his article was that Muslims were a 'violent race' with a 'radical tradition of rape, loot, violence and murder'. The second article, 'Lingering Disgrace of History', was written as a protest against the naming of Delhi roads after the Mughal Emperors, whom he calls 'lustful perverts, rapists and murderers'. He extended his criticism to argue that:

> From Mohammad Ibn Qasim, who landed in India in June 712 AD with 6000 Muslim cut-throats, to Mohammad Ali Jinnah, who cut the ancient cradle of a peace loving human race into three bleeding

> birds in August 1947, we have had 1235 years of bloodstained history in which our life has been constantly punctuated by endless raids, rapes, loots, arson and slaughter. (As quoted in the judgement of *Babu Rao Patel v. State of Delhi 1980* A.I.R. 763)

After discussing various atrocities and tyrannies of the Mughals ending with Aurangzeb, he wrote:

> To have a street named after this Mughal bastard in New Delhi, the capital of India, is not only a disgrace to the Hindus but a raging insult to the brave community of Sikhs. Had the Muslims been insulted thus, they would not only have burnt every house on the road named after the tyrant but also set fire to the whole damned city. The Muslims know how to guard their traditions.

In the Supreme Court, A. K. Sen, the counsel of the appellant, argued that if the articles were seen as a whole, it would be visible that 'A Tale of Two Communalisms' was no more than a political thesis, and the second article, 'Lingering Disgrace of History', was no more than a protest based on historical truths. It was contended that none of the articles attacked any religion, and so there was no question of promoting and attempting to promote feelings of enmity, hatred or ill-will between different religious groups. But the court rejected these arguments and held that both the articles were deliberately and maliciously written to promote feelings of enmity, hatred and ill-will between the Hindu and Muslim communities, and this, the court maintained, 'cannot be done in the guise of political thesis or historical truth'. The method applied by the court to reach this conclusion is indicative of its approach. The court discussed the content of each article in detail, citing important sections and highlighting possible interpretations. Based on an extensive analysis of the 'matter' contained in the articles, the court concluded that the possible implication of the publication was well within the scope of 153(A) and required action by the government. As we can see, both the subject-matter as well as viewpoint expressed in the publication together played a significant role in examining the consequences of the articles under controversy.

However, the pressure of statutory law is not the only reason why the courts include as part of their analysis the 'matter' of speech acts. They face extreme difficulty in maintaining a principled distinction between the 'matter' and the 'manner' of the speech act, in relation to religious offence. Can an expression be held to be offensive to the religious susceptibilities of the followers only if vile or insulting language is used to denigrate religious beliefs, a revered personage or a basic religious value system? The courts have held that freedom to criticize religion is allowed only if the criticism pertains to the practices of that religion and does not extend to its principles or basic tenets (*N. Veerabrahmam v. State of Andhra Pradesh* [1959] A.I.R.

1959 A.P. 572). Also, any criticism or questioning of the character of a religious personage or of a religious text is clearly prohibited (*Baba Khalil Ahamad* A.I.R. 1960 All. 715; *P. Ramasami* 1964 1 MLJ 147). The courts have held that even if the language used in the publication is neither aggressive nor outrageous, commentaries on these subjects have the potentiality to offend the religious sensibilities of the followers of any religion as well as promoting hatred among different religious groups. The use of restrained language or the claims of historical truth do not make the publication any less volatile, nor do they decrease the intensity of harm that such publications can cause. In such cases the reference point for the courts is the probable impact such expression could have on the religious followers.

The case of *Master Aman Preet Singh*, heard at the Punjab High Court in 1996, is reflective of this complexity. A Public Interest Litigation was filed by Master Aman Preet Singh, a class XII student of a school under the Central Board of Secondary Education (CBSE) for issuance of appropriate directions for deleting remarks alleged to be derogatory to Guru Gobind Singh (the tenth Guru of Sikhs) contained in a history textbook prescribed for Class XII students called *Modern India* (*Master Aman Preet Singh and Others v. Government of India and others* [1996] AIR 1996 PH 284). The book was written by historian Bipan Chandra and published by the National Council of Educational Research and Training (NCERT). The applicant had claimed that the chapter on Guru Gobind Singh presented the Guru in a bad light, noting in particular a reference to him being an employee of Bahadur Shah, a Mughal king. It was alleged that such references were contrary to facts and opposed to the teachings and writings of the Guru and hence 'offensive' to the Sikhs. In this case, the primary complaint was not about the 'manner' in which the subject was discussed or about the language being vile or insulting but about the content itself. A historical claim about the life of the Sikh guru (even though duly supported by historical evidence) came under controversy.

The respondents, including the publisher and the author, rejected the charge that the section deemed offensive in any way hurt the religious sentiments of any person. It was argued to be a fact based on historical research. They forwarded three arguments in favour of their position: (1) the contentious section was extracted out of context and the chapter as a whole aimed to situate the Sikh religion in perspective and to stress the popular, egalitarian and socially radical character of the Sikh religion founded by Guru Nanak; (2) the authenticity of the objectionable remarks was a matter of 'legitimate historical debate'; it was maintained that many historians disagreed with the view expressed and the truth content could only be extracted by historians alone 'by discussing it in a spirit of historical objectivity on the basis of acceptable historical evidence'; (3) the writer's view in this chapter was based on historical writings of eminent historians like Joseph Davey Cunningham (*History of the Sikhs*), William Irvine (*Later Mughals*), Sir Gukul Chand Narang (*Transformation of Sikhism*) and also upon a

Gurmukhi script, *Panth Parkash*, written by Bhai Gian Singh and a Persian work, *Umdat-ul-Twarikh*.

The court, however, remained unimpressed by the arguments of the respondents. It upheld the petition and ordered the removal of the offensive passages. It held:

> A Guru who is respected, revered and worshipped and is admitted to have fought against Moghul emperor throughout his life and sacrificed all that which was precious to him cannot be permitted to be projected to students to be an employee of Moghul emperor as the same is likely to hurt the religious feelings of the community.

The court approached the case as a question about protection of secular values of the Indian polity rather than as an infringement of freedom of speech and expression. It maintained that freedom of speech and expression could not be treated as a licence to infringe the rights or faith of others. In fact, it claimed that 'the State is under a constitutional obligation to preserve and protect the interests of Sikh Community', and therefore, 'the respondent/authorities are under an obligation to refrain from becoming a party to such controversial writing, which may ultimately hurt the feelings of the Sikh community as a whole or a part of it'.

Most significant was the observation of the court on the claim about historicity. This case was an explicit example of the blurring of the manner-matter distinction in relation to the impact of a publication. As there was no complaint about the form of expression or the language used, the decision was based strictly on the content or subject of the writing. The fact that the subject was related to a 'controversial' historical episode in the life of Guru Gobind Singh was considered reason enough to restrict the publication in the name of protecting the values of secularism. The subject-matter expressed was seen as an insult to the Guru, and though the language was neither abusive nor libellous, it was thought to be potentially offensive to the religious sensibilities of the followers of Guru Gobind Singh. The court also overlooked the fact that any kind of historical enquiry necessitated the free flow of arguments based on historical evidence. On this latter point the court held: 'The writings about religious Gurus cannot be permitted to be justified on the basis of disputed and debatable historical truths, lest it may destroy the very secular fabric of the Constitution'. Given that the author had never claimed that his views had unanimous acceptability among historians, while at the same time had shown that his statement was not bereft of historical evidences supported by several other historians, he had arguably allowed space for a view that it was aimed neither at denigrating any religious personage nor at hurting religious sentiments. But contrarily, the court suggested that 'self-restraint is expected in matters like religion, particularly when they are apprehended to affect the sentiments of a section of the society, forming part of the Indian polity'.

The above discussion shows that while interpreting statutory laws, the courts provide a very wide definition of religious offence, and this is reflected in their consideration of both 'matter' as well as 'manner' of speech acts that are seen as requiring government action. Only a restrained language and non-interference in critical aspects of religion, according to the courts, could be justified while dealing with the subject of religion. The immunity such a position provides to several aspects of religious belief, from attack or criticism, places constraints on the free exercise of freedom of speech and expression, even historical research on the subject.

Extending the Reach of Law: Separating 'Punitive' and 'Preventive' Actions

While adjudicating cases concerning contentious publications, the courts have maintained a distinction between 'punitive' and 'preventive' laws. The punitive laws like section 295(A) and 153(A) of the IPC can be used to punish authors/publishers who produce religiously offensive publications or publications that incite communal hatred, whereas the preventive law, like section 95 of the CrPC, can be used to proscribe or forfeit contentious publications. Section 95 of the CrPC empowers the government to declare any printed material forfeited which 'appears to the State Government to contain any matter the publication of which is punishable under section 124(A) or section 153(A) or section 153(B) or section 292 or section 293 or section 295(A) of the Indian Penal Code' by notification, 'stating the grounds of its opinion'. A look at the provision under section 95 would suggest that it is concomitant to the crime defined under the punitive laws, that is, the powers conferred upon the authorities to forfeit or proscribe can be used only if the conditions mentioned under other laws like section 295(A) or 153(A) are fulfilled. However, the courts have highlighted at least three important aspects in which the provisions are not only defined differently but also allow wider latitude for state action in order to prevent the circulation of publications containing religiously offensive subject-matter.

Firstly, the courts have maintained that the reference of various IPC laws in section 95 is only a description of the kind of offence required to be prevented and that the use of section 95 is not dependent on the tests mentioned for other statutory laws. Initially, some High Courts held that the law expected that cases be examined based on the tests suggested under sections 153(A) and 295(A) and only if a violation was deduced under these clauses could the action of the government to forfeit a publication be justified. This included tests such as *mens rea*, as required in the punitive laws.[8] The approach of the courts seems to have departed from this position significantly after the *Nand Kishore Singh* case. In this case, the Patna High Court argued that 'it would be somewhat fallacious to mathematically equate the proceedings under Sections 95 and 96 of the Code with a trial under Section 295-A of the Penal Code with the accused in the dock (*Nand Kishore Singh v. State of Bihar* AIR 1986 Pat 98). It held that the law under section 95 was essentially preventive in nature and to require the government be satisfied of the deliberate and malicious intention before using it was like defeating the very purpose of section 95. Also, the statute did not specify that it should be 'proved' to the state government or that the state government is 'satisfied' that all requirements of punishing section are established. All that the section expected was that it should 'appear' to the state government that the offending publication would come under the relevant section of the law. In this case the court also made it explicit that the 'clear and present danger' doctrine, as used in the US, cannot be applied in the Indian case.

This interpretation of law was significant for many reasons. On the one hand, it meant that the state government could proscribe a publication, without being satisfied about the tests like 'deliberate and malicious intention' of the author or publisher in the said case; nor was the government required to defend its decision in the courts on such grounds. On the other hand, it also allowed the state government to act towards pre-emption of the threat posed by the controversial publication. Broadly, the courts allowed a wider space for government's intervention on contentious publications, much wider in latitude than in cases under punitive laws. This interpretation of section 95 was upheld in several subsequent cases, most notably including the Supreme Court's observations in the *Sri Baragur Ramachandrappa* case and in the *Sangharaj Damodar Rupawate* case.[9]

Secondly, within the application of preventive laws, courts expect the government to spell out the 'grounds of opinion'.[10] A close analysis suggests that the courts insist that the 'ground of opinion' should include at least the citation of the offending passages (*Mohammad Khalid v. The Chief Commissioner, Delhi* [1967] A.I.R. 1968 Delhi 13) and the noting of the communities whose susceptibilities were allegedly hurt by the speech act (*Harnam Das* 1961 A.I.R 1662) as well as the 'conclusion of facts' (*Sanghraj Damodar Rupawate* Civil Appeal of 2010 [Arising out of S.L.P.(C) No. 8931 of 2007]) which led the government to forfeiture of the publication. The ground of opinion formation helped judges to understand the 'application of mind' by the authorities. The courts emphasized the importance of mentioning the grounds on which the opinion of the government was based in order to avoid arbitrary action by the government (*Lalai Singh Yadav* 1977 AIR 202),[11] and a failure on the part of the government to mention the ground of opinion could become the reason for cancellation of the notification of forfeiture (*Lalai Singh Yadav* 1977 AIR 202; *M/S Varsha Publications* Cri LJ 1446).[12] However, the courts have made this test lenient and subjective by reducing the details expected by the officials to spell out in a notification. There was the threat that the objectionable content, if declared in the notification explicitly, would ultimately be made available in the public sphere and thereby defeat the very objective of forfeiture or ban. In *Nand Kishore Singh* case, the Patna High Court took cognizance of this problem and brought some clarity on the issue. It opined:

> The declaration of forfeiture is consequently not required to be an exhaustive or self-contained document incorporating all the offending material as also each and every fact on which it is based. Any such detailed recitals or contents in a notification are neither mandated by statute nor precedent and would perhaps be incongruous in the nature of the notification envisaged by the statute.... It is amply sufficient if on the grounds of opinion, that is, the conclusions of fact being duly stated, the Government's opinion arrived at there from is clearly exhibited that the publications come within the mischief of the law.

As to mentioning the grounds of opinion, the courts held that though it was important, it did not need to include detailed exposition of the subject-matter but should exhibit the link between the conclusion of facts and the decision by the government. This is not an exception, as the courts have been consistently citing this case in order to check the validity of the notifications. The detailed notification was mandated in order to ascertain that the officials had conducted a thorough examination of the contentious publication before acting against it. The exemption pronounced in *Nand Kishore Singh*, therefore, protected the authorities from this mandatory procedure, making it easier for them to act against a contentious publication, even without a survey of the publication in question. It made it possible that the decision of authorities to act be guided more by the form of opposition or threat to public order that such publication would have attracted, and less by the content of the publication.

Thirdly, courts also held that in cases where any person appealed to the High Court against the forfeiture order, the onus of proof fell on the aggrieved, that is, it is for the petitioner in such cases to prove that the book does not contain anything disallowed in the section under which the order was passed. This followed from an interpretation of law under section 96(1) of the CrPC, which deals with the application in the High Court against forfeiture. Section 96(1) states:

> Any person having any interest in any newspaper, book or other document, in respect of which a declaration of forfeiture has been made under section 95, may, within two months from the date of publication in the Official Gazette of such declaration, apply to the High Court to set aside such declaration on the ground that the issue of the newspaper, or the book or other document, in respect of which the declaration was made, did not contain any such matter as is referred to in sub-section (1) of section 95.

Therefore, in order to challenge the order of forfeiture, the applicant would have to show that: (1) the publication in question did not contain anything 'which will offend or outrage the religious feelings of any section of the society' (*Baragur Ramachandrappa* [1998] CriLJ 3639); (2) there did not exist any intention on the part of the author to do so (*Sanghraj Damodar Rupawate* Civil Appeal of 2010 [Arising out of S.L.P.{C} No. 8931 of 2007]); and (3) the opinion of the government to proscribe the publication could not be sustained. This was in complete contradistinction to the requirements of punitive laws where the state government was expected to defend its decision to prosecute an individual by presenting evidence that not only proved the commission of offence but also pointed at 'deliberate and malicious' intention involved in the act.

Considering all these aspects together shows that if the state government follows the technical requirements, the probability of its action being upheld by the courts is quite high. It is far easier for government authorities to proscribe and forfeit a contentious publication than to punish (under statutory law) an individual attached to that publication. This also reveals the court's attitude towards the balance that it was expected to maintain between freedom of expression and claims of religious offence. Its interpretation of statutory laws provides wide space for the government's action against publications that are charged with defaming religion or promoting hatred against any religious groups. This is further confirmed by the difference the courts maintain between punitive and preventive law. The claim of freedom of expression becomes weaker with respect to controversial publications because courts do not intervene against censorship or proscription of such material in the name of public interest if the procedural aspect of law is not violated. The threat perception of government agencies becomes an important guiding point, and the interpretation of the preventive laws by the courts helps it to justify its prompt action.

The above section analyzed how courts interpret statutory laws, including the tests and doctrines they use to adjudicate on the subject of publications claimed to be religiously offensive. But an important question that still needs to be considered is why courts provide such a broad definition of religious offence, thereby making government's action justifiable in a wide range of cases.

Restricting Freedom of Expression: Courts and the Justifications for Legal Intervention

There is some general consensus that limitations to freedom of expression are acceptable if there are fears of disturbance to public order. Yet there is much less agreement on how to judge whether a specific speech act is in fact a threat to public order, and therefore deserving of prohibition. Mill's differentiation between 'advocacy' and 'instigation', as discussed earlier in this chapter, was indicative of this tension. That idea became more explicit in Justice Holmes's famous advocacy of the 'clear and present danger' doctrine that dominated American jurisprudence on freedom-of-speech questions during the last century. Justice Holmes in the *Schenck* case argued that it was largely a matter of 'proximity and degree'. He held:

> The question in every case is whether the words used are used in such circumstances and are of such a nature as to create a clear and present danger that they will bring about the substantive evils that Congress has a right to prevent.
>
> (*Schenck* 249 U.S. 47)

This approach was further fine-tuned during his dissent in the *Abrams* case, where he was joined by Justice Brandeis. In this case, Holmes opined that there should not only be 'clear and present' danger but rather the danger should be imminent and only if a direct relation could be established between the intentions of the actor and the consequence of the act would it be reasonable to punish such acts (*Abrams v. Unites States* [1919] 250 U.S. 616). In other words, it is argued that there should be a direct consequential relation between the speech act and the threat to public order.

In the Indian case, public order as a valid limitation to freedom of speech and expression was inserted in the constitution through the First Amendment in order to create a balance between 'individual freedom' and 'social freedom' as explained by Nehru in the *Statements of Objects and Reasons* for the Constitution (First Amendment) Act, 1951. The Supreme Court in its various judgements has refined the definition of the term 'public order', thereby drawing out its scope and limitations, especially when the claim of public order is used by the government to restrict freedom of speech and expression. In the *Superintendent, Central Prison, Fatehgarh* case the court defined public order as the absence of disorder involving 'breaches of local significance' (*Superintendent, Central Prison, Fatehgarh v. Ram Manohar Lohia* [1960], 2 SCR 84). The state of public order was marked as the orderly state of society or community 'in which citizens can peacefully pursue their normal activities of life'. Judges accepted that 'public order' was a wide term that might include minor 'law and order' aspects or major issues like the threat to state security such as attempts to overthrow it, and therefore asserted that the usage of the term should be precise. Emphasizing precision, the court in the *Dr. Ram Manohar Lohia* case referred to a set of three concentric circles with 'law and order' and 'security of state' in its outer- and inner-most circles, with public order in the middle (*Dr. Ram Manohar Lohia* 1966 AIR 740). The court opined that 'an act may affect law and order but not public order' and that not all cases of public disorder pose a threat to the security of the state. In the *Arun Ghosh* case, the court further asserted that the disturbances of public order needed to be distinguished 'from acts directed against individuals, which do not disturb the society to the extent of causing a general disturbance of public tranquillity'. 'It is the degree of disturbances and its effect upon the life of the community in a locality' that would determine, according to the court, 'whether the disturbance amounts only to a breach of law and order' (*Arun Ghosh v. State of West Bengal* [1969] 1970 3 SCR 288). Since the constitution of India devolves the power of maintaining law and order to the state government, it is the prerogative of the state officials to decide when a condition resembles a public-order problem and also to determine the possible ways to handle the situation. However, in order to justify its action against freedom of speech, the government was required to show (1) the speech act under question had caused or was likely to cause actual disturbance of a local significance and (2) the speech act should not only affect one or few individuals but the larger community.

Public Order and the Issue of Religiously Offensive Publications

The threat to public order posed by religiously offensive publications became the reason for the birth during the colonial period of most statutory laws that govern the freedom of speech and expression even today. In the post-Independence phase, the controversial religious content of political speeches and the printing press were thought to be playing a major role in promoting enmity and instigating violence among different communities and were therefore considered eligible for regulations.

But how and when does religious offence lead to public-order problems, and when is the government justified to act in such cases? In the context of independent India, the judiciary was expected to balance the claims of social cohesion with those of individual liberties. The fear was that the government in power could use the threat of public order for political purposes, thereby restricting freedom of speech and expression unreasonably. Contrarily, there was also fear that even small misjudgements on the part of authorities could lead to a severe public-order problem. So, courts were expected to draw the line between freedom of expression as a fundamental right to be freely enjoyed by all citizens and its misuse that threatened public order. In this regard, Pratap Bhanu Mehta (2008) is critical about the role of the judiciary. He argues that since the fundamental right to expression can be regulated on grounds of 'maintaining public order' legally, courts generally tend to allow regulation of any 'insult' to religion. This, according to him, is made possible because courts read the public-order exception in articles 19 and 25 so broadly that whenever a restriction is said to be associated with public order, they do not pursue any further questions. In the process, as Mehta argues, courts also assume that every attempt to insult religion tends to disrupt public order. This analysis of the judiciary's role, though suggestive, is not free from limitations. While Mehta's conclusion that the judiciary refrains from allowing private judgement to impede the 'legitimate purposes of the state that can be publicly justified', especially in relation to religious discourse, might be correct, his analysis of the cases to reach the conclusion is inconclusive and does not adequately do justice to the judiciary's position.

Let us consider two cases, one related to criminal prosecution for vilifying religious personage, the second related to the ban and forfeiture of a book. These examples help us to analyze the judiciary's role in questions of public order from different dimensions. In the first case, *Ramji Lal Modi*, a case that Mehta also cites, the government's action directly impacted freedom of speech and expression as well as an individual's personal freedom. In the second case, *Lalai Singh Yadav*, the government's action was limited to proscription of the controversial publication.

Case 1: As early as 1957, the Supreme Court was faced with the questions concerning an 'insult to religion' and its impact on the public-order situation. While testing the constitutionality of section 295(A) of IPC, in *Ramji Lal Modi*, the court dealt with the subject in great detail. In August 1952, a cartoon appeared in a popular Hindi daily published from Allahabad, Uttar Pradesh, *Amrit Patrika*, which caricatured the Prophet Mohammed in the form of a donkey. The state witnessed protests from the Muslim community, which turned violent in many instances. *Bandhs* and demonstrations were organized, despite prohibitory orders from the government (*The Times of India*, 14 August 1952). Repeated apologies by the editor, the publisher and the director-in-charge of the newspaper did not help to pacify the situation (*The Times of India*, 6 October 1952). It was only after government's decision to prosecute the newspaper that the situation was controlled. In the month of November, when the case was still fresh, Ramji Lal Modi, the editor and publisher of a monthly magazine called *Gaurakshak* (a magazine published to serve the cause of the Cow Protection Movement), wrote an article in the November issue questioning the protests by the Muslims. On the one hand, the article questioned the rationale behind such reactions, and on the other hand, it launched a scathing attack on the basic tenets of the Muslim religion, including popular beliefs about the Prophet. Fearing threats to law and order in the polarized communal context, the government ordered the prosecution of Ramji Lal Modi under sections 153(A) and 295(A) of the IPC. In the Sessions Court of Kanpur, the judge acquitted him of the charges under section 153(A) but found him guilty under 295(A), and thereby sentenced him to 18 months' rigorous imprisonment. Modi then appealed against the judgement before the High Court, but the court held that the article was published with a deliberate and malicious intent to outrage the religious feelings of the Muslims and hence was punishable.

The accused then approached the Supreme Court with two separate applications, one claiming a stay on the High Court order and the other, under article 32 of the constitution, urging that section 295(A) was *ultra vires* and void inasmuch as it interfered with the petitioner's freedom of speech and expression (*Ramji Lal Modi* 1957 AIR 620). The Supreme Court rejected the application for a stay and dismissed the other application, thereby upholding the action taken against Modi. During the trial, the counsel for the appellant argued that it was only in the 'interest of public order' that a 'reasonable restriction' to freedom of speech and expression could be justified, and therefore, the likelihood of public disorder 'should be a matter of proximate and not remote consideration'. He substantiated these arguments using the Supreme Court's observations in the *Romesh Thapar* and *Brij Bhushan* cases and insisted that in the present case, there was no direct threat of public disorder. Secondly, he maintained that insults to religions and religious beliefs may or may not lead to public disorder, and therefore there was always a sense of ambiguity attached to the practical implications of section 295(A), which was dangerous if allowed to curtail a fundamental right. The Court rejected both these submissions and held that section 295(A) was well within the scope of article 19(2), which set reasonable restrictions to freedom of speech and expression. The observations of the court were significant for future cases. On the first submission, the court held that after the First Amendment, Romesh Thapar's and Brij Bhushan's cases were no more relevant because the First Amendment had significantly changed the nature and scope of article 19(2). The court differentiated between two significant phrases: 'for the maintenance of' and 'in the interest of'. According to the court, the addition of the phrase 'in the interest of' public order had significantly widened the scope of article 19(2), and therefore, even if some action by the government might not be justified on the grounds of directly maintaining public order, it might still be important in 'the interest of public order'. Chief Justice S. R. Das pronounced: 'If ... certain activities have a tendency to cause public disorder, a law penalising such activities as an offence cannot but be held to be a law imposing reasonable restriction "in the interests of public order", although in some cases those activities may not actually lead to a breach of public order.' The court also rejected the claim that freedom of speech and expression could be restrained only if the threat to public order was proximate and imminent. Countering the second proposition, the court did not believe that there was any sense of ambiguity in law. It held that 'deliberate and malicious' intention was the sine qua non of section 295(A), and therefore only those acts of insult to religion or religious beliefs that were carried out with deliberate and malicious intention were punishable. Deriving a direct connection between the calculated tendency of an 'aggravated form of insult' and 'public order', the court held that such intentional vilification, aimed 'clearly to disrupt the public order and the section, which penalises such activities, is well within the protection of cl. (2) of article 19'. It meant that if government could successfully show that an act was 'deliberately and maliciously' aimed at insulting religion or religious beliefs, it would be assumed to be a threat to public order and hence punishable under law. Based on these arguments, the court held Ramji Lal Modi guilty and rejected his application.

Significantly, in the unrecorded trial of the editor and the publisher of *Anand Patrika*, who were prosecuted by the state under section 295(A) for publishing the cartoon of Prophet, the accused were acquitted by the Allahabad High Court due to the failure by the prosecution to produce enough evidence to prove that the act was done with 'deliberate and malicious' intention.[13] The contrast in both cases is evident of the court's differing approach. It is significant that the reactions to the publication of the cartoon were directly responsible for a law-and-order situation in Uttar Pradesh. The acquittal of the editor and publisher of the newspaper hinted that for criminal prosecution, it was necessary to establish a link between the intentions of the accused and the reaction of the members of religious community who claimed a feeling of 'offence'. In Modi's case, the fact that his essay was in reaction to events surrounding the publication of the cartoon helped to establish deliberate and malicious intention. The same did not apply to the editor or publisher of *Amrit Patrika*, who had continuously pleaded it to be a case of ignorance and had also publicly apologized for the same. So, it can be concluded that though the court believed that government could act based on its assessment of public-order problems and it did not compulsorily include the 'clear and present danger' test, the prosecution of individuals under criminal law required authorities to prove presence of deliberate and malicious intentions.

The above analysis hints at two important aspects of the court's position on the subject of criminalizing speech acts that contain religiously offensive subjects. First, courts allow for action if there was an aggravated form of insult, presuming that such utterances had every chance to flare up into a public-order issue. At the same time, it did not explain what could be included as an aggravated form of insult or how it is to be differentiated from insults of a general kind, which could not be punished. The reluctance of the courts to examine or provide clear directions left it largely to the prerogative of government officials to decide when to act. Secondly, the actors in these cases could be held guilty only if deliberate and malicious intention was proven. Considering the fact that the intention was to be derived from the content and language of the publication, the court tried to distance the justification of government's action from its implication for an individual's personal liberty. The only justification required for the government's action is the presumption of public-order problems. Whether prosecution in the case was legally justified or not could be left for the judiciary to decide later. Arguably, such a position enables government officials to act on the presumption of public-order threats without taking into account the reasonability of such action vis-à-vis freedom of speech and expression. This approach of the judiciary has even more serious implications in cases involving proscription or banning of the books in a territory.

Case 2: The second case is related to the proscription order of the book *Sachchi Ramayana*.[14] The case was about the Uttar Pradesh government's appeal in the Supreme Court against the Allahabad High Court's decision to strike down a government order banning *Sachchi Ramayana* or *Ramayana: A True Reading*, originally written by radical Tamil social reformer Periyar, later translated and published by Lalai Singh Yadav, a resident of Uttar Pradesh. It was a polemical text questioning the sacredness of different characters of the revered epic. Contemplating a threat to public tranquillity, the Intelligence Department sent copies of the book to Kanpur police to enquire if any action could be taken. The Magistrate then decided to forfeit all copies from Lalai Singh Yadav. Later, formal orders of forfeiture of all the copies of the book, both in Hindi as well as the English language, were notified through the *Gazette* of Uttar Pradesh on 8 December and 20 December 1969 under section 99 (A) of the CrPC.[15] The government claimed that by treating the main characters of the epic with disdain, the author and publisher had offended the religious sentiments of a majority of Hindus. However, in the notification issued for proscription, officials had not mentioned the grounds for the opinion formation, and the High Court held the notice insufficient because it did not clearly state why government believed the publication fell under section 295(A). It maintained that until an offence qualified under the tests of section 295(A) of IPC, section 99(A) of CrPC did not apply, and hence the order was struck down. The Uttar

Pradesh government approached the Supreme Court against the judgement. Though the Supreme Court upheld the decision of the High Court, it was essentially on technical grounds, and as the judgement mentions, it was not reflective of the view of the judges 'on the merits of the book or its provocative vitriol' (*State of Uttar Pradesh v. Lalai Singh Yadav* [1976] 1977 AIR 202).

In the unanimous judgement written by Justice V. R. Krishna Iyer, the approach of the court on the question of the proscription of a contentious publication under the threat of a public-order situation is discussed in great depth. Firstly, the Court made it absolutely clear that the decision to ban or forfeit a controversial publication was a legitimate power in the hands of the government and 'whoever violates by bombs or books societal tranquillity will become [a] target of legal interdict'. Secondly, it was maintained that though the 'clear and present danger' test, as popularized in American jurisprudence, was not relevant for Indian conditions, extreme caution was required on the part of the government in its judgement of how to safeguard social tranquillity. Thirdly, reiterating the views of the court in *Ramji Lal Modi*, the judges recognized a clear relationship between religious offence and public disorder. It held: 'Hatred, outrage and like feelings of large groups may have crypto-violent proneness and the State, in its well-grounded judgment, may prefer to stop the circulation of the book to preserve safety and peace in society.... The actual exercise will depend not on doctrinaire logic but practical wisdom'. The practical wisdom of government was to depend on a number of factors including the context and content of the publication. As mentioned earlier, the court rejected the application on technical grounds; however, it also pointed out that if the state government thought that the peace of the state would be disturbed by the book under consideration, it could reissue a fresh notification, keeping in mind the essential legal requirements. So, though the judgement was in favour of the publisher of the book, the court hinted that the technical aspects aside, the government was well within its legitimate capacity and powers to order proscription under the perception of a threat to public order.

Both the above cases had some significant similarities and differences. It is clear that the Supreme Court in both the cases held that government's intervention was justified and was constitutionally protected under article 19(2) if it was seen to be 'in the interest of public order'. The significance of the phrase 'in the interest of' was made explicit by the court's reference to the First Amendment, whereby the phrase was introduced to the constitution. This was in contradistinction to Mehta's assumption that the fundamental right to expression

Court reasoned that 'in the interest of public order' has a larger connotation and implications for government's action than 'for the maintenance of public order', as it allowed for intervention even if there were no direct threats to public order. Thereby courts also seemed to have rejected the application of the 'clear and present danger' doctrine in the Indian context as in the US. Furthermore, the two judgements also revealed that, unlike Mehta's proposition, the court did not base its judgement solely on the government's claims of a threat to public order. In the first case, the court held that the prosecution of an individual also required that 'deliberate and malicious intention' was proven. In this way, the court balanced an individual's personal liberty with the threat posed to public order by the contentious publication. In the second case, the court emphasized the importance of mentioning in the notification order the grounds on which the officials had based their opinion, which could reflect the application of mind by the government in making the decision to forfeit or ban a particular publication. Therefore, in such cases the threat to public order, though an important condition, was not considered as a sufficient claim for justifying the government's action under 'reasonable restriction'. However, under the looming threat to public order and the government having cogent reasons to believe it, the court held that it was totally justified in acting against the publication or the person responsible for it.

Secularism and the Protection of the Right to Conscience and Religion

One of the main dilemmas attached with laws against religious offence has centred on the role of state – concerning the scope and limitations of state intervention in such subjects. For example, a very strong justification in favour of blasphemy laws has been that it is the duty of state to preserve morality in society. This was especially true about societies where blasphemy laws were used to protect from insult the religion of the majority. For example, one of the strongest advocates of blasphemy laws in Britain, Lord Devlin justified the presence of blasphemy laws on grounds that morals and religion were intrinsically related and enforcement of morals in society was the duty of state. Therefore, according to him, the state was duty-bound to protect religion from attacks (Devlin 1965: 23–25). But in the changed context of multicultural societies, this position faced challenges from different quarters. One school of thought argues that restriction of freedom of speech and expression on the pretext of religious offence had lost its moral justification. For example, George

Letsas (2012) believes that the fact that each religious system is based on a set of 'particularities' represented in the form of doctrines, symbols or figures requires that any protection of religion would mean forcing people to accept the ethical ideas and ideals that they might not have contemplated or have been familiar with. This, according to Letsas, should not be the role of the state, and therefore any law like blasphemy could not be supported (2012: 255–257). Other critics, like Peter Jones (1980), argue that 'the protection of religion for moral purposes ceases to be feasible in a multi-religious society' because it would be detrimental to the idea of a secular state to prefer and protect a certain conception of a good life represented by the religion of the majority, and on the other hand, if the state 'tried to avoid that inequity by protecting all religions it would be supporting contradictory beliefs and beliefs which had different moral consequences' (1980: 133). So, it was asserted that the state should either not indulge in restricting freedom of expression in the name of religious offence or it should look for a more potent justification to legitimize its action, like the threat on public order. However, there were others who believed that the law of blasphemy should be extended to protect all religious subjects. It was argued that the changing nature of societies, whereby they were becoming multi-religious and plural, required a secular state to extend such protections to followers of all religions. For example, Lord Scarman, who favoured the expansion of the common law crime of blasphemy to protect the religious feelings of non-Christians in Britain, urged during the *Lemon* case[16] that the common law be changed by legislation to protect the sensibilities of all religious groups (*Whitehouse v. Lemon* [1979] 2 WLR 281). Scarman cited the example of India to build a case for the need for protection of all religions in a plural society. He said:

> In an increasingly plural society such as that of modem Britain it is necessary not only to respect the differing religious beliefs, feelings and practices of all but also to protect them from scurrility, vilification, ridicule, and contempt….When Macaulay became a legislator in India, he saw to it that the law protected the religious feelings of all. In those days India was a plural society: today the United Kingdom is also…. My criticism of the common law offence of blasphemy is not that it exists but that it is not sufficiently comprehensive.
>
> (As quoted in Post 1980: 312)

Britain abolished the offences of blasphemy and blasphemous libel from its common law in 2008 by the Criminal Justice and Immigration Act, 2008.

Looking at the history of laws against religious offence in India, one can conclude that ever since it got codified under the colonial state, it was meant to protect followers of all religions. But the question about how a secular state should behave in a multi-religious and plural society still remains a puzzle. Unlike many Western democracies, where the principles of secularism expected an approach of neutrality from the state on the issues concerning religions, in India it was expected to maintain what Rajeev Bhargava has famously called 'principled distance'. On the one hand, it meant equal treatment of all religions and non-interference in matters internal to religion; on the other hand, on subjects that affected the public in general, it had every right to assert its authority. Protection of the right to freedom of religion as guaranteed under article 25 also became a constitutional as well as a moral duty for the state to uphold in India's multi-religious society.

But how was the state expected to behave when freedom of religion was threatened by publications that vilified and insulted religious beliefs, symbols and practices? In its various judgements, courts have considered instances where freedom of speech and expression clash with other constitutional guarantees, including freedom of conscience and the right freely to profess, practice and propagate religion. It has been observed that courts in such situations attempt to preserve a balance based on two premises: first, as discussed earlier in the chapter, courts hold that wounding religious susceptibilities of other religious denominations could lead to disruptions of public order; and second, courts opine that freedom of conscience and religion needs to be protected, and it is the duty of the state to create an environment where this right can be freely enjoyed. One of the earliest examples of this attitude of the court was reflected in the *N. Veerabrahmam* case. The Andhra Pradesh High Court in this case was considering the constitutionality of section 99(A) and ban of the book *Bible Bandaram* – which was claimed to be a rationalist critique of the Bible (*N. Veerabrahmam v. State of Andhra Pradesh* [1959] A.I.R. 1959 A.P. 572). The author had pointed at incongruities and inconsistencies in the Bible, raised doubts about its authorship, and made certain controversial claims like, for instance, because nobody can be born of a virgin, Jesus was a product of an adulterous union and the Immaculate Conception theory was a cover-up. Introducing a balanced approach, the court held: 'People are at liberty to write books without offending deliberately the religious sentiments of other citizens who are as much entitled to certain freedoms as the petitioner himself.' Rejecting the argument from the counsel for the petitioner that the book was based on rational and free thinking and was therefore eligible for protection under article 19(1)(a), the court defined the boundary of such claim by arguing that free thinking did not 'involve freedom to make scurrilous attacks on the religion and religious beliefs of other sects with impunity'. 'It is not free-thinking to abuse and insult other religions', the court observed. Deliberating the subject further, judges held that 'no citizen could claim a right to insult the religion or religious beliefs of another section of the population'. They maintained that it was the duty of the state to ascertain that citizens are able to exercise freedom of religion and conscience, and according to the court, section 99(A) of the CrPC as well as section 295(A) of the IPC were legitimate powers in the hands of the government to ensure such protection for the rights of all its citizens. The emphasis on protecting freedom of conscience and religion was based on the understanding that though freedom of speech and expression was important, it did not enjoy any special status and hence needed to be balanced with competing claims based on other fundamental rights. In the final section of the judgement, the court observed that 'all the citizens of India are guaranteed freedom of religion and freedom of conscience by our Constitution and each one has a right to pursue his own way of attaining salvation, unhampered and without interference from others'. This attitude of the court provides both moral and legal protection to freedom of conscience and religion against freedom of expression. By recognizing that freedom of religion should be 'unhampered and without interference', courts provided certain immunity to religions against criticism.

This perspective is further reflected in the way courts determine what constitutes legitimate criticism when it is directed against religion. So, for example, courts have proved to be lenient against criticism of religious practices but at the same time have made explicit that any insult or vilification of a religious personage and criticism of religious texts and beliefs could not be allowed. It was based on the perception that a criticism or insult of a religious personage and of religious texts amounted to interference in the faith of others, something that could not be allowed in a secular and plural society like India. This position of the court was reiterated in the Supreme Court's judgement in the *Sri Baragur Ramachandrappa* case, where the court observed:

> [N]o person has a right to impinge on the feelings of others on the premise that his right to freedom of speech remains unrestricted and unfettered. It cannot be ignored that India is country with vast disparities in language, culture and religion and unwarranted and malicious criticism or interference in the faith of others cannot be accepted.
>
> (*Sri Baragur Ramachandrappa & Ors. v. State of Karnataka & Anr* [2007] 5 S.C.C.11)

The court emphasized that secular values needed to be protected, and the state was duty-bound to act if such values were threatened, even if it was done under the garb of freedom of expression. This position provides a justifiable reason for government's intervention by warranting a restriction on freedom of expression in cases where it is found to interrupt free exercise of the right to freedom of religion. Government's action is also justified, according to courts, in cases that include acts of vilification or wounding religious susceptibilities of followers of any religion, as they have a tendency to lead to disruption of public order. 'If there is no law authorising the executive to take necessary action ... there will be disorder in society and bitter feelings and even hatred between various sections of society which is not conducive to the maintenance of order', the court observed in the *N. Veerabrahmam* case. This was another ground on which section 99(A) was considered well within the limitations set by article 19(2) to the freedom of speech and expression. This aspect was further elaborated by Justice Krishna Iyer in the *Lalai Singh Yadav* case. He maintained that in a country like India, the secular state was obligated 'to create conditions where the sentiments and feelings of people of diverse or opposing beliefs and bigotries are not so molested by ribald writings or offensive publications as to provoke or outrage groups into possible violent action'. Justice Iyer believed that state was expected not only to protect society against breaches of peace but also to prevent the causes of such a state of order. This essentially involved proscribing publications which were deeply offensive to the religious sentiments of any section of the population. He said:

> [P]ublic power comes into play not because the heterodox few must be suppressed to placate the orthodox many but because every-one's cranium must be saved from mayhem before his cerebrum can have chance to simmer. Hatred, outrage and like feelings of large groups may have crypto-violent proneness and the State, in its well-grounded judgment, may prefer to stop the circulation of the book to preserve safety and peace in society.
>
> (*State of Uttar Pradesh v. Lalai Singh Yadav* [1976] 1977 AIR 202)

This principle of balancing counter-claims about fundamental rights along with the assumption of a threat inherent in the misuse of freedom of speech and expression allowed space for state governments to ban books that insulted or even criticized religions.

Conclusion

The decisions and observation of the courts show sensitivity towards protecting the religious sensibilities of citizens from being affronted by religiously offensive publications. In the process, courts allow wide latitude for government intervention both in its punitive as well as preventive actions. This reading of the court's attitude departs from Sorabjee's and Dhavan's studies, whereby they held that courts in general and the Supreme Court in particular has put a strong defence in favour of freedom of speech and expression. A point to note in this comparison is that both Sorabjee (1994) and Dhavan (2008) talk about freedom of speech and expression in general, and this study concentrated only on religiously offensive publications. Though Sorabjee's and Dhavan's arguments may be more generally valid, my own analysis of publications that defame religion or promote religious hatred certainly qualifies their more general claims. In fact, courts seem to maintain that there are some subjects that cannot be discussed even in mild and non-harmful language. These include criticism or insult of religious personage or denigrating religious texts or sacred beliefs. This gives some kind of covert immunity to religion from criticism, a point also made by Mehta (2008: 332). In the name of maintaining public order and protecting the ethos of secularism, the claims of religious offence have generally received a much more favourable response from the courts than do the claims of freedom of expression.

Notes

1 As Samuel Walker (1994) has shown in the case of the US, courts played a defining role in determining the scope of freedom of speech. Though the laws in India do not allow the same liberty to the courts, their role is still significant. The courts in India are expected to limit their role to checking whether the state action is based on procedure set by law rather than the 'due process' doctrine followed by American courts.

2 I have used cases from High Courts across different states of the country depending upon the importance of such cases and whether they deal exactly with the subject under discussion here, that is, religiously offensive publications.

3 Manupatra is a digital legal database which includes all the reported judgements of the Supreme Court and High Courts in India, along with Central and State Acts, Central Rules, Pending Bills in the Parliament, and Notifications of various Central Ministries.

4 Many scholars present 'offence' as a subjective experience (Collini 2010; Melville 2009). However, recently scholars like Lorenz Langer (2014) have argued that though a subjective experience, it has the potential to mobilize similar experiences of hurt.

5 Cohen-Almagor argues that 'the offence to sensibilities argument in and of itself can serve as grounds for restricting freedom of expression in extreme cases when the offense is severe and the target group cannot avoid being exposed to the offence' (2005: 107).

6 Courts have also used other expressions like 'aggravated form of insult' in the *Ramji Lal Modi* case or 'aggravated form of criticism' in the *R. V. Bhasin* case. But the intention in each of these expressions is to argue that not all forms of insult or claims of hurt can be taken into consideration while employing section 295(A). The expression 'grossly offensive' is also used by courts in several other cases like *Shiv Ram Dass Udasin* and *N. Veerabrahmam*.

7 This test was first introduced by Justice Vivian Bose in *Bhagwati Charan Shukla v. Provincial Government* A.I.R. 1947 Nagpur 1, where he held that the impact of words 'must be judged from the standards of reasonable, strong-minded, firm and courageous men, and not those of weak and vacillating minds, nor of those who scent danger in every hostile point of view'. Thereby this became an important test in Indian jurisprudence.

8 For example, in the *N. Veerabrahmam* case, the court held that 'it is only insults to religion or religious beliefs that are deliberately and maliciously made that would bring into play section 99-A criminal procedure code'. This position was reiterated in the *Baba Khalil Ahamad* case. This position continued till the *M/S*

Varsha Publications case. But since the Patna High Court's observation in *Nand Kishore Singh* case, courts have changed their position on the subject.

9 In the *Sri Baragur Ramachandrappa* case, the court agreed with the interpretation in *Nand Kishore Singh* and held: 'It will be seen that section 95 and section 96 of the code when read together are clearly preventive in nature and one designed to pre-empt any disturbance to public order. At the same time, we find that section 95 does not by itself create a criminal offence and the reference to the various sections of the penal code is merely description of the kind of offence which need to be prevented by a declaration under section 95.' This position was reiterated by courts in different cases like *R. V. Bhasin* and *Sanghraj Damodar Rupawate*.

10 In fact, courts have indicated that its only role in cases regarding forfeiture and proscription is to judge on the basis of notification whether or not the action of the government falls within the scope of 'reasonable' restrictions. See *Harnam Das v. State of Uttar Pradesh* (1961), 1961 A.I.R 1662.

11 Justice Krishna Iyer held: 'If you laze and omit, the law visits the order with voidness and this the State Government must realize especially because forfeiture of a book for a penal offence is a serious matter, not a routine act to be executed with unconcern or indifference. The wages of neglect is invalidity, going by the text of the Code. These considerations are magnified in importance when we regard the changeover from the Raj to the Republic and the higher value assigned to the great rights of the people.'

12 Courts argued that since the law allowed the victim to challenge the decision of forfeiture or ban in the High Court (under section 96 of the CrPC), it was important for the victims to know the reasons for proscription, in order to defend their position. Also, in order to decide the case, the court needed to be informed as to 'which communities were alienated from each other or whose religious beliefs had been wounded according to the Government, or why the Government thought that such alienation or offence to religion had been caused'. These details, according to court, were necessary for it to reach to a conclusion on the subject.

13 Though the judgement was not recorded, the case was closely followed in the press owing to the public-order situation it had created. See, 'Hooliganism Breaks Out Again in Kanpur: Government Decides to Prosecute Hindi Paper', *The Times of India*, 14 August 1952; 'Case against Newspaper: Police Official's Deposition', *The Times of India*, 6 October 1952; 'Allahabad Editor Acquitted: Muslim Feelings Not Wounded', *The Times of India*, 23 April 1954.

14 It was translated and published by Lalai Singh Yadav after seeking permission from Periyar. It was published at Ashok Pustakalaya: Jhinjhak, Uttar Pradesh in 1969.

15 This information was given by the then–Health Minister of UP, Krishnanad Rai, on the floor of the UP State Legislative Assembly. See *UP State Assembly Debates*, 21 May, 1969, vol. 279, part 3: 323.

16 It was a blasphemy case in the UK regarding a poem published in *Gay News* which was considered to be denigrating the image of Christ.

4

LAW AND LEGAL PROCESS AS HURDLES

In May 2015, PEN Canada and the International Human Rights Programme, University of Canada's Faculty of Law, produced a report titled *Imposing Silence: The Use of India's Laws to Suppress Free Speech* (2015). The report argued that 'vague overboard laws' and a 'corrupt inefficient justice system' have given rise to an environment in India where free speech can easily be censored. It further discussed the regulatory framework used by government officials, individuals and social and religious groups to curtail freedom of expression. The report looked at various aspects of the legal process that account for the diminishment of freedom of speech in India. Issues ranging from the filing of criminal charges and civil suits, the role of the police and judicial corruption, and questions as to the competence of the judiciary to hear cases on the subject were examined. On the one hand, the report discussed the limiting attitude of Indian law and the judicial process, and on the other hand, based on a comparative analysis with international legal provisions, it criticized India's position in protecting the freedom of speech and expression. The report also forwarded a list of suggestions, which included issues such as reform in the police and judiciary and scrapping as well as amending significant statutory laws. The sentiment embodied in the report has also been reflected earlier by scholars like Lawrence Liang (2004) and Sohini Ghosh (2004), among others, who believe that the real threat to freedom of speech and expression in the Indian context emanates from the 'slippery slope'[1] effect produced by the legal provisions. They recommend repealing of laws like section 153(A) and 295(A) in order to prevent misuse. For example, Liang (2012: 1) argues that 'once you have a law that allows for the making of legal claims on the basis of charged emotional states, you begin to see the emergence of cases that steadily cultivate a legal vocabulary of hurt sentiments'. It is in this sense that Ahmed notes that attempts to 'regulate wounded attachments and religious passions' through law may 'conversely constitute them'. Such legal construction of offence, Ahmed argues, gives space to 'social groups to organize in order to ensure the state take cognizance of blasphemous events and practices' (2009: 177). Though the slippery slope argument forwarded by these scholars holds strong ground, it fails to explain how it was

 DOI: 10.4324/9781003369257-5

a unique phenomenon attached to laws governing freedom of speech and expression. Any law could be misused in a situation where the executive was not sensitive to its usage. Further, the criticism of law forwarded by these scholars does not take into account the responsibility of the judiciary as interpreter of law in drawing the boundaries of the legal discourse. The analysis therefore suffers limitations.

In this chapter, I highlight the operative and functional inadequacies attached to the legal process, including the role of the judiciary that impacts free speech cases. Lacunae in the procedural and functional aspects of the working of law together contribute in strengthening the role of non-state actors in cases related to censorship. These weaknesses have inspired the claimants of hurt sentiments to approach the legal route as a means to censor free speech. On the other hand, the labyrinth of law and legal process produces an environment of fear and confusion for authors/publishers. Their struggle to defend freedom of speech and expression is set back due to the insecurities and uncertainties surrounding the legal process and system. It may even result in their surrender to the demands of censorship by non-state actors, in order to escape the long and exhausting legal process. The fissures in the law and legal process, therefore, act as constraints upon the free exercise of the freedom of speech and expression.

The Procedural Dimensions of the Legal Process as a Hurdle to Freedom of Speech and Expression

Procedural dimensions here refer to the process through which cases related to contentious publications arrive in courtrooms, as well as the procedural aspects related to the functioning of courts. Three aspects have particular relevance for freedom of speech and expression, and these directly or indirectly act as hurdles in its free exercise: (1) spurious charging and overcharging; (2) the tendency to file cases against the author/publisher in different parts of the country; and (3) the delay in administering justice. The first two aspects are related to the pre-courtroom phase. However, even after the case reaches the stage where the formal legal process begins in the courts, it takes a long period of time to deliver judgement, making the legal process itself a hurdle. All these together contribute to making the process tedious and demoralizing, thereby dissuading actors from seeking legal recourse when their freedom of expression is curtailed by either state or non-state actors.[2] On the contrary, the legal process becomes an easy option for non-state actors to harass the author/publisher and force them to agree to their demands for censorship.

Spurious Charging and Overcharging

The phenomenon of spurious charging and overcharging is related to vagueness of the law as well as the tendency among government authorities to react under pressure and act in order to avoid immediate threats to public order. Spurious charging refers to instances where police register cases under different sections of laws without being sure about the legal validity of such laws in the courts. Overcharging includes framing multiple accusations in a single case. It may result in charges being framed against authors and publishers under sections of law which might not even be relevant in that case. The vagueness in constitutional and statutory laws governing freedom of speech and expression (as discussed in Chapter 1) leaves the authorities unsure about which laws could be justifiably invoked in a particular case. To add to it, the pressure exerted by different socio-religious groups claiming hurt to their sentiments by the publications creates an environment of uncertainty, leaving it to the legal prerogative of the officials to decide upon the relevant sections to be invoked, and to register a First Information Report (FIR) accordingly. As many legal scholars have also noted, an important facet of statutory laws governing freedom of speech and expression in India is that the kind of offences that fall under their purview are 'cognizable' and 'non-bailable' (Bhatia 2016: 139–145; Narrain 2016a: 41–42). This means that officials do not require any form of prior approval either from the state government or the judiciary to act in such cases. Further, the 'non-bailable' nature of the offence ensures that the accused has to face trial and can only be granted bail after the matter is debated in the court. So, the investigation and opinion of the officer on duty becomes central in such cases, which have a high possibility of being guided by the pressure asserted by the complaining parties/groups. Legal commentators have observed that police use these provisions as tools to avoid any kind of altercation in the public-order situation arising due to contentious publications. At the same time, it also ensures that even if charges against the publication and the author/publisher do not stand in the court of law, the accused party could still be found guilty under some section of the law (Dhavan 2008: 145). As my reading of cases also suggests, in most cases where criminal charges were invoked, officials charged the authors/publishers of being guilty under multiple sections of the penal codes. Generally, section 153(A) was invoked together with sections 295(A) and 298 of the IPC and section 95 of the CrPC. It was left to the judiciary to decide whether the charges fell within the legal brackets defined by any of those provisions. Further, as criminal charges against the author/publisher and notification for forfeiture of their publication formed two separate cases, the accused publishers/authors had to appear for trials in both these cases separately. The criminal charges fall under the category of 'cognizable' and 'non-bailable' offense, so appearance before the court is compulsory, whereas in cases of forfeitures, it remains the prerogative of the author/publisher to approach the court under section 96 of CrPC if they want the notification to be revoked. This means extra expenditure both in terms of time and resources for the authors and publishers to defend their position.

The Liberty to Lodge a Case against the Book or Author/ Publisher in Any Part of the Country

The Code of Civil Procedure (CPC), 1908, under section 19 allows that a case may be instituted either in the jurisdiction in which the defendant resides or carries on business or where the tort was committed. This means that a publication in India could be accused of the hurting sentiments in any part of the country, and on that basis, a complaint could be lodged with the local police station of that area or a case could be filed in the local court, irrespective of the place where the author/publisher resided or where the work was published. So, if an author resided in Delhi, and such complaint or case was lodged against him/her in Mumbai, he/she would have to appear before the local courts in Mumbai for hearing. Take for example, the case of historian D. N. Jha's book *Holy Cow: Beef in Indian Dietary Conditions*. Even before the book was officially released, it became controversial due to its subject matter.[3] Jain Seva Sangh, a Hyderabad-based organization dedicated to the propagation and protection of Jainism, filed a civil suit against the author and CB Publishers, the publisher of the book, in a civil court at Hyderabad. The author, who was a professor at the University of Delhi, had to travel to Hyderabad to appear in the court to defend his position.[4] Similarly, in the controversy over NCERT textbook on history (discussed in a previous chapter, the petition was filed in Punjab and Haryana High Court, and historian Bipan Chandra, who was one of the respondents in the case and was based in Delhi, had to appear before the court at Chandigarh each time he was summoned. This legal provision therefore becomes a source of harassment. At times, as has been demonstrated by legal scholar Rajeev Dhavan (2008: 173), this legal provision is used consciously by non-state actors to put pressure on the author/publisher to either delete the controversial portions of the publication or withdraw the entire publication in order to escape the tedious legal process.

The Issue of Delay in Judgements

The amount of time each case takes in the Indian judicial process has been a significant concern for the justice delivery system.[5] In case of contentious publications, this delay also means that the relevance of the publication declines with time. In order to understand the delay in the courts, I examined a data set of 32 cases related to both punitive and preventive laws that appeared in High Courts and the Supreme Court during 1947–2010 (as explained in the introduction to Chapter 3) (see Table 4.1). These cases were related to publications that were deemed controversial owing to their comments on religious subjects. From the table given below, which indicates the date, month and year (based on availability) of government notification or registration of the case, and the date on which the respective High Court or Supreme Court delivered the final judgement in the case, it is clear that

Table 4.1 List of cases, primary statutory laws invoked in each case, year of issuance of notification, date of delivery of final judgement and time taken by courts in each case

S.No.	*Case*	*Section of IPC/ CrPC (Primary Charge as Invoked in Court)*	*Year of Notification/ Order of Arrest*	*Date of Final Verdict at High Court*	*Date of Final Verdict at Supreme Court*	*Total Time Taken in High Court*	*Total Time Taken for Judgement If Case Reaches Supreme Court*
1.	Shiv Ram Dass Udasin *v.* The Punjab State	99(A) {equivalent to 95 of current CrPC}	29/02/1952	05/04/1954	Not Applicable	2 years, 2 months	Not Applicable
2.	Ramji Lal Modi *v.* The State of UP	295(A) IPC	12/12/1952	25/10/1956	05/04/1957	3 years, 10 months	4 years, 4 months
3.	Harnam Das *v.* State of Uttar Pradesh	99(A) CrPC	30/07/1953	07/05/1957	27/04/1961	3 years, 10 months	7 years, 9 months
4.	N. Veerabrahm-am *v.* State of Andhra Pradesh	99(A) CrPC	23/03/1958	12/03/1959	Not Applicable	1 year	Not Applicable
5.	Baba Khalil Ahmad *v.*The State	99(A)	1956 (Only year mentioned)	20/04/1960	Not Applicable	4 years	Not Applicable
6.	The State of Mysore *v.* Henry Rodigues and Another	295(A)	January 1959	11/10/1961	Not Applicable	2 years, 9 months	Not Applicable
7.	Public Prosecutor *v.* P. Ramasami	295(A)	February 1961	16/10/1963	Not Applicable	2 years, 8 months	Not Applicable

8.	Mohammad Khalid *v.* The Chief Commissioner, Delhi	99(A)	27/11/1959	10/12/1962	02/03/1967	3 years, 1 month	7 years, 4 months
9.	Sant Das Maheshwari *v.* Babu Ram Jadoun and others	Writ petition under article 226	27/03/1961	06/02/1968	Not Applicable	6 years, 11 months	Not Applicable
10.	Ramlal Puri *v.* State of Madhya Pradesh	99(A) CrPC	28/09/1970	24/12/1970	Not Applicable	3 months	Not Applicable
11.	Chinna Annamalai *v.* The State of Tamil Nadu	Writ petition	12/02/1971	24/02/1971	Not Applicable	1 month	Not Applicable
12.	Babu Rao Patel *v.* State of Delhi	153(A) IPC	March 1968	14/08/1973	21/02/1980	5 years, 5 months	11 years 11 months
13.	State of Uttar Pradesh *v.* Lalai Singh Yadav	99(A) CrPC	08/12/1969	19/01/1971	16/09/1976	1 year, 2 months	6 years, 9 months
14.	Lalai Singh Yadav *v.* State of Uttar Pradesh	99(A) CrPC	26/08/1970	14/05/1971	Not Applicable	9 months	Not Applicable
15.	M/S Varsha Publications Pvt. Ltd. *v.* State of Maharashtra and Others	95 CrPC	31/07/1982	03/05/1983	Not Applicable	8 months	Not Applicable

(Continued)

Table 4.1 (Continued)

S.No.	*Case*	*Section of IPC/ CrPC (Primary Charge as Invoked in Court)*	*Year of Notification/ Order of Arrest*	*Date of Final Verdict at High Court*	*Date of Final Verdict at Supreme Court*	*Total Time Taken in High Court*	*Total Time Taken for Judgement If Case Reaches Supreme Court*
16.	Nand Kishore Singh and etc. *v.* State of Bihar and another	95 CrPC	29/10/1983	04/09/1984	Not Applicable	11 months	Not Applicable
17.	Chandmal Chopra *v.* State of West Bengal	Writ petition for proscription under sec 95 CrPC	March 1985	24/11/1987	Not Applicable	2 years, 8 months	Not Applicable
18.	Master Aman Preet Singh and others *v.* Govt. of India and others	PIL (Public Interest Litigation) for removal of content	January 1996	19/04/1996	Not Applicable	4 months	Not Applicable
19.	G. Jairaj and others *v.* State of Karnataka and others	Writ petition to apply section 95	June 1994	25/07/1997	Not Applicable	3 years, 1 month	Not Applicable
20.	Baragur Ramchandra-ppa and others *v.* State of Karnataka and another	95 CrPC	27/03/1997	16/04/1998	02/05/2007	1 year, 1 month	10 years, 2 months
21.	The Trustees of Safdar Hasmee Memorial Trust *v.* Govt. of NCT of Delhi	95 CrPC	21/08/1993	16/07/2001	Not Applicable	7 years, 11 months	Not Applicable

22.	Zac Poonen *v.* Hidden Treasure Literature	295(A) IPC	1998	27/07/2001	Not Applicable	3 years	Not Applicable
23.	Yashwant Venilal Sanghvi *v.* Sahdevsinh Dilubha Zala	295(A) IPC	January 2004	16/08/2004	Not Applicable	1 year, 7 months	Not Applicable
24.	Sujato Bhadra *v.* State of West Bengal	95 CrPC	28/11/2003	22/09/2005	Not Applicable	1 year, 10 months	Not Applicable
25.	State of Maharashtra and others *v.* Sanghraj Damodar Rupawate and others	95 CrPC	20/12/2006	26/04/2007	09/07/2010	4 months	3 years. 7 month
26.	R. V. Bhasin *v.* 2 Marine Drive Police Station	95 CrPC	09/03/2007	06/01/2010	Not Applicable	2 years, 8 months	Not Applicable
27.	Prasad Jacob (US citizen) *v.* State of Kerala	153(A) IPC	29/03/2010	06/04/2010	Not Applicable	1 month	Not Applicable
28.	Manzar Sayeed Khan *v.* State of Maharashtra	153(A) IPC	23/02/2004	06/05/2004	05/04/2007	3 months	3 years, 2 months
29.	Hulikal Nataraju *v.* State of Karnataka	PETITION-153(A) IPC	27/02/2006	13/09/2010	Not Applicable	4 years, 7 month	Not Applicable

(Continued)

Table 4.1 (Continued)

S.No.	*Case*	*Section of IPC/ CrPC (Primary Charge as Invoked in Court)*	*Year of Notification/ Order of Arrest*	*Date of Final Verdict at High Court*	*Date of Final Verdict at Supreme Court*	*Total Time Taken in High Court*	*Total Time Taken for Judgement If Case Reaches Supreme Court*
30.	Father C. R. Prabhu *v.* State of Jharkhand and another	PETITION-153(A) IPC	11/06/2010	09/04/2013	Not Applicable	2 years, 10 months	Not Applicable
31.	Maninder Singh and another *v.* State of Punjab and another	295(A) IPC	09/09/2010	02/08/2013	Not Applicable	2 years, 11 months	Not Applicable
32.	Piara Singh Bhaniara *v.* State of Punjab and another	95 CrPC	27/09/2001	11/11/2008	Not Applicable	7 years, 2 month	Not Applicable

on an average it took 2.43 years for the High Court to deliver judgement in all such cases, with an average of 2.35 years in cases under section 96 of the CrPC[6] (which is related to challenges against proscription orders of the state), and an average of 3.06 years for cases under section 295(A) and section 153(A) (both related to criminal charges against the author or the publisher). The time taken by the High Court varies from 1 month in a case to 7 years, 2 months. Similarly, if the case is further appealed in the Supreme Court, the average time taken for final judgement on the subject since the registration of case is 6.87 years. This data clearly reflects that the legal process is exhausting. The fact that in each case, the judgement of the court finally arrives after several rounds of hearings, where both plaintiff and accused need to be present, means that it is a constant source of difficulty for the author or publisher who wishes to defend himself/herself or his/her work. This process requires both – the expenditure on advocates who argue the case in the courts, as well as the loss of valuable time for the author/publisher, since he/she has to be present in the courts for the hearings – which as my evidence indicates, can continue for years.

The Functional Dimensions of the Legal Process as a Hurdle to Freedom of Speech and Expression

The issues discussed in the previous section are not unique to cases related exclusively to freedom of speech and expression, but form part of the legal process in general. The attempt is to show how these issues impact the author/publisher against whom the accusations are filed or who seeks to defend their publication against government's action. In the present section, I highlight the functional dimension of courts that act as impediments against cases related to contentious publications. Two aspects that have direct bearing on the discourse of freedom of expression include (1) low importance rendered to cases related to freedom of speech and expression by courts and (2) inconsistency in judgements, which creates confusion regarding precedent and a high degree of subjectivity.

The Court's Interest in Free Speech Cases

Abhinav Chandrachud (2012) in a study of free speech cases in the Supreme Court shows that these cases don't fall under 'high priority' status on the docket of the Supreme Court of India. Chandrachud undertook a quantitative study of 107 cases related to freedom of speech and expression under section 19(1)(a) until November 2011. His conclusions were based on a set of structural and behavioural observations related to the treatment of these cases in the apex court. Structural observations included aspects such as instances where the Chief Justice formed part of the judgement bench and the size of the panel that heard the cases. As is the general trend, the Chief Justice forms the panels for each case and includes himself in those panels that hear the cases of highest priority.[7] Chandrachud's study shows that Chief Justices have formed a part of the panel of judges in only 40.1 percent of cases related to free speech. The possibility that the Chief Justice forms a part of such a panel has significantly declined over the years – from 85.7 percent during the 1950s down to just 3.8 percent during the period 2000–2010. Similarly, Chandrachud shows that the size of the panel for hearing such cases is extremely small, and at most times it was a two-member bench that heard cases related to free speech (in 44.8 percent of cases). Constitutional benches of five or above are a rarity in such cases.[8] These observations conform to Nick Robinson and others' (2011) assessment about the size of Supreme Court benches in all cases related to constitutional subjects. While scholars tend to agree that the smaller size of benches could also be due to the increasing number of cases, they are unanimous in the view that whenever a particular case is held to be important, it is referred to a larger bench. The behavioural observations that Chandrachud gleans in his study include aspects like the judges' voting patterns in each case and the registry of concurring and dissenting opinions. A large degree of homogeneity and a smaller number of dissents or concurrence statements is traced back to the idea that the degree of deliberation is less compared to other cases and also seen as an indication that other judges concur with the senior-most judge's views, who is most often responsible for writing the judgement on behalf of the bench. Chandrachud shows that in 51.4 percent of case related to freedom of speech and expression, the senior judge writes the judgement on behalf of the bench, and only in 15.8 percent of cases do we find evidence of concurring judgements by other judges; in only 10. 2 percent cases were dissenting opinions registered. These findings of Chandrachud are indicative of the importance the apex court attaches to free speech cases. I applied a similar method to test if the conclusions reached were in conformity with studies of scholars like Robinson and Chandrachud. However, the data set – which included both Supreme Court as well as High Court cases – differed from studies by Robinson and Chandrachud because they examined only cases heard in the Supreme Court. Further, my study focused on only cases related to contentious publications on religious grounds, unlike Robinson, who provides a detailed study about constitution benches in the Supreme Court, or Chandrachud, who worked with all cases related to article 19(1)(a) of constitution.

My research suggests that Chandrachud's and Robinson's observations were indeed applicable even to free speech cases. For example, in the 32 cases (as reflected in Table 4.2), the Chief Justice formed part of the bench only six times, once in the Supreme Court and five times in High Courts. However, the conclusions about the size of the Court benches differ from other studies. Section 96 makes it mandatory that any case where the proscription notification of the government is challenged, a bench of three High Court judges will hear such pleas, and therefore most of the cases in the study consisted of three judges. But in other cases, the benches consisted of

Table 4.2 List of cases along with size of bench, presence of chief justice and whether it included opinion of judges other than the one who wrote the judgement[9]

S.No.	*Case & Year of Controversy*	*Sections of Statutory Laws Invoked*	*Size of Bench of Judges Hearing the Case*	*Was the Chief Justice a Part of the Panel? (Yes/No)*	*Whether Judges Other Than the One Writing Judgement Registered Their Concurrence/ Dissent?*
1.	Shiv Ram Dass Udasin *v.* The Punjab State (1954)	Section 99(A) (Currently section 95)	3	No	Yes. Only agreement, no explanation
2.	Ramji Lal Modi *v.* The State of UP (1956)	Section 295(A) IPC	5	Yes	No
3.	Harnam Das *v.* State of Uttar Pradesh (1957)	Section 99(A) (Currently section 95)	5	No	Yes. Each judge expressed his/her opinion and explanation
4.	Harnam Das *v.* State of Uttar Pradesh (1961)	Section 99(A) (Currently section 95)	3	No	No
5.	Baba Khalil Ahmad *v.* The State (1960)	Section 99(A) (Currently section 95)	3	No	Yes. Only agreement, no explanation
6.	N. Veerabrahmam *v.* State of Andhra Pradesh (1959)	Section 99(A) (Currently section 95)	3	Yes	Yes. Each judge expressed his/her opinion and explanation
7.	The State of Mysore *v.* Henry Rodigues and Another (1961)	Section 295(A) IPC	2	No	No
8.	Mohammad Khalid *v.* The Chief Commissioner, Delhi (1967)	Section 99(A) (Currently section 95)	3	No	No

(Continued)

Table 4.2 (Continued)

S.No.	*Case & Year of Controversy*	*Sections of Statutory Laws Invoked*	*Size of Bench of Judges Hearing the Case*	*Was the Chief Justice a Part of the Panel? (Yes/No)*	*Whether Judges Other Than the One Writing Judgement Registered Their Concurrence/ Dissent?*
9.	Public Prosecutor *v.* P. Ramasami (1963)	Section 295(A) IPC	1	No	NA
10.	Sant Das Maheshwari *v.* Babu Ram Jadoun and others (1968)	Section 295(A) IPC & Section 95	2	No	No
11.	Babu Rao Patel *v.* State of Delhi (1973) (in High Court)	Section 153(A)	1	No	NA
12.	Babu Rao Patel *v.* State of Delhi (1980) (in Supreme Court)	Section 153(A)	2	No	No
13.	State of Uttar Pradesh *v.* Lalai Singh Yadav (1976)	Section 99(A) (Currently section 95)	3	No	No
14.	Lalai Singh Yadav *v.* State of Uttar Pradesh (1971)	Section 99(A) (Currently section 95)	3	No	No
15.	Ramlal Puri *v.* State of Madhya Pradesh (1970)	Section 99(A) (Currently section 95)	3	No	Yes. Each judge expressed his/her opinion and explanation
16.	Chinna Annamalai *v.* The State of Tamil Nadu (1971)	Section 99(A) (Currently section 95)	3	No	No
17.	M/S Varsha Publications Pvt. Ltd. *v.* State of Maharashtra and Others (1983)	Section 95	3	Yes	No

(Continued)

Table 4.2 (Continued)

S.No.	*Case & Year of Controversy*	*Sections of Statutory Laws Invoked*	*Size of Bench of Judges Hearing the Case*	*Was the Chief Justice a Part of the Panel? (Yes/No)*	*Whether Judges Other Than the One Writing Judgement Registered Their Concurrence/ Dissent?*
18.	Nand Kishore Singh and etc. *v*. State of Bihar and another (1984)	Section 95	3	Yes	Yes. Each judge expressed his/her opinion and explanation
19.	Chandmal Chopra *v*. State of West Bengal (1987)	Section 95	2	Yes	Yes. Each judge expressed his/her opinion and explanation
20.	The Trustees of Safdar Hasmee Memorial Trust *v*. Govt. of NCT of Delhi (2001)	Section 95	3	Yes	No
21.	G. Jairaj and others *v*. State of Karnataka and others (1997)	Section 95	2	No	No
22.	Baragur Ramchandra-ppa and others *v*. State of Karnataka and another (1998) (in the High Court)	Section 95	3	No	No
23.	Sri Baragur Ramchandra-ppa and others *v*. State of Karnataka and another (2007) (in Supreme Court)	Section 95	2	No	No
24.	Master Aman Preet Singh and others *v*. Govt. of India and others (1996)	Section 95	2	No	No

(Continued)

Table 4.2 (Continued)

S.No.	*Case & Year of Controversy*	*Sections of Statutory Laws Invoked*	*Size of Bench of Judges Hearing the Case*	*Was the Chief Justice a Part of the Panel? (Yes/No)*	*Whether Judges Other Than the One Writing Judgement Registered Their Concurrence/ Dissent?*
25.	Zac Poonen *v.* Hidden Treasure Literature (2001)	Section 295(A), 505, 508 IPC	2	No	No
26.	Piara Singh Bhaniara *v.* State of Punjab and another (2008)	Section 95	1	No	No
27.	Sujato Bhadra *v.* State of West Bengal (2005)	Section 95	3	No	Yes. Each judge expressed his/her opinion and explanation
28.	Yashwant Venilal Sanghvi *v.* Sahdevsinh Dilubha Zala (2004)	Section 295(A), 505, IPC	1	No	NA
29.	Manzar Sayeed Khan *v.* State of Maharashtra (2007)	Section 153, 153(A), 34 IPC	3	No	No
30.	State of Maharashtra and others *v.* Sanghraj Damodar Rupawate and others (2010)	Section 95	2	No	No
31.	Hulikal Nataraju *v.* State of Karnataka (2010)	Section 153, 153(A) IPC	1	No	No
32.	R. V. Bhasin *v.* 2 Marine Drive Police Station (2010)	Section 95	3	No	No

(Continued)

Table 4.2 (Continued)

S.No.	*Case & Year of Controversy*	*Sections of Statutory Laws Invoked*	*Size of Bench of Judges Hearing the Case*	*Was the Chief Justice a Part of the Panel? (Yes/No)*	*Whether Judges Other Than the One Writing Judgement Registered Their Concurrence/ Dissent?*
33.	Prasad Jacob (US citizen) *v.* State of Kerala (2010)	Section 153(A) IPC	1	No	No
34.	Father C. R. Prabhu *v.* State of Jharkhand and another (2013)	Section 153(A) IPC	1	No	No
35.	Maninder Singh and another *v.* State of Punjab and another (2013)	Section 295(A) IPC	1	No	No

either one or two judges, with only two instances where the case was sent for hearing to a bench consisting of five members (both times in the Supreme Court in years 1957 and 1961). So, Chandrachud's observation that the sizes of benches hearing free speech cases are usually small is also borne out by my own findings. Similarly, his points about behavioural aspects were equally valid. It was found that only in five instances (all in the High Courts) did judges other than the one who wrote the judgment register their concurrence, and in only two instances (both in High Courts) did the other judges dissent. In only five such cases where the opinion was registered, it was supported by a detailed explanation of the judges' position. The list of cases where concurrence by other judges was registered includes: *Nand Kishore Singh*, *Shiv Ram Dass Udasin*, *Baba Khalil Ahmad, N. Veerabrahmam* and *Sujato Bhadra*. Out of these, in *Shiv Ram Dass Udasin* and in *Baba Khalil Ahmad*, only the concurrence of the other judges was registered, without any explanation. The two cases where a dissenting opinion was registered included one in the Andhra High Court by Justice Bheemshankaran in the *N. Veerabrahmam* case, and another in the Supreme Court by Justice Das Gupta in the *Harnam Das* case. In all other cases, judges preferred either to remain silent or were completely convinced by the opinion of the judge who wrote the judgement and his grounds for forming that opinion. The statement of concurrence or dissent is important because it helps us to understand why judges agreed or disagreed with the judge who pronounced the judgment. It can add to the description of the case and also suggest grounds on which the judgement was arrived. A complete silence on the part of other judges does not contribute to analysis of the judgement in any way, and also indicates that other judges might not have taken equal interest in the case as the judge who was expected to write the judgement on their behalf. So, based on earlier studies like those of Chandrachud and Robinson, and their appositeness to my own analysis, it is indicative that cases related to freedom of speech and expression do not invite particular interest from the judiciary.

The Problem of Conflicting and Confusing Precedents

One of the pressing problems related to the courts' position on freedom of speech and expression cases has been the issue of conflicting and confusing precedents. The 'doctrine of precedent' expects courts to provide a legal framework for individuals to plan their lives and take decisions based on settled laws. Absence of a settled precedence related to law invokes a context of confusion and doubt. Further, lack of coherence also undermines the rule of law whereby two litigants are not treated equally. This makes the operation of the law unequal and uncertain (Mehta 2005). The conflicting precedents in higher courts also cascade to lower courts and have significant impact on the decisions taken at the level of lower courts. Confusion and indeterminacy tend to produce two lines of precedents, which lead to unpredictability of outcomes of the cases. In the present section, I focus on this aspect of the courtroom and discuss the broad themes around which cases related with contentious publications are dealt with in the courtroom. The aim is to highlight the inconsistencies in judgements and their impact on freedom of expression.

The debates and decisions of courts on various cases of censorship can be categorized into two types. Firstly are the cases where the court looks into the procedural aspects as mentioned in section 95 of the CrPC. These include an examination of the operative part of the government's action as well as the scrutiny of the grounds on which the action was based. Secondly are cases where the court examines the validity and applicability of government's action in the light of the publication in question. This includes an evaluation of state government's order based on the evidence presented. It largely revolves around the questions of 'intention' of the author or *mens rea*, the nature of the subject dealt with in the book, and the assessment of the method employed in making sense of the book's contents. On all these above-mentioned grounds, courts have exhibited diverse opinions which have resulted in similar books meeting different fates. This has only served to increase ambiguity about a settled position. A more detailed analysis will show the range of variance.

The Operative Part of Government's Action

Courts have generally held that it is the prerogative of state government to decide whether a publication falls under the prohibitive sections or not. Making its position clear in this respect, the court in the *Sri Baragur Ramachandrappa* case held that as section 95 was preventive in nature, government could take action if it pre-empted any danger to public order and there was no need for the actual occurrence of such incidents. This attitude is also reflected in the cases of *Nand Kishore Singh* and *R. V. Bhasin*. But this freedom has been questioned in other cases citing section 95 of CrPC that warranted government issuance of notification for any ban or forfeiture. In such cases the content of the notification was closely examined to look at the 'application of mind' in the decision. But even in these cases there has been diverse opinion about what such notifications should contain. In different cases proscription and forfeiture orders were set aside, citing different reasons. For example, in the *Sanghraj Damodar Rupawate* case, the Supreme Court held that it was important to mention the grounds on which government formed the opinion for forfeiture. It maintained that the notification should also include a 'conclusion of facts' on which opinion was arrived so that courts could evaluate those facts to check the applicability of the decision (*Sanghraj Damodar Rupawate* Civil Appeal of 2010 [Arising out of S.L.P. {Cl No. 8931 of 2007]). However, in the *Mohammad Khalid* case, the Supreme Court had held that mere opinion or grounds of opinion were not enough. The objecting communities as well as the objectionable passages should also be clearly mentioned in order to substantiate the basis of such opinion formation, and any absence of such reference could lead to such notification being set aside (*Mohammad Khalid* A.I.R. 1968 Delhi 13). Quite contrarily, in the *N. Veerabrahmam* case and *Nand Kishore Singh* case, respective High Courts opined that though opinion should be mentioned, an absence of grounds of opinion cannot be reason for not proscribing the book. In each case it was argued that section 99-D (96 of the current CrPC) mandated the courts 'only to examine the correctness of any such order made by the government' based on evaluation of the content of the publication and not to determine the content of notification.[10] Therefore, it was held that mentioning the grounds of opinion could only be an indicative and not a conclusive aspect of the notification order. The above discussion highlights the absence of any set precedent in examining government's order for forfeiture of contentious publications.

The Evaluative Aspects of the Government's Decision

A second set of cases included those where courts evaluated the government's order in light of evidence. An important requirement of statutory laws like section 153(A) and 295(A) that govern freedom of expression in India is the presence of 'deliberate and malicious intentions' on the part of the author/publisher. Though courts broadly agree on the necessity of this clause, there are divergent views about how intentions could be extracted and what tests are to be employed for such examination. For example, in some cases, courts seem to hold that the whole book and not isolated passages should be taken into consideration while making sense of the intentions of authors/publishers (*Sujato Bhadra*, 39 A.I.C. 239; *Nand Kishore Singh*, A.I.R. 1986 Pat. 98). However, in other cases it was maintained that this did not prevent the state from taking decisions based on portions or isolated passages, the validity of which could be later judged by the court (*Sanghraj Damodar Rupawate*, Civil Appeal of 2010 [Arising out of S.L.P. {C} No. 8931 of 2007]).

On the question about how to gather the intention of author/publisher, in the *N. Veerabrahmam* case the Andhra High Court opined that 'intention of the author has to be gathered primarily from the language used'. It was similar to the position of Allahabad High Court in the *Baba Khalil Ahmad* case, which had ruled that if language was problematic, there was no need to look for any other evidences and that no defence could stand for vituperative and offensive language (*Baba Khalil Ahamad*, A.I.R. 1960 All. 715). In the *Sanghraj Damodar Rupawate* case, the court extended the test to examine the content of offending passages as well as their import. So, if passages were drawn from 'folklore, tradition or history something in extenuation could perhaps be said for the author', the judges held. In *Nand Kishore Singh* case, the court maintained that along with language, and the import of offending passages, the audience to which the publication was catered to should also be kept in mind. Similarly, in the *R. V. Bhasin* case the Bombay High Court reiterated that the recognition of the audience for whom the publication was written and published was equally important to identify the intentions of the author. Interestingly, in the *Nand Kishore Singh* case, the court had explicitly maintained that no other external evidence should be considered while judging the intention of the author/publisher. However, in the *Sujato Bhadra* case, the court's observations were drawn extensively from the external context about which the book had referred. The significance of external circumstances was also upheld in the *Manzar Sayeed Khan* case, where the Supreme Court held that the circumstances in which a book was written and published were one of the critical indicators of the author's intention (*Manzar Sayeed Khan v. State of Maharashtra* [2009] 12 S.C.C. 157). It would appear, therefore, that there are no fixed criteria about how to make sense of the intentions of the author, even though these are seen as an important aspect of law.

Further, in several cases courts have held that if intentions were proven to be deliberate and malicious, even the claims of truth and history could not be used as excuses to defend offensive writings. For example, in the *Sanghraj Damodar Rupawate* case, the Supreme Court observed:

> If the writing is calculated to promote feeling of enmity or hatred, it is no defence to a charge under section 153(A) of the IPC that the writing contains a truthful kind of past events or is otherwise supported by good authority. Adherence to the strict path of history is not by itself a complete defence to a charge under section 153(A) of the IPC.

Quite contrarily, the Bombay High Court argued in the *M/S Varsha Publications* case that these sections should not be extended so far as to affect historical research or writings criticizing religions. The court held:

> Different considerations will prevail when we are to consider a scholarly article on history and religion based upon research with the help of a number of reference books. It will be very difficult for the State to contend that a narration of history would promote violence enmity or hatred. If such a contention is accepted a day will come when that part of history which is unpalatable to a particular religion on the pretext that the publication of such history would constitute an offence punishable under S. 153A of the I.P.C.
>
> (*M/S Varsha Publications*, Cri LJ 1446)

Another test courts use to examine the validity of government's decision of proscription or forfeiture is that of 'reasonability'. It is based on the perception that impact of any publication should not be judged on the basis of reactions of a believer or an emotionally invested person; rather, the effect is 'to be judged from standard of reasonable, strong minded, firm and courageous' (*Sanghraj Damodar Rupawate*, Civil Appeal of 2010 [Arising out of S.L.P. {C} No. 8931 of 2007]). So, only works which are considered 'grossly offensive to reasonable man' should be eligible for proscription or forfeiture (*Shiv Ram Dass Udasin*, A.I.R 1955 P H 28). However, in the *Baragur Ramachandrappa*, case the Karnataka High Court made it explicit that 'we are concerned with [the] impact of the book on the minds of ordinary people with religious beliefs and not discerning intelligentsia'. Also, in the *Baba Khalil Ahmad* case, the court opined that if the content was insulting to some sacred figure, it naturally led to a feeling of offence for its followers and hence the content itself should be the guide in the subject.

The above discussions show that the jurisprudence relating to ban and forfeiture of publications has been chaotic, to say the least, and leaves considerable room for subjectivity of judges (Dhavan 2008: 145). In similar cases, courts have employed quite different yardsticks and have come up with starkly opposite and irreconcilable conclusions. Such inconsistency has significant consequences, both in terms of principles as well as practice. Its impact on the principle of precedents has already been discussed. In practical experience, it encourages non-state actors to exert pressure on government officials to issue ban orders. In the absence of a clear mandate on the subject, the magistrate and other officials consider it better to act against the publication, the validity of the action being left to be decided later in the court. Dhavan views this as 'problem solving' politics, whereby, the government 'solves' the problem of social pressure by imposing the ban, and the court later provides the 'legal' solution by taking decision on the ban (2008: 144). The lack of clarity in the judiciary's position also encourages non-state actors to file criminal cases against authors/publishers in the hope that the court's verdict could run in their favour. From the perspective of the author/ publisher, both these strategies are particularly intimidating. There is a constant fear of loss of civil liberty, punishment, and even imprisonment. Add to this the tiring legal process including the duration for a verdict, which may take decades, and the whole experience in itself can be like a punishment. Even after all that, one can never be sure about which side the court's decision would go. The tough and exhaustive legal battle in the judiciary, where free speech cases are not high in the docket of cases and which works in the context of a lack of conclusive precedent, can have a lasting impact on the experience of authors/publishers defending their freedom of expression (Liang 2012; Narrain 2016b). This also creates an environment of fear and uncertainty where authors/publishers often choose to desist from such engagement and instead give in to the demands of protesting groups either by removing controversial sections or by pulping the publication itself. The case of Wendy Doniger's *The Hindus* is an explicit example of this phenomenon.

Pulping of Wendy Doniger's *The Hindus: An Alternative History*: A Case Study

On 10 February 2014 the district court in Delhi accepted the settlement agreement between Penguin Books India Pvt. Ltd. and Dina Nath Batra[11] of Shiksha Bachao Abhiyan Samiti. After a legal battle that lasted four years, the publishers of the book, in an out-of-court settlement, succumbed to the demands of Batra. Penguin agreed to 'recall and withdraw' all copies of the book from Indian territory with immediate effect. It also promised that it would pulp all the 'recalled/withdrawn/unsold copies of the book' at their own cost. In return Batra agreed to withdraw all civil/criminal cases/complaints filed against the author or the publishers of the book.[12]

The ordeal surrounding Doniger's book *The Hindus* began in 2010 when Saraswati Research and Education Trust started an online petition claiming that the book contained factual errors about the historical past as well as vilification of Hinduism.[13] It highlighted 16 factual errors, including distortion of maps, mistakes in historical accounts and bibliographic inaccuracies among others. It also cited eight passages which it claimed to be highly derogatory, defamatory and offensive to Hindus. These concerns were reiterated in a legal notice sent by Batra to the author and publishers of the book in the same year.[14] He charged the author and publishers of the book of consciously misrepresenting the Hindu religion by quoting passages from religious books out of context, distorting facts and providing wrong information. He further claimed that the author also promoted obscenity and vulgarity through images and writings in the books, which were aimed to vilify Hinduism. Doniger's approach to the question of religion, Batra argued, was that of a 'woman hungry of sex' and the book was written with a 'Christian missionary zeal and hidden agenda to denigrate Hindus and show their religion in poor light'. The notice asked the author and the publisher to seek an 'unconditional apology', 'withdraw the said objectionable parts from book' and 'undertake not to offend the religious sentiments of the Hindus in future'. Failing that, he warned 'legal action under section 153, 153(A), 295(A), 298, 505(2) of IPC' would be initiated and that he would further ask Hindus to 'boycott the books published by Penguin Books India Pvt. Ltd'. When no action was taken in response to the legal notice, Batra took the author and publishers to court and filed several civil and criminal suits against them.[15] After battling the court cases for more than four years, the publishers finally decided to give in to Batra's demands.

The settlement agreement was criticized by several scholars and intellectuals as surrender by the book company to radical conservative forces, thereby weakening the battle for freedom of speech and expression.[16] But here I am concerned with only the debates surrounding legal aspects of the case. Penguin's submission to legal pressure generated by Batra indicates the complex role that law and the legal process play in the discourse of censorship. On the one hand, it highlights how law and the legal process could be used as legitimate tools for censorship by those claiming hurt sentiments, and on the other hand, it also shows the vulnerability experienced by authors and publishers when such pressure is exerted. In the process, the practical limits of the theoretical debates surrounding freedom of speech and expression were clearly exposed.

The Role of Law and the Legal Process in Penguin's Surrender

It was not the first time that Dina Nath Batra was using a legal route to censor historical work he considered objectionable. In 2008, Batra on behalf of Shiksha Bachao Andolan Samiti (SBAS) moved to the Delhi High Court, requesting it to issue orders to University of Delhi to remove A. K. Ramanujan's essay titled *Three Hundred Ramayanas: Five Examples and Three Thoughts on Translation* from its history syllabus taught at the undergraduate level.[17] Judges at the High Court decided not to interfere in the subject as it was an internal matter of the university and also because, according to them, the court lacked the capacity to judge academic matters. The plea was therefore rejected. But Batra filed another civil suit in the Supreme Court. Hearing the matter in July 2010, the Supreme Court asked the university to set up an expert committee competent to look into the matter. This eventually led to the removal of the essay from the syllabus.[18]

So, Batra had previous experience with how to use legitimate legal means to enforce censorship. Unlike the violent mob that threatened authors or vandalized bookstores, Batra claimed to be a law-abiding citizen, and expressed it to be his legal right to raise objections and bring it to the notice of the government and judiciary if anything denigrating his religious beliefs was published and circulated. Batra's legal counsel, Monika Arora, justified his act in an article written in *Organizer*, the mouthpiece of RSS. Arora argued that the Indian constitution did not allow for unlimited freedom of speech and expression and that 'reasonable restrictions' could be imposed, which were to be defined on case-to-case basis by the judiciary (*Organizer*, 23 February 2014). She claimed that Batra was right in bringing such cases to the judiciary and left it upon the judges to take decision about the future of such controversial publications. It is evident that people like Batra use law as a potent weapon in their battle against publications they consider hurting their religious sentiments. In fact, just after his success in the Doniger case, Batra reportedly sent similar legal notices to other publishers regarding other books that he thought were offensive to Hindus.[19]

An equally important aspect related to such incidents of censorship is the effectiveness of legal methods. When the case of settlement between Penguin and Batra became public, legal scholars and practitioners criticized the company for succumbing to legal threats and presented two sets of arguments about why the step was completely unnecessary. On one hand, some scholars argued that provisions of Indian law under which civil and criminal charges were registered did not even apply to the case. It was therefore liable to be summarily rejected by the courts. Noorani claimed that Batra was able to win the battle 'with a toy gun' (*Frontline*, 4 April 2014). He and other commentators like V. Venkatesan (*Frontline*, 7 May 2014) believed that Penguin did not receive the right legal guidance on the subject because, as Noorani held, 'the High Court is there to ensure such a dismissal even if the District Judge or the Magistrate or the police did not follow the law. If not the Supreme Court would have surely done that'. They opined that instead of surrender, Penguin should have continued the legal battle. Another set of legal scholars, like Saurav Datta, claimed that if Penguin would not have given up, it would have been assured of a legal victory, if not in the lower courts than at least in the Supreme Court (*DNA*, 4 March 2014). To substantiate his point, Datta used cases from the Supreme Court where it had handed judgements in favour of authors/publishers in similar cases.

The issues raised by both sets of commentators are significant, but the arguments that were offered by either do not seem convincing. One of the primary limitations of their analyses is that it completely overlooks Penguin's point of view. Further, these arguments, especially in the context of Penguin's action, missed some important facts. Take, for example, Datta's claim that 'the courts have [a] long tradition of protecting freedom of speech by upholding the right to express divergent and alternative views on religions even if they rile a majority of believers'. It was hailed and cited uncritically by various other scholars and journalists.[20] Datta's conclusions, however, are based on selective analysis of court cases, and suffer from a severe misreading of facts in cases that he cites as evidence for his conclusions. In the last chapter, I have shown how courts in India have favoured proscription of books claimed to be offensive to religious sentiments of different communities, and therefore Datta's position that Penguin was assured of a legal victory if they would have continued the legal battle is far from reality. Even if one agrees that criminal charges could not stand in the court of law as it would have been difficult for the counsel of the plaintiff to show 'deliberate and malicious intentions' of the author/publisher, nevertheless the civil suit could still go against them. Further, as discussed earlier in this chapter, given the fact that courts have been inconsistent in terms of doctrines used to decide each case, it is quite difficult to predict whether or not the courts would have upheld the criminal charges.

Coming back to arguments of legal scholars like Venkatesan and Noorani, we see that though it is difficult to comment whether Penguin was misled by its legal advisors, it is clear that its fear was more than just about court's position on criminal charges levelled against the author and the company. This is evident from the statements released by Doniger and Penguin India Ltd. in response to the criticism they faced after the settlement agreement. It was maintained in both responses that uncertainty over interpretation of section 295(A) was one of the primary reasons for their out-of-court settlement with Batra. Doniger called statutory laws 'the true villain' in the case, as they threatened to 'jeopardize the physical safety of any publisher, no matter how ludicrous the accusation brought against a book'.[21] The company feared that 'the Indian Penal Code, and in particular section 295(A) of that code, will make it increasingly difficult for any Indian publisher to uphold international standards of free expression without deliberately placing itself outside the law'.[22] The concern was not only with the vague and broad language used in such a law but also the ambiguity over its probable interpretations in the courts. Doniger and her publisher, Penguin, were equally worried about the ambiguity of the legal process. Doniger argues that in Indian context 'if you got the wrong judge ... you'd be convicted just for publishing a statement that you had good reason to believe might well offend someone'.[23] Penguin, on its part, pointed out that it was obligated to respect the law of land, 'however intolerant and restrictive those laws may be', but at the same time, it was also committed to protect its employees from threat and harassment. Therefore, it maintained that the decision to settle the matter after four years of legal battle was justified. Although the act was seen by many legal commentators as surrender to radical forces, the reasons forwarded by the company point to insecurities that the author/publisher faced in the absence of robust institutional structures for protection of their freedom of speech and expression.[24]

Doniger's was not an isolated incident where legal notices from groups claiming hurt sentiment had forced significant changes in the attitude of publishers. For example, in September 2008, while a case was filed in the Delhi High Court to order the removal of A. K. Ramanujan's essay from the history syllabus being taught at undergraduate level, the SBAS also served a legal notice to Oxford University Press (OUP), India, the original publisher of the essay in an edited volume, asking them to stop printing the essay.[25] The OUP not only apologized for the fact that the essay had hurt religious sentiments of Hindus, but also gave assurance that the essay was no more in print, nor did the publishers have any intentions of reprinting it.[26] Also, in case of James Laine's book *Shivaji: Hindu King in Islamic India*, the publishing house had promised, even before the case reached court, to stop printing and withdraw the publication from market due to fear of legal action against it.[27] Similarly, in case of D. N. Jha's book *Holy Cow: Beef in Indian Dietary Tradition*, the publisher, CB Publishers, refused to publish the book, due to fear of further prosecution or controversy, even after the civil court in Hyderabad lifted its stay on the publishing of the book.[28] The concern guiding each such publisher's decision to withdraw or pulp a book is almost the same, that is, to protect themselves from entering the vortex of a legal process which harms their interest both financially as well as in the form of intimidation through criminal charges against its employees.

Conclusion

It is evident from above discussion that both law and legal process can act as hurdles in the free exercise of freedom of speech and expression by creating an environment of fear of retribution. This eventually encourages what Cook and Heilmann call 'public self-censorship'. Public self-censorship is a phenomenon where the censor and the censee are two different agents 'and where the censee censors him or herself in response to this external censor' (Cook & Heilmann 2013: 186–187). Cook and Heilmann differentiate 'public self-censorship' from 'private self-censorship' based on absence of an external censor in the later case: the censor and the censee therefore being the same agent. In the case of Doniger's book, it was explicitly a case of self-censorship, where the publisher decided to pulp the book, without any such direction from either governmental institutions or the judiciary. However, in this case there were two sources of external censors. First of all, there was Dina Nath Batra, who threatened by filing civil suits and criminal charges against the author and the publisher; and second, law and the legal process played the role of another censor by creating an atmosphere of uncertainty and prolonged distress. As the external sources were not situated in any form of government order for a ban or the judiciary's pronouncement in the case, it cannot be seen as a classic case of censorship. The role of law and legal process as external sources for censorship in this case cannot be put into the same bracket of overt forms of censorship[29] (Cook & Heilmann 2013: 180–183), as it had less to do with the stated position of the law in the constitution or statutory books or even the settled interpretation of the law by the judiciary, and much more to do with the ambiguity produced by the language of the law as well as the fluctuating position of the judiciary in such cases. In Doniger's case, the decision to pulp the book by Penguin as the censee was a response to its interaction with external sources of censorship. This phenomenon precisely reflects the pressures exerted by law and the legal process in the struggle for freedom of speech and expression in the Indian context.

Notes

1 The idea of a 'slippery slope' has been an important argument for claiming extreme freedom in relation to speech and expression. It assumes that if laws are made to constrain such freedom, they can be misused in different ways to hurt the core of the value enshrined in freedom of speech and expression.

2 Dhavan uses the phrase 'process as punishment' to explain how the long legal process harasses authors/publishers/painters who are targeted by the socio-religious groups, who in the name of hurt sentiments create hurdles for their freedom of expression (Dhavan 2008: 223). The sense of alienation from the legal process is reflected in the fact that some authors/publishers, as in Wendy Doniger's case (discussed later in the chapter) agree for an out-of-court settlement of the issue with the non-state actors.

3 The book discussed, with the help of historical evidence, how beef had been an essential component of Indian dietary habits since ancient times; and this practice, he argued, was present among all religions, including Hinduism, Jainism and Buddhism. Before the book was released, a Member of Parliament from the BJP, R. S. Rawat, wrote to the union Home Ministry demanding a ban on the book and the arrest of the author and publisher. See, 'Book on Beef Eating Runs into Trouble', *The Hindu*, 9 August 2001.

4 Sheela Reddy, 'A Brahmin's Cow Tales', *Outlook*, 17 September 2001. The court issued a temporary stay on the publication of the book. Though the stay was lifted after a year of judicial process, the publisher, fearing further controversy, and prosecution, refused to publish the book. As a result, Jha had to look for another publisher, and the book was published later by London-based Verso publishers, under a new title, *The Myth of the Holy Cow*.

5 This is not unique to cases related to freedom of expression. There have been various reasons cited for such delay, like the number of judges in the judiciary, among others. For details on such concerns, see Law Commission of India's 77th Report titled *Delay and Arrears in Trial Courts*, November 1978, available at lawcommissionofindia.nic.in/51-100/report77.pdf (last accessed 28 June 2018. Also see Robinson [2011: 27] and Chandrachud [2011: 71–78]).

6 Note that the maximum time allowed for a complainant to file a case against the government's notification for forfeiture is two months from when the notification order is made public.

7 Robinson and others argue that the apex court in India is 'Chief Justice–dominant' and highlights the important role that the Chief Justice plays in the court (2011: 31).

8 As article 145(3) of the Indian constitution suggests, the 'minimum number of Judges who are to sit for the purpose of deciding any case involving a substantial question of law' has to be five.

9 The data set is of 32 cases. However, the difference in serial number is because in three cases, I have also included the data of the same cases appearing both in the High Court as well as Supreme Court. Years mentioned in table are according to the year the final judgement was delivered.

10 This position was also upheld by Justice Das Gupta in his dissenting note in the case of *Harnam Das*, 1961 A.I.R 1662.

11 Dina Nath Batra is a retired schoolmaster who now heads Shiksha Bachao Andolan Samiti (SBAS), an organization that claims to be dedicated to protecting Indian values and reforming the Indian education system. It is considered to be very close to the RSS.

12 The copy of the settlement agreement was widely available. The one here is taken from, www.outlookindia.com/article/penguin-to-withdraw-the-hindus-an-alternative-history/289467 (last accessed on 27 June 2018).

13 The online petition was started by Saraswati Research and Education Trust and addressed to the CEO and the president of Penguin Group. It was launched on the website www.petitiononline.com. However, the website has not been functional since 30 September 2014. But the content of the online petition and the attached letter can be found at www.outlookindia.com/article/the-book-promotes-prejudices-and-biases-against-hindus/289472 (last accessed on 27 June 2018).

14 Legal notice sent by Dina Nath Batra to Wendy Doniger, Penguin Group (USA) Inc. and Penguin Books India Pvt. Ltd., dated 3 March 2010 and Ref. No. 254/LN/0310 is available at www.outlookindia.com/article/your-approach-is-that-of-a-woman-hungry-ofsex/289468 (last accessed on 27 June 2018).

15 Batra pursued two forms of legal pressure building – civil and criminal. He filed a complaint under criminal charges at Hauz Khas Police Station on 29 April 2010 and another in 2013. On 19 March 2010 he also brought a civil suit in the Saket District Court at Delhi (No. 360 of 2011).

16 There were diverse reactions on the episode. Some commentators claimed it to be another case of an attack on the freedom of expression by radical fundamentalist forces. See Kenan Malik, 'Changing Landscape of Free Speech', *The Hindu*, 12 February 2014; Ratna Kapur, 'Totalising History, Silencing Dissent', *The Hindu*, 15 February 2014; 'Narrowing Horizons: Withdrawal of Doniger Book Highlights Sway of Taliban-like Forces in India', *The Times of India*, 13 February 2014. However, most commentators believed that it was surrender by the company against such forces that was an important matter of concern. The incident was followed by several public statements signed by scholars and academicians criticizing Penguin for the act. See for example, 'Statement on Withdrawal of Wendy Doniger's Book Issued by Centre of Historical Studies, JNU', available at kafila.org/2014/02/21/chs-jnu-statement-on-the-wendy-doniger-issue/ (last accessed on 27 June 2018); 'SAHMAT Statement on Wendy Doniger's Book', available at www.sacw.net/article7666.html (last accessed on 27 June 2018); Sridharan and Cerulli (2014: 274–276).

17 See *Dina Nath Batra v. University of Delhi Laws* (DLH) 2008-7-180, decided on 19 July 2008. Also see A. A. Mahaprashta, 'The Rule of Unreason', *Frontline*, 5 November 2011.

18 'Delhi University Scraps Ramanujan's Essay on Ramayana', *Deccan Herald*, 13 October 2011.

19 On 3 March 2014 Batra sent legal notice to Aleph Books demanding that the book company should withdraw another book by Wendy Doniger, titled *On Hinduism*. See 'Doniger's Book *On Hinduism* Put on Hold', *The Indian Express*, 11 March 2014. In May 2014, he also sent a legal notice to an academic publisher to halt the release of Megha Kumar's book *Communalism and Sexual Violence: Ahmedabad since 1969*. See 'Another Publisher Forced to Censor Textbooks', *The Hindu*, 3 June 2014.

20 See, for example, Sethi & Sengupta (2014: 290–299); Pallavi Polanki, 'Censorship by Other Means, Dinanath Batra Shows the Way', available at www.firstpost.com/india/censorship-by-other-means-dinanath-batra-shows-the-way-1560243.html (last accessed on 27 June 2018).

21 See Wendy Doniger's statement released by PEN India, available at www.outlookindia.com/article/i-do-not-blame-penguin-books-india/289473 (last accessed on 27 June 2018).

22 See 'Penguin India's Statement on *The Hindus* by Wendy Doniger', available at http://www.penguinbooksindia.com/en/content/penguin-india%E2%80%99S-statement-%E2%80%98-hindus%E2%80%99-wendy-doniger (last accessed on 27 June 2018).

23 See Wendy Doniger, 'India: Censorship by the Batra Brigade', *New York Review of Books*, 8 May 2014, www.nybooks.com/articles/archieves/2014/may/08/india-censorship-batra-brigade/ (last accessed on 27 June 2018).

24 This concern was also reflected by commentators like Pratap Bhanu Mehta and Shivprasad Swaminathan. Mehta held that the courts have consistently failed to protect liberal values like freedom of speech and expression and therefore have led to the silencing of 'liberal India'. See Pratap Bhanu Mehta, 'Silencing of Liberal India', *The Indian Express*, 12 February 2014. Swaminathan on a similar line showed that if the potential benefits are pitted against the hazards, the authors and the publishers ought to prefer some form of censorship in order to protect themselves from the distress surrounding legal actions. See Shivprasad Swaminathan, 'Scribblers, Scholars in the Same Boat', *The Hindu*, 25 February 2014.

25 SBAS served a legal notice to Oxford University Press in relation to the book edited by Paula Richman (1991).

26 In the Supreme Court the advocate of the publisher assured the court about this in 2010. See 'When a Department Let the University Down', *The Hindu*, 3 November 2011.

27 James Laine's book *Shivaji: Hindu King in Islamic India* was banned in Maharashtra after some Hindu groups from Maharashtra protested against it. Later the Supreme Court lifted the ban. See *Sanghraj Damodar Rupawate* Civil Appeal of 2010 (Arising out of S.L.P. [C] No. 8931 of 2007).

28 The author and the publisher faced several threats during the controversy. Jha's property was also vandalized by unknown assailants. For complete reporting of the events, see Sheela Reddy, 'A Brahmin's Cow Tales', *Outlook*, 17 September 2001.

29 Overt forms of censorship here refer to the censorship imposed by state institutions directly. Normally laws limiting freedom of expression form part of the tools used by the state to regulate speech acts. However, in cases like those mentioned here, laws do not act directly to restrict free speech.

5

NON-STATE ACTORS AS CENSORS

The Legal Position

The last two chapters discussed the attitude of courts in India towards freedom of speech and expression in general, and with regard to contentious publications in particular. It was observed that lacunae largely associated with the functioning of the courts and the ambiguities reflected in its judgements have proved counter-productive for defenders of free speech. It has resulted in not only creating an atmosphere of uncertainty and fear among authors/publishers but has also acted as a source of encouragement for people demanding censorship of publications, based on their claims of religious offence. It can be claimed that the institution of the judiciary, which was established by constitution makers as the ultimate defender of civil and fundamental rights of the citizens – especially freedom of speech and expression – has allowed curtailment of this important right in the garb of legal language and constitutional interpretations. Though some judgements seem to uphold freedom of expression, courts' general attitude of defining the limits of freedom of expression vis-à-vis public order or other values that it considered important for Indian society has resulted in producing a public context which cannot be considered favourable for free exercise of freedom of expression.

This chapter shall examine cases related to censorship where government, the judiciary and non-state actors interact. The process through which social forces collude with state power often renders subordinate the role of courts in the politics of censorship. To highlight this aspect, I focus on two types of cases: (1) cases where the use of statutory laws like the Customs Act renders an immunity to the decision of government and (2) cases where the prevailing atmosphere forced the author/publisher to censor controversial writing regardless of the fact that court had found nothing objectionable in the text and hence revoked the official ban on the book. In each of these cases we see an active role played by non-state actors (which include socio-religious groups as well as political parties). Although the main arena of contestation between claims of religious offence and freedom of expression remained outside the courtroom, demands of censorship predominantly used the language of law as its legitimizing source.

DOI: 10.4324/9781003369257-6

Trivializing the Role of the Court in the Politics of Censorship

The role of courts in censorship is significantly limited by the existence of laws that protect the executive's decisions from judicial scrutiny. For example, the Customs Act[1] is one of the notable laws that government uses to prevent import of any publication that it presumes will create problems in the country or that may be in bad taste according to the government. Historically, this law has been used to stop the import of propaganda material, political manuscripts and also publications on religion which, according to the government, have the potential to create unrest among any section of the population.[2] In many such cases, the government's act goes unnoticed as it does not become part of the popular discourse nor does the news get appropriate mediation. As early as 1956, Nehru's government decided to ban the import of Aubrey Menen's *Rama Retold*, which was believed to contain material that could hurt the sentiments of the Hindus in the country.[3] The use of the Customs Act to prevent entry of any publication in the territory of India reflects a paternal attitude on behalf of the state, where it decides for its citizens which material is readable and which could instigate sharp reactions. One of the significant cases of censorship where the Customs Act played a role was the ban on Salman Rushdie's *Satanic Verses*. The banning of *The Satanic Verses* raised several moral and normative questions about religious offence and freedom of expression, which became the subjects of intense debates within political theory. However, here I primarily discuss the debates on the subject from the perspective of law and the role played by non-state actors.

Banning The Satanic Verses *and Public Debate over Law*

Much before the formal launch of the book, there were apprehensions about the probable impact it could have on Indian readers. Khushwant Singh[4] advised the publishers of the book, Viking Penguin, not to publish the book in India as he feared that the content of the novel, especially satirical references to the Prophet and his wives, would not be received in good spirit by the country's Muslim audience. Before the launch of the book, an interview with the author, Salman Rushdie, along with some extracts from the book were published in two popular journals.[5] Syed Sahabuddin, the Member of Parliament (MP) from the Janata Party, along with other prominent Muslim representatives like Khurshid Alam Khan[6] brought the interviews of Rushdie and the extracts published in *India Today* to the notice of the government.[7] They feared that the book might create communal disturbances in the country and therefore requested that the book be banned. The Rajiv Gandhi government felt that the concerns were reasonable and hence the ban order was passed on 5 October, 1988 under section 11 of the Customs Act, which prevented any import of the book into India.[8]

The call for the ban incited controversy. It was argued that government had succumbed to demands of Muslim politicians and showed disregard for freedom of expression and misuse of the legal provisions. Some legal luminaries argued that the Customs Act did not contain any provision to ban a book on the basis of religious insults. For instance, Soli Sorabjee remarked that the law 'curiously does not impose any ban on books which insult religion or offend religious sentiment of the people, as have been erroneously assumed in some quarters'.[9] However, an official statement by the government maintained that the ban under section 11 of Customs Act (1962) was a 'pre-emptive step' to avoid 'misrepresentation' of passages of the *Satanic Verses* for 'political purposes', which it feared could lead to a public-order problem. It further held that the order did 'not detract or otherwise reflect on the artistic or literary worth of the book or its author'.[10] The government presented it as a judgement based on public-order concerns rather than on the merits or contents of the book and held that although a ban under the Customs Act was immune from any challenge in the judiciary, the decision could be justified in the public realm as pragmatic and well within the constitutional limits set for freedom of expression under article 19(2).[11]

The decision to ban the book initiated a public debate about the state of freedom of speech and expression in India. One section raised issues about the intentions of government, as it appeared that it had succumbed to pressure from some Muslim politicians.[12] The demand for the ban was raised by influential Muslim legislators and ministers, like Shahbuddin and Khurshid Alam Khan, and government was accused of responding to such demands simply to distract public attention, as well as to regain the confidence of India's Muslim population, which was lost due to its position in the Ayodhya case.[13] As a result, it was claimed by those who opposed the ban that the decision of government was arbitrary and it lacked cogent justification for imposing the Customs Act.[14] Though it was not the first time that a book was banned in India, the case of Rushdie attracted international attention owing to polarized reactions on the subject the world over. This included a fatwa by a Muslim cleric in Iran for beheading Rushdie, and an explicit position taken by governments across countries like Britain of not banning the book despite pressure from Muslim communities.[15]

On the contrary, the supporters of the ban invoked both moral as well as legal arguments. They appreciated the role of government in the entire episode and lauded it for protecting the constitutional spirit of secularism and multiculturalism.[16] Support for the ban was broadly based on three sets of arguments. The first argument was that the vilification of religious personalities contained in the book could hurt religious sensibilities. Sahabuddin argued that insulting the respected figures of Islam could not be a part of satire, and any act of casting aspersions on such pious symbols could not be tolerated. He commented:

> You depict the holy Prophet ... as an imposter and you expect us to clap for you. You have the diseased mind and the evil pen to situate the wives of the holy Prophet ... the mothers of the community, in a brothel and you expect the Muslims to prove your power of imagination.[17]

The second argument was that the book could ignite religious sensibilities, and could lead to rioting and communal disturbances. This was in contradistinction to Rushdie's belief that 'no book can cause riots'.[18] This claim was effectively rebutted by Khushwant Singh, who remarked that Rushdie was 'naïve' to think that way because Indian history was full of cases where hurt sentiments had led to communal mobilization culminating in violence and riots.[19] The third argument forwarded in support of the government's action was about violations of Indian laws. It was argued that the demand for the ban as well as the government's decision were not based on abstract principles or force; rather, they had firm support from within the legal structure of the country and were therefore justified. Salman Khurshid, a prominent Congress leader and also a lawyer, charged Rushdie with defying 'Indian laws relating to obscenity and religious practice'.[20] Laws under the IPC were quoted along with the Customs Act to convey the point that if Rushdie had been present in India, he could even be convicted under sections 295(A) and 153(A).[21] So, overall the book was found objectionable by those supporting the ban of the book on three grounds: it was considered to be 'a crime against human decency'; 'an insult to Islam'; and 'an offence under Indian law'.[22] Two lessons from the episode are significant. Firstly, it exposed the limits of courts when laws like the Customs Act are invoked by government. Though it was claimed that the book violated the law, the validity of the claim could not be tested as such laws provide immunity to government orders from being challenged in courts. Secondly, it had shown that government could be forced to order a ban on publications in the name of hurt sentiments and threats to public order. This aspect was crucial as it threw light on the role of non-state actors in censorship.

The binary created between freedom of expression and protecting the interest of religious communities in the name of the state's role in a multicultural society persisted even after *The Satanic Verses* episode. In fact, in certain cases the binary became more acute with a more direct role of non-state actors. This phenomenon was visible when Taslima Nasreen, the Bangladeshi author, was physically attacked, and under pressure from socio-religious groups, she agreed to delete controversial portions from her novel *Dwikhandito* regardless of the fact that the High Court had found nothing objectionable in it. This case not only uncovers the complexity of censorship debate in the Indian context but also shows how censorship has often become a tool for instrumental politics among the stakeholders.

The Curious Case of Dwikhandito *and the Role of the Courts*

The book *Dwikhandito* was the third volume of Nasreen's autobiographical series and discussed the author's multiple sexual relationships with some of the most prominent authors and poets both in Bangladesh and India during her youth. It first came to public scrutiny when the West Bengal High Court passed an injunction on the publication, sale, marketing and circulation of the book after a defamatory suit was filed by Syed Hasmat Jalal, one of the figures with whom Nasreen had claimed sexual relations in the book. The government of West Bengal banned the book only a week after this injunction order. Some Muslim organizations like Jamiat Ullema-e-Hind and All India Minority Forum (AIMF) had also complained about the book. They had claimed that certain passages contained insults against the Prophet and Islam.[23] Justifying the ban, Chief Minister of West Bengal, Budhadeb Bhattacharjee, said, 'I've read the book, not once but several times. I've discussed the contents with 25 people who matter and have finally decided to proscribe it.'[24] The government argued that if the book were not banned, 'it could ignite communal tension'.[25]

As in Rushdie's case, criticism of the government's decision came from those who believed that it had submitted to the demands of extremists. Some critics believed that the reaction of government was not based so much on fear of communal violence as on Nasreen's reference to sexual relationships with prominent personalities of Bengal, who as it happened were also close to the Left Front government leaders of Bengal.[26] Nasreen expressed shock at the ban order. She argued that there was nothing 'in the relevant pages of the book that might cause riots'. 'Also'. she pointedly asked, 'is it correct to underestimate Muslims so much? Are Muslims so ignorant, illiterate, intolerant, and convertible when faced with any kind of criticism about their religion?'[27] However, government had decided to ban the book, and the decision was actively supported by other major political parties. They believed that the book contained perversions of the teachings of the Quran and hence would give sustenance to anti- Islamic views. Further, it was claimed that adjectives used for the Prophet were not in good taste.[28]

A human rights activist from Kolkata, Sujato Bhadra, appealed the ban in the High Court. After almost two years, the court lifted the ban from the book, on 22 September 2005. The court's observations were crucial. It held that the intention of author, 'who herself profess[es] the same religion has to be gathered from the context of the book'.[29] It further maintained that though the book contained harsh language against the Prophet, there was no deliberate and malicious intent on the part of the author of *Dwikhandito* to outrage the religious feelings of any class of citizens of India because 'the insult to religion was not the central theme of the book, read as a whole'. It also opined that if the insult to religion is in good faith in 'his/her endeavour or object to facilitate some measure of social reform by administering such a shock to the followers of the religion, as would ensure notice being taken by any criticism so made would not attract the mischief of section 295(A)'. As the author was dealing with the specific situation in Bangladesh 'which was a theocracy and not India, which is a secular country', the court did not find any deliberate or malicious intent to hurt religious sentiments of Indian citizens. Though the court came to the defence of Nasreen's freedom of expression, one might see it as a case of 'overindulgence' with the text. For example, the court overlooked the insulting references to the Prophet because it believed that the subject of the book itself was not based on them. Further, the emphasis laid on the context rather than content was questionable, as it did not say anything about the possible fate of the text if the narrative was based in the Indian context. The observation that the author was dealing with a situation specific to Bangladesh, 'which was a theocracy and not India, which is a secular country', gives an impression that the court would have dealt with the book differently if it discussed a similar situation in India. The judgement of the court was therefore largely prescriptive. In the absence of a principled position, as discussed in earlier chapters, it remained open to interpretation in other cases. The stress placed upon the context also seemed to imply that the court did not believe that freedom of expression could be an absolute right. However, once the court held that there was nothing objectionable in the book and rejected the ban order against it, legality of her book was established beyond doubt. The state government also did not pursue the case further by either filing a review petition or pleading at the Supreme Court.

Muslim Groups and Nasreen's Submission

The controversy reignited four years later, in August 2007, during the release of the Telugu translation of another novel, *Shodh*, when Nasreen was physically attacked by a group led by three legislators of the Majlis-e-Ittehadul Muslimeen (MIM). The attackers justified their act by arguing that she could not be allowed in Hyderabad because of her objectionable writings against Islam and the Prophet.[30] The anger was primarily with respect to *Dwikhandito* which was first published in 2003 and had remained controversial since then. Interestingly, Nasreen also wrote a few articles in *Outlook* magazine in January 2007, where she criticized Muslim society for imposing a restrictive way of life on women, especially by insisting on *purdah*, and also on the Quran for enjoining such impositions. The issue caught the attention of Muslim organizations all over India, and Muslim organizations in Kolkata organized a protest against her visa extension. There was a general feeling that her attack on Islam and other religious symbols had consistently demeaned Muslims. Protests culminated into city-wide rioting on 21 November 2007.[31] Responding to the situation, government planned her secret escape to Rajasthan, and from there she was later shifted to Delhi, where she stayed in a safe house for 110 days before leaving for Sweden.[32]

In the context of charged Muslim sentiments, no political party was in a position to explicitly support Nasreen. It was the ruling Left Front government of West Bengal that decided to deport Nasreen, and the Congress-led central government provided the required logistics. The state government defended its action by maintaining that they respected individual freedom and rights, 'but it does not mean a person can hurt the sentiments ... and abuse religion'.[33] Jyoti Basu, the top leader of the ruling CPI(M) commented, 'No Muslim will stand the way she criticized the Quran and the Prophet. That is why we banned her book *Dwikhandito*.'[34] A statement was issued in the Parliament on 28 November 2007 by the Minister of External Affairs, Pranab Mukherjee, who made it clear that though government would continue to provide shelter to Ms. Nasreen, it was expected that the 'guests will refrain from activities and expressions that may hurt the sentiments of our people'.[35]

Consequently, Nasreen asked her publishers to withdraw the controversial parts from *Dwikhandito*. She issued a note that said:

> I have withdrawn some parts of my book *Dwikhandito*. Some said parts of the book were hurting the sentiments of the people. I hope after its withdrawal, there would be no more controversies.... The decision to withdraw these parts from *Dwikhandito* is to prove that I never wanted to hurt the people's sentiments.[36]

This decision was seen as an apology and welcomed by different parties, including non-state actors that were involved in the controversy.[37] Siddiqullah Chaudhary, General Secretary of the Jamiat Ullema-e-Hind, one of the prominent Muslim organizations involved in the controversy, said: 'This is a good step and we are happy that good sense has prevailed. If she had taken this step before, then a lot of conflict could have been avoided.'[38] Even Jyoti Basu issued a statement expressing that she could return to Kolkata.[39] Given the surrounding political circumstances, Nasreen's decision to delete controversial portions from her book was seen by authors, journalists and other members of the civil society, who only a few days earlier had organized a massive rally in Kolkata in her support, as forced censorship and a setback to the struggle for freedom of expression.[40]

The events leading to Nasreen's decision to herself delete controversial sections raises some important issues regarding censorship. The incidents at Hyderabad and Kolkata in 2007, which themselves qualified as crimes, produced a context where the legality of the book, even when pronounced by the court, was of no rescue to the author. The sentiment of hurt made visible in the streets of Kolkata was silenced with an act of self-censorship, where the court had no authority to sit on judgement.

This was not an isolated case in the history of censorship in India. There were other cases as well where the court in its legal submissions found nothing wrong with a publication, but social pressures forced the author to censor his/her writing. Another notable case was the withdrawal of *Agnipariksha* (The Test on Fire) from public circulation by its author, Acharya Tulsi, a Jain monk, in 1970. In September 1970, Acharya Tulsi, a respected and popular Jain preacher, reached Raipur[41] to stay at the Anuvrat Ashram[42] during the holy period of *chaturmasa*.[43] During one of the sessions of a discourse on 16 September, he referred to his work *Agnipariksha*, which was recently published and was based on Jain version of Ramayana. He was particularly referring to some episodes where the character of Sita[44] was questioned. This caught the attention of some orthodox Hindus, who claimed that such references had offended their religious sensibilities and demanded apology from the spiritual leader. Later it was argued that certain couplets were vulgar and profane and were designed to cast aspersions on Sita's character. The confrontation rapidly escalated, and there were demands for banning the book and Acharya's exit from Raipur. The following months saw a massive campaign against Acharya, led by Sanatan Dharma Sabha, a prominent Hindu organization in the area. The Sabha observed an 'anti-acharya week' during which massive protest demonstrations were organized and *hartals* (strike) and *bandhs* (closure) were held. Effigies of the Jain leaders and copies of the book were also burnt in Raipur.[45] Though the state government tried to control the situation, protesters defied the prohibitory orders and violated section 144,[46] which was imposed in the city. There were also reports about some individuals sitting on fast, demanding a ban of the book.[47]

Acharya Tulsi promised an unconditional apology if anyone could show mistakes in what he had said. He also maintained that the book did not contain any vilification as claimed by the protestors, but only an interpretation of the story as present in Jain tradition. He even offered to leave Raipur if that would restore peace. Under pressure from the protestors and in view of the fact that the law-and-order situation was continuously deteriorating, with reports coming in of demonstrations taking violent forms in several instances, state government issued notification for banning of the book and forfeiture of all copies available under section 99(A). The protestors had succeeded in preventing circulation of book in Madhya Pradesh.

The publisher of the book and its sponsor approached the court against forfeiture and ban orders of state government. The full bench of the Madhya Pradesh High Court heard the case and delivered its judgement on 24 December 1970. The court set aside the impugned order, arguing that grounds on which state government had based the order of forfeiture did not exist. The Advocate General representing the case argued that couplets used in the book were objectionable, as they hurt the sentiments of Sanatan Hindus. The applicants on the other side argued that the order contradicted their fundamental right to freedom of expression and freedom of religion as guaranteed under article 19(1)(a) and article 25 of the constitution.

The court maintained that the state had every right to interfere with fundamental rights, as both – freedom of expression and freedom of religion – were conditional to public order.[48] However, after a close reading of the controversial couplets, the court concluded that it could not find anything 'grossly offensive or provocative matter', nor did the court 'visualize any deliberate and malicious intention on the part of the author to outrage the religious feelings of Sanathani Hindus'. Both these basic requirements to charge a work under section 295(A) were found to be absent. Delivering the judgement, Justice Tare noted:

> People may have their own views and it cannot be denied that there have been different versions of Ramayana through the ages which have been prevailing at least for more than 2500 years and it may be that different people might give a version which might serve their purpose. But a propagandist version, which does not come within mischief of the law, can in no case be considered to be objectionable.[49]

The court, therefore, came to the rescue of the book against the order of the state government, and its comments on freedom of expression and freedom of religion were truly significant. The court held that such rights were subject to government's understanding of the situation at a practical level. Hence, though the order of forfeiture was set aside, the right of the state government to act in the way it did was upheld. Yet, even after the forfeiture notification was quashed by the High Court, the author decided to withdraw the book from public circulation, as it had initiated conflict among different groups, which was not his motive in writing the text.[50]

The act of censorship in cases of Nasreen and Acharya Tulsi cannot be captured through its conventional lens of understanding. There is no doubt that government was involved in banning the texts, but it is equally true that courts had come to the rescue of the author/publisher. So, the decision either to remove controversial passages of the book or the text from public circulation does not qualify as a fit case of state censorship. It also does not fall into the category of what modern theories of censorship have called 'new censorship' – a concept derived from the writings of Foucault and Bourdieu (Post 1998: 1). The category of 'new censorship' equates the phenomenon of state censorship with all other forms of censorships like that of the market (Post 1998: 4). Consequently, the analytical rigour of the concept of censorship is diluted as it becomes extremely difficult to locate the agency of the censor in such acts of censorship. But in the above-mentioned cases, the censors can be identified clearly. The decision of the authors remains primary in both cases. So, it can be seen as a case for self-censorship. But it is important to view such self-censorship as a consequence of interrelated events rather than arising from the independent judgement of the authors. In the cases of Nasreen and Acharya Tulsi, the pressures exerted by different non-state actors, including political parties, created an atmosphere where the act of censorship occurred. The dominance of a particular discourse defined what could or could not be allowed in the public sphere. This type of censorship is closely related to the category of 'public self-censorship' discussed in Chapter 4, where the censee decides to censor him/herself, but the main agent enforcing the decision stays outside the agent.

In the cases of Nasreen and Acharya Tulsi, the interplay between state and non-state actors is also clearly visible. Interventions by non-state actors compelled state agencies to respond, and as a result authors/publishers seem to be caught in a web of censorship that tests their potential to fight back. In such cases, courts are the only institutions to which the author/publisher can turn for respite. However, if the authority and views of courts are undermined in strategic ways, as occurred in these two cases due to fear of social forces, in practice the scope of freedom of speech and expression is severely limited. Political willingness to respect the position of court becomes crucial. In the above cases, even though the courts held that the publications did not contain anything objectionable according to law; government did not do enough to protect the publications from harm caused by the actions of non-state actors. In fact, it colluded with the non-state actors at different moments, as visible in the case studies. However, it cannot be claimed that government cannot resist the attack on publications. If government wants, it can restrain attempts by non-state actors to impose their will when the court has pronounced its judgement in a case. A clear example of this was the controversy in the *Sachchi Ramayana* case.[51] The text *Sachchi Ramayana* was banned in Uttar Pradesh in 1969, after which the Supreme Court held the notification order null and void on technical grounds. When the demand for its banning resurfaced in 2007, a demand led by the opposition parties in the Legislative Assembly, the Bahujan Samaj Party (BSP) government under the leadership of Chief Minister Mayawati used the court order as pretext to counter the demands.[52]

In the Indian context, the act of censorship is predominantly devised by means of an instrumental logic for the government. The legal landscape related to censorship gives primary importance to the judgement of the government in using laws. It is expressed both in the provisions of statutory laws as well as court judgements. It is assumed that the state, being the custodian and protector of law and order, would take fair decisions based on the merits of the case. However, as has been evident in the cases discussed in this chapter, the state has emphasized the need to protect the sentiments of different communities from hurt, primarily because there is a feeling that these emotions could result in public-order issues. It is further visible that collective mobilization in the name of hurt sentiments has the capacity to exert pressure on the state to act against a controversial publication. This pressure could either be asserted through public display of hurt sentiments, which includes protest and demonstrations (as in the case of Nasreen), or through the channels of political leadership (as in the case of Rushdie), or through threats of causing disruption to public order, including the use of violence (as in the case of Acharya Tulsi). The ambiguity that was reflected in the state's relationship with communities gives identity-based claims to censorship precedence over the individual's freedom of expression. Political mobilization of religious sentiments, a phenomenon that developed during the anti-colonial movement, continued in the times of electoral politics, after India became independent.[53] In the context of growing constraints developed by the pressure of highly competitive electoral democracy, no political party, either in government or in opposition, takes the risk of not attending to the claims of hurt sentiments as presented by socio-religious groups or other non-state actors (Dhavan 2008: 151; Jaffrelot 2010: 305). As there is no way in which the claim of hurt sentiments can be quantified – either in terms of the actual number of people hurt by the offensive publication, or the nature of the hurt caused – there is a constant fear that such controversy might take larger shape and affect the fortunes of political parties by diminishing their electoral support. Therefore, these parties prefer to act on claims raised by socio-religious groups about religious offence rather than to protect the individual's freedom of speech and expression.

The role of non-state actors discussed in this chapter appears to be essentially against freedom of speech and expression. It seems that non-state actors impose their will by exerting pressure, either on the state agencies or directly upon the author/publisher. But are all forms of intervention by non-state actors unjustified, or against the ethos of a democracy, where freedom of expression is held to be an important value?

The Debates over Censorship in India and the Role of Non-state Actors

A significant concern for scholars of free speech in India is the role of non-state actors (Bhowmik 2003: 3148–3152; Ghosh 2004: 453; Liang 2004: 439; Noorani 1999: 2898). Non-state actors, especially socio-religious groups, resort to both legal as well as extra-legal methods to exert pressure on the government to act against a publication (Ghosh 2016: 60). This includes mobilization and protests against a text,[54] its author[55] or publication house,[56] public burning of a book,[57] or even a physical attack on the author.[58] The legal recourse includes filing writ petitions against the author or the publication house or against the book itself. In fact, legal practitioners and scholars like Dhavan (2008) and Noorani (1995) maintain that in India free speech faces a much bigger threat from social censorship than state censorship. However, there are two significant problems with regard to this understanding about the role of non-state actors in censorship. First, there is a general tendency among scholars to relate the phenomenon of vocal and explicit forms of intervention by non-state actors (which includes the use of violent means) quite tightly with the period of growth of Hindu nationalism, especially in the late 20th century (Bose 2006; Ghosh 2004; Kapur 1996). Second, these scholars consider any form of intervention by non-state actors, either legal or extra-legal, as unwarranted. Unfortunately, these estimations are based on overly broad generalizations. For example, even if we were to agree with the claim about the connection between explicit forms of intervention exhibited by non-state actors and the rise of Hindu nationalism in the late 20th century, it does not explain convincingly some crucial aspects attached to social censorship: (1) considering that Hindu nationalism is not a new phenomenon in India, it fails to explain why social censorship took the shape it did, in the later part of 20th century; and (2) it also fails to explain why it did not remain a Hindu nationalist agenda, as we see similar kind of mobilization and protests in response to Taslima Nasreen in West Bengal and in the Akali's response[59] to the interpretations of Adi Granth in Punjab. As we have seen earlier, in Chapters 1 and 2, intervention by non-state actors on claims of religious offense is not at all a new phenomenon. Group mobilization on the subject of hurt sentiments was witnessed even before independence, particularly in the late 19th and early 20th centuries, and has since then remained a social reality in India. In fact, scholars like Gilmartin (1991) have shown how mobilizations of these kinds formed an alternative 'public' during colonial rule. Analysis of censorship after Independence also gives a similar picture, where claims of hurt sentiments were not only used to exert pressure on government to censor controversial texts but were also considered as a legitimate and democratic form of engaging with the government.[60] Nor is it the case that these mobilizations and protests were always non-violent in nature. Examining the controversy over the book *Living Biographies of Religious Leaders* (as shown in Chapter 2) and *Agnipariksha* (as discussed earlier in this chapter) reveals that explicit or even violent forms of intervention by non-state groups are not a late 20th century phenomenon, and they also cannot be directly linked to the growth of Hindu nationalism, as claimed by most scholars.[61]

The second issue is whether all forms of intervention by non-state actors is symptomatic of depleting space for democratic values. One mistake that scholars who hold this view arguably commit is to assume the primacy of freedom of speech and expression, over all other rights.[62] Further, these studies use a teleological approach to judge the intentions of non-state actors based on the consequences of such interventions, that is, the use of litigation or protest by any non-state actor as means to impose their viewpoint. It is argued that even if non-state actors take the legal route, it leads to harassment of the author/publisher and, therefore, restricts the exercise of freedom of speech and expression.[63] Some of these assumptions and conclusions need reassessment. First, as courts have held in their various judgements, freedom of speech and expression does not enjoy any primacy over other rights, including the right to religion, and therefore courts have maintained that it is the duty of state in a multicultural and secular society, like India, to balance conflicting claims based on such rights.[64] Second, on the subject of intervention by non-state actors, the practice of demonstrating or protesting against a publication claimed to be offensive or demanding the state act against such publications needs to be differentiated from other modes of expressing dissent, like those involving any form of violence, which is legally prohibited in any democratic set-up. Both these roles should be viewed differently, even if both have a tendency to restrict the scope of freedom of speech and expression, as the two modes of intervention by non-state actors exhibit a marked difference in both form and content.

There are primarily two ways in which non-state actors intervene through the legal structure. The first is by registering formal complaints in the local police station against contentious publications or mobilizing and demonstrating against the publication to express their hurt sentiments, in order to exert pressure on the state officials to act. The second mode of engagement is by filing petitions against such publications or taking part in the judicial process by filing affidavits in the court supporting the government's decision to seize or forfeit contentious publications. Although in each of these forms of participation, non-state actors play a dominant role, the ultimate decision of censorship rests with the courts. Note that even if state authorities register a formal complaint and decide to act against the publication in question, the author/publisher or any other affected party can under section 96 of CrPC approach the court against such action, and the judiciary can then decide the legality and validity of such action by state authorities. The primary responsibility to act in such cases is that of state authorities, and they are expected (as reflected in various observations of the courts) to act rationally, judging the situation based on the principles of proportionality.[65] However, even if state authorities falter in their decision-making, there is the judiciary to take the final call on such acts of censorship. Therefore, harassment caused to an author/publisher in the process is to be attributed to laws and legal process, as discussed in this chapter, rather than intervention by the aggrieved groups.

Forms of intervention that include using legal mechanisms or even use of protests and demonstration to attract the attention of the government authorities against contentious publications are considered – both by the state as well as the judiciary – as democratic and legitimate rights of citizens. However, there is an important caveat attached to this formal recognition of the democratic rights: such protests and demonstrations should not be violent in any form. The position of the state is reflected in the reaction of Prime Minister Nehru and other leaders during the controversy of the *Living Biographies of Religious Leaders*.[66] Though most leaders deplored the use of violence in the protests that followed the controversy, they were not critical of the subject of the protest itself. Not only Nehru, but even K. M. Munshi,[67] against whom most of the protests were directed, recognized that the claim of religious offence by the protesting Muslims was of a genuine concern. Therefore, the book was set aside as soon as the demands were raised without any form of engagement with the subject-matter under contention. Nehru, in his fortnightly letter to the Chief Ministers wrote:

> I can understand people objecting to some passages in that book and drawing attention to them. But, there was something much deeper, and it was obvious that mischief was afoot and had been deliberately organized. The offending passages were broadcast in cyclostyled papers by the very persons who objected to them.[68]

The real concern of the leaders was about the continuation of the protests, even after the demand for removal of the book was accepted. A clear demarcation was being proposed between claiming democratic rights, like the right to protest and demonstrate, and the illegal use of violence or incitement to violence for the purpose.

The position of the judiciary on the subject of the use of a legal route by non-state actors to express their grievances can be gathered from courts' interpretation of statutory laws, particularly section 95 of the CrPC, which deals with the power of the government officials to proscribe or forfeit controversial publications.[69] Courts have insisted that government officials should mention in the notification (issued for seizure or forfeiture of such publication) the details about the groups or communities offended, the reason for them to feel offended and how the officials reached a rational conclusion that forfeiture of the publication was necessary. The nature of the complaint registered or protests and demonstrations organized by the socio-religious groups in order to attract the attention of state officials towards their grievances are legally recognized by courts as valid grounds on which officials could justify their decision to act against the controversial publication. It can therefore be argued that these forms of intervention are held by courts as an important indicator for officials to form a conclusive opinion about whether action is required in a particular case or not.

On the other hand, the use of violence and threats to cause disturbance to public tranquillity as a means to impose censorship by non-state actors does severely limit the scope of freedom of speech and expression. As evidence suggests, these threats or use of violence have regularly forced authors and publishers to succumb to demands of non-state actors, even after courts held that the publication did not contain anything that could be legally considered offensive.[70] The use of both these means is illegal[71] and against the values of democracy. Courts have also been vigilant about non-state actors' use of threats and violence to impose censorship. They have held that the threat of disruption of public order by such groups is a violation of law and should be strictly dealt with by law-enforcing agencies.[72] Further, courts have also taken serious note of the fact that state authorities relent to the demands of non-state actors, and act erroneously at times under pressure from these groups, as in the case of threats to public order. In the *S. Rangrajan* case,[73] the Supreme Court held that the state could not plead its inability to contain violent protestors. It is the duty of the state, the court maintained, to protect freedom of expression from attack from such groups. This position was reiterated in the court's judgement in *M/S Prakash Jha Productions* case.[74] Recently, in the *S. Tamilselvan* case, related to Perumal Murugan's book,[75] the Tamil Nadu High Court raised serious objections on the way state authorities, in an attempt to maintain peace, relented to the pressure exerted by protesting groups. Though it maintained that it was the duty of state authorities to maintain law and order in their area, a 'threat to peace' could not be used as a reason for compromising anyone's freedom of speech and expression. It also noted that 'merely because a group of people feel agitated ... it cannot give them a license to vent their views in a hostile manner, and the state cannot plead its inability to handle the problem of a hostile audience'. The court has also specified a preferred procedure to be followed by state authorities while dealing with any controversial publication, if the claims about it being offensive are raised by socio-religious groups. Three points of the preferred guidelines are indicative of the approach of court: (1) 'There is bound to be a presumption in favour of free speech and expression as envisaged under article 19(1)(a) of the Constitution of India unless a court of law finds it otherwise falling within the domain of a reasonable restriction under article 19(2) of the constitution of India. This presumption must be kept in mind if there are complaints against publications, art, drama, film, song, poem, cartoons or any other creative expressions'; (2)'the state's responsibility to maintain law and order would not permit any compulsion on the artistes concerned to withdraw from his/her stand, and non-state players cannot be allowed to determine what is permissible and what is not'; and (3) 'The state has to ensure proper police protection when such artistes come under attack from a section'. The court has clearly stated that non-state actors cannot define the limits of a constitutional right, such as the right to speech and expression, and that courts are the sole authorities to decide what constitutes 'reasonable restrictions' as defined by the constitution. In the cases discussed above, it is clear that courts have exhibited a zero-tolerance approach towards the use of violence or a threat to public-order disruptions by these groups. They have further established that though it is the duty of state to maintain public order, freedom of expression of any artist or author cannot be compromised in the name of a threat to public order and that the state should deal strongly with groups that threaten disruption to public peace. It is evident from the above discussions that the two forms of intervention by non-state actors – legal and extra-legal – are essentially different in their form and content. It also has a different impact on the legal space defined for the freedom of speech and expression. In the previous form of intervention, courts are able to intervene and determine the reasonability of the action by state authorities; whereas the later form of intervention is not only illegal, the non-state actors take upon themselves to determine the permissibility of an expression.

This distinction also helps to respond to the claims of the scholars on censorship, who believe that the presence of statutory laws governing freedom of expression allows non-state actors to impose their will, by harassing the author/publisher, and on this basis, they demand that all such laws be repealed (Ghosh 2004; Liang 2004).[76] Such claims are largely based on an assumption about the 'slippery slope' tendency of laws. On the one hand, it assumes that all claims of religious offence are essentially targeted against the author/publisher and hence against the democratic values of freedom of speech and expression, and on the other hand, there is the assumption that if statutory laws are removed, it will end the arbitrariness attached to censorship due to the intervention of socio-religious groups. However, both these assumptions seem to be faulty. The assumption that all the claims of religious offence are ploys to impose the viewpoint of the non-state actors seems to overlook or ignore that some of these claims may actually be genuine. The only institution that can judge these aspects is the judiciary, and scrapping laws will only limit the powers of the courts to intervene. As Saba Mahmood (2009) and Tariq Modood (2005) have shown, some religious beliefs and practices define the identity of the religious communities, and if these beliefs or symbols are denigrated, they will feel offended. These feelings can take the form of demonstrations and protests, and in the absence of legal recourse, there are increased possibilities that these forms of expression of grievances turn aggressive.[77] Further, removal of statutory laws would also increase the arbitrary role of state officials. These officials could use other available laws to their discretion and could proscribe publications or arrest authors/publishers at will, in the name of preventing issues related to public order. After all, repealing laws governing freedom of expression does not disarm the officials of powers to act in such situations. So, unlike the assumptions of the scholars discussed above, repealing statutory laws may prove counter-productive and may, in fact, add to the threats to freedom of speech and expression and its free exercise.

A significant exception, however, are laws like the Customs Act, which was used by the government to ban import of publications like *Satanic Verses*, as the nature of these laws puts such bans beyond the purview of the judiciary. In cases like that of *Satanic Verses*, if non-state actors are able to exert pressure on government, they can get a publication banned, and even the judiciary cannot come to rescue these publications. Though this exception is significant and requires a rethink on the part of lawmakers, repealing all statutory laws is not the solution to intervention by non-state actors. The right approach would be to argue for more vigilant government machinery and a system of judiciary that is able to restrain mala fide intentions of non-state actors, and at same time take care of genuine grievances.

Conclusion

The examples of *The Satanic Verses*, *Dwikhandito* and *Agnipariksha* indicate that role of courts is made ineffective in the politics of censorship, where on the one hand, use of laws like the Customs Act places government's decision outside the purview of the court's interference, and on the other hand, the general atmosphere of violence and threat renders even positive interference by courts meaningless. Furthermore, provisions restricting free speech in Indian context (like section 295[A] and 153[A[) are classified as cognizable offences. This means that authorities can arrest suspects without judicial sanction. At the same time, there have been cases where government takes the role of mediator between conflicting claims (those of religious offence and freedom of expression) and reaches for an out-of-court solution while the case is still sub-judice.[78] Though government is well within its power to look for amicable solutions, it indicates the limits of court's intervention in such matters. The Tamil Nadu government's position during the controversy related to the movie *Viswaroopam*[79] is one such example. The problem is that in an attempt to find solutions, government often manages different claims in such a way that freedom of expression is compromised. The settlement, though claimed to be 'amicable', opens doors for more possibilities to assert the claim of hurt religious or communitarian sensibilities leading to a virtual curb on authors'/artists' freedoms. So, considering these cases, can we conclude that the role of the courts is of no use, and does not contribute at all in our understanding of freedom of expression in India? There are two ways to look at this issue. One approach is provided by Gautam Bhatia (2016), where he argues that a study of the role of court remains important as laws are used or misused because the laws exist, and despite several constitutional challenges, courts have not ruled against these laws. So, we need to understand why these laws are considered important by the courts. Secondly, Bhatia is optimistic about a situation when law and practice 'is not as cavernous' as in present times. So, it is essential for those future situations that a critical understanding of the application of these laws is understood. Another way to look at the subject is that though courts have not controlled the direction of free speech debate in India, they have always remained an important stakeholder, and their observations have guided the debates outside. Lack of consistency and procedural complexities, as discussed in the last chapter, remain a problem, but the authority of court has in many cases protected the fundamental right of expression from attack of both state and non-state actors. It is therefore an important institution, which still enjoys the confidence of citizens as the protector of their fundamental rights. This in itself is a reason good enough to not dismiss the role played by courts in the debates around censorship and free speech.

On the subject of intervention by non-state actors in the process of censorship, the two forms of interventions – one that follows the legal route and the other that is extra-legal, and includes use of threat and violence – need to be viewed differently. Both of these interventions are different in form and content. To consider both as unwarranted in a democracy would be to close all doors for even genuine expression of grievances. This distinction helps us to be more sensitive regarding the concerns of religious communities, about offensive publications, and at the same time, ensure that proper judicial scrutiny takes place before any form of censorship is enforced. It would further help in reducing arbitrariness in the process of censorship, a complaint that scholars on censorship in India consistently make, particularly with regard to the involvement of non-state actors.

Notes

1 Section 11 of the Customs Act allows for prohibition of import of any material, including publications, for maintenance of public order, standards of decency and morality and also for any other purpose conducive to the interest of public order.

2 Books whose import to India was banned under the law included *Pakistan-Pasmazarwa Pashmanza* (1950); *Cease Fire* (1950); *What Has Religion Done for Mankind* (1954); *Captive Kashmir* (1958); *The Heart of India* (1959); *Nine Hours to Rama* (1962), among others. Some of these were considered demeaning to the image of India, and others were material for political propaganda. The list of books to be banned from import owing to their commentary on religion included the likes of *Marka-e-Somnath* by Maulana Muhammad Sadiq Husain and Sadiq Siddiqui (1952), *Ayesha* by Kurt Frischler (1963) and *Early Islam* by Desmond Stewart (1975), among others.

3 Aubrey Menen's *Rama Retold* was one of the earliest books to be banned in independent India in 1955 on this ground. Menen's was a satirical work and dealt with the characters of Ramayana in a very different way than as in the popular discourse.

4 Singh was a well-known literary figure in India. The publishers of *The Satanic Verses*, Penguin, approached him for comments on the book six months before its formal release.

5 The interview with Madhu Jain was published as 'My Theme Is Fanaticism', *India Today*, 15 September 1988; Interview with Sharbani Basu was published as 'Of Satan, Archangels and Prophets', *Sunday*, 18–24 September 1988.

6 Khurshid Alam Khan was a minister in the Rajiv Gandhi government and a prominent Muslim leader of the Indian National Congress.

7 'The Day After', *Sunday*, 6–12 November 1988.

8 'Book Banning, Philistinism and Freedom of Expression', *Frontline*, 15 October 1988. Interestingly, *Satanic Verses* was released on 26 September 1988 in the UK, and advance copies had reached India soon afterwards. However, the government's notification only prevented the importation of copies of the book to India and did not say anything about the copies that had already reached Indian territories. So, even today, possession or reading of the novel in India is not legally banned.

9 Soli J. Sorabjee, 'Ban on Rushdie's Book: A Pernicious Precedent', *The Indian Express*, 14 October 1988.

10 Official statement as presented in 'Book Banning', *Frontline*, 15 October 1988.

11 This argument was also forwarded by Buta Singh, the Minister of Home Affairs. While answering one of the queries on the subject in Rajya Sabha, he justified the ban by arguing that 'the contents of the title were likely to be detrimental to the maintenance of public order'. Though legislator B. Satyanarayan Reddy had also asked about the objectionable material found in the book, the Minister chose to evade the question. See *Rajya Sabha Debates*, 3 November 1988, pp. 41–42.

12 Rushdie wrote an open letter to Rajiv Gandhi in this regard, which appeared in several news dailies. See Appignanesi & Maitland (1989: 42–45). He believed that the step of the government was senseless as his work was about a secular person's view on the ideas of religion and revelation. See '"A Senseless Step," says Rushdie', *The Times of India*, 8 October 1988.

13 Ayodhya is the place in Uttar Pradesh where it is claimed that Rama the Hindu deity was born. At the site of his birth, it was claimed that Babar, the Moghul king, had forcefully constructed a mosque after destroying an age-old temple. The Union government of Rajiv Gandhi had decided to open the doors of the deserted part of the temple so that prayers could be offered by Hindus. It created an atmosphere of tension that culminated in the destruction of the Babri Mosque by Hindu groups in 1992.
14 It was reported in several foreign newspaper of the time. For example, *The Independent*, under the title 'Rushdie Novel Banned in India' on 6 October 1988 reported: 'The Indian government, bowing to pressure from Muslim groups, yesterday banned Salman Rushdie's latest book.' A letter signed by 21 prominent arbiters led by Dom Moraes and Adil Jussawala was sent to the Prime Minister of India, Rajiv Gandhi, on 20 October 1988.
15 The details of the case and the reactions world over have been extensively discussed in Appignanesi and Maitland (1989) and Pipes (1998).
16 Shahbuddin said, 'If to seek redress of a religious grievance from the government which is the custodian of the dignity of all our people is fundamentalism in your lexicon, so be it.' See 'You Did This with Satanic Forethought, Mr. Rushdie', *The Times of India*, 13 October 1988. He applauded the responsiveness of the government and claimed that it signified that the government was not 'insensitive to the religious sentiments of the people'. See 'Ban Welcomed', *The Times of India*, 9 October 1988.
17 Syed Sahabuddin, 'No, Mr. Rushdie, You Acted with Satanic Forethought', *Muslim India*, November 1988.
18 As quoted in '"A Senseless Step", says Rushdie', *The Times of India*, 8 October 1988.
19 'A Riot Has Been Averted: Khuswant Singh', *The Times of India*, 30 October 1988. Reports suggested that such fears were not completely unfounded. After Khomeini's fatwa riots broke out in parts of western India, and 12 people were reported dead in police firings in Mumbai. Similar riots were also reported from Kashmir. It was indicative of the possible situation if the book was not proscribed. See 'Freedom of Information and Expression in India', *Article 19*, October 1990, republished in the *PUCL Bulletin of April 1991*. Also see 'Uneasy Calm in Riot Hit Areas', *The Times of India*, 26 February 1989.
20 As quoted in Kumar (1997: 202). Similarly, Shahbuddin maintained that indecent remarks about 'the Prophet's wife violated the Indian Penal Code, which prohibited any writing that hurt the religious sentiments of the people and were in bad taste'. Here Khurshid and Shahbuddin were referring to the laws within IPC like sections 295(A), and 153(A). 'Ban Welcomed', *The Times of India*, 9 October 1988.
21 'Ban Welcomed', *The Times of India*, 9 October 1988.
22 'You Did This with Satanic Forethought, Mr. Rushdie', *The Times of India*, 13 October 1988.
23 Nasreen had used terms like 'ruthless murderer', 'rapist' and 'scoundrel' for the Prophet and criticized Islam for its treatment of women as slaves.
24 'Bengal Bans Taslima's Book', *Statesman*, 29 November 2003.
25 The position was reiterated in the party organ of CPI(M), *People's Democracy*, on 7 November 2003 (Vol. XXVII, No. 49). It said: "The Bengal left front government has decided to ban Bangladeshi author Taslima Nasreen's latest book, Dwikhandito because it was feared that the book would incite communal violence."
26 See Ghosh (2004: 447–454).
27 As quoted in an interview published in *Frontline* on 31 January 2004.
28 See Ansari (2008: 15–19).

29 *Sujato Bhadra*, 39 A.I.R. 239. Unless mentioned, all the references related to the case remain the same.

30 However, some commentators believed that it was a planned strategy of MIM for publicity. It was argued that MIM was losing its Muslim base in Hyderabad because of the left's increasing popularity in the Muslim pockets of the city. Hence its legislators felt the need to rekindle its image as the authentic protector of Muslim rights. Saba Naqvi, 'No Orchids for Miss Nasreen', *Outlook*, 27 August 2007.

31 The immediate reasons for the protest and attacks were different. In this background appeared an unsigned article in the CPI(M)-backed journal *Pathasanket* which endorsed Nasreen's views on Islam and the Quran. The article argued that Nasreen's hitting out at fundamentalists from a rational and scientific point of view could not be treated as an offence. It further compared her with Galileo and even made a vitriolic attack on the Prophet over his marital life. The article shocked the Muslim community and was construed as an attack on Islam. The Muslim groups, especially the AIMF, led by Idris Ali, took strong exception to it. AIMF demanded a ban on the magazine and seizure of all copies in the market. The Muslim organizations also demanded that Nasreen's visa be revoked and that she should be sent out from India as she had time and again created communal tensions here. The state government promptly banned the autumn issue of the magazine, but the decision over her visa did not fall under its jurisdiction. However, by this time, violence had erupted again in Nandigram, where, it was alleged, the CPI(M) cadres had opened fire killing around 30 villagers. Prominent anti-left Muslim organizations, including AIMF, Jamiat Ullema-e-Hind and Furfura Sharif Muzadeedia Ananth Foundation, came together to protest against violence in Nandigram and unethical refuge to Taslima Nasreen in order to expose the government on 21 November 2007. The protests turned violent and soon took the shape of riots. The army was called in to manage the public-order situation. See 'Left Magazine's Autumn Number Banned', *The Times of India*, 9 November 2007.

32 Though there were obvious links between attacks in Hyderabad and her deportation from Kolkata owing to the similarity of the issues raised and the nature of the opposition, the immediate reasons that forced government to act were different. It was a period of intense political instability in West Bengal, owing to violence at Nandigram and Singur, where land acquisition by government for industrial expansion was being opposed by villagers. The government took a strong stand, and opposition witnessed extremes of police brutality. Nandigram was a Muslim majority area, and it took no time for violence to develop a communal logic. Government was further cornered after the controversy generated by the case of Rizwanur Rehman, who was allegedly murdered for marrying a Hindu girl belonging to a reputed trading family. His death saw a heavy backlash from Muslims in Kolkata, and a difficult law-and-order situation developed in late September. Such incidents had alienated the Muslims, and the West Bengal government was already on the defensive. See 'Exiled to the Vote Bank', *India Today*, 30 November 2007.

33 Minister Abdus Suttar, as quoted in *The Times of India*, 29 December 2007.

34 'Basu: Taslima, Welcome to Kolkata', *The Times of India*, 21 December 2007.

35 This statement was made in both houses of Parliament.

36 'Taslima Removes Controversial Lines from Book', *The Hindustan Times*, 30 November 2007.

37 This included Muslim organizations such as AIMF, Jamiat Ullema-e-Hind and Furfura Sharif Muzadeedia Ananth Foundation and political parties like AIMIM, the Congress Party and CPI(M).

38 'Taslima Withdraws Controversial Lines from *Dwikhandito*', *The Financial Express*, 1 December 2007.
39 "Taslima Can Return to Kolkata, says Basu," *Hindu*, 26 December 2007.
40 "Taslima's Surrender on 'Dwikhandito' a Great Setback: Intellectuals," *DNA*, 9 December 2007.
41 Raipur formed a part of the state of Madhya Pradesh, but after state reorganization in the year 2000, it became the capital of the newly formed state of Chhattisgarh.
42 Started by Acharya Tulsi under the *Anuvrat* movement.
43 *Chaturmasa* is a holy period of four months in the Jain tradition dedicated to simple living.
44 The wife of Rama according to revered Hindu mythology Ramayana.
45 'Anuvrat Leader to Quit RaIpur after Furor over Book', *The Times of India*, 29 September 1970.
46 A section under the IPC which when evoked makes assemblies and gatherings unlawful.
47 'Anuvrat Leader to Quit Rampur after Furor over Book', *The Times of India*, 29 September 1970.
48 Justice Singh, in *Ramlal Puri*, AIR 1971 MP 252.
49 Justice Tare, in *Ramlal Puri*, AIR 1971 MP 252.
50 'Order on Muni's Book Set Aside', *The Times of India*, 25 December 1970. The author later claimed that as a monk his primary commitment was to the ideals of non-violence and therefore he withdrew the book from circulation even after the Madhya Pradesh court had ruled in his favor. For reference, see the book co-authored by Anuvrat Anushasta Tulsi and Acharya Mahaprajna, titled *Non-violence and World Peace* (Ladnun: Jain Visva Bharti), available at http://www.jainworld.com/book/nvoilence/primarylessons.asp (last accessed on 20 July 2022).
51 The controversy attached to this text and the case has been discussed in detail in Chapter 4.
52 The demand was initiated by the BJP and supported by Mulayam Singh, the leader of the opposition Samajwadi Party on the floor of the Legislative Assembly. See 'Periyar Ramayana Arouse Flak', *Deccan Herald*, 6 November 2007. The ruling BSP was accused of supporting the book and allowing its sale in the state. The state's Parliamentary Affairs minister Lalji Verma assured that the government was not aware that the book was on sale in UP. The accusations of the opposition did not affect the government, which was, as it claimed, ignorant of the book and had nothing to do with it. He also cited that the Supreme Court had in the past found nothing objectionable with the book and therefore it would not be possible technically for the government to ban it. See, 'UP Oppn. Wants Periyar's Ramayan Banned, but Not a Copy to Buy in State', *The Indian Express*, 8 November 2007.
53 This phenomenon, its growth during anti-colonial movement and its role during electoral politics have all been discussed in Chapter 2.
54 There were protests against Ambedkar's *Riddles in Hinduism* in 1989, which were led by the Shiv Sena and its legislators. See, 'Parts of Riddles to Be Dropped', *The Times of India*, 17 November 1987.
55 In 2012, when Rushdie was to appear at the Jaipur Literature Festival, the Muslim organizations protested against his appearance on the pretext that he should apologize for his book *Satanic Verses*. 'Oppose Rushdie's Arrival', *Radiance Newsweekly* XLIX, no. 42, 21 January 2012. Most prominent Muslim organizations in India like Jamaat-i-Islami Hind, All India Imam Council, All India Milli Council, and Muslim Forum jointly addressed a press conference in Jaipur reiterating the demand. See 'Muslim Groups Oppose Rushdie's Visit to Jaipur Fest', *The Hindu*, 14 January 2012.

56 The pressure exerted on Oxford University Press to remove Ramanujan's essay *Three Hundred Ramayana*. See 'When a Department Let the University Down', *The Hindu*, 3 November 2011.
57 See 'BJP Workers Burnt Copies of Sachchi Ramayana', 30 October 2007, available at http://news.webindia123.com/news/articles/India/20071030/808600.html (last accessed on 18 July 2018).
58 The attack on Taslima Nasreen is a clear example of this.
59 The Shiromani Gurudwara Prabhandak Committee (SGPC) not only became furious at alternative interpretations of Guru Granth Sahib, but also announced punishment for the authors. See, 'SGPC Takes Exception to Book on Scriptures', *The Times of India*, 17 December 1992. Also see Singh (1996).
60 As discussed in Chapter 3 in the case of the book *Living Biographies of Religious Leaders*.
61 It is to be noted that the controversy over *Living Biographies of Religious Leaders* occurred in 1956, and violent protests were led by members of Muslim community. Similarly, the controversy over *Agniparikshа* occurred in 1970 and saw clashes between members of Hindu and Jain communities, who had different views about the book. See, 'Raipur under 24 Hour Curfew', *The Times of India*, 8 November 1970.
62 This aspect is clearly evident in the writings of Bose (2006), Ghosh (2004, 2016) and Liang (2004, 2016).
63 See for example, the writings of Kapur (1996), Rajeev Dhavan (2008) and Noorani (1995, 1999, 2008).
64 This aspect has been extensively discussed in Chapter 4.
65 The court used the absence of 'ground of opinion' in the notification as the reason to dismiss the order for forfeiture in cases like *Harnam Das*, A.I.R 1662 and *Lalai Singh Yadav*, 1977 AIR 202 only because it was held that there was no way in which the court could assess whether the official had reached a conclusion to act against publication based on rational grounds.
66 The details of this case have been discussed earlier, in Chapter 3.
67 Other than being the Governor of the state of Uttar Pradesh, where the controversy took shape, K. M. Munshi was also one of the editors of Bharatiya Vidya Bhawan, the publishers of the book.
68 See Nehru (1990: 436).
69 This aspect of the law has been discussed in greater details in Chapter 4.
70 This aspect has been discussed earlier in the present chapter.
71 Chapter VIII of the IPC deals with *Offences against Public Tranquility*, and Chapter XII of the IPC deals with the subject of *Criminal Intimidation, Insult and Annoyance*.
72 The court has observed this in various judgements like *S. Rangrajan v. P. Jagjivan Ram*, 1989 2 SCC 574; *M/S Prakash Jha Productions v. Union of India*, Writ Petition (Civil) No. 345 of 2011.
73 *S. Rangrajan*, 2 SCC 574.
74 *M/S Prakash Jha Productions*, Writ Petition (Civil) No. 345 of 2011.
75 This case and its different aspects have been discussed in detail in Chapter 1. For judgement see *S. Tamilselvan*, W.P. No. 1215 of 2015.
76 This kind of argument has been raised variously by scholars like Liang (2004) and Ghosh (2004).
77 In the Indian context, the form that such grievances could take is reflected in violence that followed the publication of *The Satanic Verses*, even after the book was banned in India.
78 Examples of this kind can be found in the case of the Maharashtra government's intervention in the *Riddles in Hinduism* case. The controversy was about the government's decision to publish this essay written by Ambedkar, which was

essentially targeting the Hindu gods Ram and Krishna. Details of the controversy are discussed in Purandare (2002: 306–314).

79 *Viswaroopam* was a 2013 film produced and directed by popular actor Kamal Hasan. The movie had acquired required certificates from authorities. But before release it was caught in a controversy where Muslim groups argued that the representation of Muslims in the film had hurt Muslim sentiments. The actor took the issue to the court, but before the court could give its final verdict, the Chief Minister of the State intervened and helped the two parties reach an amicable solution, which included deletion of some scenes and muting some portions. The film later was released. See 'Muslim Organizations Demand Ban on *Viswaroopam*', *The Indian Express* (Online Ed.), 23 January 2013, http://www.indianexpress.com/news/muslim-organisations-demand-ban-on-vishwaroopam/1063259/ (last accessed on 30 July 2018); 'Amicably Settle *Vishwaroopam* Row', *The New Indian Express* (Online Ed.), 29 January 2013, http://newindianexpress.com/states/tamilnadu/article1440303.ece (last accessed on 30 July 2018).

CONCLUSION

In the last few decades, two incidents – publication of Salman Rushdie's *The Satanic Verses* (1989) and publication of cartoons of Prophet Muhammad by Denmark based Jyllands-Posten (2005) – became the subjects of intense debate regarding freedom of expression and the issue of religious offence. These publications were repeatedly criticized for offending the religious sensibilities of Muslims and creating debate as to whether legal sanctions were justified in cases related to religiously offensive speech acts. These cases were very similar in most respects, and in fact critical discussions that followed the cartoon controversy were framed very much like those during the Rushdie affair, even drawing explicit parallels with and analogies from the latter. However, here I primarily deal with debates surrounding legal aspects attached with such controversies. Some important questions that became the subject of intense deliberation among academicians and scholars were: Can legal sanctions be invoked in the name of protecting religious sentiments in multicultural and multi-religious societies? Is the state justified in restricting freedom of speech and expression in order to prevent religious offence or to diffuse the threat to law-and-order situations that could follow such incidents? Is there any provision for a 'right not to be offended' within the liberal discourse? The opinions of scholars of law, politics and anthropology were deeply divided. Both incidents witnessed protests from members of the Muslim community all over world. It was claimed that the publications desecrated their deeply cherished religious values (Emon 2007: 303–321), offended their religious feelings (Hoarsher 2008: 1225–1253), and discriminated against Muslims, which was unacceptable (Laegaard 2007: 481–498; Modood 2006). Some commentators argued that Rushdie and Jyllands-Posten had only exercised their freedom of expression, and the call for restriction was unwarranted, no matter how much they may have disturbed or offended a particular community. Posing religion as a matter of public interest, commentators held that in a democracy, every aspect of religion should be open to scrutiny in all possible forms (Dworkin 2006; Post 2007). It was also argued that incidents like the 'Rushdie affair' tested the toleration of the community that claimed religious offence, and therefore was a good thing (Waldron 1993: 134–142). Even if it was agreed

DOI: 10.4324/9781003369257-7

that hurting religious sensibilities, as claimed in the two cases, was morally wrong and that the argument about respecting other's religious sensibilities had strong moral appeal, it could not justify the use of law in these cases.[1] Legal philosopher Ronald Dworkin opined that legal sanctions were also not justified because the claims about religious offence were sentimental and subjective and, hence, not eligible for legal protection. He further asserted that 'in a democracy no one, however powerful or important, can have a right not to be insulted or offended' (Dworkin 2006: 53). On the question about legal sanctions against freedom of speech and expression, in cases such as that of Rushdie and Jyllands-Posten, where members of one religious group were demanding such sanctions in the name of religious offence, it was argued that any such protection could lead to a slippery slope. Preventing religious groups from hurt in such cases, as free speech scholar Eric Barendt (2011) feared, could become a thin disguise for protecting religious beliefs and truths, which had been resisted during the debates against blasphemy laws.

Some scholars raised reservations about the way the debate was being posed as a binary between objection to blasphemy and free speech, and it was argued that in the name of liberal discourse, commentators often ignored and rendered unintelligible the kind of injury involved in religiously offensive speech, particularly that which vilified the sacred (Asad 2009; Mahmood 2009). Questioning those who opined that religious offence was subjective and sentimental in nature, Saba Mahmood (2009) and Talal Asad (2009) argued that religion was something that was inherited and naturalized, which got manifested in one's practices and lived social realities. Without understanding this aspect of religion, they argued, it was not possible to debate the harm caused by religious offence. However, on the question whether legal protection to religious feelings was justified, both Asad and Mahmood differed. Asad held that if 'modern secular societies do have legal constraints on communication' such as copyrights, patents and others, questions should not be raised if restrictions on free speech are advocated to prevent religious offence, even if they lead to blasphemy laws (2011: 283). Mahmood, on the other hand, believed that laws do not have capacity to provide remedy for harm suffered due to religious offense, and so she suggested that legal recourse cannot be a valid or appropriate demand on the part of the communities who protest against such offenses (2009: 82–83). A similar view was articulated by Tariq Modood (2005), who viewed it as a problem of multiculturalism, and argued that religious beliefs form the self-definition of a group, and incidents such as the Rushdie affair and cartoon controversy have a deep impact in the group's participation in society. He opined that legal restrictions might not be the most appropriate solution, and societies need to develop alternate mechanisms to ensure that oppression caused due to such incidents is avoided, but he insisted that freedom of expression could be curtailed to protect vulnerable groups and individuals from attack on their deeply held beliefs (Modood 2005: 121).

Though these scholars believed that debate around free speech should be sensitive to the sentimentalities of communities that claimed religious offence, they had different views on whether legal sanctions could really help in the situation.

An alternative view was represented by political philosophers Charles Taylor (1989) and Bhikhu Parekh (2012), who maintained that the question of restricting free speech would depend on the context in which it is being dealt. They are of a view that free speech should be balanced with other rights and values that are cherished in a society. However, 'there is no "true" way of reconciling them; it all depends', Parekh says, 'on the history, traditions, political circumstances, and so on of a society' (2000: 320). This view advocates a context-sensitive approach to the understanding of religious offence. The diversity of legal provisions and restrictions regarding freedom of speech and expression in different countries is representative of the point that Parekh and Taylor stress.

Take, for example, the legality involved in the above-mentioned cases in countries which became centres of the controversy: Britain in the case of Rushdie affair and Denmark in the case of the cartoon controversy.[2] *The Satanic Verses* was prohibited on legal grounds in numerous Muslim countries, including Saudi Arabia, Somalia, Bangladesh, Sudan, Malaysia, among others. In Britain a case was filed by Abdal Hussain Choudhury, on behalf of the British Muslim Action Front,[3] to the Chief Metropolitan Stipendiary Magistrate to issue a summons against Rushdie and his publishers for alleged blasphemous libel. When the appeal was rejected, he appealed to the Queen's Bench Division of the High Court. The High Court upheld the decision of the Metropolitan Magistrate and commented that even if the publication was religiously offensive to the sensibilities of Muslims, blasphemy law in Britain was applied only to the protection of Christian religion, and the same could not be extended to protect any other religion.[4] Choudhury took the appeal to the ECtHR. In *Choudhury v. United Kingdom*, the appellant contended that English law was prejudiced against Islam. However, the appeal was declared inadmissible by the commission as it held that there was no positive obligation on states under ECtHR laws to protect all religious sensibilities.[5] The central claim made by the appellant in these cases was that the law of blasphemy should be extended to protect all religious groups in the country and could not be limited to the protection of only the religion of the majority. Though the law at the time could not be invoked in the case, it built a larger consensus on the subject, which was also reflected in the abolition of the blasphemy law[6] and its replacement by the more egalitarian and inclusive Religious and Racial Hatred Act 2006.

In the cartoon controversy, although complaints were filed, the editors or publishers were never taken to court since the Danish Public Prosecutor decided that the cartoons did not violate any law. Danish Penal Code makes it a criminal offence 'to publicly mock or degrade the religious beliefs or worship of any legal religious community' (Penal Code 140). It also considers it an offence to utter things that are 'threatening, insulting or degrading to a group of persons due to their race, skin colour, national or ethnic origin, faith or sexual orientation' (Penal Code 266b). However, the Regional Public Prosecutor in Viborg, who was entrusted with the investigation in the cartoon case, maintained that though some cartoons had the capacity to ridicule or express disdain for Muslims' religious beliefs, as protected under the blasphemy clause, it did not constitute an infringement of the clause.[7] It further exempted it from violation of the racism clause as it only depicted an individual and could not be held to mean against the whole community. Though the Public Prosecutor maintained that freedom of expression had to be exercised with respect for other human rights, he argued that the journalists responsible for the publication of the cartoons could not be held to be in violation of the legal codes.[8] The legal question in the cartoon controversy was whether the publication of cartoons qualified as acts punishable within the Penal Codes of Denmark, and the Public Prosecutor provided a wide interpretation of law claiming exemption of such acts from law under the guise of editorial freedom. As is visible, legal provisions in Britain and Denmark differed on how to treat blasphemous libel. Britain had a law against blasphemy, but it only protected Christian religion, and although courts agreed that the novel was religiously offensive, the limitations of the blasphemy law became the justification for the courts to reject a case against Rushdie and the publishers of the novel. In Denmark, on the other hand, there existed provisions within its Penal Codes that defined religious offence in clear terms, and was applicable to all religious communities, but the Public Prosecutor did not find the law applicable to the kind of offence in the cartoon controversy. On these bases, the governments in the respective countries decided not to act legally against the publications.

Contrast this with the response to the same publications in India. As shown in Chapter 5, the Indian government pronounced a ban on the import of *The Satanic Verses* under the Customs Act, citing it as a 'pre-emptive step' to avoid public-order problems. The Customs Act used for the purpose cannot be challenged in the judiciary and hence no formidable case law followed on the subject. However, regardless of the blanket ban, communal disturbances including violence were reported from different places in India, where Muslims took to the street to protest the book and its author, Rushdie. In the case of the cartoon controversy, a few newspapers in India reprinted the controversial cartoons published by Jyllands-Posten, which included the Patna edition of *The Times of India* (Khanduri 2014). Government reacted immediately against the initial publishers, and this prevented large-scale reprints. Publishers were arrested under section 295(A) and 153(A) of the IPC, which are meant to prevent religious offence and incitement of hate. Moreover, in an official release, the Indian government made its position clear: government was 'deeply concerned about the growing controversy over the publication of cartoons that offend the Muslim community worldwide' and it was 'incumbent on all of us to be sensitive to the beliefs and sentiments of others and avoid all actions that cause hurt to them'.[9] Government was concerned in the way the protests against the cartoons had turned violent and converted to riots in different cities like Srinagar, Patna and Lucknow. Fearing strong protest and demonstrations, the Central Government also cancelled the proposed state visit by Danish Prime Minister Rasmussen.[10] The Indian government indicated that it was not satisfied with the way Denmark had handled the situation, especially refusing legal actions against Jyllands-Posten. At the same time, it had also signalled that if any one reprinted or published such cartoons, it would be dealt with strongly under the available laws.

The legal means available with the Indian government are primarily the statutory laws like section 295(A) and 153(A) of the IPC, and section 95 of the CrPC. Section 295(A) and 153(A) are punitive in nature, where violation of section 295(A) can amount to arrest of publishers or authors who are found to be deliberately engaged in outraging religious feelings or insulting religion or religious beliefs of any class, and violation of section 153(A) can lead to similar punishments for those who are found to be spreading disharmony, ill feeling or hatred between different religious groups. Section 95 of CrPC, on the other hand, is preventive in nature and pertains to seizure and forfeiture of publications in case such publications are found violating section 295(A) and 153(A) of the IPC. Indian laws, in that sense, do not just protect the enraged communities from religious hurt, but also provide strong protection to religion and religious beliefs of different communities from insults. This provides a wide net for the government authorities to act in cases where a publication is found religiously offensive and contentious. In cases of proscription and forfeiture, the only legal reprieve is section 96 of the CrPC, which allows the aggrieved party to approach the court against government's action. However, law is so framed that rather than government defending its act of seizure/forfeiture in the court, the onus of proving innocence falls on the author/publisher, where they are expected to justify that their acts do not fall under the category of offence as defined by the above-mentioned statutory laws.[11] Legal scholars opine that such laws not only make it very difficult for the advocates/defenders of freedom of speech and expression but also pave way for the executive to respond to claims of hurt sentiments, without serious examination of either the scope of the law or substantive principles laid down by various courts in such cases (Liang 2016: 823). The above discussions reflect the context-specific nature of laws and their implementation for similar cases in different societies. In every society, the nature of laws to restrict freedom of expression corresponds to the needs and challenges that led to the creation of such laws and allow its existence. In the UK, for example, a need was realized, according to changing demography and nature of society, to abolish blasphemy laws and replace them with a different set of laws that protected all religious and racial communities. In the case of India, the creations of the statutory laws bore a colonial legacy and were created to respond to a specific set of issues dominant in Indian society – to curb the tendency to ignite communal hatred that led to violence. Subsequently these laws were amended, as and when required, according to the demands of the context.

Governing Freedom of Speech and Expression in India

The British approach to laws governing freedom of speech and expression was strictly guided by an instrumental logic to serve the colonial interests. At the same time, Indians had a dubious attitude towards freedom of speech and expression in the colonial context. So, they were demanding extensive freedom of expression in order to criticize the government, an argument derived from the consequentialist theories of free speech, which claimed that free speech was necessary to arrive closer to the truth and was beneficial for governance. However, where such liberty was seen as leading to religious offence, Indians not only demanded censorship from the government, but also participated actively in the legislatures to ensure successful promulgation of new laws. In the post-Independence period, particularistic concerns like partition and the communal violence that it accompanied inspired constitution makers to severely limit fundamental rights promised under article 19(1)(a) by adding a number of caveats under article 19(2). In this split manufactured between article 19(1)(a) and 19(2), there was also an inherent dichotomy. Article 19(1)(a) imagined citizens as rational subjects capable of exercising complete autonomy in speech acts, whereas article 19(2) reflected the challenges of an affective public sphere, where citizens were seen as corruptible and prone to outrage and provocation (Liang 2016: 818). This same imagination about the majority of Indian citizens being emotional beings, who lacked 'maturity', particularly on matters related to religion, also became the rallying point for the introduction of significant amendments to the constitution and other statutory laws. Lawmakers took it as their duty to provide a safety net in order to protect common people from the misuse of freedom of speech and expression, and law was also seen as a medium to discipline citizens and inculcate values of toleration.

This overemphasis on public tranquillity and order also guided the proactive role of government agencies in censoring or forfeiting publications or arresting authors/publishers when controversies related to such publications surfaced. The underlying assumption that Indian citizens lacked the capacity to handle hurtful speech, and could easily be swayed by passions if the subject under discussion was religion, allows, as Pratap Bhanu Mehta argues, for a paternalistic role of state, where state takes part in the controversy only as protector of public order, and not as defender of free speech (2008: 330–332). This is ably reflected in the IPC, which uses language of 'outrage', 'disgust' and 'pain' to regulate speech, and also in the fact that most statutory laws regulating religiously offensive speech acts are cognizable offences[12] and are non-bailable[13] in nature. The effectiveness of these laws is further buttressed by the legal defence such laws enjoy under the aegis of article 19(2) of constitution, which represents 'reasonable restrictions' for freedom of speech and expression. Consequently, laws governing freedom of speech and expression in India have allowed a wide net for executive control, and authorities deem it prudent to play it over-safe whenever they sense a threat to law and order. The general approach is to ban publication or proscribe it and/or arrest the author/publisher at the slightest controversy where the claim of religious offence is involved. They maintain that the aggrieved person has every right to approach the relevant court and obtain a judicial verdict in his/her favour. It also helps officials to temporarily pacify the prevalent law-and-order situation, and if there is any breach of peace following the judgement from the court, the responsibility can be placed on the judgement. Authorities can thereby disclaim the responsibility of incumbent situation by citing their alertness at the earlier instance.[14]

Freedom of Speech and Expression and 'Reasonable Restrictions'

One of the central questions with which I began this book was: how have the courts in India interpreted laws and defined 'reasonable restrictions' concerning freedom of speech and expression vis-à-vis the claims of religious offence? This begs an assessment of the grounds on which the courts allow restrictions of freedom of speech and expression when the claim of religious offence is raised against a publication. Firstly, it should be pointed out that in various cases, courts in general, and the Supreme Court in particular, have upheld the constitutionality of statutory laws that the executives use to restrict freedom of speech and expression.[15] As of now, courts have taken a position that these laws fall well within the definition of 'reasonable restrictions' as provided under article 19(2). Further, primary justifications used by courts for upholding the restrictions over freedom of speech and expression include: (1) a threat to public order posed by the publication and (2) protection of values of secularism and religious pluralism. The former is primarily based on an assumption that an aggravated form of insult targeted against any religion or incitement of religious hatred would invariably lead to a problem of maintaining public order, and the authorities must take prompt action in such situation. However, courts have also evolved certain balancing and protective mechanisms with regard to executive action. For example, it has been made mandatory by the court that a notification mentioning the reasons for action should be issued by the concerned authority before any publication is seized or forfeited. Similarly, in case of an arrest of an author/publisher, authority needs to prove in the court that the act was carried out with deliberate and malicious intent. The problem with these balancing mechanisms, however, is that either of these – proving intentions of the arrested individual or the question of validity of the notification issued before forfeiture – can only be tested on the floor of the courts, which can only happen at a later stage. So, broadly it can be said that government officials can act in these cases based on their own judgement of the situation, which is often guided by the instrumental logic of acting against such publication and its author/publisher, against whom the charges of causing religious offence is made in order to maintain public tranquillity. The second argument for restricting freedom of speech and expression is that, though important, freedom of speech and expression does not enjoy any special status in the Indian context,[16] and needs to be balanced against competing fundamental rights. The doctrine of proportionality[17] reigns supreme in such cases, and courts have maintained that the right to profess, practice and propagate one's religion guaranteed under article 25 is one such provision, with which the right to free speech needs to be balanced. Other than this, courts also stress that in a multicultural secular country, like India, it is the duty of the state to protect religious interests of all citizens. This argument has been extended to protection of religious principles, religious texts and even religious personages from attack. Courts also try to construct a distinction between criticizing religious practices or rituals, and insulting its principles or symbols, by putting the former under the category of permissible speech. This distinction, however, as free speech scholars like Peter Jones (1980) and Eric Barendt (2011) have shown in another context, is very difficult to maintain and prone to dissolve, which would mean that authorities could act against any criticism of religion.

The above discussions reflects two prominent aspects about the courts' position on the subject of religious offence committed by a publication. First, courts appear to provide legal patronage to state actions through an expansive interpretation of statutory laws and constitutional limitations;[18] and second, courts practice legal paternalism, whereby it guides the citizens regarding what to say, how to say it and how much to say.[19] Together with this, the language of statutory laws provides a sense of immunity to religions from criticism. This also has deep impact on historical analysis and other scholarship related to religion. In a way, any critical publication on the subject of religion or a literary piece like a novel on the subject of religion automatically becomes subject to potential controversy, which restrains the scope for freedom of speech and expression.

The aspects of law and legal process discussed above also contribute to strengthening the role of non-state actors in censorship. These non-state actors, who primarily claim to be representing the offended community, use the language of law to justify their grievances. It is also reflected in the way law and legal process is used by the non-state actors to express their grievances. This can either be in the form of writ petitions (both civil as well as criminal) filed in the courts against the publication and its author/publisher or as a justificatory means to exert pressure on government authorities to act against the publication and its author/publisher, or it is also used as a legitimate strategic tool to create public opinion in their favour.[20] The long legal process, which could be tiring and costly, and ambiguity in legal interpretations produces an environment where the author/publisher is forced to impose self-censorship – a phenomenon that Cook and Heilmann call 'public self-censorship'. This can either result in the amendment of the original text including significant exclusions or the deletion of controversial portions or even pulping or withdrawing the publication in controversy. This undoubtedly poses the most serious threat to the scope of freedom of speech and expression in independent India.

Notes

1 Jones held that if people are offended, they are liable to express their protest, and the advocates of free speech should have no problems with that. See Jones (1993: 118). This argument has also been endorsed by Dworkin and Waldron.
2 The legal dimensions of the cases have been discussed in detail in the following books, among others. See Hunt (2002: 187–188); Langer (2014: 50–90).
3 British Muslim Action Front was a group organized to protest against the religious offence caused by the publication of *Satanic Verses*.
4 As discussed in detail in *R. v. Chief Metropolitan Stipendiary Magistrate, exp. Choudhury* (Queen's Bench Division) (1991) 1 QB 429 (1990).
5 *Choudhury v. United Kingdom* (1991) Application No. 17439/90, ECommHR.
6 The common-law offences of blasphemy and blasphemous libel in the UK were abolished by the Criminal Justice and Immigration Act, 2008.
7 *Rigsadvokaten (Director of Public Prosecutions)* (2006) J. Nr. RA-2006-41-0151.
8 Summarized in *Rigsadvokaten*, J. Nr. RA-2006-41-0151; *Kasem Said Ahmad and Asmaa Abdol-hamid v. Denmark* (2008) Communication no. 1487/2006, CCPR. The response of the Danish law in the controversy has also been presented effectively in Lagoutte (2008: 379–404).
9 There was a lot of pressure on the government to take some position, which is also reflected in the debates of the Parliament, particularly in the Rajya Sabha, where the top leaders of the opposition party like Sushma Swaraj and Ravi Shankar Prasad questioned the position of the government and criticized its inability to contain violence in different parts. See *Rajya Sabha Debates*, 20 February 2006, pp. 171–179; 8 March 2006, p. 100. The official press release is available at the website of the Prime Minister's office, 'Govt. Expresses Concern over Publication of Cartoons That Offend Religious Sentiments', available at http://archivepmo.nic.in/drmanmohansingh/ content_print.php?nodeid=389&nodetype=1 (last accessed on 30 August 2018).
10 'Cartoon Row Kills Danish PM's Visit', *The Hindustan Times*, 18 March 2006.
11 This interpretation of law has been defended by the Supreme Court in various cases like *Lalai Singh Yadav*, 1977 AIR 202; *Sri Baragur Ramachandrappa*, 5 S.C.C. 11.
12 Cognizable offence is one where the police do not require prior approval either from the state government or any warrant from the court. It can act *suo motu* in such cases.
13 Non-bailable means that the accused cannot be granted bail with the case being heard in a court of law.
14 See Dhavan (2008: 145). He calls this a 'problem solving' politics used by government authorities to counter threats on public order in such cases.
15 The constitutionality of sections 295(A) and 153(A) of the IPC and section 95 of the CrPC have been respectively upheld in *Ramji Lal Modi*, 1957 AIR 620; *Babu Rao Patel*, 1980 A.I.R. 763; and *N. Veerabrahmam*, A.I.R. 1959 A.P. 572.

16 This position is reflected among the scholars in relation to the First Amendment in the US, like Dworkin and C. Edwin Baker, among others. This view has, however, been effectively questioned, even in the context of the US; for example, see Fish (1994); Waldron (2012).

17 The doctrine of proportionality broadly means that the application of a given law should not be unreasonable in its reciprocal relationship and a sense of proportion must exist between the ends desired and the means employed. In case of competing fundamental rights, it is also used to weigh the impact of a decision by authorities whether the use of law in a case has adverse effects upon the liberties of a person. For an analysis of the complexities involved in the doctrine of proportionality in relation to human rights, see Tsakyrakis (2009: 468–493). Madhav Khosla's response to this article is equally important (2010: 298–306).

18 It is not to say that this patronage is uncritical, as exhibited in many judgements, but the overall reading gives a sense that on most occasions, courts seem to justify the state's response profoundly when there is a threat to law and order.

19 The courts' approach in using 'matter-manner' together in analysis of publications, and particularly its suggestion about precaution against language that vilifies. For example, in *Sri Baragur Ramachandrappa*, the court reminds us that 'it cannot be ignored that India is [a] country with vast disparities in language, culture and religion and unwarranted and malicious criticism or interference in the faith of others cannot be accepted'.

20 Legal opinion becomes one of the important rallying points to create public opinion in such cases.

REFERENCES

Acharya, Bhairav. 2015. 'Free Speech in India: Still Plagued by Pre-modern Laws', *Media Asia*, vol. 42, no. 3–4, pp. 157–160.

Ahmed, Asad Ali. 2009. 'Spectre of Macaulay: Blasphemy, the Indian Penal Code and Pakistan's Postcolonial Predicament'. In Raminder Kaur and William Mazzarella (eds.), *Censorship in South Asia: Cultural Regulation from Sedition to Seduction*, pp. 172–205. Bloomington, Indianapolis: Indiana University Press.

Anderson, Benedict. 1983. *Imagined Communities: Reflections on the Origin and Spread of Nationalism*. London: Verso.

Ansari, Iqbal A. 2008. 'Free Speech – Hate Speech – The Taslima Nasreen Case', *Economic and Political Weekly*, vol. 43, no.8, pp. 15–19.

Appignanesi, Lisa Maitland, and Sara Maitland (eds.). 1989. *The Rushdie File*. London: Fourth Estate.

Asad, Talal. 1999. *The Indian Constitution: Cornerstone of a Nation*. New Delhi: Oxford University Press.

———. 2009. 'Free Speech, Blasphemy and Secular Criticism'. In Wendy Brown, Judith Butler, Saba Mahmood and Talal Asad (eds.), *Is Critique Secular? Blasphemy, Injury and Free Speech*, pp. 14–57. Berkeley: The Townsend Center for the Humanities, University of California.

———. 2011. 'Freedom of Speech and Religious Limitations'. In Craig Calhoun, Mark Juergensmeyer and Jonathan VanAntwerpen (eds.), *Rethinking Secularism*, pp. 282–298. Oxford: Oxford University Press.

Austin, Granville. 2003. *Working a Democratic Constitution: A History of the Indian Experience*. New Delhi: Oxford University Press.

———. 1997. *The Indian Constitution: Cornerstone of a Nation*. New Delhi: Oxford University Press.

Bajpai, Rochana. 2010. 'Cultural Rights of Minorities during Constitution-Making: A Re-reading'. In Gurpreet Mahajan and S. Jodhka (eds.), *Religion, Community and Development: Changing Contours of Politics and Policy in India*, pp. 282–300. New Delhi: Routledge.

———. 2011. *Debating Difference: Group Rights and Liberal Democracy in India*. Oxford: Oxford University Press.

Baker, Edwin. 1989. *Human Liberty and Freedom of Speech*. Oxford: Oxford University Press.

Barendt, Eric. 2011. 'Religious Hatred Laws: Protecting Groups or Beliefs', *Res Publica*, vol. 17, no. 1, pp. 41–53.

Barrier, N. G. 1974. *Banned: Controversial Literature and Political Control in British India, 1907–1947*. Columbia: University of Missouri Press.

———. 1992. 'Vernacular Publishing and Sikh Public Life in the Punjab, 1880–1910'. In Kenneth W. Jones (ed.), *Religious Controversy in British India: Dialogues in South Asian Languages*, pp. 200–228. New York: State University of New York Press.

Bayly, C. A. 2009. 'The Indian Ecumene: An Indigenous Public Sphere'. In Arvind Rajagopal (ed.), *The Indian Public Sphere: Readings in Media History*, pp. 49–64. New Delhi: Oxford University Press.

———. 2010. 'Rammohan Roy and the Advent of Constitutional Liberalism in India'. In Shruti Kapila (ed.), *An Intellectual History for India*, pp. 18–34. New Delhi: Cambridge University Press.

———. 2012. *Recovering Liberties: Indian Thought in the Age of Liberalism and Empire*. New Delhi: Cambridge University Press.

Bhargava, Rajeev. 1999. 'Democratic Vision of a New Republic: India, 1950'. In Francine R. Frankel, Zoya Hasan, Rajeev Bhargava and Balveer Arora (eds.), *Transforming India: Social and Political Dynamics of Democracy*, pp. 26–59. New Delhi: Oxford University Press.

———. 2012. *What Is Political Theory and Why Do We Need It?* New Delhi: Oxford University Press.

Bhatia, Gautam. 2016. *Offend, Shock or Disturb: Free Speech under the Indian Constitution*. New Delhi: Oxford University Press.

Bhatia, Nandi. 2010. 'Censorship, Social Reform and Mythological Drama in Colonial India'. In Diana Dimitrova (ed.), *Religion in Literature and Film in South Asia*, pp. 191–211. New York: Palgrave Macmillan.

Bhatia, S. 1997. *Freedom of Press: Politico-Legal Aspects of Press Legislation in India*. New Delhi: Rawat Publications.

Bhattacharya, Neeladri. 2005. 'Notes towards a Conception of the Colonial Public'. In Rajeev Bhargava and Helmut Reifeld (eds.), *Civil Society, Public Sphere and Citizenship: Dialogues and Perceptions*, pp. 130–156. New Delhi: Sage.

Bhowmik, Someswar. 2003. 'From Coercion to Power Relations: Film Censorship in Post-colonial India', *Economic and Political Weekly*, vol. 38, no. 3, pp. 3148–3152.

———. 2009. *Cinema and Censorship: The Politics of Control in India*. New Delhi: Orient Blackswan.

Blom, Hansen Thomas. 2004. 'Politics as Permanent Performance: The Production of Political Authority in Locality'. In John Zavos, Andrew Wyatt and Vernon Hewitt (eds.), *The Politics of Cultural Mobilization in India*, pp. 19–36. New Delhi: Oxford University Press.

Bollinger, Lee C. 1988. *The Tolerant Society: Freedom of Speech and Extremist Speech in America*. New York: Oxford University Press.

Bose, Brinda (ed.). 2006. *Gender and Censorship*. New Delhi: Kali for Women.

Brass, Paul. 2003. *The Production of Hindu-Muslim Violence in Contemporary India*. Seattle: University of Washington Press.

Buckland, C. E. 1976. *Bengal under the Lieutenant Governors: Being a Narrative of the Principal Events and Public Measures during Their Periods of Office from 1854–1898*, vol. 2. New Delhi: Deep Publications.

Burt, Richard. 1994. *The Administration of Aesthetics: Censorship, Political Criticism and Public Sphere*. Minnepolis and London: University of Minnesota.

Butler, Judith. 1997. *Excitable Speech: A Politics of the Performative*. New York and London: Routledge.

Chandoke, Neera. 2005. 'Individual and Group Rights: A View from India'. In Zoya Hasan, E. Sridharan and R. Sudharshan (eds.), *India's Living Constitution: Ideas, Practices, Controversies*, pp. 207–241. London: Anthem Press.

Chandra, Bipan. 1990. 'Communalism and the State: Some Issues in India', *Social Scientist*, vol. 18, no. 6–7, pp. 38–47.

Chandrachud, Abhinav. 2011. 'An Empirical Study of the Supreme Court's Composition', *Economic and Political Weekly*, vol. 46, no. 1, pp. 71–78.

———. 2012. 'Speech, Structure and Behavior on the Supreme Court of India', *Columbia Journal of Asian Law*, vol. 25, no. 2, pp. 222–274.

Chatterjee, Partha. 1993. *The Nation and Its Fragments: Colonial and Postcolonial Histories*. Princeton: Princeton University Press.

Chaudhuri, Reba. 1955. 'The Story of the Indian Press', *Economic and Political Weekly*, vol. 7, no. 9, pp. 291–292.

Cohen-Almagor, Raphael. 2005. *The Scope of Tolerance: Studies on the Cost of Freedom of Expression and Freedom of the Press*. Abingdon: Routledge.

Collini, Stefan. 2010. *That's Offensive: Criticism, Identity, Respect*. London: Seagull Books.

Collini, Stephen, Donald Winch and John Burrow. 1984. *That Noble Science of Politics: A Study in Nineteenth-Century Intellectual History*. Cambridge: Cambridge University Press.

Cook, Philip, and Conrad Heilmann. 2013. 'Two Types of Self-Censorship: Public and Private', *Political Studies*, vol. 61, no. 1, pp. 178–196.

Darnton, Robert. 2001. 'Literary Surveillance in the British Raj: The Contradictions of Liberal Imperialism', *Book History*, vol. 4, pp. 133–176.

———. 2002. 'Book Production in British India, 1850–1900', *Book History*, vol. 5, pp. 239–262.

De, Rohit. 2012. 'Emasculating the Executive: The Federal Court and Civil Liberties in Late Colonial India, 1942–1944'. In Terence C. Halliday, Lucien Karpik and Malcolm M. Feeley (eds.), *Fates of Political Liberalism in the British Post-Colony: The Politics of the Legal Complex*, pp. 59–90. Cambridge and New York: Cambridge University Press.

Department of Law, University of Toronto, and PEN International and International Human Rights Program (IHRP), n.d. *Imposing Silence: The Use of India's Laws to Supress Free Speech*. Available at www.pen-international.org/wp-content/uploads/2015/05/Imposing-Silence--FINAL.pdf (last accessed on 14 July 2015).

Devlin, Patrick. 1965. *The Enforcement of Morals*. London: Oxford University Press.

Dhavan, Rajeev. 2008. *Publish and Be Damned: Censorship and Intolerance in India*. New Delhi: Tulika Books.

Donough, Walter Russell. 1911. *A Treatise on the Law of Sedition and Cognate Offences in British India*. Kolkata: Thackel Spink & Co.

Dworkin, Ronald. 2006. 'The Right to Ridicule', *The New York Review of Books*. Available at http://www.nybooks.com/articles/2006/03/23/the-right-to-ridicule/ (last accessed on 27 September 2018).

———. 2009. 'Foreword'. In Ivan Hare and James Weinstein (eds.), *Extreme Speech and Democracy*. Oxford: Oxford University Press.

Emerson, Thomas I. 1966. *Towards a General Theory of the First Amendment*. New York: Random House.

Emon, Anver M. 2007. 'On the Pope, Cartoons and Apostates, Sharia', *Journal of Law and Religion*, vol. 22, no. 2, pp. 303–321.

Eswaran, Venkat. 1992. 'Advocacy of National, Racial and Religious Hatred: The Indian Experience'. In Sandra Colliver (ed.), *Striking a Balance: Hate Speech, Freedom of Expression and Non-discrimination*, pp. 171–181. Human Rights Centre, University of Essex, London: Article 19, International Centre Against Censorship.

Feinberg, Joel. 1973. 'Harmless Immoralities and Offensive Nuisances: Reply'. In Norman S. Care and Thomas K. Trelogan (eds.), *Issues in Law and Morality: Proceedings*, pp. 111–126. Cleveland and London: Case Western Reserve University Press.

———. 1985. *Offense to Others*. New York: Oxford University Press.

Fish, Stanley. 1994. *There Is No Such Thing as Free Speech: And It's a Good Thing Too*. Oxford: Oxford University Press.

Freitag, Sandria B. 1989. *Collective Action and Community: Public Arenas and the Emergence of Communalism in North India*. Berkeley and Oxford: University of California Press.

———. 1996. 'Contesting in Public: Colonial Legacies and Contemporary Communalism'. In David Ludden (ed.), *Contesting the Nation: Religion, Community and the Politics of Democracy in India*, pp. 211–234. Philadelphia: University of Pennsylvania Press.

Gandhi, M. K. 1967. *The Collected Works of Mahatma Gandhi*, 100 vols. New Delhi: Publications Division, Ministry of Information and Broadcasting.

Ghosh, Sohini. 1991. 'Democracy, Nationalism and the Public: A Speculation on Colonial Muslim Politics', *Journal of South Asian Studies*, vol. 14, no. 1, pp. 123–140.

———. 2004. 'Censorship Myths and Imagined Harms', *Sarai Reader*, vol. 4, pp. 447–454. Available at http://archive.sarai.net/files/original/755257fc6fa5744ae93c402cd54bc039.pdf (last accessed 17 June 2020).

———. 2016. 'The Alchemy of Hate and Hurt'. In Rina Ramdev, S. D. Nambiar and D. Bhattacharya (eds.), *Sentiment, Politics, Censorship: The State of Hurt*, pp. 55–70. New Delhi: Sage.

Gilmartin, David. 1998. 'Partition, Pakistan and South Asian History: In Search of a Narrative', *The Journal of Asian Studies*, vol. 57, no. 4, pp. 1068–1095.

———. 1991. 'Democracy, Nationalism and the Public: A Speculation on Colonial Muslim Politics', *Journal of South Asian Studies*, vol. 14, no. 1, pp. 123–140.

Gopal, S. (ed.). 1991. *Selected Works of Jawaharlal Nehru*. New Delhi: Oxford University Press.

Guha, Ranajit. 1977. *Dominance without Hegemony: History and Power in Colonial India*. New Delhi: Oxford University Press.

———. 2009. 'Transmission'. In Arvind Rajagopal (ed.), *The Indian Public Sphere: Readings in Media History*, pp. 31–48. New Delhi: Oxford University Press.

Gupta, Nand Lal. 2006. *Jawaharlal Nehru on Communalism*. New Delhi: Hope India.

Habermas, J. 1992. *The Structural Transformation of the Public Sphere: An Inquiry into a Category of Bourgeois Society*. Trans. Thomas Burger. Cambridge: Polity.

———. 1996. 'Between Facts and Norms', *Journal of Philosophy*, vol. 93, no. 6, pp. 307–315.

———. 2001. 'Constitutional Democracy: A Paradoxical Union of Contradictory Principles', trans. William Rehg, *Political Theory*, vol. 29, no. 6, pp. 766–781.

Hantman, Daniel. 2014. 'Shaking Fists and Simmering Craniums: India's Tolerance for Restricting Socially Offensive and Emotionally Harmful Speech', *Indonesian Journal of International and Comparative Law*, vol. 1, no. 1, pp. 73–104.

Hart, H. L. A. 1963. *Law, Liberty and Morality*. London: Oxford University Press.

Heyman, Steven J. 2002. 'Spheres of Autonomy: Reforming the Content Neutrality Doctrine in First Amendment Jurisprudence', *William & Mary Bill of Rights*, vol. 10, no. 3, pp. 649–716.

Hoarsher, Guys. 2008. 'Rhetoric and Its Abuses: How to Oppose Liberal Democracy while Speaking Its Language', *Chicago-Kent Law Review*, vol. 83, no. 3, pp. 1225–1253.

Holquist, Michael, 1994. 'Corrupt Originals: The Paradox of Censorship', *PMLA*, vol. 9, no. 1, pp. 14–25.

Hunt, Murray. 2002. *Using Human Rights Law in English Courts*. Oxford: Hart Publishing.

Huttmann, G. H. 1837. *A Penal Code Prepared by the Indian Law Commissioners*. Kolkata: Bengal Military Orphan Press.

Iyer, R. (ed.). 1986. *The Moral and Political Writings of Mahatma Gandhi*, vol. 1. New Delhi: Oxford University Press.

Jaffrelot, Christophe. 1999. *The Hindu Nationalist Movement and Indian Politics*. Delhi: Penguin.

———. 2010. *Religion, Caste and Politics in India*. New Delhi: Primus Books.

Jaffrelot, Christophe, L. Gayer and M. Maheshwari. 2010. 'Cultural Policing in South Asia'. In Helmut Anheir and Yudhishthir Raj Isar (eds.), *Cultural Expression, Creativity and Innovation*, pp. 148–158. Los Angeles: Sage Publications.

Jalal, Ayesha. 2000. *Self and Sovereignty: Individual and Community in South Asian Islam since 1850*. London and New York: Routledge.

Jansen, Sue Curry. 1991. *Censorship: The Knot That Binds Power and Knowledge*. New York: Oxford University Press.

Jones, Peter. 1980. 'Blasphemy, Offensiveness and Law', *British Journal of Political Science*, vol. 10, no. 2, pp. 129–148.

———. 1993. 'Respecting Beliefs and Rebuking Rushdie'. In J. Horton (ed.), *Liberalism, Multiculturalism and Toleration*, pp. 114–138. Basingstoke: Macmillan.

Kapur, Ratna. 1996. 'Who Draws the Line? Feminist Reflections on Speech and Censorship', *Economic and Political Weekly*, vol. 31, no. 16/17, pp. 15–30.

Kaur, Reminder. 2003. *Performative Politics and the Cultures of Hinduism: Public Uses of Religion in Western India*. London: Anthem Press.

Kaviraj, Sudipta. 2010. *The Imaginary Institution of India*. New Delhi: Permanent Black.

———. 2011. *The Enchantment of Democracy and India: Politics and Ideas*. New Delhi: Permanent Black.

Khanduri, Ritu Gairola. 2014. *Caricaturing Culture in India: Cartoons and History in the Modern World*. Cambridge: Cambridge University Press.

Khilnani, Sunil. 2015. 'The Indian Constitution and Democracy'. In Zoya Hasan Esridharan, and R. Sudarshan (eds.), *India's Living Constitution: Ideas, Practices, Controversies*, pp. 64–82. London: Anthem Press.

Khosla, Madhav. 2010. 'Proportionality: An Assault on Human Rights? A Reply', *International Journal of Constitutional Law*, vol. 7, no. 3, pp. 298–306.

King, Christopher R. 1992. 'Images of Virtue and Vice: The Hindi-Urdu Controversy in Two Nineteenth-Century Hindi Plays'. In Kenneth W. Jones (ed.), *Religious Controversy in British India: Dialogues in South Asian Languages*, pp. 124–147. New York: State University of New York Press.

Kolsky, Elizabeth. 2005. 'Codification and the Rule of Colonial Difference: Criminal Procedure in British India', *Law and History Review*, vol. 23, no. 3, pp. 640.
Kumar, Girja. 1990. *Censorship in India: With Special Reference to 'Satanic Verses'*. New Delhi: Har-Anand.
———. 1997. *The Book on Trial: Fundamentalism and Censorship in India*. New Delhi: Har Anand.
Laegaard, Sune. 2007. 'The Cartoon Controversy: Offense, Identity, Oppression', *Political Studies*, vol. 55, no. 3, pp. 481–98.
Lagoutte, Stephanie. 2008. 'The Cartoon Controversy in Context: Analyzing the Decisions Not to Prosecute under Danish Law', *Brooklyn Journal of International Law*, vol. 33, no. 2, pp. 379–404.
LaMarche, Gara. 1991. 'Some Thoughts on Chilling Effect', *Art Journal*, vol. 50, no. 4, pp. 56–58.
Langer, Lorenz. 2014. *Religious Offence and Human Rights: The Implications of Defamation of Religions*. Cambridge: Cambridge University Press.
Lee, Simon. 1990. *The Cost of Free Speech*. London and Boston: Faber and Faber.
Letsas, George. 2012. 'Is There a Right Not to Be Offended in One's Religious Beliefs?' In Lorenzo Zucca and Camil Ungureanu (eds.), *Law, State and Religion in the New Europe: Debates and Dilemmas*, pp. 239–260. Cambridge: Cambridge University Press.
Liang, Lawrence. 2004. 'Reasonable Restrictions and Unreasonable Speech', *Sarai Reader*, vol. 04, pp. 434–440. Available at http://archive.sarai.net/files/original/e8cc962416f0a1f2da6bc009347fa387.pdf (last accessed on 7 June 2020).
———. 2012. 'Love Language or Hate Speech', *Tehelka*, vol. 09, no. 3. Available at http://archive.tehelka.com/story_main51.asp?filename=hub030312love.asp (last accessed on 10 July 2020).
———. 2016. 'Free Speech and Expression'. In Sujit Choudhary, Madhav Khosla and Pratap Bhanu Mehta (eds.), *The Oxford Handbook of The Indian Constitution*, pp. 814–833. New Delhi: Oxford University Press.
Low, D. A. 1973. *Lion Rampant: Essays in the Study of British Imperialism*. London: Routledge.
Macaulay, T. B. 1837. *A Penal Code Prepared by the Indian Law Commissioners*. Kolkata: Bengal Military Orphan Press.
———. 1866. 'Introductory Report upon the Indian Penal Code (IPC)'. In Lady Trevlyn (ed.), *The Works of Lord Macaulay*, vol. VII. London: Longmans, Green, and Co.
———. 1898. *The Complete Works of Lord Macaulay*, Albany Edition, 12 vols. Lady Trevlyn (ed.). London: Longmans, Green, and Co.
Mackinnon, Catherine. 1996. *Only Words*. Cambridge, MA: Harvard University Press.
Madok, Bal Raj. 2001. *Portrait of a Martyr: Biography of Dr. Shyama Prasad Mookerjee*. New Delhi: Rupa.
Mahajan, Gurpreet. 1998. *Identities and Rights: Aspects of Liberal Democracy in India*. New Delhi: Oxford University Press.
———. 2008. 'Religion and the Indian Constitution: Questions of Separation and Equality', In Rajeev Bhargava (ed.), *Politics and Ethics of the Indian Constitution*, pp. 297–310. New Delhi: Oxford University Press, 2008.
———. 2013. *India: Political Ideas and the Making of a Democratic Discourse*. New York and London: Zed Books.

Maheshwari, Malvika. 2011. 'Violent Regulation and Artists in India: The Transformation of Freedom of Expression', PhD diss., Institut d'Etudes Politiques de Paris, Sciences Po.

Mahmood, Saba. 2009. 'Religious Reason and Secular Affect: An Incommensurable Divide?' In Wendy Brown, Judith Butler, Talal Asad and Saba Mahmood (eds.), *Is Critique Secular? Blasphemy, Injury and Free Speech*, pp. 58–94. Berkeley: The Townsend Center for the Humanities, University of California.

Maine, H. S. 1876. *Village Communities in the East and West*. London: John Murray.

Mantena, Karuna. 2009. *Alibis of Empire: Henry Maine and the Ends of Liberal Imperialism*. Princeton and Oxford: Princeton University Press.

Mayne, J. D. 1862. *Commentaries on Indian Penal Code*. Chennai: J. Higgenbotham.

Mehta, Pratap Bhanu. 2005. 'India's Judiciary: The Promise of Uncertainty'. In Devesh Kapur and Self (eds.), *Public Institutions in India: Performance and Design*, pp. 158–193. New Delhi: Oxford University Press.

———. 2008. 'Passion and Constraint: Courts and the Regulation of Religious Meaning'. In Rajeev Bhargava (ed.), *Politics and Ethics of the Indian Constitution*, pp. 311–338. New Delhi: Oxford University Press.

Mehta, Uday Singh. 1999. *Liberalism and Empire: A Study in Nineteenth-Century British Liberal Thought*. Chicago and London: University of Chicago Press.

———. 2011. 'Constitutionalism'. In Niraja Gopal Jayal and Pratap Bhanu Mehta (eds.), *The Oxford Companion to Politics in India*, pp. 14–27. New Delhi: Oxford University Press.

Mehta, V. R., & Thomas Pantham (eds.). 2006. *Political Ideas in Modern India: Thematic Explorations*. New Delhi: Sage.

Meiklejohn, Alexander. 1966. 'Freedom of Speech'. In Peter Radcliff (ed.), *Limits of Liberty: Studies of Mill's 'On Liberty'*, pp. 18–26. Belmont, CA: Wadsworth Publishing Co.

Melville, Casper. 2009. *Taking Offence*. London: Seagull Books.

Metcalf, Barbara D. 1992. 'Imagining Community: Polemical Debates in Colonial India'. In Kenneth W. Jones (ed.), *Religious Controversy in British India: Dialogues in South Asian Languages*, pp. 229–240. New York: State University of New York Press.

Metcalf, Barbara D., & Thomas R. Metcalf. 2012. *A Concise History of Modern India*. New York: Cambridge University Press.

Metcalf, Thomas. 1994. *Ideologies of the Raj*. Cambridge: Cambridge University Press.

Michelman, Frank. 1996. 'Between Facts and Norms by Jurgen Habermas', *Journal of Philosophy*, vol. 93, no. 6, pp. 307–315.

———. 1998. 'Constitutional Authorship'. In Larry Alexander (ed.), *Constitutionalism: Philosophical Foundations*, pp. 64–98. New York: Cambridge University Press.

Mill, J. S. 1978. *On Liberty*. Indianapolis: Hackett Publishing Press.

Modood, Tariq. 2005. *Multicultural Politics: Racism, Ethnicity and Muslims in Britain*. Edinburgh: Edinburgh University Press.

———. 2006. 'The Liberal Dilemma: Integration or Vilification?' *Open Democracy*, 8 February 2006. Available at http://www.opendemocracy.net/content/articles/PDF/3249.pdf (last accessed on 19 September 2018).

Muller, Beate (ed.). 2004. *Censorship and Cultural Regulation in the Modern Age*. Amsterdam: Editions Rodopi.

Nair, Neeti. 2013. 'Beyond the 'Communal' 1920s: The Problem of Intention, Legislative Pragmatism and the Making of Section 295A of the Indian Penal Code', *Indian Economic and Social History Review*, vol. 50, no. 3, pp. 317–340.

Narrain, Siddharth. 2016a. 'The Harm in Hate Speech Laws: Examining the Origins of Hate Speech Legislation in India'. In Rina Ramdev, S. D. Nambiar, and D. Bhattacharya (eds.), *Sentiment, Politics, Censorship: The State of Hurt*, pp. 39–54. New Delhi: Sage.

———. 2016b. 'Hate Speech, Hurt Sentiment and the (Im)Possibility of Free Speech', *Economic and Political Weekly*, vol. 51, no. 17, pp. 119–126.

Nehru, Jawaharlal, 1990. *Letters to Chief Ministers*, 5 vols. G. Parthasarathi (ed.). New Delhi: Oxford University Press.

Noorani, A. G. 1995. 'Informal Censorship', *Economic and Political Weekly*, vol. 30, no. 40, p. 2472.

———. 1999. 'Free Speech and Provocation', *Economic and Political Weekly*, vol. 34, no. 41, p. 2898.

———. 2008. 'Films and Free Speech', *Economic and Political Weekly*, vol. 43, no. 18, pp. 11–12.

O'Dowd, T. John. 2013. 'Pilate's Paramount Duty: Constitutional Reasonableness and the Restriction of Freedom of Expression and Assembly'. In Sunil Khilnani, Vikram Raghavan and Arun K. Thiruvengadam (eds.), *Comparative Constitutionalism in South Asia*, pp. 267–302. New Delhi: Oxford University Press.

Pamment, Claire. 2009. 'The Police of Pig and Sheep: Representations of the White Sahib and the Construction of Theatre Censorship in Colonial India', *South Asian Popular Culture*, vol. 7, no. 3, pp. 233–245.

Parekh, Bhikhu. 1994. 'Superior People: The Narrowness of Liberalism from Mill to Rawls', *Times Literary Supplement*, February 25, pp. 11–13.

———. 2000. *Rethinking Multiculturalism: Cultural Diversity and Political Theory*. Cambridge, MA: Harvard University Press.

———. 2008. 'The Constitution as a Statement of Indian Identity'. In Rajeev Bhargava (ed.), *Politics and Ethics of the Indian Constitution*, pp. 43–58. New Delhi: Oxford University Press.

———. 2012. 'Is There a Case for Banning Hate Speech?' In Michael Herz and Peter Molnar (eds.), *The Content and Context of Hate Speech*, pp. 37–56. New York: Cambridge University Press.

Patel, Vallabhbhai. 1972. *Sardar Patel's Correspondence*, 10 vols. Durga Das (ed.). Ahmedabad: Navjivan Publishing House.

Peel, Lawrence. 1848. *Observations on the Indian Penal Code*. Kolkata: Military Orphan Press.

Philips, C. H., H. L. Singh & B. N. Pandey (eds.). 1962. *The Evolution of India and Pakistan, 1858 and 1947: Select Documents*. London: Oxford University Press.

Pinney, Christopher. 1997. 'The Nation (Un)Pictured? Chromolithography and "Popular" Politics in India, 1878–1995', *Critical Inquiry*, vol. 23, no. 4, pp. 834–867.

———. 2009. 'Iatrogenic Religion and Politics'. In Raminder Kaur and William Mazzarella (eds.), *Censorship in South Asia: Cultural Regulation from Sedition to Seduction*, pp. 29–62. Bloomington and Indianapolis: Indiana University Press.

Pipes, Daniel. 1998. *The Rushdie Affair: The Novel, the Ayatollah and the West*. New Delhi: Voice of India.

Post, Robert. 1988. 'Cultural Heterogeneity and Law: Pornography, Blasphemy and the First Amendment', *California Law Review*, vol. 76, no. 2, pp. 297–335.

———. (ed.). 1998. *Censorship and Silencing: Practices of Cultural Regulation*. Los Angeles: Getty Publications.

———. (ed.). 2007. 'Religion and Freedom of Speech: Portraits of Muhammad', *Constellations*, vol. 14, no. 1, pp. 72–90.

Purandare, Vaibhav. 2002. *The Sena Story*. Mumbai: Business Publications Inc.

Rao, B Shiva. 1966–1968. *The Framing of India's Constitution: Select Documents*, 5 vols. New Delhi: Indian Institute of Public Administration.

Richman, Paula (ed.). 1991. *Many Ramayanas: The Diversity of a Narrative Tradition in South Asia*. Berkeley and Los Angeles: University of California Press.

Robinson, Nick, et al. 2011. 'Interpreting the Constitution: Supreme Court Constitution Benches since Independence', *Economic and Political Weekly*, vol. 46, no. 9, pp. 27–31.

Rosenfeld, M. 2012. 'Hate Speech in Constitutional Jurisprudence: A Comparative Analysis'. In Michael Herz and Peter Molnar (eds.), *The Content and Context of Hate Speech: Rethinking Regulation and Responses*, pp. 242–289. Cambridge: Cambridge University Press.

Roy, Rammohan. 1925. *Raja Ram Mohun Roy: His Life, Writings and Speeches*. Madras: G. A. Natesan.

Said, Edward. 1978. *Orientalism*. London: Routledge and Kegan Paul.

Sapru, Sir Tej Bahadur. 1945. *Constitutional Proposals of the Sapru Committee*, The Sapru Report. Bombay: Padma Prakashan.

Sarkar, Sumit. 1983. *Modern India*. New Delhi: Macmillan.

Seal, Anil. 1968. *The Emergence of Indian Nationalism: Competition and Collaboration in the Late Nineteenth Century*. London: Cambridge University Press.

Setalvad, Teesta. 2011. 'When Hate Speech and Writing Infiltrate Public Discourse Segregation and Discrimination Become the Norm and Rape and War can Always Be Incited in the Name of That Hatred.' Paper presented at *the Expert Workshop for the Asia Pacific organized by the United Nations High Commissioner for Human Rights (OHCHR)*, 6–7 July. Available at http://www.ohchr.org/Documents/Issues/Expression/ICCPR/Bangkok/TeestaSetalvad.pdf (last accessed on 17 June 2018).

Sethi, Aarti, & Shuddhabrata Sengupta. 2014. 'Towards a Readers' Uprising: Reflections in the Wake of Assaults on Books and Authors in Today's India', *India Review*, vol. 13, no. 3, pp. 290–299.

Singh, Piar. 1996. *Gatha Sri Adi Granth and the Controversy*. Grand Ledge: Anant Education and Rural Development Foundation.

Smith, K. J. M. 1991. 'Macaulay's 'Utilitarian' Indian Penal Code: An Illustration of the Accidental Function of Time, Place and Personalities in Law Making'. In W. M. Gordon and T. D. Fergus (ed.), *Legal History in the Making: Proceedings of the Ninth British Legal History Conference, Glasgow, 1989*, pp. 145–164. London: Hambledon Press.

———. 1988. *James Fitzjames Stephen: Portrait of a Victorian Rationalist*. Cambridge: Cambridge University Press.

Sorabjee, Soli J. 1994. 'Freedom of Expression and Censorship: Some Aspects of the Indian Experience,' *Northern Ireland Legal Quarterly*, vol. 45, no. 4, pp. 327–342.

———. 1976. *Law of Press Censorship in India*. Bombay: N. M. Tripathi.
Sridharan, Eswaran, and Anthony Cerulli. 2014. 'Editor's Introduction to the Roundtable on Intellectual Freedom, Vigilantism and Censorship in India', *India Review*, vol. 13, no. 3, pp. 274–276.
Stephen, J. F. 1967. *Liberty, Equality and Fraternity*. Cambridge: Cambridge University Press.
———. 1883. *A History of Criminal Law of England*, vol. III. London: Macmillan and Co.
Stephen, L. 1895. *Life of Sir James Fitzjames Stephen*, 2nd ed. London: Smith, Elder & Co.
Stephens, Julia. 2014. 'The Politics of Muslim Rage: Secular Law and Religious Sentiment in Late Colonial India', *History Workshop Journal*, vol. 77, no. 1, pp. 45–64.
Stokes, Eric. 1959. *English Utilitarians and India*. Oxford: Clarendon Press.
Taylor, Charles. 1989. 'The Rushdie Controversy', *Public Culture*, vol. 2, no. 1, pp. 118–121.
———. 2012. *The Harm in Hate Speech*. London: Harvard University Press.
Thiruvengadam, Arun K. 2013. 'The Evolution of the Constitutional Right to Free Speech in India (1800–1950): The Interplay of Universal and Particular Rationales." University of Washington Trans-Pacific Comparative Constitutional Roundtable, Centre for Asian Legal Studies, National University of Singapore, Working Paper Series. Available at http://papers.ssrn.com/sol3/papers.cfm?abstract_id=2470905 (last accessed on 23 August 2020).
Thursby, G. R. 1975. *Hindu-Muslim Relations in British India*. Leiden: E. J. Brill.
Tsakyrakis, Stavros. 2009. 'Proportionality: An Assault on Human Rights', *International Journal of Constitutional Law*, vol. 7, no. 3, pp. 468–493.
Waldron, Jeremy. 1993. *Liberal Rights*. New York: Cambridge University Press.
———. 2010. 'Dignity and Defamation: The Visibility of Hate, 2009 Oliver Wendell Holmes Lectures', *Harvard Law Review*, vol 123, no. 7, pp. 1596–1657.
———. 2012. *The Harm in Hate Speech*. London: Harvard University Press.
Walker, Samuel. 1994. *Hate Speech: The History of an American Controversy*. London: University of Nebraska Press.
Wilkinson, Steven I. 2005. *Religious Politics and Communal Violence*. Oxford: Oxford University Press.
Wright, Barry. 2011. 'Macaulay's Indian Penal Code: Historical Context and Originating Principles'. In Stanley Yeo Self and Wing-Cheong Chan (ed.), *Codification, Macaulay and The Indian Penal Code: The Legacies and Modern Challenges of Criminal Law Reforms*, pp. 19–55. Surrey: Ashgate.

Government Publications

Constituent Assembly Debates, 12 vols.
Gazette of India (1927)
Lok Sabha Debates (1961, 1969, 2004, 2007)
Parliamentary Debates (1951)
UP State Assembly Debates (1969, 2005)
Rajya Sabha Debates (1961, 1969, 1988, 2006, 2007)

INDEX

Pages in **bold** refer to tables.

MIX
Papier | Fördert
gute Waldnutzung
FSC® C083411

Kolibri 360 GmbH
Ferdinand-Jühlke-Straße 7
99095 Erfurt, Deutschland
produktsicherheit@kolibri360.de

This is a unique collection of chapters explicitly addressing the urgent need for pedagogies for justice in education. Written and compiled by key leaders and members of the *Pedagogies for Justice Research Group* at the University of South Australia, this book provides a comprehensive and diverse set of accounts of researchers working with educators and students in school systems and tertiary institutions to make education a site for positive social change, especially for those who have previously been disadvantaged by the way things are. Arguing that contemporary policy shuts down real opportunities for meaningful and engaged learning, these writers point the ways for inclusive, critical education that matters. Contributors write with the wisdom and the integrity of being there, of 'getting their hands dirty' with leaders, practitioners and students in actual contexts of practices to reimagine and enact just education.

—Emeritus Professor Barbara Comber, OAM, University of South Australia

We are continually subjected to discourses about crisis in schooling. But where such crises are real, where do they actually lie? Who is responsible for them and what are solutions? This book takes forward in conceptually exciting ways the growing momentum of acknowledgement that educational crises in many places issue directly out of policy decisions and out of the refusal of governments to recognise their own failures of the last forty years. Central to this has been a failure to address, and even to actively intensify, educational inequality, while privileging particular versions of knowledge and truth. Nevertheless, while arguing all this, the focus here is on pedagogy. Through presenting the important work of the research group *Pedagogies for Justice*, here we see a focus on pedagogy that moves beyond simplistic universalist approaches, into highlighting issues around engaging disenfranchised learners, the centrality of context, and rethinking curricula and pedagogies that are 'just'. The educational archive of important research that is presented here demonstrates the fundamental importance of teacher inquiry and of curriculum redesign that engages with students' lifeworlds while demanding high intellectual challenge.

—Emeritus Professor Wayne Sawyer, Western Sydney University

Reimagining Just Education

COUNTERPOINTS

Studies in Criticality

Series Editor
Shirley R. Steinberg

VOL. 565

Edited by
Robert Hattam, Robyne Garrett, and Alison Wrench

Reimagining Just Education

PETER LANG
New York · Berlin · Bruxelles · Chennai · Lausanne · Oxford

Bibliographic information published by the Deutsche Nationalbibliothek
The German National Library lists this publication in the German National Bibliography; detailed bibliographic data is available on the Internet at https://dnb.dnb.de

Library of Congress Cataloging-in-Publication Data
Names: Hattam, Robert editor | Garrett, Robyne editor | Wrench, Alison, 1956- editor
Title: Reimagining just education / Edited by Robert Hattam, Robyne Garrett, and Alison Wrench.
Description: New York : Peter Lang, 2026. | Series: Counterpoints: studies in criticality, 1058-1634; Volume 565 | Includes bibliographical references and index.
Identifiers: LCCN 2026013973 (print) | LCCN 2026013974 (ebook) | ISBN 9783034359382 paperback | ISBN 9783034359825 pdf | ISBN 9783034359832 epub
Subjects: LCSH: Education and state--Australia | Motivation in education--Australia | Social justice and education--Australia | Culturally relevant pedagogy--Australia | Curriculum change--Australia
Classification: LCC LC96 .R45 2026 (print) | LCC LC96 (ebook)
LC record available at https://lccn.loc.gov/2026013973
LC ebook record available at https://lccn.loc.gov/2026013974

Cover image by Robert Hattam

ISSN 1058-1634
ISBN 978-3-0343-5938-2 (Print)
ISBN 978-3-0343-5982-5 (ePDF)
ISBN 978-3-0343-5983-2 (ePUB)
DOI 10.3726/ b22980

Published by Peter Lang Publishing Inc., New York, USA

info@peterlang.com

This publication has been peer reviewed.

www.peterlang.com

Contact for General Product Safety Regulation (GPSR): gpsr@peterlang.com

We dedicate this book to Michelle Hogan (1959–2023)

Acknowledgment of Country

We acknowledge that the chapters in this volume were written on Kaurna, Peramangk, Narungga, Bunganditj, and Ngarrindjeri Country, and that sovereignty for these lands has never been ceded. We pay our respects to Elders past, present, and future, and to the lands, skies, and waters, where we live, learn, and raise young people. Their generosity, wisdom, and guidance as sharers of knowledge enriches our practices, our lives, and our thinking.

Contents

Figures and Tables

Acknowledgments

We would like to acknowledge the work of our colleagues published here for their contribution over the past decade or so in sustaining the Pedagogies for Justice Research Group. This group provided a site for collaborative academic reading, co-construction of research designs, mentoring of early career researchers and doctoral students, collaborative conference presentations, access to schools for research, and negotiations for ethics with education jurisdictions. Perhaps more importantly this group provided a site for nurturing of critical educational sociology and academic friendships. As such the group contests the individualizing of academic work that is now rife across the university sector and instead is informed by the relational turn in the social sciences and a philosopher of the "good friend" (Aristotle).

This book publishes research accounts that have been funded by the Australian Research Council and these include the following:

- Rigney, L-I. & Hattam R. (2017–2019) Towards a Culturally Responsive Pedagogy (Indigenous Discovery Grant; IN170100017)
- Rigney, L-I., Hattam R., Kelly, S., M. Zembylas, Schulz, S., & Memon, N. (2022–2024) Culturally Responsive Schooling [Project ID: DP220100651]
- Rigney, L. (2006) Indigenous Research Methodologies: Frameworks toward Indigenous Intellectual Sovereignty and the Decolonisation of Research [Project ID: DI0348109]
- Stahl, G. (2017–2021) How First in the Family Males Transition to and Experience Australian University [Project Id: DE170100510].

Introduction

Robert Hattam, Robyne Garrett, and Alison Wrench

> Education may well be, as of right, the instrument whereby every individual, in a society like our own, can gain access to any kind of discourse. But we well know that in its distribution, in what it permits and in what it prevents, it follows the well-trodden battle-lines of social conflict. Every educational system is a political means of maintaining or of modifying the appropriation of discourse, with the knowledge and the powers it carries with it.
>
> (FOUCAULT, 1972, P. 227)

> That cause calls us to teach.
>
> (PINAR, 2015, P. 138)

Introducing the Pedagogies for Justice Research Group

State and federal government policy now dumbs down schooling and teacher education through various means including "cruel accounting," standards-driven codifications of good teaching, and curriculum frameworks that fail to foreground the key struggles of the age. Why isn't capitalism a topic in the national curriculum, why isn't living sustainably more prominent, and why is telling the story about Australian colonization so controversial? And in concert, governments rely heavily on the "school effectiveness" paradigm that pushes de-contextualized knowledge dressed up as a discourse of what-works best practice and over-inflated claims to provide the "right answer" for all manner of educational problems.

Australian education policy now preaches a one-size-fits-all solution for teachers and for educational leaders, assumes an unproblematic process of implementation, and then criticizes those working in so-called disadvantaged schools for failing to be "good." In the name of policy compliance, teachers are increasingly being pushed toward highly scripted and ritualized pedagogies that just do not work, as they grapple with a dissonance between policy and reality. Consequently, teachers' work is today being framed by a "dangerous incoherence" (Max-Neef, 1991, p. 109) between the language of power, the language that operates as a *regime of truth*, and the historical reality. The regime of truth in this case is produced by what Havel (1991) refers to as "evasive thinking," or "an immobile system of intellectual and phraseological schemata which ... without noticing it, separate[s] thought from its immediate contact with reality and thus cripples its capacity to intervene in that reality" (p. 11). For us, the most significant failure of policy is the intensifying of educational inequality, which is also the educational correlate of rising economic inequality (Piketty, 2022) that mostly goes un-noted or, worse, gets hidden in a culture war where those of us who raise the issues are seen to be pushing a politics of envy (Frye, 2016). This dangerous incoherence is felt most by students attending Australian public schools, who are increasingly becoming residualized.

In this edited book we argue that we are now involved in a struggle over the soul of educators and that means resisting the neoliberalizing policy regime that mostly governs through asserting a narrow, technicist, and individualistic definition of what it means to be a good teacher (Ball, 2016; Green et al., 2017). We are all now being rendered "autonomous and responsible" (Rose, 1999, p. 154) and for educators' work that means intensification, proletarianization, de-professionalization (Smyth et al., 2000), and precariatization (Jenkins et al., 2017). But then we can resist through local forms of radical collegium (Fielding, 1999). The sort of collegium that has been the context for this edited collection is informed by Fielding's (1999) critique of teacher collaboration and includes a suspicion of enforced or institutionalized collegiality designed to improve productivity and ensure policy compliance.

This edited collection takes up this possibility through reporting on the workings of the Pedagogies for Justice Research Group at the University of South Australia. This group is the latest iteration of a small group of socially critical educational researchers who collectively have an international reputation for both critical pedagogy studies, and critical practitioner research approaches. The book represents the recent development of our collective research program, which is focused on three key ideas: (1) responding to the educational disengagement of disenfranchised learners; (2) providing hopeful alternative accounts of socially critical pedagogies in different sites, including primary and secondary schools, teacher education programs, and foundation studies programs; and (3) rethinking curriculum and pedagogy across the curriculum.

This collection is novel in many ways. Perhaps most importantly, there are few attempts to bring together the research of a collection of scholars all working in one research group in a collective research program that is itself continually being co-constructed. The research reported is framed up by a *critical sensibility* that we understand in these terms: a skepticism toward common-sense and official knowledge; a sensitivity toward how power works on and through knowing and subjectivity; and a commitment to more socially just societies (Smyth et al., 2014, p. 68).

The book shares scholarship from senior researchers, mid-career, early career, and a few doctoral students. The chapters provide a place-based case study of research being conducted in one small Australian city, but also demonstrate how a collection of local qualitative studies connect to an international archive of critical educational research. Across this set of chapters, we argue for research that: (1) is committed to critical practitioner approaches and hence is conducted with students, teachers, and school leaders; and (2) argues for pedagogies that demand high intellectual challenge; are dialogic and improvisational (in the jazz sense); are committed to ensuring that classrooms are culturally safe; and develop critically literate active citizens.

The group originally formed in 2012, emerging out of a previous successful research group, the Centre for Studies in Literacy, Policy and Learning Cultures. The Pedagogies for Justice Research Group has met regularly since that time and has been affiliated with institutionally recognized research centers.[1]

This first chapter provides some context for this work by providing a brief reading of contemporary teacher education in Australia, theorizing a research group as a site for counter-conduct, locating research primarily in the northern suburbs of Adelaide, outlining a rationale, and briefly introducing the chapters. The rationale section makes the case for focusing on pedagogies for justice, which we understand to be code for our version of critical pedagogy studies, as well as a brief statement about how teacher education is being (mis)governed of late. The authors mostly work in teacher education studies, and hence a number of the chapters give an account of research that informs their own teaching but are also pertinent to others working in education, such as schoolteachers, early childhood educators, and policy actors who are willing to read outside of the very narrow archive that now informs the failing national education policy.

The Struggle Over What Constitutes Teacher Education in Australia

There have been over 100 reviews of initial teacher education (ITE) in Australia since the 1970s (Mayer, 2014). This intense evaluation of ITE suggests a deep mistrust of both the institution of ITE and teacher educators (Cochran-Smith et al., 2018). When ITE is framed by deficit discourses it is constructed as a *policy problem* requiring governmental solutions (Cochran-Smith et al., 2018; Levinsson et al., 2020; Rowe & Skourdoumbis, 2019). At issue are tensions around control, purposes, and practices of education, as well as visions of "good" (Rowe & Skourdoumbis, 2019), "classroom-ready," and "quality" teachers (Charteris & Dargusch, 2018; Hardy, 2018a, 2018b).

---

[1] At the time of writing, we are part of the Centre for Research in Educational and Social Inclusion, https://www.unisa.edu.au/research/research-in-educational-and-social-inclusion/

In recent times there has been an intensification of deficit discourses about teachers and teacher education and, concomitantly, escalation of calls for ITE reform (Cochran-Smith et al., 2018; Hardy, 2018a; Rowe & Skourdoumbis, 2019). This assault is framed by the historically contingent convergence of neoliberal discourses and neo-conservative agendas (Apple, 2004; Reid, 2020). Of consequence are policy "regimes of truth" (Foucault, 1980, p. 131) that tie education, including ITE, to national economic priorities, security, and prosperity. There is a corresponding trend toward reinforcing supposed traditional and/or national values and imperatives (Apple, 2004). This backlash agenda (Guitierrez et al., 2002) works to move education policy away from social democratic principles for just education toward more authoritarian framings (Cochran-Smith et al. 2018).

The consequences of this agenda include the development of intensified forms of accountability as technologies for governing (Zembylas, 2018). Foucault (1982) contends that to govern is to shape or direct the possible action of others relative to particular and calculated ends. Professional standards, for instance, exemplify governmental technologies, which seek to *fix*, control, and audit the conduct of ITE programs, teacher educators, and pre-service teachers in the name of national security (Charteris & Dargusch, 2018; Cochran-Smith et al., 2018; Rowe & Skourdoumbis, 2019).

Within the Australian context, graduate teacher registration is now premised on meeting three mandated requirements (Rowe & Skourdoumbis, 2019). Pre-service teachers must: pass the National Literacy and Numeracy Test (Gore et al., 2016); provide a portfolio evincing attainment of all 37 Professional Standards for Graduate Teachers (AITSL, 2020); and pass the Teaching Performance Assessment, embedded in a capstone course and practicum (Stacey et al., 2020). Such a regime unproblematically assumes that pre-service teacher learning is quantifiable in relation to measurable skills and practices (Wrench & Paige, 2020). Significant concerns include the de-professionalization of ITE via overly prescriptive and technicizing accounts of what programs and educators as well as pre-service teachers should do, improve, and enact (Gore et al., 2016; Hardy, 2018a, 2018b; Rowe & Skourdoumbis, 2019).

This regime of accountability represents a deliberate move away from reflexive and generative conceptions of teaching as well as marginalization of social justice issues and pedagogical approaches for meeting the needs of diverse student learners (Sleeter, 2008). As Bates and Townsend (2007) contend, ITE should not be tied to the dictates of the economy alone but be sufficiently independent to develop informed practices within open climates that also recognize what is needed to create a more just society. Moreover, teacher educators who adhere to socially critical perspectives call for approaches to ITE that embed principles of justice, critically reflective practices, and participatory inquiry as means to disrupt the hegemony of marketizing approaches to education (Cochran-Smith et al., 2018). We align with Cochran-Smith and colleagues (2018) in calling for the reclaiming of accountability in ITE so that it serves strong versions of equity, justice, and democracy.

Justice-oriented teacher educators understand that it is their responsibility to work with pre-service teachers in supportive and critical ways (Hagevik et al., 2012) that

- challenge the taken-for-granted and homogenizing effects of schooling
- help develop capacities to reflect and investigate pedagogical practices
- encourage collaborative learning environments where peers can be critical friends.

We argue for socially just and strongly democratic ITE programs that are capable of preparing ethical, socially critical teachers (see Wrench & Garrett, 2015; Wrench & Paige, 2020). Important here is the demand to support pre-service teachers in negotiating equity, including Indigenous perspectives and capabilities to teach in disadvantaged communities (Hattam et al., 2018). A significant challenge is countering deficit views of ITE, as well as demeaning accountability measures, including professional standards and narrow versions of literacy and numeracy. After all, as Reid (2019) argues, these only provide "proxy evidence of teaching" (p. 717) and may even work against the preparation of educators who can work well with all of Australia's children.

Additionally, the ITE policy regime pushes decontexualized truth claims about *what works*. As a counter-narrative, we argue for taking context seriously and, with that in mind, the next section briefly outlines important educational research that has been conducted in the northern suburbs of Adelaide. This region is significant, as the University of South Australia has historically served the communities of the northern suburbs where we have long-term commitments to conducting social justice–oriented research in public schools.

Researching in "the North"

The academic underachievement of students from disadvantaged backgrounds, including the northern suburbs of Adelaide, is an ongoing and unresolved problem in Australia (Goodman et al., 2012). Unfortunately, neoliberal educational policies that purport to provide "remedies" offer little insight or hope for the future. In 2018, the Australian federal government identified that: (1) "the performance of Australian students [has] declined at all levels of achievement compared to international benchmarks"; at the same time there exists (2) "an unacceptable link between low levels of achievement and educational disadvantage, particularly among students from low socioeconomic ... backgrounds" (Senate Select Committee on School Funding, 2014). While recent Programme for International Student Assessment comparisons support these downward trends (Thomson et al., 2019), there is also mounting evidence that Australia has one of the most unequal education systems among the OECD countries (Bruckauf & Chzhen, 2016). Students with backgrounds of disadvantage are significantly less likely to complete their schooling and have increased dropout rates and expulsions (Banks & Meyer, 2017). Beyond the personal, social, and economic costs to individual students and their families, there are profound costs to Australia's economic growth as a knowledge-based society.

This situation poses serious policy and practice problems for those leading and teaching in what are often referred to as "disadvantaged schools" that serve vulnerable communities with high rates of poverty. These schools face profound challenges in meeting the needs of many of their students, who do not live in economically stable middle-class families. As such, the chapters in this collection argue for contextualized understandings of schooling and specifically for thinking about *place* as context (Comber, 2015). In what follows we present a brief reading of a collection of ethnographically informed studies conducted in the northern suburbs. These schools serve one of the most socio-economically and educationally disadvantaged urban regions of Australia and hence provide a notable and global exemplar of the workings of neoliberal policy logic as well as a pressing need for reform.

The region north of Adelaide expanded into substantial suburbs after World War II and more intensely in the 1950s and 1960s with migration of "ten-pound poms." The region was often understood as a social experiment in welfare state social policy and especially public housing (Peel, 1995). A General Motors car factory and military training facilities boosted employment options. Since the 1960s, the North, as it is known colloquially, was settled by a range of immigrants and those settled in Australia through our humanitarian refugee programs, including Vietnamese, Khmer, Bosnian, and Serbian, with further settlements from Sudan, Somalia, Bhutan, and Afghanistan. The local economy of the North was hit hard by the recessions of 1981 and 1991 and more recently with the closure of General Motors such that the area is now characterized by significant poverty, unemployment, and ill health and is described as "one of the top three sites of social exclusion in Australia" (Hattam et al., 2009, p. 305).

Over this time, a number of educational research studies documented what was happening in northern schools during the emergence of neoliberalism as the dominant policy rationale for schooling. During the time of the federally funded Disadvantaged Schools Project (known as Priority Projects in South Australia) research included "Information Technology: Literacy and Educational Disadvantage Project," "100 Children go to School" (Hill et al., 1998), "Making Hope Practical" (McInerney, 2004) and "Schooling the Rustbelt Kids" (Thomson, 2002). In the last decade or so studies have included "Redesigning Pedagogy in the North" (Prosser et al., 2010), the "Aspirations Project" (Bok, 2010; Hattam et al., 2012; Smith, 2011), a series of doctoral studies in educational leadership (Rogers, 2013; Semmens, 2014), and "Literacy, Leading and Learning" (Hayes et al., 2017). Many of these studies facilitated research methods that enabled teacher inquiry and redesign of curriculum, engaged with student life-world funds of knowledge, and advocated performative expressions of learning. This archive of research provides an account of a number of continuities and discontinuities that require attention and acknowledgment. The continuities include:

- Income inequality is highly regional in nature and the socio-economic context of the northern suburbs remains one of the most disadvantaged in Australia. Also persistent is a correlation between low SES background and school failure.
- Teachers' work has intensified through demands for performativity (Smyth et al., 2000), loss of autonomy (Gerrard & Farrell, 2014), the normalizing of scripted forms of teaching (Lingard, 2007), and casualization of the teaching workforce (Standing, 2012).
- Schooling continues to reproduce social stratification and hence educational inequality (Connell, 2002; Connell et al., 1982). The neoliberal *sorting and sifting* of young people meant that the equity gains of the 1970s and 1980s have not been sustained and Australian schooling is more inequitable than ever (Teese, 2000).
- Teachers are still key actors in schools; however, they are increasingly silenced or ignored in policy debates. The paradox is that policy must be enacted by teachers who are positioned as technicians rather than intellectuals and expected to implement the "right" pedagogy developed elsewhere and out of context.
- Schools and teachers can still innovate when enabling conditions are met.

The discontinuities include:

- Neoliberal policy logic now pervades global institutions, foregrounding a marketizing logic as a key organizing principle. In educational sites, this shift is driven through demands for performativity including teacher standards and high-stakes testing of students. Schooling is seriously damaged by these policy technologies that now drive decreasing student attainment and widening inequality (Appel, 2020).

- Outside of high-stakes testing enhancement measures, professional development for teachers has diminished significantly. In particular, for those teachers working with vulnerable communities, there are few to no professional development opportunities that support them in managing the complex nature of their work.
- A considerable shift in government funding to the private sector (Rowe, 2016) during the Howard Government years has resulted in a movement of students from public to private schooling in a bid to secure better outcomes and life chances. The residualizing effect of these changes means that disadvantaged students are now concentrated disproportionately in government/public schools, thus compounding disadvantage for disadvantaged students.

It seems that contemporary times are characterized by a serious conflict between the dominant neoliberal framing of schooling policy and the existential challenges of life in schools in disadvantaged areas. While policy asserts one-size-fits-all solutions based on evidence that is decontextualized, abstracted, and allegedly universal, these assertions simply do not match the real-world sites of poverty and disadvantage. More than ever, we need critical and practical research that is dedicated solely and purely to improving educational outcomes for young people in situ.

Advocating Pedagogies of Justice

> Unless we solve the pedagogy problem, all other efforts at reconstruction … will be in vain.
>
> (BOOMER, 1999, P. 136)

In Australia today, the urgent (inter)national problem of social injustice and schooling has been ignored. Unfortunately, Australian schooling is now driven by a policy regime that is failing on four counts: (1) declining levels of achievement, as indicated by international benchmarks (Gonski et al., 2018); (2) strong links between low levels of achievement and educational disadvantage, particularly for students from low socio-economic backgrounds (Senate Select Committee on School Funding, 2014); (3) a serious teacher shortage (Mason & Poyatos Matas, 2015); and (4) fewer aspiring leaders (Thomson, 2009). More specifically, school devolution policy, which often goes by the term the "self-managing school," is subsumed by a one-size-fits-all logic that, by definition, cannot account for local context (Smyth, 2011). So too parental choice policies are increasingly detrimental to the public provision of schooling and contribute to the residualization of schools serving high-poverty communities (Teese, 2011). More importantly, pushing parental choice policies ignores the fact that many parents do not have a choice (Lamb, 2007). Meanwhile, the standardization of curriculum pushes teachers to take up highly scripted forms of pedagogy that seem unsuited to local needs, especially in schools serving high-poverty communities (Hardy, 2018a, 2018b). In addition, high-stakes testing undermines alternative measures of good practice and pushes teachers toward narrow and unproductive definitions of what counts as literacy and numeracy, at a time when Australia really needs to be advancing a highly developed knowledge economy (Comber & Woods, 2016), and producing citizens capable of critical literacy in a post-truth media landscape (Barton, 2019).

But that said, in Australia there has been a long history of social justice research in schools and for the past few decades this research has been framed in the field of curriculum studies. Putting this logic most succinctly, the curriculum is *the* site of struggle for social justice in schooling (Connell, 2002; Connell et al., 1982, 1991). This logic has been pursued in terms of a politics of "curricular justice" (Connell, 1993, p. 19). Such "curricular justice" logic, as defined by Connell (1993, p. 298), centers on: (1) the interests of the least advantaged; (2) participation and common schooling; and (3) the historical production of schooling.

But then the field has shifted recently with the emergence of what Green (2003, p. 18) calls the "New Pedagogy Studies." "These days, the big 'buzz word' is pedagogy" (Green, 2003, p. 16) and the debates about curriculum have been shifting toward thinking about pedagogical justice (Hattam & Zipin, 2009). Such a shift to pedagogy studies is also evident in the emergence of named pedagogy journals, such as *Pedagogies: An International Journal*, and the name change of the journal *Curriculum Studies* to *Pedagogy, Culture and Society*. As well, in Australian education studies, a number of large pedagogy-focused research projects were initiated such as "Pedagogies of Multiliteracies" (New London Group, 1996), "Productive Pedagogies" (Hayes et al., 2006), "Quality Teaching" (Ladwig, 2007), "Turn-Around Pedagogies" (Comber & Kamler, 2005), and "Redesigning Pedagogies in the North Project" (Hattam et al., 2009).

> Against those who would consolidate narrow views of what constitutes pedagogy—with instrumentalist claims to scientific objectivity—New Pedagogy Studies argues that pedagogy cannot be reduced to teaching methods or styles ... In thus mobilising the term

> "pedagogy" to bring into view varied frameworks for practice, New Pedagogy Studies unsettles moves to prescribe what teachers do, such as defining teaching in terms of "transmission of politically-selected knowledge with the aid of a psychological vision of what can be taught according to students' skills and capacities" (Hamilton & Zufiaurre, 2000, p. 5). (Hattam & Zipin, 2009, p. 298)

The term *pedagogy* is a keyword in the field of education and increasingly in the related fields of cultural studies, media studies, and social theory more generally (Morton & Zavarzadeh, 1991). The term pedagogy, or pedagogue, often calls up derision or gets "associated with deviancy and a profession that needed to be brought under political control" (Edwards, 2001, p. 164). But then the ubiquity of *pedagogy* makes it impossible to codify—certainly impossible to draft a universally applicable definition. In the words of Stuart Hall (1983), "[t]here is no general pedagogy, only pedagogies" (p. 6). Being pedagogical of course does not even have to be planned. Its ubiquity is most evident in the trope "learning from experience"—there is no time in which learning is not possible and hence we are in pedagogical relations with the world, so to speak. And this definitional problem is also evident if we consider the various sites of "public pedagogy" that are now so significant (Giroux, 2004). As well, all social movements are involved in political/pedagogical work (Hattam & Atkinson, 2006), as are key cultural institutions such as museums (Crowley & Matthews, 2006). Resisting a general theory of pedagogy, though, does not discount attempts to theorize the pedagogy of school teaching. Such pedagogies are planned and are understood in terms of a performance in which one can become more proficient.

With these political imperatives in mind, it seems obvious that one of the many possible theoretical and practical projects that New Pedagogy Studies presents is the urgent need to advance the notion of pedagogical justice. Unfortunately, contemporary policies seem to be going in the wrong direction with both of these imperatives (Au, 2008). To quote from Hayes et al. (2009): "the link between educational outcomes and social background continues to be misunderstood as representing some kind of 'natural' relationship between socio-economic disadvantage and school failure" (p. 252). While such deficit thinking has been comprehensively challenged (see, e.g., Hattam & Prosser, 2008; Lareau, 1987) there has still been a return "to blaming the poor for their lack of success at school" (Hayes et al., 2009, p. 252).

What do we know about "actually existing pedagogies" (Lingard, 2007, p. 246) that dominate in such schools? Without being extensive, recent Australian studies such as the "Queensland Longitudinal Study," the "Changing Schools Changing Times Project," and "Redesigning Pedagogies in the North" provide useful findings. For example, Lingard (2007) refers to the dominant pedagogies as "pedagogies of indifference" or "pedagogies of the same": summarized as being strong in care for students, but they mostly "fail to work with and across differences," and also "fail to make a difference in their lack of both intellectual demand and connectedness to the world" (p. 246) (see also Hayes et al., 2006). This view was confirmed by Hayes et al. (2009): "classroom practices are very traditional, following predictable routines, and are largely unsuccessful as far as formal learning is concerned" (pp. 251–252) (see also Connell et al., 1991). Hayes et al. (2009) argue that "these conditions may be widespread and not limited to high-poverty contexts. However, in challenging circumstances, more is riding on the efficacy of classroom practice because poor families are highly dependent on schooling for their educational resources" (p. 252). Our own research confirms that pedagogy in a normal(izing) school is characterized by an over-reliance on worksheet pedagogy; low expectations of students learning, which is compensated for by high expectations of student behavior; low levels of choice in classroom learning tasks and assessment; and little explicit teaching of school literate practices. Put simply, "normalizing" curriculum and pedagogy are often uninspiring and even alienating (Hattam & Prosser, 2008; Hattam et al., 2015; Smyth & Hattam, 2004; Smyth et al., 2003; Zipin et al., 2012).

But then, as Hayes et al. (2009) argue:

> [t]he key issue is not what kinds of pedagogies improve educational outcomes but how to support the development of the kinds of pedagogies that we have good reason to believe will work. As in the past, the sticking point remains practice. (p. 253)

They point out that the present model for improving pedagogy involves adopting the institutionally supported framework (New Basics, Quality Teaching or the Teaching for Effective Learning Framework)—all that is required is adopting the framework faithfully into your context. This model shows no sign of being successful in disadvantaged schools, as it is local knowledge about practice that largely determines what kinds of pedagogies get adopted. Consequently, "improvement relies upon being able to develop new knowledge about what is possible in these contexts and that this is primarily a pedagogical challenge associated with supporting the professional learning of teachers and leaders" (Hayes et al., 2009, p. 263).

Importantly also, the above description of normal practice does not account for the pedagogical innovations being practiced in schools. As Hayes et al. (2009) point out, "disadvantaged schools" have a few teachers who do make a difference; whose pedagogies enable students to learn challenging relevant tasks that lead to success in the mainstream game of school. In a similar vein, there are examples of teachers whose professional development experiences have led to the sorts of "turn around" documented by Comber and Kamler (2005). The idea of turnaround pedagogies involves, in the first instance, confronting deficit views of students, which then acts as a provocation for curriculum and pedagogical redesigns, leading to a subsequent turnaround of student learning. Such research points to the urgent need to study teachers who are actually making a difference in challenging school contexts, and to research "the complexities of producing sustainable pedagogical and curriculum change" (Comber & Kamler, 2006, p. 21). Simply put, we need to be researching teachers' engagement in the process of redesigning pedagogy (Bokhorst-Heng et al., 2006). In which case, the research focus is not mapping pedagogy *per se*, but instead researching the possibilities for pedagogical innovation in public schools serving low socio-economic status school communities.

The shift to a focus on pedagogy studies was also driven by a demand to reinvigorate critical pedagogy studies and hence also to advocate pedagogical justice, or the more simply named pedagogies for justice (Gur-Ze'ev, 2005; McLaren & Kincheloe, 2007; Popkewitz & Fendler, 1999; Trifonas, 2003). Critical pedagogy as an educational movement can also be understood in terms of an ongoing conceptual reinvigoration from various theoretical sources and sites of empirical research. The research program that drives the Pedagogy for Justice Research Group works with critical pedagogy as a conceptual framework that is understood as a significant educational movement that is neither monolithic nor coherent, and one that is open to ongoing reflexivity. Given that critical pedagogy draws conceptual resources from critical social theory, critical pedagogy now reflects the ongoing rejuvenation of critical social theory from sources such as feminism, postcolonial theory, antiracism, Indigenous studies, queer theory, post-structuralism, contemporary historical materialism, and liberation theology.

The broad contours of critical pedagogy are provided by Gore's (1993) analysis of two strands of "critical pedagogy": one that she rightly argues is "not critical *pedagogy*, but [rather] critical *educational theory*" (p. 42); and the other that "makes pedagogy the central concern" (p. 42). The first provides an abstract political vision and an elaboration of pedagogy as politics but provides compelling explanations for social injustice and often draws on critical policy sociology. The later "offers concrete suggestions and examples taken from … pedagogical practice" (p. 40), "that is, pedagogy as the politics of classroom practice" (p. 42) and now draws on new pedagogy studies. On a related point, borrowing from Westbury et al. (2020), the term pedagogy now operates at two distinct levels: at the level of pedagogical discourse (policy and research) and the classroom level (pedagogy as it is lived). The field of education presently suffers a disjuncture between these two in which far too little attention has been paid to how research should be "translated into a continuum that embraces curriculum-as-plan and pedagogy-as-praxis" (Hamilton & Zufiaurre, 2000, p. 4). This disjuncture also means that teachers often conflate pedagogy with teaching or teaching and learning. The term "pedagogy" is being mobilized by "critical pedagogy" to unsettle the too-easy move to conflate what teachers do to a prescription of methods, and instead, brings into view various frameworks for practice. Invoking the term pedagogy foregrounds the *why* questions, and links classroom practice explicitly to debates over purposes, and resists defining teaching in terms of transmission of knowledge in the hope of developing students' skills and capacities.

The critical pedagogy literature provides a diagnosis of a key pedagogical challenge, especially for those concerned with learning outcomes in schools serving low socio-economic status school communities, and we will rehearse that debate here.

Bourdieu (1977) argues that people enter schooling with differing qualities and degrees of "cultural capital," embodied as "habitus" (i.e., internalized subconscious dispositions acquired through practical immersion in prior social-cultural habitats of their lives). However, in schools these dispositions receive greater or lesser capital value depending on how near or far they are to standard cultural codes that dominate mainstream curriculum, pedagogy, and assessment (Bourdieu & Passeron, 1990). Delpit's (1988) theory of the "culture of power" in classrooms offers an alternative view of the way schooling works to exclude or silence students from disenfranchised/disadvantaged communities. She argues that many students experience cultural dissonance in the classroom, or in the words of Freebody et al. (1995), they experience "interactive trouble." The "trouble" arises because the vernacular knowledges and everyday experiences of some students are absent, misrepresented, or muted in the curriculum. In some cases, the trouble is obvious (e.g., for Aboriginal students having to study racist texts), but more often, the trouble is more subtle. For Delpit (1988), schools tend to naturalize and normalize the "codes and rules" of those who already have power in society, and this includes "linguistic forms, communicative strategies, and presentation of self; that is, ways of talking, ways of writing, ways of dressing and ways of interacting" (p. 283). Those students who arrive at school with the "accoutrements of the culture of power" (p. 283) are more likely to be successful at school because they already have access to the codes and rules of school literacy. For "disadvantaged" students, the gap between their vernacular literacies and school literacy requires explicit teaching, which too often is not forthcoming. For these students, the daily experiences of "interactive trouble" are explained to them in terms of their own deficits rather than the failure of school to acknowledge and respond to the cultural dissonance. Having to internalize the trouble year after year makes schooling for disadvantaged young people just impossible to bear, especially when the demands of schooling increase so dramatically in the later years. "They need to defend themselves against performance demands which may mean sabotage or silence" (Smyth & Hattam, 2004, p. 110), neither option leading to much success at school. The Bourdieu/Delpit analyses provide a clear direction for teachers committed to social inclusion through schooling, but one that that is certainly a challenge. In the first instance, quoting Delpit (1998), "we must keep the perspective that people are experts on their own lives ... they can be the only authentic chroniclers of their own experience" (p. 297). But that is not enough. Students must be "helped to acknowledge their own 'expertness'" as they are "assisted in learning the culture of power" (p. 296). Curricular and pedagogical balance must be struck between (a) inclusive use of the funds of knowledge that diverse students bring to school; and (b) effective learning of the "codes" and "rules" necessary for success in mainstream schooling (Zipin & Brennan, 2001).

For the members of the Pedagogies for Justice Research Group, the above rationale translates into the following set of questions that animate the chapters that follow:

- How can we develop better explanations for the persistent nature of educational inequality in Australia, especially related to poverty, racism, and cultural difference?
- How can we improve professional practice in high-poverty and complex educational contexts in which "normal" practice is less likely to work?
- What do we know about actually existing pedagogies?
- How might we understand education institutions as the site of reform?
- If developing new pedagogy is not a problem of adoption but of learning new practice, how might we support the professional learning of teachers and leaders through practitioner inquiry?
- In disadvantaged schools there are teachers who do make a difference: what characterizes their pedagogy?
- What are the possibilities for pedagogical innovation in educational settings serving low socio-economic status communities?
- What are the logics of educational policy, and specifically how is the idea of social justice understood?
- What are the effects of education policy on educators' work?
- How does globalization impact on education policy processes?
- How do we understand the relationships between what Bernstein refers to as the three message systems of education: curriculum, pedagogy, and assessment?

- How do we understand the identity work of educators, including pre-service, practicing teachers, academics, and educational leaders?
- What research methodologies and conceptual frameworks are capable of advancing pedagogies for justice/sustainability?
- How do educators contribute to social and ecological sustainability?
- How do we support transdisciplinary learning?

The book comprises three parts: "Engaging Disenfranchised Learners" (Part 1); "Engaging in Different Sites" (Part 2); and "Rethinking Just Curriculum and Pedagogy" (Part 3). The final chapter provides a summary of the critique offered in this collection and ends with some directions for enacting pedagogies for justice in Australian schools.

The seven chapters in Part 1 center on different groups of traditionally disenfranchised learners, including those from working-class backgrounds, first in family to university, Muslim learners, Aboriginal learners, those involved in flexible learning options and young people as twenty-first-century learners. Collectively the chapters explore different policy implications and curriculum limitations as well as the impact of deficit assumptions for groups and individuals. They direct attention to the importance of taking seriously context, emotional capital, spiritual ways of knowing, demythologizing pedagogy, program effectiveness, and drivers for educational change to create possibilities for emancipatory participation and engagement.

The six chapters in Part 2 are connected through the theme of advocating the enactment of critical pedagogies in various sites including the bodies of students and their cultural frames, contexts of superdiversity, remote communities, initial teacher education, alternative pathways to higher education, leadership, and school communities. Although the chapters focus on different contexts and locations, they present a commonality of ideas around resisting policy and practice that limit the engagement, control, and agency of learners and teachers. The chapters focus their attention on the impact of dominant conceptualizations of didactic teaching, backlash pedagogies, and explicit instruction for diverse learners to reveal more responsive and imaginative pedagogies that are vital for rebuilding pedagogy in these sites. Arguments are made for dialogic, embodied, and improvisational approaches that attend to the role of bodies and affect in learning, conceptualize an ethics of listening to young people and their communities, recognize students and their cultural and spiritual frames, navigate a neoliberal context with a progressive agenda, and seriously engage with students as researchers of their life worlds.

The eight chapters in Part 3 focus on the notion of developing progressive pedagogies that disrupt dominant approaches and reimagine just pedagogies in transformative ways. With theoretical resources broadly located across the spectrum of justice, affect, decoloniality, and cultural responsiveness, they consider how the reproduction of dominant ideas perpetuates colonizing, inequitable, and unsustainable practice. Each of the chapters brings new conceptual and practical approaches to what is (and can be) done in the name of critical pedagogy. They include pedagogical approaches that focus on justice, sustainable human living, critical visual and film analysis, embodied and visual arts, pedagogies of discomfort, and key ideas underpinning a vision of culturally responsive pedagogy. Collectively the chapters in this book make *visible* the possibilities for mobilizing and advancing a critical agenda.

Bibliography

Appel, M. (2020). Performativity and the demise of the teaching profession: The need for rebalancing in Australia. *Asia-Pacific Journal of Teacher Education*, *48*(3), 301–15.

Apple, M. (2004). Creating difference: Neo-liberalism, neo-conservatism and the politics of educational reform. *Educational Policy*, *18*(1), 12–44.

Au, W. (2008). *Unequal by design: High-stakes testing and the standardization of inequality*. Routledge.

Australian Institute for Teaching and School Leadership (AITSL). (2020). *Teaching Performance Assessment*. https://www.aitsl.edu.au/deliver-ite-programs/teaching-performance-assessment

Ball, S. (2016). Subjectivity as a site of struggle: Refusing neoliberalism? *British Journal of Sociology of Education*, *37*(8), 1129–46.

Banks, Y., & Meyer, J. (2017). Childhood trauma in today's urban classroom: Moving beyond the therapist's office. *Journal of Educational Foundations*, *30*(1–4), 63–75.

Barton, C. (2019). Critical literacy in the post-truth media landscape. *Policy Futures in Education*, *17*(8), 1024–36.

Bates, R. & Townsend, T. (2007). The future of teacher education: Challenges and opportunities. In T. Townsend & R. Bates (Eds.), *Handbook of teacher education: Globalization, standards and professionalism in times of change* (pp. 725–34). Springer.

Bok, J. (2010). The capacity to aspire to higher education: "It's like making them do a play without a script." *Critical Studies in Education*, *51*(2), 163–78.

Bokhorst-Heng, W. D., Osbourne, M. D., & Lee, K. (Eds.). (2006). *Redesigning pedagogy: Reflections on theory and praxis*. Sense.

Boomer, G. (1999) Curriculum and teaching in Australian schools, 1960–1990: A tale of two epistemologies. In B. Green (Ed.), *Designs on learning:*

Essays on curriculum and teaching by Garth Boomer (pp. 127–46). Australian Curriculum Studies Association. (Original work published 1991)

Bourdieu, P. (1977). *Outline of a theory of practice*. Cambridge University Press.

Bourdieu, P., & Passeron, J.-C. (1990). *Reproduction in education, society and culture*. Sage.

Bruckauf, Z., & Chzhen, Y. (2016). *Education for all? Measuring inequality of educational outcomes among 15-year-olds across 39 industrialized nations*. UNICEF Office of Research.

Charteris, J., & Dargusch, J. (2018). The tensions of preparing pre-service teachers to be assessment capable and profession ready. *Asia-Pacific Journal of Teacher Education*, *46*(4), 354–68.

Cochran-Smith, M., Cummings Carney, M., Stringer Keefe, E., Burton, S., Chang W.-C., Fernandez, M. B., Miller, A. F., Sanchez J. G., & Baker, M. (2018). *Reclaiming accountability in teacher education*. Teachers College Press.

Comber, B. (2015). *Literacy, place, and pedagogies of possibility*. Routledge.

Comber, B., & Kamler, B. (Eds.). (2005). *Turn-around pedagogies: Literacy interventions for at-risk students*. PETA.

Comber, B., & Kamler, B. (2006). Redesigning literacy pedagogies: The complexities of producing sustainable change. In W. D. Bokhorst-Heng, M. D. Osborne, & K. Lee (Eds.), *Redesigning pedagogy: Reflections on theory and praxis* (pp. 19–31). Sense.

Comber, B., & Woods, A. (2016). Literacy teacher research in high-poverty schools: Why it matters. In J. Lampert & B. Burnett (Eds.), *Teacher education for high poverty schools* (pp. 193–210). Springer International Publishing.

Connell, R. W. (1993). *Schools and social justice*. Pluto.

Connell, R. W. (2002). Making the difference, then and now. *Discourse: Studies in the Cultural Politics of Education*, *23*(3), 319–27.

Connell, R. W., Ashenden, D., & Kessler, S. (1982). *Making the difference: Schools, families and social division*. Allen & Unwin.

Connell, R. W., White, V., & Johnston, K. (Eds.). (1991). *Running twice as hard: The Disadvantaged Schools Program in Australia*. Deakin University Press.

Crowley, V., & Matthews, J. (2006). Museum, memorial and mall: Postcolonialism, pedagogies, racism and reconciliation. *Pedagogy, Culture & Society*, *14*(3), 263–77.

Delpit. L. (1988). The silenced dialogue: Power and pedagogy in educating other people's children. *Harvard Educational Review*, *58*(3), 280–98.

Edwards, A. (2001) Researching pedagogy: A sociocultural agenda. *Pedagogy, Culture and Society*, *9*(2), 161–86.

Fielding, M. (1999). Radical collegiality: Affirming teaching as an inclusive professional practice. *Australian Educational Researcher*, *26*(2), 1–34.

Foucault, M. (1972). *The archaeology of knowledge and the discourse on language.* Vintage.
Foucault, M. (1980). Truth and power. In C. Gordon (Ed.), *Power/knowledge: Selected interviews and other writings 1972–1977* (pp. 109–33). Pantheon Books.
Foucault, M. (1982). Afterword: The subject and power. In H. Dreyfus & P. Rabinow (Eds.), *Michel Foucault: Beyond structuralism and hermeneutics* (pp. 208–26). Harvester Wheatsheaf.
Freebody, P., Ludwig, C., & Gunn, S. (1995). *Everyday literacy practices in and out of schools in low socio-economic urban communities:Volumes 1 and 2.* Curriculum Corporation.
Frye, H. (2016). The relation of envy to distributive justice. *Social Theory and Practice*, *42*(3), 501–24.
Gerrard, J., & Farrell, L. (2014). Remaking the professional teacher: Authority and curriculum reform.*Journal of Curriculum Studies*, *46*(5), 634–55.
Giroux, H. (2004) Public pedagogy and the politics of neoliberalism: Making the political more pedagogical. *Policy Futures in Education*, *2*(3–4), 494–503.
Gonski, D., Arcus, T., Boston, K., Gould, V., Johnson, W., O'Brien, L., Perry, L. A., & Roberts, M. (2018). *Through growth to achievement: Report of the Review to Achieve Educational Excellence in Australian Schools.* Commonwealth of Australia.
Goodman, R., Miller, M. D., & West-Olatunji, C. A. (2012). Traumatic stress, socioeconomic status, and academic achievement among primary school students. *Psychological Trauma: Theory, Research, Practice, and Policy*, *4*(3), 252–59.
Gore, J. (1993). *The struggle for pedagogies: Critical and feminist discourses as truth regimes.* Routledge.
Gore, J., Barron, R. J., Holmes, K., & Smith, M. (2016). Who says we are not attracting the best and brightest? Teacher selection and the aspirations of Australian school students. *Australian Educational Researcher, 43*(5), 527–49.
Green, B. (2003). An unfinished project? Garth Boomer and the pedagogical imagination.*Journal of the South Australian English Teachers' Association*, *47*(2), 13–24.
Green, B., Reid, J.-A., & Brennan, M. (2017). Challenging policy, rethinking practice: Struggling for the soul of teacher education. In T. Trippestad, A. Swennen, & T. Werler (Eds.), *The struggle for teacher education: International perspectives on governance and reforms* (pp. 39–55). Bloomsbury Academic.
Guitierrez, K., Asato, J., Santos, M., & Gotanda, N. (2002). Backlash pedagogy: Language and culture and the politics of reform. *Review of Education, Pedagogy, and Cultural Studies*, *24*, 335–51.

Gur-Ze'ev, I. (2005). *Critical theory and critical pedagogy today: Towards a new critical language in education*. University of Haifa Press.
Hagevik, R., Aydeniz, M., & Rowell, C. (2012). Using action research in middle years teacher education to evaluate and deepen reflective practice. *Teaching and Teacher Education*, *28*(5), 675–84.
Hall, S. (1983). Education in crisis. In J. Donald & A. M. Wolpe (Eds.), *Is there anyone here from education?* (pp. 2–10). Pluto Press.
Hamilton, D., & Zufiaurre, B. (2000, April 24–28). *The new pedagogics: Revisiting curriculum and didactics* [Paper presentation]. American Educational Research Association Conference, New Orleans.
Hardy, I. (2018a). Practice theory and policy: Redesigning "quality" teacher education in Australia. In C. Edwards-Groves, P. Grootenboer, & J. Wilkinson (Eds.), *Education in an era of schooling* (pp. 197–212). Springer.
Hardy I. (2018b). Practising the public? Collaborative teacher inquiry in an era of standardization and accountability. *Journal of Curriculum Studies*, *50*(2), 231–51.
Hattam, R., & Atkinson, S. (2006). Reconciliation as a frame for rethinking racism in Australia. *Social Identities*, *12*(6), 683–700.
Hattam, R., Brennan, M., Zipin, L., & Comber, B. (2009). Researching for social justice: Contextual, conceptual and methodological challenges. *Discourse: Studies in the Cultural Politics of Education*, *30*(3), 303–16.
Hattam, R., Garrett, R., & Simons, M. (2015). Will this be just? Will we survive? The SACE Research Project. *Curriculum Perspectives*, *35*(2), 30–40.
Hattam, R., & Prosser, B. (2008). Unsettling deficit views of students and their communities. *The Australian Educational Researcher*, *35*(2), 89–106.
Hattam, R., Sawyer, W., & Gannon, S. (2018). Reclaiming educational equality: Towards a manifesto. In S. Gannon, R. Hattam, & W. Sawyer (Eds.), *Resisting educational inequality* (pp. 294–301). Routledge.
Hattam, R., Woodley-Baker, R., & Lucas, B. (2012, December). Rethinking equality/aspirations–achievement/pedagogy/university–school relations [Paper presentation]. In Symposium *Theorising and researching aspirations among young people in difficult spaces and times*. Australian Association for Research in Education Conference, Sydney.
Hattam, R., & Zipin, L. (2009). Towards pedagogical justice. *Discourse: Studies in the Cultural Politics of Education*, *30*(3), 297–301.
Havel, V. (1991). *Open letters: Selected writings 1965–1990*. Alfred Knopf.
Hayes, D., Hattam, R., Comber, B., Kerkham, L., Lupton, R., & Thomson, P. (2017). *Literacy, leading and learning: Beyond pedagogies of poverty*. Routledge.
Hayes, D., Johnston, K., & King, A. (2009). Creating enabling classroom practices in high poverty contexts: The disruptive possiiblities of looking in classrooms. *Pedagogy, Culture & Society*, *17*(3), 251–64.

Hayes, D., Mills, M., Christie, P., & Lingard, B. (2006). *Teachers and schooling making a difference: Productive pedagogies, assessment and performance*. Allen & Unwin.

Hill, S., Comber, B., Louden, B., Reid, J., & Rivalland, J. (1998). *100 children go to school: Connections and disconnections in literacy experience prior to school and in the first year of school*. Department for Education, Employment, Training and Youth Affairs.

Jenkins, K. A., Charteris, J., Bannister-Tyrrell, M., & Jones, M. (2017). Emotions and casual teachers: Implications of the precariat for initial teacher education. *Australian Journal of Teacher Education*, *42*(12), 162–79.

Ladwig, J. (2007). Modelling pedagogy in Australian school reform. *Pedagogies: An International Journal*, *2*(2), 57–76.

Lamb, S. (2007). School reform and inequality in urban Australia: A case of residualising the poor. In R. Teese, S. Lamb and M. Duru-Bellat (Eds.), *International studies in educational inequality, theory and policy. Volume 3: Inequality: Educational theory and public policy* (pp. 1–38). Springer.

Lareau, A. (1987). Social-class differences in family–school relationships: The importance of cultural capital. *Sociology of Education*, *60*(1), 73–85.

Levinsson, M., Norlund, A., & Beach, D. (2020). Teacher educators in neoliberal times: A phenomenological self-study. *Phenomenology & Practice*, *14*(1), 7–23.

Lingard, B. (2007). Pedagogies of indifference. *International Journal of Inclusive Education*, *11*(3), 245–66.

Mason, S., & Poyatos Matas, C. (2015). Teacher attrition and retention research in Australia: Towards a new theoretical framework. *Australian Journal of Teacher Education*, *40*(11), 45–66.

Max-Neef, M. (1991). *Human scale development*. Apex Press.

Mayer, D. (2014). Forty years of teacher education in Australia: 1974–2014. *Journal of Education for Teaching*, *40*(5), 461–73.

McInerney, P. (2004). *Making hope practical: School reform for social justice*. PostPressed.

McLaren, P., & Kincheloe, J. (Eds.). (2007). *Critical pedagogy: Where are we now?* Peter Lang.

Morton, D., & Zavarzadeh, M. (Eds.). (1991). *Theory/pedagogy/politics: Texts for change*. University of Illinois Press.

New London Group. (1996). A pedagogy of multiliteracies: Designing social futures. *Harvard Educational Review*, *66*(1), 60–92.

Peel, M. (1995). *Good times, hard times: The past and the future in Elizabeth*. Melbourne University.

Piketty, T. (2022). *A brief history of inequality*. Harvard University Press.

Pinar, B. (2015). *Educational experience as lived: Knowledge, history, alterity. The selected works of William F. Pinar*. Routledge.

Popkewitz, T., & Fendler, L. (Eds.). (1999). *Critical theories in education: Changing terrains of knowledge and politics*. Routledge.
Prosser, B., Lucas, B., & Reid, A. (2010). *Connecting lives and learning: Renewing pedagogy in the middle years*. Wakefield Press.
Reid, A. (2020). *Changing Australian education: How policy is taking us backwards and what can be done about it*. Routledge.
Reid, J.-A. (2019). What's good enough? Teacher education and the practice challenge. *Australian Educational Researcher, 46*(5), 715–34.
Rogers, B. (2013). *Educational leadership: Cultivating plurality in a dialogic teacher "public space"* [Ph.D. thesis]. Flinders University.
Rose, N. (1999). *Powers of freedom: Reframing political thought*. Cambridge University Press.
Rowe, E. E. (2016). *Middle-class school choice in urban spaces: The economics of public schooling and globalized education reform*. Routledge.
Rowe, E. R., & Skourdoumbis, A. (2019). Calling for "urgent national action to improve the quality of initial teacher education": The reification of evidence and accountability in reform agendas. *Journal of Education Policy, 34*(1), 44–60.
Semmens, B. (2014). *The public secondary school principal in contemporary times: Subjectivity, resistance and the limit to neoliberal sensibilities* [Ph.D. thesis]. University of South Australia.
Senate Select Committee on School Funding. (2014). *Equity and Excellence in Australian Schools: Executive summary*. Commonwealth of Australia. https://www.aph.gov.au/parliamentary_business/committees/senate/school_funding/school_funding/report/a03
Sleeter, C. (2008). Equity, democracy, and neoliberal assaults on teacher education. *Teaching and Teacher Education, 24*(8), 1947–57.
Smith, L. (2011). Experiential "hot" knowledge and its influence on low-SES students' capacities to aspire to higher education. *Critical Studies in Education, 52*(2), 165–77.
Smyth, J. (2011). The disaster of the "self-managing school"—Genesis, trajectory, undisclosed agenda, and effects. *Journal of Educational Administration and History, 43*(2), 95–117.
Smyth, J., Dow, A., Hattam, R., Reid, A., & Shacklock, G. (2000). *Teachers' work in a globalising economy*. Falmer Press.
Smyth, J., Down, B., Hattam, R., & McInerney, P. (2014). *Doing critical educational research*. Peter Lang.
Smyth, J., & Hattam, R. (2004). *"Dropping out", drifting off, being excluded: Becoming somebody without school*. Peter Lang.
Smyth, J., McInerney, P., & Hattam, R. (2003). Tackling school leaving at its source: A case of reform in the middle years of schooling. *British Journal of Sociology of Education, 24*(2), 177–98.

Stacey, M., Talbot, D., Buchanan, J., & Mayer, D. (2020). The development of an Australian teacher performance assessment: Lessons from the international literature. *Asia-Pacific Journal of Teacher Education*, *48*(5), 508–19.

Standing, G. (2012). The precariat: From denizens to citizens? *Polity*, *44*(4), 588–608.

Teese, R. (2000). *Academic success and social power: Examinations and inequality*. Melbourne University Press.

Teese, R. (2011). *From opportunity to outcomes: The changing role of public schooling in Australia and national funding arrangements*. Centre for Research on Education Systems, University of Melbourne.

Thomson, P. (2002). *Schooling the rustbelt kids: Making the difference in changing times*. Allen & Unwin.

Thomson, P. (2009). *School leadership – Heads on the block?* Routledge.

Thomson, S., De Bortoli, L., Underwood, C., & Schmid, M. (2019). *PISA 2018: Reporting Australia's Results. Volume I Student Performance*. Australian Council for Educational Research.

Trifonas, P. (Ed.). (2003). *Pedagogies of difference: Rethinking education for social change*. Routledge Falmer.

Westbury, I., Hopmann, S., & Riquarts, K. (Eds.). (2000). *Teaching as a reflective practice: The German Didaktik tradition*. Lawrence Erlbaum.

Wrench, A., & Garrett, R. (2015). Emotional connections and caring: Ethical teachers of physical education. *Sport Education and Society*, *20*(2), 212–27.

Wrench, A., & Paige, K. (2020). Educating pre-service teachers: Towards a critical inquiry workforce. *Educational Action Research*, *28*(3), 462–79.

Zembylas, M. (2018). Professional standards for teachers and school leaders: Interrogating the entanglement of affect and biopower in standardizing processes. *Journal of Professional Capital and Community*, *3*(3), 142–56.

Zipin, L., & Brennan, M. (2001). *"Cultural capital" and the literacy needs of a new generation of pre-service teachers*. Australian Curriculum Studies Association.

Zipin, L., Sellar, S., & Hattam, R. (2012). Countering and exceeding 'capital': A 'funds of knowledge' approach to re-imagining community. *Discourse: Studies in the Cultural Politics of Education*, *33*(2), 179–92.

PART I

Engaging Disenfranchised Learners

1 "They're Not Here to *Just* Teach You": Practice Architectures and Student Connectedness

Lisa Smith

Justice cannot be achieved by distributing the same amount of a standard good to children of all social classes. Education is a process operating through relationships, which *cannot* be neutralised or obliterated to allow equal distribution of the social good at their core. That "good" means different things to ruling-class and working-class children, and will do different things for them (or to them).

(CONNELL, 1993, P. 19, ORIGINAL EMPHASIS)

Rethinking Practice with Students

It is widely acknowledged that for the last 40 years Australia's public education system has been neoliberalized (Reid, 2019). With a narrowing discourse for education that is driven by the watchwords of high-stakes testing, accountability and school effectiveness, we witness public schools becoming entangled within a sticky web of corporate, decontextualized, market-driven approaches to policy and practice which do little to acknowledge, let alone alleviate, the reproduction of educational inequality for students living in high-poverty communities (Hayes et al., 2017; Lamb, 2007; Munns et al., 2013). Within this marketized model of education, schools serving working-class communities continue to be fitted up as "failing schools" (Sahlberg, 2006; Sahlberg et al., 2017). The policy rhetoric demands that teachers' work be increasingly scrutinized and scripted, and their professional autonomy undermined through an imposition of "what works" models. The banality of "what works" models (Hattam, 2018) strip away any need for a nuanced understanding of a school's context, instead replacing it with a carcass of homogeneity where "pedagogies of coercion and boredom" (Hattam, 2006, p. 4) prevail. It has been well documented (see Graham et al., 2015; McGregor et al., 2015; Smyth & Hattam, 2004) that implementing practices that are overtly dismissive of the role of context contribute to the exacerbation of student disaffection by creating a dislocation between the school curriculum and the students' aspirations and occupational and socio-cultural identities. It is clear that there is currently a pressing need to challenge the assumption that schools should operate as inert, static entities if we are to alleviate the hemorrhaging of students from mainstream schools serving working-class communities. In this chapter, I advocate developing a more nuanced understanding of school context to argue that, to create a more socially just education for students in working-class communities, there needs to be a greater understanding of what the "social good"

(Connell, 1993) means for such students and to develop the practice architectures that embrace it—this is a plea for doing schooling *with* students, not *to* them.

The chapter contains four main moves. I begin with a theorization of practice using Kemmis, Wilkinson and colleagues' (2014) concept of "practice architectures" as an alternative to other logics which prevail in current space/time moments. Second, I contextualize the research in which I have applied this theoretical framework by outlining the methodology and describing the material and socio-historical conditions of the school site in which my research was conducted. Third, I consider how one secondary school in South Australia has used practice architectures to cultivate the enabling conditions for reconnecting working-class disaffected students with mainstream schooling. Finally, I conclude the chapter with reflections on the pressing need to redesign practice architectures in schools serving working-class communities.

Practice Architectures: Letting the Light in

One of the recent attempts to provide a more robust theory of practice has been developed by an international research collaboration called Pedagogy, Education and Praxis (Kemmis, 2012; Kemmis, Wilkinson et al., 2014). This collaboration assumes that practice is *the* key site for improving schooling but then our theories of practice are poorly elaborated and too often sidelined by policy reformers (Kemmis, Wilkinson et al., 2014). The term practice here is defined as:

> A practice is a form of socially established cooperative human activity in which characteristic arrangements of actions and activities (doings) are comprehensible in terms of arrangements of relevant ideas in characteristic discourses (sayings), and when the people and objects involved are distributed in characteristic arrangements of relationships (relatings), and when this complex of sayings, doings and relatings "hangs together" in a distinctive human social project. (p. 31)

Our sayings, doings, and relatings happen within intersubjective spaces, which have three interdependent, and thus inseparable, dimensions that "hang together to create the working conditions to enable or constrain particular practices" (Goodyear et al., 2017, p. 238). They include:

> *cultural-discursive* arrangements that support the sayings of a practice, *material-economic* arrangements that support the doings of a practice, and *social-political* arrangements that support the relatings of the practice. These arrangements (cultural-discursive, material-economic and social-political) hold practices in place, and provide the resources (the language, the material resources, and the social resources) that make the practice possible. (Kemmis, McTaggart et al., 2014, p. 55)

The cultural-discursive terrain can be understood as the semantic space which enables or constrains particular sayings in schools. Kemmis, Wilkinson et al. (2014) explain that we see these at work through the "language or specialist discourse used for describing, interpreting and justifying the practice" (p. 32). For example, in the project of building school and community capacity, a constraining practice might be "the absence of shared language and understandings of key developmental structural elements (e.g., pedagogy and curriculum)" (Boyle et al., 2018, p. 426). Alternatively, these may exist, but may be constrained by the "doing" and/or "relating." The material-economic dimension can be understood as physical space-time that "make[s] possible the activities undertaken in the course of practice" (Kemmis, Wilkinson et al., 2014, p. 32). These operate through the physical set-ups of spaces and the resources that enable or constrain activities of practice. For example, the physical arrangement of a close partnership with a local university campus might enable sustained professional interactions between teachers and researchers to develop resources that better inform context-specific teacher practice. The social-political dimension operates in social space and is "encountered through the medium of power and solidarity" and the resources that make relating im/possible (Boyle et al., 2018, p. 426). For example, in secondary schools, teacher–student relationships and connectedness can be constrained by limited allocations of time to build more durable collaborations within classrooms.

These three arrangements do not predetermine practice in a particular site; instead they *shape* practices, allowing for their purposeful development within intersubjective spaces, evolving over time and adapting to changing times and localized circumstances (Hemmings et al., 2013, pp. 474–75). However, for practices to function and hang together in a purposeful and meaningful way, Kemmis, Wilkinson et al. (2014, p. 14) argue that they must be orchestrated by "teleoaffective structures," or by what they refer to elsewhere as the "*project* of a practice." This refers in part to "the intentions of those involved in the practice," the things participants take for granted, and the "*intersubjective spaces* in which we encounter one another in any particular site" (Kemmis, Wilkinson et al., 2014, p. 14, original emphasis).

While a number of researchers in the field have discussed practice architectures in relation to teachers' or leaders' practices across various educational settings ranging from early childhood to university (see Goodyear et al., 2017; Hemmings et al., 2013; Rönnerman et al., 2017), the students themselves have been omitted from this discussion. I seek to broaden the use of practice architectures here by bringing into conversation the ways in which working-class secondary students encounter, are supported by, and respond to practice architectures to secure stronger connectedness to school.

Researching Turn-Back-Around Schools and Students

This chapter reports on a single-school ethnography I conducted that examined the school-based opportunities that enabled disaffected working-class students to turn back around to school within a mainstream setting (Smith, 2024). I coin the term "turning back around," bending and borrowing from Kamler and Comber's (2005a, 2005b) concept of "turn-around pedagogies" as a terrain for exploring disaffected working-class students' turn back to school. Kamler and Comber (2005a, p. 7) have documented three broad types of turning around: (1) university researchers turning around to teachers; (2) teachers turning around to students and their families; and (3) pedagogies turning around to popular culture. What they documented through their study were the pedagogical shifts that take place by researchers and teachers. However conceptualizing students' "turning back around" to learning becomes new terrain for exploring disaffected working-class students' perspectives and how they articulate their re-mediation[1] (Gutiérrez et al., 2009) of the process of turning back to school when teachers, researchers, and pedagogies turnaround to them. In that case the challenge is not to fix deficits (re-mediation) but to re-meditate students' productive connections to school learning.

My research was a single-school ethnography at Unity High School that aimed to gain an understanding of the students' daily lives and experiences through prolonged involvement and immersion (Troman et al., 2006, p. 1). Semi-structured interviews, photographic elicitation interviews, and observations were conducted with students across one year. Leadership staff and teachers were also interviewed intermittently to develop an understanding of the school's own transition in turning around to its students and increasing student retention rates. After an initial examination of my research data, I identified recurring themes. Practice architectures were prevalent across both school staff and students' data sets. In this chapter, these themes are brought into conversation with one another to understand how they simultaneously in/form teacher practice and student connectedness.

Introducing Unity High School

Unity High School (UHS) was opened in the 1950s amidst an era of intense development in the working-class manufacturing region of the northern suburbs. Social and schooling policies at the time promoted industrial development and

---

1 I align my use of "re-mediate" with Gutiérrez et al.'s (2009) notion which involves students developing "new ways of learning, drawing on their newly expanded repertoires of practice to re-mediate the inequities of their previous schooling experiences and their identities as learners" (p. 18).

population growth, and the South Australian Housing Trust built low-cost mass housing to accommodate the influx of workers and high rates of predominantly British migrants settling in the region. The planned industrial region was viewed as an exemplar of urban policy until the 1970s when deindustrialization reduced the demand for industrial labor (Peel, 1995).

Although the area is now referred to as a "rustbelt" region (Thomson, 2002), Unity High School's student population remains steady, with the school providing a comprehensive curriculum to its nine hundred students across the year levels of 8 to 12. There has been a major drive to transform the culture of the school over the last ten years, with a significant emphasis on high expectations of students, improving behavior, schoolwork completion, academic achievement targets, student attendance and retention, South Australian Certificate of Education (SACE)[2] completion rates, and increased participation in higher education. The targets are constantly referred to throughout the school by way of electronic displays, staff meetings, information nights, and school assemblies. More notably, the Year 12 results feature prominently on the school's website homepage with the statement "100% SACE completion five years consecutively" taking center place. The school's commitment to building the capacity of its students has seen it develop a high profile among the wider northern community where it has gained a healthy reputation for its improved student retention rates and sustained academic success.

The school offers a broad curriculum in conjunction with a number of programs focused on personal growth and development. In the senior years of school there are two distinct pathways that students are encouraged to actively consider during Year 10: university and vocational. The university pathway immerses students in the life of university through sustained visits and involvement with various programs connected to the curriculum throughout their senior years of schooling. However, students also have the option to integrate a vocational education and training certificate with their university pathway or use it separately for a vocational pathway by participating in school-based apprenticeships. Planning for future pathways toward employment or further education is supported by selected school staff and recent old scholars through mentoring programs, a school-based information center, and formal and informal conversations.

[2] The South Australian Certificate of Education is the end-of-school certificate for South Australian schools.

The Distinctive Project: "Building the Capacity of Community"

In considering the wider project of delivering a socially just education for their students, UHS staff responses were characterized by discussions of their collective actions to "build the capacity of community." In their interpretations of community, staff identified that the key stakeholders are students, school staff, and parents.

Building capacity was articulated in a number of ways including "understanding the issues in the local district, inviting and taking parent voice seriously, moving away from a postcode deficit model, providing increased spaces for student voice and ownership of learning, celebrating student achievement publicly, sustaining partnerships with a local university campus, and providing ongoing professional development for staff constructed around their pedagogical needs" (Smith, 2024, p. 5). I turn next to the sayings, doings, and relatings that hold such a project of practice in place.

Creating Spaces of Relating and Resisting the Deficit

When asked in the initial interview to talk about the school's turnaround narrative, the principal, Lynne, had no hesitation in asserting that it began about ten years ago with a priority to shift the deficit discourse that had permeated the school's culture. She began by focusing on leadership staff and teachers' perceptions of their students—understood here to be the cultural-discursive arrangements that support the sayings of a practice—creating a space for what they referred to as "honest talk." Lynne reflected on the importance of resisting deficit thinking about students and their communities as an enabler of innovation and reform:

> Lynne (principal): That was the big cultural shift, was "Do you believe that the students at Unity High can achieve high achievement?" And the information that came back from honest talk was "No they can't because they come with a deficit model of learning. Because they don't have good home backgrounds, they're not bright enough." It's about what, what we believe ... what's the belief thing about this and how do we change that? That's where we realized that until the teachers believed—even last night we heard it—about "Why are they lazy?" You know that premise, it doesn't matter whether it's a category two school or seven, "It's the students' fault." So, when we had to unpack that and go through that and that's when we came back with we need teachers to understand how to teach better and [asked], "What skills do you need to be able to do that?"

As Lynne acknowledged, developing a shared understanding of what it means to resist the deficit is still an ongoing process, especially when confronted by teachers who utilize it as a default mechanism for explaining why their students have attained low academic achievement. At its most crass we hear this trope:

"I taught them, but they didn't learn" (Hattam & Sullivan, 2016, p. 56). One teacher, Natalie, who had been a practitioner at the school for eight years, also noted how difficult it is to "shift some teachers'" views of their students (i.e., the sayings) if they have little understanding of the students and their context, explaining: "When you get teachers that are not from the area, it reflects in the way that they talk to the kids and behavior manage them—it comes out in the deficit approach."

Shifting deficit thinking was often referred to by both leadership staff and teachers as resisting a "postcode mentality," having high expectations of students, and providing challenging and intellectual learning tasks. The following student excerpts convey their recognition of the school's "sayings" and how this plays out for them:

> Brooklyn (Year 11): The majority of them [teachers] have very high expectations and I like that because it's something to reach for. And then, say, you didn't reach those expectations, try again. It's quite easy for me to pick it [expectations] up personally.
>
> Zoe (Year 11): It really gets to a kid when people don't believe in them, like when they're just like, "If you don't want to do then you don't have to do it." Sometimes kids need to hear, "I *know* you can do it" and then you're like, "If *she* thinks I can do it, then I *can* do it." Then when I went to Unity High, I started hearing it and I thought, "This is cool." When you have people around you like teachers and stuff that want you to do better then it makes you want to do better for yourself.

Both students, Brooklyn and Zoe, were undertaking subjects within the school's university pathway, which is positioning the school community (students included) within a traditional elitist discourse, that is, pursuing aspirations involving a university degree are the "gold standard" in education. While elitism here needs to be contested, an aspiration for university is perhaps a positive sign of transforming a deficit school culture. We need to remember that the students from Unity High School continue to be under-represented in higher education—and that more generally students are "seven times less likely to attend university from the outer northern suburbs" (Tranter, 2005, p. 2)—so the "emphasis placed on a discourse encouraging students to pursue higher education pathways is a break from a social reproduction positioning of working-class students as better suited to "hands-on" vocational pathways" (Smith, 2024, p. 5).

Of course, this shift in the cultural-discursive dimension, and an assertion of high expectations, has a concomitant effect on the social-political space, and specifically for my analysis the student–teacher relationship. As I invited students to talk about the school-based opportunities or practices that sparked their turn back around to school, they unequivocally shared stories about their relationships with particular teachers who had managed to change their perceptions of school, and what a classroom could be. In other words, the turn back around was enabled through redesigned pedagogical encounters with specific teachers. Such pedagogical encounters are only made possible, though, when the social-political arrangements are held in place over a period of time that enables these relationships to establish and flourish.

UHS enacted an arrangement that fostered teacher–student connectedness through their pastoral care program, and within their core subject areas of mathematics, English, humanities, and science. UHS worked on transforming middle schooling, which is often a fraught time for students as they leave a primary school setting and enter secondary school where the curriculum is dismantled into separate subjects, rooms, and teachers. Such spaces and relationships can become fragmentary. Recognizing the potential disruption to teacher–student relationships, UHS assigns one pastoral care teacher to a class of students for the first three years of their secondary schooling, at that time comprising Years 8 to 10 in South Australia. Students meet with their care teacher each morning and spend one lesson a week focusing on relationship-building activities. After having the same care teacher for three years, students transition to senior secondary, where they have a different care teacher for the remaining two years of their schooling. Similarly, they have the same core subject teachers for the first two to three years before entering their senior years. The following quotations highlight the emphasis students place on the continuity of their relationships with teachers and the emotional support this offers:

> Brooklyn (Year 11): I can go into Mrs. Walker's office and say, "Look this is going on, I just wanted to let you know." And now that she's my care teacher I see her every morning. She asks, "Hey, how you doing? Did you resolve that issue?"—things like that. They're not here to *just* teach you; they're here to actually care for where you want to go in your future.
>
> Liam (Year 11): If I can't connect with a teacher, it makes it so much harder for me to work in class because I'm uncomfortable all the time.
>
> Ella (Year 10): Because of the way I was acting, none of my teachers liked me or cared enough to really delve deeper into why I was acting that way, but Miss Butters actually, you know, was very persistent, trying to understand why and what was going on and then she was that support that I was needing in order to reconnect.

These responses affirm the significance of an emotional connectedness and relational trust—including interpersonal (relating to others), intersubjective (constructing shared meanings), and interactional trust (interacting with agency and confidence) (Rönnerman et al., 2017, p. 15)—with their subject and care teachers. These students felt secure in being able to relate to their teachers and build more durable collaborations in the classroom and with the school more broadly. In some instances, re-mediated relations with teachers created the foundations that the students required to begin turning back around to school. This was especially the case for Ella, who noted that it was what she needed in "order to reconnect." Although re-mediated teacher–student relationships are positive, they are ultimately "driven by the imperative to promote learning and hence are educational relationships" (Hattam, 2006, p. 3).

In schools serving working-class communities there can be a tendency to privilege relationships over the promotion of learning. However, as discussed earlier, the teachers in my study understood that just getting along with their students was not enough. Invoking the material-economic arrangement here, that is, the spaces, activities, resources, and materials available, some of these teachers have a long history of thinking past deficit and hence have redesigned classroom practices (doings) that allow for an alternative reading of their students' knowledge. Many of the students and teachers talked of a funds of knowledge (FoK) approach, and even at times a *heavy* funds of knowledge (Archer, 2018) approach, which was evident in their classrooms. The FoK approach here can be understood as a culturally inclusive pedagogy that works with difference to respect non-dominant cultural knowledge so as "to develop a sense of active, critical and responsive citizenship—a belief in their capacities to change the world for the better" (Lingard & Keddie, 2013, p. 429). One of the school's English teachers, Natalie, is worth quoting at length here as she portrayed the way in which the doings of her practice involved drawing on a heavier FoK approach—that is, one associated with a more emotionally tumultuous side of life-world knowledge and experiences—with one of her Year 11 classes in response to a recent violent event in the community:

> Natalie (English teacher): So basically, when I did my Year 11 class there was three boys that were involved in an assault at the end of last year. It was against a community member ... and three of our kids were involved and in their school uniforms and they're in my class, at least one of them is. I struggled a little bit with that and I thought what could I do? I asked them what they were interested in doing. A lot of the kids were interested in true crime stories and I thought, "Okay, how am I going to do this?" I really love Garner and she writes these short stories about experiences that are quite extreme. I picked a small one and a positive one that ended well and then one that didn't end so well and I presented them as stories that they could read. For me the overarching message was for them to connect to that in some way and certainly not write about that event but knowing that they've had experiences in their lives that can kind of connect to *a* story or write a story of their own and, you know, talk about a message, or explore thematically what that was about. So, for me, they got to negotiate, they got to write the

> curriculum really. Then I showed them a couple of stories and then they sourced their own and then basically they came up with their own story. I was working with the boy today and he was a little bit unsure, like I think his focus was on *The Martian* and I said "Well, what if you were to change the setting?" So we ended up with a story about a boy who was in juvenile detention or prison and what would happen if he realizes ultimately that the thing that he did could serve him in a great way, like it's actually a bit of a gift because then he doesn't actually ever have to do it again—so to look at things a little bit differently. So, he's started writing that and I guess I just wanted to plant that seed.

Natalie borrowed from the FoK archive to transform the "doings" of her practice and find a balance between connecting with the repertoires of official knowledge and the diverse knowledge that students bring with them to class. A number of students appreciated their teachers taking up a similar approach to practice, providing accounts of how negotiating the learning and being valued for the funds of knowledge they bring to class enabled a sense of connectedness between their learning and their own lives. Emily's response captures this:

> Emily (Year 11): Well in Year 10 it's compulsory to do a personal project. Personal project can be anything we want, and we do it for, I think it's ten SACE credits. So, in Year 10 I did mine on Yanco[3] which is where my grandparents live so we always go up there constantly—it's just another place to call home. I did the history and the people. It took a while, but it was worth it. I just took photos and had conversations with people and emailed them. It was kind of like a small research project. Yeah, I think it was one of the best assignments I've ever done.

Enacting their own version of a funds of knowledge approach assisted teachers to take their students seriously, developing a curriculum that enabled them to "connect what they are learning to their own lives, communities, and regions" (Hattam, 2006, p. 6). For the students who encountered teachers drawing from this approach it often translated to a stronger connection and interest in what they were learning and, as Zoe (Year 11 student) explained, it removed a sense that their teachers were "talking in another language" (Smith, 2024, p. 13).

Conclusion

This chapter has argued that schools cannot hope to "fix" early school leaving and turn students back around by simply doing current policy harder. Thomson (2002) echoes a similar sentiment in her suggestion that "the capacity of disadvantaged

---

3 Yanco is a pseudonym for a rural town in the Riverland region of South Australia.

schools to make a positive difference in students' learning is specifically and generally context dependent" (p. 74). If we are to work toward alleviating the reproduction of educational inequality for students from disenfranchised communities then we must be wary of best practice models that "impose themselves without sensitivity to the existing milieu in all its complexity" (O'Donnell, 2013, p. 279). Such one-size-fits-all models constrain practice by offering up an externally prescribed and scripted framework that just does not work in disadvantaged schools. Instead, this research has shown that leaders and teachers must work to embrace and connect with working-class students' knowledge and life worlds if they are to better shape their practice and provide a much more contextualized curriculum for their students. In response, students in this study developed a greater sense of emotional connection with and relational trust in their teachers and school. Importantly, we are also talking about changes to practice and how a theory of practice architectures—the cultural-discursive, material-economic, and social-political arrangements—provides us with a conceptual frame for thinking about, enacting, and sustaining such new classroom practices. And if we are serious about creating the conditions that enable students to turn back around to school, then it follows that schools must work to develop the practice architectures that support such pedagogical adventures, particularly in working-class communities where students often experience disaffection and alienation from the project of schooling. Transforming schools thus requires redesigning practice architectures which foster democratic teaching practices. The existential challenges of educators should be the key driver for identifying the specific issues and needs of the community and the pedagogical changes required to perform this work. However, it is vital that these practices consider the primacy of the relational and involve students as key interlocutors if we are to consider how education policy and practice might proceed in doing mainstream school differently (Smith, 2024, p. 15).

Bibliography

Archer, L. (2018). An intersectional approach to classed injustices in education: Gender, ethnicity, "heavy" funds of knowledge and working-class students' struggles for intelligibility in the classroom. In R. Simmons & J. Smyth (Eds.), *Education and working-class youth: Reshaping the politics of inclusion* (pp. 155–80). Springer International.

Boyle, T., Petriwskyj, A., & Grieshaber, S. (2018). Reframing transitions to school as continuity practices: The role of practice architectures. *Australian Educational Researcher, 45*, 419–34.

Connell, R. W. (1993). *Schools and social justice*. Temple University Press.

Goodyear, V. A., Casey, A., & Kirk, D. (2017). Practice architectures and sustainable curriculum renewal. *Journal of Curriculum Studies*, *49*(2), 235–54.

Gutiérrez, K., Hunter, J. D., & Arzubiaga, A. (2009). Re-mediating the university: Learning through sociocultural literacies. *Pedagogies: An International Journal*, *4*(1), 1–23.

Graham, L. J., Van Bergen, P., & Swellar, N. (2015). "To educate you to be smart": Disaffected students and the purpose of the school in the (not so clever) "lucky country." *Journal of Education Policy*, *30*(2), 237–57.

Hattam, R. (2006, November 26–27). *Easier said than done: "Strong connectedness" in the middle years* [Paper presentation]. AARE Annual Conference, Adelaide.

Hattam, R. (2018). Researching the "North": Educational ethnographies of a suburban region. In S. Gannon, R. Hattam, & W. Sawyer (Eds.), *Resisting educational inequality: Reframing policy and practice in schools serving vulnerable communities* (pp. 214–24). Routledge.

Hattam, R., & Sullivan, A. (2016). Promoting pedagogies of engagement in secondary schools: Possibilities for pedagogical reform. In A. Sullivan, B. Johnson, & B. Lucas (Eds.), *Challenging dominant views on student behaviour at school: Answering back* (pp. 45–62). Springer.

Hayes, D., Hattam, R., Comber, B., Kerkham, L., Lupton, R., & Thomson, P. (2017). *Literacy, leading and learning: Beyond pedagogies of poverty*. Routledge.

Hemmings, B., Kemmis, S., & Reupert, A. (2013). Practice architectures of university inclusive education teaching in Australia. *Professional Development in Education*, *39*(3), 470–87.

Kamler, B., & Comber, B. (2005a). Designing turn-around pedagogies and contesting deficit assumptions. In B. Comber & B. Kamler (Eds.), *Turn-around pedagogies: Literacy interventions for at-risk students* (pp. 1–14). Primary English Teaching Association.

Kamler, B., & Comber, B. (2005b). Turn-around pedagogies: Improving the education of at-risk students. *Improving Schools*, *8*(2), 121–31.

Kemmis, S. (2012). Researching educational praxis: Spectator and participant perspectives. *British Educational Research Journal*, *38*(6), 885–905.

Kemmis, S., McTaggart, R., & Nixon, R. (2014). *The action research planner: Doing critical participatory action research*. Springer.

Kemmis, S., Wilkinson, J., Edwards-Groves, C., Hardy, I., Grootenboer, P., & Bristol, L. (2014). *Changing practices, changing education*. Springer.

Lamb, S. (2007). School reform and inequality in urban Australia. In R. Teese, S. Lamb, & M. Duru-Bellat (Eds.), *International studies in educational inequality, theory and policy. Volume 3: Inequality: Educational theory and public policy* (pp. 1–38). Springer.

Lingard, B., & Keddie, A. (2013). Redistribution, recognition and representation: Working against pedagogies of indifference. *Pedagogy, Culture & Society*, *21*(3), 427–47.

McGregor, G., Mills, M., te Riele, K., & Hayes, D. (2015). Excluded from school: Getting a second chance at a "meaningful" education. *International Journal of Inclusive Education*, *19*(6), 608–25.

Munns, G., Sawyer, W., & Cole, B. (Eds.). (2013). *Exemplary teachers of students in poverty*. Routledge.

O'Donnell, A. (2013). Unpredictability, transformation, and the pedagogical encounter: Reflections on "what is effective" in education. *Educational Theory*, *63*(3), 265–82.

Peel, M. (1995). *Good times, hard times: The past and the future in Elizabeth*. Melbourne University Press.

Reid, A. (2019). *Changing Australian education: How policy is taking us backwards and what can be done about it*. Routledge.

Rönnerman, K., Grootenboer, P., & Edwards-Groves, C. (2017). The practice architectures of middle leading in early childhood education. *International Journal of Child Care and Education Policy*, *11*(8), 1–20.

Sahlberg, P. (2006). Education reform for raising economic competitiveness. *Journal of Educational Change*, 7(4), 259–87.

Sahlberg, P., Hasak, J., Rodriguez, V., & Associates. (2017). *Hard questions on global educational change: Policies, practices, and the future of education*. Teachers College Press.

Smith, L. (2024). Agonistic freedoms: Enabling disaffected working-class students to turn-back-around to mainstream school. *Ethnography and Education*, 19(4), 353–371.

Smyth, J., & Hattam, R. (2004). *"Dropping out", drifting off, being excluded: Becoming somebody without school*. Peter Lang Publishing.

Thomson, P. (2002). *Schooling the rustbelt kids: Making the difference in changing times*. Allen & Unwin.

Tranter, D. (2005). *Why university? A case of socio-cultural reproduction in disadvantaged secondary schools* (Hawke Research Institute Postgraduate Working Paper Series No. 1). University of South Australia.

Troman, G., Gordon, T., Jeffrey, B., & Walford, G. (2006). Editorial. *Ethnography and Education*, *1*(1), 1–2.

2 Exploring Affective Relations in Disadvantaged Education Contexts: How First-in-Family Students Become University Bound

Garth Stahl and Sarah McDonald

Introducing the First-in-Family Project

This research is positioned at a point in Australian history when more students than ever are entering higher education including those from non-traditional and "disadvantaged" backgrounds. Such increases reflect a policy commitment to widening participation outlined in the Bradley Review report (Bradley et al., 2008), which pledged that by 2020, 20 % of undergraduate students should be from low socio-economic status (SES) backgrounds. As a result, there has been a significant rise in equity-focused programs for non-traditional students, such as alternative entry pathways (Harvey, 2014; Pearce et al., 2008), and university colleges (Cocks & Stokes, 2013). However, as Meuleman et al. (2015) note, "broadening entry points does not necessarily ensure inclusion or positive experience for these students" (p. 503). While the Australian Government (DEEWR, 2009) has previously asserted that students from such backgrounds require higher levels of support—including financial assistance, greater academic support, mentoring, and counseling services—how students who are first-in-family come to aspire to university study remains largely unexplored.

This chapter reports on findings from the *First-in-Family Project* and specifically explores teacher–student relationships as an affective experience, and the role these relationships play in influencing the aspirations of first-in-family students who are intending to pursue university in their first year beyond compulsory schooling. A *first-in-family* (or *first-generation*) student is defined as "no one in the immediate family of origin, including siblings or parents, having previously attended a higher education institution or having completed a university degree" (O'Shea et al., 2017, p. vii). First-in-family students are often characterized as having low levels of cultural capital, and as experiencing geographical marginalization and material and social deprivation, which contributes to them being at a disadvantage in their education. As an equity group, first-in-family students are also less likely to complete their degree due to various factors such as lack of family support, financial constraints, and inadequate academic preparation (Lowery-Hart & Pacheco, 2011). Gale and Parker (2013) suggest students from disadvantaged backgrounds "typically have diminished navigational capacities—the result of their limited archives of experience—with which to negotiate their way towards their aspirations" (p. 51). While these markers of disadvantage are certainly prevalent, recent research on low-SES students shifts the attention toward how student aspirations may be informed by school context as well as a desire for occupational futures that provide financial security (Gore et al., 2015).

The *First-in-Family Project* demonstrates the ways in which young people, who are labeled first-in-family in their secondary school environments, come to realize an aspiration for university, and how continuing their education in the tertiary sector is often a challenging journey (McDonald, 2024; McDonald & Stahl, 2024; McDonald et al., 2024; Stahl & McDonald, 2019, 2022, 2023a, 2023b; Stahl & Young, 2019; Stahl et al., 2020). We are interested in how young people come to "their own meanings, lives and futures, in the context of specific sociocultural, political and economic circumstances" (Hattam & Smyth, 2003, p. 381).

In exploring teacher–student relationships, it is crucial to consider the life worlds of both students and teachers as part of the daily processes of learning and aspiring, each with their own nuances and contradictions. On this theme, and drawing on the scholarship of Lusted (1986), Sellar and Cormack (2009) write: "Both teacher and student must continually subject their identities to a destabilising crisis that is productive of new knowledge" (p. 126). Biesta (2014) too speaks of the risks within education for both teachers and students, where "the risk is there because students are not to be seen as objects to be molded and disciplined, but as subjects of action and responsibility" (p. 1). Furthermore, drawing on the principles of critical pedagogy, Shor (1992) argues that both teachers and students relearn new ways of conceiving of education, particularly that learning is "not something done by teachers to students for their own good but is something students co-develop for themselves, led by a critical and democratic teacher" (p. 20). This chapter focuses on teacher–student relationships for disadvantaged students and how these relationships open up spaces for students to cultivate and validate their aspirations and to navigate around institutional notions of the "ideal learner" (Donnelly, 2015; Jack, 2014; Stahl, 2017; Stahl & McDonald, 2023a).

We consider interpersonal relationships as an act of "co-development" between staff and students, with direct implications for the formation of aspirations. We therefore refer to students' aspirations as both *negotiated*, *realized*, and in a *process of becoming*. The research presented here is situated within the wider study of the relationships between students, teachers, power relations, and knowledge/identity. We are interested in how understandings are produced along the affective "grapevines" between teacher and student (Ball & Vincent, 1998) and what "hot knowledge" (Ball & Vincent, 1998; Reay et al., 2005)—knowledge that has certain currency and positively shapes students' experiences—may contribute to students coming to see themselves in ways which increase the likelihood of becoming the first-in-family to attend university. Reay et al. (2005) note that middle-class young people often "have access to hot knowledge that has a far higher currency and exchange value than the knowledge of their working-class counterparts" (p. 158). Our data suggest that the hot knowledge in disadvantaged schooling contexts is fostered through teacher–student relationships and reified through emotional capital.

A critical investigation of teacher–student relationships requires drawing on theories of affect. To structure our analysis, we primarily draw on emotional capital (Nowotny, 1981; Reay, 2000; Zembylas, 2007) as a powerful constituting component of these relationships, which contributes significantly to the formation of dispositions as a *university-ready* learner. We suggest that emotional capital—as part of how teacher–student relationships are navigated and maintained—opens a space for young people to *occupy* and *perform* different identity positionings in reference to both teachers' perceptions and developing self-perceptions (Stahl, 2021b). First, the chapter briefly recounts some recent research on relational learning in disadvantaged contexts, followed by addressing the relevance of theories of affect and emotional capital to this area of scholarship. This is followed by a recapitulation of our methodology. Next, the findings section explores two main themes regarding how first-in-family students perceive their relationship with their secondary school teachers and how these relationships foster their journeys as learners: the teacher as an affect resource, and the contact zone and relational affect.

Teacher–Student Relationships in Disadvantaged Contexts

Internationally, schooling in disadvantaged contexts has been shaped by a neoliberal accountability agenda focused on standards, skills acquisition, and "learning to earn" (Comber & Nixon, 2009; Stahl, 2015). Such an agenda influences teacher–student relationships in particular ways that are often problematic (Chatelier & Rudolph, 2018; McLeod, 2017). For example, in the United Kingdom, we have seen policy initiatives explicitly requiring teachers to raise the aspirations of disadvantaged young people (Stahl, 2015). In terms of re-imagining a just education, there are persistent challenges in recruiting teachers to teach in disadvantaged contexts and these contexts have high turnover rates in Australia and internationally. We believe these turnover rates impede social justice, as research continues to demonstrate that teacher–student relationships in disadvantaged schooling contexts are integral to student wellbeing, general guidance, and the fostering of aspirations to further education (Nelson, 2019; Prosser et al., 2008; Zipin et al., 2012). This was particularly evident in the "Redesigning Pedagogies in the North" (RPIN) project, which focused on connection, belonging, and teachers engaging with students' life worlds (Sellar, 2012; Zipin, 2009; Zipin et al., 2012). Drawing on a Deleuzian approach posited by Bignall (2010), Sellar (2012) highlights a "conception of pedagogy that is all about relationships," where "the classroom teacher is embedded in a network of connections: connections with students, parents, other teachers, communities, policies, technologies, architecture, etc." (p. 69).

Teachers who work in challenging contexts are both committed to their students and committed to working against narrow policy constraints (Hayes & Comber, 2018). However, teachers who elect to teach in these contexts are often pathologized and labeled as inadequate. Furthermore, educators in low-SES areas have been marginalized for fostering paternalism which could atrophy a student's sense of independence (Whitman, 2008), though this notion of dependence has also featured in critical pedagogy—specifically in Freire's (1985) work.

In studies of first-in-family students there has been some attention to the importance of relational learning (Lowery-Hart & Pacheco, 2011) as a way of fostering a sense of belonging within educational contexts (Meuleman et al., 2015). Our analysis extends this work, focusing on teacher–student relationships as identity resources which contribute to marginalized young people "going against the grain." As our participants come to embody the first-in-family learner, we are interested in how they adapt and modify their subjectivities in relation to teacher–student relationships. We contend that these productive spaces—which may be casual, random, and even mundane—influence how they transition beyond their post-secondary schooling.

The Affective Turn and Emotional Capital

Since the late 1990s, we have witnessed the emotional turn—or the affective turn—in educational research, influenced by scholars such as Sara Ahmed, Lauren Berlant, Arlie Hochschild, and Erica McWilliam. Other researchers have been inspired by the work of Deleuze and Guattari (2008), specifically in references to assemblages where emotions structure spaces, setting the parameters and defining, as well as constraining, meaning and practice. Drawing on scholarly work on affect, Youdell and Armstrong (2011) emphasize the importance of considering the meanings and workings of educational settings, or what in Deleuzian terms are called "smooth" spaces where there "are moments and sites of possibility when and where the assemblage and its striations might be disrupted or deterritorialized"

(p. 145). We are accustomed to thinking of teacher–student relationships as hierarchical and bound by strict professional norms. However, this may not always be the case, as lines often become blurred (Stahl, 2021a). In exploring teacher–student relationships, our research is grounded in what Ahmed (2004, p. 117) calls affective economies where "emotions are not simply 'within' or 'without' but ... they create the very effect of the surfaces or boundaries of bodies and worlds." Therefore, our research builds upon Ahmed's (2004) "sociality of emotions," which challenges the normative conception that emotions are individual or private and instead posits that they are collectively realized, often around formal learning.

In thinking through affect, we draw on emotional capital (Nowotny, 1981; Reay, 2000; Zembylas, 2007) as an important structuring component. Originally introduced by Nowotny (1981), the concept of emotional capital is built on a Bourdieusian approach to capital but is centered on the bounds of affective familial relationships where, according to Nowotny, emotional capital encompasses the emotional resources that are collectively drawn upon. Nearly 20 years later, Reay (2000) expanded the concept of emotional capital, as a heuristic tool, to investigate mothers' emotional engagement with their children's education (both positive and negative). Reay conceives of emotional capital as "the emotional resources passed on from mother to child through processes of parental involvement" (p. 569), emphasizing its intergenerational nature. For Reay, emotional capital is not necessarily something that can be increased or exchanged; instead, she emphasizes the cost in terms of interpersonal relationships and personal wellbeing (p. 580).

Also researching emotions and relationships in education, Zembylas (2007), in contrast to Reay, contends that emotional capital is historically situated and often tied to unrecognized mechanisms and emotional norms, serving to maintain what Ahmed (2004) calls "affective economies." For Zembylas, emotional capital plays a vibrant role in structuring teacher–student relationships and their dialectical emotional practices. According to this interpretation, emotional capital is generated both in the habitus and in educational contexts. Furthermore, Zembylas draws attention to how individuals can *use* emotional capital to facilitate certain actions. Here, we think of the use value of emotional capital particularly around the "contact zone" (Somerville et al., 2011) between teacher and students. As emotional capital becomes operationalized—as an affective medium of communication—this echoes what Biesta (2004) calls "the construction of *shared* understanding" (p. 16, original emphasis).

Our research on relational learning seeks to make a small contribution to emotional geographies of education, as we explore subjectivity and affectivity in everyday life in schools (Stahl & McDonald, 2023b; Youdell & Armstrong,

2011). We are interested in how identities are cultivated and validated by forms of schooling (Donnelly, 2015). An important aspect of re-imagining a just education is focusing on *positive* emotions associated with connection, belonging, and inclusivity, which sits beside educational research addressing negative emotions (cf. Watkins, 2011; Zembylas, 2010).

Research Methodology

Conducted over a three-year period and involving 17 schools, the *First-in-Family Project* involved the use of semi-structured interviews which focused on identity resources as well as the identification of cultural patterns which contribute to the shaping of aspirations. Working closely with school leadership teams in areas of urban disadvantage (the northern and southern suburbs of Adelaide), we recruited a diverse selection of students (n = 48) who were identified by the school as likely to be first-in-family during their final week of Year 12. We asked, for young people living in some of the poorest urban regions in Australia, how do teacher–student relationships contribute to their positive experiences at school and the strengthening of their aspirations to be first-in-family? The use of semi-structured interviews allowed us to maintain an element of standardization while also personalizing the questions. Interviews were audio-recorded and fully transcribed and processed via the NVivo package. The qualitative analysis primarily involved content analysis focused on identifying themes and coding the data specifically in relation to how the participants produced the self as well as changes in aspiration. In this chapter, we focus our attention on how students come to *occupy* and *perform* identity positionings in reference to teachers' perceptions as well as their own developing self-perceptions.

Exploring the Affective Dimension of Teacher–Student Relationships

The Teacher as an Affect Resource

For our participants, the teacher–student relationship clearly functioned as an important identity resource where students actively sought out teachers who they perceived as caring. Surveying the data, students frequently described their favorite teachers as "funny," having the "ability to joke," "going the extra mile," and "approachable" (Stahl, 2021a, 2021b). Campbell, whose sense of self was tied to his strong religious beliefs, spoke about his small Studies of Religion class and the close connection he had to his teacher:

> There's only seven of us and we're really, really close with our teacher. We talk about everything and he always incorporates—because he's a very religious man himself. He always encompasses religion when he's—in his—in what he tells us to do. He—for example a student will ask him something about his missus or something, having problems, and then he will always help but he will keep it funny at the same time. He's a really good bloke, so yeah.

Aisha, for the most part, also formed productive relationships with her teachers. When she struggled with her English class, she called attention to the time her teacher spent with her, which improved her confidence:

> I always got really frustrated with my English teacher, but she always was really supportive. I had a few hundred breakdowns throughout the year, and she was always willing—if she had time she'd come and sit with me and explain what I was doing wrong and go through my essay or whatever it was I was doing, and she'd help me fix it and give me suggestions. And that probably boosted my—boosted—raised my grade a lot. So, I was really happy with her.

Here Aisha referenced a range of emotions (e.g., frustration, contentment) but we also see a range of strategies implemented by her teacher such as patience and personalized support. This level of caring and support was echoed by Nafisa, who had experienced multiple changes of teacher for one class and was able to discern what, for her, made a powerful teacher–student relationship:

> So, the teacher that we had beforehand, he was, like, a much more hands-on person with his students, and much more supportive, I felt, as well. There were a few instances where I would be like, I can't do this, I don't know what to do—and he will sit down with me, and he'll take me through it step by step if I needed it, or if he felt like I could do it, I just wasn't allowing myself to, he would be like, he'll give me, sort of, head starts to get my brain going.

Consistent in the data were references to students valuing patience and time, which we consider an integral aspect of emotional capital. While the demands of the curriculum may structure a certain high-stakes environment about the acquisition of knowledge and skills, it seemed what was most important to students were moments of one-to-one attention where the teacher recognized there was an issue and took the time to work through it, demonstrating a genuine desire to help students do well. Furthermore, this time also contributed to forming spaces where our participants came to both *occupy* and *perform* different identity positionings in reference to teachers' perceptions of them as well as their own developing self-perceptions.

How relationships formed around learning was, of course, significant, as it was often connected to students' aspirations beyond the secondary school environment. Tia, a passionate musician, spoke of her close relationship with her music teacher, whom she said was "always really helpful" and "always wanted me to succeed." Tia described her music teacher as having a high level of awareness and care:

> She would just know what I can do and can't do. And especially like because I did … singing through Year 12, and if I was struggling with singing, she'd tell me, "I know why you're struggling." And she'd help me with my voice and what to do and how to exercise it, as well as she, again … like a lot of other teachers kinda just give me the work. She'd give me the work and talk me through it, and then just check up on me when I'm just behind, or check on me when I'm ahead. Just any point she'd always talk to me. Even when we're not in class together, she'd kind of talk to me and ask me how everything's going, and how I'm going with my music assignment and things like that. And it just, it was really nice knowing that she really did care. You could feel that genuine care that she had. And it was really nice because, even if I was doing something, she'd leave me to do it sometimes as well. There'd be that independent learning, and she'd push it on me because she knows I can do it. And that helped me as well because, if my teacher believes in me, it just leads me to do what I can do. That just gives me a lot more confidence, and it did. It gave me a lot of confidence.

Tia's attention to "independent learning" and "genuine care" challenges research which has warned against paternalism (Whitman, 2008). Similar to Nafisa and Aisha, Oliver reflected on what makes a good teacher: the ones who are "really switched on, they want to help," where "other [teachers] are just here for money and you can really tell." Consistent with the rest of the data, Oliver spoke about his attraction to teachers he felt were "approachable" and "friendly." Oliver articulated that these teachers not only have a close relationship with students but also have a wider awareness of students' strengths and weaknesses. Tia echoed Oliver's sentiments and called attention to how, for her, good teachers make the effort to find differentiated and engaging ways to teach:

> they know that students learn in different ways and they cater to all of that. So they will do the visual learning—so, they'll have a PowerPoint up, and then they'll do audio, so they'll speak about the PowerPoint, give examples and stuff, and then there's that practical side to it as well. So, they'll do stuff in the class with students or with tennis balls or stuff to get a concept through to all those types of learners.

The range of approaches—working simultaneously with the affective labor of teaching—highlights the complex work of educators in disadvantaged contexts.

The Contact Zone and Relational Affect

The term "contact zone" is inspired by the work of Pratt (1992), who defines social space "where cultures meet, clash and grapple with each other, often in contexts of highly asymmetrical relations of power" (p. 34). While the use of "contact zone" in this way may initially seem problematic, given its genesis in imperialism and postcolonialism, we believe it has analytical purchase in the investigation of relational learning in all contexts. For our purposes we conceive of it as "the in-between space of the 'contact zone' where there is a 'space of transformative potential'" (Somerville et al., 2011, p. 6). "In-between-ness" furthers our thinking around how relationships open up spaces for first-in-family students to adapt, improvise, and modify their learner subjectivities, which has implications for their aspirational trajectories.

Vuong, a high-performing and driven student, described a good teacher as someone with good knowledge of a student's emotional wellbeing who knows how to *push* and *pull* the student toward their own success (Stahl, 2021b; see also Stahl & McDonald, 2023a). Therefore, for Vuong, the contact zone between student and teacher is a shifting zone informed by both the knowledge the teacher possesses and the versatility of roles the teacher plays which, it would appear, strengthens the relationship:

> Okay, so for me a good teacher would be someone who understands the student, as in the student might be stressful this week and they know how to compensate for that. They know how to provide the best sort of structure and framework for that student. Or for example if that student was a procrastinator, then they get the whip out and then they start to push you along. And so, teachers that are very active and passionate in what they do, and also, but also teachers who actually understand what the students' needs are...

Echoing this support, Logan spoke of one of his teachers as an individual who "makes the classroom feel like a home" where there is collaboration and attention to equal support:

> You enter that classroom, and you immediately feel like you're welcome and the amount of support she gives every student, she doesn't give one student more support than another, she's always supportive to every student in an equal manner. She's also another one of my inspirations because she provides me with guidance. She shows me that it's okay to make mistakes...

The language Logan used suggests the respect he had for this teacher was centered around notions of unconditional support and demonstrating the importance of making mistakes. The way Logan described this scenario is reminiscent of

Ahmed's (2004) arguments concerning how emotions circulate between people, how they "stick" as well as move, contributing to notions of exclusivity and inclusivity. Logan clearly felt an important connection with his teacher, which further manifested as a sense of belonging which he was able to articulate. In considering emotional capital as a relational construct, contributing to daily *actions* and *practices*, affect focuses our attention on how "emotions become attached to individuals united in their feelings for something" (Zembylas, 2010, p. 152). For Logan, this classroom space was an important assemblage where his identity was worked upon in relation to the trust he had in his teacher. Similar to Logan, Carissa, who shuffled between different schools and therefore a series of different teachers, noted that it was important for teachers to praise her effort when she underperformed. This links back to Logan's point that it is important for teachers to foster an atmosphere where students are allowed to make mistakes.

Sellar (2012) calls attention to thinking about the "affective quality of [student–teacher] relationships that constitute these assemblages and how this relates to learning" (p. 69) and, by default, the greater sense of social justice at play. However, the contact zone of teacher–student does not always need to be centered upon learning. Carissa spoke of teachers as "genuine" where "They're there to teach you but they're also there to be your friend." This notion of friendship was echoed by other students, such as Robbie, who recalled how his teacher "helped me through tough family times and all that. And she, she's more like a, a friend and stuff. And she, she's always there if I need her." Other students, like Kate, spoke of talking to her teachers about Pokémon and how this contributed to developing the informal and interpersonal side of the interaction: "my teachers learned how to talk to me. They realized how I liked being talked to and then kind of became more easier to talk to." Bella echoed this sentiment, describing her teachers as: "they're really loving and involved and want to know how you're going, not just in school but in everyday life."

We believe the contact zone is where emotional capital is fostered, which is necessary for young people from non-traditional backgrounds to develop themselves as learners to both aspire to and navigate university life. This becomes evident when we consider the absence of close, affective teacher–student relationships. For example, Khuyen described the importance of needing someone to "push us forward kind of," and spoke of how his progress dipped when a particular teacher left:

> Year 12, well it was going really well at the beginning until I heard one of the teachers left our school and then I started to lose motivation. So I just went down, and I was like, oh yeah, I don't care now. But then I started picking myself up in term 2 and started getting my work done, so yeah.

Schools in disadvantaged areas often struggle to retain staff and Khuyen's words highlight how relationships and motivation are intertwined. On a relational and affective level, trust takes time. This is a critical point when we consider how "hot knowledge" is fostered in teacher–student relationships and reified through emotional capital. Potentially, when the teacher–student relationship suffers—as hierarchical human interaction in institutions is prone to do—this hot knowledge can wither on the grapevine (to borrow and extend the wording of Ball & Vincent, 1998), especially without the necessary trust and support which has to be built over time.[1]

Discussion

Zembylas (2010, p. 152) argues that "educators need to look more carefully at how school practices and discourses are entangled with emotion." While education is now shaped by policy directives around standards and an increasingly high-stakes curriculum—which contributes to the formation of school cultures and classroom contexts—it is apparent that what was most important to the students in our research were moments of one-to-one attention, where the teacher took the time to demonstrate their capacity to care and guard against their students failing academically. We feel the data from the *First-in-Family Project* call attention to the students' acute awareness of what—in their view—makes an effective teacher within their schooling contexts. While this level of student reflexivity has implications for the role of student voice and democratic communities within education, we also draw attention back to Reay's (2004) focus on the costs to interpersonal relationships and personal wellbeing of emotional capital—it is worth considering that, while emotional capital present at the contact zone is enriching, it is also taxing.

Scholars in the field of emotional geographies (Anderson & Smith, 2001; Davidson et al., 2005) often call attention to how emotions are tied to particular places where the context structures the emotion, giving it a certain sense of validation. Teacher–student relationships—while potent in secondary school, particularly in Year 12—often lose salience as students transition to higher education where the culture and expectations are different. It could be argued that at the university level teacher–student relationships are limited as the learning is largely transactional. This begs the question of whether the affective aspects

1 Ball and Vincent (1998) note that the grapevine is a somewhat inaccurate and limiting metaphor as students are exposed to many "different grapevines and an individual's access to them is structured primarily by class-related factors" (p. 382).

of teacher–student relationships established at the secondary level continue to play an important role as students who are first-in-family transition to university. To nuance this further, perhaps the emotional capital fostered in teacher–student relationships only serve to grease the wheels for the acquisition of further capital(s) in university life—a space which continues to foreground a notion of student-hood grounded in independence and self-reliance.

Conclusion

It is unsurprising that first-in-family students find emotional resonance and inspiration in their relationships with their secondary school teachers. The evidence suggests that, when these disadvantaged young people receive personalized support, they gain the necessary confidence to "go against the grain" and further their education. However, this is not always a linear process. While this chapter has sought to document some of the ways in which teacher–student relationships enrich emotional capital, we have lingering questions regarding how such relationships contribute to students' aspirations to go to university. It is certainly not the case that students' and teachers' perceptions of their learner identities and engagement with learning are the same (McDonald et al., 2024; Stahl & Young, 2019). The evidence from the *First-in-Family Project* suggests teacher–student relationships need to be tested through moments of stress (exams, etc.) where, in the eyes of the students, teachers can go above and beyond their required employment and invest time and energy in their students (Nelson, 2019; Stahl, 2021b). It would appear these trusting relationships stave off feelings of anxiety and doubt which, for students from non-traditional backgrounds, can set in quickly. To conclude, we draw attention to Sellar (2012), who writes: "the teacher and learner are not 'totally' implicated in the pedagogical encounter. Parts of them connect and change while other parts do not" (p. 69). As our cohort transitions into university and beyond, it will be interesting to see the role affective relations play in contributing to both their learning and aspirations, given that these aspirations often require careful resourcing and maintenance.

Bibliography

Ahmed, S. (2004). Affective economies. *Project Muse*, *22*(2), 117–39.

Anderson, K., & Smith, S. (2001). Editorial: Emotional geographies. *Transactions of the Institute of British Geographers*, *26*, 7–10.

Ball, S. J., & Vincent, C. (1998). "I heard it on the grapevine": "Hot knowledge" and school choice. *British Journal of Sociology of Education*, *19*(3), 377–400.

Biesta, G. (2004). "Mind the gap!" Communication and the educational relation. In C. Bingham & A. Sidorkin (Eds.), *No education without relation* (pp. 11–22). Peter Lang.

Biesta, G. (2014). *The beautiful risk of education*. Routledge.

Bignall, S. (2010). Affective assemblages. In S. Bignall & P. Patton (Eds.), *Deleuze and the postcolonial* (pp. 78–102). Edinburgh University Press.

Bradley, D., Noonan, P., Nugent, H., & Scales, B. (2008). *Review of Australian higher education: Final report*. Commonwealth of Australia.

Chatelier, S., & Rudolph, S. (2018). Teacher responsibility: Shifting care from student to (professional) self? *British Journal of Sociology of Education*, *39*(1), 1–15.

Cocks, T., & Stokes, J. (2013). Policy into practice: A case study of widening participation in Australian higher education. *Widening Participation and Lifelong Learning*, *15*(1), 22–38.

Comber, B., & Nixon, H. (2009). Teachers' work and pedagogy in an era of accountability. *Discourse: Studies in the Cultural Politics of Education*, *30*(3), 333–45.

Davidson, J., Bondi, L., & Smith, M. (2005). *Emotional geographies*. Routledge.

Deleuze, G., & Guattari, F. (2008). *A thousand plateaus*. Continuum.

Department of Education, Employment and Workplace Relations (DEEWR). (2009). *Transforming Australia's higher education system*.

Donnelly, M. (2015). A new approach to researching school effects on higher education participation. *British Journal of Sociology of Education*, *36*(7), 1073–90.

Freire, P. (1985). *The politics of education: Culture, power and liberation*. Bergin and Garvey.

Gale, T., & Parker, S. (2013). *Widening participation in Australian higher education: Report to the Higher Education Funding Council for England (HEFCE) and the Office of Fair Access (OFFA), England*. Deakin University and Edge Hill University.

Gore, J., Holmes, K., Smith, M., Southgate, E., & Albright, J. (2015). Socioeconomic status and the career aspirations of Australian school students: Testing enduring assumptions. *Australian Educational Researcher*, *42*(2), 155–77.

Hattam, R., & Smyth, J. (2003). "Not everyone has a perfect life": Becoming somebody without school. *Pedagogy, Culture and Society*, *11*(3), 379–98.

Harvey, A. (2014). Early and delayed offers to under-represented university students. *Australian Journal of Education*, *58*(2), 167–81.

Hayes, D., & Comber, B. (2018). Research pedagogy in high poverty contexts: Implications of non-representational ontology. *International Journal of Research and. Method in Education*, *41*(4), 387–97.

Jack, A. (2014). Culture shock revisited: The social and cultural contingencies to class marginality. *Sociological Forum*, *29*(2), 453–75.

Lowery-Hart, R., & Pacheco, G. (2011). Understanding the first-generation student experience in higher education through a relational dialectic perspective. *New Directions for Teaching and Learning, 127,* 55–68.
Lusted, D. (1986). Why pedagogy? *Screen* 27, no. 5: 2–14.
McDonald, S. (2024). "I don't feel like I belong": First-in-family girls' constructions of belonging and space during the transition from secondary school into university. *Gender and Education, 36*(2), 183–97.
McDonald, S., & Stahl, G. (2024). "Girls do this, guys do that": How first-in-family students negotiate working-class gendered subjectivities during a time of social change. *Australian Educational Researcher, 51,* 973–93.
McDonald, S., Stahl, G., Nguyen, T., & Fairbairn, K. (2024). Resourcing their own aspirations: First-in-family young people and DIY career counselling. *British Journal of Educational Studies,* 72(2), 235–52.
McLeod, J. (2017). Reframing responsibility in an era of responsibilisation: Education, feminist ethics. *Discourse: Studies in the Cultural Politics of Education, 38*(1), 43–56.
Meuleman, A. M, Garrett, R., Wrench, A., & King, S. (2015). "Some people might say I'm thriving but": Non-traditional students' experiences of university. *International Journal of Inclusive Education, 19*(5), 503–17.
Nelson, J. 2019. "Relational Teaching with Black Boys: Strategies for Learning at a Single-Sex Middle School for Boys of Color." *Teachers College Record* 118: 6.
Nowotny, H. (1981). Women in public life in Austria. In C. F. Epstein & R. L. Coser (Eds.), *Access to power: Cross-national studies of women and elites* (pp. 147–56). George Allen and Unwin.
O'Shea, S., May, J., Stone, C., & Delahunty, J. (2017). *First-in-family students, university experience and family life: Motivations, transitions and participation.* Palgrave Macmillan UK.
Pearce, J., Down, B., & Moore, E. (2008). Social class, identity and the "good" student: Negotiating university culture. *Australian Journal of Education, 52*(3), 257–71.
Pratt, M. L. (1992). *Imperial writing and transculturation.* Routledge.
Prosser, B., McCallum, F., Milroy, P., Comber, B., & Nixon, H. (2008). "I am smart and I am not joking": Aiming high in the middle years of schooling. *The Australian Educational Researcher, 35,* 15–35.
Reay, D. (2000). A useful extension of Bourdieu's conceptual framework? Emotional capital as a way of understanding mothers' involvement in their children's education? *Sociological Review, 48*(4), 568–85.
Reay, D. (2004). Gendering Bourdieu's concepts of capitals? Emotional capital, women and social class. *Sociological Review, 52*(S2), 57–74.
Reay, D., David, M. E., & Ball, S. J. (2005). *Degrees of choice: Class, race, gender and higher education.* Trentham books.

Sellar, S. (2012). "It's all about relationships": Hesitation, friendship and pedagogical assemblage. *Discourse: Studies in the Cultural Politics of Education*, *33*(1), 61–74.

Sellar, S., & Cormack, P. (2009). Redesigning pedagogies in the middle-years classrooms: Challenges for teachers working with disadvantaged students. *Pedagogy, Culture and Society*, *17*(2), 123–39.

Shor, I. (1992). *Empowering education: Critical teaching for social change*. Chicago, IL: The University of Chicago Press.

Somerville, M., Davies, B., Power, K., Gannon S., & de Carteret, P. (2011). *Place, pedagogy, change*. Sense Publishers.

Stahl, G. (2015). *Aspiration, identity and neoliberalism: Educating white working-class boys*. Routledge.

Stahl, G. (2017). *Ethnography of a neoliberal school: Building cultures of success*. Routledge.

Stahl, G. (2021a). Supporting Fiamalu's education: A case study of affective alliances and Pacific Islander masculinity. *Gender and Education*, *34*(3), 362–77.

Stahl, G. (2021b). "They make time for you": Upwardly mobile working-class boys and understanding the dimensions of nurturing and supportive student–teacher relationships. *Research Papers in Education*, *37*(6), 975–91.

Stahl, G., & McDonald, S. (2019). Social capital and self-crafting: Comparing two case studies of first-in-family males navigating elite Australian universities. *International Journal of Inclusive Education*, *26*(1), 93–108.

Stahl, G., & McDonald, S. (2022). *Gendering the first-in-family experience: Transitions, liminality, performativity*. Routledge.

Stahl, G., & McDonald, S. (2023a). The first-in-family experience: Gendered and classed subjectivities in elite higher education. In R. Tierney, F. Rizvi, & K. Ercikan (Eds.), *International encyclopedia of education* (pp. 392–7). Elsevier.

Stahl, G., & McDonald, S. (2023b). Investigating the role of gender, social class and curriculum in the first-in-family higher education experience. *Educational Review*. Advance online publication. https://doi.org/10.1080/00131911.2023.2176468

Stahl, G., McDonald, S., & Stokes, J. (2020). "I see myself as undeveloped": Supporting Indigenous first-in-family males in the transition to higher education. *Higher Education Research & Development*, *39*(7), 1488–1501.

Stahl, G., & Young, J. (2019). "ACE boys": Gender discourses and school effects in how first-in-family males aspire to Australian university life. In H. Cuervo & A. Miranda (Eds.), *Youth, inequality and social change in the Global South* (pp. 67–81). Springer.

Watkins, M. (2011). Teachers' tears and the affective geography of the classroom. *Emotion, Space and Society*, *4*(3), 137–43.

Whitman, D. (2008). An appeal to authority: The new paternalism in urban schools. *Education Next*, *8*(4), 53–8.
Youdell, D., & Armstrong, F. (2011). A politics beyond subjects: The affective choreographies and smooth spaces of schooling. *Emotion, Space and Society*, *4*(3), 144–50.
Zembylas, M. (2007). Emotional capital and education: Theoretical insights from Bourdieu. *British Journal of Educational Studies*, *55*(4), 443–63.
Zembylas, M. (2010). Investigating the emotional geographies of exclusion at a multicultural school. *Emotion, Space and Society*, *4*(3), 151–9.
Zipin, L. (2009). Dark funds of knowledge, deep funds of pedagogy: Exploring boundaries between lifeworlds and schools. *Discourse: Studies in the Cultural Politics of Education*, *30*(3), 317–31.
Zipin, L., Sellar, S., & Hattam, R. (2012). Countering and exceeding "capital": A "funds of knowledge" approach to re-imagining community. *Discourse: Studies in the Cultural Politics of Education*, *33*(2), 179–92.

3 Pedagogical Justice for Muslim Learners

Dylan Chown, Nadeem A. Memon, Amaarah DeCuir, and Basma Elshayyal

Introduction

This chapter explores key justice concerns impacting on Muslim learners in public schooling across four national educational policy contexts: Australia, Canada, the United Kingdom, and the United States. We aim to contribute to a collective effort of advancing justice claims in education, and to the mobilizing of coherent alternatives to dominant approaches within teacher education. This chapter adds an important new perspective by focusing on pedagogical justice for the Muslim learner.

We begin by locating our work within the emerging manifesto for pedagogical justice advanced by the Pedagogies for Justice Research Group, University of South Australia. We highlight some synergies with our colleagues and co-contributors and draw attention to a collective alignment with key pillars of this emerging manifesto. Two of the authors of this chapter are members of this group, and we all share a commitment to justice claims in education which ensures a synergy with other contributors in this edited book. Making explicit this alignment, we concur with the provocations that shape this emerging manifesto: that pedagogy is constituted by global policy networks operating across and within state/national jurisdictions; that pedagogy as a keyword invokes a political project against the intrusion and technicizing of educators' work; that different pedagogies have different outcomes; and that pedagogy is a social justice concern and a hopeful space for opportunities for educational researchers and practitioners to mobilize alternate forms of counter-hegemonic and ethical learning.

Advancing justice in education is a political project, and our interest in culturally responsive pedagogy as a hopeful approach toward pedagogical justice for Muslim learners necessitates a critical reading of the inseparable interplay between politics, policy, and pedagogy. In the following section, we briefly outline the conceptual lens that we are using in our work. We interrogate the geopolitical forces that impose a dominant metanarrative on Muslim people and Islam, which intersects with neoliberalizing policy, which together undermine equity and justice. Our analysis reveals a gap in new pedagogy studies: the lack of acknowledgment that mandated pedagogies fail to engage with religious difference and diversity and, specifically for us in this chapter, the religious identities and ways of knowing of Muslim learners in public school settings. We conclude the chapter with some provocations for teacher education that we think corroborate strong justice claims (Memon & Chown, 2023) for marginalized Muslim learners that are enabled by enacting culturally responsive pedagogies.

Theoretical Lens: Advancing Pedagogical Justice

Our work here is located in new pedagogy studies (Hattam & Zipin, 2009), and specifically culturally responsive pedagogy (Price et al., 2020). Across several decades, critical pedagogy studies have argued for robust activism in areas of race, gender, and social inequality, but there has been a paucity of engagement with religious difference (Neumann, 2011; Sahin, 2018). Our work seeks to bring religion, as a form of difference, into conversation with culturally responsive pedagogy, specifically for Muslim learners.

Although we argue culturally responsive pedagogy offers a hopeful space for advancing culturally and religiously responsive practice premised on justice, we add that how culturally responsive pedagogy is theorized and practiced requires nuance if pedagogical justice is to extend to and be realized for Muslim learners in public schools. We argue the lack of attention to religion, religious identities, and religious ways of knowing represents a significant gap. In this regard, we are encouraged by an agile framing of *pedagogical justice* in critical pedagogy studies, and thus a willingness to open up complex vexing questions and debates (Hattam & Zipin, 2009). Our work demands that justice claims in education, traditionally associated with diversities, also intersect with religion and the religious identities and ways of knowing of Muslim learners.

Politics

There are lively debates in so-called Western nations, including Australia, Canada, the United Kingdom, and the United States, around the political implications of increasing cultural diversity and immigration, particularly of the Muslim *other*, and the threats these are perceived to pose to social cohesion (Hattam, 2016; Keddie, 2014; Miah, 2017b). Across these four countries, the political climate is increasingly poll-driven and right-wing populist (Zembylas, 2021), and therefore inclined to reactionary rhetoric and scapegoating policies that are seen to be tough on immigration and terrorism, and insistent on integration by Muslims (Tufail & Poynting, 2013). Exacerbated by volatile economic recessions and refugee crises, cultural conflicts and political uncertainties, nationalist and populist movements continue to command unprecedented levels of interest and commitment. Political and policy reductionism across the four national contexts has served to embolden and legitimize divisive discourses and vocabulary targeting

Muslims and has created space for the development of intolerant legislation, with politicians unapologetic about singling out Muslims. State enablement of divisive and inflammatory activities such as anti-Muslim marches reflects more concerted forms of harassment. Not discounting many differences across these contexts, what remains common is the central role of political leadership and national identity politics in the marginalization and othering of Muslims (Ali, 2020; Miah, 2017a).

Political climate and political leadership are not alone in shaping attitudes toward the Muslim other. Digitalized social media exacerbate political discourse and political agendas. Smith (2018) describes how the increasing polarization of public attitudes driven by global algorithms feeds into a discourse which spirals from mildly one-sided to dangerously bigoted. Scandals such as those associated with the widely discredited Cambridge Analytica demonstrate the staggering degree of involvement (and by extension responsibility) of media in generating and influencing mass political momentum based on highly invasive data gathering and personal profiling (Berghel, 2018). The results of this were apparent in the 2016 American elections, the 2016 UK referendum on leaving the European Union (Brexit) and the 2019 Australian federal election.

Further evincing the impact of political and media discourse, sharp spikes in Islamophobic hate crime have been recorded following instances of outspoken politicians' pronouncements, perceived terrorist attacks, and domestic incidents. The first *Islamophobia in Australia* report found that spikes in reported vilification coincided with terror attacks, anti-terror legislation, and negative media coverage of high-profile Muslim leaders (Iner, 2017). Arguing for a causal relationship between politicians' speech and the prevalence of hate crimes against Muslims in the United States, Levin (2017) cites the spike following presidential candidate Donald Trump's proposal to indefinitely ban all Muslims from entering the United States. As Warsi (2011) notes, Islamophobia, and anti-Muslim discourse in general, can only operate with impunity due to a combination of the above factors, and it has now gained the dubious distinction of having "passed the dinner table test" of polite society. Commenting on the Australian context, Poynting and Briskman (2018, p. 13) caution that "Islamophobia has progressed from a fringe element in Australian society to a position of respectability through its institutionalisation in public and private spheres." They argue all areas of public policy have been implicated, and the ideological scapegoating of Muslims has become so normalized and entrenched that it has been made respectable though formal and informal partnerships of government, media, and other institutional and professional actors. Alarmingly they posit that the explicit mission of the right wing has been taken up by what they term the "respectables," meaning parliamentary representatives, architects of new laws, academics, teachers, and social workers. In such a milieu, these trends threaten and diminish notions of multiculturalism, pluralism, and democracy across the four nations, while paradoxically operating under a pretext of tolerance, harmony, interfaith relations, and social inclusion (Poynting & Briskman, 2018). Explaining the contradictory pursuit of universalism and pluralism within Western countries, Keddie (2014, p. 419) asserts:

> the inadequacies of a western liberal universalism that positions itself as the progressive measure and mentor of minority cultures. Such a positioning does little to disrupt racialised patterns of power and privilege—rather, it denies the migrant experience, exaggerates cultural difference and emphasises the intrinsic worth of Anglo-Celtic values. Rather than creating social cohesion, unity and equity, this model of multiculturalism can create social division and fragmentation, especially in undermining the political autonomy and freedom of marginalised cultural groups.

The collective Muslim experience in each national context continues to bear witness to the dispossession and lack of agency visited upon marginalized communities as a result of discrimination, which is translated into "othering" social policies. These typically manifest in higher levels of unemployment, poorer housing, over-representation in penal institutions, lower incomes, and reduced educational opportunities, among other socio-economic markers. Statistical studies of Muslims across the four so-called Western contexts reveal other commonalities. In stark contrast to populist claims of "Muslims taking over," the Muslim population as a percentage of the total population across the four contexts ranges in size from 1 percent in the United States, 2.6 percent and 3.2 percent in Australia and Canada respectively, to as high as 5 percent in the United Kingdom (ABS, 2017; Statistics Canada, 2011; Pew Research Center, 2017; Office for National Statistics, 2012). Muslim communities studied across the four countries in this chapter are also consistently among the most ethnically, culturally, and linguistically diverse, and, despite stereotypes of being newly arrived, over a third of Muslims are either born in, or indigenous to, their countries (ABS, 2017; Statistics Canada, 2011; Pew Research Center, 2017; UK Census, 2011).

Aggressive foreign policy and global conflict also have a corrosive effect on both Muslim self-identity/psyche and the lens through which Muslims are viewed (Gilby et al., 2011). Responses to the international events such as September 11, the wars in Iraq, and the London and Bali bombings have played a significant role in shaping public attitudes toward ethnic and cultural diversity generally, and specifically toward Muslims in the population (Koleth, 2010). Muslims continue to endure a climate of paranoid nationalism, stereotyped as alien, foreign, and other, depicted as a monolithic group of people whose values and beliefs are incompatible with Western values and beliefs, and positioned as a potential threat to national security (Abdalla, 2012), or, as Poynting and Briskman (2018, p. 1) posit, "positioned not only as culturally incommensurate, but dangerously so: dishonest, criminally inclined, violent, misogynist, homophobic, backward, uncivilized." This dominant metanarrative has served to dehumanize and marginalize Muslims, creating a fertile atmosphere for Islamophobia, anti-Muslim sentiment, racism, and the steady rise of White supremacist groups. In Canada, within a month of 9/11, *Bill C-36 Anti-Terrorism Act* was initiated to acknowledge that terrorism is a national concern. In the United States, weeks after 9/11, Congress overwhelmingly passed the Patriot Act 2001, a national policy which subsidized law enforcement's surveillance resources, expanded definitions of terrorism, and increased penalties for those charged (Etzioni, 2004). The U.S. government allocated hundreds of millions of dollars in resources toward countering violent extremism, mostly targeting the American Muslim community through surveilling, policing, and expelling Muslims (Aziz, 2017).

Since the proclaimed War on Terror, education and schooling have become key racialized and securitized domestic sites (Farrell, 2016; Kundnani, 2009; Sian, 2017). In Canada, *Bill 60* banned the *niqab* (face veil), positioning Canadian Muslims as security threats (Bakali, 2018; Wilkins-Laflamme, 2018), and "as illiberal and antithetical to Canadian values" (Zine 2019). The Trojan Horse Affair in Britain, initially purported to be a hardline extremist plot to take over state schools in Birmingham, became a focal point for accusations of state-sanctioned Islamophobia and efforts to bolster the controversial Prevent strategy (Bi, 2020). Community groups and government officials grappled for control over the narrative, but amidst this struggle, the true victims—the Muslim learners and their families—were largely overlooked (Alam, 2022; Bi, 2020). These pupils experienced heightened anxiety due to the intense scrutiny from media, educators, and Ofsted inspectors, feeling trapped in a societal panopticon that monitored their every move (Bi, 2020). Over time, it became evident that the scandal and subsequent witch-hunt was a hoax and there was no substantiated evidence of extremism or a deliberate plot within these schools. Nonetheless, the damage was irreversible; successful schools in deprived areas were undermined (Alam, 2022), and the British Muslim community was stigmatized, casting them as suspicious outsiders in their own country (Miah, 2017b). The ongoing impact of this baseless scandal continues to affect Muslim children, parents, and educators, shaping their daily lives and future interactions with state policies (Bi, 2020; Miah, 2017b). This affair not only influenced immediate educational and security policies like Prevent, criticized as a tool for "ethnic profiling, monitoring and spying of Muslim communities" (Miah, 2017b, p. 100) but also shifted the broader discourse on Muslims in Britain from community integration and social cohesion to racial and religious vilification. This shift has long-term implications for racial and cultural dynamics within the United Kingdom, marking Muslims with a perpetual identity of otherness influenced by politics, governmental policies co-opting and cojoining educational and security policies, and societal perceptions.

The discourse on the crisis in Palestine reveals a stark disparity between addressing genocide and human rights violations of Muslims, on the one hand, and other global crises like the invasion of Ukraine, particularly within the educational settings of the United States and other Western nations (Jaffee, 2024). Muslims, Arabs, and other marginalized communities continue to face significant repercussions for advocating Palestinian rights, often being unjustly accused of antisemitism (Jaffee, 2024). Educators and students who challenge this conflation find themselves at the forefront of a crucial battle for academic and ideological freedom (Jaffee, 2024). After October 7, 2023, Muslim and Arab students in the United States have faced targeted bias and harassment from peers and educators, despite guidance from the U.S. Department of Education reminding schools of their legal obligations to address harmful speech and conduct based on students' religious identity (DeCuir, 2023; Kim, 2024). The continued conflation of legitimate criticism of Israel with antisemitism not only silences advocates of Palestinian justice, but also impedes broader social equity movements. Within schools, this double standard deeply disenfranchises marginalized Muslim learners, who perceive a betrayal of the very democratic and justice principles they are being taught, exacerbating their alienation, and eroding their trust in these institutions (Jaffee, 2024).

Without exception, all Muslim learners in public schooling across contexts belong to a post-9/11 generation, and collectively have no experience of a pre-9-11 world or a de-securitized environment (Manzoor-Khan, 2019). Born and raised under the long shadow of post-9/11 politics, the identities of Muslim learners across the four contexts have been impacted, leaving indelible marks on their schooling experience. Imposed identities advanced by tropes such as the "good" (quietest, compliant, state interlocutor) versus "bad" (cannot be co-opted or "domesticated") Muslim have become an integral and normalized part of their lived experience (Mamdani, 2002).

There are many examples, in Australia, Canada, the United Kingdom, and the United States, where education has been harnessed by the wider infrastructure of the state to target young Muslims, effectively conscripting and/or coercing practitioners to identify, report, and correct those deemed to be at risk of radicalization or who display non-conformist behaviors (Mansouri & Kamp, 2007).

This is a potent example of the interplay between politics, policy, and pedagogy. Conscripting educators to engage in surveillance and law enforcement mandates severely compromises their educative mission and precludes them from the necessary preparedness to develop asset-based respectful views and relationships as the basis for positive engagement with Muslim learners (Hope & Matthews, 2017; O'Donnell et al., 2017). The collective Muslim experience across the four national contexts is illustrative of the impact that political attitudes and national policies can have upon marginalized groups or communities.

Policy

Across all four national contexts, public schooling faces a challenging policy, media, and practical context, which has intensified over the past decade (Gannon et al., 2018). Various scholars point out that federal governments are ideologically foregrounding issues of economic management, while engaging in forms of backlash cultural politics (Chitpin & Portelli, 2019; Cochran-Smith et al., 2017; Gannon et al., 2018; Keddie et al., 2018). Both preoccupations of governments have manifested in education policy, with implications for Muslim learners in public schools. Most concerning is the climate of policy rhetoric which has weakened both vocabularies and strategic possibilities for pursuing equity and justice in education (Gannon et al., 2018).

Writing about marginalized learners in Australia for example, particularly Aboriginal learners, Morrison et al. (2019, p.11) explain that "internationally, neoliberal informed educational policies have been shown to be intimately linked with race and racism." Kohli et al. (2017, p. 189), in the United States, describe "a new form of educational racism that is masked by equity language and driven by capitalist, market driven goals." Under neoliberal logic, racism and culture do not exist (Sleeter, 2011); instead, individuals, in this case marginalized Muslim learners, are held solely responsible for success, or its lack, assessed narrowly using economic measures. In the public schooling context, the implications for Muslim learners manifest in a range of ways, including through systemic and institutional racism (Mansouri & Kamp, 2007), and discourses of privilege that exclude religion from school (Keddie et al., 2018), hence demanding Muslim learners leave their religious, spiritual, and cultural assets at the school gate. As such, schooling experience is characterized by feelings of exclusion based on religion (Johns et al., 2015).

Policy texts also frame equity and inclusive educational discourses that operate in schools and hence have implications for national and/or provincial/state-wide stances on faith-centered students in public schools. Here we juxtapose

Canadian and Australian experiences. In Ontario, Canada, the province's Ministry of Education put forward three attempts at articulating a vision and plan for creating equitable schools in the past decade. Each attempted to add a layer of guidance to school boards in actualizing policies and practices related to equity and inclusion. Barriers to equity and inclusion listed include religious discrimination and the guidelines advocate "moving beyond tolerance and celebration," while challenging a "Eurocentric perspective in education" by including "experiences, values, and viewpoints of members of racial and ethnocultural communities" (Ministry of Education, 2014, pp. 6, 11).

In Australia, several national policy texts have aimed to influence inclusive education practices in schools. For example, the Alice Springs (Mparntwe) Education Declaration (Education Council, 2019) announced a nation-wide commitment to two overarching educational goals: (1) "The Australian education system promotes excellence and equity"; and (2) "All young Australians become: confident and creative individuals, successful lifelong learners, [and] active and informed members of the community." A second policy text is the Australian Curriculum, emphasizing that students are to develop "knowledge and skills needed to reflect on culture and cultural diversity, engage with cultural and linguistic diversity, and navigate intercultural contexts" (ACARA, 2022).

Critiques of Ontario's Equity and Inclusive Education Strategy and the Alice Springs (Mparntwe) Education Declaration (including its forerunner, the Melbourne Declaration on Educational Goals for Young Australians) center on the dominant neoliberal discourse defined by economic competition within global contexts (Chitpin & Portelli, 2019; Ditchburn, 2012). They hold that one-size-fits-all curriculums prioritize economic and pragmatic concerns as the primary goal and relegate issues of curriculum provision for diverse student populations to the periphery (Ditchburn, 2012). Such critiques argue that demands for equity now play a secondary role as the drivers and rationale for national curriculum don't meaningfully feature "other goals of education—such as those around human values, about respect for difference, about the role of local contexts and engagements with community, about student and teacher identity and agency" (Ditchburn, 2012, p. 259). Despite explicit mention of religion, religious values, beliefs, and/or ways of knowing, and being responsive to students' religious backgrounds across policy texts in both contexts, little is known about enactments beyond "tolerance and celebration," as recommended in the Ontario strategy. Knowledge here implies more than decontextualized knowing about Islam and Muslims, and includes educators' orientations toward othering discourse and political tensions around "recognition and misrecognition, inclusion and exclusion, democracy and coercion, homogenization and pluralism" (Preger & Kostogriz, 2014, p. 157).

The key concern here is a potential gulf between educational policy rhetoric and actual policy enactment in schools and classrooms.

As a result of policy texts that fail to meaningfully address equity concerns, anti-Muslim racism frequently appears in schools as bullying of Muslim children based on their religion (Iner, 2019a). In the United States, according to a study conducted by the Institute for Social Policy and Understanding, 42 percent of Muslims reported bullying of their school-aged children and 25 percent of those reports were bullying by teachers (Kysia, 2018). In the United Kingdom, Muslim students remain the most vulnerable section of the community, often bearing the disproportionate burden of Islamophobia and shouldering the most toxic fallout from spikes in aggression following incidents such as "Punish a Muslim Day" (Dearden, 2019). Studies of Muslim learners in Australian schools reveal verbal and physical abuse, assaults on identity and self-worth, and structural exclusion (Mansouri & Kamp, 2007; Mansouri & Trembath, 2005; Preger & Kostogriz, 2014). Studies indicate that "[m]arkers of identity and cultural practices are scrutinized and fiercely debated and many institutions have not been able to respond effectively to racism directed towards Muslim students" (Preger & Kostogriz, 2014, p. 160; see also Iner, 2019b).

Pedagogy

Impact of Politics and Policy on Educators

Several empirical educational studies shed light on the impact of dominating metanarratives for understanding Islam and Muslims, and their implications for policy and practice as they relate to Muslim learners. Alarmingly, studies reveal that Muslim learners are subjected to discrimination by educators across Australia, Canada, United Kingdom, and the United States. Mansouri and Trembath (2005) argue that these negative effects are greatly underestimated in educational research and practice. Numerous studies in Canadian public schools raise serious concerns about negative views of Muslim learners, and outright discrimination, by Canadian teachers (Amjad, 2018; McDonough, 2003; Rezai-Rashti, 2005; Zine, 2004). In Alberta, Canada, Amjad (2018) found that only a few participants felt their teachers were willing or capable of putting forth unbiased views about Islam and Muslims. In Australia, a recent report revealed that perpetrators of Islamophobia toward Muslim learners in schools included teachers, principals, and sports coaches, who either enacted anti-Muslim sentiment or made it difficult for Muslim learners to document school bullying (Iner, 2019a). In America, Zaal (2012) described anti-Muslim discourses by educators to emphasize the need to address these concerns systemically. These multinational research findings emphasize the need for education (Australian Human Rights Commission, 2021), including teacher education programs, to foster a stronger sense of social justice and a clear vision of the role of public schools as acculturation agents in multicultural societies (Amjad, 2018). Demands for justice in education challenge educators and their role in reproducing anti-Muslim sentiment in schools and classrooms.

Thin Equity and Limitations to Inclusion for Muslim Learners

Research on Muslim learners over the previous two decades has been narrowly focused on issues of accommodation and assimilation, reflecting the othering of Muslims in society. Religious accommodations commonly refers to exemptions to observe religious celebrations, adaptions to uniform to accommodate religious parameters pertaining to modesty and dress, exemptions from classes where curriculum content conflicts with religious values (e.g., music, dance, drama), requests for prayer spaces, and advocating for Arabic to be recognized as a heritage language for instruction (McAndrew, 2010). Memon & Chown (2023; p. 2) equate "narrow conceptions of inclusion [with Muslim learners] that reduce it to accommodations and celebrations" with thin equity. Nonetheless, multiple studies about Canadian Muslim learners focus on Muslim female students and the pervasive negative stereotypes held of Muslim women, particularly associated with wearing the headscarf (Akseer, 2011; Sensoy & Stonebanks, 2009; Zine, 2001). In the United States, research on Muslim women's formative school experiences often focuses on identity struggles ascribed to covering their hair (Taylor et al., 2014).

Beyond research into religious accommodations are studies that seek to examine how Muslim learners negotiate their complex identities, both the presumed divide between religious values in secular learning, but also tensions between ethnic home values and mainstream popular culture. American scholars tend to highlight the assimilation struggles that students face in school (Abu El Haj, 2007; Basford, 2010). In Canada, the studies unpack identity narratives complicated by public school norms (Rezai-Rashti, 2005; Schlein & Chan, 2010; Shalabi, 2010). Across national contexts, these studies often conclude that students bear the responsibility of assimilating to increase their potential success in school, both academically and socially. But pedagogical justice cannot be subject to students' assimilatory practices; rather, justice must be extended to Muslim learners as a repudiation of anti-Muslim sentiment and an advancement of equity.

A further site for struggle for Muslim learners in public schooling has been around the mainstream curriculum. Although American researchers continue to propose supplemental curriculum content that includes Muslim experiences (Abu El Haj, 2006; Al-Hazza & Bucher, 2010; Moore & LeDee, 2006; Siddiqui,

2016), and in the United Kingdom, curriculum enrichment that is purported to be both faith-based and inclusive, curriculum additions do little to disrupt the inequities faced by Muslim learners, nor do they confront anti-Muslim sentiment rooted in today's public schools (Manzoor-Khan, 2019).

The Four Ss: Surveillance, Securitization, Secularism, and Standardization

The four Ss represent significant barriers to pedagogical justice for Muslim learners and reflect the inadequacy of approaches that do not disrupt racialized patterns of power. In relation to surveillance and securitization, studies reveal the sheer disproportionality in scale, funding, and focus of efforts toward Muslim learners, particularly when compared to the limited funding schools receive for holistic academic initiatives. In the United Kingdom, as of January 2019, Muslims constituted over 72 percent of securitization/surveillance referrals, with over half coming from schools and educational establishments (Abbas et al., 2023).

In relation to secularism, studies reveal tensions around the place of religion in public schooling. Although some scholars suggest that Canadian public schools reflect religious plurality (Al-Fartousi, 2015; Niyozov & Pluim, 2009), and an inclusion of religious worldviews (Niyozov, 2010), others argue they are insufficient in "combatting racism, discrimination, and Islamophobia" (Amjad, 2018, p. 327). In Australia, multiple studies have found that educators are either reluctant or refuse to engage with issues of religion in public schools (Halafoff, 2015; Halafoff et al., 2019; Keddie et al., 2018; Memon & Chown, 2023), and evidence suggests that "many teachers lack the confidence and/or expertise to engage with cultural difference in supportive and educationally productive ways" (Morrison et al., 2019, p. 57). The reluctance and/or refusal to enact educationally productive approaches undermines teachers' ability to connect with religious identities and ways of knowing. Such reluctance and/or refusal, borrowing from Keddie et al. (2018), can emanate from a common but narrow view of secularity that seeks to avoid the promotion of any one particular religious practice by rejecting all expressions of religious identity. Secularism, as respect for both religious and non-religious ways of knowing, is thereby reduced to an orientation that is by default anti-religion.

The dominant neoliberal education policy logic, across national contexts, further complicates the pursuit of pedagogical justice for Muslim learners. Neoliberalism in education maintains hegemonic norms within schools and prioritizes standardization and subsequently narrow or reductionist forms of curriculum, pedagogy, and assessment. Neoliberal policy regimes characterized by performativity and standardization dominate contemporary education across multiple national contexts. This has led to increased global pressure on schools via accountability measures for compliance. Scott-Baumann and Cheruvallil-Contractor (2016) argue that the increasing monetization of the UK educational system and constant "teaching to test" (Tobin et al., 2009) have severely eroded the curriculum's integrity and the teaching profession's ability to deliver a rounded education in any meaningful way. Connell (2013) comments on the impact of neoliberalism and educating for diversity, describing a system of testing and measures of skills and performance, narrowly defined according to dominant Anglo upper-middle-class practices of living. What is clear from broader research is that standardization, decontextualization, hyper-accountability, and high-stakes testing have been found to result in "pedagogies of indifference" and that dominant pedagogies represent "pedagogies of the same" (Lingard, 2007). Pedagogies of indifference fail to value the cultural (and religious) differences of students and lack connectedness to the world (Lingard & Keddie, 2013).

Culturally Responsive Pedagogy

Internationally, a growing body of evidence suggests that "culturally responsive pedagogies improve educational experiences and outcomes of First Nations peoples and other minoritized groups" (Morrison et al., 2019, p. 58). Culturally responsive pedagogy (CRP) encompasses broad conceptualizations of pedagogical practices that are associated with commitments to social justice and equity. CRP represents an approach to teaching and learning that utilizes "the cultural characteristics, experiences, and perspectives of ethnically diverse students as conduits for teaching them more effectively" (Gay, 2002, p. 106). We argue here that CRP has potential to advance pedagogical justice for Muslim learners through provoking teachers to: strengthen asset-based views of learners; respect cultural and religious diversity as an asset for learning (included respect for religious diversity—religion and religious identities and ways of knowing); strongly connect to the lifeworlds of learners and their families; and promote an activist orientation (Morrison et al., 2019).

The culturally responsive pedagogy archive historically advocates for racial/ethnic minority populations, but less is known about applying these pedagogical practices to marginalized faith communities. Unfortunately, the dominant normative pedagogies are at least implicitly oriented toward a narrowly defined learner cohort which then invariably sidelines religion and faith, ignoring the lifeworlds and devaluing the assets of Muslim learners. Put most succinctly, mandated pedagogies fail to connect with students' funds of knowledge (Esteban-Guitart & Moll, 2014). Recent research in a public school in Australia with a majority Muslim learner population found hopeful expressions of care and compassion toward Muslim learners and whole-community support for religious observance, but hesitation, if not refusal, to draw on the religious assets that Muslim learners carry with them in classroom inquiries (Memon & Chown, 2023). Some post-9/11 education research on American Muslim students considers how culturally responsive pedagogies could increase Muslim students' success in schools (Meymand, 2018). In the United Kingdom, a substantial body of literature on Muslim learners (Afro-Caribbean, Bangladeshi, and Yemeni) routinely demonstrates overwhelmingly positive results when students feel acknowledged, included, and respected (Miah, 2017a; Sewell, 2017). More research is needed to demonstrate how culturally responsive pedagogies can advance pedagogical justice in a political and policy context replete with anti-Muslim sentiment.

Justice Claims

Much of the extant literature examined above addresses each context almost exclusively within its own sphere. While acknowledging the presence of obvious geopolitical and educational differences across contexts, a recurrent theme revealed by this archive is the underlying similarities across contexts, demonstrating significant conceptual and experiential overlap. These include: othering discourses and the complex and accumulative effect of politics and policy on schools and educators; significant limitations to inclusion, and the failure to actively disrupt racialized patterns of power; and wicked challenges that surveillance, securitization, secularism and standardization present to advancing socially just education for Muslim learners. Drawing on our analysis of four national contexts, we corroborate and emphasize the following provocations that we hope will enable more pedagogical justice. We contend that these provocations have the potential to promote culturally responsive pedagogy for Muslim learners (Memon & Chown, 2023, p. 3):

1. Unsettling the deficit views of Muslim children/learners and including their culture or religion brings into view the demand to restructure and re-culture schooling and redesign pedagogy.
2. Ignoring religion and religious ways of knowing undermines educational justice.
3. Religious and spiritual ways of knowing are, for some Muslim learners, crucial elements of their identities, backgrounds, lifeworlds, and funds of knowledge.

In Conclusion

This chapter has outlined a critical analysis of pedagogical justice for Muslim learners in public schooling across four national educational contexts. Our attention to the interplay between politics, policy, and pedagogy, as this relates to Muslim learners, offers an urgent critical reading and takes up a new line of flight for culturally responsive teaching. Previous attention to the impact of politics and political discourse on Muslim people has rarely interrogated this from an educative perspective in relation to the impact on Muslim learners in public schooling. Neither has the complexity of combined political, public, and education policy been considered. Arguably the most significant contribution here is the attention to global policy networks operating across and within state/national jurisdictions as this relates to educational justice claims for Muslim learners.

We have challenged existing narratives and orientations of religious accommodation and curriculum supplements given the wicked challenges that surveillance, securitization, secularism, and standardization present to a just education for Muslim learners. We have argued that culturally responsive pedagogy offers a hopeful space for advancing pedagogical justice for Muslim learners, acknowledging more research is required to build upon the positive early findings of the few studies to date. Given the interplay between politics, policy, and pedagogy that serves to marginalize Muslim learners in public schools, and with the understanding that schools continue to reflect socio-cultural exclusion and marginalization, we have offered some provocations for future developments of culturally (and religiously) responsive pedagogy. We contend that this holds important implications for teacher education and for educators committed to equity and a just education.

Bibliography

Abbas, T., Awan, I., & Marsden, J. (2023). Pushed to the edge: The consequences of the "Prevent Duty" in de-radicalising pre-crime thought among British Muslim university students. *Race, Ethnicity and Education*, *26*(6), 719–34. https://doi.org/10.1080/13613324.2021.2019002.

Abdalla, M. (2012). The way forward for Muslim women: Reflections on Australia's social inclusion agenda. In T. Lovat (Ed.), *Women in Islam: Reflections on historical and contemporary research* (pp. 135–47). Springer.

Abu El-Haj, T. (2006). Race, politics, and Arab American youth. *Educational Policy*, *20*(1), 13–34.

Akseer, S. (2011). Book review: Afghan women: Identity and invasion. *Feminist Review*, *98*(1), e20–e22.

Alam, M. T. (2022, April 17). Britain's Trojan Horse: A hoax that still harms Muslims. *Al Jazeera*. https://www.aljazeera.com/opinions/2022/4/17/britains-trojan-horse-a-hoax-that-still-harms-muslims

Al-Fartousi, M. (2015). Enhancing contextualized curriculum: Integrated identity in young Shi'i Muslim Arabic-Canadian students' social worlds. *Journal of Curriculum Studies*, *48*(2), 192–225.

Al-Hazza, T., & Bucher, K. (2010). Bridging a cultural divide with literature about Arabs and Arab Americans. *Middle School Journal*, *41*, 4–11.

Ali, A. J. (2020). "Muslims as Archetypal Suspect Citizens in Australia." Australian Journal of Islamic Studies 5, Iss 2: 98–116.

Amjad, A. (2018). Muslim students' experiences and perspectives on current teaching practices in Canadian schools. *Power and Education*, *10*(3), 315–32.

Australian Bureau of Statistics (ABS). (2017, June 27). *2016 Census data reveals "no religion" is rising fast* [Media release]. https://www.abs.gov.au/AUSSTATS/abs@.nsf/mediareleasesbyReleaseDate/7E65A144540551D7CA258148000E2B85

Australian Curriculum Assessment and Reporting Authority (ACARA). (2022). *Understand this general capability: Intercultural understanding.* https://v9.australiancurriculum.edu.au/teacher-resources/understand-this-general-capability/intercultural-understanding

Australian Human Rights Commission. (2021). *Sharing the stories of Australian Muslims*. https://humanrights.gov.au/our-work/race-discrimination/publications/sharing-stories-australian-muslims-2021

Aziz, R. (2017). *Taking the strain: Second generation British Asian Muslim males and arranged marriage in London* [Ph.D. thesis]. University of London.

Bakali, N. (2018) Employing a critical race curriculum to challenge dominant discourses in Quebec educational curricula. *Religion & Education*, *45*(1), 52–72.

Basford, L. (2010). From mainstream to East African charter: Cultural and religious experiences of Somali youth in U.S. schools. *Journal of School Choice*, *4*(4), 485–509.

Berghel, H. (2018). Malice domestic: The Cambridge Analytica dystopia. *Computer*, *51*(5), 84–9.

Bi, S. (2020). The school as a double-edged panopticon—Increased anxiety and deflated Islamic identities: A child-centered perspective on the Trojan Horse affair. *Journal of Muslim Minority Affairs*, *40*(2), 332–44.

Chitpin, S., & Portelli, J. (2019). *Confronting educational policy in neoliberal times: International perspectives*. Routledge.

Cochran-Smith, M., Baker, M., Burton, S., Chang, W., Cummings Carney, M., Fernández, M., Stringer Keefe, E., Miller, A., & Sánchez, J. (2017). The accountability era in US teacher education: Looking back, looking forward. *European Journal of Teacher Education*, *40*(5), 572–88.

Connell, R. (2013). The neoliberal cascade and education: An essay on the market agenda and its consequences. *Critical Studies in Education*, *54*(2), 99–112.
Dearden, L. (2019, September 2). Islamophobic incidents rose 375% after Boris Johnson compared Muslim women to “letterboxes,” figures show. *Independent*. https://www.independent.co.uk/news/uk/home-news/boris-johnson-muslim-women-letterboxes-burqa-islamphobia-rise-a9088476.html.
DeCuir, A. (2023, October 27). An urgent message to school leaders: Your Arab and Muslim students need you. *Education Week*. https://www.edweek.org/leadership/opinion-an-urgent-message-to-school-leaders-your-arab-and-muslim-students-need-you/2023/10
Ditchburn, G. (2012). A national Australian curriculum: In whose interests? *Asia Pacific Journal of Education*, *32*(3), 259–69.
Education Council. (2019). *Alice Springs (Mparntwe) Education Declaration*. https://www.education.gov.au/alice-springs-mparntwe-education-declaration/resources/alice-springs-mparntwe-education-declaration.
Esteban-Guitart, M., & Moll, L. (2014). Funds of identity: A new concept based on the funds of knowledge approach. *Culture & Psychology*, *20*(1), 31–48.
Etzioni, A. (2004). *How patriotic is the Patriot Act? Freedom versus security in the age of terrorism*. Routledge.
Farrell, F. (2016). “Why all of a sudden do we need to teach fundamental British values?” A critical investigation of religious education student teacher positioning within a policy discourse of discipline and control. *Journal of Education for Teaching*, *42*(3), 280–97.
Gannon, S., Hattam, R., & Sawyer, W. (Eds.). (2018). *Resisting educational inequality: Reframing policy and practice in schools serving vulnerable communities*. Routledge.
Gay, G. (2002). Preparing for culturally responsive teaching. *Journal of Teacher Education*, *53*(2), 106–16.
Gilby, N., Ormston, R., Parfrement, J., & Payne, C. (2011). *Amplifying the voice of Muslim students: Findings from literature review* (BIS Research Paper No. 55). Department for Business, Innovation and Skills.
Halafoff, A. (2015). Special religious instruction and worldviews education in Victoria's schools: Social inclusion, citizenship and countering extremism. *Journal of Intercultural Studies, 36*(3), 362–79.
Halafoff, A., Singleton, A., Bouma, G., & Rasmussen, M. (2019). Religious literacy of Australia's Gen Z teens: Diversity and social inclusion. *Journal of Beliefs & Values*, *41*(2), 195–213.
Hattam, R. (2016). Citizenship, schooling, and “educational disadvantage.” In A. Peterson, R. Hattam, M. Zembylas, & J. Arthur (Eds.), *The Palgrave international handbook of education for citizenship and social justice* (pp. 27–47). Palgrave.

Hattam, R., & Zipin, L. (2009). Towards pedagogical justice. *Discourse: Studies in the Cultural Politics of Education*, *30*(3), 297–301.

Hope, A., & Matthews, J. (2017). "How not to be a terrorist": Radicalisation and young Western Muslims' digital discourses. In S. Pickard & J. Bessant (Eds.), *Young people re-generating politics in times of crises* (pp. 161–77). Palgrave Macmillan.

Iner, D. (Ed.). (2017). *Islamophobia in Australia report I (2014–2015)*. Charles Sturt University and ISRA.

Iner, D. (Ed.). (2019a). *Islamophobia in Australia report II (2016–2017)*. Charles Sturt University and ISRA. https://web.archive.org/web/20191117224318/http://www.islamophobia.com.au/wp-content/uploads/2019/11/Islamophobia-Report-2019-2.pdf

Iner, D. (Ed.). (2019b). *Islamophobia in Australia report III (2018–2019)*. Charles Sturt University and ISRA.

Jaffee, L. J. (2024). Anti-Zionism is not antisemitism: The centrality of Palestinian liberation in the struggle for anti-oppressive education. *Critical Education*, *15*(1), 29–51.

Johns, A., Mansouri, F., & Lobo, M. (2015). Religiosity, citizenship and belonging: The everyday experiences of young Australian Muslims. *Journal of Muslim Minority Affairs*, *35*(2), 171–90.

Keddie, A. (2014). Australian multicultural policy: Social cohesion through a political conception of autonomy. *Journal of Sociology*, *50*(4), 408–21.

Keddie, A., Wilkinson, J., Howie, L., & Walsh, L. (2018). "…we don't bring religion into school": Issues of religious inclusion and social cohesion. *Australian Educational Researcher*, *46*(1), 1–15.

Kim, R. (2024). Under the law: The Israel–Hamas war and U.S. classrooms. *Phi Delta Kappan*, *105*(8), 64–5.

Kohli, R., Pizarro, M., & Nevárez, A. (2017). The "new racism" of K–12 schools: Centering critical research on racism. *Review of Research in Education*, *41*(1), 182–202.

Koleth, E. (2010). *Multiculturalism: A review of Australian policy statements and recent debates in Australia and overseas* (Social Policy Section Research Paper No. 6). Parliamentary Library.

Kundnani, A. (2009). *Spooked! How not to prevent violent extremism*. Institute of Race Relations.

Kysia, A. (2018). Rethinking Islamophobia: Combating bigotry by raising the voices of Black Muslims In D. Watson, J. Hagopian, & W. Au (Eds.), *Teaching for Black lives* (pp. 330–9). Rethinking Schools.

Levin, B. (2017, July 20). Explaining the rise in hate crimes against Muslims in the US. *The Conversation*. https://theconversation.com/explaining-the-rise-in-hate-crimes-against-muslims-in-the-us-80304

Lingard, B. (2007). Pedagogies of indifference. *International Journal of Inclusive Education*, *11*(3), 245–66.
Lingard, B., & Keddie, A. (2013). Redistribution, recognition and representation: Working against pedagogies of indifference. *Pedagogy, Culture & Society*, *21*(3), 427–47.
Mamdani, M. (2002). Good Muslim, bad Muslim: A political perspective on culture and terrorism. *American Anthropologist*, *104*(3), 766–75.
Mansouri, F., & Kamp, A. (2007). Structural deficiency or cultural racism: The educational and social experiences of Arab-Australian youth. *Australian Journal of Social Issues*, *42*(1), 87–102.
Mansouri, F., & Trembath, A. (2005). Multicultural education and racism: The case of Arab-Australian students in contemporary Australia. *International Education Journal*, *6*(4) 516–29.
Manzoor-Khan, S. (2019). *Postcolonial banter*. Verve Poetry Press.
McAndrew, M. (2010). The Muslim community and education in Quebec: Controversies and mutual adaptation. *Journal of International Migration and Integration*, *11*(1), 41–58.
McDonough, S. (2003). Perceptions of the hijab in Canada. In S. S. Alvi, H. Hoodfar, & S. McDonough (Eds.), *The Muslim veil in North America: Issues and debates* (pp. 121–42). Women's Press.
Memon, N. A., & Chown, D. (2023). Being responsive to Muslim learners: Australian educator perspectives. *Teaching and Teacher Education*, *133*, Article 104279.
Meymand, P. (2018). Meeting the needs of Muslim learners in U.S. classrooms. *Threshold Education*, *41*, 118–27.
Miah, S. (2017a). The Muslim problematic: Muslims, state schools and security. *International Studies in Sociology of Education*, *26*(2), 138–50.
Miah, S. (2017b). *Muslims, schooling and security: Trojan Horse, Prevent and racial politics*. Springer International Publishing.
Ministry of Education. (2014). *Equity and inclusive education in Ontario schools: Guidelines for policy development and implementation*. https://files.ontario.ca/edu-equity-inclusive-education-guidelines-policy-2014-en-2022-01-13.pdf.
Moore, R., & LeDee, O. (2006). Supplemental instruction and the performance of developmental education students in an introductory biology course. *Journal of College Reading and Learning*, *36*(2), 9–20.
Morrison, A., Rigney, L.-I., Hattam, R., & Diplock, A. (2019). *Toward an Australian culturally responsive pedagogy: A narrative review of the literature*. University of South Australia.
Neumann, J. (2011). Critical pedagogy and faith. *Educational Theory*, *61*(5), 601–19.
Niyozov, S. (2010). Teachers and teaching Islam and Muslims in pluralistic societies: Claims, misunderstandings, and responses. *Journal of International Migration and Integration*, *11*(1), 23–40.

Niyozov, S., & Pluim, G. (2009). Teachers' perspectives on the education of Muslim students: A missing voice in Muslim education research. *Curriculum Inquiry, 39*(5), 637–77.

O'Donnell, K., Davis, R., & Ewart, J. (2017). Non-Muslim Australians' knowledge of Islam: Identifying and rectifying knowledge deficiencies. *Journal of Muslim Minority Affairs, 37*(1), 41–54.

Office for National Statistics. (2012). "Religion in England and Wales 2011." https://www.ons.gov.uk/peoplepopulationandcommunity/culturalidentity/religion/articles/religioninenglandandwales2011/2012-12-11#:~:text=In%20the%202011%20Census%2C%20Christianity,per%20cent%20of%20the%20population).

Pew Research Centre (July 2017). Demographic portrait of Muslim Americans, https://www.pewresearch.org/religion/2017/07/26/demographic-portrait-of-muslim-americans/#:~:text=With%20surveys%20like%20this%20one,adults%20and%201.35%20million%20children.

Poynting, S., & Briskman, L. (2018). Islamophobia in Australia: From far-right deplorables to respectable liberals. *Social Sciences*, 7(11), Article 213.

Preger, M., & Kostogriz, A. (2014). Multiculturalism, schooling and Muslims in Australia: From orientation to a possibility of hospitable education. In A. W. Ata (Ed.), *Education integration challenges: the case of Muslims in Australia* (pp. 157–66). David Lovell Publishing.

Price, D., Green, D., Memon, N., & Chown, D. (2020). Richness and complexity within diversity: Educational engagement and achievement of diverse learners through culturally responsive pedagogies. *Social Educator, 38*(1), 42–53.

Rezai-Rashti, G. (2005). Unessential women: A discussion of race, class and gender and their implications in education. In N. Mandell (Ed.), *Feminist issues: Race, class and sexuality* (pp. 83–99). Pearson Education Canada.

Sahin, A. (2018). Critical issues in Islamic education studies: Rethinking Islamic and Western liberal secular values of education. *Religions*, 9(11), Article 335.

Schlein, C., & Chan, E. (2010). Supporting Muslim students in secular public schools. *Diaspora, Indigenous, & Minority Education*, *4*(4), 253–67.

Scott-Baumann, A., & Cheruvallil-Contractor, S. (2016). An Islamic perspective: What does Islam offer to the contemporary debate? In S. Heap (Ed.), *The universities we need: Theological perspectives on the universities needed for today's world* (pp. 124–42). Routledge.

Sensory, O., & Stonebanks, C. (Eds.). (2009). *Muslim voices in school: Narratives of identity and pluralism*. Brill.

Sewell, T. (2017, October 11). Theresa May's race report is wrong … labels like "racial injustice" do more harm than good. *The Sun*. https://www.thesun.co.uk/news/4656785/race-disparity-audit-racial-injustice-harmful/

Shalabi, D. (2010). *A multiple case study on parents' perspective about the influence of the Islamic culture on Muslim children's daily lives* [Ph.D. thesis] University of Ottawa.

Sian, K. (2017). Surveillance, islamophobia, and Sikh bodies in the war on terror. *Islamophobia Studies Journal*, *4*(1), 37–52.

Siddiqui, K. (2016). A study of Singapore as a developmental state. In Y.-C. Kim (Ed.), *Chinese global production networks in ASEAN* (pp. 157–88). Springer.

Sleeter, C. (2011). Becoming White: Reinterpreting a family story by putting race back into the picture. *Race, Ethnicity and Education*, *14*(4), 421–33.

Smith, A. (November 2018). Pew Research Center, "Public Attitudes Toward Computer Algorithms, https://www.pewresearch.org/internet/wp-content/uploads/sites/9/2018/11/PI_2018.11.19_algorithms_FINAL.pdf.

Statistics Canada. (2011). *Canadian National Household Survey*. https://www12.statcan.gc.ca/nhs-enm/2011/dp-pd/prof/index.cfm?Lang=E

Taylor, J., Ayoub, S., & Moussa, F. (2014). The hijab in public schools. *Religion & Education*, *41*(1), 16–30.

Tobin, J. J., Hsueh, Y., & Karasawa, M. (2009) *Preschool in three cultures revisited: China, Japan, and the United States*. University of Chicago Press.

Tufail, W., & Poynting, S. (2013). A common "outlawness": Criminalisation of Muslim minorities in the UK and Australia. *International Journal for Crime, Justice and Social Democracy*, *2*(3), 43–54.

Warsi, S. (2011, January 20). *My faith*. Sir Sigmund Sternberg Interfaith Lecture, University of Leicester.

Wilkins-Laflamme, S. (2018). Islamophobia in Canada: Measuring the realities of negative attitudes toward Muslims and religious discrimination. *Canadian Review of Sociology*, *55*(1), 86–110.

Zaal, M. (2012). Islamophobia in classrooms, media, and politics. *Journal of Adolescent & Adult Literacy*, *55*(6), 555–8.

Zembylas, M. (2021). Refusal as affective and pedagogical practice in higher education decolonization: A modest proposal. *Teaching in Higher Education*, *26*(7–8), 953–68.

Zine, J. (2001). Muslim youth in Canadian schools: Education and the politics of religious identity. *Anthropology & Education Quarterly*, *32*(4), 399–423.

Zine, J. (2004). Creating a critical faith-centered space for antiracist feminism: Reflections of a Muslim scholar-activist. *Journal of Feminist Studies in Religion*, *20*(2), 167–87.

Zine, J. (2019, January 29). Islamophobia and hate crimes continue to rise in Canada. *The Conversation*. https://theconversation.com/islamophobia-and-hate-crimes-continue-to-rise-in-canada-110635

4 Educating Aboriginal Children After Massacre: Adorno in Australia

Lester-Irabinna Rigney

> I look on the blacks as a set of monkies, and the earlier they are exterminated from the face of the earth the better.
> (LETTER, *THE AUSTRALIAN*, DECEMBER 18, 1838, AS CITED IN ELDER, 2003, P. 83)

Ongoing atrocities globally including in Gaza and Ukraine raise questions about the purpose of education and the challenges of providing effective schooling. Drawing upon Theodor Adorno's (1966/1998) essay "Education after Auschwitz," this chapter investigates the role of teacher pedagogy in both the memory of Australian violence and its violence to memory.[1] Only recently in Australia has reconciliation and schooling for social transformation emerged as part of a new global discourse against centuries of colonial harm. An education for social transformation calls upon settler colonial nations to educate citizens out of conflict and discrimination, and into reconciliation, by confronting the danger of a totalitarian recurrence. The call for decolonizing schools after terrible atrocities is not new. However, unlike Australia, the German and South African education systems have acknowledged their brutal past. This is in spite of Australian massacres occurring centuries before Auschwitz. On such themes, "Education after Auschwitz" (Adorno, 1966/1998) and "Education after Abu Ghraib" (Giroux, 2004) demand that we rethink pedagogy against a denial of colonial harm so Auschwitz never happens again. For Adorno, educating against racism and denial of equality is a collective task for democratic societies, and for mature citizens.

The colonial history of massacre and dispossession built the narrative of Australia as "young" and "free." Yet the present appalling statistics of Aboriginal youth suicide, child incarceration, and decades of failed educational outcomes reveal deep denials about the past and the failed pedagogical project of our time.

This chapter is not meant to be a comprehensive history of violence but rather an examination of the role that pedagogies play in how violence is mythologized and remembered as catalyst for its transformation. This chapter critically examines the possibilities of schooling for social transformation against the unacknowledged silence about Australian massacres that, I argue, provides one

---

1 As the catalyst for this chapter, I want to thank Joanne Rigney for her generous support and gifted insights while we visited together for field research the massacre sites of Elliston, Risdon Cove, Myall Creek, Rufus River, and the shipwreck Maria.

of the key conditions for disenfranchising Aboriginal children from success at school. Second, I consider how the Aboriginal learner is denied their self-determined agency within Australian classrooms. Third, and as a contribution to arguments about a decolonizing education, I define and briefly outline principles for a *demythologizing pedagogy*, as guidelines for educating Australian Aboriginal children after massacres: massacres that have been denied, silenced, or ignored.

The Black War in Tasmania, 1823–34

According to one of the leading historians of Australian massacres, Lyndall Ryan (2010), "the Black War in Tasmania 1823–34, is widely perceived by historians as one of the best documented of all Australia's colonial frontier wars" (p. 39), yet facts are still denied, and claims disputed. Here is a brief rehearsal of that history. In 1804, the massacre at the Risdon Cove settlement involved the deaths of probably 50 members of an Aboriginal group, fired upon by settlers and soldiers (Litster & Wallis, 2011). Settler forces' attempts to corral Tasmanian Aboriginal peoples led to the infamous "Black Line." Ryan (2013) explains:

> The Black Line in 1830 in Van Diemen's Land (as the colony of Tasmania was then known) was the largest force ever assembled against Aborigines anywhere in Australia. Comprising more than two thousand soldiers and civilians and widely believed to have been the brain child of the colonial Governor George Arthur, its purpose was to drive four of the nine Tasmanian Aboriginal nations from their homelands to another part of the island and bring an end to the Black War. However, when the Line ended eight weeks later, only two Tasmanian Aborigines were reported captured and two others reported killed. (p. 3)

Highly effective guerrilla war tactics were taken up by the Tasmanian Aboriginal nations of Oyster Bay, Big River, North Midlands, and Ben Lomond. In describing the Indigenous–settler conflict in Tasmania as gruesome and systematic, Ryan (2010, p. 42) draws on schoolteacher James Bonwick's (1870/1970) accounts, published in *The last of the Tasmanians* in 1870. His accounts, collected from colonists, highlight 16 massacres, with a combined loss of at least 300 Aboriginal lives. While the attempted extermination by two thousand soldiers was unsuccessful, Ryan (2013, p. 15) concludes that the Black Line was not an "aberration of an autocratic governor" in a remote post. Rather, her findings concludes:

> The Line was a normal part of British imperial policy at the time, and other indigenous peoples across the empire could have suffered a similar dreadful fate. It is time, surely, that the history of Van Diemen's Land was reconsidered within its imperial context and more clearly connected with the fate of indigenous peoples in other parts of the empire. Only then can we understand the brutal reality of the imperial project. p. 15).

While the academic discipline of history has engaged a revisionist movement to produce counter-narratives to settler accounts, the discipline of education in Australia has been slow to investigate the role and motivations of schools in epistemicide, or the killing of other knowledge systems (Rigney, 2001). In the Australian context, I have argued elsewhere that colonialism, epistemicide, and racialized Eurocentric "reason" were the past structural means that excluded from schools the epistemologies and ontologies of Aboriginal learners (Rigney, 1999, 2001, 2006). Throughout much of Australian history, massacre and epistemicide were largely unspoken and/or forgotten, including those of Myall Creek in 1838, and Coniston in 1928. In 1968, eminent Anthropologist W. E. H. Stanner (1968), in his Boyer Lectures, challenged academics, historians, and governments on what he called "the great Australian silence." He argued that a system-led "cult of forgetfulness" toward Aboriginal peoples contributed to a longstanding denial of colonial frontier conflict, violence, and dispossession. It was, he proclaimed:

> A structural matter, a view from a window which has been carefully placed to exclude a whole quadrant of the landscape. What may well have begun as a simple forgetting of other possible views turned under habit and over time into something like a cult of forgetfulness practiced on a national scale. (p. 25)

On a related point, Attwood (2017) argues that settler societies like Australia find it "difficult to acknowledge their brutal pasts" and that a denial form of forgetfulness "was a crucial factor in creating the nation" (p. 24). While national identity is born from mythical claims to Australia by James Cook using *terra nullius* (land belonging to no-one), Black massacres challenge this foundational narrative. Narratives of White convict gulags are also little understood, but are embraced over Black atrocities. And more recently, informed by old forms of butchery, Australia advanced nuclear technology. In 1952, the Anangu Aboriginal peoples in South Australia were forced from their land so Australia and Britain could test atomic bombs with the aim to massacre millions with a single cost-effective detonation. In my view, the massacre of innocent Aboriginal nations, and the killings at Hiroshima and Nagasaki belong in the same historical context as genocide. Yet compellingly, the preservation of Stanner's cult of forgetfulness within a liberal democracy by the so-called civilized rulers was its precondition.

Distinguished historian Henry Reynolds (1989, p. xiii) stresses that, by the time Stanner spoke of "the cult of forgetfulness," historians were busy engaging in research to counter and transform these colonial silences. Today in Australia there are fierce academic debates, sometimes called the Australian history wars, that have been a catalyst for the re-examination and exposure of the extent of massacre events in Tasmania (Attwood, 2005; Blainey, 1993; Docker, 2010; Keating, 1992; MacIntyre & Clark, 2004; Ryan, 2013; Windschuttle, 2000a, 2000b, 2002).

In light of this debate, the question remains: why for the most part of Australian history didn't archaeology with its tools for producing evidence of human extermination expose the widespread cover-up? Litster and Wallis (2011), in their paper titled "Looking for the proverbial needle: The archaeology of Australian colonial frontier massacres," outline why "evidence of a forensically acceptable level is unlikely to be preserved archaeologically" (p. 113). They go on to claim that "massacre site identification" and understanding life during frontier wars requires multidisciplinary agents because of perpetrator concealment (language loss, police records, ration outposts, colonial school archives, fortified architecture) (pp. 113–14). I concur with Litster and Wallis but also argue that knowledge and its colonial transmission, via schooling, reproduces denialism, without which forgetting massacre on a grand scale would hardly have been possible.

As I claim above, Australian systems of education are not innocent; education is a key site of colonization and plays a significant role in dispossession, coercion, and the fixing of settler reason as "truth." However, that said, education has made some progress over time toward more inclusive practices, and our national curriculum has the potential to advance a national decolonizing project. This task is not without complexity and challenges! Such a project has to undermine and replace the colonial education system that produces a specific type of uneducated citizen, one who both forgets massacre and promulgates a White superiority rhetoric. To channel Adorno (1966/1998) again here, we have to struggle against "blind identification with the collective" and a "reified consciousness" (p. 195) that is blinded to our historical past.

Spring forward to 2008, and the Australia Prime Minister Kevin Rudd apologized to the Aboriginal Stolen Generations for the removal of children from their parents by policy and acknowledged the brutality of colonial histories. Eight years after the national apology, Australia's child gulag of shame—the Don Dale Youth Detention Centre—was exposed by the ABC program *Four corners* for the "mistreatment, tear-gassing" and torture of Aboriginal children (Worthington & Meldrum-Hanna, 2016). Disturbing footage emerged of Aboriginal youth Dylan Voller's legs shackled, his body and hands cruelly strapped to a medieval structure, his face covered with a black mask in Abu Ghraib style. Key contours of Australia's colonizing project became visible over again, repeated by a broken system and failed policy that reifies a school-to-prison pathway of its own choosing. But then nothing changes! Lorena Allam (2019), journalist for *The Guardian*, claimed that, "[a]lmost three years on from the royal commission into Don Dale, every single child in detention in the Northern Territory is Aboriginal." The

National Apology called for no more Stolen Generations and mistreatment. However, systems of state violence against Aboriginal children shaped by old rules were viewed as a relapse into the inhumane treatment of the past. Have the conditions that made historical violence toward Aboriginal peoples possible continued largely unchanged? What role, if any, has school played? How can educators think critically and act courageously against new formations of colonization and confront our own blind spots and knowledge limits? Such questions extend beyond the specifics of events such as the Stolen Generations and Don Dale, yet I hope they provide an opportunity to connect the dots between violent treatment of children and the task of redefining pedagogy as a demythologizing ethical practice for teachers and schools in the twenty-first century. What is the role of schooling after massacre?

Education after Massacre

As noted in my introduction, this chapter is inspired by Theodor Adorno's (1966/1998) famous essay "Education after Auschwitz," where he asserted that questions about Auschwitz have largely escaped social consciousness, and worse, the economic and social conditions that made the Holocaust possible have not diminished post-war. For fear of its recurrence, Adorno argued that the systems and structures that led to the atrocity of human extermination must be made visible for all to see. As he put it:

> When I speak of education after Auschwitz, then, I mean two areas: first children's education, especially in early childhood; then general enlightenment that provides an intellectual, cultural, and social climate in which a recurrence would no longer be possible, a climate, therefore, in which the motives that led to the horror would become relatively conscious. (p. 193)

In the Australian context, Adorno's insights illuminate how the Aboriginal learner and their disenfranchisement from the settler school has a colonial history, born from massacre and violent frontier wars. As explained by Adorno (1966/1998), education for indoctrination is connected to "old authoritarian structures and normative modes of behaviour" through what he calls "collectivisation" (p. 195). For example, Auschwitz was produced by a "manipulation of the masses" into "blind identification with the collective," led by Himmler and Eichmann, and the silencing of persecuted peoples' histories (see also Arendt, 2006). For Adorno (1966/1998), altering these conditions to confront the danger of Holocaust recurrence requires schools to work against the "predominance of collectives" while understanding how the system constitutes pedagogies that create such blind "collectivisation" (p. 195). Adorno claimed that, through pedagogical collectivization through schooling, "the inability to identify with others was unquestionably the most important psychological condition for the fact something like Auschwitz could have occurred in the midst of more or less civilised and innocent people" (p. 198). Put most bluntly, schooling failed the German nation during the 1930s and needs to be understood as a key site for the take-over by the National Socialists.

Advancing Adorno's notion of *collectivization*, Popkewitz and Lindblad (2004) argue that "the inability to identify with others" is constructed from colonial systems of "ordering and separating 'civilized' forms of reason from 'non-civilized'" (p. 232) versions. During and after Australian massacres, powerful narratives of "progress" and "degeneration" determined whose version of humanity and standards of reason were embodied in school cultural practices. Further nuancing, Ghassan Hage (1998) argues that in Australia colonial normative ideas of "progress" have been framed around how successfully the child can "accumulate Whiteness" (p. 58). In this sense, Australian massacre fulfills modernity's promise of "progress" toward a single national identity which is, by definition, void of difference. The image of the Aboriginal child as knower and holder of bilingual multiple intelligences brought to school is antithetical to the accumulation of whiteness (Moreton-Robinson 2000a, 2000b). What might it mean to rethink education to enable dialogue that questions the events of frontier wars, while engaging civic action for transforming new forms of injustice? What kind of education can construct the capable citizen who embraces pluralist identities and enriching ideas of humanity with the ability to consider different historical points of view?

Although not overly optimistic, implicit in Adorno's argument is the possibility of shifting what counts as good teaching, from promulgating a reified consciousness toward enacting pedagogies of difference and human solidarity. In Australia, there is now a consensus in the research literature that failure at school by Aboriginal children is in some significant part driven by the erasure of Aboriginal identities and childhoods at school (Morrison et al., 2019). Australian versions of Adorno's pedagogical collectivization manifest as normative and deficit constructions of the Aboriginal learner and the projection of whiteness onto their identities by structural racism in and outside of school (Rigney, 2001, 2021, Rigney et al., 2021). When Aboriginal children are defined as the problem, pedagogy and curriculum are assumed to be neutral in their (under)achievement. In this sense, the Anglo teacher is spared the discomfort of any self-reflection on how they might, on stolen Aboriginal land, contribute to debarbarization, un-possession, un-settlement, and future solidarity.

This is why demythologizing pedagogies are needed. Left alone to defend the integrity and honor of their ancient knowledges, Aboriginal children are subject to exclusionary discipline, harassment, and verbal assault rooted in perceptions that dismiss their version of history. This results in undermining Aboriginal authority over self or history and hence goes some way in explaining the school suspension practices, absenteeism, and rebellion commonly found in the Aboriginal school experience. Adorno's provocation calls for pedagogies that are informed by commitments to democratic inclusion, belonging, self-determination, and transformative engagement. Such a provocation pivots schooling away from narrow English-only standardization toward a respect for a plurality of languages and a re-centering of Indigenous localized embodied knowledge systems and hence ways of knowing and being, and environmental cosmology (Arbon, 2008; Martin, 2008; Ngũgĩ wa Thiong'o, 1986; Rigney, 2006).

In Germany today, Holocaust education is mandatory in the school curriculum, in contrast to Australian massacres, which remain outside the curriculum core. Aboriginal massacre continues to be seen as irrelevant to progress, even denied or accused of being fabrication. Yet the study of Australian atrocities as a significant historical event that promotes an understanding of the importance of universal human rights is urgent given the rise of nationalism, anti-Aboriginalism, and racism. Adorno conceded that education alone could not reform social and economic injustices, or rehabilitate power differentials within institutional cultures. Rather he believed in education for solidarity and self-reflection as individual, social, and collective agency. The capacity for self-determination is actualized when colonial ideas are pedagogically demythologized to children including empire, pioneer legend, teacher as all knower, child as incompetent subject, and school as politically neutral truth teller. For Adorno (1966/1998), "every debate about the ideals of education is trivial and inconsequential compared to this single ideal: never again Auschwitz" (p. 191).

Toward A Demythologizing Pedagogy for the Australian Frontier Wars

Megan Davis (2016) when discussing the Uluru Statement for constitutional recognition, Voice, and Treaty argues for reclaiming a truthful, demythologized account of the nation's past. What I want to propose, as the conclusion to this chapter, is an approach that I am calling *demythologizing pedagogy*, which takes up the challenge provide by both Davis and Adorno, toward an education for social transformation and specifically decolonization. An Australian decolonizing pedagogy requires reinstating other epistemic and ontological knowing in

Australian classrooms. Through my recent work, I argue that the central focus of decolonization must involve demythologizing teaching as culturally responsive pedagogical practices to improve human relationships, educating across cultural difference, unpacking the contested nature of histories, embracing multiple knowledges, and encouraging critical thinking for social change (Rigney 2006, Rigney 2021, Rigney & Kelly 2021, Kelly & Rigney 2021). Demythologizing the myths of the Aboriginal child, specifically those related to their abilities, histories, and knowledges, is also necessary to disrupt the reproduction of epistemicide. The act of establishing a decolonial *pluriverse* that cultivates both Anglo and Indigenized knowledges has to date been taken up by teachers who seek to move beyond knowledge hierarchies found in their own schools. I argue here and elsewhere that, if social change is desired, then scaling up demythologizing and culturally responsive schooling projects would need to move beyond mere inclusion toward greater teacher skills that recognizes colonial histories that build the agency and self-determination of the Indigenous learner (Rigney 2023a,b,c,d). Demythologizing pedagogies as culturally responsive teacher practices are in their infancy in both the literature and teacher practice. Despite a plethora of schooling initiatives to include Aboriginal perspectives in schools (Price, 2015), little attention has been given to demythologizing pedagogies in Australian public school classrooms and the potential of this work for advancing the goals of the Uluru Statement.

I define a demythologizing pedagogy as a culturally responsive dialogic teaching approach that involves students collaboratively working toward solidarity in the pursuit of justice and peace through the critical analysis of colonial grand narratives that mythologize the frontier, power, knowledge, race relations, the child, and the purpose of schooling. Demythologizing pedagogy requires considerable teacher investment in building safe and respectful learning environments using student-led inquiry, co-constructed by the teacher. Senior secondary levels are most suited to this approach with accompanying age-appropriate resources. Building from the work of Bedford and Wall (2020), in "Teaching as truth-telling: A demythologising pedagogy for the Australian frontier wars," I offer six principles as a first draft for a conceptual framework and by way of a brief summary.

Proposition 1. Knowledge Presented as Problematic and Socially Constructed

Students are to learn how and why knowledge is produced and its role in colonization. Teachers view all knowledge as being socially constructed and encompassing multiple forms of knowing. History is always someone's version of reality. Demythologizing knowledge in classrooms starts with teachers' self-reflections on their own practices by asking "to what degree is knowledge presented as constructed?" (Hayes et al., 2006, p. 144). Or as Apple (2004, 2012) has taught us, school curriculum is constructed knowledge that is mostly derived from the interests of dominant groups. Teachers "presenting knowledge as problematic involves an understanding of knowledge not as a fixed body of information" but recognition that it carries facts, silences, myths, and taboos (Hayes et al., 2006, p. 144). Demythologizing knowledge requires examples of Indigenous-authored school resources that provide localized views of history as alternatives to dominant ones (Rigney, 2001).

Proposition 2: Not Massacre but War

To demythologize Australian atrocities, teachers must be clear that the "Frontier Wars were wars" and that the "history of the Frontier Wars is not a history of massacres" (Bedford & Wall, 2020, p. 53). Indeed, there were "innumerable massacres...[but a] teaching approach that privileges a 'massacre narrative' incorrectly ascribes to First Nations peoples a lack of agency and a passivity that didn't exist in the face of a colonial expansion" (p. 53). Besides demythologizing war, students should be alerted to the legacies of colonialism and how they are never postcolonial, but they continue through current neoliberalizing forms of governing (Strakosch, 2015). Students today arrive to class with families and histories that are impacted by dispossession, invasion, massacre, patriarchy, Stolen Generations, native title, deaths in custody, and #Black Lives Matter.

Proposition 3: Critical Place-Based Studies

Colonial hegemony at the site of massacres overlaid a neutral, innocent discourse in the form of decontextualized and universalizing place naming. Demythologizing settler colonial narratives of place requires teachers and students to understand the diversity of local knowledges and the nexus between power, region, and place. Respectful learning relationships with Aboriginal children require understanding localized ways of caring for country and the ontological relatedness of all people to all things (Rigney and Rinaldi 2023). Re-centering in the classroom Aboriginal connection and obligations to country and sea is crucial to demythologizing colonial place narratives. Students can engage with questions about why conflict landscapes are forgotten and/or remembered. A "critical pedagogy of place aims to contribute to the production of educational discourses and practices that explicitly examine the place-specific nexus between environment, culture, and education" (Gruenewald, 2003, p. 10). Demythologizing requires critical place-based studies to analyze museums, memorials, and palimpsest land and seascapes.

Proposition 4: Reconceptualizing the Image of the Aboriginal Learner as Competent and Capable

Colonial histories of massacres construct Aboriginal people as feeble, needy, and without humanity. Demythologizing the colonial image of the Aboriginal child as *deficit*, homogenous, incompetent, and without prior knowledges requires pedagogical redesign by the teacher. Educators who embrace deficit views of children reject their culture and linguistic talents brought from home at the expense of acquiring those of the dominant culture. Commonly used deficit-oriented approaches to solving disparities involve compensatory education of low expectations and remedial English-only basic skills, which have proven ineffective. Demythologizing the image of the child requires school structures and teachers to view the child as powerful, competent, curious, and creative, full of potential with ambitious desires (Malaguzzi, 1994; Rinaldi, 1993). Demythologizing teachers connect the child's rights and funds of knowledge to learning (Dewey, 1966; Vygotsky, 1978). Educators see themselves as learners/teachers and co-researchers with children by investing in strong learning relationships and multiple forms of knowing.

Proposition 5: Culturally Responsive Pedagogies

Constraining Indigenous learning success is the projection of whiteness onto the Aboriginal learner without their permission by Euro-Western-centric pedagogies and curriculum. There is a growing body of evidence including my research that links culturally responsive pedagogies and learning improvement by children with diverse cultures (AITSL, 2011, Castagno & Brayboy 2008; Rigney et al., 2020, Rigney 2003 a,b,c,d, Rigney 2021). Culturally responsive pedagogy (also known as culturally relevant pedagogy or culturally responsive teaching, among other related terms) is an approach to teaching and learning that uses "the cultural characteristics, experiences, and perspectives of ethnically diverse students as conduits for teaching them more effectively" (Gay, 2002, p. 106).

Proposition 6: Solidarity for Change

The dignity of the child, as for all human beings, requires the right to maintain their histories, languages, and knowledges, and constitute their identities as dimensions of active citizenship, committed to strong equality and democracy. The child as bearer of these rights to their unique subjectivity, brought from home to school, forges bonds and solidarity with others through global knowledges and plural points of view. Teachers who are committed to forging such solidarities enact dialogic and democratic pedagogies that build empathy and collaborative knowledge production (Freire, 2003).

Conclusion

By way of a conclusion, I am envisioning a demythologizing pedagogy that can enable schools to become sites where dominant versions of curriculum knowledge and history are unsettled and re-evaluated. After all, Aboriginal grievances with Australia are the acquisition of a country by massacres, hidden behind the soft myth of *terra nullius*. Teachers committed to demythologizing engage students in re-examining the nature and causes of frontier wars, and the way people have struggled to overcome their damaging effects. For Adorno, the educator must struggle to ensure that Auschwitz never happens again. When applied to Australia, we urgently need a demythologizing as culturally responsive pedagogy that involves students building cross-cultural solidarity in the pursuit of justice and peace that prevents relapses into discrimination. A demythologizing pedagogy invites the student and the school to join in the struggle for a better world and to celebrate those who have stood against hate throughout history. Aboriginal children and their parents hold local repositories of knowledge where the spirit of the Uluru Statement thrives.

Acknowledgment

The data and theory used for this chapter derive from a 2017 Australian Research Council Indigenous Discovery Grant by Professor Lester-Irabinna Rigney and Professor Robert Hattam, "Toward an Australian Culturally Responsive Pedagogy" (Project ID: IN170100017); a 2021 Australian Research Council Discovery Grant by Professor Lester-Irabinna Rigney, Professor Robert Hattam, Dr. Stephen Kelly, Professor Michalinos Zembylas, Dr. Samantha Schulz, and Dr. Nadeem Memon, "Culturally Responsive Schooling" (Project ID: DP220100651). This work was also informed by a 2006 Australian Research Council Discovery Grant by Lester Rigney, "Indigenous Research Methodologies: Frameworks toward Indigenous Intellectual Sovereignty and the Decolonisation of Research" (Project ID: DI0348109).

Bibliography

Adorno, T. W. (1998). Education after Auschwitz (H. Pickford, Trans.). In T. W. Adorno, *Critical models: Interventions and catchwords* (pp. 191–204). Columbia University Press. (Original work published 1966)

Allam, L. (2019, May 31). "System is broken": All children in NT detention are Aboriginal, officials say. *The Guardian*. https://www.theguardian.com/australia-news/2019/may/31/system-is-broken-all-children-in-nt-detention-are-aboriginal-officials-say

Apple, M. (2004). *Ideology and curriculum* (25th anniversary ed.). Routledge.
Apple, M. (2012). *Education and power.* Routledge.
Arbon, V. (2008). *Arlathirnda Ngurkarnda Ityirnda: Being-knowing-doing: De-colonising Indigenous tertiary education*. Post Pressed.
Arendt, H. (2006). *Eichmann in Jerusalem: A report on the banality of evil.* Penguin Books.
Attwood, B. (2005). *Telling the truth about Aboriginal history.* Allen and Unwin.
Attwood, B. (2017). Denial in a settler society: The Australian case. *History Workshop Journal, 84*(1), 24–43.
Australian Institute for Teaching and School Leadership (AITSL). (2011). *Australian professional standards for teachers,* AITSL, Melbourne.
Bedford, A., & Wall, V. (2020). Teaching as truth-telling: A demythologising pedagogy for the Australian frontier wars. *Agora, 55*(1), 47–55.
Blainey, G. (1993). Drawing up the balance sheet of our history. *Quadrant, 37*(7), 10–15.
Bonwick, J. (1970). *The last of the Tasmanians, or, The Black War in Van Diemen's Land.* Libraries Board of South Australia. (Original work published 1870)
Castagno, A., & Brayboy, B. (2008). Culturally responsive schooling for Indigenous youth: A review of the literature. *Review of Educational Research, 78*(4), 941–93.
Davis, M. (2016). Ships that pass in the night. In M. Davis & M. Langton (Eds.), *It's our country: Indigenous arguments for meaningful constitutional recognition and reform* (pp. 86–96). Melbourne University Press.
Dewey, J. (1966). *Democracy and education.* Free Press.
Docker J. (2010). Epistemological vertigo and allegory: Thoughts on massacres, actual, surrogate, and averted—*Beersheba, Wake in fright, Australia.* In F. Peters-Little, A. Curthoys, & J. Docker (Eds.), *Passionate histories: Myth, memory and Indigenous Australia* (pp. 51–72). ANU Press.
Elder, B. (2003). *Blood on the wattle: Massacres and maltreatment of Aboriginal Australians since 1788* (3rd ed.). New Holland.
Freire, P. (2003). *Pedagogy of the oppressed.* Continuum. (Original work published 1970)
Gay, G. (2002). Preparing for culturally responsive teaching. *Journal of Teacher Education, 53*(2), 106–16.
Giroux, H. (2004). Education after Abu Ghraib: Revisiting Adorno's politics of education. *Cultural Studies, 18*(6), 779–815.
Gruenewald, D. (2003). The best of both worlds: A critical pedagogy of place. *Educational Researcher, 32*(4), 3–12.
Hage, G. (1998). *White nation: Fantasies of White supremacy in a multicultural society.* Pluto Press.
Hayes, D., Mills, M., Christie, P., & Lingard, B. (2006). *Teachers and schooling making a difference: Productive pedagogies, assessment and performance.* Allen & Unwin.

Keating, P. (1992). *Speech at Redfern Park, 10 December 1992, at the Australian launch of the International Year for the World's Indigenous People*. https://pmtranscripts.pmc.gov.au/sites/default/files/original/00008765.pdf

Kelly, S., & Rigney, L. I. (2022). Unsettling the reason of time: Indigenist epistemology and the child in the Australian curriculum. *Discourse: Studies in the Cultural Politics of Education*, *43*(3), 386–404.

Litster, M., & Wallis, L. (2011). Looking for the proverbial needle? The archaeology of Australian colonial frontier massacres. *Archaeology in Oceania*, *46*(3), 105–17.

MacIntyre, S., & Clark, A. (2004). *The history wars*. Melbourne University Press.

Malaguzzi, L. (1994). Your image of the child: Where teaching begins. *Child Care Information Exchange*, *94*(3), 52–61.

Martin, K. (2008). *Please knock before you enter: Aboriginal regulation of outsiders and the implications for researchers*. Post Pressed.

Moreton-Robinson, A. (2000a). Duggaibah or "Place of Whiteness": Australian feminists and race. In J. Docker & G. Fischer (Eds.), *Race, colour and identity in Australia and New Zealand* (pp. 240–55). University of New South Wales Press.

Moreton-Robinson, A. (2000b). *Talkin' up to the White woman: Aboriginal women and feminism*. University of Queensland Press.

Morrison, A., Rigney, L.-I., Hattam, R., & Diplock, A. (2019). *Toward an Australian culturally responsive pedagogy: A narrative review of the literature*. University of South Australia.

Ngũgĩ wa Thiong'o. (1986). *Decolonising the mind: The politics of language in African literature*. J. Currey.

Popkewitz, T., & Lindblad, S. (2004). Historicizing the future: Educational reform, systems of reason, and the making of children who are the future citizens. *Journal of Educational Change*, *5*, 229–47.

Price, K. (2015). *Aboriginal and Torres Strait Islander education: An introduction for the teaching profession*. Cambridge University Press.

Reynolds, H. (1989). *Dispossession: Black Australians and White invaders*. Allen & Unwin.

Rigney, L.-I. (1999). Internationalization of an Indigenous anticolonial cultural critique of research methodologies: A guide to Indigenist research methodology and its principles. *Wicazo Sa Review*, *14*(2), 109–21.

Rigney, L.-I. (2001). A first perspective of Indigenous Australian participation in science: Framing Indigenous research towards Indigenous Australian intellectual sovereignty. *Kaurna Higher Education Journal*, *7*, 1–13.

Rigney, L.-I. (2006). Indigenist research and Aboriginal Australia. In J. E. Kunnie & N. I. Goduka (Eds.), *Indigenous peoples' wisdom and power: Affirming our knowledge through narratives* (pp. 32–48). Ashgate.

Rigney, L.-I. (2021). *Aboriginal child as knowledge producer: Bringing into dialogue Indigenist epistemologies and culturally responsive pedagogies for schooling.* In B. Hokowhitu, A. Moreton-Robinson, L. Tuhiwai-Smith, C. Andersen, & S. Larkin (Eds.), Routledge handbook of critical Indigenous studies, Abingdon, New York, NY: Routledge, pp. 578–90.

Rigney, L-I. (2023a) On the Need for New Culturally Responsive Pedagogies. In Lester-Irabinna Rigney (ed.) 2023, *Global perspectives and new challenges in culturally responsive pedagogies: super-diversity and teaching practice*, Routledge, UK, pp. 3–10.

Rigney, L-I (2023b) Teachers cultivating Aboriginal child as knowledge producer: advancing Australian culturally responsive pedagogies. In Lester-Irabinna Rigney (ed.) 2023, Global perspectives and new challenges in culturally responsive pedagogies: super-diversity and teaching practice, Routledge, Abingdon, England, pp. 10–20.

Rigney, L-I (2023c), 'Teaching through Lifeworlds of Aboriginal Children: Australian Opportunities through Culturally Responsive Pedagogies', in Brock, C, Exley, B & Rigney, L-I (eds) 2024, International Perspectives on Literacies, Diversities, and Opportunities for Learning, 1st edn, vol. 1, Routledge, New York, NY. pp. 47–59.

Rigney, L-I (2023d), Global perspectives and new challenges in culturally responsive pedagogies: super-diversity and teaching practice, Routledge, Abingdon, England.

Rigney, L-I., & Kelly, S. (2021): *Reterritorialising pedagogies of listening: bringing into dialogue culturally responsive pedagogies with Reggio Emilia principles*, Discourse: Studies in the Cultural Politics of Education, 44, no. 1, pp. 147–61.

Rigney, L-I & Rinaldi, C, (2023), Teaching in cultural and linguistic super-diverse Australian classrooms: A north–south exploration of Reggio Emilia. In Fyfe, B, Lee-Johnson, YL, Reyes, J & Schroeder Yu, G (Gigi) 2023, Affirming the Rights of Emergent Bilingual and Multilingual Children and Families: Interweaving Research and Practice through the Reggio Emilia Approach, 1st edn, vol. 1, Taylor & Francis, United Kingdom, pp. 209–25.

Rigney, L.-I., Sisson, J., Hattam, R., & Morrison, A. (2020). *Bringing culturally responsive pedagogies and Reggio Emilia education principles into dialogue: Children learning to live together in diverse communities.* University of South Australia.

Rinaldi, C. (1993). The emergent curriculum and social constructivism. In C. Edwards, L. Gandini, & G. Forman (Eds.), *The hundred languages of children: The Reggio Emilia approach to early childhood education* (pp. 101–11). Ablex.

Ryan, L. (2010). "Hard evidence": The debate about massacre in the Black War in Tasmania. In F. Peters-Little, A. Curthoys, & J. Docker (Eds.), *Passionate histories: Myth, memory and Indigenous Australia* (pp. 39–50). ANU Press.

Ryan, L. (2013). The Black Line in Van Diemen's Land: Success or failure? *Journal of Australian Studies*, *37*(1), 3–18.
Stanner, W. E. H. (1968). *The Boyer Lectures: After the Dreaming*. Australian Broadcasting Commission.
Strakosch E. (2015). *Neoliberal colonialism in neoliberal Indigenous policy*. Palgrave Macmillan.
Vygotsky, L. S. (1978). *Mind in society*. Harvard University Press.
Windschuttle, K. (2000a). The myths of frontier massacres, Part I: The invention of massacre stories. *Quadrant*, *44*(10), 8–21.
Windschuttle, K. (2000b). The myths of frontier massacres, Part III: Massacre stories and the policy of separatism. *Quadrant*, *44*(12), 6–20.
Windschuttle, K. (2002). *The fabrication of Aboriginal history—Volume One: Van Dieman's Land 1803–1847*. Macleay Press.
Worthington, E., & Meldrum-Hanna, C. (2016, July 27). Four Corners: Dylan Voller strapped to chair multiple times, former Don Dale guard claims. *ABC News*. https://www.abc.net.au/news/2016-07-27/dylan-voller-strapped-chair-restraint-multiple-times-guard-says/7663332

5 Scaled Up "Safety-Net" Schooling and the "Wicked Problem" of Educational Exclusion in South Australia—Problem or Solution?

Andrew Bills, David Armstrong, and Nigel Howard

Introduction

In this chapter we investigate a major, long-running policy intervention to combat educational exclusion in South Australia: the Innovative Community Action Networks (ICAN)-Flexible Learning Options (FLO) policy and program agenda. ICAN was discontinued but FLO was its legacy as the only bureaucratically systematized "alternative" schooling approach to addressing the problem of early school leaving in Australia. We frame FLO using the concept of wicked problems in policy and specify how some problematic features of FLO since its inception in 2007 are predicted by this concept. Problems with FLO include: a lack of public accountability; shortcomings in the transparency of the attainment of enrolled students; and the consequent danger that public confidence in FLO could be undermined. This was borne out when a wide-ranging inquiry into suspension, exclusion, and expulsion (Graham et al., 2020) recommended the program be discontinued. The Department for Education (DfE) chose a "redesign" instead that offered little change other than a change of name to Tailored Learning Provision (TLP) and an imposition of some more guidance on schools. We offer constructive suggestions to address these weaknesses, including more conceptual policy work in partnership with collective stakeholder inquiry and research. We conclude that one ever-present danger with social inclusion initiatives like FLO and its younger redesigned cousin TLP is that they become a parallel education system for the disadvantaged and thereby corrode the principle of an inclusive mainstream education system meeting the needs of all children and young people.

The South Australian FLO program has catered for over 60,000 annual enrollments of students over a fifteen-year period at a total public enrollment cost of hundreds of millions of dollars. ICAN-FLO began as a localized policy response to the larger "wicked problem" of educational exclusion. Our analysis in what follows draws attention to problematic features of the FLO program and conceptualizes these features in terms of recent accounts which highlight flawed or inadequate policy responses to educational exclusion in Australia (Graham et al., 2015).

Wicked Problems

Horst Rittel, a designer and town planner, popularized the term "wicked problem" in the late 1960s (Protzen & Harris, 2010), drawing on earlier formulations (Churchman, 1967). He was interested in how design methodology and process analysis could be used to solve complex, multifaceted issues facing urban planning (Protzen & Harris, 2010). The term "wicked problems" was coined to describe features of these issues which often perplexed urban planners and policy makers. In a ground-breaking paper Rittel and Webber (1973) identified ten hallmark features of wicked problems, including that "there is no definitive formulation" of them; that they are "essentially unique," and also they are relational where "every wicked problem can be considered to be a symptom of another problem" (pp. 161, 164, 165). As Head and Alford (2015, p. 713) note, Rittel and Webber's (1973) critical analysis of wicked problems constitutes a radical critique of standard, linear approaches to solving public policy problems.

Early School Leaving

Early school leaving stemming from disengagement and detachment continues to present as a protracted public policy problem across Australia, Canada, New Zealand, the United States, and the United Kingdom (Slee, 2011). A variety of policy measures to prevent early school leaving of predominantly disadvantaged students to foster school completion have been trialed in recent decades, including policies directed at students, their families, and secondary schools (De Witte et al., 2013). Increasingly in Australia these students find a place or are placed in alternative education programs. In 2014, Australian researcher Kitty te Riele indicated that 74,000 students in Australia were placed in programs variously described as second-chance schools, flexible learning programs, or alternative schools. We will use the term FLO throughout this chapter as a catch-all term for these variously named endeavors.

At the turn of the century South Australian apparent retention rates in public secondary schools had fallen to under 70 %. With SA lagging behind the other mainland states, a collaborative project to investigate the issue was established. The project, published as *Listen to me I'm leaving* (Smyth et al., 2000), gathered the voices of 207 early school leavers using a critical sociological "voiced research" approach. It provided a sociological account of the nature of the early school leaving problem from the perspective of young people. Based on the analysis, the research provided a series of recommendations to address the phenomenon of early school leaving from a policy and schooling perspective. Across the *Listen to me I'm leaving* interviews, key themes emerged: young people spoke about schooling that was not inclusive, schooling that was over-disciplinary, poor teacher–student relationships, and student bullying. Key themes also indicated that school learning regimens were boring.

After the election of a progressive state government at the turn of the century and the establishment of a Social Inclusion Unit, FLO, South Australia's long-running policy and program response to the early school leaving issue, followed five years after *Listen to me I'm leaving*, and represents the only systematized flexible learning approach in Australia.

Flexible Learning Options in Australia

FLOs similar in intent to the South Australian FLO have expanded across Australia in the last 15 years (te Riele, 2014). In 2004, Smyth and Hattam indicated how cycles of suspension and absenteeism culminating in exclusion or *dropping out* of school frequently defined the educational journeys of early school leavers. What has changed since that research is that young people now have more access to FLOs nationally, through programs based on TAFE[1] campuses, in community youth centers, and inside or adjacent to secondary schools. They are described in the scholarly literature as inclusive programs characterized by affirming teacher–student relationships that help make the educational experience for young people more supportive, with a removal of the arbitrary uniform and disciplinary technologies that were negatively experienced by many young people in their previous schooling forays. In the FLOs, discipline is addressed through affirming teacher–student relationships and affirming support structures. An increasing number of these initiatives are being systematized under Commonwealth funding for Special Assistance Schools. FLOs are noted for serving predominantly disadvantaged young people, a key characteristic of the SA FLO cohorts. As young people have found their way into the maze of alternatives, apparent retention has increased without a corresponding increase in achievement (Bills & Howard, 2021).

Changing the nature of education to make it more engaging for all young people demands that the cultural geography of the FLOs is different from conventional schooling. In general, the structures, cultures, and dominant pedagogies of these "irregular" (Slee, 2011) schools manifest in smaller class sizes, more personalized learning, flexible time tabling and various forms of support for youth agency (te Riele, 2014). Teachers and leaders in the FLOs work hard to develop

1 The acronym TAFE stands for technical and further education and is used and recognized throughout Australia. TAFE SA is a Registered Training Organisation under the jurisdiction of the Australian Skills Quality Authority.

learning cultures attuned to how young people want to be treated in learning. Whether this translates into a curriculum that allows students to negotiate the next step of their transition to learning or work requires investigation.

Research Scholarship About FLOs

Across the Australian FLO research literature, examples of project and inquiry-based learning involving curriculum negotiation with students (McGregor et al., 2015) are given, but in recent years, research concerns have been expressed about where these young people end up post-program. Most notably, an Australian research article by te Riele (2006), "Youth 'at risk': Further marginalizing the marginalized?," highlighted these concerns. Smyth and colleagues produced similarly critical research articles including "Give me air not shelter" (Smyth & Robinson, 2015), and "Speaking back to educational policy: Why social inclusion will not work for disadvantaged Australian schools" (Smyth, 2010). Non-completion of the HSC (Higher School Certificate) or South Australian Certificate of Education (SACE) across the FLOs has fueled speculation about the effectiveness and rigor of the curriculum on offer (McGregor et al., 2015; Smyth et al., 2014; te Riele, 2006) and, most importantly for this chapter's purpose, consideration of the educational successes of the FLOs in terms of high school completion rates and post-program opportunities (te Riele et al., 2017).

Gaps in the FLO Research

Across the FLO research, there is an absence of quantitative data on HSC completion rates and longitudinal data pertaining to post-FLO transition outcomes. We argue these data are urgently needed for all FLOs in order to have insights into the educational and future life opportunities that these options actually provide and to address through policy and practice issues that may be working against socially just outcomes for young people. Concerns about the transparency and accountability of public provision in programs like SA FLO are amplified when their growing scale across Australia is considered, with enrollments in the tens of thousands nationally on an annual basis (te Riele et al., 2017). To advance knowledge about why this data gap exists we return to the concept of "wicked problems" in the context of the FLO initiative.

Methodology

The methodology chosen for our FLO investigation was critical policy historiography (Gale, 1999). We marshaled an extensive archive of gray policy and program literature over the life of the FLO program, predominantly from the

DfE, and placed this archive in dialectical tension with relevant contemporary research in the scholarly fields of early school leaving, alternative schooling, and post-compulsory schooling.

Data analyzed were predominantly documentary and included primary sources (such as government policy texts, records, and reports, Hansard parliamentary speeches, and media releases), and secondary sources (such as relevant academic literature and newspaper articles). Borrowing from Gale (1999), in analyzing such policy records we were interested in doing several things, but in particular to detail:

- a systematic overview of selected past events; initially through their analytical separation from present events and from those that do not contribute to an understanding of early school leaving and the wickedness of the problem but with subsequent division into distinctive historical periods; leading to
- a critical analysis of the data (quantitative and qualitative) that is concerned with an episode in the history of early school leaving ideas and, more importantly, with critical sociological questions about who benefits and who loses from the FLO schooling arrangements.

Understanding Low HSC Completion Rates in FLO

As touched on previously, resistance to solution has been identified as a typical feature of wicked problems (Briggs, 2012; Rittel & Weber, 1973). In keeping with this characterization, educational exclusion and the connected problem of early school leaving have proven to be highly resistant to the FLO solution because of the inherent complexity of the underlying wicked problem itself and the multifarious forces that work to disrupt scaled-up social policy away from its policy design intent. The flaws in the FLO program are rooted in the unintended consequences of policy designed to prevent educational exclusion.

Discussion of FLO Policy "Wickedness"

All in all, FLO has become normalized after years of operation in the political, bureaucratic, and schooling realm as the way DfE does things for young people "at risk" in SA. There is no doubt that on-the-ground staff working with FLO students are indeed passionate about their work and they work hard. This is borne out in the gray literature on the program, and our own experiences of working in similar programs. DfE-commissioned evaluations spoke highly about the wellbeing outcomes of the program for those they spoke to, even as their data pointed to uneven outcomes. This chapter is concerned with the macro policy design and the "wickedness" of this design as it presents in SACE outcomes. In

2012, 2 percent of FLO students completed their SACE (ARTD Consultants, 2013, p. 57), 5 percent in 2014 (DfE, 2016, p. 1), and a reported 12 percent of the possible Year 12 cohort in 2023 (DfE, 2023).

Addressing "wicked" public policy problems requires more grounded inquiry and research by impartial experts both within and outside an organization. In the case of FLO, tackling the wicked problem of non-school completion requires institutional transparency and willingness to re-examine the nature of the wicked public policy problem that presents. The chance to re-examine FLO in the context of the wider wicked problem of disengagement and detachment, after the Graham Inquiry recommended the program be discontinued, was lost when the department opted to redesign the current program.

Everything is Political

Back in 2010 in the state House of Assembly, then Minister for Education Jay Weatherill provided several remarkable stories of the FLO program's life-changing impact upon participating young people. Here is one of them:

> Amanda was a student who stopped going to school after she found it too hard to connect with her fellow students. Enrolled through the Flexible Learning Options in ICAN, Amanda found, through her involvement with the outdoor education program, leadership skills that she never knew she had. Engaged through V-Tech, Amanda excelled and was awarded a scholarship to attend the Australian Technical College. She has commenced a four-year automotive apprenticeship and is now excited about her future. (South Australia, 2010)

As researchers wishing to enhance life opportunities for all young people, as do all DfE employees, young people, caregivers, and parents, how can we possibly argue against such a positive life turnaround story? Of course, we cannot dispute this individual story, but from a 60,000-student enrollment, anecdotes are not evidence. From a macro policy perspective, we must question the idea that the success of a program rests on a small number of stories of "lives transformed." Amanda's story is not indicative of a successful program. An Education Department–commissioned report released in 2020 found that:

> Among leavers, former FLO students were more likely than other students to not be in employment, education or training, were less happy with what they had achieved since leaving school and were less likely to strongly agree that they had successfully made the transition from school. (ACER, 2020, p. 120)

There is an extensive body of research that maintains successful school completion lifts life opportunity post-school (Deloitte Access Economics, 2012; King,

1999; Lamb & Huo, 2017; Lamb et al., 2015). For FLO to be seen as successful Amanda's story should be every student's story.

No DfE annual report has provided a synopsis of the percentage of FLO SACE outcomes or explicit annual data on post-program employment/tertiary entrance outcomes. Rather, favorable metrics have been used, like program enrollment growth and improved retention rate, with engagement defined in the most optimistic of terms and anecdotal references to increased wellbeing outcomes and the occasional turnaround story.

The Unintended Consequences of the FLO Response to Exclusion

Briggs (2012) highlights that attempts by public policy to address wicked problems often generate consequences that were unintended and unforeseen by policy makers. The low SACE completion rate for students enrolled in FLO can be understood as one unforeseen consequence of how this initiative has developed as a form of passive exclusion (Bills & Howard, 2017). Specifically, we would suggest that this is a by-product of the low accountability and lack of transparency surrounding this initiative, which has exacerbated the low rate of completion of school for the cohorts of disadvantaged students.

Unfortunately, just under a half of public secondary school students did not successfully complete Year 12 and gain certification in 2015 and that holds every year up to 2023, the last date we have figures for. These figures are based on Year 8 students and their journey through to Year 12: the SACE completion metric used in the SACE Review (Crafter et al., 2006). However, they are at odds with the public-facing figures released by the DfE. The DfE inflates SACE completion percentages by reporting the percentage of students who present in October of their final year of schooling who then complete their SACE, who at that time (one month before school ends) are only those students able to pass the SACE with the subjects they are undertaking.

DfE reporting practices in the public realm hide how disadvantaged DfE secondary schools are really doing in terms of SACE completion. This is because the SACE Board only provides combined private and public school SACE data and because DfE uses questionable metrics that hide the significance of the problem. The actual public secondary school SACE outcomes providing a sobering account of the inequality of outcomes in public education directly related to postcodes of disadvantage in South Australia. That is, economic and social disadvantage continues to very much influence SACE outcomes.

Students who are designated as unlikely to complete SACE in disadvantaged schools are further disadvantaged when placed into FLO programs, a form of streaming, which further concentrates disadvantage and contributes to worsening outcomes (Perry & McConney, 2010; Reid, 2016, Teese, 2011). So in constructing FLO as a program for individuals with barriers to education the policy fails to address the social make-up of schools and the inadequacy of responsive curriculum design for disadvantaged students (Slee, 2013). In other words, better educational outcomes for disadvantaged young people require a movement away from the segregation of schools and by implication the segregation of FLO learning centers that cater for the most disadvantaged of the disadvantaged: "A new policy direction is needed to create a greater social mix in our schools, and to reduce the resource disparities between schools by providing more appropriate and targeted funding" (Reid, 2016, p. 4). This is all the more urgent given that the gap between the educational outcomes of students from high- and low-SES backgrounds has increased (Bonnor & Shepherd, 2014, as cited in Reid, 2016).

Dilemmas of Inclusion

Our analysis reveals a lack of institutional transparency in the public realm across years of FLO policy and practice, in relation to funding expenditure, annual SACE program outcomes, and post-program transitions. Additionally, the DfE's unwillingness in recent years to invite impartial public policy experts to train a critical policy lens on FLO public policy has hampered attempts to address the challenge (Head, 2008; Head & Alford, 2015). We argue this form of organizational behavior may have stalled policy reconfiguration for more socially just educational outcomes. This becomes apparent in relation to the later redesign of FLO, where the official consultation was confined to the existing FLO community.

Critical research into the exclusion of disadvantaged and disengaged secondary students broadly supports policy efforts designed to redress the systematic tendency of education systems to exclude. As Slee (2013) suggests, "exclusion is a political predisposition" (p. 895). These terms are, at first glance, broadly sympathetic to the core purpose of FLO as an educational option for students who exit school prematurely due to disadvantage and disengagement (Deloitte Access Economics, 2012). Considering FLO in the light of its stated core purpose as an alternative educational option and in light of the wider goal of an inclusive educational system—a goal which is central to stated public policy in SA (Select Committee on Access to the South Australian Education System for Students with a Disability, 2017)—prompts deeper critical questioning.

By providing an option for responding to chronic failure in the mainstream system, FLO could be seen as sustaining the wicked problem of exclusion in secondary schools in SA (Cooper, 2008). Furthermore, the provision of an alternative schooling option carries dangers that its alternative framing will re-enforce deficit views of already disadvantaged students. In the context of special schools,

Norwich (2009) describes this as a dilemma of difference: specialist provision might best meet the additional needs of many students with disabilities, but the "special" label often carries "negative implications or risks associated with stigma, devaluation, rejection or denial of opportunities" (p. 448). Norwich, who has written extensively on this topic (Norwich, 2007, 2013), notes "potential tensions between having good quality provision for all, providing flexibly in common schools for the diversity of children and treating all with respect" (2009, p. 466). FLO negotiates this dilemma, and the unresolved question is whether in doing so it corrodes the principle of an inclusive and unitary public education system meeting the needs of all students in SA.

Initially conceived as a collaborative effort between schools and communities to combat low retention and achievement rates, FLO underwent scrutiny in the 2020 Ministerial Inquiry into Suspension, Exclusion, and Expulsion in South Australian Public Schools chaired by Linda Graham from the Centre for Inclusive Education at the Queensland University of Technology. The report highlighted that FLO is a form of passive exclusion, identifying issues regarding attendance and compliance, and making the damming finding that "we identified patterns in the incidence of suspension and exclusion over time that strongly suggest students in FLO are not actually 'in FLO'" (Graham et al., 2020, p. 324). The report raised concerns about breaches of international conventions, prompting recommendations for research into alternative provision and the decommissioning of FLO.

After two years of inaction on the recommendations of the Graham Report the Department for Education, ignoring its own interim recommendation, opted for a program redesign while sidelining many of the concerns raised in the report and the broader context of declining retention and achievement. The redesign, as documented, did not see the issue of exclusion and early school leaving as a "wicked problem" but as an opportunity for improvement that included "a new name, a stronger structure and greater and more specific guidance and processes regarding enrolment for schools" (DfE, 2023). The consultation focused on existing FLO programs and areas for improvement, overlooking critical issues. Stakeholder consultations, predominantly involving schools, non-government organizations, educators, parents, and students benefiting from the program, resulted in recommendations biased toward affirming the program's efficacy, neglecting critical analysis.

The redesign fails to confront the comprehensive findings outlined in the Graham Report. Instead, it reframes FLO as a program that attracts stigma and lacks some oversight. It continues to categorize FLO students as having barriers to schooling without adequately addressing systemic inequities or school responsibilities in addressing these barriers. Furthermore, the report overlooks the decline in retention and achievement rates and fails to elucidate successful FLO practices or their impact on student outcomes. A trial of 12 schools was begun in 2024, under the oversight of a centralized redesign team, while for all the other schools with a FLO enrollment it was "business as usual."

In the three years between the Graham Report and the TLP trial, retention from year 11 FLO enrollment to year 12 collapsed and was below the year 11–12 transition for students in mainstream schooling. At the same time overall FLO enrollment increased (DfE 2024). FLO no. longer served its original purpose of increasing retention and segregation from mainstream schooling became an end in itself. That TLP is posited as the solution reinforces the idea that segregating students from mainstream school is the normalized way that the DfE avoids scrutiny of underachievement of disadvantaged students.

By opting to redesign and rename FLO to avoid stigma, the necessary pedagogical and curricular work to enable significantly more students to complete SACE and negotiate the next steps to career-based work and study remains unfinished. We argue the DfE should fund transparent policy and practice research by independent experts in the field on what it means to be (1) a truly inclusive secondary school, (2) proffering curriculum and pedagogies of engagement that work for all young people, and (3) ensuring key performance indicators are in place to understand progress across the research trajectory. The key research question that presents in all of this is: How can disadvantaged young people in public secondary education experience more engaging and inclusive schooling practices that enable more hopeful futures?

Conclusion

Wicked problems can be seen as a positive because they can represent an opportunity for positive change and for organizational innovation (Murgatroyd, 2010). For these positives to transpire however and translate into practice, openness to meaningful change, in the context of SA public education, is necessary at a political level and also at the level of the SA education bureaucracy (DfE). Rittel himself came to emphasize the inescapable political complexion of wicked problems and abandoned his earlier beliefs that technical rationality could plan out problems (Armstrong, 2018).

When a significant high-stakes public policy such as FLO is revealed to have policy blind spots (Bills & Howard, 2017), with unintended policy side effects (Zhao, 2017) of unacceptably low SACE completion rates, the political and institutional consequences can be damaging if not managed well. In this situation default bureaucratic and political risk aversion requires research-informed problematizing of previously under-theorized policy assumptions. This requires enormous political courage to allow institutional transparency and to publicly accept responsibility for policy failings, in order to move into a more hopeful research-informed policy trajectory. According to Armstrong (2018):

> analysis of wicked problems can be a positive generator for enlightened design of solutions … more in keeping with the "practical epistemology" ("how to know what is known") inherent in Rittel's theories and has been identified as a particularly valuable aspect of them. (p. 998)

For all of this to happen, complex FLO policy settings must be attuned to changing educational, social, health, and economic fundamentals and recalibrated to account for the unforeseen and multifarious forces that have compromised policy intent. This policy recalibration work demands repositioning the ICAN-FLO policy and careful attunement to measure program success. The most important measures of the success of the policy are: (1) school completion rates; (2) wellbeing enhancement; and (3) longitudinal post-school pathways for all students such as their take-up of career-based opportunities or tertiary study. In all three areas, the redesign of FLO has been deficient.

To address this deficiency we propose the redesign of FLO be seen as a "wicked problem" that will need continuous revision and reinvention. Any form of alternative provision should be an integral part of the educational offering for all students and the right education and support should be offered to each student. The over-representation of Aboriginal students, students with disabilities, and students under guardianship must be interrogated. A clear definition of what Tailored Learning Provision is hoping to achieve for students, which mainstream provision cannot provide, is needed.

Students who are referred to, or enroll in, Tailored Learning Provision should be assured that they will continue to get a good education that will enable them to achieve accredited learning with the support needed to negotiate that learning and the next stage of their life. Students with Tailored Learning Provision must be able to access the full curriculum and have the support and resources to complete their learning in a manner that suits them. Considering these concerns, we believe a more comprehensive approach to the development of Tailored Learning Provision is essential to address the shortcomings identified in the Graham Report. Importantly, a redesigned Tailored Learning Provision needs to engage our most vulnerable young people fully in the design of their own education. A trial of a redesigned solution and business as usual for the majority of schools does not address the complexity and "wickedness" of the problems faced.

Bibliography

Armstrong, D. (2018). Addressing the wicked problem of behaviour in schools. *International Journal of Inclusive Education*, *22*(9), 997–1013.

ARTD Consultants. (2013). *Innovative Community Action Networks (ICAN)—A sustainable, evidenced-based approach for engaging young people in learning.* Department for Education and Child Development.

Australian Council for Educational Research (ACER). (2020). *Earning and Learning Research Project: Report to the Department for Education.*

Bills, A., & Howard, N. (2017). Social inclusion education policy in South Australia: What can we learn? *Australian Journal of Education*, *61*(1), 54–74.

Bills, A., & Howard, N. (2021). *It's time to act: Making the case for a cross sectoral response to school disengagement and detachment in South Australia* (CEPSW Educational Leadership Industry Report No. 1). Flinders University.

Briggs, L. (2012). *Tackling wicked problems: A public policy perspective.* Australian Public Service Commission.

Churchman, C. *Editorial Wicked Problems* Free for All. (1967). *Management Science*, *14*(B-141-B-146. https://doi.org/10.1287/mnsc.14.4.b141

Cooper, P. (2008). Like alligators bobbing for poodles? A critical discussion of education, ADHD, and the biopsychosocial perspective. *Journal of Philosophy of Education*, 42(3–4), 457–74.

Crafter, G., Crook, P., & Reid, A. (2006). *Success for all: Ministerial Review of Senior Secondary Education in South Australia.* Government of South Australia.

De Witte, K., Cabus, S., Thyssen, G., Groot, W., & van den Brink, H. M. (2013). A critical review of the literature on school dropout. *Educational Research Review*, *10*, 13–28.

Deloitte Access Economics. (2012). *The socio-economic benefits of investing in the prevention of early school leaving.*

Department for Education (DfE). (2016). *Flexible Learning Options—Interim Service Improvement Report.* Department for Education and Child Development. (Accessed through FOI, December 2017).

Department for Education (DfE). (2023). *Flexible Learning Options redesign.* Government of South Australia. (Accessed through Freedom of Information).

Department for Education (DfE). (2024). *Senior School Retention and SACE Completion 2023.*

Gale, T. (1999). Policy trajectories: Treading the discursive path of policy analysis. *Discourse: Studies in the Cultural Politics of Education*, *20*(3), 393–407.

Graham, L., McCarthy, T., Killingly, C., Tancredi, H., & Poed, S. (2020). *Inquiry into suspension, exclusion and expulsion processes in South Australian government schools: Final report.* Centre for Inclusive Education, QUT.

Graham, L. J., Van Bergen, P., & Sweller, N. (2015). "To educate you to be smart": Disaffected students and the purpose of school in the (not so clever) "lucky country." *Journal of Education Policy*, *30*(2), 237–57.

Head, B. W. (2008). Wicked problems in public policy. *Public Policy*, *3*(2), 101–18.

Head, B. W., & Alford, J. (2015). Wicked problems: Implications for public policy and management. *Administration & Society*, *47*(6), 711–39.

King A. (1999). *The cost to Australia of early school-leaving*. Dusseldorp Skills Forum.

Lamb, S., & Huo, S. (2017). *Counting the costs of lost opportunity in Australian education*. Centre for International Research on Education Systems, Mitchell Institute.

Lamb, S., Jackson, J., Walstab, A., & Huo, S. (2015). *Educational opportunity in Australia: Who succeeds and who misses out*. Centre for International Research on Education Systems, Mitchell Institute.

McGregor, G., Mills, M., te Riele, K., & Hayes, D. (2015). Excluded from school: Getting a second chance at a "meaningful" education. *International Journal of Inclusive Education*, *19*(6), 608–25.

Murgatroyd, S. (2010). "Wicked problems" and the work of the school. *European Journal of Education*, *45*(2), 259–79.

Norwich, B. (2007). *Dilemmas of difference, inclusion and disability: International perspectives and future directions*. Routledge.

Norwich, B. (2009). Dilemmas of difference and the identification of special educational needs/disability: International perspectives. *British Educational Research Journal*, *35*(3), 447–67.

Norwich, B. (2013). *Addressing tensions and dilemmas in inclusive education: Living with uncertainty*. Routledge.

Perry, L., & McConney, A. (2010). School socio-economic composition and student outcomes in Australia: Implications for educational policy. *Australian Journal of Education*, *54*(1), 2–85.

Protzen, J. P., & Harris, D. (2010). *The universe of design: Horst Rittel's theories of design and planning*. Routledge

Reid, A. (2016). *Building our nation through public education*. Australian Government Primary Principals Association.

Rittel, H., & Webber, M. (1973). Dilemmas in a general theory of planning. *Policy Sciences*, *4*, 155–69.

Select Committee on Access to the South Australian Education System for Students with a Disability. (2017). *Report of the Select Committee on Access to the South Australian Education System for Students with a Disability*. Parliament of South Australia.

Slee, R. (2011). *The irregular school: Exclusion, schooling and inclusive education*. Routledge.

Slee, R. (2013). How do we make inclusive education happen when exclusion is a political predisposition? *International Journal of Inclusive Education*, *17*(8), 895–907.

Smyth, J. (2010). Speaking back to educational policy: Why social inclusion will not work for disadvantaged Australian schools. *Critical Studies in Education*, *51*(2), 113–28.
Smyth, J., Down, B., & McInerney, P. (2014). *The socially just school: Making space for youth to speak back*. Springer.
Smyth, J., & Hattam, R. (2004). *Dropping out, drifting off, being excluded: Becoming somebody without school*. Peter Lang.
Smyth, J., Hattam, R., Cannon, J., Edwards, J., Wilson, N., & Wurst, S. (2000). *Listen to me I'm leaving: Early school leaving in South Australian secondary schools*. Flinders Institute for the Study of Teaching, Department of Education, Training and Employment and the Senior Secondary Assessment Board of South Australia.
Smyth, J., & Robinson, J. (2015). "Give me air not shelter": Critical tales of a policy case of student re-engagement from beyond school. *Journal of Education Policy*, *30*(2), 220–36.
South Australia. (2010, November 25). *Parliamentary Debates*. House of Assembly. (Jay Weatherill).
te Riele, K. (2006). Youth "at risk": Further marginalizing the marginalized? *Journal of Education Policy*, *21*(2), 129–45.
te Riele, K. (2014). *Putting the jigsaw together: Flexible learning programs in Australia final report*. Victoria Institute for Education, Diversity and Lifelong Learning.
te Riele, K., Wilson, K., Wallace, V., McGinty, S., & Lewthwaite, B. (2017). Outcomes from Flexible Learning Options for disenfranchised youth: What counts? *International Journal of Inclusive Education*, *21*(2), 117–30.
Teese, R. (2011). *From opportunity to outcomes: The changing role of public schooling in Australia and national funding arrangements*. Centre for Research on Education Systems.
Zhao, Y. (2017). What works may hurt: Side effects in education. *Journal of Educational Change*, *18*(1), 1–19.

6 "I Always Wanted to Come to University": Afghan-Australian Girls' Pursuit of Higher Education

Snjezana Bilic

Large numbers of students from refugee backgrounds (SfRB) now participate in Australian schools and universities. As such, educators struggle to attend to the specific and unique challenges and opportunities that now characterize emergent superdiverse student cohorts. Many SfRB have faced trauma, relocation adjustments, and identity challenges while adapting to a new life in a host society. Importantly for this chapter, the education system is one of the first institutions they encounter when settling in Australia. Recent Australian research confirms that most refugee youth have also experienced interruptions in obtaining education in the past, and often face complex obstacles to successfully completing their university studies (Matthews, 2021). This paper investigates the challenges experienced by SfRBs in university enabling pathway programs and if there are other obstacles that are specific to the university setting.

This chapter shares and explores the accounts of three Afghani students of refugee background, sharing their experiences and challenges in engaging with the new host society and with higher education. Semi-structured interviews were conducted to capture the voices and insights of refugee-background students. The interviews were analyzed and I developed a series of narrative case studies which form the basis of this chapter.

These student narratives attest to the challenges they have experienced but also to their resilience and persistence. The chapter contains the following sections. Firstly, I provide an account of their aspirations to attend university, and also their families' expectations. Second, the chapter explores their experiences in university enabling pathway programs (hereafter referred to as university enabling programs). Finally, this chapter offers some recommendations about enabling pedagogies as good practice in universities that show potential to meet the complex learning needs of SfRBs.

Students from Refugee Backgrounds in Australia

Research on experiences of refugee students entering tertiary education is expanding (Baker & Irwin, 2021). The existing studies on SfRBs highlight their ambitions to succeed at university (Naidoo, 2021; Soong et al., 2022); nevertheless, they face significant challenges. Recent research outlines that this cohort of students is impacted by diverse and complex factors and educational concerns. These include those related to interrupted education (Ramsay & Baker, 2019), language proficiency (Kong et al., 2016; Sidhu, 2017), lack of understanding of the university system (Baker & Irwin, 2021; Fagan et al., 2018; Naidoo, 2021; Naidoo et al., 2018), and not being familiar with academic skills and concepts (Kong et al., 2016; Sidhu, 2017), as well as navigating competing priorities of family and study (Baker et al., 2020; Kong et al., 2016). Little is known though on whether these and other obstacles are also experienced by students of refugee background in *university enabling programs* (albeit see Bilic and Thai, 2023; Fagan et al., 2019; Hellmundt & Baker, 2017; Gray and Irwin, 2013, for notable exceptions).

University enabling programs are a key aspect of widening participation in higher education in Australia as they provide opportunities to those students from historically under-represented groups to access a tertiary education. Policies to widen participation in higher education were prompted by the landmark Bradley Review, which was instrumental in recent higher education reform, with a goal "to increase the number of 25–34-year-olds holding a bachelor's degree to 40% by 2025; and to increase the participation rate of people from low SES backgrounds to 20% by 2020" (Finn, 2023, p. 3). These aims called for more equitable university participation and, as a consequence, Australian universities have been redesigning their alternative entry processes; this chapter reports on some of the work at UniSA College,[1] at the University of South Australia.

Methodology: A Narrative Approach

After obtaining university ethics approval, participating students were sought from UniSA College, and 11 students consented to participate. They ranged in age from 17 to 30 years and all identified as students from refugee backgrounds. In this chapter, I draw on the data from three female SfRBs from Afghanistan: Asal, Nazifa, and Mervash (pseudonyms). Their ages ranged from eighteen to early twenties, and at the time of the interviews, all were students attending UniSA College.

I conducted semi-structured interviews informed by a narrative inquiry approach (Clandinin & Connelly, 2000). The voices of the students of refugee backgrounds revealed in my interviews provide a rich and detailed account of their aspirations and experiences (O'Shea et al., 2012). The interviews allowed the

1 https://study.unisa.edu.au/unisa-college/

participants to recount how intricacies of higher education unfold in students' lives. The research questions included: How do SfRBs experience and navigate their learning at university enabling programs? What are students' experiences of academic integration? In what ways can these insights be utilized to enhance academic engagement, integration, and outcomes for this cohort of students?

Emerging Themes

Aspirations to Attend University

SfRBs shape their identities through their ambitions and accomplishments. Nourpanah (2014) notes that obtaining education and educational achievements are significant factors that assist refugees to reform their identity and successfully transition into a new life. This was evident in my research, as the girls' stories reflected their aspirations and social capital. All three girls demonstrated unwavering commitment to finishing their studies, citing greater respect, higher incomes, and improved career prospects as their motivations. They displayed aspirations to realize their career goals. Moreover, being the first in family to study at university, the participants felt a profound sense of pride in this achievement.

Status and respect are considered key measures of success for students of refugee backgrounds and their families, with educational opportunities and career pathways as the means by which to attain them (King & Owens, 2018). By way of example, and as outlined in a number of studies (Cassity & Gow, 2005; King & Owens, 2018; Naidoo et al., 2015), many students of refugee backgrounds aspire to become doctors or lawyers. As one of the participants, Asal, outlined: "Yes, our society highly values education. Whether you are doctor or an entrepreneur you are highly valued."

University is often central to the aspirations and career paths of both the student and their family. As Naidoo et al. (2015, p. 51) argue in their inquiry on supporting school–university pathways for SfRBs report, "transnational families were acutely aware of the status that university education and professional qualifications would bring" and they sought to enrich "the social, cultural and symbolic capital" by educating their children. Thus, for many students their choice of a future career was based on the expectations of their family. These expectations were further elaborated by Asal: "My mum always wanted to me to be a doctor. That's how they see it ... that's how Afghan parents see it, you being a doctor or a lawyer or something like that that has a higher status..." Family and community involvement significantly contribute to students' aspirations, but students also reported experiencing hardship in fulfilling those expectations. Asal outlined that parental pressure "to do medicine" was one of the factors that impacted on her ability to do well in high school:

> I was so focused on getting into medicine or medical school so in Year 12 I chose all subjects related to it, psychology, chemistry, biology, and I had maths and it was very hard—it all came down on me, it choked me ... and so I couldn't [complete it] ... it got so hard ...

These examples illustrate the cultural and family pressures, but also challenges refugee youth may encounter in navigating multiple cultural environments that correspond to various contexts of their lives (King & Owens, 2018). Another cultural context that students have to navigate was mentioned by Nazifa, who discussed pressures to maintain cultural membership: "I want to study journalism so I can be TV host ... but the community is against cinema." Given this, she continued, "I want to do criminology rather than journalism."

Apart from expectations from the community, insufficient support and encouragement from parents, peers, and the educational system have been identified as obstacles to university participation (Harvey-Beavis & Robinson, 2000). Family support depends upon many factors, including lack of knowledge or experience of higher education. This was outlined by Mervash:

> It's really hard, cause like, since my parents are not, like, educated, they think uni is like school hours, starting time and finishing time ... they expect you to do well at uni, do well in like housework, or other stuff, or like when you're studying late they'll be like, "Where are you so late? Didn't uni finish?"

Traditional gender roles were found to shape success and opportunity among students of refugee backgrounds. This is consistent with King and Owen's (2018), and Harris et al.'s (2015) findings which suggest that African-Australian women of refugee backgrounds are also entangled in a binary choice between academic achievement for themselves, and self-sacrifice of their cultural and gendered identities. Similar challenges were reported by participants in my research. Mervash discussed the gendered division of labor in her household:

> And 'cause I am Afghan, Afghans have a lot of gatherings between their, like, other Afghans, and every night we would get home and there's like be guests, and guests coming over, and my mum is like: "Mervash bring more tea" ... and like, you didn't really have time to pay attention on studies ...'cause you're around family and stuff. I used to help to cook, I don't have any sisters, and my brothers would go out and my mum would be alone, and our house is really big, we got a big family, so I just help here around the house with housework mainly.

This supports the findings from previous research that refugee youth experience a considerable increase in family responsibilities following migration (Harris & Marlowe, 2011; King & Owen, 2018). Juggling education and family responsibilities can be overwhelming and "'overshadow' their educational aspirations and responsibilities" (Shakya et al., 2012, p. 66).

Even though family and community exert considerable influence on the goals of refugee youth, the participants spoke about their own aspirations, and they expressed a sense of agency, as Asal did here:

> I wanted to come to the college for myself. Yes, our society highly values education, whether you are doctor or an entrepreneur you are highly valued ... [but] I don't want to get married, I want to [finish uni and] be independent, businesswoman.

Asal also outlined that, despite parental pressure to become a doctor or lawyer, she is negotiating her own pathway:

> In our society whether you are doctor or an entrepreneur you are highly valued ... but I don't see it like that ... I see it like any job you have and you're successful in it, you will have a good income, so as long as you're happy doesn't matter ... so I just did it for myself so I can get into ... so I can go into a better course next year ... into the course I want to do.

Similar themes were expressed by Nazifa who, while noting that she experienced challenges studying at university, also said: "I don't want to drop out. I want to study so I can find a good job in the future." This goes beyond merely acknowledging educational achievements but, as Nourpanah (2014) in her research also observes:

> It means that these people, in becoming refugees and stepping away from their home country, are also pushing the boundaries of their home culture, which is steeped in patriarchy. They no longer conform to the norms and demands of a country where fathers, brothers, husbands, and fathers-in-law have the final and ultimate say in all decisions relating to women. (p. 62)

Ultimately, these young girls are challenging traditional gender roles and are re-negotiating cultural expectations rooted in patriarchy.

Experiences at University

Once at university, all three girls discussed putting in significant effort to belong. A notable example of this was Mervash and Nazifa reporting removing their hijab because they were bullied:

> Interviewer: And you don't wear hijab now?
>
> Mervash: No, I used to in semester 1 at uni. I used to wear it. But then, like it was really difficult 'cause I, I don't know, it's hard to fit in. I didn't have confidence, 'cause like I didn't have the confidence to go out and approach someone new and I felt like they wouldn't like me 'cause I am Muslim, 'cause the things the media shows is just … it's not good and, like, most it is not true so that's sort of why.

Nazifa also discussed negotiating cultural identity: "It is really hard to be in society but if you are from different culture, you don't know which one do you take, Australian society or your own cultural background … it's hard." Furthermore, the participants outlined differences between university and high school environments and expectations. Mervash said: "[There are] big differences between uni and high school. It's kind of hard. We want someone to tell us and help us so it's really hard."

> Interviewer: What's the difference between uni and high school?
>
> Mervash: It is so different. At uni you have to be independent, do your own thing. Nobody's going to nag you to finish your assignment; they just give you the work and it's your responsibility to sort of get it or not. It's kind of hard … like, you're not used to it, we want someone to tell us what to do.

As Mervash's experience demonstrates, many refugee-background students arriving in Australia encounter significant educational obstacles because the teaching style, language, curriculum, and communication methods may be completely different from what they know (Naidoo et al., 2015), including from their cultural ways of knowing, while their knowledge may be misrecognized (Ramsay et al., 2016). Educators need to understand and be responsive to the life worlds and life experiences of refugee-background students, which also demands contesting deficit modes of thinking about refugee students. This insight would not only foster student engagement and aspirations but would also enable the provision of academic, financial, and social supports that are necessary for meaningful participation of SfRBs at university. Furthermore, students need to be introduced to the powerful codes used in academia as these closely relate to what Lisa Delpit (1988) calls the "culture of power." Engaging students in tasks that "help them understand that they have an important voice in their own learning processes" is essential (Delpit, 1988, p. 288). In Delpit's (1988) words:

> students must be taught codes to participate fully in the mainstream of … life not by being forced to attend to hollow, inane, decontextualized subskills, but rather within the context of meaningful communicative endeavors; that they must be allowed the resource of the teacher's expert knowledge, while being helped to acknowledge their own "expertness" as well. (p. 296)

In the Australian context and specifically for the enabling contexts, research on enabling pedagogies focuses and expands on these aspects. Enabling pedagogies "work to democratise access to, and creation of, powerful knowledges" (Bennett et al., 2016, p. 9). These pedagogical approaches highlight the importance of *enabling* learning in the university context, so that students can gain insight into the cultural norms and teaching practices that are often assumed and possessed by those who already have this social and cultural capital (Bennett et al., 2016, p. 56). In the following section I include some recommendations for enabling pedagogies as a good practice approach.

A Way Forward: Enabling Pedagogies

Enabling pedagogies is an umbrella term for inclusive and distinctive approaches to teaching students in enabling programs. Enabling pedagogies are pedagogical and relational practices that foster encouraging learning environments and can aid the development of student identity and, consequently, improve student engagement and retention.

The literature on enabling pedagogies identifies several pedagogical components. First, students' sense of belonging is "fundamental to the enactment of an enabling pedagogy" (Bennett et al., 2016, p. 39). This enhances student engagement and results in positive learning outcomes (Villains, 2019). The emphasis is placed on strong peer and staff–student relationships and nurturing a sense of community (Hellmundt & Baker, 2017; Villains, 2019). The key elements of enabling approaches include connecting with student "life-worlds" (Moll et al., 1992, p. 133) and rejecting deficit framings of students (Hattam et al., 2024). Enabling educators also believe that setting high standards and goals for their students must be accompanied by showing them how to achieve them (Bunn, 2019), and demystifying the hidden curriculum is essential here. Enabling teaching is dialogic and inclusive, and recognizes the importance of scaffolding assessment for student engagement in learning and skill development (Hattam & Weiler, 2021).

Pedagogies of care and care-full practices are at the center of enabling pedagogies. Here, "being attentive to students' experiences, histories and needs is of foremost importance" (Bennett et al., 2016, p. 39). Caring is about ensuring students are respected, feel supported and secure, and that teachers are committed to students' academic as well as social development. The positive impact of these care-full practices is echoed in Nazifa's words:

> College has been the most helpful throughout all of the time I have been here. The teachers, lecturers, they even had a librarian come and give information ... whenever

> you want you want something or you don't know how do it, there's always someone to help you. So that's the most important part.

Asal also discussed these themes:

> Interviewer: When did you make decision to come to university and why?
>
> Asal: I always wanted to come to university. I heard about the college through the radio and TV. I went and researched online and then I went to orientation day where they explained everything—it was a really good place.
>
> Interviewer: How is it going for you?
>
> Asal: It is really good—every tutor or teacher I have, they're really good. They explain everything—they put their time and effort into explaining what I've missed or what I didn't understand...
>
> Interviewer: Are there any barriers to learning?
>
> Asal: I don't think there are any barriers to learning—they give you everything that you need to know, give you e-readings, lecture recordings. They pretty much give you everything so you have to take responsibility to go and do it ... 'cause they set out what you need to do, what quiz you need to do ... it's all there. You just need to find it and it's pretty much easy to find.

These excerpts show that enabling pedagogical practices prioritize and affirm "students' knowledge and cultural situatedness" (Bennett et al., 2016, p. 24), thereby fostering the development of capabilities of all students.

Inclusive environments cultivate a sense of self-worth, safety, and belonging, supporting students to establish new relationships and friendships. Educational progress and emotional wellbeing are interdependent (Hek, 2005). All three participants used the word "comfortable" to describe the nature of the enabling environment at the college. To Asal it "means being comfortable ... wanting to be here." Mervash said, similarly: "It's about how do you feel? Like if you feel comfortable or not."

This sense of comfort coexists with the significant "discomfort" of returning to education. When discussing their sense of belonging, all three participants used metaphors of "feeling comfortable" and "feeling safe," and these factors play a significant role in how students express themselves, understand their experiences, and shape the evolving narratives about their identity (Bennett at al. 2016, p. 55). Another important element contributing to students feeling that they belong was expressed when they discussed social inclusion and forming peer relationships at the college. Mervash identified that she was comfortable forming new relationships as well: "Also, in terms of a good experience, I guess meeting new people, making new friends. I am friendly with tutors." This echoes previous research (Cassity & Gow, 2005; Earnest et al., 2010) which highlights that community development strategies that establish formal and informal social networks, connecting refugee students with peers and academic/support staff, are essential for the success and retention of this cohort of students. As the stories included here reveal, students feel confident in inclusive pedagogical environments where trust is established and a sense of belonging is fostered. Such pedagogical practices not only foster ethics and practices of care but also emphasize the importance of recognizing and building upon the strengths-based understandings of students' knowledge and capabilities.

Conclusion

This chapter explored the educational experiences and obstacles related to transitioning to university for three students from refugee backgrounds. While schools ought to be a stabilizing factor for refugee-background students, many experience hardships with learning a new language, schooling systems, and cultural and societal values.

This chapter reports on the findings of research undertaken with SfRBs studying at UniSA College. The study utilized in-depth interviews to capture the perspectives and insights of the students. The purpose of the semi-structured individual interviews was to identify challenges, concerns, and issues faced by this cohort of students, as well as matters pertaining to their academic integration, learning needs, and level of engagement. The analysis reveals refugee students encounter a range of challenges and obstacles to success that universities often fail to recognize. Students with refugee backgrounds continuously adapt their identities as they move through different environments, framing their sense of self and identity through their goals and accomplishments. Attaining education was recognized as one of the most important aims for SfRBs.

My analysis also highlighted that there needs to be a greater emphasis on building confidence and a sense of capability for students from diverse and under-represented backgrounds. In light of this, the chapter promotes enabling pedagogy as an effective approach that affirms and validates all learners' identities, through a strong emphasis on demystifying the university experience and curriculum, and by utilizing strengths-based approaches that draw on the resources students bring with them.

Bibliography

Baker, S., & Irwin, E. (2021). Disrupting the dominance of "linear pathways": How institutional assumptions create "stuck places" for refugee students' transitions into higher education. *Research Papers in Education*, *36*(1), 75–9.

Baker, S., Irwin, E., & Freeman, H. (2020). Wasted, manipulated and compressed time: Adult refugee students' experiences of transitioning into Australian higher education. *Journal of Further and Higher Education*, *44*(4), 528–41.
Bennett, A., Motta, S., Hamiton, E., Burgess, C., Relf, B., Gray, K., … Albright, J. (2016). *Enabling pedagogies: A participatory conceptual mapping of practices at the University of Newcastle, Australia*. University of Newcastle.
Bilic, S., & Thai, T. (2023). "One day I will make it to university": students from refugee backgrounds in university pathway programs. *International Journal of Learning, Teaching and Educational Research*. 22(4), 217–41
Bunn, R. (2019). "We need to help students discover themselves and see into the life of things": Advice from Open Foundation lecturers. In A. Jones, A. Olds, & J. Lisciandro (Eds.), *Transitioning students in higher education: Philosophies, pedagogies and practice* (pp. 151–60). Routledge.
Cassity, E., & Gow, G. (2005). Making up for lost time: The experiences of southern Sudanese young refugees in high schools. *Youth Studies Australia*, *24*(3), 51–5.
Clandinin, D., & Connelly, F. (2000). *Narrative inquiry: Experience and story in qualitative Research*. Jossey-Bass.
Delpit, L. (1988). The silenced dialogue: Power and pedagogy in educating other people's children. *Harvard educational review*, 58(3), 280–99.
Earnest, J., Joyce, A., De Mori, G., & Silvagni, G. (2010). Are universities responding to the needs of students from refugee backgrounds? *Australian Journal of Education*, *54*(2), 155–74.
Fagan, S., Baker, S., Irwin, E., Dantas, J., Gower, S., Singh, S., & Taiwo, M. (2018). *(Re)claiming social capital: Improving language and cultural pathways for students from refugee backgrounds into Australian higher education*. Refugee Transitions.
Finn, S. (2023). *Australian University Accord: Response to discussion paper.* Navitas, https://www.education.gov.au/system/files/documents/submission-file/2023-04/AUA_tranche3_Navitas.pdf
Harris, A., Spark, C., & Watts, M. N. C. (2015). Gains and losses: African Australian women and higher education. *Journal of Sociology*, *51*(2), 370–84.
Harris, V., & Marlowe, J. M. (2011). Hard yards high hopes: The educational challenges of African refugee university students in Australia. *International Journal of Teaching, Learning and Higher Education*, *23*(2), 186–96.
Hattam, S., & Weiler, T. (2021). "Every single student counts": Leadership of professional development underpinned by social justice for sessional staff in a South Australian university. *Professional Development in Education*, *47*(1), 128–40.
Hattam, S., Weiler, T., Hattam, R., & King, S. (2024). Working on enabling pedagogies at UniSA College: Hopeful ideas. In S. Hattam, R. Hattam,

T. Weiler, & S. King (Eds.), *Enabling pedagogy and action research for higher education in Australia*. DOI Press.

Harvey-Beavis, A., & Robinson, L. (2000). *Views and influences: Tertiary education, secondary students and their advisers*. Department of Education, Training and Youth Affairs.

Hek, R. (2005). The role of education in the settlement of young refugees in the UK: The experiences of young refugees. *Practice, 17*(3), 157–71.

Hellmundt, S., & Baker, D. (2017). Encouraging engagement in enabling programs: The student's perspective. *Student Success, 8*(1), 25–33.

Gray, K., & Irwin, E. (2013). Pathways to social inclusion: The participation of refugee students in higher education. In *Proceedings of the National Association of Enabling Educators of Australia Conference; Flexibility: Pathways to participation* (pp. 1–11).

King, S. M., & Owens, L. (2018). Great expectations: African youth from refugee backgrounds and the transition to university. In C. I. Agosti & E. Bernat (Eds.), *University pathway programs: Local responses within a growing global trend* (pp. 67–84). Springer.

Kong, E., Harmsworth, S., Rajaeian, M. M., Parkes, G., Bishop, S., AlMansouri, B., & Lawrence, J. (2016). University transition challenges for first year domestic CALD students from refugee backgrounds: A case study from an Australian regional university. *Australian Journal of Adult Learning, 56*(2), 170–97.

Matthews, J. (2021). Maligned mobilities, absences and emergencies: Refugee education in Australia. *International Journal of Inclusive Education, 25*(6), 720–34.

Moll, L., Amanti, C., Neff, D., & González, N. (1992). Funds of knowledge for teaching: Using a qualitative approach to connect homes and classrooms. *Theory into Practice, 31*(2), 132–41.

Naidoo, L. (2021). Traversing the terrain of higher education: Experiences of refugee youth on the inside. *International Journal of Inclusive Education, 25*(2), 182–95.

Naidoo, L., Adoniou, M., Cunneen, R., Langat, K., Wilkinson, J., & Bolger, D. (2015). *Case study: Supporting pathways for refugee students' access and participation in tertiary education*. Office of Teaching and Learning, University of Western Sydney.

Naidoo, L., Wilkinson, J., Adoniou, M., & Langat, K. (2018). *Navigating complex spaces: Refugee background students transitioning into higher education*. Springer.

Nourpanah, S. (2014). A study of the experiences of integration and settlement of Afghan government-assisted refugees in Halifax, Canada. *Refuge: Canada's Journal on Refugees, 30*(1), 57–66.

O'Shea, S. E., Lysaght, P. & Tanner, K. (2012). Stepping into higher education from the vocational education sector in Australia: Student perceptions and experiences. *Journal of Vocational Education and Training*, *64*(3), 261–77.
Ramsay, G., & Baker, S. (2019). Higher education and students from refugee backgrounds: A meta-scoping study. *Refugee Survey Quarterly*, *38*(1), 55–82.
Ramsay, G., Baker, S., Miles, L., & Irwin, E. (2016, July 4–7). *Reimagining support models for students from refugee backgrounds: Understandings, spaces and empowerment* [Paper presentation]. Research and Development in Higher Education: The Shape of Higher Education, 39th HERDSA Annual Conference, Fremantle, Australia.
Shakya, Y. B., Guruge, S., Hynie, M., Akbari, A., Malik, M., Htoo, S., Khogali, A., Mona, S. A., Murtaza, R., & Alley, S. (2012). Aspirations for higher education among newcomer refugee youth in Toronto: Expectations, challenges, and strategies. *Refuge: Canada's Journal on Refugees*, *27*(2), 65–78.
Sidhu, R. (2017). Navigating unfreedoms and re-imagining ethical counter-conducts: Caring about refugees & asylum seekers. *Educational Philosophy and Theory*, *49*(3), 294–305.
Soong, H., Radford, D., Hetz, H., Wrench, A., Reid-Nguyen, R., & Lucas, B. (2022). Intergenerational aspirations for educational and employment success of refugee youth. *International Journal of Inclusive Education*. Advance online publication. https://doi.org/10.1080/13603116.2022.2119487
Villains, J. (2019). Tales from the borderland: Enabling students' experiences of preparation for higher education. *International Studies in Widening Participation*, *6*(1), 48–64.

7 (Dis)assembling the Twenty-First-Century Learner

Jill Colton

This chapter is located within a context where contemporary students are positioned as twenty-first-century learners and thus identified by their association with digital technologies and individual choice. According to Williams et al. (2013), the figure of the "twenty-first-century learner" emerged toward the end of the twentieth century in Australian policy documents and commercially produced texts aimed at teachers and wider public audiences. They concluded that the twentieth-century learner was chiefly a neoliberal construct, but also constituted by a competing discourse from the social democratic tradition. In this chapter the entanglement of futurist discourses with the social and material practices associated with digital technologies is teased out in order to consider the implications for pedagogical change and educational reform.

In 2009 the Australian Government released the Digital Education Revolution (DER) policy, which aimed to improve the teaching and learning outcomes achieved by students through the use of technologies (DEEWR, 2008). This policy was followed by substantial funding to Australian schools to incorporate technologies into student learning (Moyle, 2015). In schools around Australia, the funding was used to finance the construction of new buildings, improve access to Wi-Fi, and provide computer resources to students. The considerable funding that accompanied the DER policy and significant expenditure on school infrastructure embodied a belief in the power of digital technologies to improve student learning (Moyle, 2015). Even though improvement as measured by international tests has not been evident, and as Varanasi (2015) points out there has not been a transformation in Australian school education so far, claims that digital technologies will change education continue to be made.

The Twenty-First-Century Learner as Digitally Literate

In the late twentieth and early twenty-first centuries, developments in digital tools, applications, programs, and connectivity have been significant, and individuals and institutions in countries such as Australia have adopted digital technologies for a myriad of purposes and forms (Facer, 2012). In discourses surrounding educational technology these tools are represented as available, accessible, and emancipatory. They are attributed a powerful role in educational reform and get tangled up with visions of students as a new type of learner who is, in at least some ways, different from students of previous generations.

Representations of learners as digitally aligned and digitally savvy have been popular since the mid-2000s. While some of these representations, especially the notion of the "digital native," have been critiqued, they persist as a common-sense way of imagining young people. Learners in the twenty-first century have been called digital natives (Prensky, 2005a, 2005b), the i-generation (Rosen, 2010), the wired generation (Hanman, 2005), and the digital generation (Schwartz, 2013). These names imply a familiarity with and connection to digital technology and the social practices associated with technology. Even though there is evidence that one's "generation" does not determine one's approach to using technology (Kennedy & Krause, 2008, as cited in Bayne & Jandric, 2017), claims about generations of digital learners abound. Prensky (2005b) asserts that students today expect to be engaged, to be creative, and to be able to follow their own interests because of their involvement with digital technologies. Prensky's (2001) view is that most learners today are different from those of the past. The premise is that, because twenty-first-century learners are different from learners in the past, they require a different way of being schooled—because they have a different set of social practices and because life in the twenty-first century requires a different set of skills.

One of the problems with Prensky's argument is that it tends to de-privilege the teacher as it sets up a binary of native versus immigrant (Bayne & Ross, 2015). It positions young people as subjects at one with the digital environment in a way that older users—teachers—can never be (Prenski, 2001, p. 160). Selwyn (2009) challenges the notion of the digital native, arguing that it works to diminish older people especially teachers. He argues that the digital native discourse disempowers older generations as it implies that adults lack technological fluency—a claim that feeds tensions between teachers and students in ways that are unrealistic and ideologically, rather than empirically, based.

Other iterations of the twenty-first-century learner, which may be seen to take a less divisive and more generative approach, describe the relationship between young people and digital technology in terms of transition and mobility. Contemporary students have been called the transitional generation (Kress, 2009)—as they negotiate the transition from print-based to screen-based texts—and "aliens in the classroom" (Green & Bigum, 1993) as their presence in traditional schools becomes more uncomfortable for those schools. Descriptions of young people as different from the previous generation are not new but, perhaps more than ever, contemporary students are being described as a new generation "of a radically different constitution" (Green & Bigum, 1993, p. 119).

Kress (2009) says that the gap between what schools supply and what young people judge to be of relevance in the world that they experience is the basis of young peoples' alienation from school and school-based learning practices. It is therefore not surprising that schools are looking at a change agenda based around digital technology and justified in part by the representation of learners in the twenty-first century.

Selwyn (2003) used the term "mobile generation" to describe the significance of new technologies in the way that young people socially interact and use their time. Likewise, Carrington (2006) wrote about young peoples' digital literacy practices as central to what makes them different from previous generations. Twenty-first-century learners are represented as people who create, consume, and share using digital media on computers and mobile devices such as mobile phones and iPods (Rosen, 2010). It appears that the key driver of *newness* is digital technologies and what people do with them. This emphasis on practices takes us away from an essentialized view of students, or from a deterministic view of technology, to a more complex view where learners and technologies are shaping each other in practices of communication (Thompson, 2012).

Researchers writing into the field of educational technology and literacy describe a constellation of practices with digital tools and texts. Prensky (2001, 2010) reports that contemporary students are able to collaborate and network, using technology, with others across the globe in sophisticated and complex ways. They use the World Wide Web to find out what they need to know, and they remix and share with other people all over the world (Anderson-Inman, 2009; Knobel & Lankshear, 2008). According to Gee and Hayes (2011) much of their time is spent on screen and online and they are said to be in constant contact with others. Each of these practices is framed as new and intimately connected with the affordances of the digital. These accounts of young people constitute them in particular ways: as creators, consumers, sharers, collaborative, networkers, global, mobile, sophisticated, and independent in their acquisition of knowledge. These constitutions work to put pressure on schools and teachers to inscribe and enact change.

There is a substantial body of literature which explores digital technologies as agents of change. The most generative of this literature considers the socially shaping aspects of these technologies. In their discussion of digital literacies, Jones and Hafner (2012) propose that digital technologies have a significant role in the way people communicate, find information, create, share, play, and learn. As they explain, iPods, Wikis, blogs, and SMS messages have become new spaces of communication and representation. Other scholars such as Sheridan and Rowsell (2010) find that using the web, using photographs and video, and recording sounds and voices have become common learning practices in a range of contexts. More recently, Bhatt (2017) has explored classrooms as sites where "new technological dynamics are rapidly displacing classic pedagogies" (p. 127). The claim is that, with these new communication practices, new literacies emerge and these become embodied in new social practices—ways of working in new or transformed forms of employment, new ways of participating as a citizen in public spaces, and even perhaps new forms of identity and personality (Cope & Kalantzis, 2009, p. 167).

It appears that the mesh of digital technologies with new literacies may produce opportunities for change in educational contexts. As Street (2003) states, literacy practices are "particular ways of thinking about and doing reading and writing in cultural contexts" (p. 79). In the twenty-first-century cultural context, digital technologies play a significant part in the way that literacy is practiced (Mills, 2016). This is well established by empirical studies of digital literacies (Bhatt, 2017; Gourlay & Oliver, 2018; Ito, 2010). What resonates across these studies and others (see below) is the association of new literacies with educational change. Bhatt (2017) explores classroom digital literacies that he contextualizes as emergent and new. He writes about the new textual practices that digital media afford—a claim supported by Ito (2010) in her examination of new literacy practices with digital media.

There has been a considerable amount of research into the inclusion of digital media texts in the school curriculum (Beavis, 2004; Gee, 2003; Knobel & Lankshear, 2008). New ways of working with text have been researched and analyzed as new literacy practices. An example of this is found in the work of Potter (2012), who adopted the term "curatorship" to explain the way that meanings are made in digital media using sound, text, image, and clips. Explorations into new types of texts and ways of producing texts are often about the way that experiences with text outside of the school are permeating what is known as text in school. They are also about the transfer into the school of pedagogies that students experience outside of school such as game-based pedagogy and remixing with digital media in social networking sites and media apps (Burnett & Merchant, 2015).

Literacy is a key field in which the *new* is evoked as a provocation for imagining learners in the twenty-first century as different from those in the past. Sefton-Green et al. (2009) write that "the ways in which young people learn and use technologies in informal situations clearly draw on modes of teaching and learning that are very different from teacher–student roles conventionally found in schools" (p. 121). In their discussion, digital technology serves to "create more student-centred learning environments." This is not just about what texts are permitted in schools, but about moving away from teacher-centered control and allowing students to take more control of what and how they learn (Hedberg, 2011). It is significant that Sefton Green et al. and Hedberg link digital technologies with the changing roles of teachers and students. The alignment of digital technologies with changing subjectivities has implications for the way that students and their teachers are positioned by their use of digital technologies, especially in a context where the relevance of schools and the roles of teachers are being questioned.

The Twenty-First-Century Learner as a Neoliberal Subject

When Williams et al. (2013) deconstructed the figure of the twenty-first-century learner in their policy genealogy they found that corporate and market discourses were delineating the desirable skills, dispositions, and capabilities of the contemporary student as particularly twenty-first century. This has implications for the way that teachers and students are subjectified in policy networks, which impacts on the way that teaching and learning are conceptualized, purposed, and organized.

Neoliberalism is a set of practices built on the assumption that human wellbeing is best advanced by "liberating individual entrepreneurial freedoms and skills within an institutional framework characterized by strong private property rights, free markets, and free trade" (Harvey, 2005, p. 2). These economic and political perspectives have implications for the way that students are positioned and constituted as self-managing individuals in charge of their own learning, and of their own success. In the context of neoliberalism, schools are purposed and organized as places where people are made into future workers for market-driven global and digital economies. Practices of neoliberalism, while complex and not easily defined, can be characterized as motivated by the market and resonant with corporate economics and structures (Williams et al., 2013). This works to produce the figure of the twenty-first-century learner as a neoliberal subject whose key role is to be economically productive by being enterprising and responsible. The implication is that we are offered the opportunity to succeed and, if we do not, it is our own fault—"making us into neo-liberal subjects enmeshed in the 'powers of freedom'" (Ball, 2012, p. 145).

I propose that the adoption of digital technologies in schools transpires in tandem with a neoliberal ideology that engenders a type of individualism where individuals are responsible, self-directed, and competitive citizens. As Selwyn (2016) explains, it is not unusual to see students in the twenty-first century positioned as self-contained individuals who have personal/individual choice, and to see this linked with technologies as the key enabler of this choice in contemporary texts about education and technology. For example, in the New Media Consortium (NMC) Horizon Report published in 2011, individualism and innovation are interwoven in an imaginary of twenty-first-century learning that privileges individual students' needs and student choice (Johnson et al., 2011). This imaginary motivates the prioritization of customized and personalized instruction and these priorities are seen to be met with new technologies that provide the solution to meeting students' needs and allowing for student choice.

In the NMC Horizon report mentioned above, prioritizing the individual and casting education as customizable are combined with the materiality of *new technologies* and the social valuing/practices of student choice and control (Johnson et al., 2011; see also Buckingham, 2007). This constitutes the institution of school as a type of market where people are regarded as consumers, while emphasizing individual management of one's own life/schooling/education in unstable contexts (Bialostok et al., 2012). An emphasis on each student's unique needs is an effect of risk management, where each individual must succeed in order to secure their own and our future. Individual success is represented as the result of the individual's capacity to manage themselves and direct their own learning with the enablement of technological tools (Yates, 2012). This gives digital technologies a specific role in the school as mechanisms that enable student self-management and self-directed learning.

In the late twentieth century, Levin (1998) argued that a common theme in calls for educational change focused on economic imperatives. The notion of twenty-first-century learners as workers for the future and the focus on twenty-first-century skills as necessary for global economic competitiveness can be seen as a continuation of that economic rationale. Digital technology is often closely implicated in the creation of a new kind of economy that is described as post-industrial and knowledge based (Rizvi & Lingard, 2010). In the post-industrial knowledge economy, the individual is not only linked with digital technology but also positioned as self-determining, entrepreneurial, and innovative. Gee and Hayes propose that young people in "the digital age … take on the identity of lifelong learners, comfortable with technical matters and with technology … They become portfolio shape shifting people and the new 'upper class' in the global world" (2011, p. 110). Digital technology is clearly implicated in preparing workers for the future and also in the way that individuals are required to adopt the competitive dispositions of the market.

The figure of the twenty-first century learner satisfies an urgent need to prepare for a prosperous economic future through the production of an entrepreneurial and self-managing worker and citizenry. As Giddens (1991) and Beck (1992) argued, the late twentieth century can be viewed as a period of late modernism where individuals must respond to the social and environmental problems caused by industrialization. Late modernism is characterized by what Giddens (1991) calls a "dis-embedding" from tradition where structures fragment and the individual becomes the central unit of society and as such makes choices but also has responsibilities. Beck (1992) argues that people living in late modernity are always negotiating risk and their social practices are framed through the concept of risk. As Beck explains, "risk may be defined as a systematic way of dealing with hazards and insecurities" (1992, p. 21). This concept of risk has implications for the way that futures are imagined—and these imaginaries impact on the way that learners and learning in the early twenty-first century are conceptualized.

There is much interest in what is *new* when the future is imagined and when future risks are being managed. Interest in new technologies, new pedagogies, and new educational spaces is motivated, in part, by a vision of the future where competition and digital networks frame a global knowledge economy (Facer, 2011). This is a kind of future where individual security means being able to work in digital environments and being able to access and use knowledge to be more productive, more competitive, and more innovative (Loveless & Williamson, 2013). This imaginary of the future constitutes the twenty-first-century learner as a digital learner, inquiring knowledge worker, and productive innovator. Education is seen as the key player in securing economic and social security (Bialostok et al., 2012).

In the twenty-first century, arguments for school change based on the imaginary of the twenty-first-century learner continue to reference the past and the future as disparate. A binary of the old as traditional (and of the past) and the new as innovative (and of the future) recurs as a key device in problematizing schooling and in making claims for change. The *new* is an important trope because, as Macleod and Wright (2012) write: "the promise of the new ... underpins much educational reform discourse, from utopian strands and grand gestures to the more formulaic rhetoric found in declarations of new policies for new times" (p. 283). However, problematizing schooling is not new, and neither is a student-centered, personalized, individualistic, and open approach.

The Twenty-First-Century Learner as a Progressive Figure

If we turn to the history of progressive schooling we can see how "discourses from the social democratic tradition of schooling which emphasizes equity, social justice and collective responsibility" can also be traced in the way that the twenty-first-century learner is imagined (Williams et al., 2013, p. 799). The student subject of progressive education movements in the nineteenth and twentieth centuries was constituted as self-managing and responsible, and a student-centered approach, where the individual is in charge of his/her own learning, can be traced through many aspects of progressive education movements in which individual freedom, curiosity, active learning, and child-centered pedagogies have been transferred and applied (Howlett, 2013).

This is another form of individualism, based on a belief in democracy as a powerful alliance of individuals and in the role of education as a mechanism of social progress and reform. Perhaps the most well-known proponent of the curious and self-directed student subject was John Dewey. In Dewey's (1959) view, education was responsive to children's interests and curiosity and the teacher acted to shape and connect the student's experience rather than dictating content. Dewey's case for classrooms of self-directed learners all working at their own pace on individual projects in different content areas using different materials and resources was an argument against the industrial-style schooling that dominated the first half of the twentieth century (Moran, 2012). It appears that a discontent with traditional education is not particular to the twenty-first century and perhaps the past is not so disparate from the future.

Reassembling the Twenty-First-Century Learner

Current calls for pedagogical change, framed as twenty-first-century learning, come out of a multifarious network of discourses and socio-material practices with digital technology, which cohere around the figure of the twenty-first-century learner. Moves to change education are partly a response to changes in economic conditions and associated perceptions of future risk. In the twenty-first century, fears about the future are translated into school management practices and curriculum regimes, and at the same time those risks are being induced to justify the imperatives for student choice, personalization, freedom, and openness associated with twenty-first-century learning, where students must be prepared for future workplaces where they will operate as self-managing workers. Notions of freedom and choice in the figure of the twenty-first-century learner can also be traced from the progressive education movements in the social democratic traditions of the twentieth and twenty-first centuries. These notions get twisted into the mix and so the twenty-first-century learner seems to shimmer in and out of focus, as do concepts of individualism, responsibility, and freedom. Digital technologies, as socio-material mechanisms for communicating, learning, interacting, and performing identities, emerge and re-emerge as agents of change in tandem with the young people who use them. What matters is how that change is enacted. When the main driver of educational change is seen to be the roll-out of digital technology for the purposes of increased student choice and preparation for future work, then we are in danger of missing opportunities for student-centered pedagogies that build on the affordances of digital technologies to create possibilities for emancipatory participation and engagement.

Bibliography

Anderson-Inman, L. (2009). Thinking between the lines: Literacy and learning in a connected world. *On the Horizon*, *17*(2), 122–41.

Ball, S. (2012). *Global Education Inc: New policy networks and the neo-liberal imaginary*. Routledge.

Bayne, S., & Jandric, P. (2017). From anthropocentric humanism to critical posthumanism in digital education. *Knowledge Cultures*, *5*(2), 197–216.

Bayne, S., & Ross, J. (2015). Guest editors' notes. *TechTrends*, *59*(1), 3–5.

Beavis, C. (2004). Critical perspectives on curriculum and ICTs: The 3D model, literacy and computer games. *Interactive Educational Multimedia*, *9*, 77–88.

Beck, U. (1992). *Risk society: Towards a new modernity*. Sage.

Bhatt, I. (2017). Classroom digital literacies as interactional accomplishments. In M. Knobel & C. Lankshear (Eds.), *Researching new literacies: Design, theory and data in sociocultural investigation* (pp. 127–50). Peter Lang.

Bialostok, S., Whitman, R., & Bradley, W. S. (2012). *Education and the risk society: Theories, discourse and risk identities*. Sense Publishers.

Buckingham, D. (2007). *Beyond technology*. Polity Press.

Burnett, C., & Merchant, G. (2015). The challenge of 21st century literacies. *Journal of Adolescent and Adult Literacy*, *59*(3), 271–4.

Carrington, V. (2006). *Rethinking middle years: Early adolescents, schooling and culture*. Allen and Unwin.

Cope, B., & Kalantzis, M. (2009). Multiliteracies: New literacies, new learning. *Pedagogies: An International Journal*, *4*(3), 164–95.

Department of Education, Employment and Workplace Relations (DEEWR). (2008). *Success through partnership: Strategic plan to guide the implementation of the Digital Education Revolution initiative and related initiatives*.

Dewey, J. (1959). *Experience and education*. Macmillan.

Facer, K. (2011). *Learning futures: Education, technology and social change*. Routledge.

Facer, K. (2012). Taking the 21st century seriously: Young people, education and socio-technical futures. *Oxford Review of Education*, *38*(1), 97–113.

Gee, J. P. (2003). *What video games have to teach us about learning and literacy*. Palgrave Macmillan.

Gee, J. P., & Hayes, E. (2011). *Language and learning in the digital age*. Routledge.

Giddens, A. (1991). *Modernity and self-identity: Self and society in the late modern age*. Stanford University Press.
Gourlay, L., & Oliver, M. (2018). *Student engagement in the digital university: Sociomaterial assemblages*. Routledge.
Green, B., & Bigum, C. (1993). Aliens in the classroom. *Australian Journal of Education*, *37*(2), 119–41.
Hanman, N. (2005, November 10). Growing up with the wired generation. *The Guardian*. http://www.guardian.co.uk/technology/2005/nov/10/newmedia.media
Harvey, D. (2005). *A brief history of neoliberalism*. Oxford University Press.
Hedberg, J. G. (2011). Towards a disruptive pedagogy: Changing classroom practice with technologies and digital content. *Educational Media International*, *48*(1), 1–16.
Howlett, J. (2013). *Progressive eduction: A critical introduction*. Bloomsbury.
Ito, M. (2010). *Hanging out, messing around, geeking out: Living and learning with new media*. MIT Press.
Johnson, L., Adams, S., & Haywood, K. (2011). *The NMC Horizon Report: 2011 K–12 edition*. New Media Consortium.
Jones, R., & Hafner, C. (2012). *Understanding digital literacies: A practical introduction*. Routledge.
Knobel, M., & Lankshear, C. (2008). Remix: The art of endless hybridization. *Journal of Adult and Adolescent Literacy*, *52*(1), 22–33.
Kress, G. (2009). Comments on Cope and Kalantzis. *Pedagogies: An International Journal*, 4, 205–12.
Levin, B. (1998). An epidemic of education policy: (What) can we learn from each other? *Comparative Education*, *34*(2), 131–41.
Loveless, A., & Williamson, B. (2013). *Learning identities in a digital age: Rethinking creativity, education and technology*. Routledge.
Macleod, J., & Wright, K. (2012). The promise of the new: Genealogies of youth, nation and educational reform in Australia. *Journal of Educational Administration and History*, *44*(4), 283–93.
Mills, K. (2016). *Literacy theories for the digital age: Social, critical, multimodal, spatial, material and sensory lenses*. Multilingual Matters.
Moran, P. W. (2012). Efficiency, standardization and mitigating risk: The strange career of scientific management in American education, 1890–2010. In S. Bialostok, R. Whitman, & W. Bradley (Eds.), *Education and the risk society: Theories, discourse and risk identities in education contexts* (pp. 55–74). Sense Publishers.
Moyle, D. (2015). "Are we there yet?" Revisiting the Digital Education Revolution. *Curriculum Perspectives*, *35*(2), 64–9.
Potter, J. (2012). *Digital media and learner identity: The new curatorship*. Palgrave Macmillan.

Prensky, M. (2001). *Digital game-based learning*. Paragon House.
Prensky, M. (2005a). "Engage me or enrage me": What today's learners demand. *Educase Review*, *40*(5), 60–5.
Prensky, M. (2005b). Listen to the natives. *Educational Leadership*, *63*(4), 8–13.
Prensky, M. (2010). *Teaching digital natives: Partnering for real learning*. Corwin.
Rizvi, F., & Lingard, B. (2010). *Globalizing education policy*. Routledge.
Rosen, L. D. (2010). *Rewired: Understanding the igeneration and the way they learn*. Palgrave Macmillan.
Schwartz, K. (2013, March 8). Remixing Melville: Moby Dick meets the digital generation. *MindShift*. https://www.kqed.org/mindshift/27552/remixing-melville-moby-dick-meets-the-digital-generation
Sefton-Green, J., Nixon, H., & Erstad, O. (2009). Reviewing approaches and perspectives on "digital literacy." *Pedagogies: An International Journal*, *4*(2), 107–25.
Selwyn, N. (2003). Schooling the mobile generation: The future for schools in the mobile networked society. *British Journal of Sociology in Education*, *24*(2), 131–44.
Selwyn, N. (2009). The digital native—Myth and reality. *Aslib Proceedings*, *61*(4), 364–79.
Selwyn, N. (2016). Minding our language: Why education and technology is full of bullshit … and what might be done about it? *Learning, Media and Technology*, *41*(3), 437–43.
Sheridan, M. P., & Rowsell, J. (2010). *Design literacies: Learning and innovation in the digital age*. Routledge.
Street, B. (2003). What's "new" in new literacy studies? Critical approaches to literacy through theory and practice. *Current Issues in Comparative Education*, *5*(2), 77–91.
Thompson, T. L. (2012). (Re/dis)assembling learning practices online with fluid objects and spaces. *Studies in Continuing Education*, *34*(3), 251–66.
Varanasi, R. (2015). The evolution after the (digital education) revolution. *Curriculum Perspectives*, *35*(2), 77–80.
Williams, C., Gannon, S., & Sawyer, W. (2013). A genealogy of the "future": Antipodean trajectories and travels of the "21st century learner." *Journal of Education Policy*, *28*(6), 792–806.
Yates, L. (2012). "My school, my university, my country, my world, my Google, myself"…What is education for now? *Australian Educational Researcher*, *39*(3), 259–274.

PART II

Engaging in Different Sites

8 Affect, Embodiment, and Critical Pedagogy

Robyne Garrett

Introduction

The global impact of neoliberalism and its ongoing manifestation in schooling is a seemingly relentless pursuit (Wrigley et al., 2012). While educational policy is redefined to serve economic interests, centralized control over curriculum and pedagogy is sustained through ongoing surveillance, testing, and audit. The dominant story in mainstream schooling has become one that defaults to particular ways of valuing knowledge and assumptions about "intelligence" that are deeply flawed and prejudiced (Savage, 2017). Students who have not been afforded the cognitive, cultural, and social skills to engage as competitive learners are systematically disadvantaged and constructed as "undeserving" (Wilkins, 2012).

While teachers are denied professional responsibility for what goes on in classrooms, they are still left with the overwhelming task of addressing structural inequity (Biesta, 2004). In normalizing testing regimes, they are encouraged to take up technical modes of teaching that assume certainty and efficiency. Most worrying is the narrowing of pedagogic practice to explicit teaching, with a view of learning as the memorization of facts and a one-size-fits-all approach (Donahue & Stuart, 2008; Smyth, 2011). Despite an ongoing rhetoric of raising standards, learning for many young people has ultimately become fast, shallow, and completely divorced from lived experience, bodies, or pleasure (Wrigley et al., 2012).

In these contexts, schooling becomes a form of alienated labor, where students are told what to do, what to think, and what to write. They submit "work" to teachers who assess it and allocate "marks" as a proxy measure of achievement (Hayes, 2019). In the process, bodies are examined, passed, graded, hurt, applauded, praised, encouraged, and coerced (Corrigan, 1988; Gore, 2018) by pedagogical processes that are observed, sensed, felt, and have affect.

Despite all, change does happen, and innovation can occur, especially where teachers utilize the small spaces of freedom to develop *enabling* rather than *fickle* pedagogies that buy compliance and deliver little (Comber, 2016). Central to this chapter are socially just pedagogies that engage with bodies and creativity as instruments for learning. In attempting to support young people to become more human (Wrigley et al., 2012), the chapter begins by drawing on principles and theories from the rich legacy of critical pedagogy. It then turns to theories of affect and embodiment that are generative in developing a theoretical case for incorporating the body and creativity in educational practice. Next, examples are provided of how principles of critical pedagogy can be mobilized through a creative and body-based learning initiative. In conclusion, I argue for a theory of critical pedagogy that takes seriously the role of affect and embodiment in learning, as well as the need to bridge the gulf between educational theory and the real worlds of young people.

Critical Approaches

Critical pedagogy has evolved from theoretical principles around critical theory as well as practices that serve the transformative ideals of democratic schooling (McLaren, 2017). It recognizes that inequalities are deeply embedded in the institutional structures of exclusion, marginalization, and relations of power. As the previous chapters suggest, the challenges associated with addressing inequity call for versions of schooling that empower disenfranchised students as well as those traditionally excluded from schooling. The emerging body of evidence suggests that, in moving past deficit views of students, critical pedagogy can improve academic success for all young people.

When engaging with critical pedagogies teachers are asked to confront their beliefs and taken-for-granted assumptions. They are encouraged to interrogate their practice to identify the knowledge and skills being valued, the groups being privileged, and the control of communication in their classes (Smyth, 2001, 2011). Theoretical orientations draw attention to knowledge and power (Delpit, 2006; Giroux, 1985; Gore, 1995), including where power sits within the classroom (Freire, 1996); connection to the life worlds of students (González et al., 2006; Thomson, 2002; Vygotsky 1964); and pedagogies that are dialogic and multimodal (Boal, 1974; Freire, 1996).

However, while critical pedagogy makes sense in principle, putting critical pedagogies into practice in complex and ever-changing educational environments presents many challenges (Gore, 2018). Hence, there is a need for theorists to *translate* their notions and visions into practice—to directly address what might go on in the classroom in the name of critical pedagogy. In contributing to the broad intersections between theory and practice, this chapter presents an argument for a theory of critical pedagogy that amplifies bodily conceptions of human existence and acknowledges the role of the body, senses, and imagination in learning.

Affect, Embodiment, and the Arts

Early educational theorists including Dewey (1938) strongly advocated a multimodal approach to education as well as bringing disciplinary knowledge together with life experience. However, while schools and classrooms are clearly bodied spaces where the *control* of bodies is central to managing classrooms, less common is a focus on the body as a productive site of learning. In drawing on ideas around the body's capacity to affect (Massumi, 2002); the body as a pedagogic device (Ivinson, 2012); and embodied pedagogy (Nguyen & Larson, 2015), I argue for an understanding of embodiment that focuses on the body's *power* to feel, sense, respond, and imagine; thus, its capacity to construct meaning. Most significantly, bodily activity is intimately connected to both affect and intellect.

Despite their various articulations, affect theories question the boundaries drawn between mind, body, affect, and experience, and call us to think about the role of senses, feelings, and emotions in learning. Understood as both capacities and forces, affect enables us to articulate the non-linguistic modalities, energies, sensations, and intensities that guide our action and impact how we think (Kinnunean & Kolehainen, 2019; Massumi, 2002; Robinson & Kutner, 2019). It is a means to acknowledge how meanings are made and power is felt, imagined, or contested within the body (Skattebol, 2010). For Zembylas (2007) in particular, affect and cognition are inextricably linked in the process of student learning. Thought itself is embodied and moments of affective intensity activate cognitive processes that create meaning (Tomkins, 1995). From a socially critical perspective, all young people have bodies, and all young people are capable of original ideas. In picking up and utilizing these universal capabilities (Bingham & Biesta, 2010) potential exists for bodies and affect to support young people in accessing the powerful codes of schooling.

Encounters with the arts also generate sensations of feeling, sensing, imagining, and of being in motion (Eisner, 2004). They provide a means to give form to feeling or concepts in ways that transcend the limitations of language (Greene, 1995; Osei-Kofi, 2013). Arts practice involves both *making* and *viewing*, both of which are deeply embodied. By their very nature, arts experiences ignite affect and imagination with unique potential for developing critical awareness and imaginative capacities (Greene, 1995). The arts also recognize the importance of co-construction and consciousness raising with strong connections to active citizenship that challenge dominant discourses, analyze power, and provide for a collective re-imagining of life worlds (Franks et al., 2014; Thomson et al., 2019). Put simply, the arts offer a range of opportunities for making meaning beyond the rational and cognitive, to encompass the imaginative, the corporeal, and the haptic (McDonnell, 2017). They allow young people to explore and communicate in ways that bring bodies, sensations, and feelings into the learning experience (Osei-Kofi, 2013). Thus, there is significant potential for a corporally centered pedagogy that demands creativity and imagination to mobilize and put into action principles of critical pedagogy.

Creative and Body-Based Learning

The above conceptual resources led to the development of a creative and body-based learning (CBL) initiative which encompasses a range of pedagogical approaches that put embodiment, creativity, and imagination at the center of the educational experience. In drawing on foundational strategies of drama-based pedagogy (Dawson & Kiger Lee, 2018), CBL extends these approaches to include multiple artistic and movement forms. Guided by the principle of praxis, CBL represents a set of *provocations*, rather than a specific set of practices, which are designed to help teachers reimagine pedagogical practice in ways that utilize the body and creativity to access the curriculum and represent learning. The intention is to provide an embodied pedagogy that facilitates exploration, creative energy, and *felt* understanding.

Additionally central to the approach is a describe-analyze-relate (DAR) reflection process that fosters student understanding through opportunities to *describe* actions, *analyze* learning and *relate* to life worlds (Dawson & Kiger Lee, 2018). This is intended to provide cycles of reflection that facilitate collective understandings and regard for the standpoints of others. In summary, CBL represents an interactive production of knowledge that emerges from physical and creative *encounters*, where senses and feelings give rise to the embodied understanding of curriculum concepts.

Mobilizing Critical Pedagogy Through CBL

From Giroux (1985) we understand that critical pedagogy aims to bring change for learners—it is about transformative practice that places *inclusion* in learning as central to practice. However, in moving toward praxis we need to move beyond theorizing toward seriously considering implications for teacher pedagogy. In the following sections, a series of creative and body-based approaches are used to illustrate how principles of critical pedagogy including connecting to life worlds, addressing issues of power, and multimodal learning can be enacted, embodied, and brought to life.

Connecting to Students' Life Worlds and Bodies

Knowledge that is grounded in the learners' life worlds is seen as having significant potential to connect young people to schooling. Pedagogies that draw on student worlds as sources of rich visceral knowledge can be seen in approaches including "strengths-based" approaches (Lingard & Mills, 2011); "funds of knowledge" (González et al., 2006); working with local knowledge (Zipin, 2017); "virtual schoolbag" (Thomson, 2002), and "culturally responsive pedagogy"

(Ladson-Billings, 1995). In these approaches, new knowledge is attached to what students bring to school and is grounded in learners' life worlds and identity. They represent epistemological inclusion, where lives and bodies have symbolic capital that is respected, scaffolded, and connected to something new (Wrigley et al., 2012).

In mobilizing these kinds of connections, CBL practice is essentially embodied. Strategies ask students to move, think, talk, imagine, and create with their bodies. In drawing on drama-based pedagogy (Dawson & Kiger Lee, 2018) strategies that *activate dialogue* are used to encourage talking and sharing as well as the development of vocabulary and connections between new learning and prior understandings. This is exemplified in a "poster dialogue" activity where students move around the room and individually respond to prompts in written or visual form on posters that might require them to recall what they know or identify what they are interested in knowing about a particular topic. They can visually see other responses and can read, add, or tick as needed. A teacher then synthesizes each poster to provide an overview of the collective knowledge/inquiry in the room. *Games* are used to rehearse curriculum material, and to develop fluency and recall. In an example that resembles a form of musical chairs, a "truth about me" strategy requires an individual in the center of the group to make a statement that is true for themselves, a number, an animal, or topic, thus calling on their own knowledge and life world. Everyone for whom that statement is true is then required to move to a different place. The activity is active, it uses imagination and activates affect. It also acknowledges differences and similarities between individuals, concepts, and ideas. *Image work* strategies utilize the body or artifacts to create material or corporeal representations of curriculum concepts. This might be through the creation of a 3D model or the body itself in statue or movement. Finally, *role play* strategies are used to create problem-solving scenarios that connect real-world situations to learning. They involve teachers and/or students taking up imaginary roles such as that of a reporter, shop assistant, or marginalized student. Collectively the strategies engage with the body, affect, and the life worlds of students. They give form to curriculum concepts where embodied knowledge is brought into dialogue with disciplinary knowledge, thus scaffolding access to powerful learning. By engaging students' lives, bodies, and senses, thoughts and memories are created and stored deeply within the embodied self.

Addressing Issues of Power and Justice

Also important to critical pedagogy is a focus on power, agency, and perspective. Transformative practice requires a change in power relations between teachers and students such that knowledge is co-constructed, and learners emerge as more powerful, independent, and agentic (Delpit, 2006; Giroux, 1985; Gore, 1995). Learning becomes a series of *acts of cognition* rather than a one-way transfer of information (Freire, 1996). In this way, democratic citizenship and social responsibility can be *lived* rather than abstractly conceptualized and students can build awareness of the social realities that shape their lives (Wrigley et al., 2012).

CBL can enact a transforming pedagogy through sequences and strategies, as outlined above. Students can begin to view themselves in ways that are relational to the broader context in which they are located. For example, using arts-based approaches, such as role play, tableau, or 3-D model making, students can engage in their own way to give form to abstract concepts and construct themselves in relation to what they already know and what they are learning.

CBL is also informed by the work of Augusto Boal (1974) and his "Theatre of the Oppressed." His work offers insight into scenarios that replicate real-life oppressions. "The Great Game of Power" is one such strategy that encourages participants to see the machinations of power from multiple standpoints. The task involves one student positioning four chairs and a water bottle in a way that represents a particular power relationship they experience. Other students are asked for their perspective and understanding of this formation depending on where they stand in the space, thus activating powerful meaning making from multiple points of view. Once participants identify what they see as the power relationship, they can re-create an image of what a more ideal relationship might look like. In tasks such as this, students can locate themselves in relation to a broader context, and understandings can emerge collectively with the perspectives of others. Agentic possibilities are then created for a re-telling of young people's experience of power.

Learning that is Dialogic and Multimodal

Another key tenet of critical pedagogy is meaning making that is *visible* and shared between teachers and learners. Freire (1996) warns against an educational "banking system" that constrains students' creative power and advocates a system of learning through dialogic and interactive approaches. Broader symbol systems can operate as tools for understanding and access to powerful codes can be made possible via multimodal (physical, verbal, and visual) sensorial and lived experiences (Dewey, 1938; Merleau-Ponty, 2002). This kind of corporeally centered pedagogy invites a more democratic participation into the meaning-making process where students from historically marginalized social groupings can construct their own symbolic metaphors of meaning (Berdayes, 2004).

CBL strategies invite students to actively co-construct learning where the body, objects, and experiences serve as both text and tool (Perry & Medina, 2011). The sense-making process is made visible as an intentional, shared process between teachers and learners (Dawson & Kiger Lee, 2018). During the strategies, students' embodied feelings and perspectives are actively sought through a describe-analyze-relate (DAR) reflection process. Here, students engage in a ritualized cycle of reflection and connection to life worlds. In asking generative questions that draw on their sensorial experience, the teacher can build knowledge through collective sense making. The initial emphasis is on drawing out affective and embodied states from learners by asking: What did you do? How did you feel? How were you successful? Generally, this is followed by questions that ask students to interpret their experiences in relation to curriculum goals (What does this mean? What did we learn?) and then to relate this learning to broader contexts (Where else would this be useful?). These interactive exchanges are intended to include all students in dialogic conversation as well as to encourage deep listening and collective understanding.

While many teachers attempt to draw out students' knowledge, sometimes this is difficult to achieve through words alone. Embodied and creative practices provide a different mode of knowing that is not reduced to the written word, but instead is experienced and understood through the body. Material entities interact to produce new knowledge that can be both empowering and enabling. Simply put, CBL approaches are designed to engage the body, games, image work, and role play to activate dialogue and promote understanding that is held within senses, feelings, and thought.

Conclusion

As we encounter multiple versions of "critical pedagogy," this book is about sharing our various orientations and building a meso-level set of key characteristics for curriculum, pedagogy, and assessment. This represents a reference point for our shared commitment to understanding what is possible in the name of critical pedagogy.

In this chapter I have discussed principles and theories of critical pedagogy before turning to theories of affect and embodiment in order to generate a theoretical case for a creative and body-based learning initiative. Specific principles of critical pedagogy then provided a framing for moving beyond theorizing to seriously consider how embodied and creative approaches can mobilize and enact transformative pedagogies. Through this work I argue that important pedagogies are lived, relational, and embodied practices that call affect into play. They operate in visual, aural, and physical ways that far exceed the limits of prescribed criteria, tests, or specific forms of thinking. Rather, they draw attention to the body, spoken or visual images, gestures, movement, sound, or silence (Mills & Dooley, 2018).

Dimensions of critical and transformative pedagogy can be achieved through strategies that bring affective, aesthetic, and embodied responses into dialogue with disciplinary knowledge. It is here that the relationships between emotion, cognition, and the body become central to learning. These efforts challenge the erasure of the body in academic endeavors and acknowledge that important knowledge is not only cerebral but can be drawn from senses, feelings, and physical acts (Osei-Kofi, 2013).

In CBL, students can see themselves in relational ways and engage in communication of ideas or concepts through the body and artistic constructions. The co-construction of these enactments is a deep reflective practice that makes the invisible visible and understanding embodied. These pedagogical approaches represent an epistemological shift from those that routinely privilege certain students toward a collective community of learners that centralizes dialogue and exchange of ideas (Biesta, 2017).

In arguing for a version of critical pedagogy that attends to the embodied and situated nature of students' lives, CBL provides *spaces of freedom* for all students to be positioned as capable, knowledgeable, and imaginative. It recognizes the primacy of active, sensing, and sometimes silent bodies to communicative action and meaning making. Learning becomes a series of sensed and creative encounters that not only allow access to curriculum knowledge but multiple ways to share, show, and communicate that knowledge. If the ultimate power of critical pedagogy is to help young people to "become more human," we must see purposes of education beyond the passing of exams and tests toward a deeper embodied sense of what is real, imagined, and important.

Bibliography

Berdayes, V. (2004). The body and educational practice: Some themes in the work of Paolo Freire. In V. Berdayes & L. Esposito (Eds.), *The body in human enquiry: Interdisciplinary explorations of embodiment* (pp. 217–31). Hampton Press.

Biesta, G. (2004). Education, accountability, and the ethical demand: Can the democratic potential of accountability be regained? *Educational Theory, 54*(3), 233–50.

Biesta, G. (2017). *The rediscovery of teaching.* Routledge.

Bingham, C., & Biesta, G. (2010). *Jacques Rancière: Education, truth, emancipation*. Bloomsbury Publishing.

Boal, A. (1974). *The theatre of the oppressed.* Theatre Communications Group.

Comber, B. (2016). Poverty, place and pedagogy in education: Research stories from front-line workers. *Australian Educational Researcher, 43*(4), 393–417.
Corrigan, P. (1988). The making of the boy: Meditations on what grammar school did with, to, and for my body. *Journal of Education, 170*(3), 142–61.
Dawson, K., & Kiger Lee, B. (2018). *Drama-based pedagogy: Activating learning across the curriculum*. Intellect.
Delpit, L. (2006). *Other people's children: Cultural conflict in the classroom*. New Press.
Dewey, J. (1938). *Experience and education*. Macmillan.
Donahue, D., & Stuart, J. (2008). Working towards balance: Arts integration in pre-service teacher education in an era of standardization. *Teaching and Teacher Education, 24*(2), 343–55.
Eisner, E. W. (2004). What can education learn from the arts about the practice of education? *International Journal of Education & the Arts, 5*(4), 1–13.
Franks, A., Thomson, P., Hall, C., & Jones, K. (2014). Teachers, arts practice and pedagogy. *Changing English, 21*(2), 171–81.
Freire, P. (1996). *Pedagogy of the oppressed*. Penguin Books.
Giroux, H. A. (1985). Critical pedagogy, cultural politics and the discourse of experience. *Journal of Education, 167*(2), 22–41.
González, N., Moll, L. C., & Amanti, C. (2006). *Funds of knowledge: Theorizing practices in households, communities, and classrooms*. Routledge.
Gore, J. (1995). On the continuity of power relations in pedagogy. *International Studies in Sociology of Education, 5*(2), 165–88.
Gore, J. (2018). On the limits to empowerment through critical and feminist pedagogies. In D. Carlson, & M. Apple (Eds.), *Power/knowledge/pedagogy: The meaning of democratic education un unsettling times* (pp. 271–88). Routledge.
Greene, M. (1995). *Releasing the imagination: Essays on education, the arts, and social change*. Jossey-Bass.
Hayes, M. (2019). Education as utopian method: Reimagining education for a post-alienated labor world. In M. Peters, P. Jandric, & A. Means (Eds.), *Education and technological unemployment* (pp. 329–42). Springer.
Ivinson, G. (2012). The body and pedagogy: Beyond absent, moving bodies in pedagogic practice. *British Journal of Sociology of Education, 33*(4), 489–506.
Kinnunean, T., & Kolehainen, M. (2019). Touch and affect: Analysing the archive of touch biographies. *Body and Society, 25*(1), 29–56.
Ladson-Billings, G. (1995). Toward a theory of culturally relevant pedagogy. *American Educational Research Journal, 32*(3), 465–91.
Lingard, B., & Mills, M. (2007). Pedagogies making a difference: Issues of social justice and inclusion. *International Journal of Inclusive Education, 11*(3), 233–44.
Massumi, B. (2002). *Politics of affect*. Polity Press.

McDonnell, J. (2017). Political and aesthetic equality in the work of Jacques Rancière: Applying his writing to debates in education and the arts. *Journal of Philosophy of Education*, *51*(2), 387–400.
McLaren, P. (2017). Critical pedagogy: A look at the major concepts. In A. Darder, M. Baltoddano, & R. Torres (Eds.), *The critical pedagogy reader* (pp. 69–96). Routledge Falmer.
Merleau-Ponty, M. (2002). *Phenomenology of perception*. Routledge.
Mills, K., & Dooley, J. (2018). Sensory ways to indigenous multimodal literacies: Hands and feet tell the story. In J. Rennie & H. Harper (Eds.), *Literacy education and Indigenous Australians: Theory, research and practice* (pp. 1–21). Springer.
Nguyen, D. J., & Larson, J. B. (2015). Don't forget about the body: Exploring the curricular possibilities of embodied pedagogy. *Innovative Higher Education*, *40*, 331–44.
Osei-Kofi, N. (2013). The emancipatory potential of arts-based research for social justice. *Equity & Excellence in Education*, *46*(1), 135–49.
Perry, M., & Medina, C. (2011). Embodiment and performance in pedagogy research: Investigating the body in curriculum experience. *Journal of Curriculum Theorizing*, *27*(3), 62–75.
Robinson, B., & Kutner, M. (2019). Spinoza and the affective turn: A return to the philosophical origins of affect. *Qualitative Inquiry*, *25*(2), 111–17.
Savage, G. C. (2017). Neoliberalism, education and curriculum. In B. Gobby & R. Walker (Eds.), *Powers of curriculum: Sociological perspectives on education* (pp. 143–65). Oxford University Press.
Skattebol, J. (2010). Affect: A tool to support pedagogical change. *Discourse: Studies in the Cultural Politics of Education*, *31*(1), 75–91.
Smyth, J. (2001). *Critical politics of teachers' work: An Australian perspective*. Peter Lang.
Smyth, J. (2011). The disaster of the "self-managing school"—Genesis, trajectory, undisclosed agenda, and effects. *Journal of Educational Administration and History*, *43*(2), 95–117.
Thomson, P. (2002). *Schooling the rustbelt kids: Making the difference in changing times*. Allen & Unwin.
Thomson, P., Hall, C., Earl, L., & Geppert, C. (2019). Towards an arts education for cultural leadership. In S. Riddle & M. Apple (Eds.), *Reimagining education for democracy* (pp. 174–89). Routledge.
Tomkins, S. (1995). *Exploring affect: The selected writings of Silvan S. Tomkins*. University Press.
Vygotsky, L. S. (1964). Thought and language. *Annals of Dyslexia*, *14*(1), 97–8.
Wilkins, A. (2012). The spectre of neoliberalism: Pedagogy, gender and the construction of learner identities. *Critical Studies in Education*, *53*(2), 197–210.

Wrigley, T., Lingard, B., & Thomson, P. (2012). Pedagogies of transformation: Keeping hope alive in troubled times. *Critical Studies in Education*, *53*(1), 95–108.

Zembylas, M. (2007). The specters of bodies and affects in the classroom: A rhizo-ethological approach. *Pedagogy, Culture & Society*, *15*(1), 19–35.

Zipin, L. (2017). Pursuing a problematic-based curriculum approach for the sake of social justice. *Journal of Education (University of KwaZulu-Natal)*, *69*, 67–92.

9 The Culturally Responsive Listener

Stephen Kelly

Introduction

This chapter discusses the effects of a pilot action research project intended to support the generation of a school-wide culture of listening and respect for cultural diversity. The two teachers whom I report on were challenged to use diversity as a curriculum resource, while exploring strategies of active listening in attempts to respond to cultural diversity. The teachers involved in the project work at a large rural Kindergarten to Year 12 Catholic College. Prior to the commencement of the project the school had already made commitments to engage with the Reggio Emilia philosophy, well known for its influence in early years education. The challenge the school's leadership had posed for its staff was to explore how the tenets of the Reggio Emilia philosophy, as promoted by Rinaldi (2006), might translate to primary and secondary education.

In projecting the principles of Reggio Emelia, the school's leadership had made commitments to see the child as someone who possesses the rights of democratic citizenship. The leadership group were intent on promoting a view of the child as an already competent and capable learner from birth. For this team, the capable child is therefore already critically active toward their own intellectual, emotional, imaginative, and civic aspirations. These leaders were concerned that their beliefs and aspirations for the children in their school were not evident in daily practices. The school wished to address: (a) perceptions that students were deferring the work of thinking and speaking to teachers, and (b) the lack of recognition of the capabilities of a complex, culturally diverse community. The leaders aimed to respond by establishing an ethics of listening, which provided students with opportunities to act upon their interpretations of "things in the world."

As Rinaldi (2013) argues, knowledge for the child is understood to be contingent, and open to the child's experience. As an active participant, the child works with a collective of other children and members of the community to generate many possible interpretations of those things under investigation. This seemingly situates the teacher as a partner who works with children to enable or project educational conditions. This view implies a relation of equality between the child and her adult teacher: each subject possesses the right to speak and be heard (Rancière, 2007). The teacher as *progettazione*, the one who assists children in projecting their next steps, engages with children in educational research using processes of observation, documentation, and interpretation.

The approach imagines the child as an outsider, not already schooled in the ways of the world. For the teacher, this means being alert to how they socialize students into worldly practices. As Foucault (1972) might suggest, there is no way of escaping the world. The child born into the world is subject to systems of thought, the disciplinary practices of schooling being among them. The teacher, as a culturally responsive listener, is aware of the disciplining effects of socializing. The teacher can also be aware that the child new to the disciplines of schooling stands at the threshold of these discourses and is capable of thinking anew (Foucault, 2010). As a person other than adult, the child is capable of disrupting common-sense understandings. For the listening teacher this involves working toward an emergent practice between children and adults where the student claims their experience as subject.

There the teacher and child stand together at the threshold of an expansive discourse, where both teacher and student assert the right to feel and think otherwise (Foucault, 2010). In this case the learner is able to demonstrate the capability of speaking to what they feel, see, and hear, but in regard to the thinking of others. To link pedagogies of listening to cultural responsiveness begs the questions this chapter investigates: What conditions of learning enable the capacity to observe, speak, and listen with integrity? In what ways can we place demands on all students to democratically engage in the practice of being observers, listeners, and speakers? What happens when a school connects their view of the child as already capable to the challenges of being culturally responsive? In the remainder of the chapter, I begin by conceptualizing an ethics of listening and its connection to cultural responsiveness. I then frame the research, before moving to the teachers' responses to the research undertaken, finishing with some observations about the characteristics of the culturally responsive listener.

The Ethics of Listening

When discussing what she means by listening, Rinaldi (2013) emphasizes its active quality. Listening requires being present to the speaker. It is not an act that can be fixed in time, but unfolds as ongoing, perpetual activity. Listening, then, is a form of becoming when in relation to others. For Rinaldi, to listen requires the gift of time that opens a space where one is sensitive to others, while attendant to the dance of thoughts within. Listening is not to be captured by teleological demands that drive the participant to given ends, which exclude other possibilities (Derrida, 2000). Listening is a form of hospitality, requiring a responsibility to others and to oneself. This responsibility to others also requires a welcoming attitude that is open to difference, other points of view/

theories/meanings, and interpretation. If knowledge of things in the world is contingent and open, participants need to suspend judgment and embrace and use uncertainty when acting with others. In this sense listening is a pedagogical disposition that offers ways of studying things in the world as collective, collaborative, and democratic action.

It is only when acting in relation to others and allowing oneself to be supplemented by the action of others that the human subject appears (Biesta, 2013). Here, the task is to provide an opportunity for students to be political subjects when practicing their democratic responsibility to others (Kelly, 2018). This is an education that creates conditions that are open to plurality and difference. As Rancière (2010) suggests, to appear as a political and democratic subject does not just require one to listen; it demands the right to be heard through the act of speaking.

Connecting Listening to a Culturally Responsive Pedagogy

If the action research sought to bridge the school's commitment to a pedagogy of listening with culturally responsive pedagogies, then it was to foster the sense of the child as a capable speaking subject. The child in culturally responsive schooling can be described as an active member of an extended family and communal structure (Castagno & Brayboy, 2008). Children are apprenticed into the social, economic, spiritual, and political life of the culture, and are expected to be competent and make contributions to the life of the community. This is not to deny the possibility of multiple subjectivities across cultural contexts. Castagno and Brayboy (2008) argue that Indigenous Native American children observe from nature, and from the examples of elders, siblings, and peers, and exercise a capacity to learn through reciprocal processes of listening. The capacity to take time to apprehend and discern prior to acting is a characteristic of practicing being a competent member of the community. What might appear as a reticence or delay in communicating engagement is an act of the ethical subject taking part in public life. Gay (2002) makes similar observations when speaking of the child's collaborative nature in African, Asian, and Latino contexts. For Gay (2002), children of colored communities demonstrate the capability of subordinating their individual needs to the welfare of the group. It is a characteristic of these children to competently engage in collective discourse. Individual achievement is subordinated to group success. Gay argues that children from these communities are active speakers and listeners. They are partners in a dynamic community who place demands on each other through "providing prompts, feed-back, and commentary" (Gay, 2002, p. 111). Their patterns of exchange are both polyphonic and dialogic, demonstrating the capacity to switch role and pass the baton of expertise in "fluid and interchangeable ways" (Gay, 2002, p. 111).

In reporting these characteristics, we are invited to see children's capability to communicate and structure ideas as the emergent property of participating in complex narrative events. Making meaning is accomplished through participating in oral or written discursive chains characterized by providing a lot of background information; being passionately and personally involved with the content of the discourse; using indirectness (such as innuendo, symbolism, and metaphor) to convey ideas; weaving many different threads or issues into a single story; and embedding talk with feelings of intensity, advocacy, evaluation, and aesthetics (Gay, 2002, p. 112).

If other ways of knowing and being are to be culturally validated, then we need to take into account the conversational nature of pedagogic discourse and the demand this places on listeners to resonate with the other. Whether children silently discern or actively engage in discourse we need to avoid making assumptions about how they are building knowledge. To acknowledge, in all their heterogeneity, the diverse qualities of childhood within and across cultures offers the conditions of possibility for listening. Culturally responsive schools might be characterized as spaces where the child, who resonates with others, is competent and able to exercise cultural knowledge grounded in the cultural heritage and traditions of their community. When listening, the child builds on the knowledge and skills of the local cultural community as a foundation from which to achieve personal and academic success. She actively participates in various cultural environments; engages effectively in learning activities that are based on traditional ways of knowing and learning; and demonstrates an awareness and appreciation of the relationships and processes of interaction of all elements in the world around her.

As in Reggio contexts, these rich descriptions help us to think of children as cooperative beings who take pride in being competent. Equally, the child is accorded the right to contemplate and speak their mind when in dialogic relation to others. In a culturally responsive pedagogy, the child has a capacity to use their tactile, visual, oral, spiritual experience of the world to make holistic sense of their culture. This child seeks choice and self-determination over the pace and means of producing cultural knowledge and exercising their citizenship within their world.

To generate a culturally responsive and listening practice the action research work drew on Gay's (2002) proposal that culturally responsive teaching acknowledges the learner's right to access "their own cultural frames" (2002, p. 9) when grappling with the demands of mainstream curricula. In responding to the CRP literature, the teachers in this project aimed to make links to the principles of Reggio Emelia that had been informing initiatives at the school.

The Action Research

The concept of a listening school offered a number of challenges to teachers and students, particularly in the upper primary and secondary years. The Reggio Emelia project seemed particularly relevant to the needs of early years educators but not, for example, to the demands and expectations placed on senior secondary teachers. To lay the ground for future inquiry, the school wanted teachers to imagine how a pedagogy of listening might be characterized at each stage of learning. To borrow from Foucault, to imagine and enact these constructs from Reception to Year 12 demanded a learning community that required students who are prepared to speak fearlessly about things that they feel, see, perceive, and interpret. Paradoxically, this required teachers and students to listen with intent.

A key to this work would be the shift toward a disposition of education as research, to enable a pedagogy of listening to take hold within the school. The strategy used for *scaling up* a pedagogy of listening, relevant to teachers at each stage of schooling, was to enlist two key leaders to engage in the process of action research: in effect to build leadership capacity through practitioner research. Two leader/teachers were identified and were asked to join a project initiated by the Catholic Education Office of South Australia, where I was working at the time.

The participants used the action research process to respond to conjecture that the disposition of the listening teacher, who researches pedagogy and curriculum with children, is a powerful technology in developing the knowledges and practices required for culturally responsive pedagogies. The teachers began by linking constructs emerging out of readings of Gay, Ladson-Billings, and Castagno and Brayboy, to question what it means to be culturally responsive and to live in democratic relation to others.

The action research project asked participants to respond to the challenges of combining listening and cultural responsiveness. We were interested in how teachers and students might act, interact, and reflect when they focused on deploying their own experiences and engaged in deep listening. Here we asked how emergent learning might be founded on: (a) a principle of equality between students and teachers, and (b) students and teachers who, when observing, speaking, and listening, experience the plurality and difference in community as an opportunity for thinking anew the limits of discourse. Using Hattam and his colleague's (2009) approach to action research, the teachers were engaged in a research cycle that asked them to be challenged by readings, rethink and redesign their curriculum, teach the redesign while generating data, analyze data, and publish findings in a public performance of the research.

The approach supports Biesta's (2006) notion that "education should be conceived as a space where individuals can act, where they can bring their beginnings into the world" (p. 137), but in a way that does not "obstruct the opportunities for others to bring their beginnings into the world" (p. 138). This is a space where students and teachers reframe the curriculum in such a way that it provides opportunities for students and teachers to bring into being a subjectivity supplemented by the other. As Rancière (2007) suggests, the task is to avoid the effects of the master explicator dividing his intelligence against the novice. Rather, what is required is a demand placed on the student for "absolute attention for seeing, and seeing again, saying and repeating" (p. 23). Rancière's (2007) challenge is to exercise a certain liberty, to respond to the demand to exercise one's intelligence by speaking to questions that address "what do you see? what do you think about it? what do you make of it?" (p. 23). In turn I rework these questions to read how the teachers in this project have framed their curriculum, so that the student's capacity for thought will be used to speak with attention to their:

- observations: the data (things in the world) that the student senses, generates, and collects;
- questions: how students attune with each other and pose questions to critically examine things they have observed/sensed/felt;
- interpretations: how students move from affective responses to produce their knowledge/view of the world.

My reading of the teachers' reflections below draws on interviews conducted in school visits, regular reports from the teachers in research meetings and PowerPoint presentations delivered at an end-of-year conference organized by the school.

Interpreting the Teachers' Work

In responding to the challenges of reading and making links between listening and culturally responsive pedagogies, the teachers began to rethink their approach to curriculum and pedagogy. Teacher One, a Year Eleven religious education teacher, was focused on how a relation of equality (Rancière, 2007) could be established with students in her Year 11 religious education class and how dialogic practices might enhance this aim. She was interested in questioning how relationships can drive the curriculum; and how being in dialogue with students can influence the curriculum choices and add to a student's sense of connection to the class. The second teacher, of a Year 11 English as an additional language and dialect class, focused on how listening to students' experience facilitates the choice of text and how this might improve students' learning outcomes. The question reflected her interest in how offering choice to her Year 11 EALD class figured in providing opportunity for students to demonstrate their funds of knowledge (Moll et al., 1992) and capability.

When rethinking her practice, Teacher One was interested in how she might negotiate tasks around aspects of student subjectivity, the role of personal narrative, and the exchange of ideas in a discursive learning community. This involved the sharing of individual interests and themes across the class to promote connection between students. Her focus emphasized how dialogue with students enabled deeper insights into their life worlds, offering their experience as a curriculum resource and hopefully providing the base for linking student inquiry to curriculum. These aims placed strong demands on participants to create a space for listening. And finally, the teacher was interested in documenting the effects of changed practices in a target research group. The target research group reflected the ethnic diversity in her class made up of students from Indigenous, African, Indian, and Anglo backgrounds. She identified the members of this group as:

- Student A (LL), female, 16, Indigenous Australian
- Student B (MM), male, 17, Zimbabwean EAL, three years in Australia
- Student C (PK), male, 16, Congolese EAL, six years in Australia
- Student D (AN), male, 16, Indian EAL
- Student E (JR), male, 16, Anglo-Celtic Australian.

Teacher Two rethought her practice by valuing student experience and prior learning, providing opportunities for students to use autobiography as a curriculum resource for their task, taking time to listen to the students' reasons for choosing their themes and songs. She wished to understand the significance of culture in providing a strong foundation for social, emotional, and intellectual development and demonstrate the ability to build on that understanding in her teaching. The class comprised students from Chinese, African, Caribbean, and Indian backgrounds.

Observation: Speaking to What is Felt and Seen

In observing how she provided opportunities for students to speak to what they see, Teacher One reported that, when given opportunity to negotiate topics, her students chose racism and the Syrian refugee crisis. While the means of producing cultural knowledge was connected to the students' interest in racism, modes of representation and dissemination potentially enabled engagements with networks of cultural practice, both within the community and beyond. The teacher also identified the need to negotiate the presentation mode. Here, students in the target group created a website and an app using the principle of choice to connect the mode of representation to themes they were exploring. When concerned about the level of cultural safety operating across the class, the teacher encouraged dialogue about the level of comfort students experienced when discussing and investigating their chosen topics. She felt that this encouraged students to draw on their experiences when speaking. By attuning to their feelings, students were able to use their affective responses to speak their thoughts. This became particularly relevant for the Indigenous girl in the target group who reported experiences of racism.

Teacher Two reported weaving into the demands of the task personal choice, time, and funds of knowledge as curriculum resources. This involved the selection of songs based on a theme of their choosing, the identification of personal, social, and cultural perspectives using the song lyrics, drawing on personal experience, and making connections to the life worlds of others. The teacher's use of students' experiences moved beyond reporting on events as narrative chains. Rather she aimed to highlight the affective dimensions of students' perceptions, understanding "the significance of the role of cultural identity in providing a strong foundation for all social, emotional, intellectual and spiritual development and demonstrate the ability to build on that understanding in their teaching" (Teacher Two). The students seemed to use these processes to generate and communicate their thoughts. When given opportunity and space to draw on domains of sensory experience and to link these felt experiences to abstract concepts, students were able to connect their choices and emerging ideas to the mandated curriculum.

Questioning: Speaking to Questions Posed

Teacher One's target group pursued the topic of racism through collecting data through a survey and semi-structured interviews, providing the basis for fertile discussion within the group and across the class. The students' research process indicated higher perceptions of racism in the school and community than anticipated.

The students' representation of the data unearthed perceptions that racism in the school was less prevalent than in the local community and across Australia. While they used a straightforward research instrument, the data generated by an Anglo boy in the target group had the effect of providing a culturally safe space for the Indigenous girl in the group, while still enabling room for addressing her feelings and experience.

Teacher Two reported individual and class discussions which involved reciprocal exchange between the students and herself. The teacher grouped the discursive foci of the discussion under the headings of affect, subjectivity, observation, and cultural knowledge. According to Teacher Two:

> This action research allowed me to observe the increased engagement once the students had thought of their life connections and how these experiences can inform their learning, can on their learning, including sharing with me. The time I invested in listening to their stories also contributed to their engagement.

Students were able to engage in dialogue that posed questions about their personal experiences and emotional connections to their chosen songs; their thoughts about sharing their feelings and its impact in developing relationships and understanding; and how the strength of their feelings may lead to wanting to act or advocate about new perceptions or ideas. Students also posed questions about the autobiographical connections they made to the songs, the sound resonating within, which in turn led to discussions about their feelings about themselves and their sense of how their subjectivities had been produced through their cultural experience: the sound resonating beyond. Each of the cultural groups reported instances of dissonance between the primary discourse of home and the plurality of intercultural secondary discourses in educational settings. Students were able to use their affective responses to the songs to make observations about their own lived experience and their observations about the experience of others. These discussions enabled students to pose questions about the differences and similarities between cultures and the experience of cultural belonging: in effect to expand the dimensions of their sonorous, discursive space.

Interpretations: Speaking to What They Feel and Think

When reporting on the target group's responses to racism, Teacher One commented that students acknowledged that they were venturing into topics that were experienced and recognized, but often avoided. While Teacher One suggested that "It was difficult to name and address my feeling of unease with such topics," she also reported students struggling with and naming their affective response to racism. Nevertheless, the heuristic work, which revealed the presence of racism in the community, helped to build the "value of purposeful questioning and reflection in building relationships with students." The enhancement of discursive relationships surfaced questions of plurality and difference and enabled students to respond to these questions in ways that were culturally safe. Being sensitive to cultural safety became important when confronting forms of cultural violence and exclusion experienced by class members. Importantly, the teacher reported that students felt enabled to "drive" the curriculum.

In Teacher Two's class, students completed their investigation with an oral presentation. The students' presentations addressed diverse issues/themes they found important. A common thread in these presentations was the struggle of diaspora, contextualized and reinforced through representing specific experiences of drug abuse, courtship, grieving, personal confidence, and academic success. The teacher conducted a debriefing after the oral presentation where the students contrasted previous learning experiences with the one they had just completed. Teacher Two reported that students "indicated that they consolidated their connection with their lived experience and their choice of songs in the pre-task discussion." The idea that their own lives could be seen to be the subject of knowledge reinforced the value they placed on exploring and using feelings and previous experiences as a resource for the assessed curriculum.

The Culturally Responsive Listener

In reflecting on their research, the teachers reported the value of using action research to explicitly focus on cultural diversity as a curriculum resource. This enabled the use of affective processes which valued the students' social world and plurality of experience. In this chapter, I have argued that, when teachers value students' experience of "things in the world," students and teachers are equally able to enter into discursive relationships about matters which affect their lives.

To be a culturally responsive listener, the teacher and the student must both be aware of the other as a sonorous presence, each observing their own senses resonating, but opening up the space to enunciate and affect the other. Teacher One explicitly used cultural diversity as a curriculum resource, then the opportunity to negotiate racism as a topic for investigation arose out of the foreclosure of difference being sensed in the presence of each other's alterity. This led to the disclosure of racism in the community as a substantive knowledge that affected their experience of curriculum and themselves. Students in Teacher Two's class, who came from Chinese, Indian, and African backgrounds, found themselves observing (as a function of feeling, as well as seeing) and disclosing personal tensions in their experience of hybridity. The demand to listen ushered in an immediacy to each other's presence. The songs that they drew upon helped them to temporally locate a personal grieving that centered on feelings of alienation from: (a) an experience of schooling that devalued a social world, and (b) a code of ethics which devalued affective experience, particularly those related to a sense of loss or insufficiency. When present to each other's text, the sense of the culturally responsive listener's loss came also with a sense of expectation of a new subjectivity.

In moving from sensing to action, the students in each class negotiated and posed difficult questions. If students in both classes produced questions that focused on their affective experience, these class texts became a resource for examining shifts and tensions in cultural values. The culturally responsive listener oscillates between the observed, the spoken, and the heard. In both classes the questioning of plural experiences and differences between people led to evaluating ethical and political implications of making new beginnings in relation to others. Here, the culturally responsive listener positions their self, but is simultaneously exposed to others. Each self receives the inscriptions of the other, is attendant to co-emergence of subjectivities, and in their own enunciation echoes, re-inscribes, and supplements their own subjectivity.

When interpreting things in the world the culturally responsive listener is attendant to a polyphony of wills. Each listener is present to the space the other occupies and is opened by their listening. In occupying a space, the embodied listener displaces space and time, and forces a movement which demands the other to speak. This pedagogy of bringing each other into the world values students' and teachers' sense and perception. The affective dimensions of emergent thought become resources for each subject to be recognized as a truth maker. This is to say that students can be a source of authoritative knowledge and capable citizens in their own right, suggesting further possibilities for researching students' experience of their being, in epistemologically plural settings, as a pedagogy for making curriculum.

Conclusion

In this chapter I have suggested that it is possible to bring a listening and culturally responsive pedagogy together. In such a pedagogy, both student and teacher enact the subjectivity of a culturally responsive listener. Conscious of living in diversity, they create an affective environment out of diversity, which is sensitive to the capability of each subject, their civic aspirations, and the democracy they both wish to live in. Each person is a feeling and thinking subject that brings to the sonorous pedagogical space a complex, plural, onto-epistemic experience. Rather than allow curriculum to police, they enact a pedagogy that makes curriculum. In this refusal of given systems of thought, they stand at the thresholds of discourse and are present to the expansive unfolding of what they feel, see, and speak. As one to the other, they extend the gift of hospitality, and bring each other into being.

Acknowledgments

This collaborative research project, was funded by the Australian Research Council for 2022–2024 (Project ID: DP220100651), between the Centre for Research in Educational and Social Inclusion University of South Australia, the University of Adelaide, and Open University of Cyprus. The Research team includes Lead Chief Investigator Lester-Irabinna Rigney Robert Hattam, Nadeem Memon, Sam Schulz, Stephen Kelly, Michalinos Zembylas, Abigail Diplock (Research Assistant), Mikayla King (Ph.D. Candidate) and 30 participating teachers, 4 Principals.

Bibliography

Biesta, G. (2006). *Beyond learning.* Routledge.

Biesta, G. (2013). *The beautiful risk of education*. Paradigm.

Castagno, A., & Brayboy, B. (2008). Culturally responsive schooling for Indigenous youth: A review of the literature. *Review of Educational Research, 78*, 941–93. https://doi.org/10.3102/0034654308323036

Derrida, J. (2000). Hostipitality. *Angelaki—Journal of Theoretical Humanities, 5*(3), 3–19.

Foucault, M. (1972). *The archaeology of knowledge and the discourse on language.* Pantheon Books.

Foucault, M. (2010). What is enlightenment? In P. Rabinow (Ed.), *Michel Foucault: The Foucault reader* (pp. 32–50). Vintage Books.

Gay, G. (2002). Preparing for culturally responsive teaching. *Journal of Teacher Education*, *53*(2), 106–16.

Hattam, R., Brennan, M., Zipin, L., & Comber, B. (2009). Researching for social justice: Contextual, conceptual and methodological challenges. *Discourse: Studies in the Cultural Politics of Education*, *30*(3), 303–16.

Kelly, S. (2018). *Governing literate populations: The political uses of literacy in securing civil society.* Routledge.

Moll, L., Amanti, C., Neff, D., & Gonzalez, N. (1992). Funds of knowledge for teaching: Using a qualitative approach to connect homes to classrooms. *Theory Into Practice*, *31*(2), 132–41.

Rancière, J. (2007). *The ignorant schoolmaster* (K. Ross, Trans.). Stanford University Press.

Rancière, J. (2010). *Dissensus: On politics and aesthetics*. Continuum.

Rinaldi, C. (2006). *In dialogue with Reggio Emelia: Listening, researching and learning.* Routledge.

Rinaldi, C. (2013). *Re-imagining childhood: The inspiration of Reggio Emilia education principles in South Australia*. Government of South Australia.

10 Re-*placing* Aboriginal Voices in Policy Making and Practice in Remote Aboriginal Education

Sam Osborne

Introduction

Aboriginal and Torres Strait Islander education in Australia has been a key site of social policy enactment from early eras of exclusion and assimilation (1788–1960s), through to an era of land and civil rights, self-determination, and reconciliation (1960s–early 2000s), followed by an era of intervention and Closing the Gap (mid 2000s–present) (Buckskin, 2009; Guenther et al., 2016; Partington & Beresford, 2012). The current policy era could be described as the twilight of an era of recognition and voice, where more than a decade of policy focus and advocacy has not resulted in constitutional recognition of Aboriginal and Torres Strait Islander peoples, treaty, or a representative voice in Indigenous policy making in the federal parliament (Pearson, 2014, 2017; Referendum Council, 2017).

Reports reviewing remote Aboriginal and Torres Strait Islander education policies question the effectiveness and outcomes of significant Commonwealth investment in three main focus areas of the previous decade: boarding school scholarship programs, a school attendance initiative (Remote Schools Attendance Strategy), and Direct Instruction (an English language instruction program) (Department of the Prime Minister and Cabinet, 2017; Guenther, 2019; Guenther & Osborne, 2020; Guenther et al., 2022; House of Representatives Standing Committee on Indigenous Affairs, 2017). These initiatives largely funded organizations based outside of the local remote community and outside of the school gates, and frustrations over a lack of evidence-informed policy making and disappointing outcomes are repeated throughout these reviews (Guenther et al., 2023). This moment of reflection offers a chance to reconsider the importance of *place* in policy making and actions—that is, to lift the curse of the externally imagined (Osborne, 2023), and instead draw on the latent assets of family, local community, local languages, histories, knowledges, and aspirations as a process of re-*place*-ment.

Central to strengthening and drawing on local communities as rich and irreplaceable sites of support for young people is a need to move away from current power-laden, universalist approaches to policy making in remote education (Osborne, 2015; Zipin & Brennan, 2018). This requires rejecting current invocations of historical colonialism, and to pursue what Haraway (1988, p. 589) terms "power-sensitive" dialogue. This means that Aboriginal and Torres Strait

Islanders living in "local-remote" communities must be primary voices in shaping the nature of education for their children (Guenther et al., 2015, 2017; Osborne & Guenther, 2013; Osborne et al., 2018).

The Context of Indigenous Education Policy

The International Context of Indigenous Education

Indigenous scholars across the globe have railed against historical policies, attitudes, and actions in colonial settler states. Indigenous peoples share experiences of violence and massacres, removal and relocation, separation from and institutionalization of their children, forced acquisition of land and natural resources, and large-scale Anglicization and Christianization. These systematic and oppressive enactments were fueled by prevailing Western scientific social Darwinist views (Bishop, 2011; Nakata, 2007; Smith, 1999; Wallace Adams, 1995; Welch, 1988; Wilson & Yellow Bird, 2005). Education has been utilized as a key instrument in the execution of a broader agenda of land acquisition and wealth creation for the colonial power. In North America and Canada, the policy catchphrase "Kill the Indian, save the man" (Grande, 2004, p. 14) summarizes the intent of the prevailing policies designed to remove Native children from their families, communities, land, and languages as a form of colonialist intervention couched in sentiments of *helping*, or being *nice* (Castagno, 2014). As Grande explains, this slogan summarized "a hidden curriculum that not only advocated the termination of Indian-ness, but also of Indians" (2004, p. 14), an expansive program of both assimilation and extermination. Using Grande's (2004) language of "Red pedagogy," the North American approach featured removing Native children from their families and educating them with a view to assimilation into the dominant culture. The ultimate aim of absorbing the population, their land, and natural resources (assets) stands in contrast to what might be considered contemporaneous "Black pedagogy." This practice of acquiring African slaves as cheap (or free) labor insisted on segregation from Western society and education, an approach aimed at exploiting *human* resources (assets) to benefit the colonial power (Pinkney, 2016; Reece & O'Connell, 2016; Wallace Adams, 1995).

The era of trading African slaves and policies to remove Native children may have ended, but lingering attitudes of racial superiority and power maintenance—including in the positioning of education—have led a growing body of Indigenous scholars to argue for the decolonization of research and education for Indigenous young people (Mignolo, 2009; Nakata et al., 2012; Rigney, 1999; Smith, 1999). These arguments have strong connections to the work of critical race theorists who challenge the White hegemonic structures and assumptions of *other* as lesser that shape Western education and classroom practice (Delpit, 1993; Ladson-Billings, 1999; Milner, 2008).

A pedagogical ally for engaging student life worlds in education beyond mere recognition is the funds of knowledge movement. This work has developed from the early work of Mexican Americans arguing that the assets of family, languages, knowledges, and community need to be reflected and drawn upon in classrooms where their children attend (Moll et al., 1992). These arguments have been taken up in global communities (Howard, 2001; Zipin, 2013) and strengthen the claims Indigenous scholars are making for decolonial approaches in education for their children.

In its origins, the funds of knowledge movement tended toward relatively homogenous socio-cultural groups and an argument is made for more nuanced pedagogical tools for diverse classrooms and communities. Culturally responsive pedagogies (Brayboy & Castagno, 2009; Morrison et al., 2019) builds on the philosophical foundations of funds of knowledge and is being explored internationally and in Australia as an approach that shifts teachers from needing to be an expert knower about other cultures to developing pedagogical skills for making diverse student life worlds, experiences, and communities curricular (Osborne et al., 2014; Zipin, 2013).

The Australian Context of Indigenous Education

In Australia, early eras of exclusionary and interventionist approaches shifted toward placing importance on Indigenous participation and voice in policy making and education. By the 1990s (a period referred to as an era of reconciliation), a number of forums were established for Aboriginal and Torres Strait Islander participation in education decision making including the National Aboriginal Consultative Group (NACG, an advisory body to the Commonwealth Government), Aboriginal Education Consultative Groups (AECGs, state and territory based), and school-based Aboriginal decision-making groups (Aboriginal Student Support and Parent Awareness or ASSPA) (Buckskin, 2009). From the mid-2000s, however, the approach reverted to a logic of intervention and Closing the Gap with one noticeable outcome being the disestablishment or virtual abandonment of Aboriginal education decision making forums including ASSPA, the NACG, and AECGs.

From 2013, carriage of Indigenous education administration was moved away from Indigenous participatory models, but also from education itself, instead being housed within the remit of Prime Minister and Cabinet as part of the broader Closing the Gap policy program. Measures of success for Indigenous education currently focus on student attendance, Year 12 completion, and the attainment of (minimal) benchmarks in English language, literacy, and numeracy (see Morrison, 2019).

For very remote students, the Closing the Gap policy approach has included investment in three key areas: the Remote Schools Attendance Strategy ($128.5M initially, with a further $78.4M in 2019), Direct Instruction, an English language instructional program (more than $30M across three installments, see Guenther & Osborne, 2020), and boarding school scholarship investment including the Australian Indigenous Education Fund ($83M to 2018), Yalari (roughly $2–3M per year) and the Commonwealth government's Indigenous Youth Leadership Program. The Prime Minister committed a further $200M to this sector in his 2019 Closing the Gap address (Morrison, 2019). While Year 12 attainment was recognized as being on track, these figures mask poor access, participation, and completion rates and "limited value" (Stewart, 2015, p. 209), including questionable flow-through benefits on completion for very remote students (Guenther, 2020; Osborne et al., 2019). A recent parliamentary review of Indigenous education found patchy or inconclusive evidence relating to all three focus areas of remote education investment and these are likely to come under further scrutiny (House of Representatives Standing Committee on Indigenous Affairs, 2017).

A key concern is a misalignment between the aspirational, epistemological, axiological, and ontological contexts of remote communities and those who apply their own (externally located) values and assumptions to education policy making. The Remote Schools Attendance Strategy employs local people to make sure children go to school, DI metes out what Delpit (1993) would likely term "less-powerful codes" through focused repetition of the mechanical aspects of basic English, and the boarding school model relocates students to geographically and culturally remote sites of learning, an approach that has long been viewed as the "only hope" (Benveniste et al., 2015) of educational success for Indigenous students. These values and assumptions are visible in the language applied, such as in the Commonwealth Government's 1967 Referendum 50th Anniversary Indigenous Education Package (Commonwealth of Australia, 2017) announcing $138M of investment, primarily into boarding schools, football clubs, and role model/mentoring programs. It included statements such as, "The Government is investing in our next generation of Australia's leaders by *encouraging Indigenous students to dream*; to *have big*, bold *aspirations* and *to succeed*," and "Assist secondary students to complete their studies by *providing mentoring* and *high-quality leadership*." Italics have been added here to emphasize the assumption that remote Indigenous students are without dreams, aspirations, or any chance to "succeed." There is also an assumption that the family and local community is unfit to provide mentoring and high-quality leadership. In perhaps a final insult to both local communities and remote educators more broadly, the policy allocates some

$17M to football clubs to "Provide access to *high quality educational facilities* in major centres through accommodation and scholarship assistance."

So how might the locus of power and voice in remote education provision shift from the colonial imagination (Commonwealth of Australia, 2017; Forrest, 2014; Penfold, 2013) toward a closer alignment with the philosophical foundations and aspirations of local communities?

Re-"placing" Family and Community in Aboriginal and Torres Strait Islander Education

Remote communities are often framed in deficit terms of disadvantage, being behind, or simply "failing" (Hughes & Hughes, 2012; Hunter & Stephenson, 2013; Wilson, 2014). However, the very nature of geographical isolation has provided some distance between these communities and the colonial project, a distance that was not afforded to Aboriginal populations in less arid areas. To this end, many remote communities enjoy a raft of advantages in that many are still living on their traditional lands and continue long-standing social structures of kin and relatedness, practice their traditional religion (law and culture), and have retained their language (Guenther et al., 2014). These languages, however, exist in various states of health and change as interactions with colonialism and the global-digital era shape the socio-cultural context (Simpson, 2019). These are powerful elements in shaping identity and building confidence in young people as they engage with Western schooling and the wider world (Burton & Osborne, 2014; Minutjukur & Osborne, 2014; Osborne et al., 2014; Tjitayi & Osborne, 2014). A̲nangu Education leader Katrina Tjitayi describes the importance of student confidence and rethinking Closing the Gap in this way:

> There are many gaps in our children's spirits and they can't close them on their own. Schools can do much to help all the children, both young and older. Children can't find their future on their own … When a child is afraid, he can't learn. This is the way we can close the gaps.
>
> The child is in the middle and his family are around him. When the family surrounds the child, they can help him. Only his family can help him to change to a positive way of thinking …
>
> Our children need to learn together with us as one spirit. Our spirits are like a solid rock for them to stand on. It is only when they are standing together with us that they can stand firm without falling. (Osborne et al., 2014, p. 12)

Tjitayi's logic places the assets and advantages of family, language, culture, and Country that young people are "placed" (Somerville & Perkins, 2010) within as central to educational success. A̲nangu education leader Rueben Burton also sees the role of family as central to building aspiration and a *future*, rather than a project to be outsourced to teachers, boarding schools, and football programs:

> as an Anangu educator and as a father, it is very important that I show my children a future; that I am courageous and confident in what I do so that I can give that future to my children …
>
> The parents hold the future for the children. Piranpa [non-Aboriginal] teachers hold "keys" to the future, but they don't understand Anangu ways, so it's Anangu that give the future to their children. (Burton & Osborne, 2014, p. 36)

Outsider educators, researchers, and policy makers need to ensure that the core ingredients that position young people in remote Aboriginal communities for success are foundational to education policy and practice. Apple (2017) highlights the important role of education leaders in bringing community values and life worlds into dialogue with education administration and leadership. He argues the importance of "advocacy leadership" and reawakening a "more activist tradition" where education leaders work toward a more inclusive and, by implication, more just education (p. 249). Apple (2017) draws on Macherey's (2006, as cited in Apple, 2017) notion of the "absent presence" in shaping meaning making in education, stating, "what is *not* there is often just as significant as what is there" (p. 251). This leads him to suppose:

> it would be useful to see what the traditions of leadership were in the racially segregated schools of the south in the United States or in First Nation schools in Canada, or in Maori schools in New Zealand, where everyday leadership had to often fight against an interventionist and racialising state. Did a more community-based and responsive form of leadership evolve? What contradictions and compromises had to be engaged in? Thinking more historically and internationally about such things is crucial. (p. 249)

These are poignant questions for leaders of remote schools who are committed to working toward culturally responsive leadership and pedagogical models. They are also important questions at the system and policy-making level. I have previously proposed a model for ethical listening (*kulini*) and responsibility for action (Osborne, 2017), drawing on Delpit's (1993) assertion that "it is those with the most power … who must take the greater responsibility for initiating the process of moving from ethical listening towards justice-oriented action" (p. 139).

Structuring Local Voices and Aspirations in Remote Education Provision

The South Australian and Northern Territory Education Departments have recognized frustrations at the lack of progress in remote schools and have announced shifts toward re-engaging local languages, increased local Aboriginal participation and voice in education, and culturally responsive pedagogies (Department for Education, 2019; Department of Education, 2018). But it is not enough to write a policy document and then continue to rely on power-laden structures of policy enactment. It is important that local Aboriginal voices are re-"placed" at the center of informing and shaping the nature and purpose of education for their children. These voices and aspirations must then be resourced and sustained over a long period to rebuild local engagement at the core of education in local-remote Aboriginal communities in Australia. This requires redefining measures of success pertinent to the re-placed educational structures and remaking education to better enable the strengthening of local aspirations for and by young people in remote education (Osborne & Guenther, 2013; Osborne et al., 2018).

Conclusion

For more than a decade, significant restructuring and investment in remote Aboriginal education has worked from a position of colonial re-inscription—where externally imagined solutions to the "problem" of remote Aboriginal education are resourced and then enacted on local-remote communities. The evidence is now more than clear that this approach has failed on many levels. The need to re-"place" local Aboriginal voices as central to approaches that center the assets of local languages, knowledges, families, and communities is now urgent. This need has been recognized in the release of new state and territory policy documents, but the road ahead remains largely unconstructed. Careful attention to the dynamics of power, and applying a locally centered, culturally responsive frame is vital for rebuilding local-remote Aboriginal schooling approaches.

Bibliography

Apple, M. W. (2017). Dialogue, field, and power. *Journal of Educational Administration and History*, *49*(3), 247–55.

Benveniste, T., Guenther, J., Dawson, D., & Rainbird, S. (2015, November). *Deciphering distance: Exploring how Indigenous boarding schools facilitate and maintain relationships with remote families and communities* [Paper presentation]. Australian Association for Research in Education Conference, Fremantle, WA.

Bishop, R. (2011). *Freeing ourselves*. Sense Publishers.

Brayboy, B., & Castagno, A. (2009). Self-determination through self-education: Culturally responsive schooling for Indigenous students in the USA. *Teaching Education*, *20*(1), 31–53.

Buckskin, P. (2009). Hawke and Ryan: An acceleration of Indigenous education policy. In G. Bloustien, B. Comber, & A. Mackinnon (Eds.), *The Hawke legacy* (pp. 83–95). Wakefield Press.

Burton, R., & Osborne, S. (2014). At the heart of learning (series paper 4 of 4): Kuranyu-kutu nyakula nyaan nyanganyi? Imagining the future. *Alter Native: An International Journal of Indigenous Peoples*, *10*(1), 33–44.

Castagno, A. (2014). *Educated in Whiteness: Good intentions and diversity in schools*. University of Minnesota Press.

Commonwealth of Australia. (2017). *1967 Referendum 50th Anniversary Indigenous Education Package*. https://nacchocommunique.com/wp-content/uploads/2017/05/nrw-education-package.pdf

Delpit, L. (1993). The silenced dialogue: Power and pedagogy in educating other people's children. In L. Weis & M. Fine (Eds.), *Beyond silenced voices: Class, race, and gender in United States schools* (pp. 119–41). State University of New York Press.

Department of Education. (2018). *Strategic Framework 2018–2022*. https://education.nt.gov.au/__data/assets/pdf_file/0009/460944/educationnt-strategic-plan-a03.pdf

Department for Education. (2019). *Aboriginal Education Strategy 2019 to 2029*. https://www.education.sa.gov.au/docs/curriculum/aboriginal-education/dept-ed-aboriginal-education-strategy-2019-2029.pdf

Department of the Prime Minister and Cabinet. (2017). *Study away review: Review of support for Aboriginal and Torres Strait Islander secondary students studying away from home*. Commonwealth of Australia. https://www.niaa.gov.au/sites/default/files/documents/publications/study-away-review_0.pdf

Forrest, A. (2014). *The Forrest review: Creating parity*. Commonwealth of Australia. https://apo.org.au/sites/default/files/resource-files/2014-07/apo-nid40734.pdf

Grande, S. (2004). *Red pedagogy: Native American social and political thought*. Rowman and Littlefield Publishers.

Guenther, J. (2019, December 2). Evidence on what doesn't work for very remote schools (attendance strategies) and what does. *EduResearch Matters*. https://www.aare.edu.au/blog/?p=4797

Guenther, J. (2020). Taken for a ride? The disconnect between high school completion, employment and income for remote Australian First Nations Peoples. *Race, Ethnicity and Education*, *24*(1), 132–47.

Guenther, J., Bat, M., & Osborne, S. (2014). Red dirt thinking on remote educational advantage. *Australian and International Journal of Rural Education*, *24*(1), 51–67.

Guenther, J., Disbray, S., & Osborne, S. (2016). *Red dirt education: A compilation of learnings from the Remote Education Systems project*. Ninti One. https://www.nintione.com.au/resource/RedDirtEducation_CompilationLearningsRES_EBook.pdf

Guenther, J., Halsey, J., & Osborne, S. (2015). From paradise to beyond: Geographical constructs and how they shape education in the bush. *Australian and International Journal of Rural Education*, *25*(3), 62–79.

Guenther, J., McRae-Williams, E., Osborne, S., & Williams, E. (2017). Decolonising colonial education researchers in "near remote" parts of Australia. In G. Vass, J. Maxwell, S. Rudolph, & K. Gulson (Eds.), *The relationality of race in education research: Local/global issues in education* (pp. 108–19). Routledge.

Guenther, J., & Osborne, S. (2020). Did DI do it? The impact of a programme designed to improve literacy for Aboriginal and Torres Strait Islander students in remote schools. *Australian Journal of Indigenous Education*, *1*(8), 163–70.

Guenther, J., Osborne, S., Corrie, S., Rigney, L-I., & Lowe, K. (2022). The Remote School Attendance Strategy (RSAS): Why invest in a strategy that reduces attendance? *Australian Journal of Indigenous Education*, *51*(2), 1–22.

Guenther, J., Rigney, L.-I., Osborne, S., Lowe, K., & Moodie, N. (2023). The foundations required for First Nations education in Australia. In N. Moodie, K. Lowe, R. Dixon, & K. Trimmer (Eds.), *Assessing the evidence in Indigenous education research: Implications for policy and practice* (pp. 265–84). Springer International Publishing.

Haraway, D. (1988). Situated knowledges: The science question in feminism and the privilege of partial perspective. *Feminist Studies*, *14*(3), 575–99.

House of Representatives Standing Committee on Indigenous Affairs. (2017). *The power of education: From surviving to thriving. Educational opportunities for Aboriginal and Torres Strait Islander students*. Commonwealth of Australia. https://www.aph.gov.au/-/media/02_Parliamentary_Business/24_Committees/243_Reps_Committees/Indigenous/EducationalOpportunities/Committee_Report_-_Final.pdf

Howard, T. (2001). Powerful pedagogy for African American students: A case of four teachers. *Urban Education*, *36*(2), 179–202.

Hughes, H., & Hughes, M. (2012). *Indigenous education 2012*. Centre for Independent Studies.

Hunter, B., & Stephenson, N. (2013). *Less is more: Reflections on the Overcoming Indigenous Disadvantage reports*. Centre for Aboriginal Economic Policy Research, Australian National University. https://caepr.cass.anu.edu.au/sites/default/files/docs/TI2013_01_Hunter_Stephenson_OID_0.pdf

Ladson-Billings, G. (1999). Preparing teachers for diverse student populations: A critical race theory perspective. *Review of Research in Education*, *24*(1), 211–47.

Mignolo, W. D. (2009). Epistemic disobedience, independent thought and decolonial freedom. *Theory, Culture & Society*, *26*(7/8), 159–81.

Milner, H. R. (2008). Disrupting deficit notions of difference: Counter-narratives of teachers and community in urban education. *Teaching and Teacher Education*, *24*(6), 1573–98.

Minutjukur, M., & Osborne, S. (2014). At the heart of learning (series paper 2 of 4): Witulya mulapa nganana mantjintjaku: From cultural devastation to cultural reinvention. *AlterNative: An International Journal of Indigenous Peoples*, *10*(1), 15–22.

Moll, L., Amanti, C., Neff, D., & Gonzalez, N. (1992). Funds of knowledge for teaching: Using a qualitative approach to connect homes and classroom. *Theory into Practice*, *31*(2), 132–41.

Morrison, A., Rigney, L., Hattam, R., & Diplock, A. (2019). *Towards an Australian culturally responsive pedagogy: A narrative review of the literature*. University of South Australia.

Morrison, S. (2019). *Statement to the House of Representatives–Closing the Gap 2019*. https://nacchocommunique.com/wp-content/uploads/2019/02/prime-minister-close-the-gap-speech.pdf.

Nakata, M. (2007). *Disciplining the savages: Savaging the disciplines*. Aboriginal Studies Press.

Nakata, M., Nakata, V., Keech, S., & Bolt, R. (2012). Decolonial goals and pedagogies for Indigenous studies. *Decolonization: Indigeneity, Education & Society*, *1*(1), 120–40.

Osborne, S. (2015). Families as foundation: Anangu perspectives on what else matters in remote education. *UNESCO Observatory Multi-Disciplinary Journal in the Arts*, *4*(2), 1–25.

Osborne, S. (2017). Kulini: Framing ethical listening and power-sensitive dialogue in remote Aboriginal education and research. *Learning Communities: International Journal of Learning in Social Contexts*, *22*, 26–37.

Osborne, S. (2023). Kulini: Ethical listening and the curse of the externally imagined. An argument for culturally responsive pedagogies in Anangu schools. In L.-I. Rigney (Ed.), *Global perspectives and new challenges in culturally responsive pedagogies: Super-diversity and teaching practice* (pp. 149–61). Routledge.

Osborne, S., Benveniste, T., Rigney, L., Disbray, S., & Guenther, J. (2019). Mapping boarding school opportunities for Aboriginal students from the Central Land Council region of Northern Territory. *Australian Journal of Indigenous Education*, *48*(2), 162–78.

Osborne, S., & Guenther, J. (2013). Red dirt thinking on aspiration and success. *Australian Journal of Indigenous Education*, *42*(2), 88–99.

Osborne, S., Guenther, J., King, L., Lester, K., Ken, S., & Lester, R. (2018). *Centring Anangu voices: A research project exploring how Nyangatjatjara College might better strengthen Anangu aspirations through education*. Ninti One. http://www.nintione.com.au/resource/NR005_CentringAnanguVoices.pdf

Osborne, S., Lester, K., Minutjukur, M., & Tjitayi, K. (2014). *Red dirt curriculum: Reimagining remote education* (Sidney Myer Rural Lecture 3). Flinders University.

Partington, G., & Beresford, Q. (2012). The context of Aboriginal education. In Q. Beresford, G. Partington, & G. Gower (Eds.), *Reform and resistance in Aboriginal education* (pp. 35–84). University of Western Australia Press.

Pearson, N. (2014). A rightful place: Race, recognition and a more complete Commonwealth. *Quarterly Essay*, *55*, 1–72.

Pearson, N. (2017, December 1). Betrayal: The Turnbull government has burned the bridge of bipartisanship. *The Monthly*. https://www.themonthly.com.au/issue/2017/december/1512046800/noel-pearson/betrayal#mtr

Penfold, A. (2013, June 1). Strong leadership, not motherhood statements, will improve Indigenous education results. *The Weekend Australian*. http://www.theaustralian.com.au/national-affairs/in-depth/strong-leadership-not-motherhood-statements-will-improve-indigenous-education-results/story-fnia28mo-1226654727211b

Pinkney, A. (2016). The role of schools in educating black citizens: From the 1800s to the present. *Theory & Research in Social Education*, *44*(1), 72–103.

Reece, R., & O'Connell, H. (2016). How the legacy of slavery and racial composition shape public school enrolment in the American south. *Sociology of Race and Ethnicity*, *2*(1), 42–57.

Referendum Council. (2017). *Uluru statement from the heart*. https://ulurustatement.org/the-statement/view-the-statement/

Rigney, L. (1999). Internationalization of an Indigenous anticolonial critique of research methodologies: A guide to Indigenist research methodology and its principles. *Wicazo Sa Review*, *14*(2), 109–21.

Simpson, J. (2019, January 21). The state of Australia's Indigenous languages—And how we can help people speak them more often. *The Conversation*. https://theconversation.com/the-state-of-australias-indigenous-languages-and-how-we-can-help-people-speak-them-more-often-109662

Smith, L. (1999). *Decolonizing methodologies: Research and Indigenous peoples*. Zed Publishing.

Somerville, M., & Perkins, T. (2010). *Singing the coast*. Aboriginal Studies Press.

Stewart, R. (2015). Book review: Australian Indigenous Education Foundation compendium of best practice for achieving successful outcomes with Indigenous students in Australian boarding schools. *Australian Journal of Indigenous Education*, *44*(2), 207–09.

Tjitayi, K., & Osborne, S. (2014). At the heart of learning (series paper 3 of 4): Kurunta kanyintja: Holding knowledge in our spirit. *AlterNative: An International Journal of Indigenous Peoples*, *10*(1), 23–32.

Wallace Adams, D. (1995). *Education for extinction: American Indians and the boarding school experience, 1875–1928*. University Press of Kansas.

Welch, A. R. (1988). Aboriginal education as internal colonialism: The schooling of an Indigenous minority in Australia. *Comparative Education*, *24*(2), 203–15.

Wilson, A., & Yellow Bird, M. (2005). *For Indigenous eyes only: A decolonization handbook*. School of American Research.

Wilson, B. (2014). *A share in the future: Review of Indigenous education in the Northern Territory*. Department of Education.

Zipin, L. (2013). Engaging middle years learners by making their communities curricular: A funds of knowledge approach. *Curriculum Perspectives*, *33*(3), 1–12.

Zipin, L., & Brennan, M. (2018). Transforming the curriculum frame: Working knowledge around problems that matter. In S. Gannon, R. Hattam, & W. Sawyer (Eds.), *Resisting educational inequality: Reframing policy and practice in schools serving vulnerable communities* (pp. 245–56). Routledge.

11 Recognition and Belonging in Enabling Education

Sarah Hattam

Introduction

As an enabling educator at a South Australian university, my educational project has involved making sense of the transition between secondary school and first year undergraduate study where I have sought to understand how we might prepare students for university. Enabling programs are defined as award programs that incorporate enabling subjects or modules designed to develop academic skills in order to facilitate the transition of students into higher level award programs (National Association of Enabling Educators in Australia, 2020). I have come to recognize the important role of enabling education in disrupting a number of pedagogical problematics in secondary schools and universities such that young people, who have previously been denied, can access and participate in higher education (Hattam & Bilic, 2019).

Over the last decade, the enabling sector has flourished across Australia and practitioners and educators have begun to define a distinctive approach to teaching students in preparatory and university programs. Attention to a scholarship of teaching in enabling education has culminated in a collective teaching philosophy informed by pedagogies for social justice that are increasingly known as "enabling pedagogy" (Bennett et al., 2016; Hattam & Stokes 2019; Stokes, 2014). Although embedded within higher education institutions, the *enabling* space is distinct to traditional higher education due to the higher representation of students from recognized equity groups (Bennett et al., 2016; Crawford, 2015; Stokes, 2014).

Our enabling program at UniSA College (at the University of South Australia) was created to closely align with Australia's widening participation targets, specifically the 2020 target that "20 per cent of undergraduate enrolments in HE should be students from low socio-economic backgrounds" (Bradley et al., 2008, p. xiv). Sixty four percent of students who enroll in our pathway programs belong to a defined equity group, with 56.5 percent of the 2019 student cohort coming from low socio-economic status (SES) groups. It is here that equity categories often intersect, and students experience intersectional marginalization (Burke et al., 2017).

The UniSA College programs offer an alternative pathway into university for students who have either not achieved the entry score needed for a bachelor program or have not completed Year 12 at high school. The program is supported through adequate resourcing both institutionally and federally, with a full cross-disciplinary suite of courses that are taught by experienced teaching academics with postgraduate qualifications. The program currently sits outside the Australian Qualification Framework and South Australian Certificate of Education (SACE) requirements, so this allows a significant level of freedom over our curriculum development. The most popular pathway program in terms of volume of students is the Foundation Studies program, which is completely open access and fee free. The twelve-month program offers a range of academic literacy courses as well as discipline-specific courses to prepare students for their destination degree. The numbers have grown from approximately 300 commencing students in 2011 to over 1,000 commencing new students each year since 2016. The college also offers a suite of two-year diploma programs as well as an Aboriginal Pathway Program, which is offered in the metropole and five regional sites.

My own professional inquiry has led me to question why students do not take a traditional pathway to university. I am interested in what occurs during their secondary years that limits or inhibits their completion of schooling as well as what we might do differently in the enabling space that better engages the disengaged. As a sociologist, I am concerned with the social reproduction function of education (Bourdieu & Passeron, 1977) and the inequality created within and by the system. This documented inequality reveals that more young people from middle- and upper-class backgrounds enroll into and complete tertiary study than those from lower socio-economic backgrounds (Lamb et al., 2015). In a just society, all young people should have the opportunities to reap the benefits of further study (Atherton et al., 2016, p. 10).

However, from anecdotal discussions with students in our enabling programs, I have developed an understanding that some high schools in South Australia engage in a range of "exclusionary" (Sibley, 1995 p. ix, as cited in Smyth et al., 2004, p. 10) practices that contribute to students' decisions to leave school early. These discussions led to a formal inquiry into students' experiences of enabling education, in comparison with their secondary schooling. I interviewed ten students who self-identified as early school leavers. In this chapter, I discuss research findings from two of the interviews as well as advancing the concept of "critical" enabling pedagogy by aligning it with critical pedagogy and emotional work enacted by enabling educators in higher education as "emotional champions" (O'Shea, 2019). The students' accounts are located inside the cultural geography of a school (Smyth et al., 2004) and aligned with Fraser's "parity of participation," which describes feelings of misrecognition/recognition.

The "Widening Participation" Agenda

Despite a neoliberal logic that is increasingly shaping the sector, universities have an established and widely accepted agenda of widening participation in education for under-represented groups (Bennett et al., 2012). The federal government reports an increase in high school retention over the last twenty-plus years with a jump from 66.9 percent apparent retention in 1997 (as cited in ABS, 1997) to 84 percent apparent retention in 2019 (as cited in ABS, 2019). However, problems remain around lower school completion rates and the possibilities of entering university for students from low-SES backgrounds. Other studies provide a more nuanced account according to demographic factors and show that 26 percent of young people do not complete Year 12 by age 19, with 40 percent of low-SES young people not completing Year 12 by age 19 (Lamb et al., 2015).

Widening participation initiatives have increased the participation of students from lower socio-economic backgrounds in undergraduate programs. Between 2008 and 2015, there was an increase of 50.4 percent of student enrollments from lower socio-economic groups into university programs (NCSEHE, 2017), with a significant number entering via enabling pathways. However, completion numbers according to socio-economic band reveal a disparity as only 68.9 percent of students from lower SES backgrounds complete their university degree compared with 77.7 percent of students in the higher SES band (Edwards & McMillan, 2015, p. 6). While a deficit explanation would attribute the lower completion number of low-SES students to a lack of resilience or low aspirations (Burke, 2002), there are strong and continuing arguments regarding problems with higher education pedagogy.

Pedagogical Problems in Higher Education

Widening participation policy is focused on increasing access and entry routes into higher education. Burke et al. argue the policy should pay attention to the "ways that higher education pedagogies might also be complicit in the reproduction of inequalities *even after entry* to higher education has been achieved" (2017, pp. 1–2). Participation and inclusion of diverse identities focuses on:

> transforming the individual student subject, which is constructed through discourses of "neediness" and connected assumptions of lack and deficiency, to become a particular kind of (neoliberal) participant that is "independent", "resilient", "confident" and "employable". (p. 2)

It seems that higher education pedagogy relies significantly on the "banking method" of education (Freire, 1973), with one-way communication from teacher to student typically in a lecture format or online reading. The problems with higher education pedagogy are not just symptomatic of the power dynamic between teacher and students but also the way that universities define who belongs to its exclusive culture (Habel & Whitman, 2016). Traditionally, a "proper" university student (read legitimate) is confident and independent, and someone who has a voice (but knows when to be quiet) (Burke et al., 2017). The subject position of the legitimate university student is constructed along class, ethnic, and gendered lines, and according to these qualities is more likely to be white, middle class, and male (Burke et al., 2017). Academics frame the problem of difficulties of "fitting in with the university culture" as a deficit of non-traditional students (O'Shea et al., 2016, p. 324).

Moving beyond the deficit framing, Burke et al. (2017, p. 3) propose that higher education institutions should work toward "pedagogic participation" that "considers the relationship between formations of difference and higher education participation in and across contested pedagogical spaces." Adopting Nancy Fraser's parity of participation with attention to *redistribution*, *recognition*, and *representation* could produce such outcomes. Significantly, for the pedagogic interventions that have occurred in enabling education programs, "*participation* is more than having access to financial and material resources or cultural and social capitals" (Burke et al., 2017, p. 31) and also includes measures that enable the "person to be recognized and have access to representation as a fully valued member of the community" (Burke et al., 2017, p. 31). They argue that processes of misrecognition are driven by "institutional values and judgements that are imposed on the misrecognized person in ways that effectively exclude her/him from parity of participation" (Burke et al., 2017, p. 31) in universities. Enabling educators have attempted to shift attention away from "deficit discourses to directing attention to transforming institutional spaces, systems and practices, which are implicated in reproducing exclusions and inequalities at cultural, symbolic and structural levels" (Burke et al., 2017, p. 30). The outcomes of this shift away from deficit framings are explored in this chapter.

Advancing Research Designs

Looking at the problem of early school leaving, prominent South Australian education scholars John Smyth and Robert Hattam (Smyth et al., 2004) provide an in-depth account of the reasons young people do not complete high school. Between 1997 and 1999, Smyth and Hattam interviewed over two hundred early school leavers on their experiences of secondary school. This research was significant because it aimed to shift the framing of the retention "problem" away from a "students-at-risk" frame in order to give students a "voice" (Smyth & Hattam, 2001). Smyth and Hattam revealed student voices that expressed a myriad of "gatekeeping" mechanisms and strategies implemented within schools, illustrating the ways educational participation is complicated by class, socio-economic status, and other inequalities. As Sibley argues, paying attention to "exclusionary practices are important because they are less noticed and so the ways in which control is exercised in society are concealed" (Sibley, 1995, p. ix, as cited in Smyth et al., 2004, p. 10).

Smyth et al. (2004) offer useful conceptual tools that describe a "cultural geography" of schools that is either *active*, *passive*, or *aggressive* and is a contributing factor in students' choices to leave school early. Their *active-culture* approach recommends that students are *listened to* empathetically and teachers actively connect with students' lives. Educators are also urged to focus on ensuring that students develop a sense of belonging and can negotiate the curriculum, content, and assessment. The cultural geography approach (summarized in Table 11.1) is thus a useful framework that highlights the importance of the cultural messages of schools.

Table 11.1: School Cultural Geography Around Leaving School

Dimension	Aggressive	Passive	Active
Inclusion/exclusion	Troublemakers removed	"Ease out" those who do not fit	Those who traditionally fit the least are most welcome
Students' lives/ emotions	No space for dealing with emotions	Acknowledges them but deals with them immaturely	Students are listened to. Atmosphere of trust.
Pedagogy	Condescending way of treating students	Uninteresting classroom practice	Enlarges cultural map of students. Negotiation of content and assessment.

My study also attempts to give *voice* to students' experiences of secondary school that have contributed to their decision to leave school early by focusing on two aspects. Firstly, I investigate whether the students experienced gatekeeping mechanisms in secondary school and if educators misrecognized (Burke et al., 2017; Fraser, 2003) the capabilities, traits, or behavior of the students that might enable them to continue with their studies at secondary schools or aspire for a place in higher education. Misrecognition is described here by Burke (2015) as the

> processes in which a pathologizing gaze is projected on to Other bodies that have historically been constructed as a problem, and as suffering from a range of deficit disorders (e.g., lack of aspiration, lack of motivation, lack of confidence and so on). Through such processes, Other bodies become marked as different through (often implicit and subtle) reference to racialized, gendered and classed discourses. The injuries of misrecognition are embodied, through the internalization of shame, and are tied to the emotional level of experience. (p. 394)

This study provides space for students to reflect on the process of misrecognition (Burke et al., 2017) in their high schools as well as an account of how a cultural geography approach might be a useful framework to explain the participants' experiences and feelings that led to them leaving school early.

A Pedagogical Intervention

While the team of teaching-focused academics at UniSA College had experience of teaching undergraduate students, it was quickly understood that teaching these students with the same pedagogy found in undergraduate teaching could lead to increased attrition, reduced student satisfaction, and negative experiences of higher education (Bennett et al., 2016). We concur with Olds et al. (2019) that "transitional education is a unique space that often places academics in a pedagogical pastiche that layers multidisciplinary knowledge with academic skills development, and elements of pastoral care" (p. 47).

The academic team in our enabling program have developed their curriculum, assessment, and pedagogy to align with critical teaching approaches. The aim of the *critical* enabling educator is to create an inclusive and care-full (Motta & Bennett, 2018) learning environment that is democratic and in which dialogue is shared (Shor & Freire, 1987). In addition, assessment is scaffolded, curriculum is negotiated, the tasks are challenging and clearly explained, the diversity of individuals is valued, and effort is made to connect to the students' life worlds (Moll et al., 1992). Through enabling pedagogy, the student is recognized for their strengths and the processes of learning are adapted.

In contrast to the traditional "banking" style of higher education, we adopt a dialogic approach to teaching that sets out to "not talk knowledge at students but talk with them" (Shor, 1992, p. 85). In this way the program adopts an *active* culture across all student interactions, from orientation to enrollment and right through to the academic review process (see Hattam et al., 2018). Also deemed necessary was that teaching staff had knowledge of enabling pedagogies through a series of professional development opportunities (see Hattam & Weiler, 2021).

The core teaching team have also collectively engaged in three years of action research in enacting enabling pedagogies across our courses.

My study involved conducting semi-structured interviews with ten students who self-identified as early school leavers. The interview questions provided an opportunity for the participants to reflect on their experiences at high school as well as their experiences at university, and specifically their studies in our enabling program. I conducted a thematic analysis of the interview data to detect the common themes regarding the dimensions detailed in the cultural geography framework of inclusion/exclusion, students' lives and emotions, and pedagogy. For the purposes of this chapter, I will provide accounts of two student voices. These accounts demonstrate some of the gatekeeping processes occurring in secondary schools where specific teachers enact their own doubts and assumptions about students' motivations and capabilities (Cuconato et al., 2015).

Student Voices of Misrecognition, Disconnection, Recognition, and Belonging

In the broader study, students gave voice to the processes of misrecognition/recognition they experienced as they traversed from secondary school to enabling education, often with a significant lapse in time between engagement in education. In line with Burke et al. (2017) this work takes on an understanding of misrecognition as the students are discounted from a university pathway years before the opportunity presents itself because their *difference* at the age of 15 or 16 is viewed as *high risk* and threatening to academic standards (Burke et al., 2017). The students' experiences also speak to the generation and enactment of a *passive* or *aggressive* school culture.

Lillian's Story

Lillian grew up in a lower socio-economic suburb of South Australia in a single-parent household. Her mother struggled with Lillian's older sibling's drug and behavioral issues and Lillian described that her mother "was working as hard as she could and wouldn't be able to afford to put me in any [university] courses and I didn't really know about HECS [delayed payment for higher education through the tax system] as an option so didn't really think I could go anyway." She did not complete the SACE but rather was advised by her teachers to attend a Technical and Further Education (TAFE) college in order to complete a hairdressing certificate. She described the coercion she felt to enroll in the TAFE program when in Year 11 by her school and the sense that they

> gave up a little bit once I was in that course 'cause they thought, "Oh, she's doing something now. She's got something. We don't really need to spend any extra time with her." I feel like they almost set us up for failure. Now that I think about it, it was almost like they were succeeding, still getting us into TAFE courses and they were getting us into jobs. But they in turn weren't because they were not really giving us, really, any other choices.

The process of misrecognition that occurred in secondary school for Lillian is reflected in her feelings that the school *aggressively* (Smyth et al., 2004) moved her out of the secondary schooling system because she was seen as a "ratbag." Her teachers did not present tertiary study as an option for her or lead her to feel as though she was recognized as a legitimate student who would be able to complete the SACE and participate in a university context. She compared her experience of secondary schooling with enabling education as like "night and day." She described her sense of belonging and feelings of recognition as a legitimate university student as "being treated like an adult compared to being treated like a child." Her reflection speaks to the adoption of democratic approaches to the curriculum and *dialogic* elements of Shor's (1992) framework as he emphasizes that "an empowering teacher does not talk knowledge at students but talks *with* them" (p. 85, emphasis in original).

Lillian also reflected on feelings of being supported by the UniSA educators: "I don't think I would've been able to do it if I didn't have the support that I did." Having left her marriage due to domestic violence, Lillian enrolled in the program as a single parent of two young children under the age of three. She communicated that she was able to juggle study with caring for her children due to the support shown by the academics for bringing the children to classes, which made her feel really "comfortable." The recognition of the importance of the affective domains in critical enabling pedagogy is evidenced here where educators often take on the role of "emotional champion," as described by O'Shea (2019). O'Shea argues that access to "productive relational networks" contributes to students' persistence to complete higher education. Lillian's comments reflect an *active* (Smyth et al., 2004) culture enacted through processes and actions of the educators to reach out to students and create a sense of belonging in the university spaces, through the curriculum and the focus on communicating an ethos of care across the program.

Fatima's Story

In a second example of misrecognition, Fatima, a Muslim student, experienced Islamophobia at her regional high school and chose to leave her family and community to move to a city and enroll in the Foundation Studies program.

Fatima's dream is to get into a law degree, which she "is realizing every single day with getting high grades, that I never thought I would get." Whereas Lillian experienced an *aggressive* school culture that contributed to her leaving school early, Fatima recounted that her school "didn't care whether I was attending the classes or not" and worked as a *passive* school culture that contributed to her not sitting for exams in Year 12 and limiting her options for a university degree:

> They were encouraging people that didn't want to go to university not to do the exam, even though they were able to do it. Like, I was able to do it because I studied like Year 12 head on, but because they were saying that, "If you don't want to go to university then don't do the exams." But you see, like, how the exams, one person's marks can affect another person's, and then the overall reputation of the high school.

Fatima also reflected that teachers did not invest time or attention in her learning because she was seen as a "rebel" and put in detention a few times in her earlier years of secondary schooling. Her interview echoed Lillian's account of *misrecognition* as her youthful misbehavior was interpreted as academic disinterest, or incapability of achieving academic success. Neither Lillian nor Fatima were treated as legitimate students deemed worthy of investment of school resources and time. Fatima provided further examples of a *passive* culture at her school in their lack of response to Islamophobic comments from other students:

> when there were two girls that were always picking on me, and saying like "Take off your turban, take off your curtains. Why are you wearing a curtain on your head?" She [teacher] would hear all that stuff, but she would never intervene.

Fatima consequently completed Year 12 without a tertiary entrance score due to the advice of her teachers not to sit exams. She reflected on this period as quite dark, where she felt like "there was nothing, my life had no purpose." After hearing about the enabling program through a family member, Fatima left her family and moved to Adelaide.

Once within our program, Fatima spoke positively of the critical enabling pedagogy approaches implemented such as connection between real-world examples or assessment tasks and academic themes, for example "writing a radio script" in one of her English classes. She recognized a key difference between secondary school and foundation studies in being told: "You're capable of doing this, you're capable" as well as the "continuous encouragement" by UniSA educators and identified this as being key to her motivation to study. Her message to other students also demonstrates the significance of emotional championing in enabling programs:

> Even if you think you are not smart like I thought, or you can't do it, you are going to be able to do it, because you will have so much support, and everyone will be there standing behind you and telling you that you can do it.

These words to other students demonstrate feelings of *recognition* as a legitimate participant in the university context, and as a young Muslim woman who has previously experienced misrecognition and marginalization.

The Way Forward

While the research participants revealed themes of exclusion like those offered in Smyth and Hattam's study from the late 90s, this study offers a counter-narrative that emanates from the implementation of a widening participation policy agenda since 2008 such as the Review of Australian Higher Education (Bradley et al., 2008). This chapter shows that a focus on *cultural geography* (Smyth et al., 2004) through cultural messages about who belongs as well as the enactment of a *critical* enabling pedagogy have clear potential to develop feelings of *recognition* for students in our enabling program.

Despite the issues with how the widening participation agenda has been implemented across the university sector, my hopeful idea is that opportunities for "radical teaching" (Hattam & Stokes, 2019; Shor, 2007) and pedagogical interventions in enabling education might influence mainstream undergraduate and postgraduate pedagogies to become more inclusive. This chapter offers a positive intervention or disruption to the framing of the problem of high school retention rates as the study provides an account of "what works" for previously disengaged students who have chosen to re-engage with education.

In accordance with Burke et al. (2017), I have emerged from this study thinking that "the project of changing pedagogical spaces in higher education is necessarily long-term and challenging because it is about eradicating deeply entrenched, historical inequalities and misrecognitions" (p. 142). It is possible if teachers and leaders in higher education take seriously the role they have to play in widening participation, such that it is not just the concern of those working in enabling education, the *radical teachers*, or social justice warriors.

The findings in this study demonstrate that playing the role of an emotional champion (O'Shea, 2019) through enabling pedagogical approaches can have a significant impact on the confidence and motivation of the student, not only in terms of engagement, but also feelings of *recognition* and belonging, with ultimate articulation into a university undergraduate program. Smyth and Hattam's study was conducted before the growth of enabling education offerings so this contribution marks a hopeful "turn back around" (Smith, 2017) to educational experiences that inspire aspiration.

In conclusion, I advocate that critical enabling pedagogy can be applied across all levels of education to disrupt social reproduction and work toward Fraser's (2003) parity of participation. To borrow from Burke et al. (2017), I do not mean inclusion in the sense of molding and shaping our diverse students to take on the middle-class, mono-cultural practices, identities, and norms inherent in universities, but in recognizing and valuing differences that encompass the intersectional identities of the student cohort. The findings reported here suggest that, despite disengaging from the secondary system, marginalized students can experience a moment of "turning back around" to education with the enactment of an *active* culture that embraces critical enabling pedagogies and provides *recognition* for students so that they develop a strong sense of belonging at university.

Bibliography

Atherton, G., Dumangane, C., & Whitty, G. (2016). *Charting equity in higher education: Drawing the global access map*. Pearson.

Bennett, A., Motta, S. C., Hamilton, E., Burgess, C., Relf, B., Gray, K., Leroy-Dyer, S., & Albright, J. (2016). *Enabling pedagogies: A participatory conceptual mapping of practices at the University of Newcastle Australia*. University of Newcastle.

Bennett, A., Hodges, B., Kavanagh, K., Fagan, S., Hartley, J., & Schofield, N. (2012). "Hard" and "soft" aspects of learning as investment: Opening-up the neo-liberal view of a programme with "high" levels of attrition. *Widening Participation and Lifelong Learning*, *14*(3), 141–56.

Bourdieu, P., & Passeron, C. (1977). *Reproduction in education, society and culture*. Sage.

Bradley, D., Noonan, P., Nugent, H., & Scales, B. (2008). *Review of Australian higher education*. Department of Education, Employment and Workplace Relations.

Burke, P., Crozier G., & Misiaszek, L. (2017). *Changing pedagogical spaces in higher education: Diversities, inequalities and misrecognition*. Routledge.

Burke, P. J. (2002). *Accessing education: Effectively widening participation*. Trentham Books.

Burke, P. J. (2015). Re/imagining higher education pedagogies: Gender, emotion and difference. *Teaching in Higher Education*, 20(4), 388–401

Cuconato, M., du Bois-Reymond, M., & Lunabba, H. (2015). Between gate-keeping and support: Teachers' perception of their role in transition. *International Journal of Qualitative Studies in Education*, *28*(3), 311–28.

Crawford, N. (2015). Practical and profound: Multi-layered benefits of a university enabling program and implications for higher education. *International Studies in Widening Participation*, *1*(2), 15–30.

Edwards, D., & McMillan, J. (2015). *Completing university in Australia: A cohort analysis exploring equity group outcomes*. Australian Council for Educational Research.

Fraser, N. (2003). Social justice in the age of identity politics: Redistribution, recognition and participation. In N. Fraser & A. Honneth (Eds.), *Redistribution or recognition? A political-philosophical exchange* (pp. 7–109). Verso.

Freire, P. (1973). *Education for critical consciousness*. Seabury.

Habel, C., & Whitman, K. (2016). Opening spaces of academic culture: Doors of perception; heaven and hell. *Higher Education Research & Development*, *35*(1), 71–83.

Hattam, S., & Bilic, S. (2019). "I can be powerful as an individual agent": Experiences of recently homeless women in an enabling program, transformative pedagogies and spaces of empowerment in higher education. *Journal of International Studies in Widening Participation*, *6*(1), *65–79*.

Hattam, S., & Stokes, J. (2019). Liberation and connection: Fostering critical students as active agents of their own learning. In A. Jones, A. Olds, & J. Lisciandro (Eds.), *Transitioning students into higher education: Philosophies, pedagogies and practice* (pp. 25–35). Routledge.

Hattam, S., Stokes, J., & Ulpen, T. (2018). Should I stay or should I go? Understanding student subjectivity, institutional discourse and the role enabling academics can play in empowering students within the system. *International Journal of Educational Organisation and Leadership*, *25*(1–2), 1–14.

Hattam, S., & Weiler, T. (2021). "Every single student counts": Leadership of professional development underpinned by social justice for sessional staff in a South Australian university. *Professional Development in Education*, *47*(1), 128–40.

Lamb, S., Jackson, J., Walstab, A., & Huo, S. (2015). *Educational opportunity in Australia 2015: Who succeeds and who misses out*. Centre for International Research on Education Systems, Mitchell Institute.

Moll, L. C., Amanti, C., Neff, D., & González, N. (1992). Funds of knowledge for teaching: Using a qualitative approach to connect homes and classrooms. *Theory into Practice*, *31*(2), 132–41.

Motta, S., & Bennett, A. (2018). Pedagogies of care, care-full epistemological practice and "other" caring subjectivities in enabling education. *Teaching in Higher Education*, *23*(5), 631–46.

National Association of Enabling Educators in Australia. (2020). *Enabling education*. https://enablingeducators.org/enabling-education/

National Centre for Student Equity in Higher Education (NCSCHE). (2017). *Successful outcomes for low-SES students in Australian higher education*. Curtin University.

Olds, A., Jones, A., & Lisciandro, J. (2019). The Social Justice League: Philosophies of flourishing and emancipation in enabling education. In A. Jones, A. Olds, & J. Lisciandro (Eds.), *Transitioning students into higher education: Philosophies, pedagogies and practice* (pp. 45–53). Routledge.

O'Shea, S. (2019). *Creating a capitals/capabilities-based persistence framework on university student persistence: A framing paper*. Unpublished manuscript.

O'Shea, S., Lysaght, P., Roberts, J., & Harwood, V. (2016). Shifting the blame in higher education—Social inclusion and deficit discourses. *Higher Education Research & Development*, *35*(2), 322–36.

Shor, I. (1992). *Empowering education: Critical teaching for social change*. University of Chicago Press.

Shor, I. (2007). A disruptive student, *The Radical Teacher*, 80, 44–5.

Shor, I., & Freire, P. (1987). *A pedagogy for liberation: Dialogues on transforming education*. Bergin & Garvey.

Smith, L. (2017). *Class disaffection and turning back around: Exploring working class students turning back around to learning within a mainstream school* [Ph.D. thesis]. University of South Australia.

Smyth, J., & Hattam, R. (2001). Voiced research as a sociology for understanding "dropping out" of school. *British Journal of Sociology of Education*, *22*(3), 401–15.

Smyth, J., Hattam, R., with Cannon, J., Edwards, J., Wilson, N., & Wurst, S. (2004). *Dropping out, drifting off, being excluded: Becoming somebody without school*. Peter Lang.

Stokes, J. (2014). New students and enabling pedagogies: Supporting students from diverse backgrounds through a university enabling program. *International Journal of Diversity in Education*, *13*, 115–24.

12 Advancing Social and Religious Equity in Super-Diverse Classrooms: Reflections for Initial Teacher Education

Hannah Soong, Dylan Chown, Nadeem A. Memon, and Mahmood Nathie

Challenges for Initial Teacher Education: The Reality of Super-Diverse Classrooms

A common feature of contemporary Australian classrooms is a high degree of cultural, religious, linguistic, economic, and class diversity, which researchers now describe as "superdiversity" (Vertovec, 2007). Acknowledgment of this diversity, in the form of policy and curriculum drivers, weighs heavily on initial teacher education (ITE) providers in order to prepare pre-service educators (PSEs) with culturally responsive pedagogies. This chapter engages with religion as an under-researched area within the superdiversity of contemporary student cohorts as well as the unique responses and understandings PSEs offer regarding religious diversity. In so doing, we highlight some of the broader issues in this area and how they might be approached in a teacher education program. Throughout this chapter we focus on Muslim learners as a group that is marginalized and often misunderstood.

Social tensions and challenges around negotiating religious pluralism are often mirrored in education. This is reflected in a deep sense of discomfort for many PSEs. Some hold a theory of secularization (Rasmussen, 2010) that views religious faith as irrelevant to school learning. Others avoid explicit acknowledgment of religious ways of knowing when promoting notions of intercultural understanding for example, that are meant to encourage learning from diverse worldviews (ACARA, n.d.). Far from genuinely seeing religious knowledge and experience as a potential strength for learning, subscribers to strong forms of secularism view religion as a *barrier to overcome* in order for valued learning to occur.

The authors of this chapter are all involved in initial teacher education including in delivery of pedagogy courses that directly address social justice and equity, with a specific focus on learners from diverse backgrounds including Muslim learners. Together, we offer a nuanced understanding of the teacher education–religion nexus by more fully accounting for how the issue of difference and diversity is differentially experienced and contested, and for how the education of Muslim learners maintains contradictions and Muslim learners continue to be positioned as "other."

This work draws on our collective experiences as well as qualitative data from a Critical Perspectives of Education graduate entry ITE course, which is aimed at preparing pre-service educators to respond to super-diverse teaching contexts. The course is structured within a critical framework, and reflexive practice is built into assessment. The data for this chapter include anecdotal evidence, field notes and course artifacts. In particular, we highlight narratives from Christina (pseudonym), one of the PSEs in the course. The quotations are largely drawn from her final assessment for the course and are illustrative of many of the attitudes and ambivalences surrounding religion among the course cohort.

Christina, who had a clear aspiration to be a social justice–oriented educator, was an engaged and enthusiastic course participant. However, the topic of "spirituality, religion and world view" brought up significant challenges. While she had previously been able to use the intersections between her cultural background and schooling norms as starting points for critical reflection, her response to this topic was particularly negative. In workshops, she shared her memories of religion "being forced down my throat" as a child, which had left her with "a complete personal distaste for religion." She took the stance that Australian public schools were secular, and that religion or spirituality had no place in schools at all. She commented: "this is a good thing, because it means students cannot be brainwashed or indoctrinated." As with many others in the course, Christina's engagement and willingness to commit to reflexivity led to some level of rethinking and shifts in her previously closed position. In a "hindsight" reflection piece for her final assessment of the course, she wrote:

> [P]rior to this course I held some pretty damaging views—not intentional but they simply did not acknowledge my ignorance. I feel after this course that ignorance is dangerous. It leads to assumptions, misguided thinking, and does not benefit anyone. But approaching a topic with a willingness to learn, especially where it represents a topic that is frequently the subject of misunderstanding, that the benefits will be immense.

Christina is now keen to develop her own culturally and religiously responsive pedagogies, although she still has some "pretty big questions" about how to address religious diversity in her own teaching. We begin this chapter with an overview of Australian multiculturalism as well as related policy and curriculum drivers for ITE providers. This is followed by a discussion of the growing resistance to migration and multiculturalism in Australia, including a strong anti-Muslim stance, which appears to be gaining traction in the general community and is reflected in some of our PSE cohort like Christina. We then describe a sociological foundations course in diversity called Critical Perspectives of Education which strives to galvanize our PSEs to develop culturally responsive pedagogies in the face of increasingly super-diverse educational settings. This is followed by a discussion of PSEs' orientations toward, and impediments to, inclusive practice as socio-critical educators. In conclusion, we argue for the necessity of recognizing and drawing on religion in pedagogical practice in PSE preparation.

Australian Multiculturalism

Australia, as a colonialist settler nation, relied on government control and policy to exclude the dehumanized other, primarily First Nations people, and extending to all "othered" people of color. The 1901 *Immigration Restriction Act*, commonly known as the White Australia Policy, was one of the very first Acts of the newly formed parliament and deliberately designed to further the utopian dream of a "civilized" White Australia (Jupp, 2018). Largely unacknowledged until very recently was the genocidal intent that accompanied this colonial project. Watson (2014) describes a purposeful and deliberate ongoing genocide, a literal attempt to exterminate the colored other. This was coupled with the forceful assimilation of lighter-skinned children, who became known as the Stolen Generations. Over a century later, former prime minister Paul Keating (1996) described this myth of monoculture as a great tragedy, the "lie that we can retreat to."

From such exclusionary beginnings, Australia now has one of the highest overseas-born populations of any settler nation and is often touted as one of the most successful multicultural countries in the world (Hassan, 2018). Alternative perspectives, however, point out an ongoing conflict that is overt, symbolic, and structural, particularly in relation to Australia's First Nations Peoples but also with regard to religious diversity. Colonial legacies are enduring and have been made evident over time from historically downplayed and denied frontier violence, which decimated Aboriginal populations at colonization (Rogers & Bain, 2016), through to recent debates about constitutional recognition more than two hundred years after colonization. Australia's First Nations Peoples remain at the mercy of an exclusionary constitution which historically could not prevent the Stolen Generations and the Northern Territory Intervention (Australian Human Rights Commission, 2023). Poor outcomes in terms of health, education, and political representation measured against non-Aboriginal people and over-representation in the justice system also continue (Australian Human Rights Commission, 2008).

Conflict is also evident in terms of Australia's recent policy and practice around refugee detention and treatment (Refugee Council of Australia, 2020) with a clear intent to stop asylum seekers from seeking refuge in Australia. Consequently, while the policy move to multiculturalism is often presented as relatively smooth and uncontested, there has in reality been serious contestation around issues of migration, which has occurred in waves over time. The more prominent waves have included vilification of Chinese working the goldfields during the gold rushes, to resentment of Greek and Italian immigrants, Vietnamese "boat people" fleeing war, to increased anti-Muslim sentiment and, more recently, moral panic around African gangs, particularly pointed at Sudanese teenagers. It is clear that tolerance toward immigrants has not been automatically forthcoming. The 1996 federal election marked a significant change to anti-immigration and anti-multiculturalism policy moves. As well, a distinctly anti-Muslim stance intensified following 9/11, 2001 (Iner et al., 2017; O'Donnell et al., 2017). Generally, in Australia immigrants of various nationalities have endured racism and "otherness," and acceptance has often been conditional and part of a promise of generational change.

While it has been argued that in comparison to other countries—rarely identified—Australia appears to be a cohesive and inclusive nation, alternative perspectives suggest that this has only been the case for those who possess the privilege of belonging in the dominant White culture (McIntosh, 1990). It is also increasingly evident that such perceived stability is being shaken (Hassan, 2018, p. 8), with rising levels of Islamophobia "fuelled by ignorance of both the religion and its adherents and stoked by world events, the news media and political actors" (O'Donnell et al., 2017, p. 41).

Political leadership and national identity politics have been central to tensions around immigration, social cohesion, and multiculturalism. These political discourses have generated a questioning of compatibility between wider Australian values and those held by Muslims (Iner et al., 2017). In doing so they "gave voice to existing anxieties about the commitment of portions of the Australian population to the 'core values' of Australian society" (Koleth, 2010, p. 33). Tracing the fluctuating shifts, policy appears to have traveled a full circle from an emphasis on assimilation and integration to multiculturalism, and in the present a return to assimilation and integration (Koleth, 2010). Australia is not alone in political and policy reductionism, and lively debates continue among Western nations around the unprecedented cultural diversity and immigration, particularly of the Muslim "other," and associated threats to social cohesion (Keddie et al., 2018).

The dramatic shifts in political discourse and policy around multiculturalism, combined with other factors, are an important backdrop for education policy and the experiences of Muslim learners in Australian public schools. The broad moves in Australia's response to cultural diversity outlined above have been reflected in educational policies. They range from assimilation through to various forms of multiculturalism, with the current language being that of inter-culturalism. Yet little is known regarding how current policy directives relating to ITE, which emphasize the importance of preparing pre-service educators to respond effectively to the super-diversity in Australian schools, are translated into practice. This gap is highlighted in the following section.

While the school curriculum has always been contested due to cultural politics, Hattam (2016, p. 30) argues that "it has now become a battlefield." The current policy processes of neoliberalism include the mobilization of a culture war, Hattam argues, and this includes schooling policy as a key site for the production of culture and identity. In Australia, a standardized National Curriculum was implemented for the first time in 2010, after an intensive consultation and writing process, by the federal Labor Government. One of the first actions of the 2013 incoming Liberal National coalition government was the instigation of a highly contentious review of the Australian Curriculum, headed by Professor Ken Wiltshire AO and Dr. Kevin Donnelly. Donnelly had a long pre-existing association with the federal Liberal Party and conservative media outlets as an "expert commentator" on Australian education, despite having no peer-reviewed research publications at the time (Hattam, 2016). Donnelly styles himself as a "cultural warrior" (Donnelly, 2020) and has long been an outspoken critic of what he terms "left-wing political correctness" (Donnelly, 2018). It is not surprising, then, that the final report included the following in Recommendation 15:

> ACARA revise the Australian Curriculum to place more emphasis on morals, values and spirituality as outlined in the Melbourne Declaration, and to better recognise the contribution of Western civilisation, our Judeo-Christian heritage, the role of economic development and industry and the democratic underpinning of the British system of government to Australia's development. (Donnelly & Wiltshire, 2014, p. 246)

This privileging of Western, Judeo-Christian orientations noticeably works to marginalize learners from diverse backgrounds, including those not of Judeo-Christian religious backgrounds.

Pre-service Educators' Orientations Toward, and Impediments to, Inclusivity

That we live in a time of unparalleled social and political polarization cannot be disputed. These tensions and polarizations are often directly related to education (Apple, 2018) and are evident, to varying degrees, in our PSE cohort. While left-leaning activists and proponents work toward inclusivity and equity, there is also a pronounced rise of right-wing ideology, whose proponents argue that they are being silenced and excluded, both in the broad community and in terms of education policy and practice.

Over the course of our time in teacher education, we have witnessed how some PSEs have expressed cognitive dissonance in their approach to diversity. While paying lip service to valuing diversity, many see aspects of religion in particular as being in opposition to curriculum learning. Most struggle to articulate pedagogical approaches that mobilize the culturally and religiously formed funds of knowledge (Moll et al., 2009) that their own students possess. The language of Thomson's (2002) "virtual schoolbag" is commonly used within courses in our program and this terminology is used easily by our PSE cohort to demonstrate an awareness of the knowledge and experiences diverse learners bring with them. This awareness is coupled with recognition that, because it is not valued by the "official knowledges" in the form of curriculum, such knowledge tends to remain largely unseen and unacknowledged in the school context. While they can see the injustice of such approaches, our PSEs still struggle to recognize the learning assets culturally and religiously diverse students bring from their life worlds (Zipin, 2009), let alone to see such funds of knowledge as strengths for learning. This is perhaps not surprising given the strong focus on curriculum knowledge and transmission throughout their program, which itself is driven by gatekeepers and neoliberal policy imperatives which prioritize human and economic capital.

A clear concern, coming through in tutorial discussions, is that PSEs do not want to inadvertently offend or cause hurt but feel unprepared for the tensions of teaching in religious schools or teaching students who actively functionalize their religious identities, knowledges, and ways of knowing. Their second, and arguably greatest, fear is teaching Muslim students. Common concerns center on potential conflicts between standard teaching practices, such as mixing genders in activities, physical education activities such as dancing, and teaching science, that may be in conflict with religious beliefs, such as evolution versus creationism. This collection of insecurities is illustrative of the wider concerns about the place of religion in schools.

Current PSEs are very likely to be teaching in super-diverse schools, including Muslim learners in their classrooms. Unproblematized, biased, and stereotypical views create a strong likelihood that, at best, their Muslim learners will be subjected to a "culturally defined, economically driven and politically motivated" form of inclusion (Barry, 1998, p. 9, as cited in Chown, 2019, p. 384) and, at worst, excluded and marginalized, confined to the edges of academic and social participation in schools. It is important to note that the notion of inclusion has strong political connotations, being linked to neo-conservative policy imperatives

(Gidley et al., 2010) and significant tensions. Used in this way, inclusion can become a normalizing process which overlooks or fails to recognize the deep knowledge, experiences, and identities of marginalized students of diverse ethnic, linguistic, and religious groups (Chown, 2019). The outcomes of inclusion policies have often been underwhelming for culturally and religiously diverse peoples and, for some communities, are a reason for suspicion due to implicit connotations of assimilation (Flahavin, 2008, as cited in Gidley et al., 2010).

In Australia, as elsewhere in the world, Muslims are subject to negative and stereotypical news media and social media attention. Research has identified the adverse effects of such attention, including rising Islamophobia, racism, acts of violence, and linking Islam with terrorism (O'Donnell et al., 2017). Studies of Australian people who do not identify as Muslim report a lack of knowledge of Islam as well as the diversity among Muslims, which can lead to *confirmation bias*, a phenomenon in which people tend to select new information that aligns with a previous position, rejecting that which is discomfiting (Johnston, 1996). This results in an increased confidence in the stereotypical belief or, as relevant to this chapter, confirming bias against Muslims and the teaching of Islam. Furthermore, tendencies toward confirmation bias are amplified by the currently ubiquitous nature of technology, and in particular social media. While some of our PSEs recognize this bias and are able to engage critically with such social media, others fall into a dangerous space of resisting stereotype change, prioritizing information which confirms prior biases. An emphasis on free speech has also been an emerging theme of far-right activists who denounce leftist "political correctness" as stifling free speech and shutting down legitimate discussion.

Our Experience of "Diversity" Courses: The Importance of Religion

Critical Perspectives of Education is grounded in the sociology of education, incorporating the teaching–research nexus, using recent research in the field. The premise of the course is that all learners have strong life-world knowledge and experiences which can be used as resources for learning. However, such knowledges are often sidelined if they do not exhibit the normed middle-class, White, colonial knowledge that education demands (Ferfolja et al., 2015; Santoro, 2009; Thomson, 2002). While courses preparing PSEs for teaching in diverse contexts include topics on race, gender, sexuality, ethnicity, and linguistic diversity, religion has not been commonly included. Until very recently, most research around religion in schools was directly related to faith-based schools, or in the United States to questions about whether religion could be included in the school curriculum. White (2009) was one of the first researchers to question why religion was being silenced within teacher education classes especially where students were invited to deconstruct the way other aspects of identity impacted on teaching and learning.

In recognition of the increasing importance of religion in the public sphere (Rasmussen, 2010) the topic "religion, spirituality, and world view" was incorporated into the course this chapter is based on. At this point, there was a dearth of research about religion in schools, or even acknowledgment of the importance of religion in terms of understanding identity. A critical perspective was taken, which meant engagement with questions of power and privilege as they relate to religion, spirituality, and world view. Tutorial activities focused on unpacking the overlaps between religion, spirituality, and world view along with the way this can influence both students' and educators' approaches to learning and teaching. Relevant educational policy was also examined.

The lecture for this topic takes a strongly pedagogical stance on treating religious identities (whole student), knowledges (including beliefs, traditions, and values), and ways of knowing as a strength for learning. The course literature also encourages a critical perspective on religion (Wang, 2013). The anecdotal response from our PSE cohort to the lecture was largely positive and it has become the basis for a critical engagement with the place of religion in education.

As with Christina, many students' assessment pieces acknowledged that they initially felt religion was irrelevant to their developing pedagogies and practices, moving to a ready acceptance of the importance of spirituality in identity development. The most common understanding of spirituality centered on a search for inner self-awareness and wellbeing, which is not necessarily linked to formal religion or religious practice (Wright, 2000) Christina's views correlated with this idea, writing in her final assessment that "spirituality is more of an organic set of beliefs and attitudes about life without being tied to any particular doctrine" and that "I believe the days of promoting Christianity or any other form of organized religion in mainstream education has come to an end. But to ignore religion altogether would be detrimental." Christina's ambivalence was typical of the cohort. While most hold strong social justice orientations and accept the need for culturally responsive pedagogies in teaching diverse populations, they continue to hold reservations about religion.

The critical lens taken by the course helped some PSEs, including Christina, to articulate ways of recognizing and availing religion or spirituality into their teaching in ways that did not foreground any one way of living as being more acceptable than others, instead being inclusive of all. Christina's final assessment writing included the following:

> To promote a critical exploration of world views allows "exposure to multiple realities of living" (Wang, 2013) and I see this as holding great potential for engagement of students in a non-threatening way. Knowing the lived realities of students in the classroom can help in determining a curriculum that is relevant or of interest to the students. I would not seek to exert my own opinions on any one religion or engage disparaging views. Instead, a focus would be placed on critical thinking, exploration, and teasing apart and critical reflection on student understandings and reactions.

While Christina used the terminology of "world views," possibly being less "threatening" than spirituality or religion, responses such as these hearten us, in that they clearly accept the centrality of students' lived experiences to their learning. We do not know how Christina will translate her learning from the course into her classroom but remain positive that it has helped shape her teaching pedagogies.

Conclusion

Through Christina's story, we have used this chapter to situate the concerns and hopes of our PSE cohort in the context of current times, although including historical influences on responses to diversity. Including our "religion, spirituality and world view" topic in the course was a brave but seemingly necessary move at a time when the topic was only just beginning to be recognized as important for educators to consider and a focus for research.

While it is clear that some of our PSEs continue to pay lip service to discussions of inclusion and exclusion, most engage seriously with the complexities raised by the concepts they engage with. We are heartened by the acknowledgment in many of their assessment pieces that they leave the course with more questions than they came with. Rather than seeing these new questions as a negative, they acknowledge that these questions come from a new level of awareness and understanding. They recognize that the ongoing search for answers will probably be a career-long pursuit, which reminds us of all of the need to continuously develop socially just and equitable pedagogies and practices throughout our teaching careers.

Acknowledgment

We would like to acknowledge our former colleague Helen Ovsienko for her great leadership and effort in leading the research project and her contribution to the book chapter before she transitioned to new directions and her new space.

Bibliography

Apple, M. W. (2018). The critical divide: Knowledge about the curriculum and the concrete problems of curriculum policy and practice. *Nordic Journal of Studies in Educational Policy, 4*(2), 63–6.

Australian Curriculum Assessment and Reporting Authority (ACARA). (n.d.). *Intercultural understanding.* https://www.australiancurriculum.edu.au/f-10-curriculum/general-capabilities/intercultural-understanding

Australian Human Rights Commission. (2008). *A statistical overview of Aboriginal and Torres Strait Islander peoples in Australia: Social justice report 2008.* https://humanrights.gov.au/our-work/statistical-overview-aboriginal-and-torres-strait-islander-peoples-australia-social

Australian Human Rights Commission. (2023). *Constitutional reform: Fact sheet—Recognising Aboriginal and Torres Strait Islander people in the Constitution.* https://humanrights.gov.au/our-work/constitutional-reform-fact-sheet-recognising-aboriginal-torres-strait-islander-people

Chown, D. (2019). Culturally responsive pedagogy: Respecting the diversity of learners studying humanities and social science. In D. Green & D. Price (Eds.), *Making humanities and social sciences come alive* (pp. 379–99). Cambridge University Press.

Donnelly, K. (2018). *How political correctness is destroying Australia: Enemies within and without.* Wilkinson Publishing.

Donnelly, K. (2020). *Kevin Donnelly.* https://kevindonnelly.com.au/

Donnelly, K., & Wiltshire, K. (2014). *Review of the Australian curriculum: Final report.* Department of Education.

Ferfolja, T., Jones-Diaz, C., & Ullman, J. (2015). *Understanding sociological theory for educational practices.* Cambridge University Press.

Gidley, J. M., Hampson, G. P., Wheeler, L., & Bereded-Samuel, E. (2010). From access to success: An integrated approach to quality higher education informed by social inclusion theory and practice. *Higher Education Policy, 23*(1), 123–47.

Hassan, R. (2018). *Australian Muslims: The challenge of Islamophobia and social distance.* International Centre for Muslim and Non-Muslim Understanding, University of South Australia.

Hattam, R. (2016). Citizenship, schooling, and educational disadvantage. In A. Peterson, R. Hattam, M. Zembylas, & J. Arthur (Eds.), *The Palgrave international handbook of education for citizenship and social justice* (pp. 27–47). Palgrave Macmillan.

Iner, D., Briskman, L., Latham, S., Matthews, Z., Pearson, C., Poynting, S., Krayem, G., Vergani, M., & Yasmeen, S. (2017). *Islamophobia in Australia 2014–2016.* Centre for Islamic Studies and Civilisation, Charles Sturt University and ISRA.

Johnston, L. (1996). Resisting change: Information-seeking and stereotype change. *European Journal of Social Psychology*, *26*(5), 799–825.

Jupp, J. (2018). *An immigrant nation seeks cohesion: Australia from 1788*. Anthem Press.

Keating, P. (1996, November 11). *For the new Australia* [Speech]. http://www.paulkeating.net.au/shop/item/for-the-new-australia---11-november-1996

Keddie, A., Wilkinson, J., Howie, L., & Walsh, L. (2018). "...we don't bring religion into school": Issues of religious inclusion and social cohesion. *Australian Educational Researcher*, *46*(1), 1–15.

Koleth, E. (2010). *Multiculturalism: A review of Australian policy statements and recent debates in Australia and overseas* (Research Paper No. 6). Department of Parliamentary Services, Parliament of Australia. https://www.aph.gov.au/About_Parliament/Parliamentary_Departments/Parliamentary_Library/pubs/rp/rp1011/11rp06

McIntosh, P. (1990). White privilege: Unpacking the invisible knapsack. *Independent School*, *49*(2), 30–6.

Moll, L. C., Amanti, C., Neff, D., & Gonzalez, N. (2009). Funds of knowledge for teaching: Using a qualitative approach to connect homes and classrooms. *Theory into Practice*, *31*(2), 132–41.

O'Donnell, K., Davis, R., & Ewart, J. (2017). Non-Muslim Australians' knowledge of Islam: Identifying and rectifying knowledge deficiencies. *Journal of Muslim Minority Affairs*, *37*(1), 41–54.

Rasmussen, D. M. (2010). Conflicted modernity: Toleration as a principle of justice. *Philosophy & Social Criticism*, *36*(3–4), 339–52.

Refugee Council of Australia. (2020). *Australia's asylum policies*. https://www.refugeecouncil.org.au/asylum-policies/

Rogers, T. J., & Bain, S. (2016). Genocide and frontier violence in Australia. *Journal of Genocide Research*, *18*(1), 83–100.

Santoro, N. (2009). Teaching in culturally diverse contexts: What knowledge about "self" and "others" do teachers need? *Journal of Education for Teaching*, *35*(1), 33–45.

Thomson, P. (2002). *Schooling the rustbelt kids: Making the difference in changing times*. Allen & Unwin.

Vertovec, S. (2007). Super-diversity and its implications. *Ethnic and Racial Studies*, *30*(6), 1024–54.

Wang, C.(2013). Fostering critical religious thinking in multicultural education for teacher education. *Journal of Beliefs & Values*, *34*(2), 152–64.

Watson, I. (2014). *Aboriginal peoples, colonialism and international law: Raw law*. Routledge.

White, K. R. (2009). Connecting religion and teacher identity: The unexplored relationship between teachers and religion in public schools. *Teaching and Teacher Education*, *25*(6), 857–66.
Wright, A. (2000). *Spirituality and education*. Routledge/Falmer.
Zipin, L. (2009). Dark funds of knowledge, deep funds of pedagogy: Exploring boundaries between lifeworlds and schools. *Discourse*, *30*(3), 317–31.

13 Toward the Knowledge-Producing School

Robert Hattam

> Why is it that, in spite of the fact that teaching by pouring in, learning by passive absorption, are universally condemned, that they are still so entrenched in practice? That education is not an affair of "telling" and being told, but an active constructive process, is a principle almost as generally violated in practice as conceded in theory.
>
> (DEWEY, 1916/1966, P. 38)

Connecting Lives and Learning

This chapter has been drafted as a thought experiment, or as a provocation to school leaders and teachers to reimagine their curriculum and pedagogical work. I am assuming that local school-based curriculum development is not entirely defunct and that in some schools there is still a commitment by educators to connect the Australian Curriculum to the unique contexts and communities that each school serves (Prosser et al., 2010). School-based curriculum development is, after all, still a key part of the published rationale for the Australian Curriculum, as noted in the following key proposition for the Australian Curriculum (ACARA, 2013, p. 11):

> j) Jurisdictions, systems and schools will be able to implement the Australian Curriculum in ways that value teachers' professional knowledge, reflect local contexts and take into account individual students' family, cultural and community backgrounds. Schools and teachers determine pedagogical and other delivery considerations.

That said, there are serious policy pressures on school leaders and teachers that are undermining their professional autonomy (Biesta, 2015) and so this chapter is also a call to educators to reclaim their right to make significant decisions about what goes on in their schools and classrooms, and specifically to take up Dewey's call outlined in the opening quotation. Put simply, they need to resist the demand to adopt *teaching by pouring in*, which entails decontexualized and ritualized performances or pedagogies of indifference (Lingard, 2007). Instead, I am arguing here for teaching approaches that connect lives and learning and hence entail negotiating the curriculum with our students. The book *Negotiating the curriculum* (Boomer et al., 1992) here provides a generative frame for leaders and teachers to think past the idea of curriculum as pre-packaged, involving "lock-step teaching sequences" (Boomer, 1992b, p. 5) experienced as "an almost self-perpetuating chain of subjections" (p. 5). Instead, educators' work is "a jointly enacted composition" (Boomer, 1992a, p. 24), or a co-construction with their unique cohort of students:

> Every day, and at almost every moment of their teaching lives, they have to make delicate choices in order to avoid the classroom equivalents of reefs, shallows, squalls and looming cliffs. In this sense teaching has always been a matter of "negotiating the curriculum." The physical environment, the set syllabus, the nature of the local community, the available resources, the school policies and the children themselves all present challenges that must be accommodated. Teachers need artistry, experience, knowledge and their own reliable maps to find a way. (Boomer, 1992a, p. 24)

Importantly for this chapter, we need to be reclaiming *the* school as the site for reform and hence we need to think out how a school can develop and sustain the artistry of negotiating curriculum in a critical mass of classrooms.

Against Backlash Pedagogy

School teachers and school leaders in Australia are now being fitted up with policy logics that are failing them, their students, and the nation. As a system, Australian schooling now has falling student achievement as measured by international comparisons (Senate Select Committee on School Funding, 2014), and we have one of the most unequal schooling systems in the OECD (Bruckauf & Chzhen, 2016). In this chapter, I want to pursue a reading of this policy failure as a backlash policy.

After decades of neoliberalizing logics (Hattam, 2016), our nation is trending toward more authoritarian governing (Lazzarato, 2014) and a noticeable de-democratizing (Brown, 2015). I borrow the metaphor of the backlash from Faludi (1991), who proposed we are witnessing a "powerful counter-assault on women's rights," and an "attempt to retract the handful of small and hard-won victories that the feminist movement did manage to win for women" (p. 12). Faludi argues that the backlash is "largely insidious" by claiming that social movement struggles are in fact the cause of contemporary hardships and social problems.

> The backlash is at once sophisticated and banal, deceptively "progressive" and proudly backward. It deploys both the "new" finding of "scientific research" and the sentimental moralizing of yesteryear; it turns into media sound bites both the glib pronouncements of pop-psych trend watchers and the frenzied rhetoric of the New Right preachers. (p. 12)

This critique of backlash politics has been taken up by Gutierrez et al. (2002), who use the term to critique the "techniques of persuasion" (Lowenthal & Guterman, 1949) used by neoliberal education policy activists who have been, for decades now, justifying education policies that strengthen the reproductive function of schooling. Gutierrez et al. (2002) push this argument to invoke a notion of "backlash pedagogy." Put simply here, the backlash in education policy deliberately undermines the social justice gains of the last century, especially around struggle to redefine curriculum and pedagogy. Post-World War II, social justice activists in education argued for a range of projects including: crashing the gate between secondary school and university; questioning the notion that mandated school knowledge is somehow free of power/knowledge; supporting local school curriculum decision making and raising the professional autonomy of teachers; and, perhaps most importantly, developing many forms of dialogic pedagogy, in contrast to didactic monological classroom relationships in which students get *done to* by teachers. Backlash pedagogy here names those versions of teaching that are now being pushed onto teachers and that reassert forms of didactic teaching, such as explicit instruction, back-to-basics, and approaches pushed by literacy fundamentalists (Luke, 2004). But then, running in a parallel to neoliberal versions of "what works" (Biesta 2007; Wrigley, 2012), there is an alternative archive of educational research, with its own evidence and truth claims. It is to that archive that I now turn.

Toward Dialogic and Improvisational Pedagogies

In the first instance we need to understand how inequality works, and Delpit's (1988) theory of the "culture of power" in classrooms offers an explanatory theory of the way schooling works to exclude or silence students from disenfranchised communities. She argues that many students experience a cultural dissonance, or "interactive trouble" (Freebody et al., 1995) in their classrooms. The "trouble" arises because the vernacular knowledges and everyday experiences of some students are absent, misrepresented, or muted in the lived curriculum. In some cases, this trouble is obvious, as in the case for Indigenous students having to study racist texts, but more often the trouble is more subtle.

> For Delpit, schools tend to naturalise and normalise the "codes and rules" of those who already have power in society, including "linguistic forms, communicative strategies, and presentation of self; that is, ways of talking, ways of writing, ways of dressing and ways of interacting." (Hattam et al., 2009, p. 307, citing Delpit, 1988, p. 283)

Those students who arrive at school with the "accoutrements of the culture of power" (Delpit, 1988, p. 283) are most likely to be successful at school because they already have access to the codes and rules of school literacy. For "disadvantaged" students, the gap between their vernacular literacies and school literacy requires translation, or explicit teaching, which too often is not forthcoming. For these students, the daily experiences of "interactive trouble" are explained to them in terms of their own deficits rather than a systemic failure to acknowledge and respond to the cultural dissonance. Having to internalize the trouble year after year makes schooling for disadvantaged young people just impossible to bear, especially when the demands of schooling increase so dramatically in the later years of secondary school: "They need to defend themselves against performance demands which may mean sabotage or silence" (Smyth et al., 2004, p. 110), neither option leading to much success at school. Delpit's (1988) analysis provides a clear direction for teachers committed to interrupting social stratification: "we must keep the perspective that people are experts on their own lives ... they can be the only authentic chroniclers of their own experience" (p. 297). But that is not enough.

> I suggest that students must be *taught* the codes needed to participate fully in the mainstream of ... life, not by being forced to attend to hollow, inane, decontexualized subskills, but rather within the context of meaningful communicative endeavors; that they must be allowed the resource of the teacher's expert knowledge, while being helped to acknowledge their own "expertness" as well. (Delpit, 1988, p. 296)

Delpit's argument foregrounds tensions around what knowledge counts in the official curriculum. This question has been at the center of decades of debates in curriculum and pedagogy studies, and more recently has been taken up again by the so-called "social realists." An exemplary text is Young's (2008) *Bringing knowledge back in*. To summarize the social realist argument, they establish a neat "binary orientation" (Zipin et al., 2015, p. 22) to the problem of school knowledge and argue for a definitive separation between "school-privileged disciplinary knowledge from life-world knowledge" (p. 22) rather than the more dialectical interrelation invoked by Delpit above. Put simply, Young valorizes *disciplinary* as against *everyday* knowledge. As Young (2014, p. 62) puts it: "[Curriculum that] celebrates the experience of pupils, whatever that may be...[goes against] the idea that the purpose of schools is to introduce them to knowledge beyond their experience" (as cited in Zipin, 2017, p. 72).

Those of us who are arguing against Young, and the broader policy push for backlash pedagogies, now recognize that the challenge for teachers committed to advancing dialogic approaches is to treat student life-world knowledges seriously in a curricular and pedagogical sense. Previous related research (Comber & Kamler, 2004; Kamler & Comber, 2005) indicates that, when teachers take the opportunity to learn about young people and their families as an integral part of curriculum design, then what results is new-found respect for students as learners, workers, and citizens, directly contesting pervasive deficit assumptions (Egan-Robertson & Bloome, 1998). When communication between teachers' and students' communities is enacted in the form of more relevant curriculum design with higher academic expectations, teachers can expect improved pedagogical relations and enhanced student outcomes (Gonzalez & Moll, 2002). As an example, the "Redesigning Pedagogies in the North Project" (Hattam et al., 2009) found that, when teachers treat students seriously in a curricular and pedagogical sense, their pedagogy is characterized by

- finding creative ways to learn about what is most existential for their students;
- being able to negotiate with students the themes to study, learning processes, and assessment practice;
- establishing the classroom as a research center and teaching students to conduct their own inquiries;
- providing space for students to develop their capacity as canny theorists of the cultures they inhabit; and
- providing opportunities for students to take an active role in addressing the specific social issues they have identified and to critically reflect on the action taken.

The dialectical approach being foregrounded here demands a theory of pedagogy. For the sake of my discussion, let us start with the view that pedagogies are planned and are often understood in terms of a performance in which one can become more skillful or proficient. This performance of the teacher, or their repertoires of classroom practice, is what we refer to as *pedagogy*. And while the term pedagogy directs our attention to teaching practices, the term pedagogy cannot be reduced to teaching methods or styles. Against narrow instrumentalist and economic framings of pedagogy, I want to foreground instead that pedagogies have histories, are used to advance political projects, involve technologies, and produce identities and national imaginaries, and the term also invokes the *why* questions and links classroom practices explicitly to debates over purposes, and hence also to visions for the future (Luke, 2006). A useful starting point for defining pedagogy was provided by Lusted (1986):

> What pedagogy addresses is the process of the production and exchange … [and] the transformation of consciousness that takes place in the interaction of three agencies—the teacher, the learner and the knowledge they together produce.
>
> [The term pedagogy] … draws attention to the process through which knowledge is produced. Pedagogy addresses the "how" questions involved not only in the transmission or reproduction of knowledge and also in its production. Indeed, it enables us to question the validity of separating these activities so easily by asking under what conditions and what means we "come to know." How one teaches is therefore of central interest but, through the prism of pedagogy, it becomes inseparable from what is being taught and, crucially, how one learns. (pp. 2–3)

While this view has its problems (Green, 1998), it does foreground the relationships between student, teacher, and the mediation of knowledge and leaves open the possibility of significant negotiation on the roles of teacher and student, especially who is teaching and who is learning and what constitutes worthwhile knowledge. As such, it provides a generative model for those of us who are arguing for less reified views of pedagogy. As well, this definition is open to ongoing revision, such as adding on Cummins' (2003) insight that pedagogy not only produces knowledge, but also certain kinds of teacher and student identities. With Lusted then we can map out the role of students and teachers as they engage with knowledge.

A key aspect of the approach being advocated here often goes by the term "students-as-researchers" (Egan-Robertson & Bloome, 1998; Fielding, 2007; Thomson & Gunter, 2007). Against common practice, which involves students learning knowledge that has already been codified in books, on websites, on videos, etc., the students-as-researchers approach involves the production of knowledge by students researching their own life worlds and the concerns of their communities. Rather than being consigned to an undemanding repetitive curriculum, student-as-researchers are positioned both as knowledgeable people, and as knowledge producers. But then this form of students-as-researchers can only work if teachers are seriously inquisitive about the life worlds of their students and the concerns of their communities. By *life world* I mean that site in time and space in which we all live, sometimes referred to as *everyday life* (Hattam & Howard, 2003). Such curiosity not only rejects taken-for-granted views, but also "deficit storylines" (Comber & Kamler, 2004, p. 294) about students and their families. The seriously inquisitive teacher I refer to as the "teacher-as-ethnographer." Ethnography here, drawing on Marcus (1998), can be thought of as "predicated upon attention to the everyday, an intimate knowledge of face-to-face communities and groups" (p. 83). The ethnographer studies relationships, language in use, and the "circulation of cultural meanings, objects and identities" (p. 79).

The ethnographic work I am speaking of is integral to curriculum and pedagogy and involves the students being researchers of their own situations. Applied to the teacher, being an ethnographer means being both expert in their field of academic knowledge or in their subject discipline, and also expert in the lives of their students. The teacher-as-ethnographer, as defined here, is also an improviser, in the jazz sense of the word, as opposed to a scripted teacher. Scripted teachers are heavily institutionalized in the way they relate to students and hence "without meaning to ... are engaged in a fairly mechanical repetition of gestures that have almost no connection to the daily life of the school" (Kaplan, 2000, p. 391) or their students. The teacher-as-improviser understands the "act of teaching and learning is not so much about enacting someone's else script, designed in another place and time, but co-authoring a script through a dialogic process" (Smyth et al., 2003, p. 190). In which case, teachers support students to conduct their own research, which involves research training, gathering data, making meaning, and devising representations of their findings. Without being exhaustive, the following subsections discuss some ways that teachers negotiate with their students.

Funds of Knowledge

This approach explicitly confronts the deficit views that teachers have of some disenfranchised communities. Instead, there is an assumption that "people are competent and have knowledge, and their life experiences have given them that knowledge" (Gonzalez & Moll, 2002, p. 625). Rather than the traditional curriculum that either misrepresents or ignores far too many communities, the funds of knowledge approach represents "communities in terms of the resources, the wherewithal they do possess, and a way to harness these resources for classroom teaching" (p. 625). The approach involves household analysis, the creation of study groups or lab settings with teachers, and the development of curriculum and pedagogy. Thus, the approach enables the use of the funds of knowledge of historically marginalized communities to make household assets "pedagogically viable" (Moll, 2005, p. 278) and to reduce the "insularity of classrooms" (Moll et al., 1992, p. 139). The aim is to provide classroom instruction "that far exceeds in quality the rote-like instruction these children commonly encounter in schools" (p. 132). A local South Australian variation, the "Redesigning Pedagogies in the North Project" (Hattam et al., 2009) asked teachers to research their students' life worlds, rather than family households, as a basis for curriculum and pedagogical design, and to focus on curriculum design that provides opportunities for students to be researchers of their life worlds and their communities.

Place-Based Studies

Place-based education has emerged as a key word for a collection of curriculum designs that enables "students to connect what they are learning to their own lives, communities, and regions" (Smith, 2002, p. 587). From a standpoint of local knowledge, this approach analyses more *abstract* knowledge from familiar places. It documents regional cultures, maps community assets, researches local environmental phenomena, gets students to identify and investigate school/community issues, and creates internship and entrepreneurial opportunities for students to think through relations between vocations and place. Of course, there are many possible elements to studying place, including socio-cultural, discursive, and ecological. With a socio-cultural approach it would be possible to study communities, identities, histories, or industries. With a focus on discursive elements of place, it would be possible to study knowledges, meta-narratives, institutions, authorities, subject positions, texts, or vocabularies. By considering the ecological elements of place it would be possible to study flora, fauna, landscape, geology, or climate. There are various models for place-based education, including Cameron's (2004) idea of "learning place responsiveness"; Smith's (2002) "learning to be where you are"; and Gruenewald's (2003) "multidisciplinary framework for place-conscious education."

Local Literacies

A local literacies approach (Barton & Hamilton, 1998; Luke et al., 1994; McLaughlin, 1996; Street, 1994) holds that part of the problem of the cultural dissonance that gets played out in too many classrooms is that the traditional school curriculum often ignores the rich literacy practices extant in non-elite communities. A local literacies approach seeks to access and validate those vernacular literacies closely associated with non-elite communities and youth subcultures that are marginal, misrepresented, or absent in school. Thinking about literacies in this way opens up the possibility of studying the keywords students use in their vernacular language, their local dialects, the vernacular languages of local youth subcultures, the sorts of texts they read outside of school, or their engagement with popular culture, as just a few examples. Taking up an interest in local literacies, teachers recognize "their students as master interpreters and canny theorists of the culture they inhabit" (McLaughlin, 1996, p. 154) and look for their students' theories in the vernacular mode: "theory that would never think of itself as 'theory'" (McLaughlin, 1996, p. 5). The vernacular here refers to "the practices of those who lack cultural power and who speak a critical language grounded in local concerns" (pp. 5–6). This type of knowledge is subjugated knowledge and hence is mostly overlooked or even denied. For McLaughlin, "[t]here are theorists everywhere in our culture, an unacknowledged community of sceptics and questioners. We need to know as much about each other's methods as we can" (p. 165). A local literacies approach provides students with opportunities to make connections between their linguistic, cultural and world knowledge and their experience, and the topics, skills, and competencies demanded by the official curriculum. As stated earlier, the challenge is to find ways to integrate local literacies with the official literacies of school in ways that do not trivialize either.

Popular Culture

While youth and popular culture are commonly used terms, their meanings are not always clear and not everyone uses them the same way. Some use youth culture and popular culture as one term that roughly equates to music and television media. Duncan-Andrade (2004) proposes a useful definition: "[b]roadly defined, youth popular culture includes the various cultural activities in which young people invest their time, including but not limited to: music, television, movies, video games, sport, Internet, text messaging, style and language practices" (p. 313). Keeping the definition broad in scope enables teachers to include not only the influence of media on young people, but also the important role of youth subcultures, their involvement in non-media activities (such as sport or religion), and the tendency of young people to resist or adapt (rather than accept) what is transmitted to them. With this definition in mind, how might youth and popular culture be a resource in teaching? While not an exhaustive list, I have identified the following approaches:

- engagement in new forms of textual practice and media culture (Durrant & Green, 2000)
- emphasizing literate practices within popular culture resources, such as professional wrestling (Alvermann et al., 2004)
- using critical literacy techniques with digital texts and web pages (Kerin & Nixon, 2004)
- studying new communication literacies (Knobel & Lankshear, 2003)
- studying young people's engagement with movies, fashion, or out-of-school learning sites as important resources for exploring youth identity (Atkinson & Nixon, 2005; Dimitriadis & McCarthy, 2000).

Of course, there are challenges for those teachers attempting to integrate student life-world knowledges and the official curriculum. Firstly, educators cannot assume that students are passive receptors of media, popular culture, or youth culture (Dimitriadis & Weis, 2001; Mraz et al., 2003), nor can we assume that they will be interested in any part of youth culture (Alvermann et al., 2004; Mraz et al., 2003). Second, there is a risk that popular culture is used to engage or entertain students, but it does not stretch them academically. Curriculum planning needs to consider how studying youth and popular culture will teach skills and provide academic rigor. Third, the power of popular culture needs to be open to critique.

Toward the Knowledge-Producing School

What I want to propose as the conclusion to this think piece is a whole-school approach to redesigning curriculum and pedagogy that takes up the broad rationale outlined above. As noted, this set of projects can be collectively referred to as the knowledge-producing classroom, and to date this approach has been taken up by individual teachers, often against the dominant culture of the schools they work in. What I want to suggest here is scaling up these projects to the *knowledge-producing school.* Such an idea has yet to really get any traction in the literature and in practice. This seems strange given the focus on whole-school change in the sociology literature (Connell et al., 1990; Smyth et al., 2014; Tyack & Tobin 1994), but to date whole-school change advocates have yet to make a compelling case for the knowledge-producing school and what that might mean for school-based curriculum and professional development. Before proceeding, this gap demands revisiting briefly a rationale for the school as *the* site for reform:

- Schools are sites for policy enactment and hence are sites of interpretation and resistance.
- "Actually existing pedagogies arise in response to locally diagnosed problems and are sustained as an 'ongoing practical accomplishment' (Freebody & Freiberg 2012, p. 80), constituted out of the 'practical reasoning' or 'practical theorising' (p. 80) at the local school level" (Hayes et al., 2017, p. 58).
- While individual teachers continually demonstrate they can reform their classroom practices, the long-term sustainability of these reforms are often undermined by the lack of enabling conditions at the school level.

Bigum's (2003, 2004) work on the "knowledge-producing school," and Smyth et al.'s (2010) "relational school" do provide a start to devising a conceptual framework. By way of a brief summary:

- "[S]chools have always acted largely as *consumers* of knowledge and information but there are some examples of 'schools as *producers of knowledge*'" (Bigum, 2003, p. 24).
- Knowledge-producing schools develop new types of relations with the world outside of school and especially with their local communities and focus mostly on community-based research projects. "The school views its community as an asset with a reserve of skills, talents and gifts to enrich learning for students" (Smyth et al., 2010, p. 205).
- Learning tasks are designed that shift decision making to the students, require significant negotiation, and derive from local community needs or interests. "Teachers are seen as allies and advocates for students and communities in processes of community renewal and reinvigoration" (Smyth et al., 2010, p. 205).
- The work of students produces a product of some kind, usually an artifact or a performance, but there are other options such as building gardens, and these products "are directed at audiences beyond the school" (Bigum, 2004, p. 61) and are "valuable to a community or group in the community" (p. 60).

"Schools are significant neighbourhood assets with resources to promote civic engagement and strengthen social and cultural fabric of local communities" (Smyth et al., 2010, p. 204).

What I have in mind are schools that become sites for "knowledge production, accumulation and dissemination" (Bigum, 2004, p. 63) and become known as repositories of knowledge about their local communities, which includes knowledge about the local environment, history, geography, economy, political economy, migration, and (de)colonization, and the list goes on. Schools would be known as local research centers with capacity-building resources for doing research of many kinds. The school curriculum would transform from providing opportunities for young people to jump through hoops for future learning and work to places where they learn how to learn and conduct their own research that contributes to making their communities better places to live.

Bibliography

Alvermann, D. E., Huddleston, A., & Hagood, M. C. (2004). What could professional wrestling and school literacy practices have in common? *Journal of Adolescent and Adult Literacy, 47*, 532–40.

Atkinson, S., & Nixon, H. (2005). Locating the subject: Teens online @ninemsn. *Discourse: Studies in the Cultural Politics of Education*, *26*(3), 387–409.

Australian Curriculum, Assessment and Reporting Authority (ACARA). (2013). *The shape of the Australian Curriculum Version 4.0*. https://acaraweb.blob.core.windows.net/resources/The_Shape_of_the_Australian_Curriculum_v4.pdf

Barton, D., & Hamilton, M. (1998). *Local literacies*. Routledge.

Biesta, G. (2007). Why "what works" won't work: Evidence-based practice and the democratic deficit in educational research. *Educational Theory*, *57*(1), 1–22.

Biesta, G. (2015). What is education for? On good education, teacher judgement and educational professionalism. *European Journal of Education*, *50*(1), 5–87.

Bigum, C. (2003). The knowledge-producing school: Moving away from the work of finding educational problems for which computers are solutions. *Computers in New Zealand Schools*, *15*(2), 22–6.

Bigum, C. (2004). Rethinking schools: The knowledge producing school. In S. Marshall, W. Taylor, & Y. Xinghou (Eds.), *Using community informatics to transform regions* (pp. 51–66). Idea Group Publishing.

Boomer, G. (1992a). Curriculum composing and evaluating: An invitation to action research. In G. Boomer, N. Lester, C. Onore, & J. Cook (Eds.), *Negotiating the curriculum: Educating for the 21st century* (pp. 24–39). Falmer.

Boomer, G. (1992b). Negotiating the curriculum. In G. Boomer, N. Lester, C. Onore, & J. Cook (Eds.), *Negotiating the curriculum: Educating for the 21st century* (pp. 4–13). Falmer.

Boomer, G., Lester, N., Onore, C., & Cook, J. (Eds.). (1992). *Negotiating the curriculum: Educating for the 21st century*. Falmer.

Brown, W. (2015). *Undoing the demos: Neoliberalism's stealth revolution*. Zone Books.

Bruckauf, Z., & Chzhen, Y. (2016). *Education for all? Measuring inequality of educational outcomes among 15-year-olds across 39 industrialised nations*. UNICEF Office of Research.

Cameron, J. I. (2004). Sandstone stories: Place writing and education. *Southerly*, *64*(2), 33–8.

Comber, B., & Kamler, B. (2004). Getting out of deficit: Pedagogies of reconnection. *Teaching Education*, *15*(3), 293–310.

Connell, R., White, V., & Johnston, K. (1990). *Poverty, education and the Disadvantaged Schools Program (DSP): Project overview and discussion questions*. Macquarie University.

Cummins, J. (2003). Challenging the construction of difference as deficit: Where are identity, intellect, imagination, and power in the new regime of truth? In P. Trifonas (Ed.), *Pedagogies of difference: Rethinking education for social change* (pp. 39–58). Routledge Falmer.

Delpit, L. (1988). The "silenced dialogue": Power and pedagogy in educating other people's children. *Harvard Educational Review*, *53*(3), 280–98.

Dewey, J. (1966). *Democracy and education*. Free Press. (Original work published 1916)

Dimitriadis, G., & McCarthy, C. (2000). Strangers in the village: Baldwin, popular culture and the ties that bind. *Qualitative Inquiry*, *6*(2), 171–87.

Dimitriadis, G., & Weis, L. (2001). Imagining possibilities with and for contemporary youth: (Re)writing and (re)visioning education today. *Qualitative Research*, 7(2), 223–40.

Duncan-Andrade, J. (2004). Your best friend or your worst enemy: Youth popular culture, pedagogy, and curriculum in urban classroom. *Review of Education, Pedagogy and Cultural Studies*, *26*(4), 313–37.

Durrant, C., & Green, B. (2000). Literacy and the new technologies in school education: Meeting the li(IT)eracy challenge. *Australian Journal of Language and Literacy Education*, *23*(2), 89–108.

Egan-Robertson, A., & Bloome, D. (Eds.). (1998). *Students as researchers of culture and language in their own communities*. Hampton Press.

Faludi, S. (1991). *Backlash: The undeclared war against women*. Chatto & Windus.

Fielding, M. (2007). Beyond "voice": New roles, relations, and contexts in researching with young people. *Discourse: Studies in the Cultural Politics of Education*, *28*(3), 301–10.

Freebody, P., & Freiberg, J. (2012). Ethnomethodological research in education and the social sciences: Studying "the business, identities and cutlures" of classrooms. In L. Markauskaite, P. Freebody, & J. Irwin (Eds.), *Methodological choice and design: Scholarship, policy and practice in social and educational research* (pp. 79–92). Springer.

Freebody, P., Ludwig, C., & Gunn, S. (1995). *Everyday literacy practices in and out of schools in low socio-economic urban communities*. Curriculum Corporation.

Gonzalez, N., & Moll, L. (2002). Cruzando el Puente: Building bridges to funds of knowledge. *Educational Policy*, *16*(4), 623–41.

Green, B. (1998). Teaching for difference: Learning theory and post-critical pedagogy. In D. Buckingham (Ed.), *Teaching popular culture: Beyond radical pedagogy* (pp. 177–97). UCL Press.

Gruenewald, D. A. (2003). Foundations of place: A multidisciplinary framework for place-conscious education. *American Educational Research Journal*, *40*(3), 619–54.

Gutierrez, K., Asato, J., Santos, M., & Gotanda, N. (2002). Backlash pedagogy: Language and culture and the politics of reform. *Review of Education, Pedagogy, and Cultural Studies*, *24*, 335–35.

Hattam, R. (2016). Citizenship, schooling, and "educational disadvantage." In A. Peterson, R. Hattam, M. Zembylas, & J. Arthur (Eds.), *The Palgrave international handbook of education for citizenship and social justice* (pp. 27–48). Palgrave.

Hattam, R., & Howard, N. (2003). Engaging lifeworlds: Public curriculum and community building. In A. Reid & P. Thomson (Eds.), *Rethinking public education: Towards a public curriculum* (pp. 75–94). PostPressed.

Hattam, R., Zipin, L., Brennan, M., & Comber. B. (2009). Researching for social justice: Contextual, conceptual and methodological challenges. *Discourse: Studies in the Cultural Politics of Education*, *30*(3), 303–16.

Hayes, D., Hattam, R., Comber, B., Kerkham, L., Lupton, R., & Thomson, P. (2017). *Literacy, leading and learning: Beyond pedagogies of poverty*. Routledge.

Kamler, B., & Comber, B. (2005). Turn-around pedagogies: Improving the education of at-risk students. *Improving Schools*, *8*(2), 121–31.

Kaplan, A. (2000). Teacher and student: Designing a democratic relationship. *Journal of Curriculum Studies*, *32*(3), 377–402.

Kerin, R., & Nixon, H. (2004). Middle years English/literacy curriculum: The interface of critical literacy and digital texts. *Literacy in the Middle Years Journal*, *13*(1), 20–35.

Knobel, M., & Lankshear, K. (2003). Planning pedagogy for i-mode: From flogging to blogging via Wi-Fi. *English in Australia*, *139*, 78–102.

Lazzarato, M. (2014). *Signs and machines: Capitalism and the production of subjectivity*. Semiotext(e).

Lingard, B. (2007). Pedagogies of indifference. *International Journal of Inclusive Education, 11*(3), 245–66.

Lowenthal, L., & Guterman, N. (1949). *Prophets of deceit: A study of the techniques of the American agitator.* Harper and Brothers.

Luke, A. (2004). Literacy and educational fundamentalism: An interview with Allan Luke. *English Quarterly Canada, 36*(4), 11–17.

Luke, A. (2006). Editorial introduction: Why pedagogies? *Pedagogies: An International Journal, 1*(1), 1–6.

Luke, A., O'Brien, J., & Comber, B. (1994). Making community texts objects of study. *Australian Journal of Language and Literacy, 17*(2), 139–49.

Lusted, D. (1986). Why pedagogy? *Screen, 27*(5), 2–14.

Marcus, G. (1998). *Ethnography through thick and thin.* Princeton University Press.

McLaughlin, T. (1996). *Street smarts and critical theory: Listening to the vernacular.* University of Wisconsin Press.

Moll, L. (2005). Reflection and possibilities. In N. Gonzalez, L. Moll, & C. Amanti (Eds.), *Funds of knowledge: Theorizing practices in households, communities and classrooms* (pp. 275–87). Lawrence Erlbaum.

Moll, L., Amanti, C., Neff, D., & Gonzalez, N. (1992). Funds of knowledge for teaching: Using a qualitative approach to connect homes to classrooms. *Theory into Practice, 31*(2), 132–41.

Mraz, M., Heron, A. H., & Wood, K. D. (2003). Media literacy, popular culture and the transfer of higher order thinking abilities. *Middle School Journal, 34*(3), 51–56.

Prosser, B., Reid, A., & Lucas, B. (Eds.). (2010). *Connecting lives and learning: Action research in the middle years.* Wakefield Press.

Senate Select Committee on School Funding. (2014). *Equity and Excellence in Australian Schools: Executive Summary.* Commonwealth of Australia. https://www.aph.gov.au/parliamentary_business/committees/senate/school_funding/school_funding/report/a03

Smith, G. A. (2002). Place-based education: Learning to be where we are. *Phi Delta Kappan, 83*(8), 584–94.

Smyth, J., Down, B., & McInerney, P. (2010). *Hanging in with kids in tough times: Engagement in contexts of educational disadvantage in the relational school.* Peter Lang.

Smyth, J., Down, B., & McInerney, P. (2014). *The socially just school: Making space for youth to speak back.* Springer.

Smyth, J., Hattam, R., with Cannon, J., Edwards, J., Wilson, N., & Wurst, S. (2004). *"Dropping out," drifting off, being excluded: Becoming somebody without school.* Peter Lang.

Smyth, J., McInerney, P., & Hattam, R. (2003). Tackling school leaving at its source: A case of reform in the middle years of schooling. *British Journal of Sociology of Education*, *24*(2), 177–98.

Street, B. (1994). What is meant by local literacies? *Language and Education*, *8*(1–2), 9–17.

Thomson, P., & Gunter, H. (2007). The methodology of students-as-researchers: Valuing and using experience to develop methods. *Discourse: Studies in the Cultural Politics of Education*, *28*(3), 327–42.

Tyack, D., & Tobin, W. (1994). The "grammar" of schooling: Why has it been so hard to change? *American Educational Research Journal*, *31*(3), 453–79.

Wrigley, T. (2012). Rethinking school effectiveness and improvement: A question of paradigms. *Discourse: Studies in the Cultural Politics of Education*, *34*(1), 31–47.

Young, M. (2008). *Bringing knowledge back in: From social constructivism to social realism in the sociology of education*. Routledge.

Zipin, L. (2017). Pursuing a problematic-based curriculum approach for the sake of social justice. *Journal of Education (University of KwaZulu-Natal)*, *69*, 67–92.

Zipin, L., Fataar, A., & Brennan, M. (2015). Can social realism do social justice? Debating the warrants for curriculum knowledge selection. *Education as Change*, *19*(2), 9–36.

PART III

Rethinking Just Curriculum and Pedagogy

14 Socially Critical Orientations and Pedagogies for Justice in Health and Physical Education

Alison Wrench and Robyne Garrett

Introduction

Issues related to student diversity, equity, and inclusion have featured in the development of Health and Physical Education (HPE)[1] curriculum in Australia for over 20 years (Whatman & Singh, 2015). However, school-based HPE continues to be framed by inequitable practices and understandings around gender, sexuality, culture, ethnicity, class, overweight/obesity, and (dis)ability, among other socially constructed categories of difference (see Cale & Harris, 2013; Evans & Davies, 2014; Macdonald et al., 2002; Whatman & Singh, 2015). At issue are marginalizing, alienating, and low-demand pedagogical practices and HPE curricula through which some students acquire "less privileged and privileging forms of … knowledge, skills and bodily dispositions" (Whatman & Singh, 2015, p. 215).

Challenges associated with addressing student diversity, equity, and inclusion are evident in global calls for Initial Teacher Education (ITE) programs to develop socio-critical pedagogical orientations among pre-service teachers learning to teach HPE (see Hill et al., 2018; Tsangaridou & Kyriakides, 2018; Wrench, 2018). However, as we have previously reported, the adoption of socially critical orientations is neither neat nor guaranteed (see Garrett & Wrench, 2011; Wrench & Garrett, 2015).

These concerns are central to this chapter. We first address critical pedagogies and socially critical orientations to HPE before introducing emotional connectivity and Raymond Williams' (1977) "structures of feeling." We then turn to the social construction of inequity and engage with Nancy Fraser's (2010) notions of justice. Our next move brings Fraser's theoretical perspectives into dialogue with a range of pedagogical considerations for developing socio-critical orientations for HPE. In foregrounding socially critical, affective, and just orientations to HPE we present practice exemplars along with orienting pedagogical questions. In conclusion, we argue that an engagement with socio-cultural perspectives and critical orientations to pedagogy is crucial if HPE is to lead to inclusion and justice outcomes for all students. We also argue for the adoption of "an ethics

1 Physical Education (PE) and Health are standalone learning areas outside of Australia and New Zealand. In this chapter our discussion of HPE incorporates PE in the global sense.

of discomfort" by teachers, which incorporates questioning certainties around HPE and problematizing that which is taken for granted (Foucault, 1988b, 2007).

Critical Pedagogies and HPE

The development of socio-critical framings for HPE has unsettled structures, understandings, and pedagogical practices commonly associated with the learning area (Cliff, 2012). Within the Australian context, the merging of the two previously discrete learning areas of physical education (PE) and health into HPE has been significant. Consequences of this integration include increased purchase of discourses that problematize inequitable and damaging forms of PE and prioritize the connection of health and physical activity to the cultural and social contexts of students' life worlds (Cliff, 2012).

Traditionally, pedagogical practices have privileged instrumental, linear processes, whereby teachers transmit knowledge and expertise to be unproblematically received by students in HPE classes (Tinning, 2010). Perceptions that teachers should control decision-making processes while imparting valued skills and knowledge to homogenous student cohorts within neutral learning environments have been influential. Of further significance has been the normalization of curricular offerings and pedagogical practices informed by rational truth claims of bio-medical discourses of human movement science and psychology (Cliff, 2012; Tinning, 2010).

Broader orientations to pedagogy recognize the interrelationships and connections between teachers, students, learning environments, and curricula as well as the influence of personal and cultural perspectives (Cummins, 2006; Lusted, 1986). From this standpoint pedagogical practices of HPE are more than imparting knowledge and skills. They have a potential to impact on students' identity, engagement, achievement, and positioning in relation to societal and cultural assumptions (Tinning, 2010). Socio-critically oriented HPE pedagogies can provide means for working against the grain, rather than regulating and classifying young people in relation to Anglo-Saxon, middle-class male norms (Wright, 2004).

Critical pedagogies have long been associated with the work of Brazilian educationalist Freire (1996) and subsequently a heterogeneous movement of authors and theorists around radical social thought and progressive educational practices (McArthur, 2010). While theorization of critical pedagogy is disparate, accord exists in relation to the premise that education and society are inextricably linked. Consensus is also evident around commitments to schooling practices that improve the justice outcomes for all students (Darder et al., 2016; McArthur, 2010).

Educators engaging with critical pedagogies, hence, recognize and confront links between power, knowledge, the existing social order, and schooling (Smyth, 2001). They question taken-for-granted assumptions and practices which support the dominant culture, while simultaneously marginalizing the cultures, knowledges, and lived experiences of students from less powerful social positions (Smyth, 2001). A strong sense of purpose exists around change "within education, through education and throughout society" (McArthur, 2010, p. 493).

Utopian claims attributed to critical pedagogies for transformation, empowerment, and emancipation have, however, been questioned and in turn problematized (Gore, 1992; McArthur, 2010; Tinning, 2010). Critique has focused upon tendencies toward abstract rhetorical theorization, which bears little relation to practicalities and implementation dilemmas experienced in actual classrooms. Exclusionary language and claimed emancipatory possibilities have also been deemed problematic (see Biesta, 1998; Ellsworth, 1989; Kohli, 1998; Lather, 1998; Lingard & Keddie, 2013; Tinning, 2002). Moreover, concerns have been raised about Eurocentric, universalizing, patriarchal, and Enlightenment assumptions, which work to privilege White middle-class male perspectives (Biesta, 1998; Gore, 1992; Kohli, 1998; Lather, 1998). Against this background of concern and critique, calls have been made for less utopian pedagogies that do not make unrealistic promises of emancipation for all (Gur-Ze'ev, 1998), are more practical or pragmatic (Gabel, 2002), and even modest (Tinning, 2002).

In arguing for "modest pedagogies" for HPE, Tinning (2012) does not suggest a reified set of practices, but rather seeks to orient ways of thinking. Of importance is the development by pre-service and in-service teachers of an embodied emotional commitment to the values, ideals, and practices of the socio-critical project. For Tinning (2002, 2012) a modest critical pedagogy of HPE also recognizes and takes into account the embodied subjectivities of students and teachers. Of significance are the ways in which pre-service and in-service teachers of HPE "learn to *think* and *feel* about education, social justice, physical activity, bodies and health" (Tinning, 2012, pp. 235–36).

Emotions, Affect, Structures of Feeling, and HPE

In this work we draw on Tinning's notions of "modest pedagogies" and "embodied emotional commitment." We also locate ourselves with scholars such as Zembylas (2016) who contend that *affect* as a category incorporates emotions and feelings, which are historically constructed and embodied in actions and practices. However, emotions and feelings are perceived as marginal attributes in comparison to rational ways of thinking and being in the field of

HPE (Dowling, 2008; Larson & Silverman, 2005; Tinning, 2012). Despite this, we assert that modest pedagogies that engage emotions and affect (thinking and feeling) can enable HPE educators to "reflexively re-evaluate closely held assumptions, values, and beliefs" (Zembylas & Boler, 2016, p. 27) developed within the dominant framings of HPE. Of significance are possibilities for "*knowing differently*, as well as knowing different things or knowing difference" (Hemmings, 2012, p. 151).

Raymond Williams' (1977) "structures of feeling" assists in making sense of generalized feelings and connections to the social and cultural institution of HPE and its pedagogical practices. According to Williams, structures of feeling embody "affective elements of consciousness and relationships: not feelings against thought, but thought as felt and feeling as thought: practical consciousness of a present kind, in a living and interrelating continuity" (p. 132). Williams (1977) maintains that practices, feelings, values, and meanings carry residual, dominant, and emergent cultural forms that pervade institutional spaces such as HPE and teacher education. The resilience, for instance, of sports and games in defining HPE programs and pedagogical practices exemplifies how a *residual*—previously dominant—cultural element continues to shape values, meanings, and practices. Aspects of this active and idealized residual element fit comfortably with dominant cultures of HPE as informed by rational discourses of sport and human movement sciences. In contrast, *emergent* cultural forms, such as those associated with socio-critical orientations to HPE, are less readily articulated and enacted than residual or dominant forms. An explanation for this is that they are incipiently in processes of formation and consequently not yet captured in institutional codes, language, and practices.

These tensions permeate the means by which we attempt to develop socio-critical orientations among pre-service and in-service teachers of HPE. Pre-service teachers, for instance, bring their biographies, emotional connections, and understandings about identities, bodies, health, and physical activity to their university ITE studies. These are informed by social and cultural elements of their experiences of school-based HPE and work to mediate processes of becoming HPE teachers (Garrett & Wrench, 2007; Wrench & Garrett, 2015a). HPE learning spaces are, hence, framed by shared affective, residual, generalized, and inexplicit knowledge that circulates beneath the surface (Berlant, 2015).

Importantly, spaces of shared life such as HPE are not essential or irrefutably given. Activities that disturb or challenge the established hegemonic social order and regimes of truth can lead to new ways of thinking, feeling, and seeing (Berlant, 2015; Zembylas, 2002). It is this potentiality that we engage with in the chapter in relation to developing socio-critical orientations among teachers of

HPE. Questioning *why*, *how*, and *what* is taught in HPE is critical for reframing *thinking* and *feeling* in relation to enhancing educational justice effects of schooling. With this and the above challenges in mind we turn next to Nancy Fraser's theorization of justice in relation to HPE.

Just Pedagogies for HPE

Fraser argues that justice equates with "social arrangements that permit all to participate as peers in social life" (2010, p. 16). From Fraser (2010), the achievement of justice and improved equity outcomes for all students requires approaches that incorporate the interrelated dimensions of *recognition*, *redistribution*, and *representation*. The politics of *recognition*, especially as this relates to gender, ability, and ethnicity, has been a priority for socio-critical HPE research and policy agendas (Devine, 2016). Meanwhile, socio-economic status or class and political barriers, including in terms of overweight/obesity and religion, as well as student voice, have not received the same attention (Evans & Davies, 2008, 2014).

Cognizant of these inclinations, we turn next to exploring *recognition*, *redistribution*, and *representation* in relation to affective, socio-critical orientations, and modest pedagogies for HPE. Exemplars of how these dimensions of equity might be played out in the context of HPE are presented. We also identify pedagogical questions designed to provoke emotional connections, critical reflection, and concomitantly emergent "structures of feeling" in HPE.

Recognition

Recognitive justice involves addressing socio-cultural hierarchies created through knowledge, skills, and ways of being associated with the dominant culture. Of significance are socially and culturally constructed categories of difference such as gender, class, ethnicity, overweight/obesity, and disability, among others, which work against equity in participation (Fraser, 2010).

As HPE is commonly framed by Anglo-Saxon middle-class male norms, attributes associated with traditionally male team sports such as speed, strength, and aggression are privileged (Wrench & Garrett, 2021). Consequences include the marginalization of attributes associated with aesthetic activities as well as movement forms from Indigenous and ethnic minority cultures. It follows that *recognitive* justice is premised on a willingness to reflect critically upon *how* and in *what ways* HPE pedagogical practices and curricula privilege particular student cohorts. This extends to reflecting upon how socially and culturally constructed groupings are (re)presented in texts, teaching materials, movement experiences, and understandings of ability and corporeality in HPE.

Recognizing and valuing the cultural resources, abilities, and understandings that students from non-dominant cultural groupings bring to HPE is a pedagogical and curricular imperative. The challenges associated with *recognition* include incorporating cultural resources, frames of reference, knowledge, and experiences that are informed by gender, sexuality, ethnicity, Indigeneity, class, corporeality, and ability including in their intersectionality (Lingard & Keddie, 2013). Specifically, in relation to HPE, pedagogical action for *recognition* involves respecting diversity, differences, and similarities, as well as appreciating breadth in perspectives, movement forms, and performance styles (Wrench & Garrett, 2018).

Reflection and awareness building are also vital in developing what Tinning (2002, 2012) refers to as an "emotional commitment" to the socio-critical project. Of interest are possibilities that arise through HPE curriculum and pedagogies that recognize and account for the embodied subjectivities of all students (Tinning, 2002). This is made possible when students' cultural resources and knowledge are drawn on in teaching and learning activities.

An example is a secondary HPE teacher's pedagogical decision to commence an Indigenous games unit with students' reflections about cultural, community, and familial practices around health and physical activity. The foregrounding of cultural practices underpinned subsequent student research into selected Indigenous games and peer teaching. With the aims of enhancing engagement and learning, pedagogical practices enacted by this teacher established affective relationships between health, physical activity, and culture for all students (see Wrench & Garrett, 2021).

A further example of recognition is when teachers commence with what students with disabilities *can do* rather than what they *cannot do* in negotiating learning experiences and adapting pedagogical practices in HPE. Teachers who commence with what students *can do* are able to make suitable accommodations to rules, equipment, and playing areas. Specific examples include using brightly colored equipment and balls with bells in them for vision-impaired students and providing extra time to complete tasks and modifying distances to ensure engagement, participation, and student success (see Overton et al., 2017).

Pedagogical questions that support these examples and extend the *thinking* and *feeling* of HPE educators to enable *recognitive* justice in HPE might include:

- Are learning environments safe, supportive, and inclusive of all?
- Is there balance between competitive, cooperative, and aesthetic activities?
- Whose knowledge and skills are prized and who is privileged through these value orientations?

- Is it possible for all students to develop a positive sense of self in relation to physical activity, health, and their body?
- In what ways do pedagogical practices build and utilize connections to students' life worlds?

Redistribution

Redistribution focuses on economic and material barriers to full and fair participation (Fraser, 2010). Providing access for students from less powerful social/cultural positions to educational goods and cultural capital is a crucial aspect of projects of *redistributive* justice (Lingard & Keddie, 2013).

In times marked by the logic of neoliberalism, and concomitant discourses of individualized responsibility for self-management, socio-economic class has been hidden in the shadows of HPE policy, practice, and research agendas (Evans & Davies, 2008; Smyth et al., 2014). Class does matter and, like no other socio-cultural category, it "forces us to think again about the nature of 'ability' and how the purposes and values of education are configured and distributed, to whom, where and why" (Evans & Davies, 2008, p. 200). At issue are low-demand, less privileging forms of HPE experienced by socio-economically and socio-culturally disadvantaged students (Whatman & Singh, 2015). Specifically, these are HPE tasks and activities that are designed to keep students busy, while bereft of any form of intellectual demand and rigor. Importantly it is disadvantaged and marginalized students who are heavily reliant on formal schooling for their educational resources (Hayes et al., 2009) including as these relate to physical activity, health, and wellbeing.

Developing capacities and dispositions toward actioning *redistributive* justice requires consideration of whether and how curriculum and pedagogies of HPE provide access to powerful forms of knowledge, skills, and critical thinking. Abandoning deficit views of students in preference to believing in the capacity of all students to learn, achieve, and be successful is significant to *redistributive* justice outcomes. Learning experiences and pedagogies that build engagement across the affective, cognitive, and operative (or behavioral) domains (Munns & Sawyer, 2013) are also essential if students are to procure educational resources for realizing positive outcomes in terms of health, physical activity, and bodies.

As a means of illustration we draw on an example from a senior secondary Skill Acquisition unit of study where a HPE teacher re-designed traditional learning activities and jettisoned teacher-directed pedagogical practices to include embodied movement challenges, guided discussions, and student-led problem solving (see Garrett & Wrench, 2016; Wrench & Garrett, 2015b). In this example, students' embodied movement experiences evoked feelings which framed initial group discussions. Through carefully crafted facilitative questioning and guided discussions, the teacher used students' experiences to introduce disciplinary discourses of skill acquisition and, hence, scaffold students' acquisition of scientific literacy required for academic success in senior secondary HPE.

Reflection, curricular action, and pedagogical practices for *redistributive* justice are also premised on an *emotional commitment* to the socio-critical project as this specifically relates to possibilities and embodied subjectivities of students (Tinning, 2012). Pedagogical questions that evoke this emotional commitment as well as different kinds of thinking and feeling for redistributive justice in HPE might include:

- Are high expectations held and communicated to all students?
- Are learning experiences engaging across the affective, behavioral, and cognitive domains?
- How is rigor ensured without relying on tools for comparison and measurement, which privilege "performance" and corporeal perfection?
- How is success defined and demonstrated? In what ways/how will learning improve the life chances of students?
- Are multiple points of entry, forms of achievement, and success recognized?

Representation

Representation is the political dimension of justice, concerned with who is included/excluded and merits "just distribution and reciprocal recognition" (Fraser, 2010, p. 17). It is predicated upon acknowledging and (re)presenting the knowledges and identities of students in ways that support their full and active participation in schooling, including HPE. Of consequence are top-down approaches to policy, curriculum, and pedagogies, which ignore circumstances at the local level (Devine, 2016). Safe, supportive learning environments, characterized by mutual respect, as well as positive student–student and student–teacher relationships are essential (Lingard & Keddie, 2013). Pedagogical practices of negotiation, encouraging student input and critical inquiry, are also important in enabling *representative* justice (Lingard & Keddie, 2013). Mobilizing the principles of *representative* justice in the context of HPE entails validating students as knowledgeable and capable in understanding and enacting their own health and active practice.

Specific examples include HPE teachers negotiating with students in curricular and learning activity design (see Wrench & Paige, 2020). In one example pre-service teachers negotiated practitioner inquiry undertakings that were informed by social justice discourses, inclusion of diverse learners, and just schooling outcomes. A second example is provided by a primary HPE teacher who problematized her reliance on direct instruction, which alienated her male students from Dance. In drawing on her students' interests in hip hop and the expertise of older male students, she utilized cross-age peer teaching to develop a dance unit that made connections to students' cultures and life worlds (see Garrett & Wrench, 2017; Wrench & Garrett, 2016). These pedagogical practices validated students as knowledgeable and offered opportunities for investigating connections to meaningful forms of movement.

Representative justice reflects Tinning's (2002) call for developing embodied emotional commitment in students and engaging with emotional commitment to change. Pedagogical practices for *representation* involve students in decision making about movement experiences, framing activity participation (for example cooperative, nature of competition, indicators of success, modifications to support multiple levels of participation and success), assessment, and the performance of learning. Pedagogical questions to encourage the kinds of *thinking* and *feeling* that will support representative justice include:

- What are the connections between HPE and students' communities and life worlds?
- Is decision making shared between teachers and students?
- How do pedagogical practices encourage student input, negotiation, and decision making?
- How are students' knowledges valued and respected in HPE?

Conclusion

In this chapter we have discussed socially critical orientations as modest pedagogies of HPE. We turned to Raymond Williams' structures of feeling as an explanatory framing of socially critical orientations and pedagogies as *emergent* rather than *dominant* with the field of HPE. Nancy Fraser's theorization of justice provided an additional framing for practices, examples, and the questions we might ask in our endeavors to implement socio-critical pedagogical practice.

We contend that the adoption of socially critical orientations to HPE curricula and pedagogies represents ethical, affective, and political action. This is action that deliberately seeks to make a real difference for students from less powerful socio-cultural positions. It requires an emotional connectivity to students, taking risks and operating with an "ethic of discomfort" (Foucault, 2007). We suggest that the examples and questions we have posed in relation to *recognitive*, *redistributive*, and *representative* justice represent means for developing these dispositions. These questions are not offered as a definitive list; rather we advocate their use in guiding critical reflection and in developing different kinds of *thinking* and *feeling* that evoke an embodied emotional commitment to making a difference for all students.

We believe that these questions can disrupt or unsettle residual and dominant structures of feeling founded on common-sense practices, curricula, and cultures of HPE, which limit or constrain embodied subjective possibilities for students from less powerful social positions. These disruptive or unsettling questions are essential for developing emergent structures of feeling or cultural forms, such as those associated with socio-critical orientations toward HPE.

Finally, we argue that in supporting the development of socio-critical orientations we can normalize the questioning of pedagogical assumptions and inferred curriculum potentialities which reinforce hegemonic norms in relation to physicality, ability, bodies, and health. Foucault provokes us to "question over and over again what is postulated as self-evident, to disturb people's mental habits, the way they do and think things, to dissipate what is familiar and accepted" (1988a, p. 265). We argue that the development of social, cultural, and educational resources of all students is a responsibility of HPE teachers and teacher educators. There is an urgent need for HPE teachers and teacher educators to adopt pedagogical practices and curriculum that endorse knowledge founded in the communities and cultures of students, so as to build health and physical activity capacities and dispositions that can actually make a difference to students' lives.

Bibliography

Berlant, L. (2015). Structures of unfeeling: Mysterious skin. *International Journal of Politics, Culture and Society*, *28*(1), 191–213.

Biesta, G. J. J. (1998). Say you want a revolution: Suggestions for the impossible future of critical pedagogy. *Educational Theory*, *48*(4), 499–510.

Cale, L., & Harris, J. (2013). "Every child (of every size) matters" in physical education! Physical education's role in childhood obesity. *Sport, Education and Society*, *18*(4), 433–52.

Cliff, K. (2012). A sociocultural perspective as a curriculum change in health and physical education. *Sport, Education and Society*, *17*(3), 293–311.

Cummins, J. (2006). Identity texts: The imaginative construction of self through multiliteracies pedagogy. In O. Garcia, T. Skutnabb-Kangas, & M. E. Torres-Guzman (Eds.), *Imagining multilingual schools* (pp. 51–68). Multilingual Matters.

Darder, A., Mayo, P., & Paraskeva, J. (2016). The internationalization of critical pedagogy: An introduction. In A. Darder, P. Mayo, & J. Paraskeva (Eds.), *International critical pedagogy reader* (pp. 1–14). Routledge.

Devine, C. (2016). Sex, sport and justice: Reframing the "who" of citizenship and the "what" of justice in European and UK sport policy. *Sport, Education and Society*, *21*(8), 1193–1212.

Dowling, F. (2008). Getting in touch with our feelings: The emotional geographies of gender relations in PETE. *Sport, Education and Society*, *13*(3), 247–66.

Ellsworth, E. (1989). Why doesn't this feel empowering? Working through the repressive myths of critical pedagogy. *Harvard Educational Review*, *59*(3), 297–324.

Evans, J., & Davies, B. (2008). The poverty of theory: Class configurations in the discourse of physical education and health (PEH). *Sport, Education and Society*, *13*(2), 199–213.

Evans, J., & Davies, B. (2014). Physical education PLC: Neoliberalism, curriculum and governance. New directions for PESP research. *Sport, Education and Society*, *19*(7), 869–84.

Foucault, M. (1988a). The concern for truth. In L. D. Kritzman (Ed.), *Michel Foucault: Politics, philosophy, culture* (pp. 255–67). Routledge.

Foucault, M. (1988b). Politics and reason. In L. D. Kritzman (Ed.), *Michel Foucault: Politics, philosophy, culture* (pp. 57–85). Routledge.

Foucault, M. (2007). *The politics of truth*. Semiotext(e).

Fraser, N. (2010). *Scales of justice: Reimagining political space in a globalizing world*. Columbia University Press.

Freire, P. (1996). *Pedagogy of the oppressed*. Penguin.

Gabel, S. (2002). Some conceptual problems with critical pedagogy. *Curriculum Inquiry*, *32*(2), 177–201.

Garrett, R. & Wrench, A. (2007). Physical Experiences: Primary Student Teachers' Conceptions of Sport and Physical Education, *Physical Education and Sport Pedagogy*, 12(1), 23–42.

Garrett, R., & Wrench, A. (2011). Making physical education a fairer, safer, and happier place: Putting critical practices into action. *Asia-Pacific Journal of Health, Sport and Physical Education*, *2*(2), 239–55.

Garrett, R., & Wrench, A. (2016). If they can say it they can write it: Inclusive pedagogies for senior secondary physical education. *International Journal of Inclusive Education*, *20*(5), 486–502.

Garrett, R. & Wrench, A. (2017). Redesigning pedagogy for boys and dance in physical education. *European Physical Education Review*, *24*(1), 97–113.

Gore, J. (1992). What we can do for you! What can "we" do for "you"? Struggling over empowerment in critical and feminist pedagogy. In C. Luke & J. Gore (Eds.), *Feminisms and critical pedagogy* (pp. 54–73). Routledge.
Gur-Ze'ev, I. (1998). Toward a non-repressive critical pedagogy. *Educational Theory*, *48*(4), 463–86.
Hayes, D., Johnston, K., & King, A. (2009). Creating enabling classroom practices in high poverty contexts: The disruptive possibilities of looking in classrooms. *Pedagogy, Culture and Society*, *17*(3), 251–64.
Hemmings, C. (2012). Affective solidarity: Feminist reflexivity and political transformation. *Feminist Theory*, *13*(2), 147–61.
Hill, J., Philpot, R., Walton-Fisette, J. L., Sutherland, S., Flemons, M., Ovens, A., Phillips, S., & Flory, S. B. (2018). Conceptualising social justice and sociocultural issues within physical education teacher education: International perspectives. *Physical Education and Sport Pedagogy*, *23*(5), 469–83.
Kohli, W. (1998). Critical education and embodied subjects: Making the poststructural turn. *Education Theory*, *48*(4), 511–19.
Larson, A., & Silverman, S. J. (2005). Rationales and practices used by caring physical education teachers. *Sport, Education and Society*, *10*(2), 175–93.
Lather, P. (1998). Critical pedagogy and its complicities: A praxis of stuck places. *Educational Theory*, *48*(4), 487–97.
Lingard, B., & Keddie, A. (2013). Redistribution, recognition and representation: Working against pedagogies of indifference. *Pedagogy, Culture and Society*, *21*(3), 427–47.
Lusted, D. (1986). Why pedagogy? *Screen*, *27*(5), 2–14.
Macdonald, D., Kirk, D., Metzler, M., Nilges, L. M., Schemp, P., & Wright, J. (2002). It's all very well, in theory: Theoretical perspectives and their applications in contemporary pedagogical research. *Quest*, *54*(2), 135–56.
McArthur, J. (2010). Achieving social justice within and through higher education: The challenge for critical pedagogy. *Teaching in Higher Education*, *15*(5), 493–504.
Munns, G., & Sawyer, S. W. (2013). Student engagement: The research methodology and the theory. In G. Munns, W. Sawyer, & B. Cole (Eds.), *Exemplary teachers of students in poverty* (pp. 14–32). Routledge.
Navigating culturally responsive pedagogy through an Indigenous games unit. *Sport, Education and Society*, *26*(6), 567–78.
Overton, H., Wrench, A., & Garrett, R. (2017). Pedagogies for inclusion of junior primary students with disabilities in PE. *Physical Education and Sport Pedagogy*, *22*(4), 414–26.
Smyth, J. (2001). *Critical politics of teachers' work*. Peter Lang.

Smyth, J., Mooney, A., & Casey, M. (2014). Where has class gone? The pervasiveness of class in girls' physical activity in a rural town. *Sport, Education and Society*, *19*(1), 1–18.

Tinning, R. (2002). Toward a "modest pedagogy": Reflections on the problematics of critical pedagogy. *Quest*, *54*(3), 224–40.

Tinning, R. (2010). *Pedagogy and human movement: Theory, practice, research*. Routledge.

Tinning, R. (2012). A socially critical HPE (aka physical education) and the challenge for teacher education. In B. Down & J. Smyth (Eds.), *Critical voices in teacher education: Explorations of educational purpose* (pp. 223–38). Springer Sciences & Business Media.

Tsangaridou, N., & Kyriakides, E. (2018). Pre-service primary physical teacher education. In G. Griggs & K. Petrie (Eds.), *Routledge handbook of primary physical education* (pp. 98–111). Routledge.

Whatman, S. L., & Singh, P. (2015). Constructing health and physical education curriculum for Indigenous girls in a remote Australian community. *Physical Education and Sport Pedagogy*, *20*(2), 215–30.

Williams, R. (1977). *Marxism and literature*. Oxford University Press.

Wrench, A. (2018). Hope, spaces and possible selves: Processes of becoming socially critical teachers. In W. Sawyer, S. Gannon, & R. Hattam (Eds.), *Resisting educational inequality* (pp. 140–49). Routledge.

Wrench, A., & Garrett, R. (2015a). Emotional connections and caring: Ethical teachers of physical education. *Sport, Education and Society*, *20*(2), 212–27.

Wrench, A., & Garrett R. (2015b). "If they can say it they can do it": Redesigning pedagogies in senior secondary physical education. *Journal of Educational Enquiry*, *14*(2), 45–58.

Wrench, A., & Garrett, R. (2016). Pedagogies for justice in health and physical education. *Asia-Pacific Journal of Health, Sport and Physical Education*, *7*(3), 235–50.

Wrench, A., & Garrett, R. (2018). Diversity and inclusion. In G. Griggs & K. Petrie (Eds.), *Routledge handbook of primary physical education* (pp. 134–44). Routledge.

Wrench, A., & Paige, K. (2020). Educating pre-service teachers: Towards a critical inquiry workforce. *Educational Action Research*, *28*(3), 462–79.

Wright, J. (2004). Poststructural methodologies: The body, schooling and health. In J. Evans, B. Davies, & J. Wright (Eds.), *Body knowledge and control: Studies in the sociology of physical education and health* (pp. 19–31). Routledge.

Zembylas, M. (2002). "Structures of feeling" in curriculum teaching: Theorizing the emotional rules. *Educational Theory*, *52*(2), 187–208.

Zembylas, M. (2016). Making sense of the complex entanglement between emotion and pedagogy: Contributions of the affective turn. *Cultural Studies of Science Education*, *11*(3), 539–50.

Zembylas, M., & Boler, M. (2016). Interview with Megan Boler: From "feminist politics of emotions" to the "affective turn." In M. Zembylas & P. A. Schultz (Eds.), *Methodological advances in research on emotion in education* (pp. 17–30). Springer International Publishing.

15 Eco-social Justice Education in the Anthropocene

Kathryn Paige, David Lloyd, and Richard Smith

Introduction: Why Eco-socially Just Education?

For most of the last century, our models of economic growth have assumed an uncontested abundance of natural resources. We mined our way to growth and burned our way to prosperity. We believed in consumption without consequences. Those days are gone! That model is now clearly a recipe for national disaster (Ehrlich et al., 2012; Hunter & Hewson, 2020; Slaughter, 1996) and, we suggest, also global disaster. On the evidence, all societies must move toward more sustainable human living and valuing the welfare of all species and ecosystems, a pursuit at the heart of this chapter.

We need to challenge the dominance of a neoliberalizing agenda. As Klein (2014, p. 9) argues: "finding new ways to privatize the Commons and profit from disaster is what our current system is built to do; left to its own devices, it is capable of nothing else." Kolbert (2014, p. 266) similarly says that it "doesn't matter much whether people care or don't care. What matters is that people change the world." Our approach to this challenge has been informed by the work of many current scholars, including Figueres and Rivett-Carnac (2020), Kopnina (2017), Laszlo and Dennis (2013), Singer (2010, 2016), and Suzuki and McConnell (1997). These scholars argue that all societies must move toward ways of valuing and acting that make possible longer and more comfortable lives for all beings and living systems. There is also evidence that, in this largely unplanned and uncontrolled human experiment on Earth, humanity is at high risk of crossing one or more hard-wired system thresholds with irreversible consequences (Rockstrom et al., 2018).

To end the Western world's profiteering tradition of economic and technological colonization, and the consequent slow environmental degradation, we need an eco-social justice vocabulary and practice that can better steer us beyond contemporary ways of living (Bowers, 2017). Much of humanity's current approach turns out to be more naïve than enlightened, a world view lacking any comprehensive expression of empathetic holism. More specifically, "developed" countries' human-centered and colonizing modernity can be characterized by its separation of three cultural value spheres:

- arts-aesthetics, representing the interior-subjective or the "I" domain of thinking and knowing;
- religion-morals, representing the interior, inter-subjective, cultural, or "We" domain; and,

- empirical science, representing the exterior-objective or "It" domain (Esbjörn-Hargens & Zimmerman, 2009; Settelmaier & Taylor, 2001).

The tendency of those operating within this modernity (that is, most of "us") to separate these value spheres to pursue their own selection from them without interference from the others omits serious consideration of the idea that Earth is an integrated entity with no internal boundaries. Moreover, the separation of these value spheres is taken too far and seen as absolute.

In response to global environmental challenges, arising largely because modern humans separate rather than integrate these value spheres, we have developed a set of guiding principles for our own teaching. We believe that they promote learning which views Earth as an internally unbounded, coherent whole, and that values the integrity of all living and non-living aspects of the place we call our home (Paige et al., 2016, 2019).

We have demonstrated (see Paige et al., 2019) that initial teacher education (ITE) programs *can* contribute to eco-social justice learning by introducing, and making explicit, the ethical and sustainability necessity of valuing all aspects of Earth systems. To this end, our ITE science specialization and curriculum courses provide conceptual frameworks, mobilize student participation (Ferreira et al., 2015), and enable direct action (Hodson, 2003) that is essential for healthy, resilient communities and ecosystems. We have focused primarily, but not exclusively, on the natural world aspects of eco-social justice education and its application to the places in which we live—that is, our local situations. Educational experiences in natural settings have been of fundamental importance to the development of our own approaches to active citizenship (Paige et al., 2016), as they have been for many other people's activism (Lloyd & Deans, 2017; Lloyd & Paige, 2022). We wish to provide our students with their own opportunities to realize we are all a part of, and responsible for, a world ecology (Paige et al., 2016, 2019).

We have developed a set of eight eco-social justice education principles which have informed our approaches in ITE and contribute to a framework for curriculum-based action research projects with teachers. In earlier work we have used the term "eco-justice"; here we use "eco-social justice" to emphasize the inextricable interconnectedness of ecological and social justice. This interconnectedness underpins our guiding principles:

- *Identify and challenge* current world views and behaviors.
- Develop a *community of learners* with a disposition to knowing and valuing with compassion natural, including human, systems.

- Invite students to *engage collaboratively* in working toward creating eco-socially just and sustainable communities.
- Assist students in their development as *role models* who value the commons, partnerships, quality of life, and material adequacy.
- Promote students' acquisition of *eco-social wisdom*—ways of thinking, feeling, and acting within places which they inhabit.
- Help students to develop a respect for long-term rather than short-term thinking through historical and *futures studies*.
- Provide opportunities for students to *reflect critically* on what they have learnt.
- Prioritize *culturally responsive* pedagogy and Indigenous perspectives.

In order to give these principles form, we focus here on a specific case study, our Water Literacies Project, which provides practical insights into and evidence of the application of the above principles. Five teachers were involved in this year-long action research project in three primary schools (see Paige et al., 2018). The chapter finishes with a reflection and discussion of key emerging themes and approaching futures.

Case Study: Transdisciplinary STEM: Eco-social Justice Education Principles in a Water Literacies Project

The aim of the year-long Water Literacies Project was to provide professional learning opportunities for teachers which would enable them more skillfully to assist their primary-aged co-learners to build understandings of the importance and finite availability of natural resources. The recognition by all co-learners, that is both teachers and students, of their personal impact on the Earth through their natural resource use in an overdeveloped world and their "unfair" ecological footprint was also central. The project focused specifically on developing scientifically and mathematically literate citizens with the confidence to make informed decisions and participate in working toward a democracy that values a whole Earth for this and future generations. The specific natural resource we focused on was fresh water (Paige et al., 2018).

The Water Literacies Project is an example of an eco-social-justice-driven, transdisciplinary STEM program, developed in collaboration with academic researchers and enacted by primary teachers. The transdisciplinary units of work developed were intended to support primary teachers to be more explicit about discipline-based knowledge in science, mathematics, and English, while engaging students in sustainability-oriented learning that focused on possible/preferable futures.

The Water Literacies Project also incorporated an action research approach (see Grundy, 1994; Kemmis, 2008) with three phases over a year: 1) orientation and provocation (one term); 2) enactment (two terms); and 3) evaluation (one term). Practitioners were central to these investigations and transformations of educational practices. Teachers were supported to critically examine their pedagogical practices as well as their own and their co-learners' development. Data were elicited through recorded interviews with teachers, analysis of student work samples, and documentation of teachers' planning, for example units of work and photographs of learning experiences. Links between the eight eco-social justice education principles, teachers' pedagogical practices, and students are described below.

The first principle incorporates identifying and challenging current world views and assumptions that direct thoughts and behaviors. This is captured by the notion that "we seldom consider ourselves as [a] species among species" (Berry, 1988, p. 21). In the Water Literacies Project this process included relearning the values central to living well with sufficient resources and valuing the limited resource of fresh water. We believe that world views can be effectively challenged if educators share complex open-ended activities that stress authentic links to their lived experiences with their learners. Equally important is providing opportunities for exploring and experiencing the kind of connectedness that reflects life outside of school. We also advocate employing pedagogies that invite all involved to *engage collaboratively* in working locally toward creating socially and ecologically just and sustainable communities.

This project on freshwater environs also adopted a transdisciplinary approach that went beyond subject-specific areas to include, art, literature, poetry, and spiritual experiences, as well as the "usual" bio-physical sciences, humanities, and social sciences (see Arvay, 2018; Balsiger, 2015; Haggerty, Paige & O'Keeffe, 2023). That is, we adopted an integral approach (Wilber, 2006), inclusive of all aspects of knowing, feeling, and doing (cognitive, affective, spiritual, and intentional) to address, in our case, the issue of sustainability and ecojustice with a particular focus on fresh water.

The participating teachers introduced ideas from a range of disciplinary concepts, including trophic feeding levels in ecosystems, soil types, composition, and soil erosion (earth science). They also addressed aquatic macroinvertebrates, salinity, pH and other aspects of water quality (bio-physical sciences). Further considerations included changing appreciations of "place" (history), local species, and mass of sandbags (mathematics). The teachers and their co-learners talked about real projects and problems in their local places. They also arranged meetings with several people such as council workers, Natural Resources Management Board (now Green Adelaide) educators, fishers, farmers, environmental activists, and passionate citizens. Collectively, all contributed to the deep curriculum experienced by the students and were critical to the success of the learning that took place.

The second principle involves encouraging the development of a community of learners with a common disposition to value with compassion natural systems and human systems (the commons) (Awbrey et al., 2006). In our project this meant enhancing the connection to nature of all co-learners and promoting "knowing our place" and where, in this case, ten-year-old children "fit" as Earth citizens. We developed participants' appreciation of species and their interconnections in ecosystems through regular visits to the local wetlands.

Co-learning community members developed confidence as citizen scientists capable of responding to threats to their local wetlands. This involved collecting a wide range of knowledge about the biodiversity of the wetlands and issues associated with stormwater pollution. Their research included weekly monitoring of water quality, through macroinvertebrate assessment, recording physical parameters such as pH, and bird species using the wetlands. They responsibly disposed of rubbish collected in their monitoring of litter in and around the wetlands and developed understandings and viewpoints about how they could be involved in significantly reducing the amount of pollution from litter and other sources.

Letters written by the students showed their considerable skills as communicators, able to use properly researched information to protect their "place." They were also able to articulate how its loss would affect them as they struggled to imagine their community without a healthy wetland. What we describe above is, hopefully, the early stages of the development of vibrant activism for eco-social equity, expressed in collaborations that foster a better, fairer Earth society in their particular place and the wider world (Team Ecohustler, 2011).

Employing the third principle necessitated assisting our co-learners to work collaboratively to enhance an eco-socially just and sustainable community of people and other living things (Bache, 2008). This meant working in groups while accessing community and local experts as well as spending time in their special places in the wetland—sometimes together, sometimes alone (Laszlo & Dennis, 2013). One school invited a local conservationist, known colloquially as the "carp lady," to present ways of making productive use of carp when they were caught. Possibilities included as a food, as a fertilizer, and as carp leather, which could be produced in the classroom. Congruent with this third principle, several sessions were led by project officers from a local Natural Resources Management Board education team. These skilled educators visited the classes regularly to assist co-learners in the identification of aquatic macroinvertebrates, water quality testing, monitoring bird species, and rubbish collection.

In experiencing the fourth principle in action, the co-learner teams acted as eco-social justice role models in their personal and educational communities. The enacted water literacy curriculum was about more than the cognitive and, hence, more than "knowing about." It was transdisciplinary and used different lenses to explore an issue in depth. Another powerful aspect of this project was the work co-learner teams did in the general community. This is exemplified by the letters they wrote to school leaders, and to politicians inviting them to visit their classrooms. Further examples include the establishment of a system of peer leaders and engagement with local government. The teams also set up displays in local main streets and shopping centers, and expos in the school hall/classrooms. In doing so they operated within the inter-subjective domain and active cognitive, affective, social, and cultural elements. With the aim of making a difference, students learnt about their local environments and engaged with their ecological and social values. These experiences reflect the exterior-objective as well as the interior-subjective domains, evinced by their attachment to their wetland. Most importantly, they shared their learning with the community at an expo, which provides evidence of "being activists."

Teachers as leaders in the co-learner teams also acted in the cultural domain in their activism within their professional educational communities. For example, teacher participants, in discussions with their peers, not only made specific reference to how much they had learnt about new pedagogical approaches to art and other subject areas, but also how to use this approach to structure student learning when teaching a transdisciplinary unit of work (Kemmis, 2008; Wilber, 2000).

The fifth principle aims to assist learners to develop ways of thinking, feeling, and acting with eco-social wisdom in places that we inhabit. This principle also incorporates recognizing and relating to a wisdom that necessarily includes ecological systems thinking, and scientific knowledge, skills, and practices. Perhaps the most significant outcome of the Water Literacy Project was the enhanced connection of children to an aspect of their "place," the wetlands (Paige, Haggerty & Comber, 2022). This was evidenced in their visiting it on weekends, sometimes taking parents or grandparents. The children seemed never to tire of weekly walks or bus rides to the wetlands and expressed a real sense of ownership. Involving a significantly different set of expertise, that of the artist referred to above, enabled the classes to further explore their "place" as a creative space, as well as recording observations through drawing and models.

The sixth principle addresses developing a respect for long-term rather than short-term thinking through historical and futures studies (Bateson, 2002; Hicks, 2002; Lloyd & Wallace, 2004; Paige et al., 2018; Slaughter, 2012). This approach was pursued primarily through futures scenario writing. Specifically, co-learners imagined what they thought the wetlands could look like in 30 years' time, based on their new appreciation and attachment to it. Gidley (2017, p. 206) argues that "we need to imbue our futures thinking with human agency and our concepts of time with urgency, because we are living in a planetary emergency."

Student co-learners were encouraged to write and draw what they envisaged and were supported by teacher co-learners who openly valued the development of children's futures thinking and enactment. As Bateson (2002, p. 13) points out, "if the world be connected … thinking in terms of stories must be shared by all minds." Students could write as themselves, a fictitious person, or as an animal that lived in the wetlands. Stories ranged in their contexts, with some projecting themselves as educators, scientists, or aged versions of themselves, while others used animals to tell their stories of new, improved wetlands.

The teachers believed that their co-learners' interest in the project, as well as their futures thinking and writing, was strongly influenced by weekly visits to the wetlands and the creation of a sense of belonging to place. They listened to children's visions and supported them in taking action to get there. Students created narratives that captured creative and visionary futures of possibilities for the wetlands. Children were able to discuss the wetland's importance, including what its loss could mean to themselves and the community. Our observations led us to concur with the teachers' view that connection to their wetland made it possible for children to imagine a positive future.

In their futures writing the children identified many of the problems involved in sustainably maintaining and improving their local wetland, their place. They developed a working understanding of wetland ecosystems and the need to value all the species that live there including humans. This is evidence of them adopting an ecojustice mindset (Figueres & Rivett-Carnac, 2020; Gidley, 2017). Our analysis suggests that the issue children felt most strongly about was keeping the wetlands healthy and vibrant with abundant flora and fauna for future generations. Importantly they did not want the wetlands turned into a drain or a housing estate.

The seventh principle requires co-learners to be provided with opportunities to reflect critically on what they have learnt, the impact this learning has had on their perspectives, and how this could influence future behavior (Cochran-Smith, 2004). In our project it involved children being enabled to establish a peer group committee and valuing student voice by encouraging them to take issues to the school leadership team. In another development, one of the schools was offered a plant voucher to create natural gardens and to research what to plant to attract butterflies. They also volunteered to host the next Natural Resources Management Education student voice summit and have continued to make presentations on their sustainability work to staff, parents, and the wider community. Another group presented a workshop at the Adelaide Botanic Gardens during World Environment Day. Critical reflection occurred when children were:

- journaling about their experiences to identify ones that helped them to see themselves, others, and the rest of the Earth through "new eyes"
- discussing something they wanted to do that they had not thought of before
- telling others what they had done that was new for them, why they did it, and what they hoped their actions would achieve
- presenting their learning at expos, and on the video made by Natural Resources Management Education.

In addressing the eighth principle, educators implemented culturally responsive pedagogies (Castagno & Brayboy, 2008; Ladson-Billings, 1995). In this project, co-learners listened to Aboriginal Elders and explored how natural materials such as reeds were used to make fish traps (see Paige et al., 2016, 2019) in the wetlands under study. In order that Aboriginal communities and Elders were able to share their knowledge and narratives of local histories and environments on their own terms, a long-term view of building relationships and trust with communities needed to be taken. Providing co-learners with access to a wide range of Aboriginal texts and authors (see Abdulla, 2014; Morgan & Kwaymullina, 2016; Pascoe, 2019) proved to be a successful strategy. This did not simply mean finding a Dreaming story about a place or an animal in order that the cross-curriculum priority of Aboriginal and Torres Strait Islander histories and perspectives would be addressed. Rather, it meant introducing Aboriginal authors and voices through a wide range of texts, including poetry, fiction, personal accounts, non-fiction texts, and contemporary narratives. Also available were historical narratives that are often whitewashed from official curriculum and knowledge. Collectively these showcased Aboriginal perspectives of hope, humor, and place-based meaning and identity making. On occasions when co-learning leaders lacked confidence or needed help in locating community-based resources, Aboriginal school-based support staff, local government staff, and local Aboriginal organizations, including land councils, provided support in working with local Aboriginal communities, including guidance in developing respectful relationships (Paige & Lloyd, 2023).

On Reflection: Water Literacy Case Study

In summary, the eight eco-social justice principles were evident in the extended unit of transdisciplinary work enacted in all three sites and their communities. Co-learners' enthusiastic involvement in the work reported here suggested to us that the transdisciplinary pedagogy we employed was a productive and in-depth way to learn. Our own reflections identified four key findings:

- Participants in the project were involved in *real* environmental learning in their local natural environments. For those called "co-learners" in the above discussion—often separately designated "teachers" and "learners/students" as though teachers do not learn and students do not teach—the *problem* involved them in becoming more informed and capable agents within their *place*. As citizens of the wider community, they sought to maintain and improve the state of their wetland. As members of the school community, they identified how to maintain and improve the workings of the educational ecosystem in class and beyond.
- All participants—intended and unintended—were co-learners. Members of the local community and researchers developed understandings, motivations, and capabilities in circumstances where interactions were "real."
- Place-based inquiry "connected" or "wired-up" co-learner participants, their schools and local communities, including Aboriginal, settlers, and "out-of-townies" with novel interests and skills. All were woven a little more beautifully together in the process of enjoying histories and continuing narratives of place. What potent educational opportunities these are.
- The action research model we used demanded extended time for co-learners in their various, but connected, places. There were multiple opportunities for deep learning through connection to and caring for their place. Teacher participants were able to indulge themselves and their inquisitive minds in deep experiences, thinking, connecting, acting, learning, and sharing. Teachers and researchers experienced (as well as observed, recorded, analyzed, and shared) the impact of their professional work through action research.

Recommendations for Moving Forward

Five themes have emerged as recommendations for advancing eco-socially just education. These themes are elephant recognition and management; ecological knowing and acting; humans as part of nature; future studies; and co-learner change through action research.

- *Elephant recognition and management:* Common-sense notions suggest that all is well and that everyone and everything will be OK if humans just proceed with getting ahead and being entertained. We believe, however, that it is abundantly clear that this is not the case. Humans are "the elephant in the room." More importantly, there is much that communities of co-learners can do to realize more eco-socially responsible and enjoyable lives, within current curriculum prescriptions.

- *Ecological knowing and acting:* Educators who wish to make useful contributions to future situations that are more sustainable than our present ones have a clear responsibility to make explicit to themselves, and all those in the formal education and community development spheres in which they have influence, the need to bring about eco-socially useful changes. Our approaches have been primarily local, in "our places," and lean toward landscapes of larger dimensions where citizens seek to be effective actors for better worlds. We believe that committed educators who choose to employ similar pedagogical strategies will discover that they are capable of shifting the axes of present eco-social inequities.
- *Humans as part of nature:* We hope that our contribution will remind all readers, in mutually respectful and professional ways, that we are but one species among several other millions. Unfortunately, ours is the species which is, in some ways, "the elephant in the room-that-is-Earth." There is much on Earth to love and hence a need to work cooperatively toward reducing the impact of our footprint, so that it might become less ego-centered, and more whole-Earth-community nurturing. On our better, more eco-socially attuned days, humans can be capable nurturers. We think application of Earth-centered eco-social justice approaches to education, like those we have discussed, can address this need.
- *Futures studies:* The purpose and value of futures scenario writing resides in its explicit and systematic enquiry, and intention to be agents in "making the best of" what we can make. Futurists clarify goals and values. They also analyze and interpret the recent past and present as well as exploring projections of current trends. This requires them to carry out systematic studies of possible, probable, and preferable futures. In formulating plans they seek out insights from communities about what constitutes desirable futures and the best ways to create these. A challenge for educators is to value and employ futures scenarios construction as an integral aspect of their pedagogy. It is from such a position that it becomes possible for them and their co-learners to learn the wisdom and enjoyment of deeply valuing the place that they are an integral part of, including its ecosystems.
- *Co-learner development through action research:* Teachers' roles in education continue to evolve. As the world changes, so teachers and their co-learners need to develop ways of interacting with the Earth's environments that are

more likely to affect positive eco-social changes. We would encourage teacher-researchers committed to tackling complex ecological, social, and ethical questions in relation to local issues, like those discussed in the Water Literacies action research project, to adopt approaches similar to ours.

We believe that an eco-social justice–oriented world view is appropriate. Specifically, this is one that pursues an integration of value spheres by promoting an informed awareness of the natural world (of which humans are a part) through studying science/ecology. Equally important is the acquisition of collective (cultural) values that place humans within ecosystems. Finally, we advocate the provision of opportunities for humans to appreciate the importance of always thinking and acting within the cognitive, affective, and intentional domains (Martusewicz et al., 2015). Our grandchildren, theirs and theirs, we think, expect no less of us. We optimistically envisage interconnected communities of all humans, together with all our biodiversity companions, living with, not on, each other. We envisage an Earth on which our intentional compass points unfailingly toward compassion between and within generations, and between humans and other species. We consider that the eight principles we set out here provide muscular support for such a project.

Bibliography

Abdulla, I. (2014). *As I grew older*. Working Title Press Australia.

Arvay, C. (2018). *The biophilia effect: A scientific and spiritual exploration of the healing bond between humans and nature*. Sounds True.

Awbrey S., *Dana*, D., *Miller*, V., Robinson, P., Ryan, M., & Scott, D. (Eds.). (2006). *Integrative learning and action: A call to wholeness*. Peter Lang.

Bache, C. (2008). *The living classroom: Teaching and collective consciousness*. State University of New York Press.

Balsiger, J. (2015). Transdisciplinarity in the classroom? Simulating the co-production of sustainability knowledge. *Futures*, *65*, 185–94.

Bateson, G. (2002). *Mind and nature: A necessary unity*. Hampton Press.

Berry, T. (1988). *The dream of the Earth*. Sierra Club Books.

Bowers, C. A. (2017). Educational reforms for survival. *Tikkun*, *32*(4), 25–32.

Castagno, A., & Brayboy, B. (2008). Culturally responsive schooling for Indigenous youth: A review of the literature. *Review of Educational Research*, *78*, 941–93.

Cochran-Smith, M. (2004). Defining the outcomes of teacher education: What's social justice got to do with it? *Asia-Pacific Journal of Teacher Education*, *32*(3), 193–212.

Ehrlich, P. R., Kareiva, P. M., & Daily, G. C., (2012). Securing natural capital and expanding equity to rescale civilization. *Nature, 486*, 68–73.
Esbjörn-Hargens, S., & Zimmerman, M. (2009). *Integral ecology: Uniting multiple perspectives on the natural world*. Integral Books.
Ferreira, J., Ryan, L., & Davies, J. (2015). Developing knowledge and leadership in preservice teacher education systems. *Australian Journal of Environmental Education, 31*(2), 194–207.
Figueres, C., & Rivett-Carnac, T. (2020). *The future we choose: Surviving the climate crisis*. Manilla Press.
Gidley, J. M. (2017). Imbuing futures and time with agency and urgency: Reframing concepts for a planetary emergency. *World Futures Review, 9*(4), 201–07.
Grundy, S. (1994). Action research at the school level: Possibilities and problems. *Educational Action Research, 2*(1), 23–37.
Haggerty, B., Paige, K., *&* O'Keeffe, L. *(2023)*. A transdisciplinary approach to teaching citizen science in a primary classroom. Teaching Science: *Australian Journal of Association of Science Teachers Vol 2, p. 11–20.*
Hicks, D. (2002). *Lessons for the future: The missing dimension in education*. Routledge.
Hodson, D. (2003). Time for action: Science education for an alternative future. *International Journal of Science Education, 25*(6), 645–70.
Hunter, A., & Hewson, J. (2020). Our survival as a species requires urgent action. https://reporter.anu.edu.au/all-stories/our-survival-as-a-species-requires-urgent-action Australian National University.
Kemmis, S. (2008). Critical theory and participatory action research. In P. Reason & H. Bradbury (Eds.), *The SAGE handbook of action research: Participative inquiry and practice* (pp. 121–38). Sage.
Klein, N. (2014). *This changes everything*. Penguin.
Kolbert, E. (2014). *The sixth extinction: An unnatural history*. Bloomsbury.
Kopnina, H. (2017). Future scenarios for sustainability education: The future we want? In P. Blaze Corcoran, J. Weakland, & A. E. Wals (Eds.), *Envisioning futures for environmental and sustainability education* (pp. 129–39). Wageningen Academic.
Ladson-Billings, G. (1995). Toward a theory of culturally relevant pedagogy. *American Educational Research Journal, 32*(3), 465–91.
Laszlo, E., & Dennis, K. L. (2013). *Dawn of the Akashic age: New consciousness, quantum resonance, and the future of the world*. Inner Traditions.
Lloyd, D., & Deans, J. A. (2017). Building on the buzz: Community learning about and valuing native Australian bees. *International Journal of Interdisciplinary Environmental Studies, 12*(1), 1–33.
Lloyd, D., & Paige, K. (2022). Learning science locally: Community gardens and our future. *Frontiers in Education*, 7, 1–13.

Lloyd, D., & Wallace, J. (2004). Imaging the future of science education: The case for making futures studies explicit in student learning. *Studies in Science Education*, *40*, 139–78.

Martusewicz, R., Edmundson, J., & Lupinacci, J. (2015). *Eco justice education: Towards diverse, democratic, and sustainable communities* (2nd ed.). Routledge.

Morgan, S., & Kwaymullina, A. (2016) *Dream little one, dream*. Penguin Books Australia.

Paige, K., Caldwell, D., Elliott, K., O'Keeffe, L., Osborne., S, Roetman, P., Lloyd, D., Comber, B., & Gosnell, S. (2018). *Fresh water literacies: Transdisciplinary learning for place and eco justice. Final report*. University of South Australia.

Paige, K., Haggerty, B., Comber, B. (2022). Water Literacies: Co-researching, Learning, and Acting for the Wetlands. In: Häggström, M., Schmidt, C. (eds) *Relational and Critical Perspectives on Education for Sustainable Development. Sustainable Development Goals Series*. pp 53–66 Springer.

Paige, K., & Lloyd, D. (2023). Eco-justice and transdisciplinary approaches to education in the era of the Anthropocene: Advances towards teaching and learning in a diverse world. In L.-I. Rigney (Ed.), *Global perspectives and new challenges in culturally responsive pedagogies: Superdiversity and teaching practice* (pp. 20–36). Routledge.

Paige, K., Lloyd, D., & Smith, R. (2016). Paths to "knowing places" and ecojustice: Three teacher educators' experiences. *Australian Journal of Environmental Education*, *32*(3), 260–87.

Paige, K., Lloyd, D., & Smith, R. (2019). *Intergenerational education for adolescents toward liveable futures*. Cambridge Scholars Publishing.

Pascoe, B. (2019). *Young dark emu: A truer history*. Magabala Books.

Rockstrom, J., Xuemei, B., & de Vries, B. (2018). Global sustainability: The challenge ahead. *Global Sustainability*, *1*(6), 1–3.

Settelmaier, E., & Taylor, P. C. (2001). *Ken Wilber's integral philosophy and educational research: Fleshing out the seventh moment (and beyond?)*. Australian Association for Research in Education.

Singer, P. (2010). All animals are equal. In D. R. Keller (Ed.), *Environmental ethics: The big questions* (pp. 169–75). Wiley-Blackwell.

Singer, P. (2016). *Ethics in the real world: 87 brief essays on the things that matter.* Text Publishing Company.

Slaughter, R. A. (1996). *The knowledge base of futures studies*. DDM Media Group.

Slaughter, R. A. (2012). Welcome to the Anthropocene. *Futures*, *44*, 119–26.

Suzuki, D., & McConnell, A. (1997). *The sacred balance: Rediscovering our place in nature*. Allen & Unwin.

Team Ecohustler (2011, June 18). From Ego to Eco a New Sense of Self. *Ecohustler*. https://ecohustler.com/article/from-ego-to-eco-a-new-sense-of-self
Wilber, K. (2000). *Integral psychology: Consciousness, spirit, psychology, therapy*. Shambhala.
Wilber, K. (2006). *Integral spirituality*. Integral Books.

16 Unsettling Settler Colonialism in Teacher Education

Jenni Carter

Introduction

This chapter draws on the experience of a class of final year initial teacher education students studying English curriculum as a major area of their practice. It examines how teacher educators furthered student teachers' understanding of settler colonialism through a critical visual analysis of the picture book *The rabbits* (Marsden & Tan, 1998). Specifically, the chapter explores the pedagogical process employed to deepen students' understanding of the colonizing of Australia, and as such the political context of the culture and histories of Aboriginal and Torres Strait Islander Peoples. This is significant in the Australian Curriculum: English, where it is stated that it is "through the study of English that individuals gain increasing control over language to analyse, understand, communicate and build relationships with others and with the world around them" (ACARA, 2024b).

The final year curriculum major courses shared a focus on culturally responsive approaches to curriculum and pedagogy, with an interest in whether initial teacher educators feel competent and confident in their teaching of Aboriginal and Torres Strait Islander histories and cultures (O'Keeffe et al., 2019). This interest arose from the demand to prioritize Aboriginal and Torres Strait Islander content in the eight learning areas of the Australian Curriculum and as a cross-curriculum priority (ACARA, 2024a). The English curriculum states that "The Australian Curriculum: English also helps students to engage imaginatively and critically with literature to expand the scope of their experience" (ACARA, 2024c). Specific reference is made to the ways in which "Aboriginal and Torres Strait Islander Peoples have contributed to Australian society and to its contemporary literature and its literary heritage through their distinctive ways of representing and communicating knowledge, traditions and experience" (ACARA, 2024c). Pre-service teachers had indicated in the course in the previous year that they did not feel they had the depth of understanding to be able to teach the content required.

The Australian Institute for Teaching and School Leadership introduced professional standards for teachers in 2011 and initial teacher education providers must be able to demonstrate how the graduate teacher level is met as a condition of the accreditation of their programs and courses. These standards include demonstrating knowledge, understanding, and respect for Aboriginal and Torres Strait Islander histories, stories, and culture, and promoting reconciliation (AITSL, 2011).

Moodie and Patrick (2017) warn that there is a danger that standards about Aboriginal and Torres Strait Islander cultures, histories, and reconciliation "are interpreted in ways that perpetuate an essentialised and ahistorical understanding of Indigenous peoples and perspectives" (p. 439). Further, they argue that engaging with concepts and practices of reconciliation without a "sociological approach that recognised the ongoing impact of colonialism" can limit the how these issues are attended to for both Indigenous and non-Indigenous students (p. 440). Rather, they suggest that the content for the standards be examined within an anticolonial framework, where the concept of settler grammars provides a lens through which to disrupt myths "of Indigenous homogeneity and subordinate positions of Othered knowledge" and to contribute to the political project of reconciliation (p. 440). The intention is to understand colonial discourses in Indigenous histories and education and to investigate how these continue to be shaped and affirmed through policies and practices.

Settler Colonialism

Settler colonialism describes the ongoing project of colonialism, where settlers come to stay, and establish a new social, cultural, and political order that is informed by what the settlers have left behind, erasing and forgetting the already established ways of living of the Indigenous inhabitants. As described by Veracini:

> Of course, while the colonies settlers build for themselves are either independent or politically subordinate to the colonising metropole, a capacity to establish a new society that replicates the original one (without its perceived shortcoming), is inevitably premised on the possibility of controlling and dominating indigenous peoples. (2013, p. 314)

The dismissal of Indigenous ways of knowing and living as inferior is a feature of settler colonialism (Andreotti, 2011; Moodie & Patrick, 2017). In Australia, the formal schooling system is inherited from British schooling. This continues to be seen in the architecture of schools, the privileging of Western Eurocentric knowledges in the content of the curriculum, approaches to pedagogy, and the organization of the school's management and school day. Aboriginal and Torres Strait Islander knowledges have been presented as a separate topic for study or as events and customs to learn facts about, rather than being a focus that values engagement with multiple epistemologies and ontologies.

Steinman (2020) argues that settler colonialism should not be seen as a historical event, but a structure that provides an underlying logic that continues the domination of settler interests, such that they are portrayed as normative and superior. Furthermore, policies and public discourses about Indigenous peoples continue to entrench systemic and institutional racism. There is a concomitant attempt to render invisible the violences that are deeply embedded within social and cultural norms and practices about the relationship between Indigenous peoples and settlers. Moodie and Patrick (2017) and Andreotti (2011) suggest a way forward is for educators to imagine knowledge and learning beyond the paradigms of colonialism, demanding an understanding of the coloniality of power, and its ongoing constitution of colonial epistemologies. Further, educators should examine the mechanisms that continue to secure colonialism, including those that are deeply embedded in the schooling system.

In research conducted with educators, Moodie and Patrick (2017) found that, when educators do not feel prepared or proficient in their knowledge or the politics of Aboriginal cultures and histories, or the context and issues surrounding reconciliation, they are reluctant to teach Aboriginal content. A further issue for educators is a view that perhaps Indigenous education should be best left to Indigenous scholars. O'Keeffe et al. acknowledge this tension, stating:

> we believe that there is an imperative to ensure the next generation of teachers is well prepared to teach both Indigenous and non-Indigenous students effectively as well as being confident to incorporate Indigenous knowledges and ways of knowing across learning areas. (2019, p. 157)

Providing a similar viewpoint, Hogarth (2022), argues that there is an urgency for non-Indigenous Initial teacher education providers to begin critical conversations that will inform their role in preparing pre-service teachers. While acknowledging the issue of settlers teaching about settlers is complicated and potentially problematic in terms of the possibility of maintaining colonial positions, Steinman (2020) argues that non-Indigenous educators must unsettle settler colonialism "where they are." It follows that all educators must be accountable for unsettling the mechanisms and violences of settler colonialism in their own context. Further, this should be done through establishing and maintaining respectful alliances of Indigenous and settler peoples in order to bolster meaningful relationships and facilitate justice and healing. The notion of alliances is significant here as teacher educators can work with Aboriginal scholars, teachers, and community members, rather than feeling that as non-Indigenous educators they should be experts and, if they are not, they should do nothing.

The following challenges for educators have been identified by Andreotti (2011). Educators should consider how to "engage with different epistemologies ethically, responsibly and critically without homogenising, essentialising or romanticising them" (p. 394). Such an engagement demands "interrupt[ing] one's own assumptions in order to engage with other epistemologies on their own terms" (p. 394). Importantly such approaches demand "a pedagogical emphasis on 'dissensus'…to [be able to] hold paradoxes and not be overwhelmed by complexity, ambiguity, conflict, uncertainty and difference" (p. 395). These challenges center on building positive and respectful approaches to curriculum and pedagogy.

The Pedagogical Process

Having completed courses in previous years that included knowledges about Aboriginal histories and cultures, feedback from initial teacher education students indicated an uncertainty about the legitimacy and limits of their own knowledges and understandings. This became visible as the students participated in a visit to the Art Gallery of South Australia. With a focus on visual storytelling and text analysis, they were asked to examine a range of artworks that depicted encounters between colonial settlers and Aboriginal people in the 1800s. One of the paintings selected by students depicted a settler's farmhouse, and Aboriginal people and settler families standing and talking together outside the front door, while the second painting was of colonial soldiers watching a corroboree from the shadows of surrounding trees. The dominant interpretation by the students was that these demonstrated "harmony," or an interest in getting to know another culture. They did not identify the political context of imperialism in these works, and the social and political structures embedded within the portrayal of relationships. A notion of reconciliation was expressed as accepting others' points of view or ways of life.

The initial teacher education students in this course discussed the range of experiences they had in learning about Indigenous issues, histories, cultures, and knowledges. Some shared that they had seen the movie *Rabbit-proof fence* every year in their secondary schooling. Discussion about the film focused on the historical events, where there was a consideration of the ethical issues involved in taking the children; however, there was less understanding of how this was aligned with ongoing political processes to dehumanize Aboriginal people. Others told of learning about Dreaming stories as curious texts, ignoring the significance of these in an oral culture in terms of sharing knowledges and culture. Further points involved looking at Aboriginal art as dot paintings to be copied in a classroom art lesson, rather than their importance in sharing local knowledges and culture.

Country is a site of identity for Aboriginal Australians. However, with a limited understanding of the significance of Country as a spiritual, cultural, and pedagogical location, opportunities to engage with Aboriginal ways of knowing and being may not be developed. Limited understandings provided most students with an awareness of Aboriginal histories and cultures; however, their main point of reference, particularly in regard to reconciliation, was their own beliefs. Absent from their dialogue was a deeper understanding of the history of colonialism and the mechanisms this produced by positioning the ways of knowing and living of Aboriginal people in a political context.

As a pedagogical strategy to more deeply engage with settler colonialism as a lens to consider Indigenous issues, the picture book *The rabbits* was selected for a text study. Specific pedagogical practices included drawing on a *visual critical literacy approach*, and its features as a literary text. Critical literacy is a way of reading "not just to grasp the text's meaning but to also think more deeply about the ideas and values being put forward by the authors" (Papen, 2020, p. 3). Visual critical literacy includes how visual tools, such as color or gaze, are included in a critical interrogation of a text. Students had been introduced to visual analysis in previous courses, analyzing visual grammar (Callow, 2017; Kress & van Leeuwen, 2005) to develop their knowledge of the ways in which semiotic choices made through the visual elements of the texts work to create meaning. In picture books, illustrators' stories are often regarded as secondary. In the instance of *The rabbits*, it is the artwork that provided opportunities for a depth of critique, where reading only the text would diminish the available meanings in the book (Unsworth & Wheeler, 2002).

The development of a visual metalanguage provides students with new repertoires for critical literacy, including a concern for the ways in which power relations are both represented and exercised through different forms of text and image. (Luke, 2000; Luke & Freebody, 1999). Following a functional semiotic approach to visual analysis, as outlined by Callow (2013), the ideational, interpersonal, and textual purposes and functions of the text are examined. The ideational function is concerned with what is happening in the text and who or what is involved. Analysis attends to the *action* qualities of the text, how line and shape represent people, objects, events, and places. The interactional function is concerned with the ways in which *interaction* is made within the image, examining gaze, shot distance, angles, and color. The textual function examines the *design and layout* of the image with a focus on salience, reading paths, placement, layout, and framing (Callow, 2013). Examining how these three dimensions work together to produce meaning provided a language with which to explain the features of the text and how the story is told. Students further considered the literary elements referred to in the Australian Curriculum: English, again a feature of their studies in previous courses. These provided conceptual resources to consider the social, cultural, and political purposes and context of the text, as well as the different repertoires readers bring to responding to a text (McDonald, 2013).

The Book: The rabbits

The rabbits, with written text by John Marsden and visual text by Shaun Tan (1998), is an allegory of the colonization of Australia. It was selected as the Children's Book Council of Australia's Picture Book of the Year in 1999. Marsden, an established Australian author for children and young people, is well known for inviting a different perspective on the relational dimension of growing up, the advent of war, and the experiences of refugees. *The rabbits* was chosen as a text for study to provide an opportunity to open up students' understandings of the concepts and practices of settler colonialism. The book examines the history and relationships between British settler colonialism and Australian Aboriginal Peoples and country.

In the book, the central characters are "rabbits," invaders of a country already inhabited by "numbats." These choices by Marsden and Tan are significant. Numbats are Australian native animals, while rabbits are an introduced species that have overrun the non-urban environment. The rabbits are initially depicted in colonial clothing, in tweed suits, and then, as the country becomes more industrialized, in the bureaucratic black and white indicative of the British public service. The numbats are initially portrayed as observers, then participants in moves to retain their place, and then as the book progresses they become harder to detect, or are invisible in the images.

Tan provides vivid illustrations, described by Unsworth and Wheeler (2002, p. 71) "as surreal, provoking uncertainty and unsettling the reader." They suggest his use of strong, vivid colors is central to establishing the relationship with the reader. Each of the double-page images can be read in many different ways. Layers of images constitute different perspectives, while highlighting the plight of the numbats as the rabbits move to take over and settle on the lands. They establish dominant new ways of living together, traveling, farming, and agriculture, establishing industry, spreading disease, and bringing about environmental degradation.

The book begins with an image recognizable as belonging to an Australian landscape. Over a double page, the right page is dominated by a vivid blue sky, the center features a cave, with several large snakes curled up on the bottom, colored in the vivid reds of the outback sand, while on the left, in darkness, are spiral snail-like shapes, appearing as rock art on the wall of the cave. The accompanying text, located on the wall of the cave, reads "The Rabbits came many Grandparents ago." The book proceeds as a historical recount describing the events that occurred in the meetings of the numbats and rabbits, from the perspective of the numbats, located in rich and detailed visual depictions of the changes to the landscape. It tells that there were only a few rabbits initially, but then more came over the water in large ships. The rabbits made their own kind of houses, while their talk could not be understood by the numbats, who watched from the trees where they lived. The rabbits brought with them new food and other animals, and they spread across the country, not to be stopped by mountains, deserts, or rivers. While more and more came, there were fights, but nothing could stop the rabbits; there were too many and the numbats lost the fights. The rabbits ate the grass, chopped down trees, scared away friends, and stole the numbats' children. Eventually there were millions of them, everywhere you looked. Meanwhile the land became bare and brown, with the wind blowing over empty plains (Marsden & Tan, 1998).

The Pedagogical Experiences

Before engaging with the picture book, students were asked to read Moodie and Patrick's "Settler grammars and the Australian Professional Standards for Teachers" (2017). Each student selected two passages to share, one relating to how they felt about meeting the professional standards and their own knowledge, and one that identified the implications for classroom practice. The most commonly selected passages related to a lack of confidence in teaching Aboriginal and Torres Strait Islander content, expressing concerns about their own understandings and knowledges, and identifying with the following statement:

> Particularly notable were expressions of feelings of ineptitude or ignorance, or discussion of the marginal knowledge of Indigenous issues that teacher candidates possess when they arrive at university. These issues tended to override substantive issues of concern to Indigenous people, such as sovereignty and epistemological equality. (Moodie & Patrick, 2017, p. 442)

Commonly, the responses indicated political awareness of issues of racism and not wanting to offend Indigenous students, parents, and community members by saying something that could be considered offensive or was incorrect. Some responses indicated assumptions about the homogeneity of Aboriginal culture, and ideas of assimilation that dominate conservative public discourses. At the same time, students expressed a strong sense of wanting to teach Indigenous knowledges and issues well with a commitment to social justice and, as they described it at the time, being fair.

In *The rabbits*, it is the visual text that reveals the deep meanings of the text, more so than the written narrative. The deeply metaphorically images by Tan are both aesthetically compelling and, upon close examination through the lens of settler colonialism, highly emotive for the students. Students were asked to choose an image from the book to "read closely" through an analysis of visual grammar and then to consider and discuss the story being told.

One of the images selected by many students is that depicting the Stolen Generations, where young Aboriginal children who were considered to be of mixed race were taken from their families into state care. Across a double page, the image depicts baby numbats, in white box-shaped kites, tethered together with strings. The words provided by Marsden were "And Stole Our Children." The discussion considered the power of the colors selected by Tan, with the whiteness of the kites in stark contrast to the vast, blue sky, and the punctuation of the written text. The spatial layout of the images, where the sky was filled with baby numbats floating and disappearing into the horizon, provided an overwhelming image of the number of children that were subjected to removal.

The taking of children was a eugenics-inspired program, the violence of which was described in the *Bringing them home report* by the National Inquiry into the Separation of Aboriginal and Torres Strait Islander Children from Their Families in 1997. Much community and political debate followed as to the responsibility of current generations when in 2008 then Prime Minister Kevin Rudd, fulfilling an election commitment, issued a parliamentary apology to those who had suffered the violence of these government policies. The students in our course would have been in primary school at this time, and hence this was seen as an event in history, rather than a focus of divisive political debate, but also a moment of healing in the politics of reconciliation. Our students said their understandings of the Stolen Generations were informed by viewings of the movie *Rabbit-proof fence* in their secondary schooling. As reported above, repeated viewings of this movie often provided the major content of their Australian or Aboriginal studies units.

The movie depicts the experiences of three young Aboriginal girls who were taken from their families in the early 1930s as part of government policies to remove children who were said to have White blood, now referred to as the Stolen Generations. The girls returned to their families by following the rabbit-proof fence, built to protect pastoral and agricultural lands in Western Australia from the rabbit pests of the east.

The response of one student was particularly memorable. With tears in her eyes she stated, "Now I get it, all those children." Other students discussed how their emotional responses were engaging with their personal responsive repertoires, but that this was also insufficient. They were able to read with more meaning through knowing more about the experiences of settler colonialism and discussed how the policy assumptions and mechanisms depicted in the image were still at play in current times.

The other image that was selected by many students divides the double page horizontally. A narrow strip at the top depicts above the ground populated with multiple flags of the colonizers, and an image of a rabbit bureaucrat. The depiction of what is under the ground dominates the two pages, in dark black and brown, covered with the snail-like images of the grandparents from the first image in the book. In the bottom left-hand corner, there is a smaller image of what appears to be an underground cell, with numbats chained together with their backs to the wall, being guarded by a rabbit. The text reads: "We lost the fights." Discussion of this image focused on the burying of the ancestors, specifically moving them from visibility on the cave walls, as presented in the first image of the book, to underground to become buried. They were, hence, no longer contributing to the ways of knowing of those who lived upon the lands, now populated with the knowledges and ways of living of those flying the flags of the colonizers. This image points to the Eurocentric epistemological traditions of the school curriculum, and the oppression of those of Indigenous peoples.

Having a theoretical lens through which to "read" critically is important pedagogically. As O'Sullivan (2006) states, merely responding to a text in ways that identify with your own knowledge, beliefs, and values is a confirmation of something that is already in place. He argues that a genuine encounter, in this case a critical reading, should disrupt, where "our typical ways of being in the world are challenged, our systems of knowledge disrupted" (p. 1). Further, an encounter that ruptures "also contains a moment of affirmation, the affirmation of a new world, in fact a way of thinking and seeing this world differently" (p. 1).

The students acknowledged that their reading of *The rabbits* was disruptive. It challenged some of the ways they thought about Australia's history, the experiences of Indigenous peoples, and their own responsibilities as educators. As such it deepened their understanding of critical visual analysis, particularly the significance of the interpersonal meta-function and the capacities of multimodal text to invoke a multi-layered approach to meaning making.

As Marsden and Tan are not Aboriginal, their role could be considered as allies; hence pointing to the demand to engage with the narratives of Australia's colonization differently. Further elements of the course introduced the students to texts and resources written and produced by Aboriginal and Torres Strait Islander authors. Rather than being seen as interesting artifacts, these became important resources for learning about Indigenous epistemologies and pedagogies, the politics of race in Australian history, and how these can be embedded and valued across the curriculum, rather than stand-alone topics. Through engaging with

Aboriginal stories, songs, poems, and art, new ways of attending to histories, cultures, and reconciliation were explored. This was evident in student planning for classroom practice including ensuring that planning for teaching in schools is developed with the local community, drawing on language and stories of Country.

Conclusion

This chapter has examined how furthering an understanding of settler colonialism through a critical visual analysis of the picture book *The rabbits* provided a pedagogical process through which to deepen initial teacher education students' understanding of the colonizing of Australia. As a pedagogical process, it aimed to provide students with a lens through which to examine their own knowledges and practices in teaching Aboriginal cultures, histories, and reconciliation, as required by the Australian Curriculum: English and the Australian Professional Standards for Teachers. The students' analysis of the book *The rabbits* pointed to the significance of their own positions. Only through developing an understanding of the politics and mechanisms of colonialism does it become possible to establish the importance of teachers working with Aboriginal communities to develop approaches to their own teaching that are inclusive and respect multiple epistemologies and pedagogies.

Bibliography

Andreotti, V. (2011). (Towards) decoloniality and diversality in global citizenship education. *Globalisation, Societies and Education*, *9*(3–4), 381–97.

Australian Curriculum, Assessment and Reporting Authority (ACARA). (2024a). *Cross-curriculum priorities*. https://v9.australiancurriculum.edu.au/f-10-curriculum/f-10-curriculum-overview/cross-curriculum-priorities

Australian Curriculum, Assessment and Reporting Authority (ACARA). (2024b). *English, Foundation–Year 10 (Version 8.4)*. https://www.acara.edu.au/curriculum/foundation-year-10/learning-areas-subjects/english-foundation-to-year-12

Australian Curriculum, Assessment and Reporting Authority (ACARA). (2024c). *English: Rationale*. https://www.australiancurriculum.edu.au/f-10-curriculum/english/rationale/

Australian Institute for Teaching and School Leadership (AITSL). (2011). *Australian Professional Standards for Teachers*. http://www.aitsl.edu.au/australian-professional-standards-for-teachers

Callow, J. (2013). *The shape of text to come*. Primary English Teaching Association Australia.

Callow, J. (2017). “Nobody spoke like I did”: Picture books, critical literacy, and global contexts. *Reading Teacher, 2*, 231–37.
Hogarth M. (2022) An analysis of education academic’s attitudes and preconceptions about Indigenous Knowledges in initial teacher education. *Australian Journal of Indigenous Education. 51*(2), 1–18.
Kress, G., & Van Leeuwen, T. (2005). *Reading Images: The grammar of visual design*. Routledge.
Luke, A. (2000). Critical literacy in Australia: A matter of context and standpoint. *Journal of Adolescent & Adult Literacy, 43*(5), 448–61.
Luke, A., & Freebody, P. (1999). A map pf possible practices: Further notes of the four resources model. *Practically Primary, 4*, 5–8.
Marsden, J., & Tan, S. (1998). *The rabbits*. Lothian.
McDonald, L. (2013). *A literature companion for teachers*. Primary English Teaching Association Australia.
Moodie, N., & Patrick, R. (2017). Settler grammars and the Australian Professional Standards for Teachers. *Asia-Pacific Journal of Teacher Education, 45*(5), 439–54.
O’Keeffe, L., Paige, K., & Osbourne, S. (2019). Getting started: Exploring pre-service teachers’ confidence and knowledge of culturally responsive pedagogy in teaching mathematics and science. *Asia-Pacific Journal of Teacher Education, 47*(2), 152–75.
O’Sullivan, S. (2006). *Art encounters Deleuze and Guattari: Thought beyond representation*. Palgrave Macmillan.
Papen, U. (2020). Using picture books to develop critical visual literacy in primary schools: Challenges of a dialogic approach. *Literacy, 54*(1), 3–10.
Steinman, E. (2020). Unsettling as agency: Unsettling settler colonialism. *Settler Colonial Studies, 10*(4), 558–75.
Unsworth, L., & Wheeler, J. (2002). Re-valuing the role of images in reviewing picture books. *Literacy, 36*(2), 68–74.
Veracini, L. (2013). “Settler colonialism”: Career of a concept. *Journal of Imperial and Commonwealth History, 41*(2), 313–33.

17 Visualizing Curriculum: Arts, Film, and Critical Pedagogy

Dino Murtic

In wider socio-political settings, the struggle for socio-liberal egalitarianism is becoming an endangered concept. Its previous achievements and further promises are, on one hand, under assault from neoliberal rationalities, which in a search for financial profit have strengthened totalitarian capitalism and its consequent geo-political expansion. On the other hand, the cosmopolitan appeal of egalitarianism is damaged by irreparable fragmentation of the democratic left, which for a long time has been engaged in a maniacal quest for new identities and their specific problematization. Combined with continuing exploitation and the consequent erosion of the habitable spaces on our planet, neoliberal greed and the absurdity of the contemporary priorities of the left have triggered the awakening of monsters from the past. The 1920s European example is a fine historical lesson, which teaches us that there is a clear connection between populism and fascism, as one complements the other. Against this backdrop, practices that insist on *just* education, embedded in learning practices that insist on a critical paradigm and cosmopolitan humanism, are a predictable casualty.

With a fragmented left, neoliberal profit-driven politics are well positioned to frame the curricula of educational institutions. For instance, in Australia, policy and curriculum developers support teaching practices that favor *skilled* over *knowledgeable* students. In June 2020 the Australian federal government, used the backdrop of COVID-19, proposed doubling university fees for future students willing to study degrees related to arts and humanities. This sent a clear message to students and their parents alike: in times to come, there shall be no space and time for progressive humanist visions heightened by critical thought as developed through arts and humanities. Instead, tendencies which favor simplistic slogans over contextual critique when explaining the contemporary human condition become the prevailing discursive practice (Hattam, 2020). In societies dominated by simplistic mottos and skill-centered approaches in the classroom, invigorating practices of "social vision," as McLaren labeled it back in 1991, are the first casualty. Consequences include depriving students of opportunities to comprehend and engage with egalitarian ideals through "reflective process, critical thinking and deliberation" (McLaren, as cited in Ferneding, 2004, p. 54).

If there are no signifiers in curricula which suggest the possibilities of just worlds, students, soon to be adults, have little choice but to learn the *skill* of the day, considered essential for the profit-based priorities of neoliberal communities.

A pessimist would say that students and adults alike, who are deficient in social vision and/or failing in implanting themselves in neoliberal economic practices, might eventually turn their frustration toward the "other." The "other" might one day be an overly liberal politician or artist resisting or ridiculing their Duce or, on another day, a fellow unprivileged human being, who is blamed for their own unskilled misery. The underprivileged "other" with different cultural practices or skin color is the first to blame, but everyone else who dares to think otherwise is soon scrutinized.

In these circumstances, "reinvigoration of critical pedagogy ... both theoretically and practically" is a necessity (Hattam, 2020, p. 80). Until the time it becomes the norm, such stipulation should and could be exercised, even in classrooms that offer little or no space for critical examination of contemporary social conditions. Thus, and until the time when classrooms are sites that encourage the accumulation of critical knowledge, this chapter proposes the inclusion and use of artistic practices, specifically film art, as a thought-provoking supplement to the preferred *skill-based* curricula. Specifically, the chapter will engage theoretically with the possibilities of cinematic vision as a form and tool for critical pedagogy. Once the theoretical aspect of its argument is established, the chapter will shift focus to the practical implementation of critical pedagogy in a socially and culturally diverse transitioning classroom. In this class the educator is first and foremost asked to teach the skilled (mechanical) aspects of knowledge.

Art, Cinema, and Critical Pedagogy

In an ideal setting, curriculum design should be a balancing act between abstract concepts, and sensory and lived experiences (Wrigley, 2018). The benefit of the arts in such a process, as Bell and Desai (2014) indicate, is in their aesthetic and sensory elements, which bear a capacity to enable students to rediscover lived experiences and/or imagine alternatives. The arts are also linked to enriching students' reasoning and higher-order thinking capacities (Garrett et al., 2018). Adams and Owens (2015) insist on the significance of allocating and using art form(s) capable of provoking creative and critical explorations within particular learning contexts. Thus, appreciating, viewing, learning, and teaching arts should not be reserved for those considering arts as their profession of choice. Rather, artistic practices should be seen as providing an opportunity to understand current times and imagine the worlds of tomorrow.

At this moment, one may want to consider offering preferential status to film art in classrooms. It is a popular, hence recognizable and allegedly easily comprehended, artistic practice. For Parry (2013), some films aimed at children have the possibility to create affective and ideological spaces in which "children can distance themselves from adults, developing their own playful, imaginative and transgressive responses" (p. 14). In Perry's extensive, monographic argument there is a clear link between children's interpretation of filmic narratives and enhancement of literacy skills. What is appropriate for children's classrooms could also be applied to young adult and adult learning settings. A six-year-old child who has been encouraged to watch and eventually became amazed by the nature-celebrating animated fantasy *My neighbor Totoro* (Miyazaki, 1988), as a young adult may equally, but in different ways, be affected by the Holocaust-themed movie *Life is beautiful* (Benigni, 1997).

The art of filmmaking is a complex process that involves not only artistic imagination, but also a time-consuming and expensive production negotiated within the complex web of political and profit-based decisions. Consequently, before inclusion in the classroom a teacher should, for instance, understand that, due to its multifaceted procedure of creation and distribution, film art is often annexed into the connotatively richer term of cinema. It is cinema which signifies film through genre, style, aesthetic, productions, and reception (Kellner, 2010). Given this proposition, Grubba (2020) argues that notions of cinema seem to be "self-explanatory and, now a day, the great form of popular art, reaching social sectors that other art, such as painting and literature, cannot break into with such intensity" (p. 87).

As Alain Badiou (2009) argues, film's advantage is its capacity to absorb all other art forms. In other words, film feeds on other art forms such as literature, painting, theater, and photography. Similarly, William Costanzo (2004) believes that in some ways filmic art may seem richer than pure literary forms. Yet, Costanzo is sensible when he underlines that this is not because film is somehow superior to literature. On the contrary, "literary codes are far more precise and elaborately developed than those in film" (Costanzo, 2004, p. 4). For Costanzo, however, the great advantage of film art over literature is film's ability to cover a "wider range of direct sensory experience" (p. 4). Hence, affective or sensory stimulation is crucial when films are used in classrooms. As Anne Rutherford (2003) explains, not every dancer is able to provoke in a "spectator the feeling of the limbs unleashed from their sutures to the spine, of the spine unshackling itself from its bony frame to become molten liquid." What is true for the art of dance may also be true for other artistic expressions. Not every film director, for instance, can lead a project that will stimulate the senses of its audience (Rutherford, 2003). Thus, when considering the inclusion of filmic narrative, the teacher should comprehend that a film may contribute both to abstract and lived concepts (Wrigley, 2018). While its first task is awakening the sensory experiences among students, the teacher must consider more than sensory pleasures when deciding on films to use.

Walter Benjamin (1936/1973) pioneered meditation on film art as a potential exposer of otherwise inapprehensible aspects of the viewer's own time in history. Benjamin perceived film aesthetics as one means to re-imagine and renew our social worlds. Yet, Benjamin was aware of the possibility that a filmic re-imagination of the world can swing in more than one direction. In Benjamin's time, which was framed by the rise of Nazism and fascism in pre-World War II Europe, one direction led to the politicization of art (communism), the other to the aestheticization of politics (fascism). For Benjamin, art practices are the battleground for politics, and neither their tendencies nor outcomes can be predicted in advance. Benjamin's contemporary Douglas Kellner (1998) argued that films incorporate "raw material of social history and of social discourse and process them into products which are themselves historical events and social forces" (p. 355). Kellner (2010) extended this critical pedagogical potential of film by asserting that film provides artistic visions of the world that might exceed the social context of the moment and articulate future possibilities, both positive and negative.

One of those filmic visions was grasped by a politically active underground group of information technology savvy individuals known as Anonymous. To conceal their identity when engaged in verbal communication to the public, the Anonymous wear Guy Fawkes masks, immortalized in the present time by the film *V for vendetta* (McTeigue, 2005). While the future possibilities of Anonymous are yet to be fully understood or defined, another movement, which also adopts a specific signifier promoted in film art, is sitting on the extreme side of emerging populism in Europe.

This far-right political cross-national cluster, commonly named the Identitarian Movement, opposes globalization and multiculturalism, and tends to defend cultural hegemony inside the nations of Europe (Virchow, 2015). The most recognizable emblem of its first and foremost Islamophobic political platform is the Greek letter lambda, depicted in black and yellow. Using this letter from the Greek alphabet is a reference to Spartan warriors who fought against the Persians at Thermopylae (Vejvodová, 2014). The black lambda on a yellow background was borrowed from the feature movie *300* (Snyder, 2007) in which the Spartans, who gave their lives in defense against the eastern invaders, carry this sign on their shields. This Hollywood-made fantasy, with its distorted vision of factual events, is praised as the fifth best conservative movie by the influential conservative magazine *National Review* (NR Staff 2009). Being able to recognize artistic visions with treacherous tendencies is, hence, a skill that should be developed by students and their teachers alike.

In his essay "The author as producer," Benjamin (1934/1978) names three features of an author's task: to help organize the proletariat, to make the proletariat active, and to weaken their enemies. Here, Benjamin underlined his previous stance that no art can avoid being political, even if it tries to be non-political. There is little doubt that Benjamin's argument is based on the postulation that political predisposition is inherent to artistic endeavor. Thus, for Benjamin, an author should not focus on writing alone but on the teaching and organizing of readers (teachers and students) and other writers (students and teachers). While constantly improving in aesthetic vigor, artistic practices in general and film art, in particular, should always be centered on emancipatory and socially engaged themes. In such settings, the artifact and its creator are in permanent engagement with those present in the classroom. An emancipatory artifact should become praxis for critical pedagogy, which is, according to Freire (as cited in Firdaus & Mariyat, 2017, p. 35), "reflection and action upon the world in order to transform it."

Using Film in a Classroom Setting: An Example

Let us imagine that you teach the mechanics of academic research and writing. For this exercise, you could teach students in a high school or the first year of a bachelor's degree program. The example below illustrates experiences of using film in a class located in an enabling program within a large metropolitan Australian university (see Hattam & Stokes, 2019; Stokes, 2018). The diverse student cohort, mostly from low socio-economic or refugee backgrounds, are in a transitional phase, hoping to enroll in a bachelor-level degree at this Australian university.

Understanding the research and writing process for tertiary-level study is important for these students. A significant reason many of the students have been unable to enroll in a bachelor-level degree in the first place is real, sometime supposed, and, quite often, deficit postulations about their capability to perform well within educational spaces. As their academic tutor your task is to equip these students with the requisite academic skills/tools. You are also hoping to embed in their consciousness the essence of critical confidence. You have been trying to use this combined approach for almost two months. Today, in the middle of the semester, your task is to teach your students effective writing strategies for introducing segments of an essay or report.

You begin your lesson by introducing an inverted triangle. This, upside-down but still easily recognizable geometrical object is an appropriate visual representation of the structure of an essay introduction. It starts, you tell your students, by catching the readers' attention. You encourage students to use an anecdote or event that will offer a general overview of the essay or research topic. You continue by pointing to the mid part of the inverted triangle, as there is a need to narrow the general into the specific, hence identifying the main task of the essay or research report. The very tip of the inverted triangle, you may wish to excitedly announce, is reserved for the essay topic or research thesis.

At this moment, you may want to underline the significance of an effective introduction. It must attract the reader, make them want to continue reading, and engage with the ideas or argument of the essay/research report. Inform your students that the ideas they are presenting will eventually enter contested and competitive territories. Competition is prominent in a profit-driven economy. A clichéd example could be a junior adviser in a large company who is competing against the other rising employees for the executives' attention. Or, for some of your students, and you are wishful here, such competition may happen in university where a research project will be in competition against the research proposals of other enthusiastic scholars willing to change the world, you hope, for the better.

Once you have established the significance of the introduction, it is the right moment to introduce artistic and cinematic practices into your academic essay writing lesson. You might inform students that an essay introduction is similar to the opening minutes of a movie. This pedagogical practice centers on asking students to predict what the movie is about and why they would continue watching after viewing the introductory scenes. You will need to be cautious to avoid picking out any of the cinematic narrative. Curating art for your students is like creating a well-informed curriculum to use in your day-to-day teaching.

If you are teaching students in Australia, I suggest you choose the opening scenes of Down under, a film directed by Abe Forsythe (2016). Its genre is black comedy, and the opening scene is creative in an unusual way. Overall, the film tackles the important topic of antagonism between two groups of young men from different ethnic backgrounds. Avoid informing your students about this as you do not want to spoil the plot. Nevertheless, warn them about the violence and coarse language.

The introductory scene of *Down under* encompasses footage of Sydney Harbour, swiftly replaced with picture-postcard scenes of an Australian summer, including bodies of young people in constant movement in and around seawater. The non-diegetic score that accompanies these sunny scenes is a cheerful carol. Your next pedagogical move is to pause the movie and question students to promote conversation about what they think the movie is about and where it is filmed. It may be obvious from the landmarks that the movie is set in Sydney, but it is less likely students are ready or willing to predict the movie's plot. From past experiences some might assume it is about having a Christmas party on the beach. You then press the play button again. In a matter of seconds, the idyllic Sydney summer seashore scene is replaced by masses of young, Caucasian bodies carrying Australian flags, but also unofficial national signifiers such as fighting kangaroos and beer bottles. There is also a dramatic visible police presence! At this moment, diegetic sounds of helicopter propellers and human chanting start to take over from the cheerful Christmas carol. Soon, the racist chanting, coming from the chest and throats of young men, becomes the dominant sound. Quite a few of these young men are topless. One of these torsos is decorated clearly and boldly with the words "We grew here, you flew here." Another young male has used black marker to ornament his developing chest with the words "Shire Boyz." Instead of inscribing his body, a third one proclaims "Ethnic Cleansing Unit" on the back of his white T-shirt.

At this moment, pause the movie and repeat your questions about predicting the movie's plot. If students suggest that the movie is about the "Cronulla riots," you may nod in approval and press the play button again. Even if the students are silent, which is more than likely, continue showing the introductory scene of *Down under*, as it is not finished yet. After all, an unfinished introduction for an essay may diminish reader interest or effort to continue further in the text. The same could be said for a movie's introduction.

Returning to the movie, the chanting of racist slogans intensifies. Scenes of violence follow with the mob of noisy young males involved in bashing those whom they call "wogs" or "lebos" and police officers using force in efforts to disperse the attackers and protect the attacked. At this moment, the final rhymes of the cheerful Christmas carol begin to dissolve into the raw, diegetic sound from Cronulla and nearby streets. Instantly, the wide aerial footage of Sydney's shore reappears accompanied by the news-style narration reflecting on the immediate aftermath of the Cronulla riots. At this moment, you press the stop button for good and then turn toward the students. You might realize that some of them are expressing facial feature signifying uneasiness. Others may seem excitedly impatient, a feeling well known to anyone who cannot wait to talk.

So, they talk. To your great surprise, many students in your Adelaide-based classroom, born at the turn of the twenty-first century, will inform you they are not aware of the December 2005 Cronulla riots in Sydney. Then you may ask both groups—the Cronulla aware and those who are not—if they would continue watching the movie after they have seen its opening scene. Many students may say yes, but the others may remain silent. If asked in an encouraging way, the "yesses" may also let you know that using news footage to open a feature movie on a real-life topic is good idea. If that happens, you should agree. *Down under* is a black comedy directly inspired by the Cronulla riots. Using the brutality of news footage supplemented with the innocence of carol tunes provides a superlative introduction for a feature film that aims to problematize ethnic animosities entrenched behind the façade of the irresistible aesthetic attractiveness of Sydney Harbour.

Lessons From Critical Pedagogy

If asked to critically examine the skill needed to create an artifact, one may declare with confidence that *Down under* has a catchy and memorable introduction. Consequently, such qualities, if evident in an essay introduction written by the students you teach, would provoke a satisfying feeling of accomplishment for you and students alike.

However, showing the opening sequences of *Down under* to your students also represents an opportunity for enactment of critical pedagogy within an otherwise resistant curriculum. A critically aware teacher may hope that brushing up the mechanical aspects of how to write an essay introduction with the "Cronulla riots" could provoke a classroom discussion on class and cultural divisions within Australian society. Perhaps, a teacher could become wishful here, as thoughtful questioning may initiate students' reflections about their own place and status within Australian society.

The discussion to follow could be a space to explore the notion that ethnic ghettoization, as seen in Sydney, could harm everyone (Collins et al., 2000). Mostly, it hurts those who are ghettoized and/or isolated and left to live in imagined or real poverty (Noble & Tabar, 2017). Such segregation, however, can also make those living on the other side of class or ethic borders across Australia's largest city uncomfortable, if not fearful. The Cronulla riots first and foremost exposed the vulnerability of marginalized Middle Eastern or Muslim communities. Nevertheless, the Cronulla riots also unsettled previously established and relatively well-off communities. These are communities whose lack of engagement with and, hence lack of knowledge of, newly arrived subjects was underpinned by a fear of the unknown and of losing privileges that are both real and imagined (Moore, 2019). Perhaps, *Down under* and similar artistic interventions have started to build symbolic, yet welcoming gates across divisive socio-economic borders in Sydney. In times to come, with the assistance of such films, just education may contribute to the dismantling of visible and invisible class, ethnic, or racial fences which separate those living in Sydney and other Australian urban areas.

The narrative of *Down under*, the movie you have used to supplement your teaching about writing an academic essay introduction, actually begins on the day after the riot. It portrays the parallel paths of a group of four young Anglo-Australian men from the Shire who wish to "protect" their turf, and a corresponding group of four young Lebanese-Australian men from the western suburbs seeking revenge for the events of the previous day. Both groups are grotesque caricatures of underlying ethnic and, perhaps, racial animosities within broader Sydney.

Film scholars and critics, however, described the film as "no laughing matter" (Krayem, 2017) and a "superficial examination of race and racism" (McGrath, 2017). Moreover, for De Bruyn (2016), *Down under* is exploitative entertainment that "does not deliver any insights into the racism at their core." Perhaps, they are all correct. But *Down under* is also a tragi-comedy of the underclass which exposes the absurdity of racial antagonism, fueled by educational inequities and gaps in critical knowledge. In such distributions, heterogenous underclasses, regardless of their ethnicity, are potential losers.

Instead of a Conclusion

This chapter began by acknowledging the uncomfortable fact that the educational curriculum in Australia is in danger of obliterating teaching and learning practices framed by critical pedagogies. The convergence of conservative and profit-based neoliberal agendas within political establishments works to normalize notions that skills-based education is the priority. For the current political class, everything else, including public media outlets and humanist-centered professions critical of neoliberal logic, are an unnecessary burden for those paying taxes.

In spite of this, one should not stop resisting. Whenever possible, critically oriented decision makers and creators of the school curriculum must work across all levels and fields of education in ways that include pedagogies described as critical. In this chapter, I have argued for the inclusion of artistic practices, and film art in particular, in classroom settings that are comprised of diverse and disadvantaged students. The current decision makers of the day may reject such ideas. Their reasons for rejection could center on a lack of funding and the insistence that creating or analyzing socially engaged arts is a skill that will not increase the employment prospects of students.

Despite this predictable answer, one should not be discouraged. As this chapter elaborated, there are possibilities for embedding artistic imaginary in a curriculum that is seemingly artless. For instance, the opening scenes of a specific feature film could significantly supplement the lesson on writing an essay introduction. Moreover, what is crucial for preserving the flame of critical pedagogy in a classroom where there is no obvious place for it is the content and seductiveness of a visual narrative that may be used to encourage students to critically reflect upon their own existence in society.

If critical pedagogy is to be practiced across classrooms in a society interested in reaching the elusive potential of socio-liberal egalitarianism, socially engaged arts can make a significant contribution. Teachers and curriculum designers are, hence, encouraged to use particular filmic visions for educational purposes. These practices should supplement "pedagogical practices that promote political engagement, that challenge conventional ways of thinking … use films as a cultural text to bridge the gap between the academic discourse of the classroom and those issues and public concerns that animate larger society" (Giroux, 2011, p. 693).

My hope is that the day will come when socially engaged artistic practices are common signifiers in just curricula. Until that moment, even the occasional fragments of inspiring artistic practices can preserve this hope. It is up to teachers to recognize them and share them with their students.

Bibliography

Adams, J., & Owens, A. (2015). *Creativity and democracy in education: Practices and politics of learning through the arts*. Routledge.

Badiou, A. (2009). Cinema as a democratic emblem (A. Ling & A. Mondon, Trans.). *Parrhesia, 1*.

Bell, L., & Desai, D. (Eds.). (2014). *Social justice and the arts*. Routledge.

Benjamin, W. (1973). *Illuminations*. Fontana. (Original work published 1936)

Benjamin, W. (1978). *Reflections: Essays, aphorisms, autobiographical writing*. Schocken Books. (Original work published 1934)

Benigni, R. (Director). (1997). *Life is beautiful* [Film]. Melampo Cinematografica.

Collins, J., Noble, G., Poynting, S., & Tabar, P. (2000). *Kebabs, kids, cops and crime: Youth ethnicity and crime*. Pluto.

Costanzo, W. V. (2004). *Great films and how to teach them*. National Council of Teachers.

De Bruyn, D. (2016, July 29). The tragi-comedy *Down under* appropriates Cronulla rather than offering insight. *The Conversation*. https://theconversation.com/the-tragi-comedy-down-under-appropriates-cronulla-rather-than-offering-insight-63259

Ferneding, K. (2004). The discourse of inevitability and the forging of an emergent social vision: Technology diffusion and the dialectic of educational reform discourse. In W. M. Reynolds & J. A. Webber (Eds.), *Expanding curriculum theory: Dis/positions and lines of flight* (pp. 47–63). Erlbaum Associates.

Firdaus, F. A., & Mariyat, A. (2017). Humanistic approach in education according to Paulo Freire. *At-Ta'dib*, *12*(2), 25–48.
Forsythe, A. (Director). (2016). *Down under* [Film]. Wild Eddie.
Garrett, R., Dawson, K., Meiners, J., & Wrench, A. (2018). Creative and body-based learning: Redesigning pedagogies in mathematics. *Journal for Learning through the Arts*, *14*(1). https://escholarship.org/uc/item/5396b47c
Giroux, H. A. (2011). Breaking into the movies: Public pedagogy and the politics of film. *Policy Futures in Education*, *9*(6), 686–95.
Grubba, L. S. (2020). Cinema, human rights and development: The cinema as a pedagogical practice. *CINEJ Cinema Journal*, *8*(1), 87–123.
Hattam, R. (2020). Untimely meditations for critical pedagogy. *Asia-Pacific Journal of Teacher Education*, *48*(1), 79–92.
Hattam, S., & Stokes, J. (2019). Liberation and connection: Fostering critical students as active agents of their own learning. In A. Jones, A. Olds, & J. G. Lisciandro (Eds.), *Transitioning students into higher education: Philosophies, pedagogies and practice* (pp. 45–53). Routledge.
Kellner, D. (1998). Hollywood film and society. In J. Hill & P. C. Gibson (Eds.), *The Oxford guide to film studies* (pp. 354–62). Oxford University Press.
Kellner, D. (2010). *Cinema wars: Hollywood film and politics in the Bush-Cheney era*. Blackwell.
Krayem, M. (2017). Down and out for "Down under": Critiquing race representation in Abe Forsythe's satire. *Metro Magazine: Media & Education Magazine*, *191*, 14–19.
McGrath, K. (2017). Riot and revenge: Symmetry and the Cronulla riot in Abe Forsythe's *Down under. Alphaville: Journal of Film and Screen Media*, *13*, 13–32.
McLaren, P. (1991). Critical pedagogy: Constructing an arch of social dreaming and a doorway to hope. *Journal of Education*, *173*(1), 9–34.
McTeigue, J. (Director). (2005). *V for vendetta* [Film]. Warner Bros. Pictures.
Miyazaki, H. (Director). (1988). *My neighbor Totoro* [Film]. Studio Ghibli.
Moore, T. (2019). Once as tragedy and again as farce: Hansonism, backlashers, and economic nationalism after 20 years. In B. Grant, T. Moore, & T. Lynch (Eds.), *The rise of right-populism: Pauline Hanson's One Nation and Australian politics* (pp. 203–16). Springer.
Noble, G., & Tabar, P. (2017). Wounded detachments: Cronulla, social memory and the injuries of racism. *Journal of Intercultural Studies*, *38*(3), 271–83.
NR Staff (2009, February). The Best Conservative Movies. *National Review*. https://www.nationalreview.com/magazine/2009/02/23/best-conservative-movies/
Parry, B. (2013). *Children, film and literacy*. Springer.
Rutherford, A. (2003). Cinema and embodied affect. *Senses of Cinema*, *25*. https://www.sensesofcinema.com/2003/feature-articles/embodied_affect/

Snyder, Z. (Director). (2006). *300* [Film]. Warner Bros. Pictures.
Stokes, J. (2018). Students on the threshold: Commencing student perspectives and enabling pedagogy. In C. I. Agosti & E. Bernat (Eds.), *University pathway programs: Local responses within a growing global trend* (pp. 223–42). Springer.
Vejvodová, P. (2014). *Transnational forms of contemporary neo-Nazi activity in Europe from the perspective of Czech neo-Nazis*. Nakladatelství Masarykovy Univerzity.
Virchow, F. (2015). The Identitarian Movement. In P. A. Simpson & H. Druxes (Eds.), *Digital media strategies of the far right in Europe and the United States* (pp. 177–91). Lexington Books.
Wrigley, T. (2018). "Knowledge," curriculum and social justice. *Curriculum Journal*, *29*(1), 4–24.

18 Visual Arts Curriculum: A Pluralist and Embodied Perspective on Shifting Points of View

Bindi MacGill

Introduction

Visual arts education in Australia has routinely focused on Western art movements such as Impressionism, Cubism, and Expressionism to inform students' cultural knowledge. Many art teachers struggle to include Aboriginal and Torres Strait Islander perspectives in their curriculum, due to an absence of knowledge about the diversity of Indigenous art and the history of colonization. This chapter offers insights into how to address this through adopting a decolonial relational ethic (Bourque Bearskin, 2011). It describes approaches that reflect a decolonizing approach to curriculum design and building relational knowledge through embodied strategies in visual art classrooms. Specific visual arts strategies enacted with Australian university arts education pre-service teachers (PST) who are preparing to teach visual arts in primary schools are outlined in this chapter.

The Australian Curriculum invites teachers to embed the cross-curriculum priorities (CCPs) of Aboriginal and Torres Strait Islander Histories and Knowledges, Sustainability, and Asia and Australia's Engagement with Asia into their curriculum. Eighty percent of the PSTs in this arts education course come from Anglo-Australian backgrounds, have limited understanding of cultural knowledge apart from their own, and often describe themselves as culture-less (Aveling, 2004). However, the student cohort also includes Aboriginal and Torres Strait Islander PSTs and those from various locations around the globe. The funds of knowledge (Moll, 2005) approach adopted within the learning design of the course is informed by an ethics of care. The aim was to create safe spaces for dialogue, to co-create artwork, and to build a community of learners that supports pluralism, de-centers "whiteness," and generates a decolonizing approach to learning design.

This chapter argues that a "pedagogy of care" plays a pivotal role in unpacking PSTs' understanding of their standpoints (Harding, 2004). This can be achieved through centralizing relational ethics as an embodied and reciprocated engagement with each other as a community of learners (Lave & Wenger, 1991). Making visible the colonial narratives and omissions in art history that have perpetuated the central location of "whiteness" creates discomfort on multiple levels (Zembylas & Boler, 2016). A key practice in the arts education course is that all PSTs navigate their location as we resolve to unpack race blindness and use art as the vehicle for this work.

The challenges PSTs collectively and individually face as they transition epistemologically through collaborative strategies are addressed. Additionally, I explore how making visual art provides possibilities for "un-learning" normative assumptions about education. Finally, the chapter explores the framework of a "pedagogy of care" that supports PSTs as they move toward a decolonizing approach to curriculum design. This compositional approach relies on the affective, cognitive, and aesthetic domains that are built within a framework of trust and care (Dawson & Kiger Lee, 2018; Rankin et al., 2021).

A Pedagogy of Care

The concept of a pedagogy of care emerged from feminist ethics of care theory. Historically, ethics of care theory centralized interpersonal relationships between the carer and cared for (Noddings, 1984, 1992, 2002). Typically, this was within a mother–child or patient–doctor dichotomy that was limited by normative caring structures reflective of the White middle class. The political and cultural arrangements of care were subsequently challenged by Thompson (1998), Rolon-Dow (2005), and others who explored a "black ethics of care" (cited in MacGill, 2008), and were later extended to incorporate a post-humanist conception of care. This move allowed for examination of an Indigenous ethics of care that included both human and non-human relations grounded in reciprocity and responsiveness (Rose, 2003, as cited in MacGill, 2008).

A pedagogy of care in visual arts education is a different form of engagement within the teaching/learning cycle through material and embodied strategies that will be outlined below. These strategies are designed to unveil PSTs' standpoints and understandings of the world and target the contact zones of intersectionality that shift binary canonical thought (Biesta, 2017). Disrupting PSTs' world views is complex and creates discomfort (Zembylas & Boler, 2016), and therefore requires a strong ethic of care that is grounded in dialogic meaning making.

Communities of Practice Model as the Frame for a Pedagogy of Care

A community of learners is built through a collaborative approach that positions teachers and students within a communities of practice model (Lave & Wenger, 1991). A CoP model is an approach to develop cultural safety and it uses "the metaphor of a landscape [that] ensures we pay attention to boundaries, to our multi-membership in different communities and to the challenges we face as our personal trajectories take us through multiple communities" (Hutchinson et al., 2015, p. 2). Students and educators create space for their students in a way that is supportive of their funds of knowledge (Moll, 2005). It is a site of reciprocity that is built through care and grounded in emotional intelligence.

As part of this learning journey, students navigate their standpoints (Harding, 2004) whilst at the same expanding their ontologies and epistemologies through embodied relational strategies known as creative and body-based learning (henceforth CBL). CBL is an extension of drama-based instruction developed by Dawson and Kiger Lee (2018) that utilizes gameplay, image work, role play, and dialogic meaning-making strategies to engage students in learning. CBL strategies are used to examine students' standpoints and epistemologies including sociometrics where students position their bodies on a continuum about what they know, their understandings about funds of knowledge, and their confidence in creative curriculum design informed by pluralism. PSTs are also asked to consider how they might learn more deeply about the intersection of White race privilege and knowledge production. This deconstruction process is not bound by guilt but instead hinges on the question: "What has been made absent in my own schooling that has erased multiple knowledge systems such as Muslim art or Aboriginal and Torres Strait Islander histories?"

Interestingly, in the topic of Teaching Visual Arts for Primary School, students navigate ways to address the CCPs. Many of the PSTs were stuck with their lack of knowledge about Aboriginal and Torres Strait Islander perspectives, and their starting point for lesson planning was dot painting, which is generic and homogenizing. This reductive approach is not surprising given the absence of education in the school curriculum and the general assumption by many non-Indigenous people that all Aboriginal art is dot painting.

There was a sense that PSTs felt that sustainability was a concept that was easy to integrate (e.g., asking students to recycle materials). However, the deeper conversations around "response-ability" and connection to the land from a post-humanist perspective (Rose, 2003) unraveled layers of thinking and positioning from the PSTs. Some students explored the theme of Asia and Australia's engagement with Asia. However, there was a tendency to view manga as the only Japanese art form, similar to how many non-Indigenous people assume all Aboriginal art is dot painting. Using art to illustrate how we construct knowledge through binaries was useful in unpacking the practices of Western knowledge production. This was coupled with "activating dialogue strategies," which involved students voicing their experiences of how they learn and are taught to think.

Reflective dialogue sparked "aha" moments as we contemplated how students absorb information. Incorporating relational methods and visual thinking strategies (Harvard Graduate School of Education, 2022) proved influential, particularly when juxtaposing an arabesque design with Reko Rennie's 2012 mural "Always

ways always will be." Describing visual rhythm, color, line, shapes, and repetition fostered dialogue and offered a new approach to connecting overarching concepts and themes about culturally responsive pedagogy. Teachers are required to teach through these elements and principles of art from Foundation to Year 12. Importantly, these elements can be mobilized in simple and yet powerful ways to build insight into images and how they sit in relation to each other. We then moved on to key aspects of point of view, as well as principles of philosophy, religion, and design. This enabled new ways to think through curriculum design and how this process is linked to knowledge production.

Curriculum design underpins what is going to be taught and is therefore inextricably linked to knowledge production. Two main issues arise throughout the process of curriculum design. Firstly, the majority of the students have limited knowledge of Aboriginal and Torres Strait Islander perspectives, Islamic art, Australia's relationship with Asia in the arts, and sustainability. Secondly, for many students, tensions arise between understandings informed by their predominantly White Anglo-Saxon heritage, which they bring to the course, and the broader perspectives introduced. The latter includes First Nations sovereignty, imperialism, settler notions of belonging, the privilege of whiteness, and the ethics of building a socially just education (Tannoch-Bland, 1998). Creating a learning journey that does not compromise students who are Aboriginal or Torres Strait Islander, or from areas defined as part of Asia, is built into the ethics of care model and learning design for this course, through the use of strategies that draw on students' funds of knowledge.

CBL Strategies: Deep Listening. Printmaking and the Watercolor Conversation

Both the ethics of care and post-humanist/feminist new materialist ethics regard ontology (theory of being), epistemology (theory of knowing), and ethics as interconnected and inseparable from each other (Barad, 2007, as cited in Bozalek, 2016, p. 81). When PSTs consider the complexity of Aboriginal and Torres Strait Islander knowledges, Asia and Australia's engagement with Asia, and sustainability from a pluralist perspective, epistemologies become entangled and inseparable from the knowledge-making work they do in their curriculum design. Therefore, the work and assessment tasks, which on the surface appear relatively simple, become complex as PSTs unpack ways of knowing through embodied and dialogic strategies that make their standpoints and learning visible.

When PSTs begin to weave the CCPs through the process of using CBL strategies coupled with their art-making skills, such as painting with watercolors, they see links between the CCPs. Both the ethics of care and post-humanist ethics are firmly located in the *doing process* and sit within a relational ontology, which includes listening and maintains that humans or entities do not exist before or outside of relationships (Barad, 2007). Moreover, "human agency (the potential to think and act morally) can only be considered as a performance within a relationship either between humans and non-humans, non-human animals or the material world" (Bozalek, 2016, p. 82). The challenge is how to teach listening as an active tool for learning.

The "watercolor conversation" developed by Beth Link (2019) is a strategy used as a practice for deep listening. Listening is a decolonizing approach that connects to Levinas' notion of "I see you" (Levinas, 2012; Strahan, 2012). During this watercolor strategy, PSTs check in with themselves and consider how they are feeling. Music is turned on and PSTs *listen* to each other in pairs but do not speak as they paint. Instead, they make marks on shared 300 gsm watercolor paper—as if in conversation. As they listen to the other and add layers of color the session leads to a final blended watercolor piece, represented in the demonstration example below (see Figure 18.1).

Figure 18.1: Watercolor Conversation Demonstration Example.
Source: Bindi MacGill.

As Levinas states:

> To approach the other in conversation is to welcome his expression, in which at each instant he overflows the idea a thought would carry away from it. It is therefore to receive from the Other beyond the capacity of the I, which means exactly: to have the idea of infinity. (2012, p. 51)

Watercolor conversations attune one's ear to others as a practice of "deep listening" (Ungunmerr-Baumann et al., 2022), which requires both care and attentiveness (Thompson, 1998). Listening is an acquired skill. Foucault (2005) draws on the ancients to explore the skill of listening as a method of *atonement*. The practice of listening is underpinned by the principle of living in one's truth. To authentically listen involves truth telling that includes, in this context, the mechanisms of colonization that have interrupted Aboriginal and Torres Strait Islander knowledges and histories. Throughout the semester, the strategies employed become a process by which to examine *true* discourse and its connection to the ethical responsibility around knowledge production in the curriculum. Whilst the "watercolor conversation" is a process of listening and learning, practices of *attunement* make visible how Aboriginal and Torres Strait Islander knowledges often sit outside of students' consciousness. These understandings prompt many non-Indigenous PSTs to think about pluralism within curriculum design. Similarly, Kompridis (2013) defines this practice as becoming *unclosed*, which "[u]nlike some abstract, free-floating openness to anyone or anything … involves struggle, a struggle with ourselves to open up what is now closed, or what has never been open" (pp. 20–21).

An ethics of care includes recognition of each other in a community of practice context, and these strategies not only build community but highlight how non-Anglo-Saxon identities, cultures, and knowledges have historically been *othered* and *misrecognized* within the Australian curriculum. As Fraser states:

> To be misrecognized … is not to suffer distorted identity or impaired subjectivity as a result of being depreciated by others. It is rather to be constituted by institutionalized patterns of cultural value in ways that prevent one from participating as a peer in social life. (in Fraser & Honneth, 2003, p. 29)

By making art through this lens of cultural erasure, it becomes possible to understand differences inside of pluralism where normative models are decentered (Fraser & Honneth, 2003). In the context of this work, the right to recognition is used as one of the underlying principles of pluralism.

Different kinds of encounters for students engaged in CBL strategies include breaking habits and ways of learning in restricted learning spaces. The *encounter*

(Deleuze, 2004) produces the moment of cognitive transition from recognition to a new understanding. Cascading patterns of knowledge are created through strategies that are informed by aesthetics (Greene, 1995). These emerge from using visual art to understand colonial representational fields and decolonial methods of engaging with art. This process links ontological shifts with relational subjectivity, such as occurs through the watercolor conversation.

Biesta's (1994) notion of relational subjectivity in teaching and learning is significant here. It is not a:

> one-way process in which culture is transferred from one (already acculturated) organism to another (not yet acculturated) organism, but ... a co-constructive process, a process in which both participating organisms play an active role and in which meaning is not transferred but produced. (pp. 311–312)

CBL strategies provide a framework for students and teachers to co-create through dialogic meaning that is made explicit in the final steps of deconstruction identified as DAR (describe, analyze, relate).[1] In the deconstruction of strategies and their content knowledge students articulate their positions through their interpretation in the form of a personal discovery (Biesta, 2014). This new beginning is consciousness about pluralism within curriculum design. Students' final images in printmaking, for example, center on a collective piece that they construct through collaborative storytelling (see Figure 18.2). This is inspired by the prints of Wiradjuri printmaker Kevin Gilbert, who builds narrative into his images. Students do not appropriate artists but are informed by the art-making process when building their own narratives in group work. They are required to think deeply about the broad themes represented in Gilbert's work. Students then relate these themes and art-making practices to their collective narrative and work toward a final product. At the end of each class, we have mini-exhibitions and use the DAR process to weave art making, theory, artist's inspiration, and future curriculum design ideas as a practice of integrating the CCPs.

---

1 Describe—describe what you see (What did you do?); analyze—infer based on observations or prior knowledge and link observations to interpretations (Why did we do this? What did we learn?); relate—connect sense making and textual/visual evidence to a wider context or human experience (Where could we use this or where do we see this happening in our lives?).

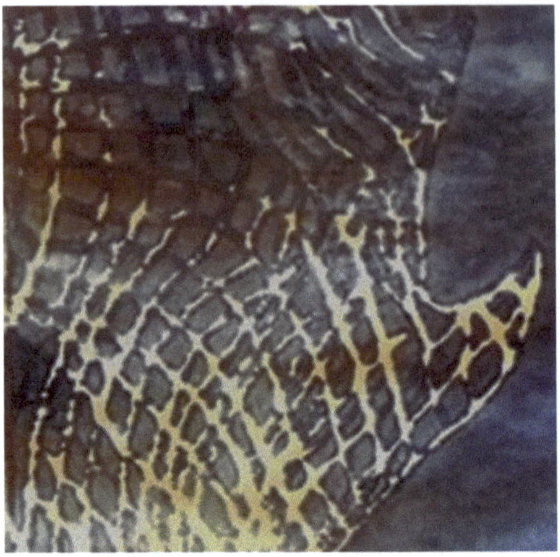

Figure 18.2: Printmaking: Sustainability and Belonging Demonstration Example.
Source: Bindi MacGill.

Navigating Pluralism in the Field of Visual Arts Through Embodied and Visual Thinking Strategies

In visual arts, students are required to understand how images produce knowledge within a semiotic and discursive field (Hall et al., 2013). Many PSTs are familiar with working through binaries, such as Black–White and male–female, in their history of learning. To shift this approach to understanding, it is necessary to also shift the epistemological and ontological systems that have shaped students' understanding of themselves, their ideas about nationalism, and how they see themselves in relation to the world. Discomfort around not knowing how to embed a pluralist approach to the CCPs is the first phase that requires careful "attunement."

I make explicit how knowledge is produced within the curriculum and support students in their discomfort as a key factor of "unlearning." I begin with how and why many non-Aboriginal and Torres Strait Islander people do not know these histories and make explicit how these omissions and erasures are produced through a colonizing curriculum.

We use 3-D models (Dawson, 2024a), where students make an object out of a range of materials to explore their teaching philosophy about inclusion and "truth" telling. This practice of 3D model making is meditative, as students wrestle with materials such as wire, bark, plasticine, and sticks whilst considering their teaching philosophy (see Figure 18.3). This is followed by DAR, where students unpack the link between their teaching philosophy and the notion of "truth telling," where things can be made visible or invisible. This is followed by another strategy called "constellations," which invites students into a productive, community-focused, and co-created space through various provocations. Constellations involve students moving around the room to music, encouraging them to explore and demonstrate connections within a group, as well as reflecting on their identity and sense of belonging through visible interpersonal connections (Dawson, 2024b).

Figure 18.3: 3D Model: Teaching Philosophy Demonstration Example.
Source: Bindi MacGill.

PSTs are encouraged to border cross (Giroux, 2005) to unknown sites of content knowledge as well as shifting their standpoints as they unpack and recognize similarities and differences that occur through dialogic meaning-making practices. They are challenged to understand ways to teach in areas that they may have not yet learnt. They begin to understand the complexities of difference without "othering" or reproducing power hierarchies that privilege one set of knowledge over another when they embed the CCPs, particularly when they use DAR to explain the complexity of their artworks.

We use visual thinking strategies (VTS) to enable new ways of interpreting artwork conceptually. This guided strategy's strength lies in its dialogic meaning-making process, which reveals multiple perspectives through aesthetics and visual arts language. By understanding how meaning is constructed through images, PSTs can align their thinking with the curriculum.

Implementing dialogic meaning-making strategies like VTS serves to challenge fixed notions of culture while shedding light on how privilege operates within dominant cultures. This approach shifts focus away from blaming individuals and instead illuminates how discursive regimes shape knowledge production. By engaging in this pedagogy, PSTs can navigate a space that encourages both safety and intellectual challenge as they develop curriculum content.

In this visual art education topic, meta-thinking is developed by using codes for interpretation within the visual arts context, juxtaposing two stories of Australia and using embodied strategies—such as "vote from your seat" (Dawson, 2024c)—to consider how they are culturally located through semiotic fields (Hall et al., 2013). We unpack semiotic fields by juxtaposing contemporary art such as Paddy Bedford's *Two women looking at the Bedford Downs massacre burning place* (2002) with Tom Robert's iconic nationalistic oil painting *A breakaway* (1891). When juxtaposed they offer two very clear but starkly different codes and narratives of colonization. By juxtaposing the codes from these two images through VTS, we drill deeper into the meaning of each image and how they sit semiotically in relation to each other. Bedford's aerial picture plane offers insight into points of view and speaks of a massacre site, in contrast to Robert's linear perspective, which privileges the White male horse rider who is steering sheep away from the dam and symbolizes control and ownership of the land. It reveals the way "fields of codes" are produced through positioning and how the "circuit of culture" (Hall et al., 2013, p. 45) within national narratives has historically privileged the Western perspective. Aboriginal narratives from the margins provide a richer account of the nation, challenging dominant narratives and promoting a more inclusive perspective (Phillips & Bunda, 2018, p. 107).

PSTs unpack how their knowledge systems have been produced and we, as a collective, reflect on how we construct mental maps through images and stories that are hierarchical and reproduced through the "circuit of culture" (Hall et al., 2013). Over the semester, PSTs re-create and offer "shared maps of meaning" (Hall et al., 2013, p. 14) that are co-created in group work, with a focus on pluralist curriculum frameworks. The CBL strategies create discomfort for many students because the process of unveiling unconscious bias is part of the work toward becoming allies of liberal citizenship education (Boler, 1999; Callan, 1997; Kumashiro, 2002). Using CBL strategies grounded in an ethics of care "draws students into dialogue with the world" (Biesta, 2019, p. 15) as they focus on their responsibility as educators and their role in creating inclusive curriculum design and pedagogy. This transformational work operates in the cognitive, affective, and aesthetic domains and therefore must be conducted with care (Dawson & Kiger Lee, 2018).

Conclusion

An ethics of care is a moral philosophy that demands critical thinking around knowledge production. PSTs acknowledge and then shift their unseen raced, classed, and gendered views when they are made visible through CBL strategies. Through using embodied and dialogic meaning-making strategies, PSTs can be supported to explore perspectives and ways of thinking that are different from their own.

The danger arises when PSTs seek to insert themselves into the narrative of the image, often unconsciously engaging in a proprietary form of knowledge that oscillates between "othering" and asserting ownership and control over knowledge. A pedagogy of care in this context emphasizes the importance of recognizing and addressing these potential pitfalls, allowing PSTs to navigate new content knowledge with awareness and sensitivity. It also highlights standpoints through dialogic meaning-making strategies and brings to light patterns of the knowledge–power nexus. When the image is not located within the artist's discourse but instead re-located into a "romantic" or "spiritual" context without recognition of the conditions and context from where the image emerges, we run the risk of re-colonizing work. Deconstructing the image through contextual, historical, and socio-policy frameworks enables PSTs to see the problematics of education and offers a way to positively centralize pluralist positions within their curriculum rather than at the margins.

Through dialogic meaning-making strategies, we use dialogue to unravel divergent voices, concerns, and emotional blocks. Socio-metric strategies use the body to enable PSTs to work together as a collective within a safe space as a community of learners. Visual thinking strategies provide an opportunity to unpack ways in which knowledge is produced through visual arts. As examples, the watercolor conversation and the 3-D model offer ways PSTs can represent and describe how they operate within an ethical framework. At each point there is a choice where PSTs turn toward a particular focus of representation and misrepresentation in the visual text. At no point are they made to feel blame, but the emotion of guilt is unpacked around a past that continues to reinforce practices of retro-assimilation in the present.

Flattening out relations of power through CBL invites PSTs to reflect and speak in ways that produce insights into divergent viewpoints. Slowing down teaching and learning, coupled with creating a safe space, enables insights into the interrelationship of emotion and context by which knowledge is produced. A pedagogy of care in the arts informed by a post-humanist aesthetic foregrounds opportunities for transformation that are clearly required in the current social, political, and environmental context.

Bibliography

Aveling, N. (2004). Critical whiteness studies and the challenges of learning to be a "White ally." *Borderlands E-Journal: New Spaces in the Humanities*, *3*(2).

Barad, K. (2007). *Meeting the universe halfway: Quantum physics and the entanglement of matter and meaning*. Duke University Press.

Biesta, G. (1994). Education as practical intersubjectivity: Towards a critical-pragmatic understanding of education. *Educational Theory*, *44*(3), 299–317.

Biesta, G. (2014). Pragmatising the curriculum: Bringing knowledge back into the curriculum conversation, but via pragmatism. *Curriculum Journal, 25*(1), 29–49.

Biesta, G. (2017). *Letting art teach*. ArtEzPress.

Biesta, G. (2019). Trying to be at home in the world: New parameters for art education. *Artlink, 39*(3), 10–16.

Boler, M. (1999). *Feeling power: Emotions and education*. Routledge.

Bourque Bearskin, R. L. (2011). A critical lens on culture in nursing practice. *Nursing Ethics, 18*(4), 548–59.

Bozalek, V. (2016). The politics of ethics of care and feminist posthuman ethics: Contributions to social work. In R. Hugman & J. Carter (Eds.), *Rethinking values and ethics in social work* (pp. 80–96). Palgrave Macmillan.

Callan, E. (1997). *Creating citizens: Political education and liberal democracy*. Clarendon.

Dawson, K. (2024a). *3-D models*. Drama-Based Pedagogy. https://dbp.theatredance.utexas.edu/teaching-strategies/3-d-models

Dawson, K. (2024b). *Constellations*. Drama-Based Pedagogy. https://dbp.theatredance.utexas.edu/teaching-strategies/constellations

Dawson, K. (2024c). *Vote from your seat*. Drama-Based Pedagogy. https://dbp.theatredance.utexas.edu/teaching-strategies/vote-your-seat

Dawson, K., & Kiger Lee, B. (2018). *Drama-based pedagogy: Activating learning across the curriculum*. Intellect.

Deleuze, G. (2004). *Difference and repetition*. A & C Black.

Fraser, N., & Honneth, A. (2003). *Redistribution or recognition? A political-philosophical exchange*. Verso.

Foucault, M. (2005). *The hermeneutics of the subject: Lectures at the College de France 1981–1982*. Picador.

Giroux, H. (2005). *Border crossings: Cultural workers and the politics of education* (2nd ed.). Routledge.

Greene, M. (1995). *Releasing the imagination: Essays on education, the arts, and social change*. Jossey-Bass.

Hall, S., Evans, J., & Nixon, S. (2013). *Representation* (2nd ed.). Sage.

Harding, S. (2004). *The feminist standpoint theory reader: Intellectual and political controversies*. Routledge.

Harvard Graduate School of Education. (2022). *Project Zero: MoMA's visual thinking curriculum project*. http://www.pz.harvard.edu/projects/momas-visual-thinking-curriculum-project

Hutchinson, S., Fenton-O'Creevy, M., Goodliff, G., Edwards, D., Hartnett, L., Holti, R., MacKay, E., McKeogh, S., Sansoyer, P., & Way, L. (2015). Introduction: An invitation to a conversation. In E. Wenger-Trayner, M. Fenton-O'Creevy, S. Hutchinson, C. Kubiak, & B. Wenger-Trayner (Eds.), *Learning in landscapes of practice: Boundaries, identity, and knowledgeability in practice-based learning* (pp. 1–10). Routledge.

Kompridis, N. (2013). Recognition and receptivity: Forms of normative response in the lives of the animals we are. *New Literary History*, *44*(1), 1–24.
Kumashiro, K. (2002). Against repetition: Addressing resistance to anti-oppressive change in the practices of learning, teaching, supervising, and researching. *Harvard Educational Review*, 72(1), 67–93.
Lave, J., & Wegner, E. (1991). *Situated learning: Legitimate peripheral participation*. Cambridge University Press.
Levinas, E. (2012). *Totality and infinity: An essay on exteriority*. Springer.
Link, B. (2019). White lies: Unravelling whiteness in the elementary art curriculum. *Journal of Cultural Research in Art Education*, *36*(3), 11–28.
MacGill, B. (2008). *Aboriginal education workers in South Australia: Towards equality of recognition of Aboriginal and Torres Strait Islander ethics of care practices* [Ph.D. thesis]. Flinders University.
Moll, L. (2005). Reflection and possibilities. In N. Gonzalez, L. C. Moll, & C. Amanti (Eds.), *Funds of knowledge: Theorizing practices in households, communities, and classrooms* (pp. 275–87). Lawrence Erlbaum Associates.
Noddings, N. (1984). *Caring: A feminine approach to ethics and moral education*. University of California Press.
Noddings, N. (1992). *The challenge to care in schools: An alternative approach to education*. Teachers College Press.
Noddings, N. (2002). *Educating moral people*. Teachers College Press.
Phillips, L., & Bunda, T. (2018). *Research through, with and as storying*. Routledge.
Rankin, J, Garrett, R., & MacGill, B. (2021). Critical encounters: Enacting social justice through creative and body-based learning. *Australian Educational Researcher*, *48*, 281–302.
Rolon-Dow, R. (2005). Critical care: A color(full) analysis of care narratives in the schooling experiences of Puerto Rican girls. *American Educational Research Journal*, *42*, 77–111.
Rose, D. B. (2003). Decolonising the discourse of environmental knowledge in settler societies. In G. Hawkins & S. Muecke (Eds.), *Culture and waste: The creation and destruction of value* (pp. 53–72). Rowman & Littlefield.
Strahan, A. (2012). *Levinas, subjectivity, education: Towards an ethics of radical responsibility*. Wiley-Blackwell.
Tannoch-Bland, J. (1998). Identifying White race privilege. In Foundation for Aboriginal and Islander Research Action, *Bringing Australia together: The structure and experience of racism in Australia* (pp. 33–8). Foundation for Aboriginal and Islander Research Action.
Thompson, A. (1998). Not the color purple: Black feminist lessons for educational caring. *Harvard Educational Review*, *68*, 522–53.
Ungunmerr-Baumann, M.-R., Groom, R. A., Schuberg, E. L., Atkinson, J., Atkinson, C., Wallace, R., & Morris, G. (2022). Dadirri: An Indigenous

place-based research methodology. *AlterNative: An International Journal of Indigenous Peoples*, *18*(1), 94–103.

Zembylas, M., & Boler, M. (2016). Interview with Megan Boler: From "feminist politics of emotions" to the "affective turn." In M. Zembylas & P. A. Schultz (Eds.), *Methodological advances in research on emotion in education* (pp. 17–30). Springer International Publishing.

19 Culturally Responsive Pedagogies of Discomfort: Engaging with the Difficult Knowledges of Racism

Melanie Baak and Robert Hattam

This chapter presents a case study of how a secondary teacher at a rural school in South Australia redesigned her classroom practices. Historically, rural areas in Australia have been significantly less culturally diverse than metropolitan cities. More recently, classrooms and schools in some rural areas have diversified beyond predominantly White-Anglo student cohorts. This has resulted in some teachers beginning to rethink how they teach, especially themes related to migration and racism (Forrest et al., 2017). The case study takes up this theme and discusses the experiences of Amy, a White Australian secondary teacher in a rural school as she reflects on her enactment of culturally responsive pedagogy (CRP) to explore issues and experiences of racism with students of African, Aboriginal, Indian, and Anglo-Saxon heritage.

Through the case study, we explore how pedagogical approaches that de-center "whiterarchy" (Housee, 2008, p. 427) can be "inclusive of black experiences" and voices, and use them "to question the structures, relations and processes of power found in whiterarchy" (p. 428). Drawing on the idea of pedagogies of discomfort (Boler & Zembylas, 2003; Zembylas, 2015), we also consider how CRP may be a productive approach to working with culturally and linguistically diverse students in relation to content that may be discomforting for students and teachers, or what others have referred to as difficult knowledges (Britzman, 1998; Keddie, 2012; McConaghy, 2003; Montgomery, 2013; Pitt & Britzman, 2003).

We begin by briefly introducing CRP and pedagogies of discomfort as conceptual tools to frame our reading of Amy's narrative. Amy was involved in a collaborative action research project which aimed to support teachers to enact and reflect on their use of CRP in their classrooms. She described a history of avoiding hard conversations and controversial topics. Amy also reflected on how she enacted ideas from an archive of CRP and worked with emerging tensions while learning about racism in a culturally diverse classroom. The archive she worked with includes the variations of CRP outlined in the next section.

Culturally Responsive Pedagogy

We take, as a starting point, a description of pedagogy as "a practice within which one acts with the intent of provoking experience that will simultaneously organize and disorganize a variety of understandings of our natural and social world" (Simon, 1992, p. 56). While we acknowledge the slipperiness of the term "culture," we build on work by scholars in Indigenous and critical race pedagogies calling for the use of CRP as an approach that uses "the cultural characteristics, experiences, and perspectives of ethnically diverse students as conduits for teaching them more effectively" (Gay, 2002, p. 106). CRP should not be rendered as an instructional technique (Villegas & Lucas, 2002b) and, hence, reduced to a series of steps to be implemented in classrooms. Rather we understand CRP to be a mindset (Milner, 2011; Morrison et al., 2019), a way of being (Ladson-Billings, 2006), and/or "a paradigm for teaching and learning" (Sleeter, 2012, p. 569).

Ladson-Billings (1995a, 1995b, 2009) was one of the first academics to define CRP. She has worked primarily to improve learning for African-American children and her version of CRP was developed in that context. Ladson-Billings identifies three key components of CRP. Firstly, she argues that culturally responsive teachers connect school learning to the life worlds of students (Zipin et al., 2012), but they also teach them what Delpit (2006) calls the "codes of power." Academic success at school is defined by being able to demonstrate these powerful codes, but for children whose families and communities have historically been marginalized by schooling systems, this is often not possible without strong life-world connections. Secondly, Ladson-Billings (1995a) suggests that students need to experience a degree of cultural integrity in classrooms to achieve academically. Thirdly, she argues that "students must develop a broader socio-political consciousness that allows them to critique the cultural norms, values, mores, and institutions that produce and maintain social inequities" (p. 162).

Villegas and Lucas (2002a, 2002b, 2007) build on Ladson-Billings' work to develop notions of the culturally responsive teacher. They identify six characteristics of a culturally responsive teacher:

- socio-culturally conscious, that is, recognizes that there are multiple ways of perceiving reality and that these ways are influenced by one's location in the social order;
- affirming views of students from diverse backgrounds, seeing resources for learning in all students rather than viewing differences as problems to be overcome;
- sees themself as both responsible for and capable of bringing about educational change that will make schools more responsive to all students;
- understands how learners construct knowledge and capable of promoting learners' knowledge construction;
- knows about the lives of his or her students; and

- uses their knowledge about students' lives to design instruction that builds on what they already know while stretching them beyond the familiar (Villegas & Lucas, 2002b).

Below we see ways in which Amy endeavors to utilize and develop these characteristics to work with her culturally diverse class.

Pedagogies of Discomfort

Burns (2019) suggests that "the duality of acknowledging one's own complicity in the system while at the same time working against its unfairness requires an ethic of discomfort for instructors, not just students" (p. 798). For Amy, teaching about racism entailed an element of discomfort for her as a teacher, while also acknowledging discomfort for students. On this theme, Zembylas and Papamichael (2017) suggest that a pedagogy of discomfort "is grounded in the assumption that discomforting emotions are important in challenging dominant beliefs, social habits and normative practices that sustain stereotypes and social injustice and in creating openings for empathy and transformation" (p. 3). CRP alone is not sufficient to understand Amy's pedagogical work in teaching the "difficult knowledges" of racism with her culturally diverse class. As such, we suggest bringing together CRP with understandings of pedagogies of discomfort to better understand how Amy did this work.

Amy illustrates below how a fear of teaching about topics like racism had previously meant that she avoided or skirted over these conversations in the classroom. Using CRP gave her the courage to venture into a space of pedagogical discomfort.

Methodology

Amy participated in a two-year cycle of action research alongside teachers from a range of rural and metropolitan schools. Each year consisted of a four-stage cycle: provocation, redesigning, doing, and reflecting. Participants engaged in workshops facilitated by Robert Hattam that included collective readings and discussion about CRP and supported teachers to enact an action research approach. At the conclusion of the two years, Melanie Baak undertook in-depth interviews with the participants. This enabled Amy and the other teachers to reflect on their experiences of action research and CRP. Melanie then engaged in a process of composing personal experience narratives from the interview transcripts (McCormack, 2004). Using primarily the words of the participants from their interview transcripts, Melanie crafted a narrative portrait that illustrated each participants' experience of engaging with action research and chronologically detailed their projects. Using this portraiture approach enabled us "to remain faithful to the participants' intentions, create a space for their ideas, and retain their vernacular language" (Smyth & McInerney, 2013, p. 14). Below, we extensively incorporate the section of Amy's portrait that related to her use of CRP to teach about racism in her classroom.

Amy: "CRP Can be a Tool to Navigate Difficult Content"

Amy is a secondary teacher with over 25 years' teaching experience. Amy teaches a subject called "Integrated Learning" for students in the senior secondary years at a Catholic school. This subject provides opportunities for students to study topics related to religious education and Catholic identity. Amy acknowledged that it "is definitely a subject that you can do things differently in." Amy admitted that she was quite new to teaching students from culturally and linguistically diverse backgrounds. She also acknowledged that the school has a very low number of Aboriginal or Torres Strait Islander students and there has only been an increase in students from culturally and linguistically diverse backgrounds in the past five years.

> I chose to use CRP in classes with foci like racism and migration. We have always looked at these topics within our religious education curriculum. Previously I think I would have steered clear of the hard conversations, the controversial topics, or probably wouldn't have engaged in discussion as much, just at risk of someone feeling different or feeling like we were talking about them. I didn't want to be the expert, but was nervous about opening that up for conversation. By changing the lens, I took to these topics and, using CRP, I found working in small groups and hearing the voice of every person did make a difference. Using CRP enabled me to recognize the students as experts.
>
> In working with a group of Year 11 students I developed a research question to explore how dialogue with students can drive the curriculum and add to a student's sense of connection in the class. The topic that they were about to do was racism. I was really aware that there were students in the class who would have experienced racism and I hadn't. It sat uneasily with me to be the expert standing up there teaching about racism. So that was where the question or the pedagogical challenge came out around what I needed to do differently so that I was actually hearing their voice without them being highlighted as being different.
>
> I talked to colleagues about how I was going to do that, and we considered working in small groups and hearing their voice through small groups. Strategies I used included:
>
> - negotiating tasks around aspects of identity and encouraging the personal narrative
> - bringing individual topics back to the class to promote connection
> - regular individual one-on-one or small group dialogue
> - using the experiences of individuals to connect to the curriculum.

So much knowledge is actually trapped in the students, so CRP gave strategies on how to unpack that and how to tap into that knowledge through the conversations and dialogue. Really stressing that if the story's there, we can change our pedagogy to bring those stories out. In that Year 11 group, I keep thinking about an Aboriginal girl who said, "I didn't think my story was so different." Using CRP perhaps enabled students to use their voice more. The other students also identified how much they appreciated hearing those stories. The diversity of their stories and experiences highlighted that no one person is the same but if we're in dialogue with each person and we're actually listening to their story and valuing their experiences, what we do best will come out of that.

I worked really closely with five students as part of the larger class. They were all from different cultural backgrounds: an Aboriginal girl, two boys from African countries, a boy from India, and an Anglo-Australian boy. I worked with them to express their thoughts and experiences about forms of racism they had experienced. One student did a survey of student experiences of racism, then we used that data as the data that the rest of the class looked at. We tried to explore that idea of—you don't know if racism exists unless you're the one on the receiving end of that, but then how does that look?

One of the really interesting things that came out of that was a focus on sporting communities and how these students felt in our community. That was probably the space where they experienced most racism, either on the receiving end or as bystanders. At the beginning of that first Year 11 class there were quite a lot of students who really believed that there was no racism. There was a lot of "football boys" in the class and when the conversation came up around racism in sporting venues and things that are said and the sorts of banter that's around, they said, "But that's just a joke." Those sorts of engrained thinking that you have to undo. So, I guess one of the challenges in dealing with Year 11 and 12 students is that if they're not culturally aware or haven't had much to do with other cultures, you have to kind of unlearn some things and challenge them. Instead of the class saying, "Well no, racism doesn't exist," they had to acknowledge that actually it does and sometimes it's in the spaces I'm in and I'm not recognizing it and how do I deal with that?

There's a bit of an art in challenging students of that age in a way that keeps it a dialogue. I say to them, "If we listen it doesn't mean you have to take on that other person's point of view, but it should change you in some way. If you're listening to someone's point of view that's different to yours, it should move you to a different place even if it's not much of a move. If you're talking to someone and you're not doing the listening, you're actually doing the talking, you're not talking to try to change that person's point of view but to take them to a different place of understanding." That was a good discussion with those Year 11 and 12 students about conversation and dialogue not being about criticizing, it's not about someone being right and someone else being wrong, but it's about listening to that person's experience. If it is their experience, then it is. It's real because it's theirs. I think those Year 11's really moved to a different place from that conversation. There were some mutual understandings that grew out of some of those students that I hope made a difference to the people they are.

Through my action research projects and using CRP, I learnt that CRP can contribute to cultural safety and a positive classroom environment in diverse classrooms. CRP can be a tool to navigate difficult content and leads to more effective pedagogies, stronger relationships, and practices that give all students a voice. Using CRP requires planning and reflection, and I did lots of reflection after those lessons—because in the back of my mind, there's always that aim of not wanting to highlight the "otherness" of students from culturally diverse backgrounds more than what it already is. But through the dialogue that my CRP action projects enabled I learned that teachers and students can become co-creators of the curriculum and shared knowledge.

Understanding Amy's Enactment of a Culturally Responsive Pedagogy of Discomfort

We now turn to more critically unpack the work that Amy was doing. There are three particular elements of Amy's portrait that we draw attention to and unpack in light of notions of discomfort and CRP in teaching about racism. These are:

- experiencing and negotiating teachers' discomfort in teaching about racism
- balancing CRP and discomfort, through bringing students' life worlds and experiences of racism into the classroom
- enabling spaces for speaking, listening, and hearing for all students.

Teachers' Discomfort in Teaching about Racism

Amy described that, prior to learning about and using CRP in the classroom, she would have "steered clear of the hard conversations, the controversial topics." She did not want to "be the expert" but was "nervous about opening that up for conversation." Applebaum argues that, when exploring aspects of racism and shaken by their own experiences of White fragility, "[s]ometimes educators want to avoid conflict in the classroom or do not have the tools to deal with conflict" (2017, p. 867). Similarly, Montgomery suggests that White teachers "express a fear for their own safety or career if they were to take up what they deem to be such 'controversial topics' in the classroom" (2013, p. 11). For Amy, moving away from viewing herself as having to be the expert on racism to viewing the students as experts in their own experiences, which CRP requires, enabled her to feel less discomfort, while also recognizing that some discomfort was necessary and useful. Amy was not specifically aware of a "pedagogy of discomfort"; however, she seemed to recognize some of the central tenets, where "this approach assumes that discomforting emotions play a constitutive role in challenging dominant beliefs, social habits and normative practices" (Zembylas & McGlynn, 2012, p. 41). Amy was conscious of her own discomfort relating to racism, but also of the need to acknowledge and work within the confines of the discomfort of White students and students of color. Amy was aware of the risks that are inherent in schooling White discomfort (Zembylas, 2018), but recognized the inherent value in working with her students to explore notions of race, racism, and whiteness. As she concluded, her CRP projects enabled her to learn "that teachers and students can become co-creators of the curriculum and shared knowledge" and that they are a "tool to navigate difficult content."

Balancing CRP and Discomfort

Applebaum (2017), in her article exploring whether comforting discomfort equates to complicity with White fragility, asks: "Is it possible to support white students without recentering the emotional crisis of white students, without disregarding the needs and interests of students of colour, and without reproducing the violence that students of colour endure?" (p. 862). Amy was constantly negotiating the tensions between these questions. She balanced the CRP tenet of bringing students' life worlds to the classroom with practicing pedagogies of discomfort which require consideration of who experiences the discomfort, particularly within a diverse classroom. Amy acknowledged the complexity of having an open dialogue about racism in a classroom where some students have experienced racism and others believe racism does not exist. She recognized the need for a degree of discomfort for the White students but was conscious of the need to do this so that students of color did not bear the brunt of this discomfort or so that their experiences of racism were dismissed. She was particularly wary of reproducing violence against students of color. She was conscious of the tendency of approaches to multicultural education to exoticize and essentialize the experience of the other—furthering the self–other dichotomy and highlighting the abyssal lines (De Sousa Santos, 2007). As she described, she wanted to find ways of "actually hearing their voice without them being highlighted as being different." In fact, she recognized "there is pedagogical violence that is being perpetrated against marginalized students, because the teaching approaches that are used ... who is seen to be the holder of knowledge, and the pedagogies that flow from that are also colonial" (Martin et al., 2017, p. 244).

To counter this risk of pedagogical violence, Amy engaged a range of strategies. She utilized small group work, where she strategically organized all the students of color and one White student into one group. The students of color were able to test and discuss their own emerging understandings of racism within the relative "safety" of the small group before taking the ideas they chose for discussion to the entire class.

Through working with this small group, Amy enabled the students to undertake a survey of experiences of racism in the broader community. This meant that none of the individual students were required to become or speak as experts based simply on their own experiences. The "data" from the survey spoke in a way that did not require the students of color to speak about their experiences of racism and, hence, become the "voice" of racism. Through this Amy acknowledged the needs of the students but endeavored not to reproduce the violence. While space was given for the students to voice their own experiences, there was scope for the students to be able to "retreat" to the safety of data if they needed. The survey data were a quantitative starting point from which to begin conversations that offered the students of color some protection from having to be the "cultural experts" or from having to encounter the risk of their personal experiences of racism being dismissed and/or ridiculed.

Enabling Spaces for Speaking, Listening, and Hearing

Amy suggested that her use of CRP gave students permission to use their voice more. CRP also gave Amy the impetus to provide space to enable and value the telling of the stories of students of color in her classroom. Amy highlighted the impact of this on the students of color, remembering the Aboriginal student who did not realize her story was so different (presumably from those of the White students in the class). However, perhaps even more poignantly Amy emphasized the value of White students hearing the stories of students of color. It is this hearing of the stories that we think is critical to a culturally responsive pedagogy of discomfort. Simply telling and listening, which can be inherently passive, will not necessarily enable the change desired by a pedagogy of discomfort. Taylor focuses on multiple ways of listening, arguing that "listening in the pedagogy of discomfort directly challenges didactive listening both in its emphasis on listening as a political and ethical act … listening involves students' challenging of their own preconceived assumptions, expectations and emotional responses to others' differences" (2015, p. 115). We take this slightly further to suggest that ensuring White students are open to and actually able to hear the stories of students of color is a critical part of these pedagogies, particularly when learning about racism (Baak, 2016). Amy poignantly articulated the importance of being able to hear when she reflected on telling the students, "If we listen it doesn't mean you have to take on that other person's point of view, but it should change you in some way."

In recounting the challenge of reporting the survey findings, which emphasized the prevalence of racism in sporting venues, spaces which in rural Australia normalizes strong forms of White, heteronormative masculinity, Amy reflected that the football boys in the class responded with, "But that's just a joke." This kind of response embodies White fragility where "white people react with a range of defensive moves that compensate for even the slightest distress caused by the challenges to their racial worldviews and/or to their racial innocence"

(Applebaum, 2017, p. 866). Recognizing that expressions of White fragility can shut down classroom conversations about racism, Amy worked hard to find ways to keep the dialogue open. As she described, "There's a bit of an art in challenging students of that age in a way that keeps it a dialogue." She used this as an opportunity to teach about dialogue and spaces of listening and hearing, which became so much more than simply a discussion of racism. Through that moment she taught about "conversation and dialogue not being about criticizing, it's not about someone being right and someone else being wrong, but it's about listening to that person's experience. If it is their experience, then it is. It's real because it's theirs."

Through ethical listening (Delpit, 2006) and actually hearing, Amy was able to facilitate what Zembylas and Papamichael (2017) refer to as "[s]trategic empathy … the use of empathy by the teacher in strategic ways, that is, in ways that empathise with the 'difficult' knowledge learners carry with them, even when this knowledge is disturbing to others" (p. 4).

Conclusion

It is important to note the limits of this chapter. We include a portrait of Amy's own reflections on her own practice. We did not engage in classroom observations, nor did we talk to any of the students who were in Amy's Year 11 classroom. As such, we have presented a fairly narrow reflection on this particular example of enacting a culturally responsive pedagogy of discomfort when teaching about racism. Nonetheless, we argue that Amy's reflections contain valuable insights into how she, as a White teacher, navigated this space. Amy's work with her Year 11 class only explored notions of overt or obvious racism (Montgomery, 2013). However, this was a starting point for a teacher in an historically monocultural rural town with a strong history of settler narratives and particular views of "Australian identity" to explore difficult knowledge with a group of students who are beginning to understand aspects of racism.

Amy used CRP as something of a decolonial project which positions "the work of liberation in the structures of colonisation that need to be dismantled" (Zembylas, 2018, p. 96). She also recognized the abyssal thinking and the "othering" that can occur and become reified in discussing racism and strategically worked against these. Her narrative clearly demonstrates what Zembylas (2018) argues, drawing on the work of Gaztambide-Fernández (2012): "[d]ecolonised pedagogies of discomfort entail making subjugated knowledges key points of reference in the curriculum and engendering pedagogies of solidarity that reject racial essentialisms, while confronting how white supremacy continues to inform what legitimate knowledge is in schools" (p. 98). We acknowledge the critiques of CRP, in which some have identified that

> the term culturally responsive is commonly interpreted from a mainstream, multicultural perspective, as teachers needing to be responsive to the cultures of others while continuing to be ignorant of their own culture and how it is bound up with white privilege and superiority. (Martin et al., 2017, p. 245)

While this acknowledgment is important, Amy's narrative illustrates that this is not cause to disregard CRP as an important tool to assist White teachers to engage with difficult knowledge. In coupling CRP with pedagogies of discomfort, it is clear that many of the strategies that are advocated in CRP can enable productive and beneficial conversations about difficult knowledge such as racism, particularly when engaged with in a way that enables critical reflection on the teacher's own positionality. Amy demonstrated the ways in which a culturally responsive pedagogy of discomfort might operate as "a site of intersubjective encounters that entail transformative possibilities" (Zembylas, 2007, p. xiii).

Bibliography

Applebaum, B. (2017). Comforting discomfort as complicity: White fragility and the pursuit of invulnerability. *Hypatia*, *32*(4), 862–75.

Baak, M. (2016). *Negotiating belongings: Stories of forced migration of Dinka women from South Sudan*. Brill Sense Publishers.

Boler, M., & Zembylas, M. (2003). Discomforting truths: The emotional terrain of understanding difference. In P. P. Trifonas (Eds.), *Pedagogies of difference: Rethinking education for social change* (pp. 107–30). Routledge.

Britzman, D. P. (1998). *Lost subjects, contested objects: Toward a psychoanalytic inquiry of learning.* State University of New York Press.

Burns, E. A. (2019). Ethic of discomfort: Is asking for nude lipstick racist? *Race, Ethnicity and Education*, *22*(6), 788–801.

De Sousa Santos, B. (2007). Beyond abyssal thinking: From global lines to ecologies of knowledges. *Review (Fernand Braudel Center)*, *30*(1), 45–89.

Delpit, L. (2006). *Other people's children: Cultural conflict in the classroom*. New Press.

Forrest, J., Lean, G., & Dunn, K. (2017). Attitudes of classroom teachers to cultural diversity and multicultural education in country New South Wales, Australia. *Australian Journal of Teacher Education*, *42*(5), 17–34.

Gay, G. (2002). Preparing for culturally responsive teaching. *Journal of Teacher Education*, *53*(2), 106–16.

Gaztambide-Fernández, R. A. (2012). Decolonization and the pedagogy of solidarity. *Decolonization: Indigeneity, Education & Society*, *1*(1), 41–67.

Housee, S. (2008). Should ethnicity matter when teaching about "race" and racism in the classroom? *Race, Ethnicity and Education*, *11*(4), 415–28.

Keddie, A. (2012). Poetry and prose as pedagogical tools for addressing difficult knowledges: Translocational positionality and issues of collective political agency. *Pedagogy, Culture & Society*, *20*(2), 317–32.

Ladson-Billings, G. (1995a). But that's just good teaching! The case for culturally relevant pedagogy. *Theory into Practice*, *34*(3), 159–65.

Ladson-Billings, G. (1995b). Toward a theory of culturally relevant pedagogy. *American Educational Research Journal*, *32*(3), 465–91.

Ladson-Billings, G. (2006). "Yes, but how do we do it?" Practicing culturally relevant pedagogy. In J. Landsman & C. W. Lewis (Eds.), *White teachers, diverse classrooms: A guide to building inclusive schools, promoting high expectations, and eliminating racism* (pp. 29–42). Stylus.

Ladson-Billings, G. (2009). *The dreamkeepers: Successful teachers of African American children*. John Wiley & Sons.

Martin, F., Pirbhai-Illich, F., & Pete, S. (2017). Beyond culturally responsive pedagogy: Decolonizing teacher education. In F. Pirbhai-Illich, S. Pete, & F. Martin (Eds.), *Culturally responsive pedagogy: Working towards decolonization, indigeneity and interculturalism* (pp. 235–56). Springer.

McConaghy, C. (2003). On pedagogy, trauma and difficult memory: Remembering Namatjira, our beloved. *Australian Journal of Indigenous Education*, *32*, 11–20.

McCormack, C. (2004). Storying stories: A narrative approach to in-depth interview conversations. *International Journal of Social Research Methodology*, *7*(3), 219–36.

Milner, H. R. (2011). Culturally relevant pedagogy in a diverse urban classroom. *Urban Review*, *43*(1), 66–89.

Montgomery, K. (2013). Pedagogy and privilege: The challenges and possibilities of teaching critically about racism. *Critical Education*, *4*(1).

Morrison, A., Rigney, L.-I., Hattam, R., & Diplock, A. (2019). *Toward an Australian culturally responsive pedagogy: A narrative review of the literature*. University of South Australia. http://researchoutputs.unisa.edu.au/11541.2/138335

Pitt, A., & Britzman, D. (2003). Speculations on qualities of difficult knowledge in teaching and learning: An experiment in psychoanalytic research. *Qualitative Studies in Education*, *16*(6), 755–76.

Simon, R. I. (1992). *Teaching against the grain: Texts for a pedagogy of possibility*. Greenwood Publishing Group.

Sleeter, C. E. (2012). Confronting the marginalization of culturally responsive pedagogy. *Urban Education*, *47*(3), 562–84.

Smyth, J., & McInerney, P. (2013). Whose side are you on? Advocacy ethnography: Some methodological aspects of narrative portraits of disadvantaged young people in socially critical research. *International Journal of Qualitative Studies in Education*, *26*(1), 1–20.

Taylor, A. (2015). Listening in the pedagogy of discomfort: A framework for socially just listening. In L. Waks (Ed.), *Listening to teach: Beyond didactic pedagogy* (pp. 113–36). State University of New York Press.

Villegas, A. M., & Lucas, T. (2002a). *Educating culturally responsive teachers: A coherent approach*. State University of New York Press.

Villegas, A. M., & Lucas, T. (2002b). Preparing culturally responsive teachers: Rethinking the curriculum. *Journal of Teacher Education*, *53*(1), 20–32.

Villegas, A. M., & Lucas, T. (2007). The culturally responsive teacher. *Educational Leadership*, *64*(6), 28–33.

Zembylas, M. (2007). *Five pedagogies, a thousand possibilities: Struggling for hope and transformation in education*. Sense Publishers.

Zembylas, M. (2015). "Pedagogy of discomfort" and its ethical implications: The tensions of ethical violence in social justice education. *Ethics and Education*, *10*(2), 163–74.

Zembylas, M. (2018). Affect, race, and White discomfort in schooling: Decolonial strategies for "pedagogies of discomfort." *Ethics and Education*, *13*(1), 86–104.

Zembylas, M., & McGlynn, C. (2012). Discomforting pedagogies: Emotional tensions, ethical dilemmas and transformative possibilities. *British Educational Research Journal*, *38*(1), 41–59.

Zembylas, M., & Papamichael, E. (2017). Pedagogies of discomfort and empathy in multicultural teacher education. *Intercultural Education*, *28*(1), 1–19.

Zipin, L., Sellar, S., & Hattam, R. (2012). Countering and exceeding "capital": A "funds of knowledge" approach to re-imagining community. *Discourse: Studies in the Cultural Politics of Education*, *33*(2), 179–92.

20 Culturally Responsive Pedagogy: Five Key Ideas

Abigail Diplock, Anne Morrison, Lester-Irabinna Rigney, and Robert Hattam

Acknowledgment of Country

We acknowledge that this chapter was written on Kaurna and Peramangk Country, and that sovereignty for this land has never been ceded. We pay our respects to Elders past, present, and future, and to the lands, skies, and waters, and acknowledge the sophistication of the teachings of People and Country that have been here for millennia, and that have so much to offer today.

Introduction

Across Australia, culturally and linguistically diverse Aboriginal Peoples have engaged in sophisticated educational practices for tens of thousands of years. Moreover, like many post-industrial nations, Australia is becoming increasingly culturally and linguistically diverse, and this demographic shift is reflected in public school classrooms across the country. Although incoming cultural groups bring with them a range of sophisticated philosophies and practices, these valuable resources are often unrecognized and under-utilized in a schooling system which is framed by its imperial roots and dominated by White Eurocentric curriculum and pedagogy (Vass, 2014, 2016). As a consequence, school communities are missing out on the richness that cultural diversity offers. Furthermore, students from cultural and linguistic backgrounds that are positioned as "different" are often marginalized and thereby disenfranchised, while those from Anglo-European backgrounds are privileged. Culturally responsive pedagogy (CRP) offers a hopeful countermeasure to this marginalization and accompanying deficit discourses that frame those who are not considered part of the "mainstream."

At the outset, we wish to make clear that CRP is not to be confused with *cultural competence*. Significantly, while acknowledging the central position of culture in education, CRP challenges the possibility of teachers *knowing* the cultures of their students. Cultures are understood to be "organic and constantly changing, constructed within particular socio-historical times and places" (Dean, 2001, p. 625). They vary across individuals and communities, depending on their backgrounds and circumstances. Rather than conceptualizing culture in generalized and totalizing ways, our version of CRP focuses "on practices, on how people come to live and learn within their concrete social circumstances"

(Moll, 2013, p. 155). CRP therefore demands much more than a "fragmented and superficial treatment of diversity" (Villegas & Lucas, 2002, p. 20). It highlights potential issues around essentialized and static constructions of culture (Harrison & Greenfield, 2011; Vass, 2018), recognizing students and communities as the experts in their own cultural identities.

Often, the notion of a culturally responsive pedagogy (also known as culturally relevant pedagogy, among other terms) is attributed to Gloria Ladson-Billings (1995, 1998), who drew from critical race theory to identify pedagogies that help disrupt the systemic disadvantage experienced by students of color in the United States. According to Ladson-Billings (1995), CRP is based on "a theoretical model that not only addresses student achievement but also helps students to accept and affirm their cultural identity while developing critical perspectives that challenge inequities that schools (and other institutions) perpetuate" (p. 469).

While Ladson-Billings' influential work focused on the schooling experiences of African-American students, it has inspired research in other settler colonial contexts.[1] As we found when reviewing the literature a few years ago, there was (and continues to be) a "growing body of evidence that culturally responsive pedagogies *do* improve educational experiences and outcomes of First Nations peoples and other minoritised groups" (Morrison et al., 2019, p. 58; see also Schulz et al., 2023). At the time however, there had been few advocates for CRP in Australia, and in 2018–2020 we ran a three-year project to address this gap.

The Project: Toward an Australian Culturally Responsive Pedagogy[2]

The ARC research project "Toward an Australian Culturally Responsive Pedagogy" was designed to develop a theoretically informed and empirically substantiated Australian version of CRP available to Australian educators working in schools, and to those preparing new teachers. This research brought together 13 self-selected primary and secondary teachers from schools in metropolitan Adelaide to form a professional learning community with the aim of developing a version of CRP that makes sense in the Australian context.

1 Foundational North American work includes Castagno and Brayboy (2008), Gay (2010), Sleeter (2012), Villegas and Lucas (2002), and the Assembly of Alaska Native Educators (1998). Bishop and colleagues have conducted significant research in New Zealand (Bishop, 2019; Bishop et al., 2007, 2014).

2 For more about the Toward an Australian Culturally Responsive Pedagogy project see: https://culturallyresponsivepedagogy.com.au

At the start of the project, the university researchers introduced the teachers to four tentative and relatively abstract "key ideas" that they considered to be foundational to culturally responsive practice. The teacher researchers were then supported to use these key ideas to redesign pedagogy and curriculum, and to try them out in practice. In the course of two action research cycles conducted over two years, the teachers interpreted, augmented, and, in some cases, remodeled these key ideas in various innovative ways. Meanwhile, the university researchers conducted an extensive review of the academic literature and educational policy documents, engaged in professional conversations with teachers during workshops convened twice each term, and supported teachers on site when requested. Interviews with teachers and principals were conducted at the end of each year. As a consequence, the teacher/researcher team collaboratively reworked the initial ideas of CRP to move toward the *five key ideas* that we present in this chapter. For more on the development of the five key ideas see Hattam (2023); Morrison et al. (2023); Rigney (2021, 2023a, 2023b, 2024); and Rigney and Rinaldi (2023). These works, when read collectively, are evidence of the evolution of the five key ideas for teacher pedagogy and school systems to improve practice.

Respecting teachers' professionalism was central to our research methodology, taking seriously the observation by Hayes and colleagues (2006) that "there is a real need to value teachers, their knowledges and ongoing learning" (p. 24). By recognizing that teachers are intellectuals, we do not mean to romanticize their work, but rather we understand their role at the nexus of theory and practice, where a myriad of complex decisions are made in the everyday milieu of the classroom. On this theme, we concur with Thomson (2015), who writes that, "in order to produce change, knowledge production has to occur at the local level—again and again" (p. 310).

In this chapter we share a version of the five key ideas that the teacher researchers found productive in working toward culturally responsive practices in their own classrooms. Culturally responsive teachers:

- strongly connect to students' life worlds
- view cultural difference as an asset for learning
- offer high challenge
- foster a critically conscious/activist orientation
- enable students to learn, and to express their learning, multimodally and beyond the classroom.

These key ideas are not intended as a definitive list, and they are deliberately framed in ways that leave them open to multiple interpretations. In this way, we hope that these ideas can act as provocations for pedagogical innovation across multiple local settings. These key ideas are not intended as a checklist, and do not prescribe "how to do CRP." Rather, they are offered as generative points of departure to be borrowed, adapted, and built upon in ways that work in local contexts.

We do note that our set of five key ideas for culturally responsive teachers does not include building meaningful educational relationships. As we have noted elsewhere, "The nurturing of trusting, respectful and caring relationships—between students and teachers, between students and their peers, and between teachers and the families and communities of students—is considered a vital element of CRP" (Morrison et al., 2019, p. 21). Importantly for us, educative relationships move beyond *just* friendship or therapy (Lingard, 2007). In the context of teaching across cultural difference, productive educative relationships are reciprocal, meaning that teachers learn from their students and vice versa. Many times throughout the project, the research team considered whether to include relationships as a sixth key idea. We see relationships as transcending or being embedded in the other key ideas, and hence the theme of relationships is not articulated as a distinct key idea.

Lastly, it is important to note that each of the key ideas is insufficient if taken in isolation from the others. Rather, they work with and through each other. In the following sections, we elaborate on each of the five key ideas that emerged from our research.

Strongly Connect to Students' Life Worlds

Almost a century ago, Vygotsky (1926/1997) wrote:

> Ultimately only life educates, and the deeper that life, the real world, burrows into the school, the more dynamic and the more robust will be the educational process. That the school has been locked away and walled in as if by a tall fence from life itself has been its greatest failing. (p. 345)

Arguably, this failing is particularly acute for those students who do not see their life worlds reflected in the "official" curriculum (Apple, 2000). Commonly, underlying the official curriculum is a hidden curriculum which ensures that "ways of arranging, utilising and transmitting knowledge to students, [are] generally based within the framework of a dominant culture" (Rahman, 2013, p. 661). Thus, for those students who sit outside of White cultural norms, schooling is often disconnected from their experiences of the world. CRP recognizes that students' life-world experiences form who they are both socially and as learners and are thus crucial to the educational process. Students' out-of-school lives are not "left at the school gate" but rather come into the classroom as "virtual schoolbags" (Thomson, 2002, p. 1).

Furthermore, connecting to students' life worlds is not merely a "hook" to the official curriculum. This would constitute an assimilatory education that reifies White constructions of knowledge as an "epistemological *a priori*" (Moreton-Robinson, 2004, p. 75), whereby "cultural inclusion [could become] just another form of lulling Indigenous peoples into assimilation and further colonialism" (Battiste, 2017, p. vii). Nevertheless, connecting to students' life worlds does not imply an abandonment of the codes of power. As Delpit (1988) observes, "to act as if power does not exist, is to ensure that the power status quo remains the same" (p. 292). Rather, powerful codes "can be more easily reflected upon and deliberately manipulated" (Moll, 2013, p. 35) when students are able to connect them with their own life worlds. In this way, the various knowledge systems present in the classroom are far from distinct; rather they inform each other. Drawing from Zipin's (2017) notion of *problems that matter*, curricular and life-world knowledges can be brought into conversation to enliven both and recognize them as of equal worth:

> The idea is *not* that schooling can make initial use of life-based knowledge, to "meet learners where they start from," but then leave everyday concepts behind as learning progresses to specialist knowledge of "higher worth." Rather, in educative processes, specialist concepts acquire meaning and significance, and contribute to powers of matured thought, *only by virtue of* growing into domains of life experience—the conceptual fabric—and *not* by tearing away. (p. 74, emphasis in original)

This can be significant, not only for the identities and educational outcomes of students, but also for the education system as a whole. CRP moves beyond individual change to problematize and shift our understanding of schooling. Rich resources to develop and support this process include Indigenous and other epistemologies and ontologies that are so often marginalized from dominant discourses. This redesign work involves confronting deficit assumptions, which imply that Indigenous students have much to learn from White cultures, but that White cultures have little to learn from Indigenous cultures (Hynds & Sleeter, 2011).

View Cultural Difference as an Asset for Learning

In all forms of CRP, cultural difference is understood as an asset for learning, rather than a deficit that must be remediated. This theme builds onto the previous key idea that schooling should strongly connect to students' life worlds. We suggest that the major distinction between these two key ideas is that, while connecting to students' life worlds has a broad curricular focus, viewing cultural difference as an asset foregrounds specifically the diverse cultural knowledges, experiences, languages, and practices students bring to the classroom. Cultural differences are a specific aspect of students' life worlds. They can be grist for redesigning curriculum and pedagogy that has more of an identity focus, and hence implications for learning.

Historically, deficit perceptions of cultural (and socio-economic) difference have permeated Western education systems, and these perceptions remain pervasive to this day (Weuffen et al., 2023). According to a deficit view of cultural difference, the perceived educational challenges experienced by minoritized students are due to factors inherent in their communities and cultures. Meanwhile the structural biases in education systems that privilege Anglo-European knowledges, understandings, and behaviors are rendered invisible (Bertrand, et al., 2015; Bonner et al., 2017). Cultural deficit explanations for students' "underachievement" may be overt or may be normalized and naturalized. Regardless, "[d]eficit notions render the skills and strengths of minoritized students and families invisible and unimaginable. For a teacher with this mindset implications include not recognizing prior knowledge and experiences of students that could support relevant new learning" (Hogg, 2015, p. 1).

Anti-deficit pedagogical approaches that explicitly focus on the strengths or cultural assets of students and their communities include:

- *funds of knowledge*: "historically accumulated and culturally developed bodies of knowledge and skills essential for household or individual functioning and well-being" (Moll et al., 1992, p. 133)
- *funds of identity*: "the historically accumulated, culturally developed, and socially distributed resources that are essential for a person's self-definition, self-expression, and self-understanding" (Esteban-Guitart & Moll, 2014, p. 31)
- *turn-around pedagogies*: "[involving] a physical and embodied turn by the teacher—moving to see the child and their families in different contexts with a new lens" (Kamler & Comber, 2005, p. 125).

We want to argue for a strong version of viewing cultural difference as an asset for learning, and hence it is important to move beyond tokenistic celebrations of visible and often stereotyped cultural markers such as "food, folk dancing, festivals and fashion" (Harbon & Moloney, 2015, p. 15). Watkins and Noble (2019) problematize ubiquitous Australian school events such as Multicultural Day and Harmony Day as a form of "lazy multiculturalism" which "may entail simplistic understandings of culture that reproduce essentialised understandings of difference" (p. 296). Culture is instead understood as fluid, hybrid, and dynamic. In reference to culturally *sustaining* pedagogy, Alim and Paris (2017) speak of the need to avoid "static, unidirectional notions of culture and race that center only on longstanding cultural practices of communities without also attending to continual shifts and cultural reworkings" (p. 12). We suggest that viewing cultural difference as an asset should include at least the following three dimensions:

- Teachers view their students' cultures as assets.
- Students view their peers' cultures as assets.
- Students view their own cultures as assets.

In relation to Aboriginal or Torres Strait Islander students in Australian schools, Rahman (2013) notes that, in order to negotiate formal schooling, many students have had to relinquish their cultural heritage (p. 666). For students who have been historically marginalized, achievement in formal education should not compromise their cultural integrity (Ladson-Billings, 1995). There is much research to show that, where cultural difference is seen as an asset, developing a strong cultural identity supports high academic achievement (Herbert, 2012; Rahman, 2010; Sarra, 2014) without sacrificing the cultural identity of the student.

Offer High Challenge

Deficit views of minoritized students most often impact on the learning tasks they are offered. A substantial body of literature supports the premise, first advanced more than 50 years ago by Rosenthal and Jacobson (1968), that teachers' expectations influence students' achievement (see, e.g., Johnston et al., 2019; Peterson et al., 2016). Put simply, the learning tasks that teachers offer are influenced by their expectations of their students (Peterson et al., 2016). Teachers who hold deficit views of particular students or student groups based on social factors, such as ethnicity, socio-economic status, or gender (Bishop, 2003; Bishop & Berryman, 2006), are less likely to offer learning tasks that are as challenging or rigorous as the tasks they offer students who are perceived to be members of non-stigmatized groups. For example, in settler colonial societies, persistent deficit stereotypes of Indigenous peoples are often replicated in the classroom, resulting in low academic and social expectations of students (Sarra et al., 2018).

Low-challenge pedagogies are intellectually, socially, creatively, or affectively undemanding and include what Comber (2015) refers to as "fickle literacies" such as "copying and coloring in, which foster compliance and quiet, but little else" (p. 365). Lingard and Keddie (2013) identified what they termed *pedagogies of indifference*, where teachers show high levels of care for their students but lower their expectations in doing so. In reference to the schooling of Aboriginal and Torres Strait Islander students, Rose (2012) describes this lack of rigor as an insidious form of racism: "In the classroom, 'racism by cotton wool' can be exhibited in execution of codes of discipline, standards of work, grading, professional distance and acceptable boundaries of school culture by 'going soft' on Aboriginal and Torres Strait Islander students" (p. 71). This is not to say that teachers should withhold understanding and empathy, but rather their ethic of care must include high expectations for all students, or to be "caring demanders" (Daniels-Mayes, 2016, p 227). In terms of high intellectual challenge, Morrison et al. (2008) note: "simply providing challenging curricula does not ensure culturally relevant pedagogy is occurring. Culturally relevant teachers understand that offering a rigorous curriculum rarely results in student achievement if students are not supported throughout the process of learning" (p. 436).

In relation to affective challenge, CRP engages both teachers and students in the affective dimensions of social justice issues. Following Boler (1999), Zembylas and McGlynn (2012) refer to a *pedagogy of discomfort* which "pushes students and teachers to move outside of their 'comfort zones'" (p. 55). They explain: "Pedagogically, this approach assumes that discomforting emotions play a constitutive role in challenging dominant beliefs, social habits and normative practices that sustain social inequities and in creating possibilities for individual and social transformation" (p. 41). They note that "engaging in a discomforting pedagogy is not without complications, and the ethics of doing so must be carefully considered by teachers" (p. 56). They continue: "Students need to know that they are emotionally and intellectually supported in their efforts to gain greater clarity about their emotional investments and increase their ability to account for their values and their effects on others" (pp. 56–57).

Foster a Critically Conscious/Activist Orientation

A critically conscious or activist orientation is also foundational to CRP's focus on educating for social justice. An activist orientation has the potential to contest the reproductive, colonizing function of schooling, and instead to contribute to socio-political change toward greater social justice and decolonization. This means that, while CRP aims to enable individual students' achievement, it also has a broader function that addresses power imbalances in ways that go beyond individual students' successes. As Ladson-Billings (1995) explained over 20 years ago:

> This work [of culturally relevant pedagogy] is important for its break with the cultural deficit or cultural disadvantage explanations which led to compensatory educational interventions. A next step for positing effective pedagogical practice is a theoretical

> model that not only addresses student achievement but also helps students to accept and affirm their cultural identity while developing critical perspectives that challenge inequities that schools (and other institutions) perpetuate. I term this pedagogy, *culturally relevant pedagogy*. (p. 469)

Thus, a strong version of CRP promotes a critical problematizing of the systems and structures of education. In problematizing the way broader systems perpetuate inequities, CRP seeks to unsettle and restructure curriculum and pedagogy. This situates CRP as a form of critical pedagogy which proceeds from the premise that education can be a means of creating a more socially just world through the development of critical thinking and by rewriting dominant discourses about the society in which we live (Shor & Freire, 1987). To be culturally responsive in these terms teachers need to be aware of the ways that historical and political processes and discourses of power construct a racialized landscape for their practice (Vass, 2014, 2016). This contrasts with "neoliberal reforms that purport to address racialised achievement gaps [yet] treat racism and culture as if they do not exist" (Sleeter, 2011, p. 8). In relation to Indigenous students, Castagno and Brayboy (2008) call for teachers to develop their understandings of racism, sovereignty, and Indigenous epistemologies. And in one of the systematic reviews from the extensive Aboriginal Voices Project, Vass et al. (2019) state that an "explicit engagement with efforts to foster (anti)racist and/or colour-conscious skills and knowledges" is the "foundation that actively works toward equipping teachers with the understanding, ability and confidence to critically engage with and reject deficit theorising" (p. 356; see also Moodie et al., 2019).

In addition to teacher awareness, students need to be supported to develop a critical consciousness of the social, cultural, economic, and political dimensions of their life worlds (Ladson-Billings, 2017, p. 146). Further to this, students need to be offered opportunities to take action toward solving the problems and challenges that matter in their lives (Ladson-Billings, 2021; Maher, 2023). Culturally responsive teachers support students as active citizens in their communities who can "engage productively with their lives, both now and in the future'" (Hayes et al., 2006, p. 174).

Enable Students to Learn, and to Express Their Learning, Multimodally and Beyond the Classroom

Our framing of CRP acknowledges the plurality of ways in which people express themselves and make meaning, opening up pedagogy to diverse ways of communicating in the classroom. These "multiliteracies" include "the burgeoning variety of text forms" (New London Group, 1996, p. 61) and the "increasing multiplicity and integration of significant modes of meaning-making, where the textual is also related to the visual, the audio, the spatial, the behavioural, and so on" (p. 64). Here, meaning making is framed beyond language, to encompass multiple modes of representation. As Stein (2008) explains, "the forms of representation through which students are permitted to make their meanings is a critical component in constructing classrooms as hybrid, democratic spaces which value diversity and difference" (p. 144), with digital literacy, in particular, crucial for being active, agentive citizens in our internet-mediated world (Rigney, 2018).

Finding a genuine audience for students to share their learning (Cormack et al., 1998; McArthur, 2023) is also important. The strategy decenters the role of the teacher and encourages students to participate in challenging learning activities by offering an authentic purpose for their work. When students are expected to produce high-quality work with significant academic or intellectual demands, having an audience for their learning renders it more meaningful. This not only creates an intrinsic reason for rigor, but also enables their work to have impact beyond the classroom. Several methods have been developed for this purpose, including but not limited to exhibitions, blogs, podcasts, social media campaigns, publishing in school newspapers or local magazines, multimedia presentations, and creating books. As Comber and Hill (2000) argue, we need to "equip young people with complex repertoires of practices—ways of thinking, analysing, communicating, designing and so on—that assist them to deal with (and in) changing media and modes, new contexts and problems" (p. 80).

Conclusion

Our version of CRP reframes cultural diversity from a perceived deficit to an asset that enriches school and societal spaces. This reframing requires both a critical consciousness of teachers and students, and the development of ways to connect classroom learning to students' funds of knowledge. Classroom dynamics are democratic, power is shared with the students, and students are positioned as active, agential participants in the world. In culturally responsive practice, classroom relations are re-imagined so that "young people's sense-making processes (cultures) are incorporated and enhanced, where the existing knowledges of young people … are seen as 'acceptable' and 'official,' and where the teacher interacts with students in such a way that new knowledge is co-created" (Bishop 2003, p. 221). In this way, CRP has the potential to open up "*what* counts as knowledge … *where* education might take place…[and] what counts as *pedagogy*" (Martin et al., 2017, p. 244, emphasis in original).

To put CRP in perspective, we are "clear that our activities as ... educator[s], will not be enough to change the world ... but ... by doing something inside the space of the school we can make some good contributions" (Shor & Freire, 1987, p. 180). We are hopeful that, by drawing on some of the key ideas outlined above, education can contribute to creating citizens who are more empowered to contribute to "intellectual, political, social and economic emancipation" (Rigney, 2006, p. 42).

Acknowledgment

The data used for this chapter derives from a 2017 Australian Research Council Indigenous Discovery Grant by Professor Lester-Irabinna Rigney and Professor Robert Hattam, "Toward an Australian Culturally Responsive Pedagogy" [Project ID: IN170100017]; a 2021 Australian Research Council Discovery Grant by Professor Lester-Irabinna Rigney and Professor Robert Hattam, Dr. Stephen Kelly, Professor Michalinos Zembylas, Dr. Samantha Schulz, and Dr. Nadeem Memon, "Culturally Responsive Schooling" [Project ID: DP220100651]. This work was also informed by a 2006 Australian Research Council Discovery Grant by Lester Rigney, "Indigenous Research Methodologies: Frameworks toward Indigenous Intellectual Sovereignty and the Decolonisation of Research" [Project ID: DI0348109].

Bibliography

Alim, H. S., & Paris, D. (2017). What is culturally sustaining pedagogy and why does it matter? In D. Paris & H. S. Alim (Eds.), *Culturally sustaining pedagogies: Teaching and learning for justice in a changing world* (pp. 1–21). Teachers College Press.

Apple, M. W. (2000). *Official knowledge: Democratic Education in a Conservative Age*. Routledge.

Assembly of Alaska Native Educators. (1998). *Alaska standards for culturally responsive schools*. Alaska Native Knowledge Network.

Battiste, M. (2017). Foreword. In F. Pirbhai-Illich & F. Martin (Eds.), *Culturally responsive pedagogy: Working towards decolonization, Indigeneity and interculturalism* (pp. vii–xi). Palgrave Macmillan.

Bertrand, M., Perez, W. Y., & Rogers, J. (2015). The covert mechanisms of education policy discourse: Unmasking policy insiders' discourses and discursive strategies in upholding or challenging racism and classism in education. *Education Policy Analysis Archives*, *23*, Article 93.

Bishop, R. (2003). Changing power relations in education: Kaupapa Māori messages for "mainstream" education in Aotearoa/New Zealand. *Comparative Education*, *39*(2), 221–38.

Bishop, R. (2019). *Teaching to the north-east: Relationship-based learning in practice*. NZCER Press.

Bishop, R., & Berryman, M. (2006). *Culture speaks: Cultural relationships and classroom learning*. Huia Publishers.

Bishop, R., Berryman, M., Cavanagh, T., & Teddy, L. (2007). *Te Kōtahitanga (Phase 3) Whānaungatanga: Establishing a culturally responsive pedagogy of relations in mainstream secondary school classrooms*. Ministry of Education, New Zealand.

Bishop, R., Berryman, M., & Wearmouth, J. (2014). *Te Kotahitanga: Towards effective education reform for indigenous and other minoritised students*. NZCER Press.

Boler, M. (1999). *Feeling power: Emotions and education*. Routledge.

Bonner, P. J., Warren, S. R., & Jiang, Y. H. (2017). Voices from urban classrooms: Teachers' perceptions on instructing diverse students and using culturally responsive teaching. *Education and Urban Society, 50*(8), 697–726.

Castagno, A. E., & Brayboy, B. M. J. (2008). Culturally responsive schooling for Indigenous youth: A review of the literature. *Review of Educational Research, 78*(4), 941–93.

Comber, B. (2015). Critical literacy and social justice. *Journal of Adolescent & Adult Literacy, 58*(5), 362–67.

Comber, B., & Hill, S. (2000). Socio-economic disadvantage, literacy and social justice: Learning from longitudinal case study research. *Australian Educational Researcher, 27*(3), 79–97.

Cormack, P., Johnson, B., Peters, J., & Williams, D. (1998). *Authentic assessment: Implications for teaching and learning*. Australian Curriculum Studies Association.

Daniels-Mayes, S. (2016). *Culturally responsive pedagogies of success: Improving educational outcomes for Australian Aboriginal students* [Ph.D. thesis]. University of South Australia.

Dean, R. (2001). The myth of cross-cultural competence. *Families in Society: The Journal of Contemporary Social Services, 82*(6), 623–30.

Delpit, L. (1988). The silenced dialogue: Power and pedagogy in educating other people's children. *Harvard Educational Review, 58*(3), 280–99.

Esteban-Guitart, M., & Moll, L. C. (2014). Funds of identity: A new concept based on the funds of knowledge approach. *Culture & Psychology, 20*(1), 31–48.

Gay, G. (2010). *Culturally responsive teaching: Theory, research, and practice*. Teachers College Press.

Harbon, L., & Moloney, R. (2015). "Intercultural" and "multicultural," awkward companions: The case in schools in New South Wales, Australia. In H. Layne, V. Trémion, & F. Dervinches (Eds.), *Making the most of intercultural education* (pp. 15–33). Cambridge Scholars Publishing.

Harrison, N., & Greenfield, M. (2011). Relationship to place: Positioning Aboriginal knowledge and perspectives in classroom pedagogies. *Critical Studies in Education*, *52*(1), 65–76.

Hattam, R. (2023). Towards a decolonising Australian culturally responsive pedagogy? In L.-I. Rigney (Ed.), *Global perspectives and new challenges in culturally responsive pedagogies: Super-diversity and teaching practice* (pp. 75–88). Routledge.

Hayes, D., Mills, M., Christie, P., & Lingard, R. (2006). *Teachers and schooling making a difference: Productive pedagogies, assessment and productive performance*. Allen & Unwin.

Herbert, J. (2012). Delivering the promise: Empowering teachers to empower students. In K. Price (Ed.), *Aboriginal and Torres Strait Islander education: An introduction for the teaching profession* (pp. 35–50). Cambridge University Press.

Hogg, L. (2015). Funds of knowledge: A tool for New Zealand teachers to reimagine the lives of minoritized students. *International Journal of Learner Diversity and Identities*, *22*(4), 1–16.

Hynds, A., & Sleeter, C. E. (2011). Professional development from teacher and facilitator perspectives. In C. E. Sleeter (Ed.), *Professional development for culturally responsive and relationship-based pedagogy* (pp. 91–113). Peter Lang.

Johnston, O., Wildy, H., & Shand, J. (2019). A decade of teacher expectations research 2008–2018: Historical foundations, new developments, and future pathways. *Australian Journal of Education*, *63*(1), 44–73.

Kamler, B., & Comber, B. (2005). Turn-around pedagogies: Improving the education of at-risk students. *Improving Schools*, *8*(2), 121–31.

Ladson-Billings, G. (1995). Toward a theory of culturally relevant pedagogy. *American Educational Research Journal*, *32*(3), 465–91.

Ladson-Billings, G. (1998). Just what is critical race theory and what's it doing in a nice field like education? *International Journal of Qualitative Studies in Education*, *11*(1), 7–24.

Ladson-Billings, G. (2017). The (r)evolution will not be standardized: Teacher education, hip hop pedagogy, and culturally relevant pedagogy. In D. Paris & H. S. Alim (Eds.), *Culturally sustaining pedagogies: Teaching and learning for justice in a changing world* (pp. 141–56). Teachers College Press.

Ladson-Billings, G. (2021). Race, research, and urban education. In H. R. Milner & K. Lomotey (Eds.), *Handbook of urban education* (2nd ed., pp. 9–25). Routledge.

Lingard, B. (2007). Pedagogies of indifference. *International Journal of Inclusive Education*, *11*(3), 245–66.

Lingard, B., & Keddie, A. (2013). Redistribution, recognition and representation: Working against pedagogies of indifference. *Pedagogy, Culture & Society*, *21*(3), 427–47.

Maher, K. (2023). Culturally responsive movements for climate justice: Learning from and with student activism. In L.-I. Rigney (Ed.), *Global perspectives and new challenges in culturally responsive pedagogies: Super-diversity and teaching practice* (pp. 131–48). Routledge.

Martin, F., Pirbhai-Illich, F., & Pete, S. (2017). Beyond culturally responsive pedagogy: Decolonizing teacher education. In F. Pirbhai-Illich, S. Pete, & F. Martin (Eds.), *Culturally responsive pedagogy: Working towards decolonization, indigeneity and interculturalism* (pp. 235–56). Palgrave Macmillan.

McArthur, J. (2023). Rethinking authentic assessment: Work, well-being, and society. *Higher Education*, *85*(1), 85–101.

Moll, L. C. (2013). *L. S. Vygotsky and education*. Routledge.

Moll, L. C., Amanti, C., Neff, D., & González, N. (1992). Funds of knowledge for teaching: Using a qualitative approach to connect homes and classrooms. *Theory into Practice*, *31*(2), 132–41.

Moodie, N., Maxwell, J., & Rudolph, S. (2019). The impact of racism on the schooling experiences of Aboriginal and Torres Strait Islander students: A systematic review. *Australian Educational Researcher*, *46*(2), 273–95.

Moreton-Robinson, A. (2004). Whiteness, epistemology and Indigenous representation. In A. Moreton-Robinson (Ed.), *Whitening race: Essays in social and cultural criticism* (pp. 75–88). Aboriginal Studies Press.

Morrison, A., Rigney, L.-I., Hattam, R., & Diplock, A. (2019). *Toward an Australian culturally responsive pedagogy: A narrative review of the literature*. University of South Australia.

Morrison, A., Rigney, L.-I., Hattam, R., & Diplock, A. (2023). Advancing culturally responsive pedagogy in an Australian context. In L.-I. Rigney (Ed.), *Global perspectives and new challenges in culturally responsive pedagogies: Super-diversity and teaching practice* (pp. 211–21). Routledge.

Morrison, K. A., Robbins, H. H., & Rose, D. G. (2008). Operationalizing culturally relevant pedagogy: A synthesis of classroom-based research. *Equity & Excellence in Education*, *41*(4), 433–52.

New London Group. (1996). A pedagogy of multiliteracies: Designing social futures. *Harvard Educational Review*, *66*(1), 60–93.

Peterson, E. R., Rubie-Davies, C., Osborne, D., & Sibley, C. (2016). Teachers' explicit expectations and implicit prejudiced attitudes to educational achievement: Relations with student achievement and the ethnic achievement gap. *Learning and Instruction*, *42*, 123–40.

Rahman, K. (2010). Addressing the foundations for improved Indigenous secondary student outcomes: A South Australian qualitative study. *Australian Journal of Indigenous Education*, *39*(1), 65–76.

Rahman, K. (2013). Belonging and learning to belong in school: The implications of the hidden curriculum for Indigenous students. *Discourse: Studies in the Cultural Politics of Education*, *34*(5), 660–72.

Rigney, L.-I. (2006). Indigenist research and Aboriginal Australia. In J. E. Kunnie & N. I. Goduka (Eds.), *Indigenous peoples' wisdom and power: Affirming our knowledge through narratives* (pp. 32–48). Ashgate.

Rigney, L.-I. (2018). Defining culturally responsive digital education for classrooms: Writing from Oceania to build Indigenous Pacific futures. In E. McKinley & L. T. Smith (Eds.), *Handbook of Indigenous education* (pp. 1–17). Springer.

Rigney, L.-I. (2021). Aboriginal child as knowledge producer: Bringing into dialogue Indigenist epistemologies and culturally responsive pedagogies for schooling. In B. Hokowhitu, A. Moreton-Robinson, L. Tuhiwai-Smith, C. Andersen, & S. Larkin (Eds.), *Routledge handbook of critical Indigenous studies* (pp. 578–90). Routledge.

Rigney, L.-I. (2023a). On the need for new culturally responsive pedagogies. In L.-I. Rigney (Ed.), *Global perspectives and new challenges in culturally responsive pedagogies: Super-diversity and teaching practice* (pp. 3–10). Routledge.

Rigney, L.-I. (2023b). Teachers cultivating Aboriginal child as knowledge producer: Advancing Australian culturally responsive pedagogies. In L.-I. Rigney (Ed.), *Global perspectives and new challenges in culturally responsive pedagogies: Super-diversity and teaching practice* (pp. 10–20). Routledge.

Rigney, L.-I. (2024). Teaching through lifeworlds of Aboriginal children: Australian opportunities through culturally responsive pedagogies. In C. Brock, B. Exley, & L.-I. Rigney (Eds.), *International perspectives on literacies, diversities, and opportunities for learning* (pp. 47–59). Routledge.

Rigney, L.-I., & Rinaldi, C. (2023). Teaching in cultural and linguistic super-diverse Australian classrooms: A north–south exploration of Reggio Emilia. In B. Fyfe, Y. L. Lee-Johnson, J. Reyes, & G. Schroeder Yu (Eds.), *Affirming the rights of emergent bilingual and multilingual children and families: Interweaving research and practice through the Reggio Emilia approach* (pp. 209–25). Routledge.

Rose, M. (2012). The "silent apartheid" as the practitioner's blindspot. In K. Price (Ed.), *Aboriginal and Torres Strait Islander education: An introduction for the teaching profession* (pp. 64–80). Cambridge University Press.

Rosenthal, R., & Jacobson, L. (1968). *Pygmalion in the classroom: Teacher expectation and pupils' intellectual development*. Rinehart and Winston.

Sarra, C. (2014). *Strong and smart—towards a pedagogy for emancipation: Education for First Peoples*. Routledge.

Sarra, C., Spillman, D., Jackson, C., Davis, J., & Bray, J. (2018). High-expectations relationships: A foundation for enacting high expectations in all Australian schools. *Australian Journal of Indigenous Education*, *49*(1), 32–45.

Schulz, S., Morrison, A., Blanch, F. R., Buckskin, J., & Corrie, S. (2023). *Improving schooling and outcomes for Aboriginal and Torres Strait Islander learners in South Australian Catholic schools and centres: A narrative review of the literature*. University of Adelaide and Flinders University.

Shor, I., & Freire, P. (1987) *A pedagogy for liberation: Dialogues on transforming education*. Bergin & Garvey.

Sleeter, C. E. (2011). An agenda to strengthen culturally responsive pedagogy. *English Teaching, 10*(2), 7–23.

Sleeter, C. E. (2012). Confronting the marginalization of culturally responsive pedagogy. *Urban Education, 47*(3), 562–84.

Stein, P. (2008). *Multimodal pedagogies in diverse classrooms: Representation, rights and resources*. Routledge.

Thomson, P. (2002). *Schooling the rustbelt kids. Making a difference in changing times*. Allen & Unwin.

Thomson, P. (2015). Action research with/against impact. *Educational Action Research, 23*(3), 309–11.

Vass, G. (2014). The racialised educational landscape in Australia: Listening to the whispering elephant. *Race, Ethnicity and Education, 17*(2), 176–201.

Vass, G. (2016). Everyday race-making pedagogies in the classroom. *British Journal of Sociology of Education, 37*(3), 371–88.

Vass, G. (2018). "Aboriginal learning style" and culturally responsive schooling: Entangled, entangling, and the possibilities of getting disentangled. *Australian Journal of Teacher Education, 43*(8), 89–104.

Vass, G., Lowe, K., Burgess, C., Harrison, N., & Moodie, N. (2019). The possibilities and practicalities of professional learning in support of Indigenous student experiences in schooling: A systematic review. *Australian Educational Researcher, 46*(2), 341–61.

Villegas, A. M., & Lucas, T. (2002). Preparing culturally responsive teachers: Rethinking the curriculum. *Journal of Teacher Education, 30*(1), 20–32.

Vygotsky, L. (1997). *Educational psychology*. St. Lucie Press. (Original work published 1926)

Watkins, M., & Noble, G. (2019). Lazy multiculturalism: Cultural essentialism and the persistence of the Multicultural Day in Australian schools. *Ethnography and Education, 14*(3), 295–310.

Weuffen, S., Maxwell, J., & Lowe, K. (2023). Inclusive, colour-blind, and deficit: Understanding teachers' contradictory views of Aboriginal students' participation in education. *Australian Educational Researcher, 50*, 89–110.

Zembylas, M., & McGlynn, C. (2012). Discomforting pedagogies: Emotional tensions, ethical dilemmas and transformative possibilities. *British Educational Research Journal, 38*(1), 41–59.

Zipin, L. (2017). Pursuing a problematic-based curriculum approach for the sake of social justice. *Journal of Education (University of KwaZulu-Natal), 69*, 67–92.

21 Inclusive Pedagogies of Obscenity: Critical Literacy Takes on Offensive Language in the Classroom

Penelope Bateman

> Young people are not inert materials to be prodded, poked and pontificated upon—they are active, live agents that have viewpoints, aspirations, and designs for their futures, which they are not at all reticent in speaking vociferously into existence ... Young people are the most salient witnesses of what occurs in schools and classrooms, yet at the same time, they are the most marginalized and excluded.
>
> (SMYTH & MCINERNEY, 2012, PP. 1, 3)

A Prologue of Sorts

This chapter is a report of my pre-service teacher inquiry learning project, which was part of a mandatory assessment for the Teachers Registration Board. To become a qualified teacher in Australia, pre-service teachers must pass the Teacher's Performance Assessment (TPA) (AITSL 2017).[1] The TPA demands pre-service teachers conduct and document their own inquiry project to provide evidence of their practical skills and knowledge, and to demonstrate we can link our classroom practice to an evidence base. We choose our own topic, engage in a small action research project, and document the results. In my case, my university teachers have encouraged me to publish a polished version of my TPA report, in part because the case study makes a unique contribution to the published archive of funds of knowledge approaches (Moll, 2014, 2019; Rodriguez, 2013). As well, there are too few published accounts of the inquiries of pre-service teachers, who are now required to demonstrate a "teacher as researcher" capacity. As such the chapter also provides teacher educators and pre-service teachers with a narrative account of reflective practice conducted by a pre-service teacher, grappling with teaching in a "disadvantaged school" context (Hattam, 2016).

The idea for my inquiry project was the result of a combination of factors that began the day I received confirmation of my teaching placement. I would be teaching in the "'northern suburbs of Adelaide,' or 'the North' as we like to call it in our abbreviated Australian vernacular" (Hattam, 2018, p. 215). The

1 The Teacher's Performance Assessment is as assessment of reflective practice (planning, teaching, and assessing) completed by pre-service teachers using evidence collected in the final year professional experience (AITSL, 2017).

notion of vernacular language here became the focus of my inquiry, as it became apparent early on in my placement that, to communicate effectively with my students, I needed to acknowledge their "local literacies" (Luke et al., 1994). It just so happened that my students were particularly well-versed in swearing or obscene language.

The public school where this inquiry project took place sits within a multicultural and high-poverty catchment zone in the northern suburbs of Adelaide. While for the most part the students work harmoniously together, this melting pot of social backgrounds and cultures does boil over on occasion. Importantly for me, a racially motivated brawl between a large number of students took place at the school the week before my placement started. As offensive language was one of a number of factors that led to this brawl, I thought it would be appropriate to address the negative impact of such language in a monitored classroom environment. Offensive language was already in use in the yard, the hallways, and the classrooms, so it made sense to channel it into more appropriate teaching and learning. Therefore, the focus of this inquiry was to re-contextualize the students' understanding of offensive language through an inclusive pedagogy of obscenity.

I took up the challenge of reframing obscene language into critical learning and my reading of the critical pedagogy literature—the notions of "dark funds of knowledge" (Zipin, 2009), "pedagogies of obscenity" (Wolgemuth et al., 2020), and "inclusive pedagogies" (Woods et al., 2015)—provided a conceptual framework for my deliberations. What follows is a short review of this conceptual framework, a report on my inquiry, and some conclusions that provide a contribution to a classroom challenge that is too often considered a behavior problem rather than a worthwhile learning opportunity.

The Context: The North

My mother is from the North and she was a British immigrant, or "10-pound pom," who settled in the area in the late 1950s and early 1960s (see Hattam, 2018). She was the eldest of six children from a proud working-class family who shared fond memories of friendly neighbors, well-tended homes, and delicious hot chips from the local store. In her late teens, my mother left school to study nursing and moved away from the area. One day, years later, when we were in the area, my mum decided to take our family for a drive past her childhood home. After a few wrong turns we found a run-down house with peeling paint and a sagging couch on the front porch. The garden was completely overgrown and there was a rusted car parked in the long grass. Furthermore, most of the other houses on the street were versions of the same. It was not what any of us had expected and my mother was forced to consider whether she was looking back through rose-tinted glasses or whether the North had really changed that much.

So what happened in those intervening years (Peel, 1995)? Major industries were shut down and people lost their jobs (Thomson, 2003). For years, I remember listening to the local news forecasting the closure of General Motors, specifically of the Elizabeth plant, in which 1,600 manufacturing jobs were lost in as little as five years (Hambides, 2013). The North became known as a "rustbelt" characterized by intergenerational unemployment (Thomson, 2003). Coinciding with this period, the North became a destination for further waves of immigration, mostly from Australian humanitarian refugee programs, including refugees from Vietnam, Cambodia, Bosnia, and Serbia, and more recently from Sudan, Somalia, Bhutan, and Afghanistan (Hattam, 2018, p. 215). The North is thus now more culturally diverse and language barriers make it harder to find work and engage in school and community activities.

In the past decade or so, the North has been cited as a prime example of: regional income inequality (Senate Community Affairs References Committee, 2014); a high proportion of jobless families (Bankwest Curtin Economics Centre, 2014); and one of the top three areas of social exclusion in Australia (Social Inclusion Unit, 2007). Put simply, those living in the North are less likely to have the economic and social resources, opportunities, and capabilities to learn, work, engage, and have a voice (Australian Social Inclusion Board, 2012). Specifically on education, the:

> northern suburbs schools serve one of the most socio-economically disadvantaged regions in Australia, and so not surprisingly, when measured by any metrics, these schools demonstrate what is a persistent correlation between low SES background and lack of success at school. (Hattam, 2018, p. 217)

Conceptual Framing

Offensive Language as Critical Literacy

Research into "multiple literacies" has long argued for the inclusion of "vernacular literacies" (McLaughlin, 1996). Vernacular here refers to "the practices of those who lack cultural power and who speak a critical language grounded in local concerns" (p. 56). A previous study into middle years pedagogy in the northern suburbs, the "Redesigning Pedagogy in the North Project" (see Hattam et al., 2009; Prosser et al., 2010), recognized "the possibilities of studying local dialects, vernacular languages of local youth subcultures, or rap music, as just a few examples" (Hattam et al., 2009, p. 311). As many young people living in the northern suburbs of Adelaide bring their local literacies to school, it is through their vernacular literacies that they communicate their thoughts and opinions to others. For me, a focus on offensive language would be a logical extension of that definition.

Teaching literacy, regardless of whether it is traditional or local, requires the development of critical literacy skills. According to Luke et al. (1994), classrooms should provide a forum whereby students can talk critically about community texts, including "the opportunity to see and weigh the cultural, gender and social class perspectives, possibilities and opinions of texts and readings" (pp. 148–49). Although their work did not include offensive texts, such "morally and politically loaded language" would provide a wealth of material for these types of critical discussions (p. 149). Furthermore, it is through discussions that students could become aware of some of the racist, homophobic, misogynistic, and other connotations of such language.

Funds of Knowledge: From North America to South Australia

González et al. (2005) have introduced a "funds of knowledge" approach that assumes "that the educational process [could] be greatly enhanced when teachers [connect with] their students' everyday lives" (p. 6). The original study employed teachers and ethnographers to unearth "historically accumulated and culturally developed … skills" which could be used in the classroom to better connect the educational process with the everyday lives of students (Moll et al., 2005, p. 72).

The funds of knowledge approach was borrowed and bent by the "Redesigning Pedagogies in the North (RPiN) Project," which investigated how northern suburbs public teachers could redesign their pedagogies through making strong connections with the life worlds of their students (Zipin et al., 2012). The RPiN project reasoned that "traditional school curriculum ignores the rich literate repertoires practiced in non-elite communities, thus treating people with structurally less powerful local knowledge" (Hattam et al., 2009, p. 311) as deficit (Hattam & Prosser, 2008).

> On this theme, there are a number of variations that offer resources: *Negotiating the curriculum* (Boomer et al., 1992); a *funds of knowledge* approach (Moll et al., 1992; Gonzalez et al., 2005); a *local literacies* approach (Street, 1994; Luke et al., 1994); *"place-based" pedagogies* (Kerkham & Comber, 2012); *multiliteracies* (New London Group, 1996); and *situated pedagogy* (Shor, 1988). (Hattam, 2023, p. 81)

The RPiN project borrowed the funds of knowledge concept but did not conduct ethnographies of northern suburbs communities that were shared with teachers. Rather, the project team supported teachers to design pedagogies that built students' capabilities to research their own life worlds and communities (Zipin et al., 2013). Teachers were ethnographers of their own teaching and students were researchers of their own life worlds. The original funds of knowledge approach focused on knowledge assets that circulated in communities but more recently Zipin (2009) has proposed focusing on what he calls "dark funds of knowledge."

Zipin (2009) has reasoned that students not only bring positive assets of community life into the classroom, but also the more "troubling" aspects of community life. Hence, acknowledging the more complex reality of their lives is not deficit thinking necessarily, but offers a more realistic understanding of funds of knowledge. Indeed, rather than shy away from these dark funds of knowledge, Zipin argues that teachers could be "offering curricular potentials to 'fund' revitalised curricula that engage students by meeting them 'where they live'" be used as funds for curricula that arouse vital and meaningful senses of life-relevance" (p. 322). This idea provided some validation and a generative framework for my unit on offensive language, which was taught within the South Australian Certificate of Education (SACE) curriculum. My task was to work out how I could connect productively with my students' troubling offensive language as a way to improve both their academic and social learning.

Pedagogies of Obscenity for Classroom Management

Aware that this more "difficult knowledge" (Zembylas, 2014) had to be taught with careful consideration, I sought out Wolgemuth et al.'s (2020) article "(In defence of) pedagogies of obscenity." They proposed classroom management strategies that, rather than restricting the classroom discussion, left room for frank expression. Their notion of limits explained this well: "a hard limit: what must not be done, ever. Soft limit, something that can be done but only in a certain way" (p. 32). I explained this concept to my class and we agreed that offensive hate speech was a hard limit (not to be used under any circumstances), whereas other swear words were a soft limit (could be discussed under appropriate circumstances). Indeed, the admittance of such language added to and prompted critical classroom discussion. I believed that I now had the theoretical foundations and the management strategies for the offensive language topic.

Inclusive Pedagogies in the English Classroom

My challenge though was to develop curriculum and pedagogies that would both promote inclusivity (Woods et al., 2015) and achieve the critical understandings of text which my students needed to achieve in their SACE. Specifically, I wanted to focus on "how texts work to represent the world in particular ways and not others" (p. 45). To this end, I chose a variety of texts that contained offensive language.

In studying these texts, I used inclusive pedagogies of "situated practice, overt instruction, critical framing and transformed practice" (p. 59). I used situated practice to connect their difficult knowledge to the topic of offensive language. I used overt instruction to make explicit the links between my students' prior knowledge of offensive language and alternative perspectives on such language. I used critical framing through key inquiry questions to motivate my learners to reflect on "what they have come to know and assume" about offensive language (Woods et al., 2015, p. 60). Transformed practice, in the form of a co-constructed task, then provided my students with the opportunity to articulate their newfound understanding of offensive language in multiple contexts.

Methodology

My inquiry project was framed by the following questions:

- What role did inclusive pedagogies of obscenity play in supporting students in a Year 11 English class who had evidenced low literacy and disengagement in the past?
- How did pedagogies of obscenity (Wolgemuth et al., 2020) help me to access my students' dark funds of knowledge (Zipin, 2009) and subsequently improve their engagement in classroom activities?
- What inclusive pedagogies (Woods et al., 2015) supported the students who had evidenced low literacy in the past?
- What data demonstrated that the impact of inclusive pedagogies of obscenity on the students was positive, both in terms of their engagement and academic outcomes?

I engaged an action research design over the course of a four-week block in a SACE Stage 1 Essential English class. I collected evidence of my students' learning progression from three key learning moments at the beginning, middle, and toward the end of the project. I also conducted two case studies on students whom I believe represented their cohort most accurately.

Context and Participants

The class I chose to study had a community of 21 learners, all of whom had struggled with school literacy. Thirteen students had additional needs and one had special needs. For two students, English was an additional language and three students identified as Aboriginal and Torres Strait Islander. Eleven of the students had SACE Special Provisions. Attendance was approximately 75 percent and homework was often not completed by students. Two-thirds of the class were boys and they exhibited unproductive behaviors such as talking in class, using offensive language, and throwing stationary. They were challenging to engage with traditional teaching pedagogies, such as explicit teaching, because they were easily distracted. The girls in the class were quiet and withdrawn, in the sense that they did not voluntarily participate in class discussion. Given the gender differences, I chose case study students to represent two different facets of my class: an outspoken boy (Case 1), and a quiet girl (Case 2). Both students scored well below average in standardized literacy testing, as did the majority of their peers.

Key Learning Moments and Data

During this four-week inquiry, I planned the three main data collection points around the three key learning moments.

Moment 1: I introduced the topic of offensive language briefly through overt instruction (Woods et al., 2015). First, to ascertain prior knowledge, I had the students undertake a class poll and complete an individual survey on offensive language. I then asked the students to write down three swear words, and to categorize these words according to how offensive they found them: mild, medium, or severe. The students then used sticky notes to put their answers on a table I had projected onto the board. I pointed out how many of the words appeared across two or more categories, and facilitated a class discussion about how meaning was embedded into language. We also spoke about *hard* and *soft* limits on offensive language in the classroom (Wolgemuth et al., 2020), predominantly citing the words that frequently appeared under the severe categorization.

Moment 2: At the beginning of the lesson, I projected a cartoon onto the board. The cartoon itself contained no offensive words, but depicted Aboriginal and Torres Strait Islander Peoples unfavorably. I asked the students if the cartoon was an offensive text and most of them said no. I explained more about the context of the cartoon, and then asked them whether this new knowledge had changed their opinion of the text. Most of them said yes. I then engaged the whole class in an in-depth text study, using a mix of overt instruction and critical framing instruction (Woods et al., 2015), whereby we identified and explained the text features present. I then tasked the students with a short text response whereby I explained the function of Twitter, provided scaffolded instructions, and modeled how to write a tweet. The students then *posted* their tweets on the whiteboard to share with the rest of the class. I combined their #hashtags into a mind cloud to display in the classroom.

Moment 3: I projected the rubric for the students' summative assessment interview on the board. I handed out copies of the rubric between pairs of students and tasked them with highlighting the key words. I then modeled how to incorporate a key word into an interview question. Afterwards, I allocated a key word to each pair, and had them create their own interview question. I collated the questions and talked the class through choosing the best ones. I then handed each student a user-friendly rubric and explained how to mark it. My supervisor and I then modeled the interview to the students using the questions they had written. We made sure to include a good example and a poor example. The students graded us and gave us a mixture of excellent and ruthless feedback.

Data Analysis and Findings

There was significant evidence to show that the impact of inclusive pedagogies of obscenity on my class was positive. At the beginning and end point of the unit I asked the students two questions and graphed their responses. The first question was "Do you use offensive language?" and the second was "Do you think it is offensive to do so?" Largely, all students except one admitted that they still used offensive language. However, only two students thought it was offensive to do so the first time, whereas 13 students thought it was offensive to do so the second time. This marked increase evidenced their understanding that some of the language they use is considered offensive. Hence, I was able to access their dark funds of knowledge and turn these into "learning assets" through my pedagogy (Zipin, 2009, p. 321). Feedback from my supervising teachers on learning moment 2 mentioned that "critical questions worked well—made students reconsider and in some cases change their opinions of the text." In learning moment 3, according to my own notes, students went from having "no idea about the rubric to enthusiastically marking myself and my supervisor." This was a clear learning progression. In the final assessment 55 percent of students achieved a B-grade or higher, and none of the students who participated in the interview failed. Feedback sheets at the conclusion of the unit also detailed what they had learnt about the effect offensive language could have on people, and explained how the course had made them re-think their use of such language. Hence, the class as a whole achieved both academic success and social understanding of offensive language in context.

Case 1 was an engaged participant over the course of the unit. The first learning moment saw him access his dark funds of knowledge (Zipin, 2009) through situated learning (Woods et al., 2015) via the student survey and the class categorization activity. His survey told me that he heard offensive language from his family, at school, and in his workplace. He also used offensive language himself. In the first activity, he needed a reminder about hard limits (Wolgemuth et al., 2020). My reflective notes refer to a moment when he asked loudly "What's wrong with the word c*nt?" He was not trying to be offensive, but I explained how he might have offended others who had categorized the word as severe, and he was receptive to this. This led me to believe that his use of offensive language was not due to any ill intent, but more a lack of understanding about the meaning embedded in this language.

Learning moment 2 had a clear impact on Case 1. His initial response when I showed the cartoon was confusion: "but there's no swearing in it." However, his opinion of this changed after a mix of critical framing and overt instruction (Woods et al., 2015). His comprehension sheet was evidence of how he took this learning on board, specifically in how he mentioned the context and answered how the cartoon could have been seen as offensive. His tweet response further detailed how he thought the cartoon was "racist," evidencing his understanding that offensive language is not always overt, but that it can be implied as well.

Case 1 achieved a B overall for his final interview response. He was prepared for the interview after co-constructing the assignment with his peers (Woods et al., 2015). He spoke about context, and about the purpose and function of offensive language. Furthermore, in response to a question about language features he responded, "I didn't really understand them until you went through them." Thus, he directly spoke to the positive impact of my pedagogy on his understanding. In Case 1's final feedback form he wrote: "It hasn't made me re-think using swearwords, but it has made me be more aware of my surroundings and who I'm with or who's near me so I don't make racist or homophobic comments." Hence, my inclusive pedagogies of obscenity changed his mind set about offensive language.

Case 2 was quietly engaged during learning moment 1. She accessed her dark funds of knowledge (Zipin, 2009) in her student survey and participated in the class activity. Although she admitted to using such language herself, she recognized that it was not always appropriate to do so. However, she still thought that it was okay to use offensive language "at school with your friends," or when "explaining something." When called upon, she did explain why she had categorized her terms into mild, medium, and severe but she seemed uncomfortable doing so.

Though Case 2 remained quiet and considered, she spoke up more over the course of the unit. In learning moment 2 one of the boys in the class asked, "What's a stereotype?" She replied, "It's when you judge a group of people by the worst thing about them." The fact that she did so without prompting shows how familiar my students were becoming with classroom discussion. Her short text response then called the cartoon out for being "racist." Hence, she clearly understood how offense could be embedded into a text.

In learning moment 3, Case 2 was involved in transformed practice when she came up with the interview question "How is the text meaningful to you?" (Woods et al., 2015). In her final interview she responded with: "Just be nice to everyone, don't be so rude, and you don't have to swear at everyone to know that we think you're cool, and that we respect ya..." Through colloquial language she effectively described the purpose of my inquiry project. Evidence of her academic understanding of offensive language texts, specifically of language in context, was clear in her transcript and B-result. In Case 2's final feedback form she wrote: "Lately I've been trying to cut down how much I swear at school and home because I'm starting to think I should only use it making sure everyone is okay with it before just straight up using it." Hence, my inclusive pedagogies of obscenity changed her mind set about offensive language.

If Not at School Then Where?

During my teaching of this unit I did make some changes to my pedagogical encounters, informed by the inclusive pedagogies framework mentioned earlier. By design, I engaged my students' difficult knowledge through connecting the learning to their own life worlds. During my first lesson, some students were speaking out of turn when I used basketball questions as critical framing (Woods et al., 2015). During the second lesson I explained the concept of critical framing to the students before the class discussion. I also learnt to keep my overt instructions short to hold my students' interest. To do so, I interspersed more class discussion through critical framing. Hence, rather than follow the inclusive pedagogies framework exactly, I mixed up the stages according to the learning needs of my students on any given day.

Some of my better teaching was organized around "teachable moments" (McInerney, 2010, p. 28). As an example, I planned a class yarning circle (Mills et al., 2013, p. 287) to read aloud a text from Aboriginal actor Meyne Wyatt (2022). The class read the text line by line together and this lesson created an environment where the Aboriginal and Torres Strait Islander students felt that they could share their own experiences of racism in Australia. Not only did this add to our understanding of the wider context of the text, it also spoke to the effect of such language on members of our community. And when I sought student feedback about their favorite lesson in the course, many students mentioned this one.

In regard to pedagogies of obscenity, although the students understood the hard and soft limits on offensive language, in the classroom they occasionally transgressed. On one occasion a student yelled "f*ggot" across the classroom at another student. Initially, when we spoke about what had transpired he was not contrite at all. Two weeks later, when I was helping him with his classwork, he apologized for what had happened and explained that his dad used that sort of language "all the time." When I asked him what that meant for him moving forwards in this course he replied, "I want to be better than that." This conversation, combined with feedback from the majority of the class that they wanted to re-think their use of offensive language, meant that collectively my planning and practice had a positive effect on the students.

Although my research and planning had equipped me with strategies to make the most of this context, I was not fully prepared for how to productively engage my students' difficult knowledge. It made me recognize my own privilege and sharpened my focus on this research inquiry. And I borrowed from Comber's (2016) notion of "optimistic narratives" that could reposition teachers and students as positive agents in their own future (p. 398).

Pedagogies that Matter

Unfortunately offensive language in the classroom is not taken up as a curriculum or pedagogical provocation but is treated as a classroom behavior problem. Swearing at school can even be the main reason schools make for suspensions and exclusions (Smyth et al., 2004). When teachers respond punitively to students swearing in class the usual logic is to reassert a culture of power (Delpit, 1988), rather than working on how to constructively address offensive language in the classroom.

For clarity's sake, I am not advocating embracing all types of offensive language in the classroom. This chapter is not about dropping behavioral standards but about improving the quality of teaching. First and foremost, students are genuinely interested in this topic, which is half the battle for students who do not see school as *for them* (Thomson, 2003). My case study demonstrates how teachers can provide the opportunity for their students to become "canny theorists" in classroom discussions (McLaughlin, 1996, p. 154). Indeed, the students in my so-called *low-literacy* class took the initiative to research and suggest new texts to study. Offensive language appears in such a variety of text types and genres that teachers should be able to tailor it to a range of different social and learning contexts.

That said, I expect that not all schools will be able or willing to dedicate an entire unit to the subject of offensive language. Like it or not, students will always provide teachers with opportunities to address offensive language in the classroom. Instead of reprimanding students, we can instead try taking away the shock value by asking them critical questions about their word choices. In my experience they will either put up (and engage in critical conversation) or shut up (and stop disrupting the class). Furthermore, over time these interactions should improve their critical understanding of offensive language, and of how it functions in different contexts.

I would be remiss to finish this article without a final commentary on the funds of knowledge concept (González et al., 2005). There is a wealth of research into *light* funds of knowledge, but very little scholarship on so-called *dark* funds of knowledge (Zipin, 2009). Given how productive I found offensive language to be, I could not help but wonder about the potential of other dark funds of knowledge, such as homelessness, incarceration, drug use, among others. Is it that we are not addressing these topics in our classrooms, or are we just not talking about how we are doing so? Perhaps it could be a bit of both. From personal experience, I know that I would have benefited from other accounts of *dark* topics, if only so that I could have begun my project with greater confidence. It is my intention that, through sharing this research, I might convince others to join the *dark* side and publish the results of their research too.

However, I think we ought to consider using different terminology when discussing this compelling topic. Given the context of this discussion, I prefer to use other adjectives rather than the word "dark," and I have already mentioned "troubling," "difficult," and "vernacular" as alternatives. As teachers we are also lifelong learners and the events of the past decade have imparted us with a greater sensitivity toward language choices. Hence, it is my proposal that we consider using an alternative term moving forwards. After much consideration, I think "authentic funds of knowledge" speaks to our students' truths, in the sense that it honors and prioritizes their realities. Furthermore, "authentic" serves as a worthwhile reminder to educators to teach authentically, in the sense that they should be focused on valuing and extending their students' knowledge in the classroom. With that in mind, I propose that we be more forthcoming in sharing our own experiences of teaching in the classroom, if only so that we can help one another and our students more in the future.

Bibliography

Australian Institute for Teaching and School Leadership (AITSL). (2017). *Teaching Performance Assessment*. https://www.aitsl.edu.au/deliver-ite-programs/teaching-performance-assessment

Australian Social Inclusion Board. (2012). *Social inclusion in Australia: How Australia is faring*. Commonwealth of Australia. https://apo.org.au/sites/default/files/resource-files/2012-08/apo-nid30582.pdf

Bankwest Curtin Economics Centre. (2014). *Falling through the cracks: Poverty and disadvantage in Australia* (Focus on the States Report Series No. 1). Curtin University. http://business.curtin.edu.au/local/docs/BCEC-Falling-through-the-cracks-Report.pdf

Comber, B. (2016). Poverty, place and pedagogy in education: Research stories from front-line workers. *Australian Educational Researcher, 43*(4), 393–417.

Delpit, L. (1988). The silenced dialogue: Power and pedagogy in educating other people's children. *Harvard Educational Review*, 58, 280–98.

González, N., Moll, L. C., & Amanti, C. (2005). Introduction: Theorizing practices. In N. González, L. C. Moll, & C. Amanti (Eds.), *Funds of knowledge: Theorizing practices in households, communities and classrooms* (pp. 1–24). Lawrence Erlbaum Associates.

Hambides, Z. (2013, December 27). Elizabeth, South Australia: A city devastated by General Motors Holden. *World Socialist Web Site*. https://www.wsws.org/en/articles/2013/12/27/eliz-d27.html

Hattam, R. (2016). Citizenship, schooling, and educational disadvantage. In A. Peterson, R. Hattam, M. Zembylas, & J. Arthur (Eds.), *Palgrave handbook of citizenship and social justice* (pp. 27–47). Palgrave.

Hattam, R. (2018). Research the "North": Educational ethnographies of a (sub)urban region. In S. Gannon, W. Swayer, & R. Hattam (Eds.), *Resisting educational inequality: Reframing policy and practice in schools serving vulnerable communities* (pp. 214–24). Routledge.

Hattam, R. (2023). Towards a decolonising Australian culturally responsive pedagogy? In L.-I. Rigney (Ed.), *Global perspectives and new challenges in culturally responsive pedagogies: Super-diversity and teaching practice* (pp. 75–88). Routledge.

Hattam, R., Brennan, M., Zipin, L., & Comber, B. (2009). Researching for social justice: Contextual, conceptual and methodological challenges. *Discourse: Studies in the Cultural Politics of Education, 30*(3), 303–16.

Hattam, R., & Prosser, B. (2008). Unsettling deficit views of students and their communities. *Australian Educational Researcher, 35*(2), 89–106.

Luke, A., O'Brien, J., & Comber, B. (1994). Making community texts objects of study. *Australian Journal of Language and Literacy, 17*(2), 139–49.

McInerney, M. (2010). Implications of 21st century change and the geography curriculum. *Geographical Education, 23*, 23–31.

McLaughlin, T. (1996). *Street smarts and critical theory: Listening to the vernacular.* University of Wisconsin Press.

Mills, K. A., Sunderland, N., & Davis-Warra, J. (2013). Yarning circles in the literacy classroom. *Reading Teacher, 67*(4), 285–89.

Moll, L. (2014). *L. S. Vygotsky and education*. Routledge.

Moll, L. (2019). Elaborating funds of knowledge: Community-oriented practices in international contexts. *Literacy Research: Theory, Method, and Practice*, 68, 130–38.

Moll, L., Amanti, C., Neff, D., & González, N. (2005). Funds of knowledge for teaching: Using a qualitative approach to connect homes and classrooms. In N. González, L. C. Moll, & C. Amanti (Eds.), *Funds of knowledge: Theorizing practices in households, communities and classrooms* (pp. 71–87). Lawrence Erlbaum Associates.

Peel, M. (1995). *Good times, hard times: The past and the future in Elizabeth.* Melbourne University Press.

Prosser, B., Reid, A., & Lucas, B. (2010). *Connecting lives and learning: Renewing pedagogy in the middle years.* Wakefield Press.

Rodriguez, G. (2013). Power and agency in education: Exploring the pedagogical dimensions of funds of knowledge. *Review of Research in Education*, 37, 87–120.

Senate Community Affairs References Committee. (2014). *Bridging our growing divide: Inequality in Australia. The extent of income inequality in Australia.* Commonwealth of Australia.

Smyth, J., Hattam, R., with Cannon, J., Edwards, J., Wilson, N., & Wurst, S. (2004). *Dropping out, drifting off, being excluded: Becoming somebody without school.* Peter Lang.

Smyth, J., & McInerney, P. (2012). *From silent witnesses to active agents: Student voice in re-engaging with learning.* Peter Lang.

Social Inclusion Unit. (2007). *Experiencing success: SRAP Stage 3 Evaluation Report.* D

Thomson, P. (2003). *Schooling the rustbelt kids: Making the difference in changing times.* Routledge.

Wolgemuth, R., Koro-Ljungberg, M., & Barko, T. (2020). (In defence of) pedagogies of obscenity. *Power and Education*, *12*(1), 23–8.

Woods, A., Comber, B., & Iyer, R. (2015). Literacy learning: Designing and enacting inclusive pedagogical practices in classrooms. *Inclusive Pedagogy Across the Curriculum*, 7, 45–71.

Wyatt, M. (2022). *Maku.* Pan Australia.

Zembylas, M. (2014). Theorizing "difficult knowledge" in the aftermath of the "affective turn": Implications for curriculum and pedagogy in handing traumatic representations. *Curriculum Inquiry*, *44*(3), 390–412.

Zipin, L. (2009). Dark funds of knowledge, deep funds of pedagogy: Exploring boundaries between lifeworlds and schools. *Discourse: Studies in the Cultural Politics of Education*, *30*(3), 317–31.

Zipin, L., Sellar, S., Brennan, M., & Gale, T. (2013). *Educating for futures in marginalized regions: A sociological framework for rethinking and researching aspirations.* Educational Philosophy and Theory, *47(3), 227–46.*

Zipin, L., Sellar, S., & Hattam, R. (2012). Countering and exceeding "capital": A "funds of knowledge" approach to re-imagining community. *Discourse: Studies in the Cultural Politics of Education*, *33*(2), 179–92.

22 Conclusion: Reimagining Pedagogies for Justice

Robert Hattam, Robyne Garrett, and Alison Wrench

This edited collection provides lines of flight into a huge archive of critical educational research that has mostly been ignored for many decades by those governing what constitutes education in Australia (Biesta, 2015; Denzin, 2008; Lather, 2006; Lingard & Gale, 2010). Governing education demands specific forms of knowledge assembled as *regimes of truth* or official narratives that simultaneously privilege particular voices and close down critique or counter-memory. Such actions are pivotal in creating *conditions of possibility* for directing the conduct of teachers and students in relation to specific ends. As Foucault observed, "[t]he education of children was the fundamental utopia, crystal and prism through which problems of conduction were perceived" (2007, p. 231).

Biesta (2012) argues that education has long been tied to broader political issues of population and citizenship. It follows that ignoring critical educational research is a political decision. Put simply, critical education research demands a skeptical attitude toward common sense and official knowledge, has sensitivity to the way power works, and is committed to struggling for more socially just societies and hence to resist the adoption of neoliberalizing policy. In response to neoliberalized "conditions of possibility," Biesta (2014) argues for investigations and practices that work at the intersection of education and politics. We similarly argue for critical education research that ponders questions such as: In whose interests is this operating? How come things got to be this way? How can we resist being governed in this way? This is a call for critical educational research that attempts to unravel a politics of truth.

Engaging in a politics of truth requires *seeing* two games of truth that are constantly in play. On the one hand, we are all engaged in discerning what is true and what is false. We are all asserting our own truth claims into various knowledge networks. But then behind that game there is another, one that "examines how truth itself is authorised, how what counts as truth now gets to hold sway, and always in a heterogenous field of claims" (Hattam, 2022, p. 1227). From a politics of truth perspective, "teachers are now being fitted up with the 'truth' of good practice as defined by the so-called learning sciences (Eacott, 2017)—that game of truth that suits the logic of neoliberalising social policy" (Hattam, 2020, p. 80). Unfortunately, for Australian teachers and students, and our future economic prosperity, social/cultural cohesion, and good governance, policy makers have assembled and continue to push a policy regime that is spectacularly failing.

The Failure of Schooling Policy in Australia

In Australia, the urgent (inter)national problem of social injustice and schooling has been rendered invisible by those responsible for the policy regime. Australian schooling is now governed by a policy regime understood as an assemblage of neoliberalizing axioms that elevates a "what works" learning science as the gold standard for evidence-based practice (Hattam, 2020). Examples of these axioms include: the universalization of market-based social relations; deregulation of education markets; re-regulation of governance; foregrounding consumer "choice"; and framing accountability in terms of demands for evidence of "quality." As indicated in our opening chapter, educators in Australia now have their work constituted inside of a reform agenda that is increasingly under duress, and it is failing on multiple counts:

- Australian students' achievement is declining compared to international standards (Gonski et al., 2018).
- Striving for decontextualized standardization and homogeneity (Slee, 2018) has failed to address the complexity of contemporary classrooms, instead exacerbating a growing student–teacher diversity gap. This is exemplified by teachers routinely expressing concerns about their preparedness to meet the needs of students whose cultural and linguistic resources differ from the cultural majority (Santoro, 2013; Vass, 2017; Warren, 2018), who are deemed to have "special educational needs" (Fanshawe et al., 2023; Slee, 2018), along with other demarcations of "otherness."
- There are concerning and enduring links between low levels of educational outcomes and students living in poverty (Senate Select Committee on School Funding, 2014).
- Australian schooling systems are so inequitable (Bruckauf & Chzhen, 2016) that the social justice gains in education evident in the later decades of the twentieth century have unraveled (Reisch, 2014).
- The workforce is shrinking due to teacher attrition (Mason & Matas, 2015).
- There are fewer aspiring leaders (Thomson, 2009).
- Falling retention and completion, together with increasing student alienation, exclusions and suspensions, are now blamed on students' poor behavior (OECD, 2023), whilst ignoring the research on disengagement (Bills & Howard, 2021).

Whilst there is an emerging consensus regarding the key elements of the crisis, what is now moot are the policy responses. There has been a failure to understand the interconnected elements of the crisis. Rather, policy makers continue to focus on only one element at a time (e.g., teacher attrition, see Lampert et al., 2021, or student behavior: Sullivan et al., 2016, 2022), while either refuting or ignoring the problem of inequality for the past decade (Gannon et al., 2018; Riddle & Hickey, 2023; Riddle et al., 2022; Slee, 2018). This set of troubles has been clear for many years, and arguably needs to be treated as a problem complex. These issues are not separate but interrelated and operate as a constellation, with the reproduction of inequality being a central driving policy logic. We note that, in the past three to four years, governments have investigated or reviewed the teacher shortage problem, the declining student achievement problem, and the challenging behaviors of young people in schools. As well, we have seen two recent reviews of initial teacher education (ITE) (Teacher Education Expert Panel, 2023). In all cases, the problem is isolated from its context and a positivist, scientistic form of analysis dominates across all educational jurisdictions. In this way education policy is constituted in a knowledge paradigm that decontextualizes and cannot think ecologically nor get free of its commitment to the market being the solution to all policy problems. Consequently, we continue to witness its failure to value equality over marketization.

More importantly, federal and state policy makers have yet to grapple with the failures of the Global Education Reform Movement (GERM), which now operates as "a global orthodoxy in education policy" (Fuller & Stevenson, 2019, p. 1), having been in place in Australia for at least two decades. Sahlberg et al. (2017) argues that there are two variations of the GERM: (i) in Nordic countries, Canada, and Germany, governments "view education primarily as public good over market competition" (p. 4); and (ii) in Australia, the United Kingdom, and most of the United States, governments have pursued market-based or neoliberal policy regimes, standardization of curriculum, and "high-stakes" formats of accountability (Lingard, 2013). The work of Australian teachers, schools, and teacher educators is now constituted in policy which can only conceive of declining performance and inequality as a problem of school and teacher quality, rather than a problem of policy being removed from reality.

Further to this, Australian schooling policy fails because school *devolution* or the *self-managing school* proposes a one-size-fits-all logic that does not consider or acknowledge local contexts (Smyth, 2011). This marketized version of devolution centralizes parental choice, even when none exists (Lamb, 2007; Teese, 2011). Collectively this is increasingly detrimental to the public provision of schooling by residualizing schools serving high-poverty communities. In contrast, Biesta and colleagues (2022) argue for the retrieval of education as a public rather than private good or commodity. Reid (2019) similarly argues for socially and ethically just public education that enables all children to flourish.

While no government is willing to take on the independent schools and the Catholic education lobbies, inequality continues to intensify. Policy is framed by a logic of *standardization* of curriculum that demands that teachers and teacher educators implement didactic and explicit pedagogies that are ill suited to the needs of schools serving demographically complex, diverse, and high-poverty communities (Hardy, 2020; Hardy & Lewis, 2017). *High-stakes testing* marginalizes alternative pedagogical practice and drives teachers toward narrow, unproductive literacy and numeracy outcomes. Significantly this is occurring at a time when Australia needs to be supporting students to be capable of "critical literacy in the post-truth media landscape" (Barton, 2019, p. 1024). A further failing logic has many names including learning science, "school effectiveness," or "what works," all adjectives for a positivist paradigm of educational truths.

"What works" discourse is sold to us as *the* learning science, with claims there are forms of effective teaching that are rendered as "best practice." "What works" is then packaged as a series of decontexualized and universalized claims about what constitutes effective teaching, whilst bracketing out "classroom life," social class, poverty, and economic resources in families and communities (Hattie, 2009, pp. viii–ix). Importantly, "what works" discourses narrow what counts as worthwhile educational research to so-called evidence-based practice, which has allowed policy makers to elide concerns for inequality, highlighted in decades of curriculum and pedagogy studies (Green et al., 2021). Such is the hegemony of the "what works" discourse that there is no consideration of *who* is privileged and *why*. The adoption of the so-called learning sciences by those governing has literally expunged decades of worthwhile educational knowledge from its policy archive, including knowledge that takes context seriously and frames its truth claims in concerns about inequality. Rather, "what works" discourses are predicated on a crude scientism, pretending to be scientific and confidently proposing to be working on "the scientific fixing of pedagogy or the determination of universal and generalisable teaching and learning processes" (Luke, 2006, p. 2). In this way, systems now push a "pedagogic universalism": the belief that models of skill, intelligence, stimulus/response, cognition, or intrinsic patterns of development are species specific and not context specific (Cole, 1996).

Unfortunately, those with the policy levers either misunderstand the crisis, or are deliberately directing attention away from the failure of policy by blaming teachers, ITE programs, school leaders, and even students themselves. Either way, those governing what goes on in schools are trapped in a policy regime that does not have the conceptual resources to even diagnose the trouble.

We never hear anyone in governments discussing the failure of a marketized view of school devolution and correcting perverse school funding is seen as impossible. Rather, standardization is now Teflon coated and untouchable, and high-stakes testing is beyond critique, despite the fact there is no evidence that these logics actually improve learning, even framed in the narrowest of terms. The constant call for evidence-based practice is hollow when we do not have evidence-based policy.

For those of us working in education, we now find ourselves struggling over what constitutes science in a politics of truth that parades under the auspices of evidence-based practice. All government jurisdictions claim relentlessly, but without much conviction, that we must have evidence-based policy and practice. As noted earlier, governments are demanding that teachers and teacher educators implement the "evidence," but then the policy logics that frame governing do not have any evidence that they improve learning. The trick here, though, is what counts as evidence, and what this inevitably comes down to is what counts as science. We see some positivist researchers purporting to rely on the "learning sciences" as a political tactic to claim the "truth" about educational practices including what counts as worthwhile knowledge, good teachers, and good leaders. The advocates of these learning sciences propose knowledge, rendered as "what works" distilled from research approaches in epidemiology (randomized classroom trials) as the gold standard (McKnight & Morgan, 2020). Meanwhile the Australian Education Research Organisation, funded by the Australian and state governments (Rowe, 2022), acts as a knowledge broker for evidence-based practice, without *any* scientific rationale, by asserting that the meta-analysis of randomized classroom trials is *the* most reputable form of knowledge about teaching!

This kind of arrogant knowing about how good teaching works (against the practical wisdom of good teachers who would never make such claims) is asserted in the form of generalizable propositions that are at best banal but still fail to account for context. By way of an example, poverty is not a statistical notion that can be conveniently put to one side when claiming "truth" about good teaching. There are real differences between teaching at a school that serves high-poverty communities and at one in the high-end independent sector. Practitioners of the learning sciences with limited self-reflexivity also claim to be purveyors of value-free, unbiased, and objective knowing about education. However, such claims either betray their ignorance of about a century of philosophy of science, or perhaps are a willful and deliberate tactic to satisfy demands for governing and control.

Mapping the Damage

Critical educational research has a long history that outlines how schooling reproduces inequality. Importantly, such research is suspicious of deficit discourses that either silence, malign, or speak for the lives of those who live in non-dominant communities, and of those forms of educational knowledge that attempt to bracket out context in the name of universal truth claims. As noted above, poverty is not background that can be statistically elided, nor are cultural, ethnic, language, religious, (dis)ability, gender, or sexuality differences. For Sellar and Lingard (2014), such bracketing is perpetuated by contemporary neoliberalizing policy and is characterized by "the absent presence of socioeconomic context in order to focus policy attention on improving the performance outcomes of students and teachers" (p. 1).

How can we think past or better still get past reproduction (Hattam & Smyth, 2015)? For us, the key involves pushing back against all manner of deficit discourses (Hattam & Prosser, 2008) that belittle working-class intelligence (Rancière, 1991, 2010), including from educational psychology, the media, anthropology, and educational sociology (Biesta, 2010). Such deficit talk is so embedded in the reality of schooling for students who fail and get to blame themselves! But then we can unsettle deficit thinking when we realize that schooling normalizes certain repertoires of literacy practices, and on that basis evaluates as deficit all students who are lacking such a repertoire (Nixon & Comber, 2006). Inequality works through the ways that schools naturalize or normalize specific ways of speaking, ways of writing, ways of dressing, and ways of relating that are embodied as dispositions acquired through practical immersion in everyday life (Zipin et al., 2012).

Schools tend to assume that all students possess the cultural capital of families that are middle class and/or with histories of successful educational experiences. But young people enter schooling with differing funds of knowledge (González & Wyman, 2011). For too many young people, there is a substantial gap between what is assumed by the school and the cultural capital of their families. As an example, many young people experience an "interactive trouble" (Freebody et al., 1995) at school because of the gap between what counts as school literacy and their own vernacular literacy practices. Freebody et al. (1995) describe interactive trouble as "situations where there are breakdowns in communication" when students do not understand the cues within teacher talk; teachers fail to hear cues in student talk; teachers apply overly subtle criteria with little explicit explanation; or students misread what is going on in the context of the classroom. Too many young people experience schools as alienating "because of a significant mis-match between their struggles to 'become somebody'... and the narrowly defined identity that schools expected" (Smyth & Hattam, 2004, p. 191). For those students the gap between their vernacular literacies and school literacy requires *translation*, or explicit teaching, which too often is not forthcoming. To make matters worse, the daily experiences of interactive trouble are often explained to them in terms of their own deficits rather than the school's failure to acknowledge and respond to the cultural dissonance. Having to internalize the trouble year after year makes schooling for disadvantaged young people near impossible to bear, especially when the demands of schooling increase so dramatically in the post-compulsory years.

But Teaching is a Social Practice

The teaching profession, and especially those working in schools, are now being fitted up with all manner of truths that ignore the most basic of facts: that *teaching is a social practice*. For decades now, the teaching profession has been distorted by a version of educational psychology, with a fetish for measurement and support for testing regimes to control teachers' work. Unfortunately, this has meant that teaching and learning are rendered as psychological; and hence characterized as purely internal mental events. We are offered lock-step theories of child development; adolescent behavior due to hormones; and the need to dumb down activities because of cognitive limits to brains. Simply put, teaching and learning in classrooms cannot be understood by reducing pedagogical encounters to individualized psychological events.

Additionally, those who think we need to discipline the profession even more are foisting brain science on teachers as a means to validate their so-called evidence-based practice. Brain science cannot validate any claims to good teaching practices. It is not possible to jump from brain scans to claims about social practices. The causal links are just not that simple (Rose & Abi-Rachid, 2013). Brain science is still in its infancy and its claims to truth are at best banal and do not offer teachers much by way of advice about how to teach well. Brain plasticity proves we can all learn. However, brain science cannot be relied on for claims to support explicit instruction or some version of visible learning. And linking brain science with cognitive load theory does not get you there either. Cognitive load theory does not have reliable claims to advocate any social practices (Ellerton, 2020). It only offers the trivial insight that we all have limits to our cognition (Perry et al., 2021).[1] These are more banal truths that do not help teachers with

---

1 See Wyse and Bradbury (2022) for critiques of the truth claims being made about phonics.

the struggles they have in their classrooms. Brain science with or without cognitive psychology does little to support teachers with existential challenges such as how to engage their students in meaningful learning, and how to connect official knowledge with the funds of knowledges that their students bring to class. Education systems in Australia now:

> purport to offer the *right method*; and … many policies … purport to use a "scientific" evidence base to steer educational systems and engineer student outcomes. The risk is, inter alia, a narrowing rather than an expanding pedagogic repertoire and classroom practice. (Luke, 2006, p. 3)

Hopeful Alternatives

In the opening of this chapter, we argued that this edited collection provides lines of flight into a huge archive of critical educational research that has been mostly ignored for many decades. A key strength of this archive is the decades of research into context-sensitive accounts of what works in schools or, as we prefer to say, *hopeful alternatives* to dumbed down teaching that policy now demands. Significantly this archive is also committed to a frame that is concerned about unsettling educational inequality and not statistically pushing inequality out of that frame. We can only too briefly point to some of the archive that we have activated in this collection. All archives can be mapped by their vocabulary and, in our case, this book speaks through keywords/terms such as: unsettling deficit, practice architectures, student connectedness, culturally, linguistically and religiously responsive, the knowledge-producing school, affective and relational, twenty-first century learner, safety-net schooling, Aboriginal voice, belonging, socially critical, eco-justice, settler colonialism, semiotic representation, discomforting and difficult knowledges, dialogic, performing identities, demythologizing pedagogy, and embodied and co-constructed curriculum. And, to paraphrase Foucault (1977), words do not just name the world; they *constitute* it, in which case, the vocabularies we activate not only name things and practices, but they constitute the world we live in.

Vocabulary is, hence, important because we quite literally make the world up (Hacking, 1986) through the words we use. Moreover, our words do not come with *a priori* meanings but get worked on to do specific political/pedagogical work. So, for the Pedagogy for Justice Research Group, it is not only the vocabulary that is important but the meanings we invoke when we activate our vocabulary. Those struggling for just schooling are having to do political work on the terms we want to use, to load our meanings onto those terms, and to contest any attempts by others to depoliticize our terms.

We accept that pedagogy, understood here as a keyword for the practices of educators—and specifically for us early childhood educators, schoolteachers, and university teachers—is crafted and enacted with/against official and institutionalized remits for educators' work. We assume that the term pedagogy is a keyword in educational studies and hence operates as a place marker for a whole series of debates about the practices of educators. The idea of a keyword we borrow from Raymond Williams (1976), who understood that keywords present a cluster of interlocking, contemporary senses whose interaction remains unresolved across a range of fields of thought and discussion. "Interaction between the senses can lead to cross purposes and confusion in public debate" (Durant, 2006, p. 4). Put more simply, the notion of pedagogy as a keyword worries the over-simplistic rendering of pedagogy by the "what works" discourse. As a keyword, there is no one right definition and that is not the purpose of educational research anyway. The keyword is a place marker for a set of debates, and signifies also that significant terms, as keywords, are also sites for political/pedagogical work. The term pedagogy as a site for political work is being worked on by education systems with a view to strangling the definitional debates and controlling teachers' work. Importantly, however, the term pedagogy is also "the key rallying point for teachers, teacher educators and researchers, and activists and policymakers committed to reclaiming the arts and sciences of teaching from narrow instrumentalist and economic agendas" (Luke, 2006, p. 1).

The resiliency of particular forms of pedagogy signals more than the stubbornness of the profession or the conservatism of schools. Ubiquitous patterns of classroom talk (e.g., initiate–response–evaluate) and curriculum focus (e.g., alphabetic knowledge) are forms of cultural exchange and ritual that have historically evolved to establish and maintain particular social relations, epistemic authority, gender relations, and so on. The question, then, is not whether these pedagogic practices are old or new, right or wrong, nor is it a simple matter of embodied student habitus subordinated by *dominant cultures* or *symbolic violence*. The larger, more complex question is about what these potentially volatile moments of cultural exchange produce: the variable social and cognitive, individual and collective consequences of pedagogy and curriculum. Different pedagogies interact with students' cultural knowledge and practice to selectively shape distinctive kinds of knowledge, capital, and identity (Bernstein, 1996). Against the din that proclaims explicit instruction is *the* evidence-based answer we advocate—the ongoing reinvigoration of critical pedagogies (Hattam, 2020). In this edited collection we promote various takes on critical pedagogy, including culturally and religiously responsive, relational, artistic and affective, embodied, eco-justice oriented, and enabling.

Culturally and Religiously Responsive Pedagogy

We argue that there is an urgent need to investigate how schools, understood here as cultural and affective communities, enact policies and practices that are more responsive to Australia's increasingly culturally, religiously, and linguistically diverse student populations. Importantly, these populations include Aboriginal children who continue to be disenfranchised by mainstream schooling in Australia as well as the children of recent migrants and refugee families. Internationally, there is an emerging consensus that attests to the potential of culturally responsive pedagogies to improve learning outcomes for all students, and in particular children of the First Nations (Bishop et al., 2007; Castagno & Brayboy, 2008; Ladson-Billings, 1995; Sleeter, 2011; Villegas & Lucas, 2002). But recent analysis of CRP in Australia indicates only limited and weakly developed versions of policy and practice when compared to culturally responsive approaches in other settler colonial societies. A "cult of forgetfulness" concerning race relations, invasions, and massacres continues to haunt the Australian psyche and is forged in ongoing pedagogies of assimilation. Importantly, there *is* research that takes up the challenge of enacting culturally responsive pedagogy in classrooms but there is a serious gap in our knowledge about how schools become more culturally responsive. Australian school leaders and their school communities do not have access to well theorized Australian exemplars of *good practice* in this area, which undermines the national effort to address fragile relations in our super-diverse communities and compound educational disadvantage, particularly for Indigenous students (Morrison et al., 2019). Additionally, Australian research into CRP approaches have yet to seriously engage with the affective dimensions or whole-school pedagogical reforms. If such processes are to lead to an improved experience of schooling and personal and collective achievement, we argue this requires new knowledge about the complexities of sustaining whole-school engagement in the process of redesigning pedagogy.

Embodied and Artistic Pedagogies

We also argue for pedagogies that are lived, relational, creative, and embodied practices that call affect into play. They operate in visual, aural, and physical ways that far exceed the limits of prescribed criteria, tests, or specific forms of thinking. Rather, they give value to the body and creativity as instruments of learning and means of communication where spoken words, visual images, gestures, movement, sound, or silence are all included in pedagogical practice (Mills & Dooley, 2019). We argue that transforming pedagogy involves bringing artistic, affective, and embodied responses into dialogue with disciplinary knowledge and hence the relationship between emotion, cognition, and the body becomes central to learning. These insights challenge the erasure of the body that is so evident in Australian schooling and acknowledge that meaning and understanding are not only cerebral but physical and emotional (Osei-Kofi, 2013). In arguing for a pedagogy that attends to the embodied nature of student lives, we make it possible for all students to *become more human* and be positioned as capable, knowledgeable, and imaginative.

Eco-Justice Pedagogies

For most of the last century, our models of economic growth have assumed an uncontested abundance of resources and a belief in ongoing consumption without consequences. The overwhelming evidence now demands we move toward more sustainable human living as well as valuing the welfare of all species and ecosystems. There are now hopeful approaches for ITE programs that *can* contribute to eco-social justice learning by making explicit the ethical and sustainability necessity of valuing all Earth systems. Our version of eco-social justice learning is framed by a set of guiding principles that promotes learning which values the integrity of all living and non-living aspects of our sphere (Lloyd et al., 2019). We believe that educational experiences in natural settings are fundamental to the development of active citizenship where students can come to realize we are all a part of, and responsible for, a world ecology. We assert that pedagogy must include the acquisition of collective values that place humans *within* ecosystems. It is here that interconnected communities of human and non-human can live *with*, not *on*, each other.

Enabling, Relational, and Affective Pedagogies

Enabling pedagogies aim to develop academic skills to facilitate the transition of students into higher education. They disrupt a number of pedagogical problematics in secondary schools and universities by shifting attention away from deficit discourses and toward transforming institutional spaces, systems, and practices. The aim of a *critical* enabling educator is to create an inclusive environment where dialogue is shared, curriculum is negotiated, assessment is scaffolded, and tasks are challenging and connected to students' life worlds (Moll et al., 1992). In contrast to the traditional "banking style" of higher education, students are recognized for their strengths and the dialogic approach to teaching sets out to "not talk knowledge at students but talk *with* them" (Shor, 1992, p. 85). Enabling pedagogies take seriously a demand for widening participation to not just higher education but all education. This does not necessarily mean molding and shaping diverse students to take on middle-class practices and identities, but rather recognizing and valuing differences that encompass the intersectional identities of all students. Affective and relational experiences play a crucial role in nurturing aspiration. By fostering "practices of connectedness" it *is* possible to turn back around students who are not engaging productively in school. Such approaches not only help to develop a strong sense of belonging but the realization that they *are* knowledgeable and smart.

Against the banality of *quality teaching*, we are arguing for approaches that are negotiated and dialogic; contribute to self-transformation of students and teachers; are improvisational; are affectively available; and provide students with opportunities to be researching their own lives, their communities, and significant global challenges with a view to making their own communities better places to live. We are arguing for conceptualizing pedagogy in terms of the teacher as improviser or virtuoso, in which *good* pedagogy is not defined by regular productions of ritualized techniques, but instead "requires exquisite sensitivity to the characteristics of particular situations" (Garfield, 2007, p. 288) and, put simply, negotiates with the unique singularity of every classroom that can only be *known* in situ.

By way of a summary, the sorts of pedagogies we are advocating can be defined by what pedagogy needs to do:

- provide high intellectual challenge
- connect strongly to student life worlds
- recognize cultural difference as a positive asset for learning
- support the performing of learning and multimodal literacies
- enable an activist orientation
- enable cultivation of knowledge and values that place humans *within* ecosystems
- bring affective and embodied responses into dialogue with disciplinary knowledge
- nurture an ethics of care
- provide skillful scaffolding to enable success.

What To Do Now?

In closing we request that those governing Australian schooling consider the following proposals:

- Dislodge the narrowly defined version of learning science that is now literally dumbing down the nation, damaging educators' work and putting at risk the future of Australian prosperity.

- Review and reconceptualize the remit of the Australian Education Research Organisation, whose modus operandi pushes a narrow view of what counts as evidence that has no scientific basis, severely limits the educational knowledge base, and hence undermines the future of schooling.
- Reimagine the professional autonomy of teachers and especially strengthen the practice of local curriculum translation.
- Move away from claiming that policy knows the right answers and instead cultivate systems that co-construct practice knowledge about teaching with teachers.
- Promote a curriculum that supports our students to produce their own knowledge about their own communities as the basis for local community activism.

If schooling and ITE are to counter the rising inequality in educational outcomes evident in Australia and to include those students from less privileged social positions, there is an urgent need to question *why*, *how*, and *what* is taught in the name of education (Zipin, 2024). We need to question the normative pedagogical practices that marginalize or "other" students around race, gender, class, (dis) ability, and other classifications of difference including in their intersectionality, and to realign the focus and priorities of in-service and pre-service teacher education. As the chapters of this book have demonstrated, the realignment we call for incorporates the acquisition and development of dispositions and pedagogical practices capable of recognizing and responding to the diverse contextual, embodied, cultural, and societal factors that frame contemporary classrooms. The ultimate challenge is to move beyond weak or superficial adherence to educational justice toward the creation of contexts, relationships, and practices though which all students can flourish.

Bibliography

Barton, C. (2019). Critical literacy in the post-truth media landscape. *Policy Futures in Education*, *17*(8), 1024–36.

Bernstein, B. (1996). *Pedagogy, symbolic control and identity: Theory, research, critique*. Taylor and Francis.

Biesta, G. (2010). *Good education in an age of measurement: Ethics, politics, democracy*. Routledge.

Biesta, G. (2012). Becoming public: Public pedagogy, citizenship and the public sphere. *Social & Cultural Geography*, *13*(7), 683–97.

Biesta, G. (2014). Making pedagogy public: For the public, of the public or in the interest of publicness. In J. Burdick, J. A. Sandlin, & M. P. O'Malley (Eds.), *Problematizing public pedagogy* (pp. 5–26). Routledge.

Biesta, G. (2015). On the two cultures of educational research, and how we might move ahead: Reconsidering the ontology, axiology and praxeology of education. *European Educational Research Journal*, *14*(1), 11–22.

Biesta, G., Heugh, K., Cervinkova, H., Rasinski, L., Osborne, S., Forde, D., Wrench, A., Carter, J., Säfström, C. A., Soong, H., O'Keeffe, S., Paige, K., Rigney, L.-I., O'Toole, L., Hattam, R., Peters, M. A., & Tesar, M. (2022). Philosophy of education in a new key: Publicness, social justice, and education, a South–North conversation. *Educational Philosophy and Theory*, 54(8), 1216–33.

Bills, A., & Howard, N. (2021). *It's time to act: Making the case for a cross-sectoral response to school disengagement and detachment in South Australia*. Flinders University.

Bishop, R., Berryman, M., Cavanagh T., & Teddy, L. (2007). *Te Kōtahitanga Phase 3: Whānaungatanga: Establishing a culturally responsive pedagogy of relations in mainstream secondary school classrooms*. Ministry of Education, New Zealand.

Bruckauf, Z., & Chzhen, Y. (2016). *Education for all? Measuring inequality of educational outcomes among 15-year-olds across 39 industrialized nations*. UNICEF Office of Research.

Castagno, A., & Brayboy, B. (2008). Culturally responsive schooling for Indigenous youth: A review of the literature. *Review of Educational Research*, *78*(4), 941–93.

Cole, M. (1996). Interacting minds in a life-span perspective: A cultural-historical approach to culture and cognitive development. In P. B. Baltes & U. M. Staudinger (Eds.), *Interactive minds: Life-span perspectives on the social foundation of cognition* (pp. 59–87). Cambridge University Press.

Denzin, N. K. (2008). The new paradigm dialogs and qualitative inquiry. *International Journal of Qualitative Studies in Education*, *21*(4), 315–25.

Durant, A. (2006). Raymond Williams's keywords: Investigating meanings "offered, felt for, tested, confirmed, asserted, qualified, changed." *Critical Quarterly*, *48*(4), 1–26.

Eacott, S. (2017). School leadership and the cult of the guru: The neo-Taylorism of Hattie. *School Leadership & Management*, *37*(4), 413–26.

Ellerton, P. (2022). On critical thinking and content knowledge: A critique of the assumptions of cognitive load theory. *Thinking Skills and Creativity*, *43*, 1–7.

Fanshawe, M., Barton, G., Mandarakas, M., Cain, M., & Todd, N. (2023). Enablers and barriers to equitable participation for students with blindness or low vision in Australian mainstream secondary schools. *International Journal of Inclusive Education*. Advance online publication. https://doi.org/10.1080/13603116.2023.2265915

Freebody, P., Ludwig, C., & Gunn, S. (1995). *Everyday literacy practices in and out of schools in low socio-economic urban communities*. Centre for Literacy Education Research, Griffith University.

Foucault, M. (1977). *Archaeology of knowledge*. Routledge.

Foucault, M. (2007). *Security, territory, population: Lectures at the College de France 1977–1978*. Palgrave Macmillan.

Fuller, K., & Stevenson, H. (2019). Global education reform: Understanding the movement. *Educational Review*, *71*(1), 1–4.

Gannon, S., Hattam, R., & Sawyer, W. (2018). *Resisting educational inequality: Reframing policy and practice in schools serving vulnerable communities*. Routledge.

Garfield, J. (2007). Educating for virtuoso living: Papers from the Ninth East–West Philosophers' Conference. *Philosophy East and West*, *57*(3), 285–89.

Gonski, D., Arcus, T., Boston, K., Gould, V., Johnson, W., O'Brien, L., Perry, L., & Roberts, M. (2018). *Through growth to achievement: Report of the review to achieve educational excellence in Australian schools*. Commonwealth of Australia.

González, N., & Wyman, L. (2011). The past, present, and future of "funds of knowledge." In B. A. U. Levinson & M. Pollock (Eds.), *A companion to the anthropology of education* (pp. 479–94). Blackwell Publishing.

Green, B., Roberts, P., & Brennan, M. (Eds.). (2021). Curriculum challenges and opportunities in a changing world. Palgrave.

Hacking, I. (1986). Making up people. In T. Heller, M. Sosna, & D. Wellbery (Eds.), *Reconstructing individualism: Autonomy, individuality, and the self in Western thought* (pp. 222–36). Stanford University Press.

Hardy, I. (2020). *School reform in an era of standardization: Authentic accountabilities*. Routledge.

Hardy, I., & Lewis, S. (2017). The "doublethink" of data: Educational performativity and the field of schooling practices. *British Journal of Sociology of Education*, *38*(5), 671–85.

Hattam, R. (2020). Untimely meditations for critical pedagogy. *Asia-Pacific Journal of Teacher Education*, *48*(1), 79–92.

Hattam, R. (2022). Towards a politics of truth for education studies. In G. Biesta et al., Philosophy of education in a new key: Publicness, social justice, and education: a South-North conversation. *Educational Philosophy and Theory*, *54*(8), 1226–27.

Hattam, R., & Prosser, B. (2008). Unsettling deficit views of students and their communities. *Australian Educational Researcher*, *35*(2), 89–106.

Hattam, R., & Smyth, J. (2015). Thinking past educational disadvantage, and theories of reproduction. *Sociology*, *49*(2), 270–86.

Hattie, J. (2009). *Visible learning: A synthesis of over 800 meta-analyses relating to achievement*. Routledge.

Ladson-Billings, G. (1995). Toward a theory of culturally relevant pedagogy. *American Educational Research Journal*, *32*(3), 465–91.

Lamb, S. (2007). School reform and inequality in urban Australia: A case of residualising the poor. In R. Teese, S. Lamb, M. Duru-Bellat, & S. Helme (Eds.), *International studies in educational inequality, theory and policy* (pp. 672–709). Springer.

Lampert, J., McPherson, A., Burnett, B., Armour, D., Browne, S., & Tomkins, S. (2021). *Research into initiatives to prepare and supply a workforce for hard-to-staff schools*. La Trobe University.

Lather, P. (2006). Paradigm proliferation as a good thing to think with: Teaching research in education as a wild profusion. *International Journal of Qualitative Studies in Education*, *19*(1), 35–57.

Lingard, B. (2013). Policy borrowing, policy learning: Testing times in Australian schooling. In B. Lingard, *Politics, policies and pedagogies in education: The selected works of Bob Lingard* (pp. 68–85). Routledge.

Lingard, B., & Gale, T. (2010). Defining educational research: A perspective of/on presidential addresses and the Australian Association for Research in Education. *Australian Educational Researcher*, *37*(1), 21–49.

Lloyd, D., Paige, K., & Smith, R. (2019). *Intergenerational education for adolescents towards liveable futures*. Cambridge Scholars Publishing.

Luke, A. (2006). Editorial introduction: Why pedagogies? *Pedagogies: An International Journal*, *1*(1), 1–6.

Mason, S., & Matas, P. (2015). Teacher attrition and retention research in Australia: Towards a new theoretical framework. *Australian Journal of Teacher Education*, *40*(11), 45–66.

McKnight, L., & Morgan, A. (2020). A broken paradigm? What education needs to learn from evidence-based medicine. *Journal of Education Policy*, *35*(5), 648–64.

Mills, K. A., & Dooley, J. (2019). Sensory ways to Indigenous multimodal literacies: Hands and feet tell the story. In J. Rennie & H. Harper (Eds.), *Literacy education and Indigenous Australians* (pp. 33–50). Springer Nature.

Moll, L. C., Amanti, C., Neff, D., & Gonzalez, N. (1992). Funds of knowledge for teaching: Using a qualitative approach to connect homes and classrooms. *Theory into Practice*, *31*(2), 71–87.

Morrison, A., Rigney, I.-L., Hattam, R., & Diplock, A. (2019). *Toward an Australian culturally responsive pedagogy: A narrative review of the literature*. University of South Australia.

Nixon, H., & Comber, B. (2006). Differential recognition of children's cultural practices in middle primary literacy classrooms. *Literacy*, *40*(3), 127–36.

Osei-Kofi, N. (2013). The emancipatory potential of arts-based research for social justice. *Equity & Excellence in Education*, *46*(1), 135–49.

OECD. (2023). *Education policy outlook in Australia* (OECD Education Policy Perspectives No. 67). OECD Publishing. https://www.oecd.org/publications/education-policy-outlook-in-australia-ce7a0965-en.htm

Perry, T., Lea, R., Jørgensen, C., Cordingley, P., Shapiro, K., Youdell, D., Harrington, J., Fancourt, A., Crisp, P., Gamble, N., & Pomareda, C. (2021). *Cognitive science in the classroom: Evidence and practice review*. Education Endowment Foundation.

Rancière, J. (1991). *The ignorant schoolmaster*. Stanford University Press.

Rancière, J. (2010). *Dissensus*. Continuum.

Reid, A. (2019). *Changing Australian education*. Allen and Unwin.

Reisch, M. (2014). *Routledge international handbook of social justice*. Routledge.

Riddle, S., Heffernan, A., & Bright, D. (Eds.). (2022). *New perspectives on education for democracy: Creative responses to local and global challenges*. Routledge.

Riddle, S., & Hickey, A. (2023). Reclaiming relationality in education policy: Towards a more authentic relational pedagogy. *Critical Studies in Education*, *64*(3), 267–82.

Rose, N., & Abi-Rachid, J. M. (2013) *Neuro: The new brain sciences and the management of the mind*. Princeton University Press.

Rowe, E. (2022). The assemblage of inanimate objects in educational research: Mapping venture philanthropy, policy networks and evidence brokers. *International Journal of Educational Research*, 114, Article 102005.

Sahlberg, P., Hasak, J., Rodriguez, V. & Associates. (2017) *Hard Questions on Global Educational Change: Policies, Practices, and the Future of Education*, Teachers College, Columbia University.

Santoro, N. (2013). The making of teachers for the twenty-first century: Australian professional standards and the preparation of culturally responsive teachers. In X. Zhu & K. Zeichner (Eds.), *Preparing teachers for the 21st century: New frontiers of educational research* (pp. 309–21). Springer-Verlag.

Sellar, S., & Lingard, R. (2014). Equity in Australian schooling: The absent presence of socioeconomic context. In S. Gannon & W. Sawyer (Eds.), *Contemporary issues of equity in education* (pp. 1–21). Cambridge Scholars Publishing.

Senate Select Committee on School Funding. (2014). *Equity and Excellence in Australian Schools: Executive summary*. Commonwealth of Australia. https://www.aph.gov.au/parliamentary_business/committees/senate/school_funding/school_funding/report/a03

Shor, I. (1992). *Culture wars: School and society in the conservative restoration*. University of Chicago Press.

Slee, R. (2018). Educational exclusion? It's what we do and it's always been thus. In S. Gannon, R. Hattam, & W. Sawyer (Eds.), *Resisting educational inequality: Reframing policy and practice in schools serving vulnerable communities* (pp. 225–35). Routledge.

Sleeter, C. (Ed.). (2011). *Professional development for culturally responsive and relationship-based pedagogy*. Peter Lang.

Smyth, J. (2011). *Critical pedagogy for social justice*. A&C Black.

Smyth, J., & Hattam, R. (2004). *"Dropping out," drifting off, being excluded: Becoming somebody without school*. Peter Lang.

Sullivan, A., Down B., Johnson, B., Manolev, J., Robinson, J., & Tippett, N. (2022, August 4). Australian schools want to improve student discipline, they need to address these 5 issues. *The Conversation*. https://theconversation.com/if-australian-schools-want-to-improve-student-discipline-they-need-to-address-these-5-issues-187993

Sullivan, A., Johnson, B., & Lucas, B. (Eds.). (2016). *Challenging dominant views on student behaviour at school: Answering back*. Springer.

Teacher Education Expert Panel (2023). *Strong Beginnings: Report of the Teacher Education Expert Panel*. https://www.education.gov.au/quality-initial-teacher-education-review/resources/strong-beginnings-report-teacher-education-expert-panel

Teese, R. (2011). *From opportunity to outcomes: The changing role of public schooling in Australia and national funding arrangements*. University of Melbourne. https://apo.org.au/sites/default/files/resource-files/2011-09/apo-nid27999.pdf

Thomson, P. (2009). *School leadership—Heads on the block?* Routledge.

Vass G. (2017). Preparing for culturally responsive schooling: Initial teacher educators into the fray. *Journal of Teacher Education*, 68(5), 451–62.

Villegas, A. M., & Lucas, T. (2002). *Educating culturally responsive teachers: A coherent approach*. SUNY Press.

Warren, C. (2018). Empathy, teacher dispositions and preparation for culturally responsive pedagogy. *Journal of Teacher Education*, *69*(2), 169–83.

Williams, R. (1976). *Keywords: A vocabulary of culture and society*. Croom Helm.

Wyse, D., & Bradbury, A. (2022). Reading wars or reading reconciliation? A critical examination of robust research evidence, curriculum policy and teachers' practices for teaching phonics and reading. *BERA Review of Education*, *10*(1), Article e3314.

Zipin, L. (2024). Curriculum for living structural crises towards socially just futures: Bringing diverse funds of knowledge into participatory-democratic action around lifeworld problems that matter. *Curriculum Perspectives*, *44*, 249–62. https://doi.org/10.1007/s41297-024-00250-1

Zipin, L., Sellar, S., & Hattam, R. (2012). Countering and exceeding "capital": A "funds of knowledge" approach to re-imagining community. *Discourse: Studies in the Cultural Politics of Education*, *33*(2), 179–92.

Notes on Contributors

David Armstrong (PhD) is Associate Professor Inclusion and Specialist Education, La Trobe University, Melbourne. He advocates for children and young people with a disability in education and passionately supports inclusive, high-quality education for all. His research interests are exclusion of students with a disadvantage, and what can be done about it, tackling occupational violence in schools, and better understanding educational trends. Dave also researches how to enable greater academic success for students with dyslexia, ADHD, or similar learning differences. https://orcid.org/0000-0002-9683-1524

Melanie Baak (PhD) is an Associate Professor in the School of Education, Adelaide University. Her research and teaching are underpinned by understandings of how systems and structures work to marginalize sections of the population, particularly Afro-diasporic peoples and those from refugee backgrounds in settler colonial Australia. She currently holds an ARC DECRA Fellowship where she is exploring understandings of un/belonging for Afro-diasporic youth in Australia, particularly in schools. https://orcid.org/0000-0002-0745-1352

Penelope Bateman is a Curriculum Leader in English at a large coeducational secondary school in northern Adelaide. Prior to becoming a teacher Penelope completed a Bachelor of Creative Arts (Creative Writing), Honors, and a Master of Teaching degree. Penelope continues to develop her pedagogical practices and understanding of curriculum. Her research interests extend to better understanding how pedagogical practices can utilize students' funds of knowledge to enhance literacies skills and practices.

Snjezana Bilic (PhD) is a Senior Lecturer in the Pathways and Participation Unit at Adelaide University. She coordinates and teaches sociology courses in the Foundation Studies and diploma programs. Snjezana's research is grounded in social justice initiatives and equitable access to higher education for all students. Her specific research interests include making more visible the perspectives of students from refugee backgrounds who undertake enabling courses. https://orcid.org/0000-0001-8833-2760

Andrew Bills (PhD) is an Educational Leadership Consultant and an adjunct researcher at Flinders University. He lectures, leads research, and consults in the areas of policy, politics, and practice with a particular interest in socially just reform in school communities struck hard by disadvantage. He was previously an educational leader, a special education teacher, and an Education Department leadership consultant. He works within the research traditions of critical policy sociology, emancipatory action research, and lived experience phenomenology. https://orcid.org/0000-0002-3347-6123

Jenni Carter is a researcher and lecturer in literacy and English education. Her current research focuses on decoloniality, culturally responsive pedagogies, and children's literature. https://orcid.org/0000-0002-5904-9509

Dylan Chown is a lecturer in the Centre for Islamic Thought and Education (CITE), Adelaide University. Dylan serves as the Curriculum Advisor (program lead) for the Graduate Certificate (Islamic Education) at UniSA – Australia's first recognised and accredited teacher education program based on Islamic Pedagogy. He is also member of UniSA's, Centre for Research in Educational and Social Inclusion (CRESI). His research focuses on teacher education with emphasis on Islamic Pedagogy and culturally and religiously responsive pedagogy. https://orcid.org/0000-0002-3790-7656

Jill Colton (PhD) researches literacy, technology, and learning spaces from a relational socio-material perspective, drawing on actor network theory to study the "intra-actions" of humans and materials in teaching and learning practices. She is an English specialist with expertise in digital media, inclusive education, and inquiry approaches, who lectures in in the primary and secondary teacher education courses at Adelaide University. Jill's doctoral study was a critical analysis of the "twenty-first-century learner." https://orcid.org/0000-0003-0694-8794

Amaarah DeCuir (EdD) is an educator, researcher, and antiracist pedagogy fellow, and a faculty member at the School of Education, American University, and affiliate faculty member of its Antiracist Research and Policy Center. Her scholarship spans antiracist pedagogy, Muslim student experiences, prophetic pedagogy, faith erasure, equity, antiracism and social justice, education leadership, teacher education, and faculty development. A highly regarded educator, Dr. DeCuir teaches education studies and social justice, education leadership, and an Antiracist Research Methods course she co-designed.

Abigail Diplock (PhD) (she/her) is a settler Australian originally from the UK and currently living on unceded Kaurna and Peramangk Country. Abigail's research interests include culturally responsive pedagogies, First Nations education, teacher professionalism and affect theory. She has been involved in the ARC Discovery Projects *Culturally Responsive Schooling* and *Toward an Australian Culturally Responsive Pedagogy* and is currently working as a postdoctoral research fellow with the *Culturally Nourishing Schooling* project. https://orcid.org/0000-0002-9116-2958

Basma Elshayyal (MA) is a Fellow of the Chartered College of Teachers, and currently part of a team pioneering holistic and progressive curricula at nascent schools in Qatar Foundation. She serves as trustee and board governor at faith, independent, and state schools in the UK in addition to advising on national teacher training programs. Her doctoral research focuses on the relationship between ethical leadership and successful curriculum design/implementation.

Robyne Garrett (PhD) is an Associate Professor of Education in the School of Education, Adelaide University. She teaches in physical education, dance, teaching methodologies, and research. Her research interests include gender, critical pedagogies, embodiment, and affective and arts-based pedagogical approaches. Current projects include creative and body-based learning, socially just pedagogies for disadvantaged students, oracy, agency, and constructions of gender around movement and physical activity. Her research methodologies include action research, narrative storytelling, and ethnographic and arts-based approaches. https://orcid.org/0000-0002-9604-458X

Robert Hattam (PhD) is an Emeritus Professor for Educational Justice in the School of Education, Adelaide University. His research has focused on teachers' work, critical and reconciliation pedagogies, refugees, and socially just school reform. He has been involved in Australian Research Council–funded projects on teachers' learning in the devolving school; early school leaving; "Re-thinking Reconciliation and Pedagogy in Unsettling Times"; "Redesigning Pedagogies in the North"; educational leadership and turnaround literacy pedagogies;

and "Towards an Australian Culturally Responsive Pedagogy." https://orcid.org/0000-0002-0645-5685

Sarah Hattam (PhD) has worked in enabling education for fifteen years and is now Director of Domestic Pathways at Adelaide University. Sarah has expertise in the areas of widening participation policy, enabling curriculum, retention and engagement strategies, alternative education pathways, and secondary school retention. She is nationally recognized for her leadership in professional development of enabling and inclusive pedagogies. Most recently, Sarah has been advancing a theory of "critical enabling pedagogy." https://orcid.org/0000-0002-0645-5685

Nigel Howard has worked as a teacher, education activist, and school leader for the last thirty years and has been primarily concerned with students in poverty on the edge of schooling. His interest in school retention and achievement of secondary students stems from his membership of the Senior Secondary (2S) Team, where he was one of the major architects of SACE Community Studies. His work as an innovative teacher and leader has been well documented. https://orcid.org/0000-0003-0129-0823

Stephen Kelly (PhD) has recently retired and holds the title of adjunct at Adelaide University. Dr Kelly's research is influenced by post-structuralist/post-humanist approaches to education, and he has drawn on Foucault studies to pursue interests in the politics, policies, history, and philosophy of education and their connection to contemporary educational practice. He applies these sociological and philosophical approaches to research curriculum and its connection to the subjectivities of educators and children, and arts and literacy education. https://orcid.org/0000-0001-5414-1413

David Lloyd (PhD) is a retired science and environmental educator with particular interests in futures education and transdisciplinary approaches to learning. He has worked in middle and senior secondary schools in South Australia and the University of South Australia, in primary and middle school initial teacher education. He developed and taught six science and environments general studies courses designed for pre-service teachers.

Bindi MacGill (PhD) is a Senior Lecturer in arts education in the School of Education, Adelaide University, and she is also a contemporary artist. Her diverse research interests include contemporary art, Indigenous education, postcolonial theory, visual methodologies, arts pedagogy, and critical race theory. Dr MacGill's scholarly pursuits focus on decolonization through arts-based practices and creative methodologies. Her recent research projects have explored the potential of virtual reality, aesthetics, and learning design theory. https://orcid.org/0000-0002-3486-6721

Sarah McDonald (PhD) is a Senior Lecturer in the School of Education, Adelaide University. Her doctoral research focuses on how the intersection between gender and class interacts with higher education, and how this interaction impacts upon the construction of feminine identities for young women transitioning into university. She is interested in gendered subjectivities, social mobility, social barriers, and inequalities in education. https://orcid.org/0000-0002-0454-4983

Nadeem Memon (PhD) is an Associate Professor at the Centre for Islamic Thought and Education in the School of Education, Adelaide University, and Course Coordinator for the Graduate Certificate in Education (Islamic Education). His research focuses on teacher education with particular emphasis on Islamic pedagogy, comparative faith-based schooling, philosophy of religious education, and culturally responsive pedagogy. Nadeem is a Chief Investigator on an Australian Research Council Discovery Grant (2022–25) on culturally responsive schooling. https://orcid.org/0000-0002-0205-0736

Anne Morrison is a white Australian of Anglo lineage, with a PhD in the discipline of professional writing and communication. She was research assistant on the ARC-funded project "Toward an Australian Culturally Responsive Pedagogy" and provided research assistance for the project "Culturally and Linguistically Responsive Pedagogies in Early Childhood Education" (funded by the Lillian de Lissa Trust Fund). Anne has co-authored several publications in the broad fields of culturally diverse and First Nations education. https//orcid.org/0000-0002-5929-4790

Dino Murtic (PhD) is a lecturer in the Pathways and Participation Unit at Adelaide University who teaches primarily in the enabling sector of higher education, focusing on literacy. His research interests encompass the cultural and political dimensions of the arts and media, and their integration into educational settings. Dino has published a monograph on film texts in the post-Yugoslav context as both historical references and sources of emancipatory potential, reflecting his commitment to understanding the wider socio-cultural implications of artistic expression. https://orcid.org/0000-0001-8929-2836

Mahmood Nathie (PhD) was one of the founders of the National Centre of Excellence in Islamic Studies at Griffith University and also of the Centre for Islamic Thought and Education at the University of South Australia. Now retired, his research focuses on financial literacy and knowledge-based problems within disadvantaged communities. He has published on Islamic finance literacy and Islamic schooling. Presently, he is working on developing software applications designed to address financial illiteracy among unbanked communities. https://orcid.org/0000-0002-0851-2110

Sam Osborne (PhD) is an Associate Professor at Adelaide University and has worked as a teacher, principal, researcher, and lecturer. He is the Associate Director for Regional Engagement (APY Lands) and coordinates the Pitjantjatjara Yankunytjatjara Language and Culture programs and the "Ananguku Kulintja: Anangu Languages and Knowledges in Higher Education" project. He maintains a research interest in Aboriginal languages and the work of remote Aboriginal educators, culturally responsive pedagogies, and the development of high-quality first language resources for remote schools. https://orcid.org/0000-0002-0158-0292

Kathryn Paige (PhD) is an Adjunct Associate Professor in educating for sustainability in the School of Education, Adelaide University. She previously taught in primary classrooms in a range of schools in Australia and the United Kingdom. Kathryn's current research interests include pre-service science and mathematics education, eco-justice, place-based education, culturally responsive pedagogy, citizen science, connecting children to the natural world, and Indigenous ways of knowing. https://orcid.org/0000-0001-9238-0765

Lester-Irabinna Rigney AM (PhD) is Professor of Education in the Pedagogies for Justice Research group in the Centre for Research in Educational and Social Inclusion, based in the School of Education, Adelaide University. He is a citizen of the Narungga Nation Aboriginal peoples of South Australia. He is a recognized expert on Aboriginal and inclusive education of the Pacific. https://orcid.org/0000-0002-4756-2399

Lisa Smith (PhD) has a background in secondary school teaching and leadership and is currently a Research Fellow with Adelaide University's Education Futures Academy, where she co-leads the qualitative research team within a program of university–school partnered research. Her research focuses on equitable schooling practices, social class analysis, democratic school reform and relational pedagogies, with a commitment to improving educational outcomes for students in disadvantaged communities. https://orcid.org/0000-0002-2276-4429

Richard Smith has contributed to the practice and curriculum development of teacher education and sustainability education courses for 25 years, working across all areas. He has combined this with senior roles in professional associations and eco-socially regenerative civil society non-government organizations. His interests continue to be in the promotion of problem- and place-based pedagogical practice, and improvements in eco-social literacy and equity.

Hannah Soong (PhD) is a sociologist of education and an Associate Professor in the School of Education, Adelaide University. Hannah is a course coordinator of sociological courses in undergraduate and postgraduate teaching degrees. Her research interests lie in the empirical studies and theorization of the education–migration nexus of refugee, migrant, and international students. Hannah is a Chief Investigator on an Australian Research Council Discovery Grant (2020–24) "Parent Involvement Goes Online: New Ecologies of School–Home Relations." https://orcid.org/0000-0002-1798-4881

Garth Stahl (PhD) is an Associate Professor in the School of Education at the University of Queensland. His research interests lie at the nexus of neoliberalism and socio-cultural studies of education, identity, equity/inequality, and social change. Currently, his research projects and publications encompass theoretical and empirical studies of learner identities, gender and youth, sociology of schooling in a neoliberal age, gendered subjectivities, equity and difference, and educational reform. https//orcid.org/ 0000-0002-1800-8495

Alison Wrench (PhD) is an adjunct Senior Lecturer in Health and Physical Education Studies in the School of Education, Adelaide University. Alison's research program centres on socially critical and culturally responsive pedagogies in health and physical education studies, inclusion, and just schooling outcomes. Her research interests extend to in-service and pre-service teacher practitioner inquiry and student-led inquiry into localized health and physical activity issues "that matter." https://orcid.org/0000-0002-6407-3503

Author Index

Subject Index

COUNTERPOINTS

Studies in Criticality

Series Editor

Shirley R. Steinberg

Counterpoints publishes the most compelling and imaginative books being written in Education and Cultural Studies today. Grounded on the theoretical advances in critical theory, feminism, and postcolonialism in the last two decades of the twentieth century, Counterpoints engages the meaning of these innovations in various forms of educational expression. Committed to the proposition that theoretical literature should be accessible to a variety of audiences, the series insists that its authors avoid esoteric and jargonistic languages that transform educational scholarship into an elite discourse for the initiated. Scholarly work matters only to the degree it affects consciousness and practice at multiple sites. The editorial policy of *Counterpoints* is based on these principles and the ability of scholars to break new ground, to open new conversations, to go where educators have never gone before.

For additional information about this series or for the submission of manuscripts, please contact:

Shirley R. Steinberg, Series Editor
msgramsci@gmail.com

To order other books in this series, please contact our Customer Service Department:

peterlang@presswarehouse.com (within the U.S.)
orders@peterlang.com (outside the U.S.)

Or browse online by series:

www.peterlang.com

FSC www.fsc.org
MIX
Papier | Fördert gute Waldnutzung
FSC® C083411

Kolibri 360 GmbH
Ferdinand-Jühlke-Straße 7
99095 Erfurt, Deutschland
produktsicherheit@kolibri360.de

Druck:
CPI Druckdienstleistungen GmbH
im Auftrag der
Kolibri 360 GmbH
Ferdinand-Jühlke-Str. 7
99095 Erfurt